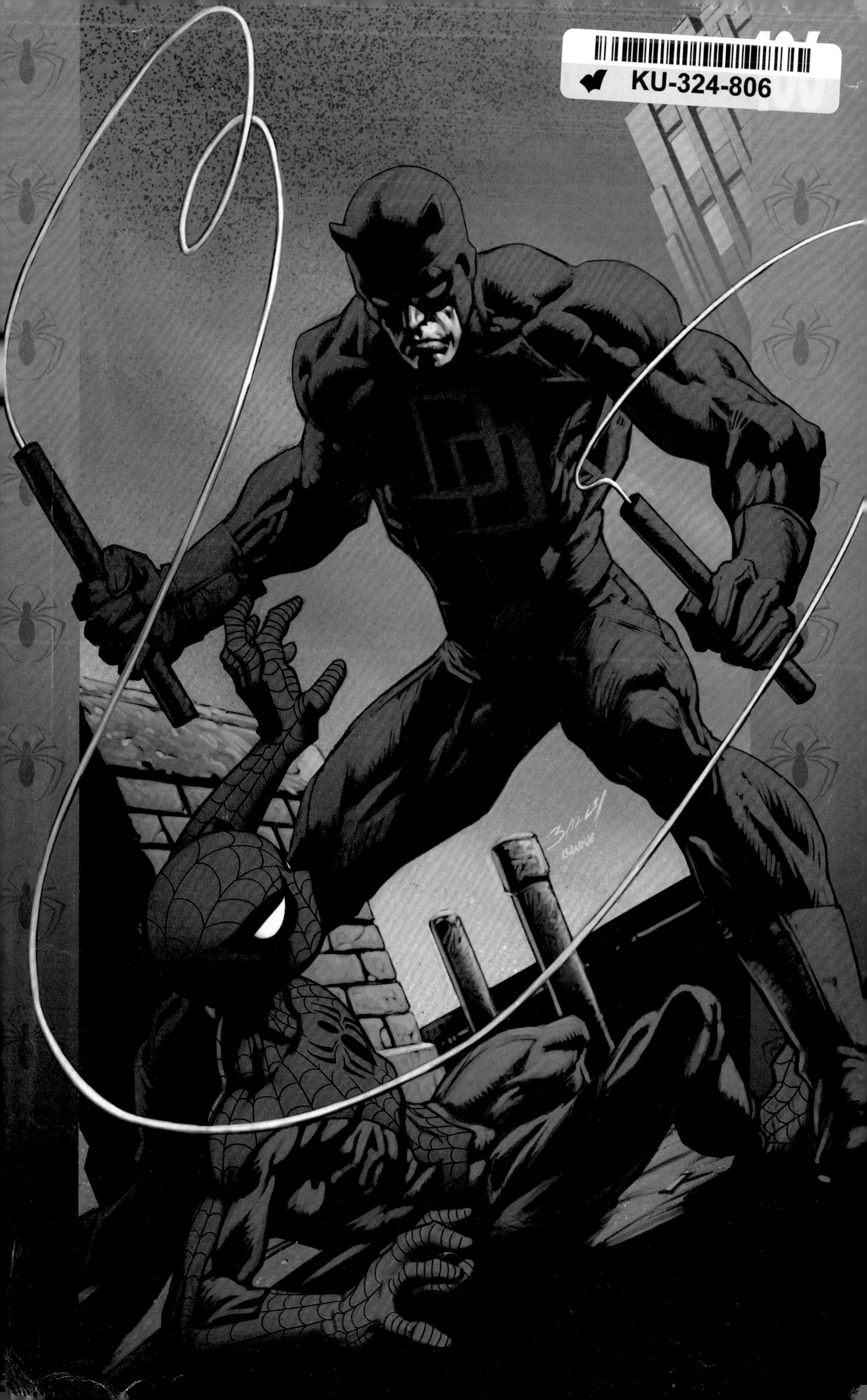

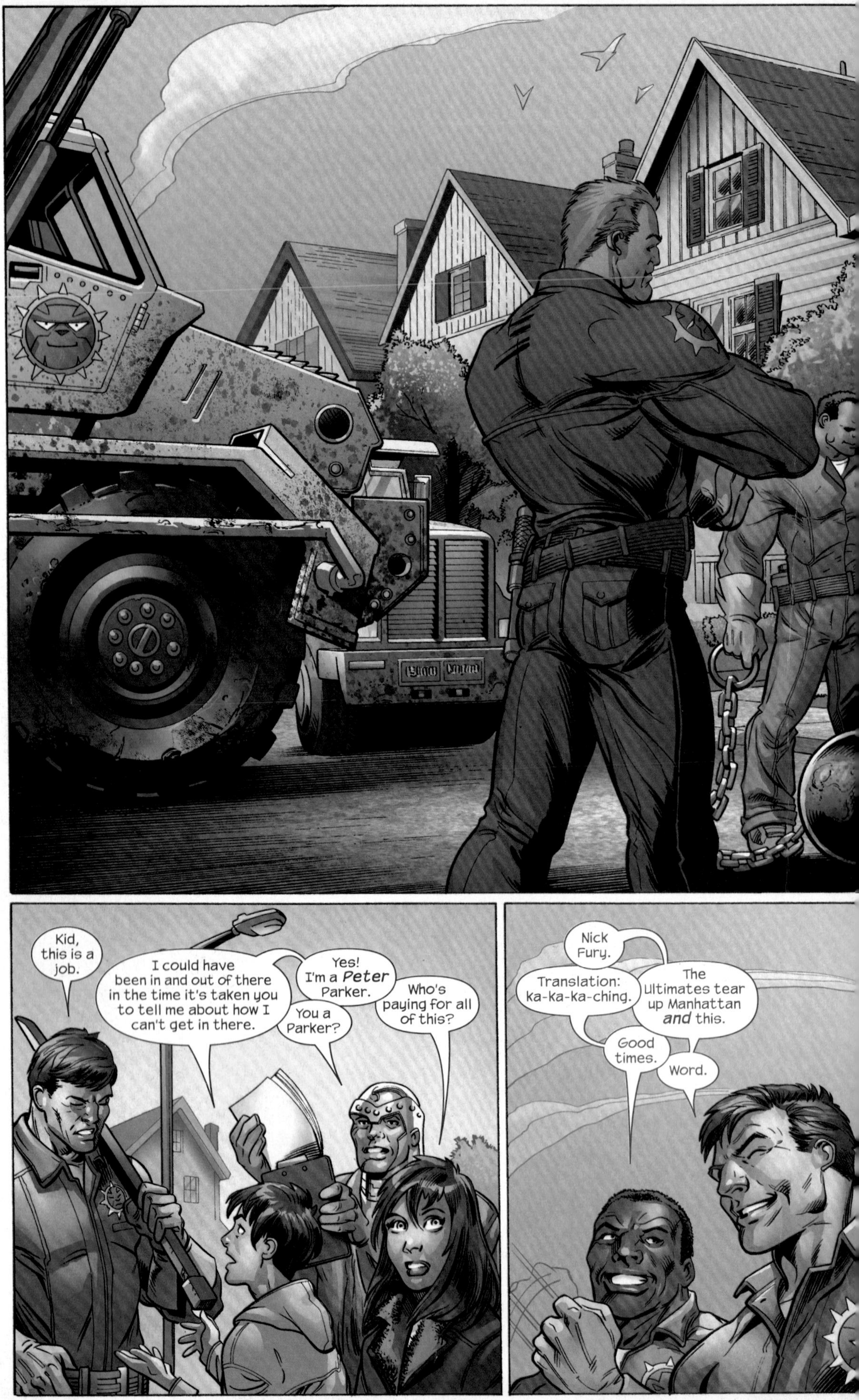
Kid, this is a job.
I could have been in and out of there in the time it's taken you to tell me about how I can't get in there.
You a Parker?
Yes! I'm a *Peter* Parker.
Who's paying for all of this?
Nick Fury.
Translation: ka-ka-ka-ching.
The Ultimates tear up Manhattan **and** this.
Good times.
Word.

ULTIMATE
# SPIDER-MAN

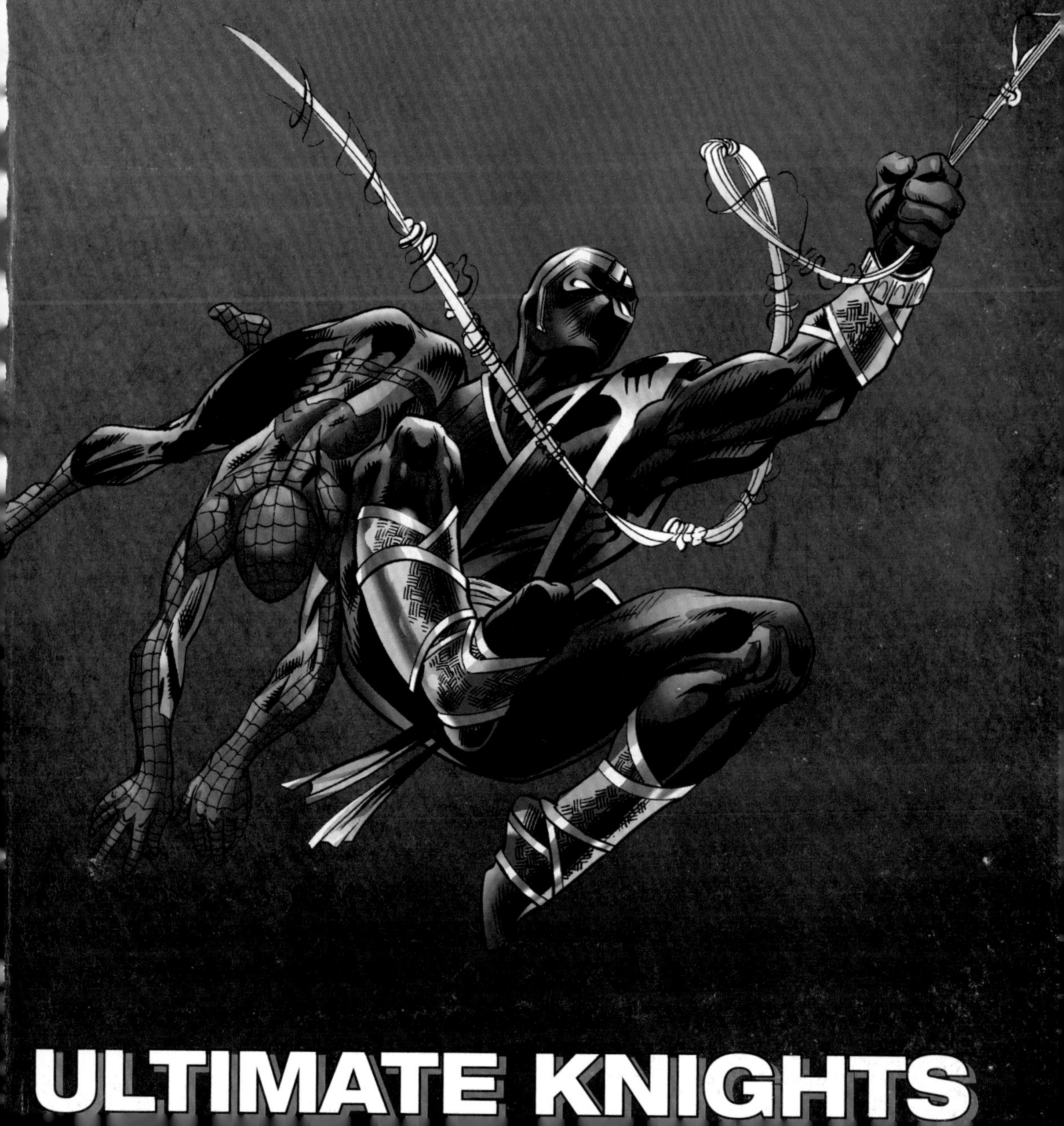

# ULTIMATE KNIGHTS

# ULTIMATE SPIDER-MAN

## ULTIMATE KNIGHTS

writer: **BRIAN MICHAEL BENDIS**
pencils: **MARK BAGLEY**
with STUART IMMONEN (Issue #111, pages 11-16)
inks: **DREW HENNESSY**
with WADE VON GRAWBADGER (Issue #111, pages 11-16)
colors: **JUSTIN PONSOR**
letters: **VIRTUAL CALLIGRAPHY'S CORY PETIT**
cover art: **MARK BAGLEY & RICHARD ISANOVE**
editors: **JOHN BARBER** with **BILL ROSEMANN**
senior editor: **RALPH MACCHIO**

collection editor:
**JENNIFER GRÜNWALD**
assistant editors:
**CORY LEVINE & MICHAEL SHORT**
associate editor:
**MARK D. BEAZLEY**
senior editor, special projects:
**JEFF YOUNGQUIST**
senior vice president of sales:
**DAVID GABRIEL**

production:
**JERRON QUALITY COLOR**
vice president of creative:
**TOM MARVELLI**

editor in chief:
**JOE QUESADA**
publisher:
**DAN BUCKLEY**

## PREVIOUSLY:

The bite of a genetically-altered spider granted high school student Peter Parker incredible, arachnid-like powers! When a burglar killed his beloved Uncle Ben, a grief-stricken Peter vowed to use his amazing abilities to protect his fellow man. He learned the invaluable lesson that with great power must also come great responsibility...

Recently, Doctor Octopus was secretly making clones of Peter Parker. The clones escaped from their laboratory and made a mess out of the real Peter's life. In the bedlam that followed, the clones destroyed the Parker home, MJ was injected with the Oz Formula (the substance that mutated the spider that gave Peter his powers), and Aunt May suffered a near-fatal heart attack after discovering Peter's double life as Spider-Man.

Reed Richards (super-genius leader of the super-hero team, the Fantastic Four) seems to have cured MJ of any mutations caused by the Oz Formula, and Peter and MJ have gotten back together, meaning that Peter's troubled relationship with Kitty Pryde (of the mutant team, the X-Men) is effectively in shambles.

Since gaining his powers, Spider-Man has had several confrontations with New York crime boss Wilson Fisk (A.K.A. the Kingpin of Crime) and a couple of run-ins with the guardian of Hell's Kitchen

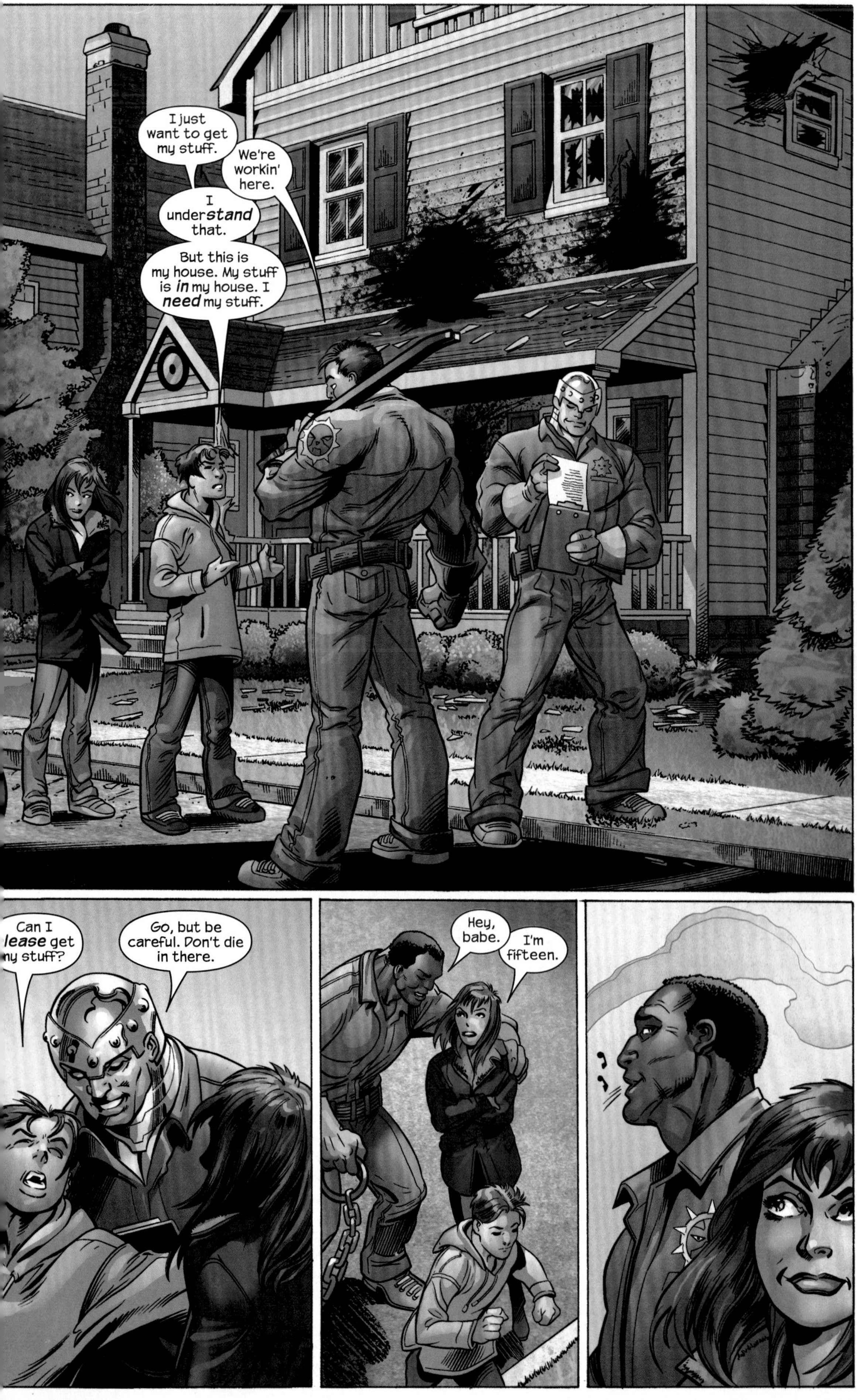
I just want to get my stuff.
We're workin' here.
I understand that.
But this is my house. My stuff is in my house. I need my stuff.
Can I lease get ny stuff?
Go, but be careful. Don't die in there.
Hey, babe.
I'm fifteen.

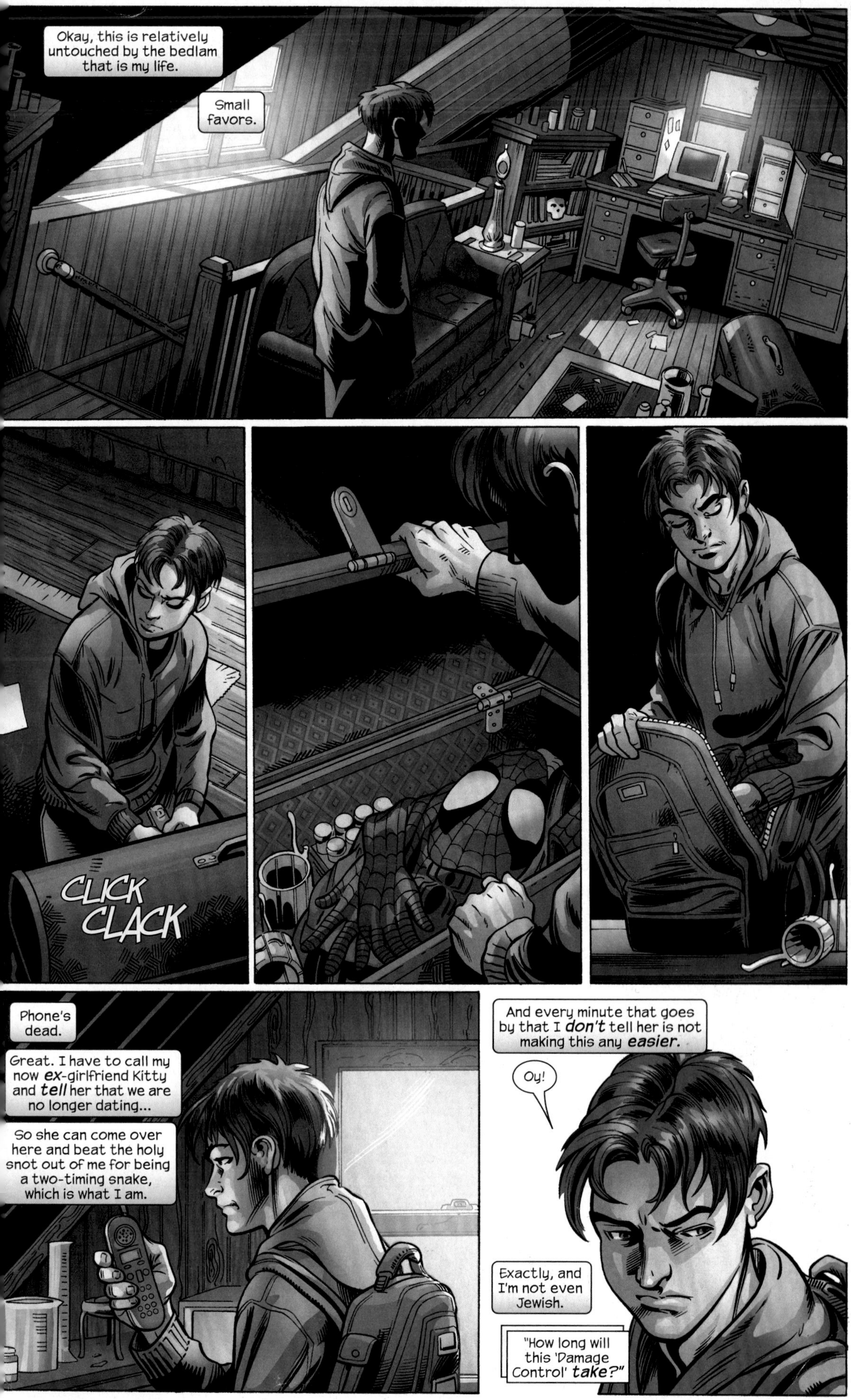

Okay, this is relatively untouched by the bedlam that is my life.
Small favors.
CLICK CLACK
Phone's dead.
Great. I have to call my now ex-girlfriend Kitty and tell her that we are no longer dating...
So she can come over here and beat the holy snot out of me for being a two-timing snake, which is what I am.
And every minute that goes by that I don't tell her is not making this any easier.
Oy!
Exactly, and I'm not even Jewish.
"How long will this 'Damage Control' take?"

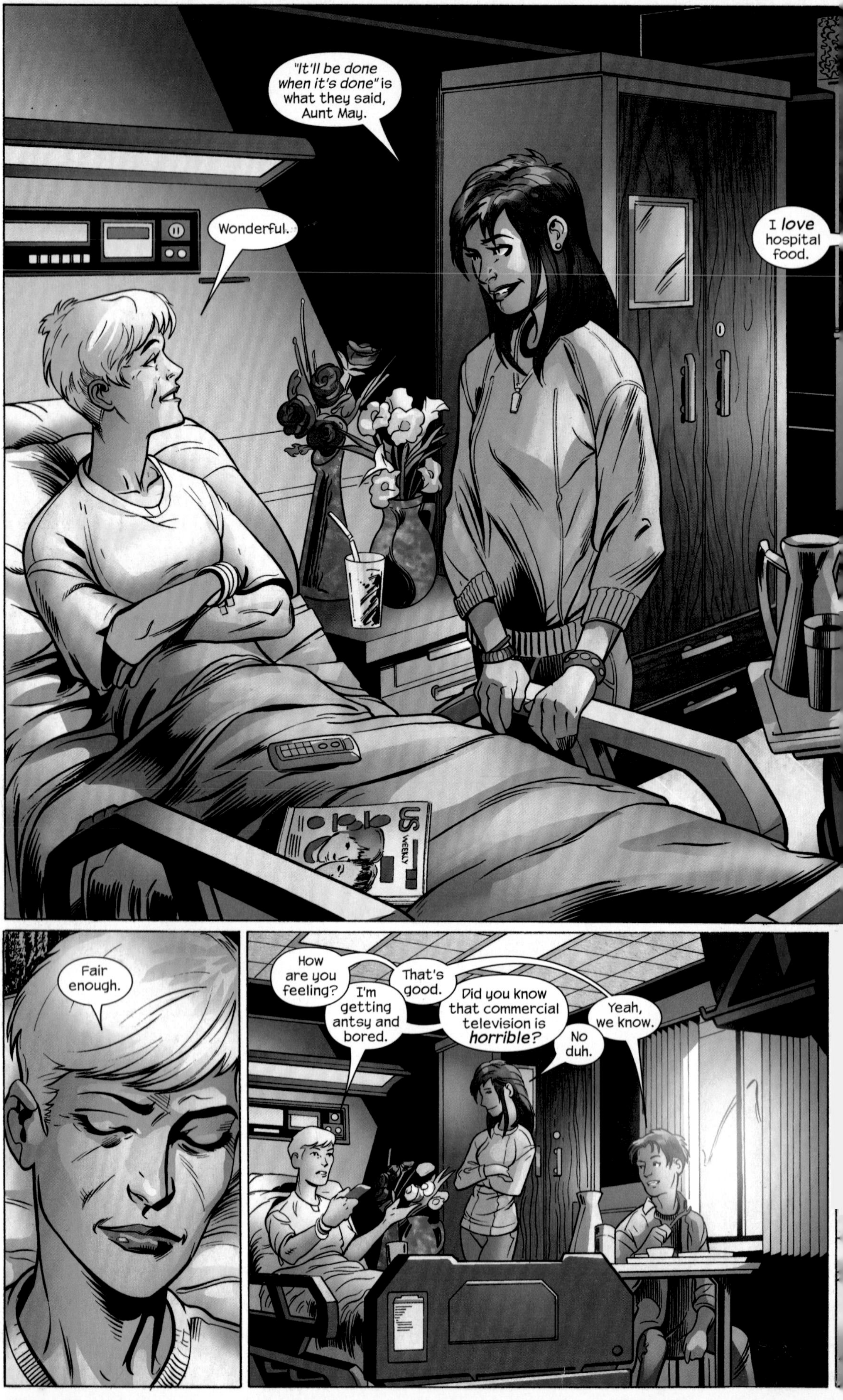
"It'll be done when it's done" is what they said, Aunt May.
Wonderful.
I love hospital food.
US WEEKLY
Fair enough.
How are you feeling?
I'm getting antsy and bored.
That's good.
Did you know that commercial television is horrible?
No duh.
Yeah, we know.

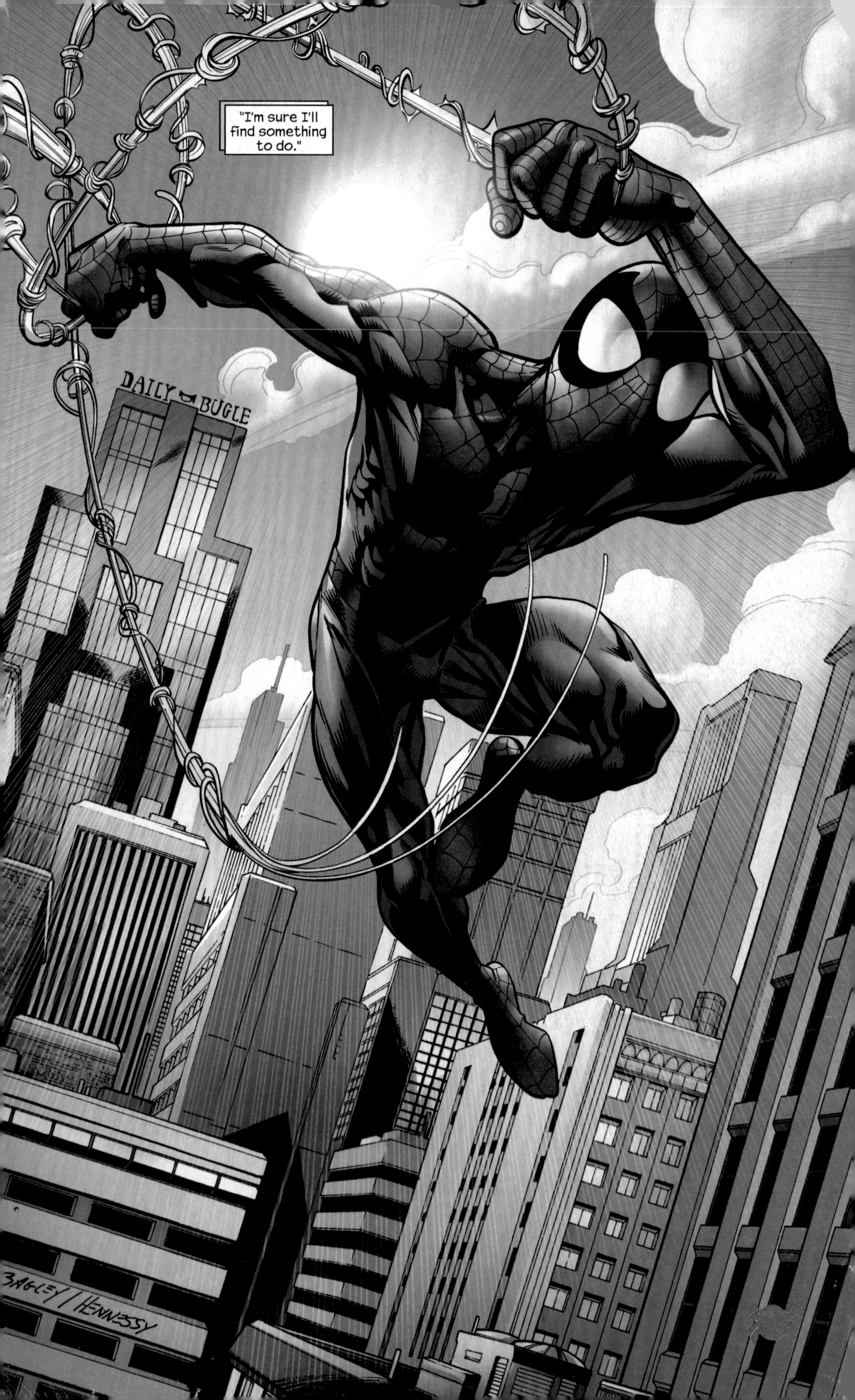
"I'm sure I'll find something to do."
DAILY BUGLE
BAGLEY / HENNESSY

# ULTIMATE SPIDER-MAN

So this is it, my last issue of Ultimate Spider-Man! Saying I'm conflicted about walking away from this project would be a vast understatement, but I really believe that the time has come for me to move on. I leave knowing that the book is in great hands with Stuart Immonen taking over the penciling chores. I don't think a better choice could have been made.

I'd first like to thank Bill Jemas for insisting I take this job over my idiotic objections. Ultimate Spidey came along at a real crossroad point in my comics career, and it is no exaggeration that it has become the most fulfilling and rewarding professional experience of my life. I'd like to thank Dan Buckley, Joe Quesada, Ralph Macchio, Nick Lowe, John Barber and all the folks in editorial who have had my back for all these years. I've never had an easier, more professional group of people to work with than you guys, and you'll always have my respect and gratitude.

Thanks and praise also to all my artistic collaborators whose talent made my work shine. Art Thibert, Steve Buccellato, Marie Javins, J.D. Smith, Scott Hanna, Justin Ponsor, Richard Isanove, John Dell and Drew Hennessy. I'm sure I'm forgetting a few (it was a looong run). All contributed to make this book as terrific looking as possible.

I have nothing to say about Brian Michael Bendis because words cannot express the deep appreciation and respect I have for the brilliance and talent, and the commitment he brings to this book. It has been my honor to be part of telling his stories, and I'm sure that Ultimate Spider-Man would be a shallow shadow without him.

Finally, to you fans — you guys rock! To have a book like this, in this day and age, remain this supported by y'all for this long is nothing short of astounding. There is not a day that goes by that I am not humbled and grateful for your support.

-Mark Bagley

# INTRO
BY Max Allan Collins

When I was first approached to write a pair of novels based on a new TV series called *CSI: Crime Scene Investigation*, I began by lying through my teeth.

Of course, I had seen the new show — it was *great*, my *favourite* show in years! In truth, I hadn't seen it yet. In my defence, it was only a few weeks into the new television season — though *CSI* was on a very short list of new shows I intended to give a look.

I'd seen promos for the new show, and the strikingly visual style of the series attracted me, but more than that, there was the presence of William Petersen. I'd been a fan of Petersen for years, having seen him in various stage productions in Chicago, as well as such films as *To Live and Die in L.A.*, *Long Gone* and of course *Manhunter*, the Michael Mann version of *Red Dragon*, which this new *CSI* series seemed to be, in part, invoking — both through the casting of Petersen and the grim yet clinical look at crime scenes and homicide.

Despite Petersen's presence, however, and some shared subject matter, *CSI* turned out to be its own very specific animal, with little or no debt to Michael Mann's neo-noir thriller (though a nice wink at the film was provided by casting *Manhunter*'s Tom Noonan as a villain on the show). When I looked at the video tapes that the publishers forwarded to me, I quickly realised that the greatest debt the series owed was to Sir Arthur Conan Doyle: quirky Gil Grissom was clearly a modern-day Sherlock Holmes, interpreting evidence the way a psychic reads tea leaves. Around this Holmes were numerous gifted Watsons in the form of his CSIs, all in awe of the Great Detective, if occasionally appalled by his people skills.

I've written a number of so-called 'tie-in' novels in the last ten years or so. And I've been lucky to have mostly excellent properties from film and TV to interpret — *Saving Private Ryan*, *In the Line of Fire* and *NYPD: Blue* among them. Doing a TV tie-in can be much more rewarding than a movie novel, because rather than 'novelise' previously existing scripts, the writer gets to come up with his own yarn featuring the familiar, popular characters from a show.

Frankly, though, whenever I'm approached, I'm always a little nervous — a lot of Hollywood movies, no matter how big the stars and other talent involved, are dreadful; and much of TV is dreck (no snobbery meant — most popular culture isn't very good). So when I discovered just how terrific the *CSI* concept was, I was thrilled. The characters were strong, too,

particularly Grissom — but the show was cleverly stingy about background details, really making the viewer work to get to know these people, and giving the actors latitude to put flesh, blood and sinew on the bones. Initially I found this challenging, and watched the early episodes with a pencil in hand, scribbling down any 'personal' morsel.

As *CSI* blossomed from surprise hit to phenomenon, I realised how lucky I was to have been asked aboard at so early a stage. I've been blessed to become sort of the 'road show' *CSI* writer — with four *CSI* novels to date, plus two *CSI: Miami*, and another four books coming. In addition, there have been two Ubi Soft *CSI* video games for which I did the dialogue and co-plotting; and of course three serialised graphic novels, the second of which you hold in your hands (the third, *Demon House*, is in progress). And it looks like I'm going to be writing two *CSI* jigsaw puzzles next!

Of the various projects, the comics hold a special place in my heart. My fifteen years as the writer of the *Dick Tracy* comic strip were solid preparation for the *CSI* assignment: *Tracy* creator Chester Gould is the virtual inventor of the police procedural, and for all the crazy villains and wacky inventions, a strong element of forensic science was always present in Gould's strip (and my continuation of it). The editorial staff came up with the brilliant notion of using two artists, one (Gabriel Rodriguez) for the realistically portrayed investigatory work with the familiar TV faces; another (Ashley Wood) for expressionistically-depicted flashbacks and re-enactments. Both are terrific, and the approach parallels the striking visual style of the show — something that can only be suggested in a prose novel. Despite their differences, film and comics are, after all, both visual mediums.

*Bad Rap* deals with the music scene and reflects my longtime interest in that branch of popular culture. *CSI* creator Anthony Zuiker suggested the neo-punk aspect of this story, for which I thank him. Editor Jeff Mariotte hung in there when last-minute revisions proved necessary. And, of course, my collaborator Matthew V. Clemens must take a bow — he does the hard work, the forensics research, then gets his hands dirty in the co-plotting stage.

Or he would, if we weren't both wearing latex gloves. Hey, we're *CSI* guys.

**Max Allan Collins**
January 2, 2004

chapter one

# Rotten Rules

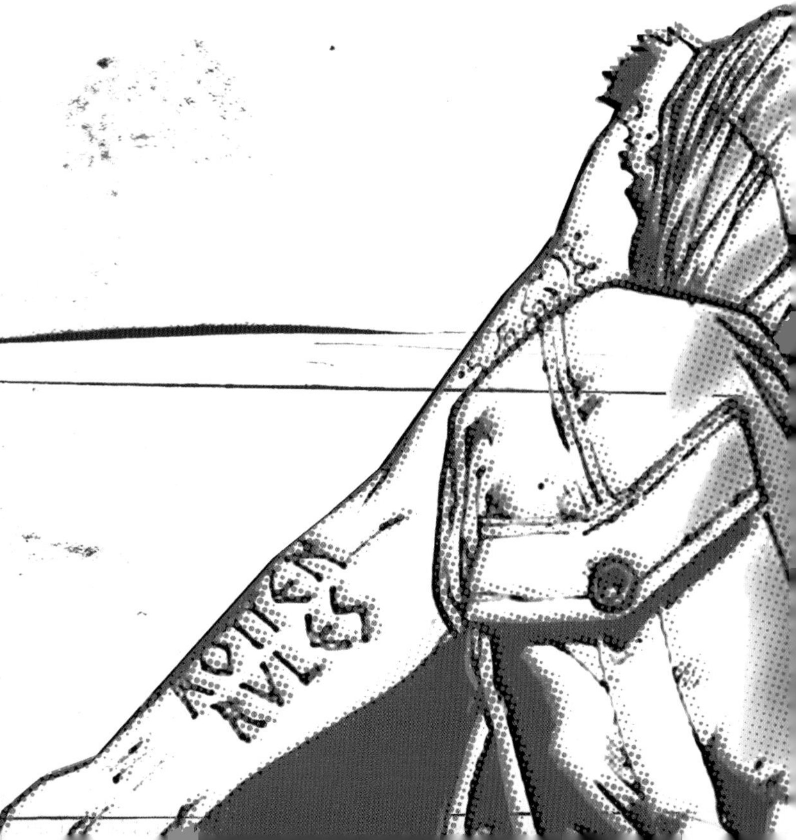
ROTTEN
RULES

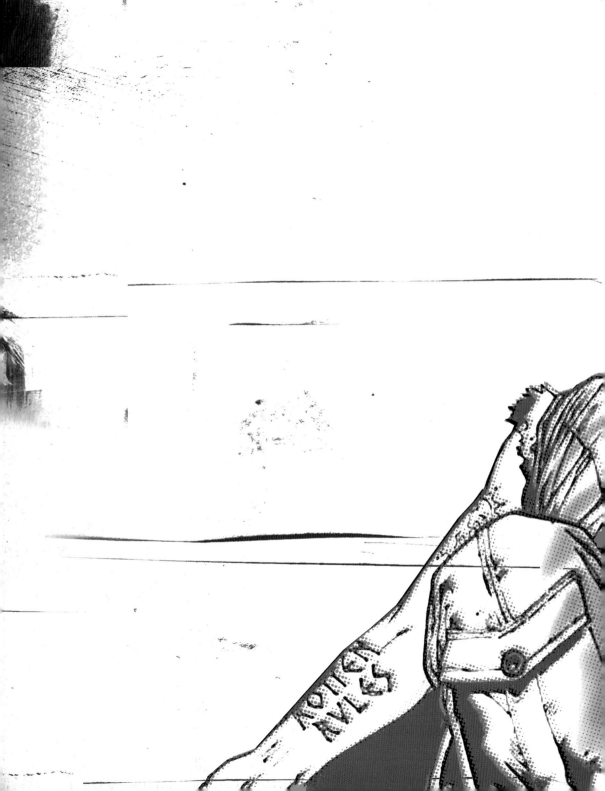

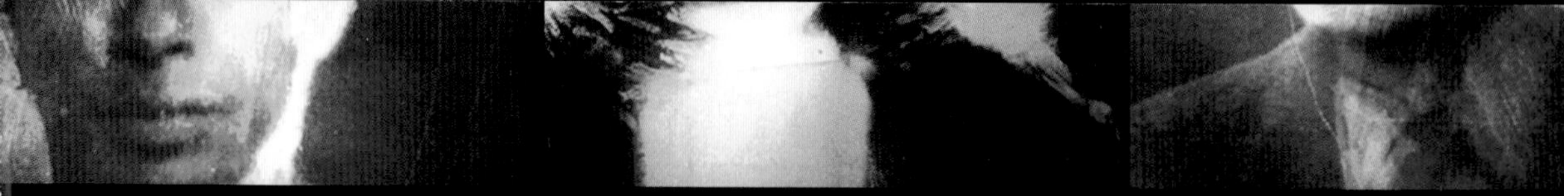

# CSI:

## CRIME SCENE INVESTIGATION™

# BAD RAP

Collins · Rodriguez · Wood

**TITAN BOOKS**

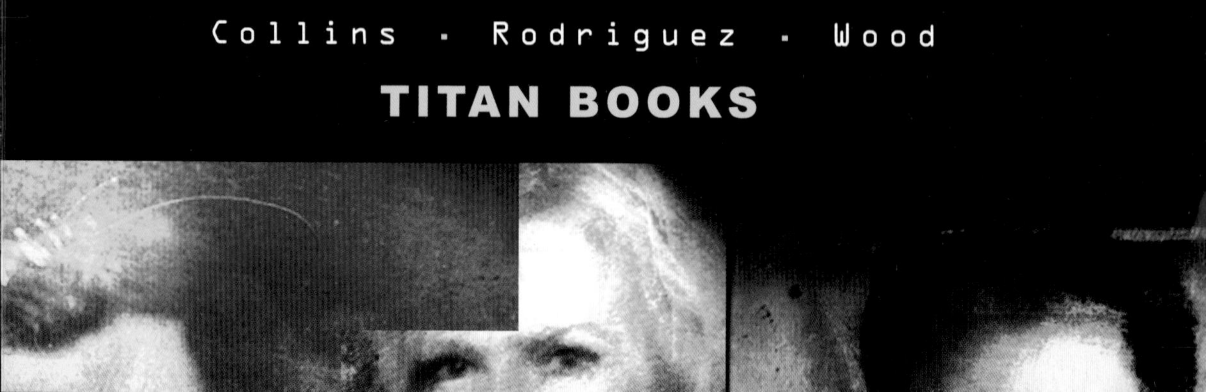

**CSI: CRIME SCENE INVESTIGATION**
Created by Anthony E. Zuiker

Licensed to IDW by CBS Consumer Products

# "BAD RAP"

ISBN 1 84023 799 6

Written by **Max Allan Collins**

Forensics Research/Plot Assist by **Matthew V. Clemens**

Pencils and inks by **Gabriel Rodriguez**

Colours by **Fran Gamboa**

Painted Artwork by **Ashley Wood**

Lettered by **Robbie Robbins**

Edited by **Jeff Mariotte**

Design by **Robbie Robbins**

Published by
**Titan Books**
A division of Titan Publishing Group Ltd.
144 Southwark St
London SE1 0UP

First edition: March 2004

10 9 8 7 6 5 4 3 2 1



A CIP catalogue record for this title is available from the British Library.

Printed in Italy.

Also available from Titan Books:
*CSI: Crime Scene Investigation* – Serial (ISBN: 1 84023 771 6)

What did you think of this book? We love to hear from our readers. Please email us at: readerfeedback@titanemail.com, or write to us at the above address.

You can also visit us at **www.titanbooks.com**

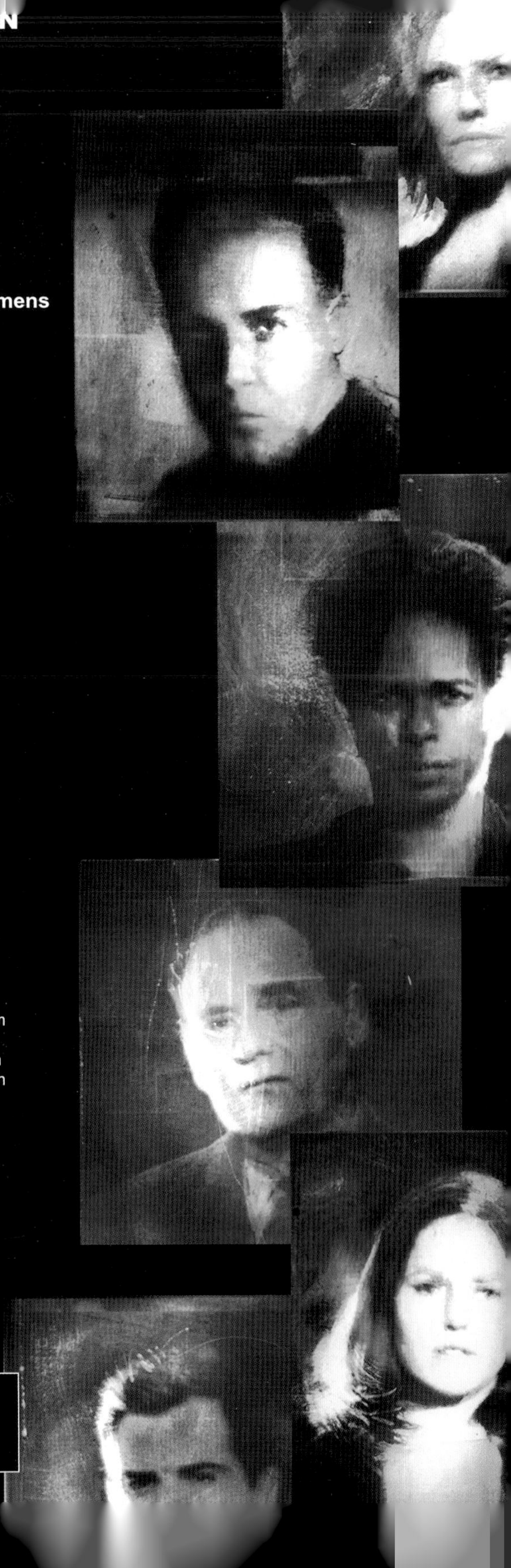

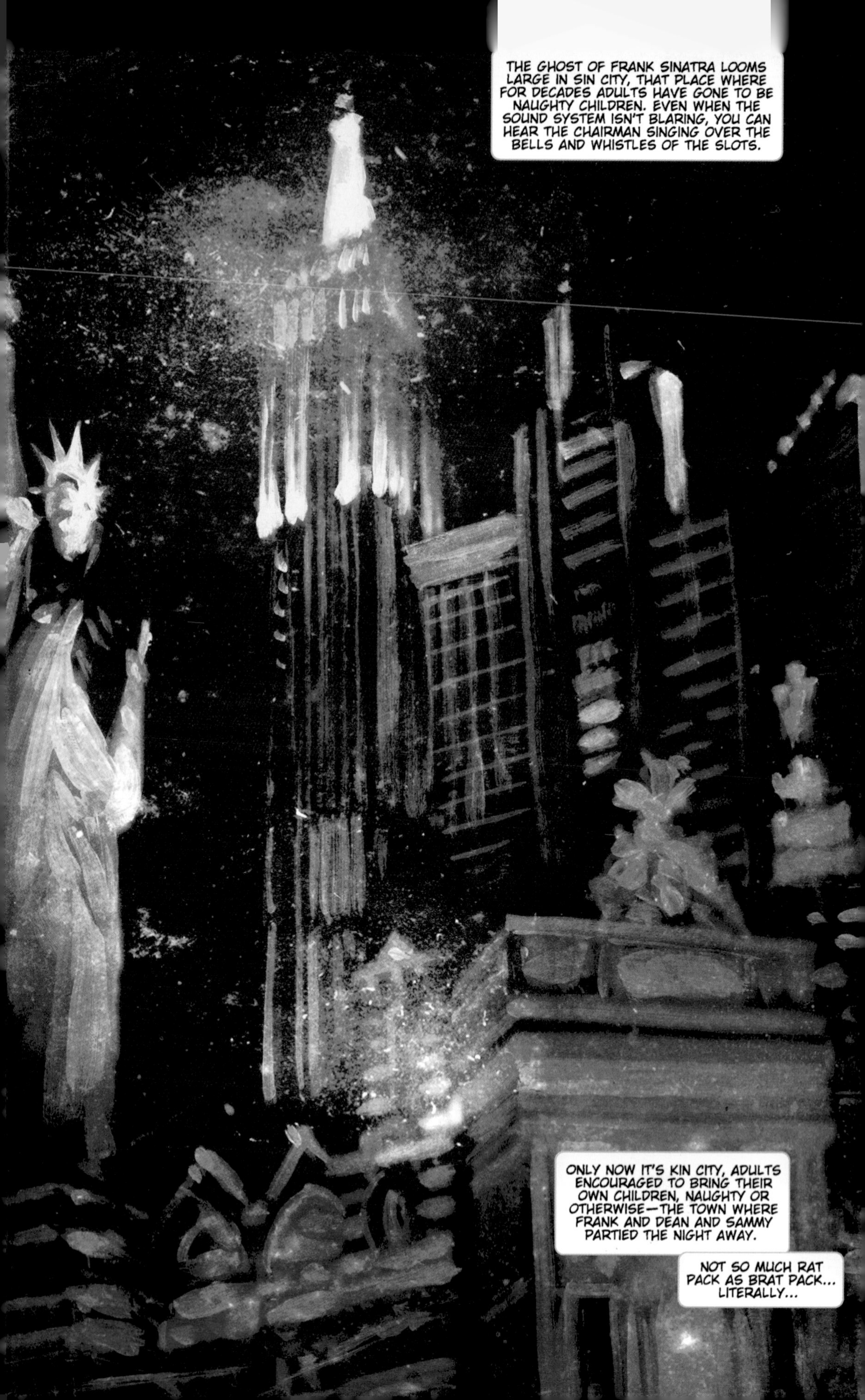
THE GHOST OF FRANK SINATRA LOOMS LARGE IN SIN CITY, THAT PLACE WHERE FOR DECADES ADULTS HAVE GONE TO BE NAUGHTY CHILDREN. EVEN WHEN THE SOUND SYSTEM ISN'T BLARING, YOU CAN HEAR THE CHAIRMAN SINGING OVER THE BELLS AND WHISTLES OF THE SLOTS.
ONLY NOW IT'S KIN CITY, ADULTS ENCOURAGED TO BRING THEIR OWN CHILDREN, NAUGHTY OR OTHERWISE—THE TOWN WHERE FRANK AND DEAN AND SAMMY PARTIED THE NIGHT AWAY.
NOT SO MUCH RAT PACK AS BRAT PACK... LITERALLY...

"SPEND YOUR DAYS WITH THE KIDS," THE TRAVEL AGENTS SAY, "AND YOUR NIGHTS IN THE CASINO." A ROLLER-COASTER RIDE BY SUNLIGHT PROVIDES THRILLS...

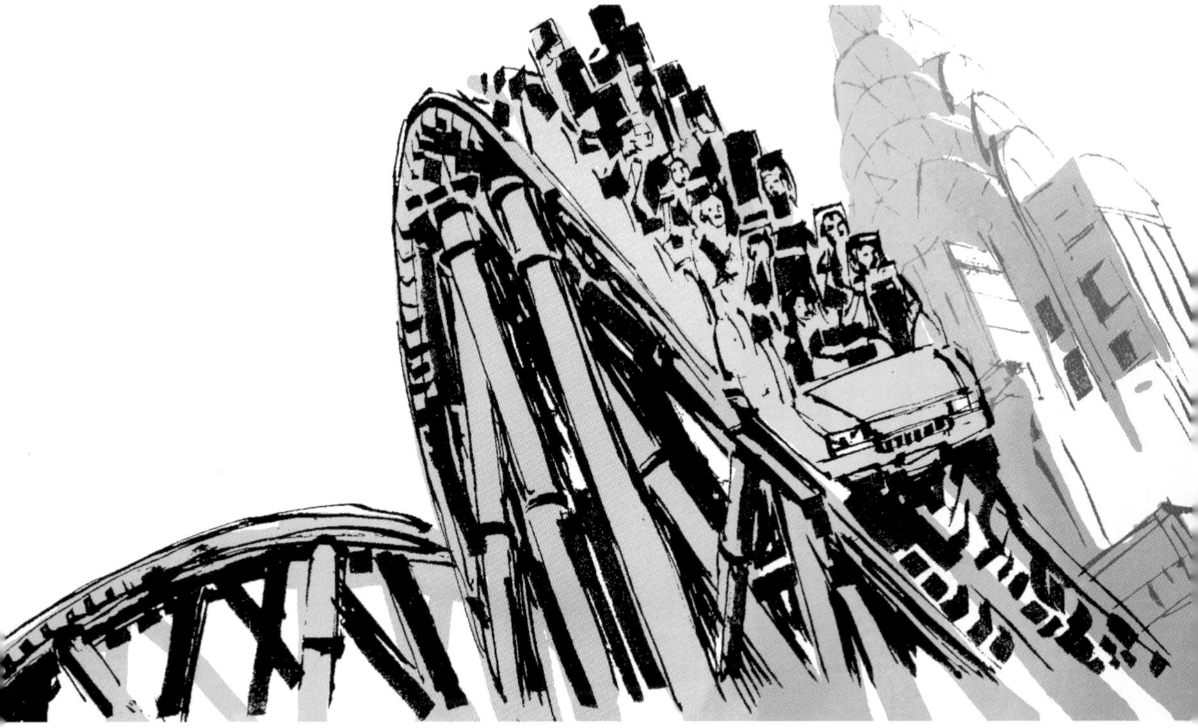

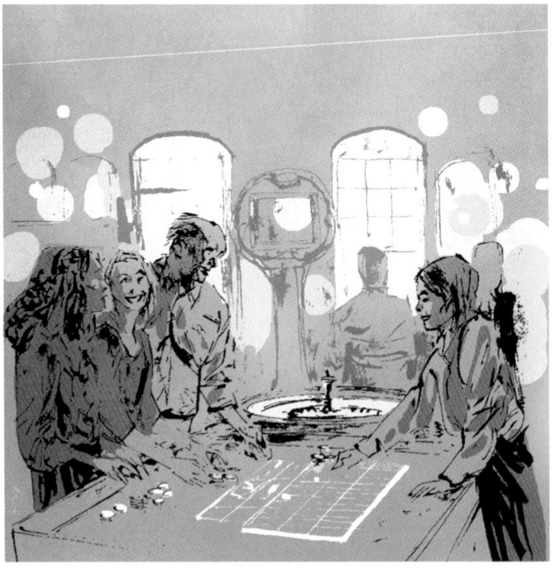
...WHILE AT NIGHT, AT THE TABLES, MOM AND DAD TAKE THEIR OWN RIDE (OR PERHAPS ARE TAKEN FOR ONE).

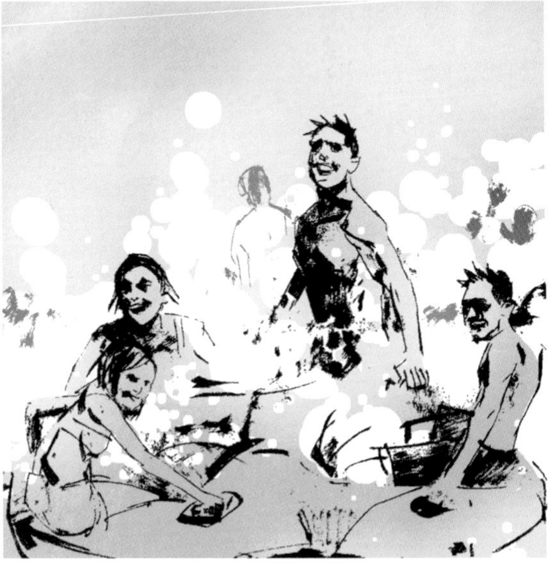
AND THE PARENTS MAY HIT THE WET BAR IN THEIR SUITE, BUT NOT BEFORE THE KIDS HIT THE WATER PARK... IT'S A FAMILY-FRIENDLY, ALL-AMERICAN TOWN.

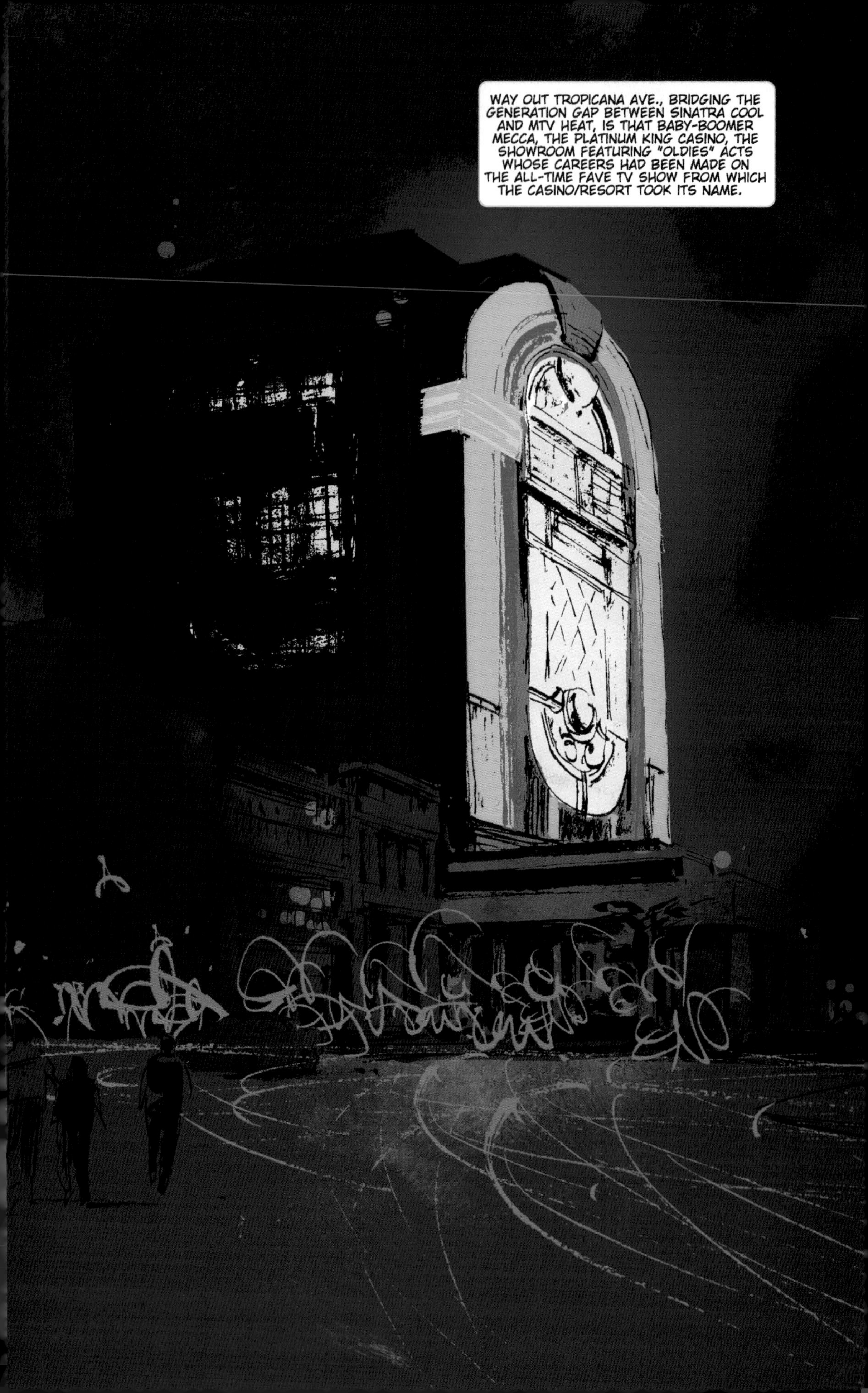
WAY OUT TROPICANA AVE., BRIDGING THE GENERATION GAP BETWEEN SINATRA COOL AND MTV HEAT, IS THAT BABY-BOOMER MECCA, THE PLATINUM KING CASINO, THE SHOWROOM FEATURING "OLDIES" ACTS WHOSE CAREERS HAD BEEN MADE ON THE ALL-TIME FAVE TV SHOW FROM WHICH THE CASINO/RESORT TOOK ITS NAME.

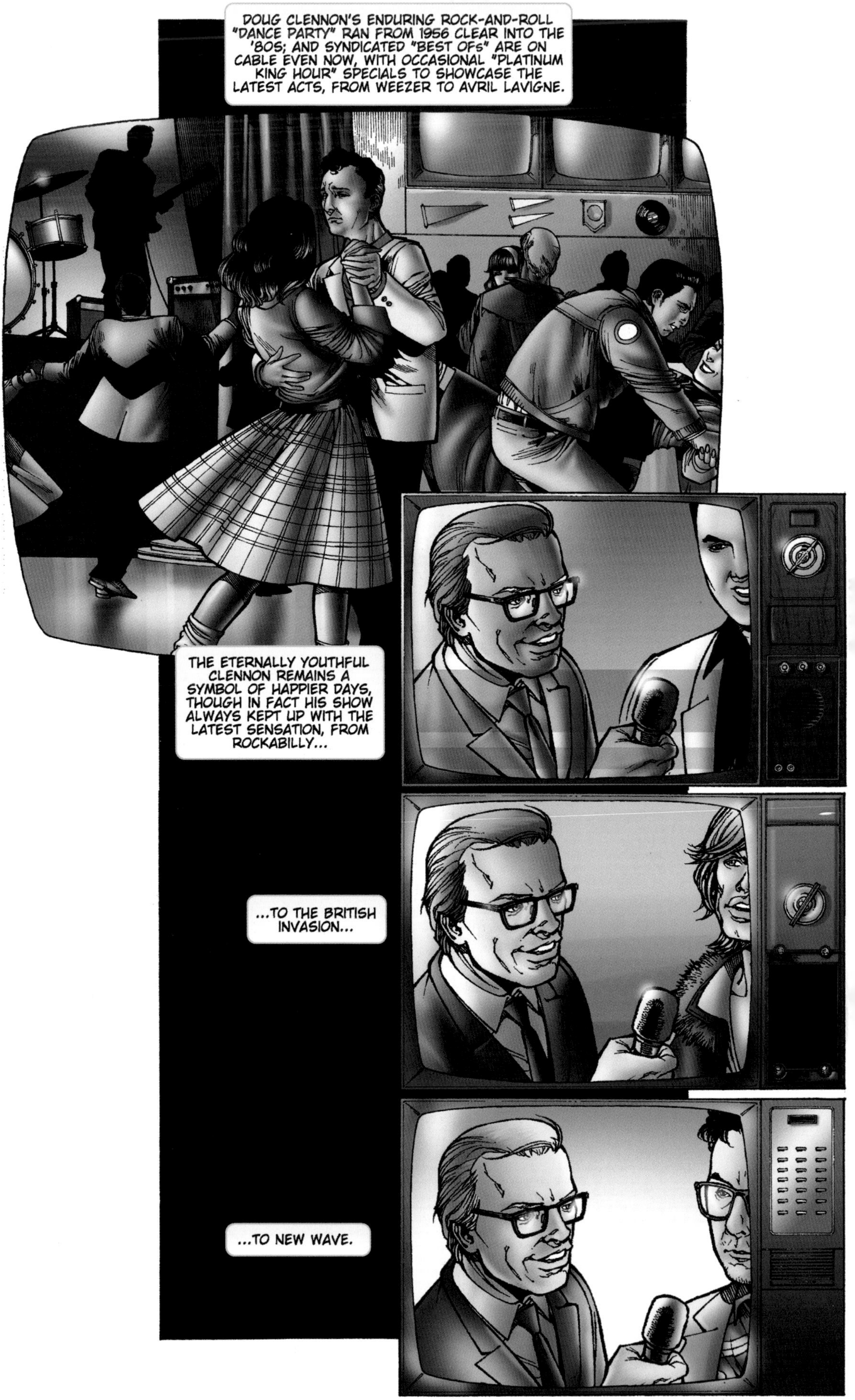
DOUG CLENNON'S ENDURING ROCK-AND-ROLL "DANCE PARTY" RAN FROM 1956 CLEAR INTO THE '80S; AND SYNDICATED "BEST OFs" ARE ON CABLE EVEN NOW, WITH OCCASIONAL "PLATINUM KING HOUR" SPECIALS TO SHOWCASE THE LATEST ACTS, FROM WEEZER TO AVRIL LAVIGNE.
THE ETERNALLY YOUTHFUL CLENNON REMAINS A SYMBOL OF HAPPIER DAYS, THOUGH IN FACT HIS SHOW ALWAYS KEPT UP WITH THE LATEST SENSATION, FROM ROCKABILLY...
...TO THE BRITISH INVASION...
...TO NEW WAVE.

MR. CLENNON, WHAT MAKES YOUR OLDIES OLYMPICS A SPECIAL EVENT AND NOT JUST ANOTHER NOSTALGIA SHOW?

WELL, CINDY, IT'S SIMPLY THE FIRST TIME TWENTY... *TWENTY*... OF THE TOP ACTS OF THE '50S AND '60S HAVE APPEARED TOGETHER ON THE SAME STAGE.

**OLDIES OLYMPICS!** ALL-STAR LINE UP!

"WE HAVE ROCKABILLY SUPERSTARS OF THE '50S, TEEN IDOLS FROM THE EARLY '60S, AND THE GREATEST DOO WOP ACTS, ALL WITH SURVIVING ORIGINAL MEMBERS, RE-GROUPING FOR THE EVENT...

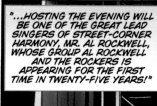

"...HOSTING THE EVENING WILL BE ONE OF THE GREAT LEAD SINGERS OF STREET-CORNER HARMONY, MR. AL ROCKWELL, WHOSE GROUP AL ROCKWELL AND THE ROCKERS IS APPEARING FOR THE FIRST TIME IN TWENTY-FIVE YEARS!"

AND, AS YOU KNOW, CINDY, SOME OF TODAY'S MOST EXCITING PERFORMERS ARE EMERGING RIGHT HERE IN LAS VEGAS.

YOU DON'T MEAN THE LOCAL RETRO-PUNK MOVEMENT, DO YOU, DOUG? *PUNKS AND RAPPERS,* AT THE PLATINUM KING?

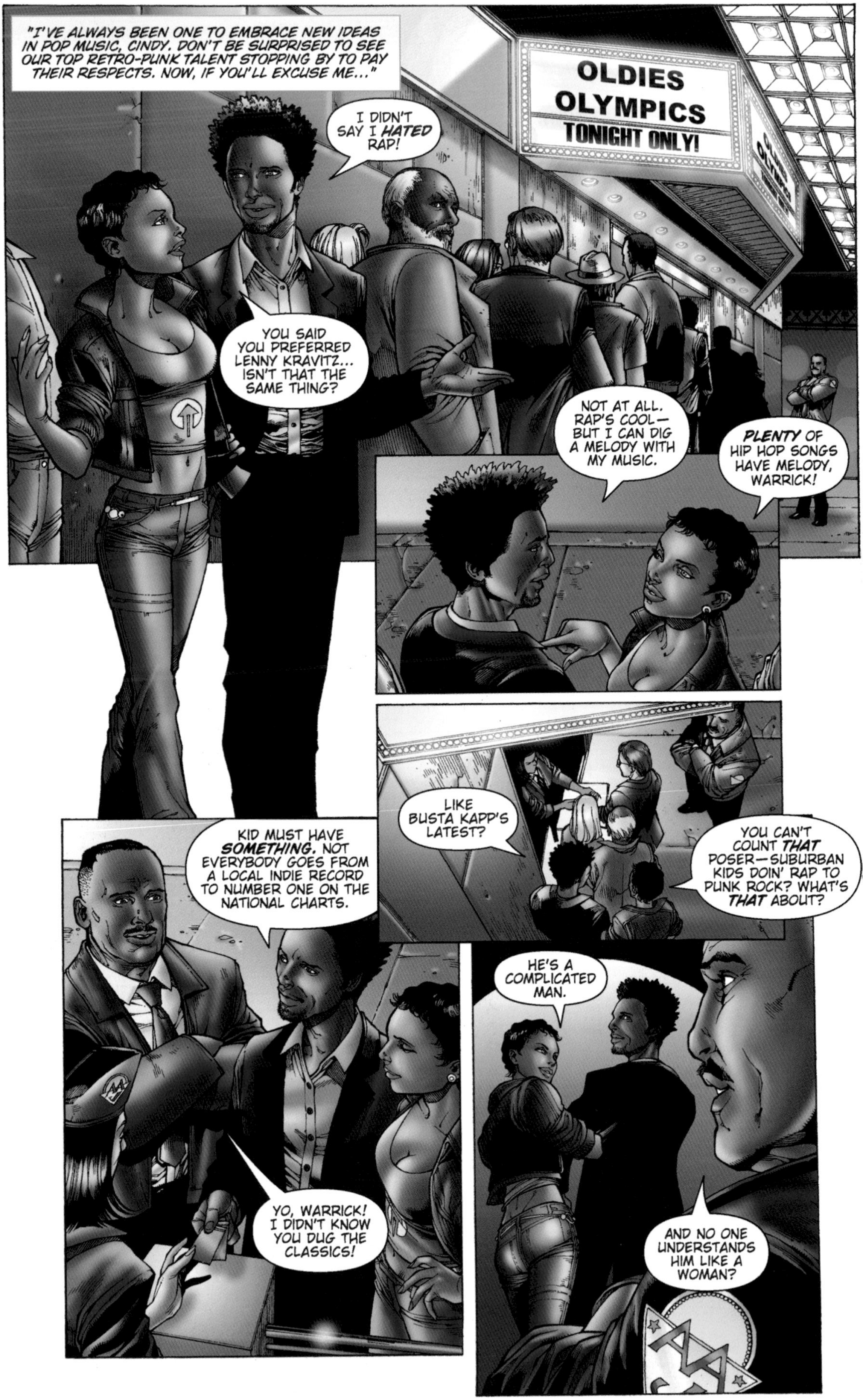
"I'VE ALWAYS BEEN ONE TO EMBRACE NEW IDEAS IN POP MUSIC, CINDY. DON'T BE SURPRISED TO SEE OUR TOP RETRO-PUNK TALENT STOPPING BY TO PAY THEIR RESPECTS. NOW, IF YOU'LL EXCUSE ME..."
OLDIES OLYMPICS TONIGHT ONLY!
I DIDN'T SAY I HATED RAP!
YOU SAID YOU PREFERRED LENNY KRAVITZ... ISN'T THAT THE SAME THING?
NOT AT ALL. RAP'S COOL— BUT I CAN DIG A MELODY WITH MY MUSIC.
PLENTY OF HIP HOP SONGS HAVE MELODY, WARRICK!
LIKE BUSTA KAPP'S LATEST?
YOU CAN'T COUNT THAT POSER—SUBURBAN KIDS DOIN' RAP TO PUNK ROCK? WHAT'S THAT ABOUT?
KID MUST HAVE SOMETHING. NOT EVERYBODY GOES FROM A LOCAL INDIE RECORD TO NUMBER ONE ON THE NATIONAL CHARTS.
YO, WARRICK! I DIDN'T KNOW YOU DUG THE CLASSICS!
HE'S A COMPLICATED MAN.
AND NO ONE UNDERSTANDS HIM LIKE A WOMAN?

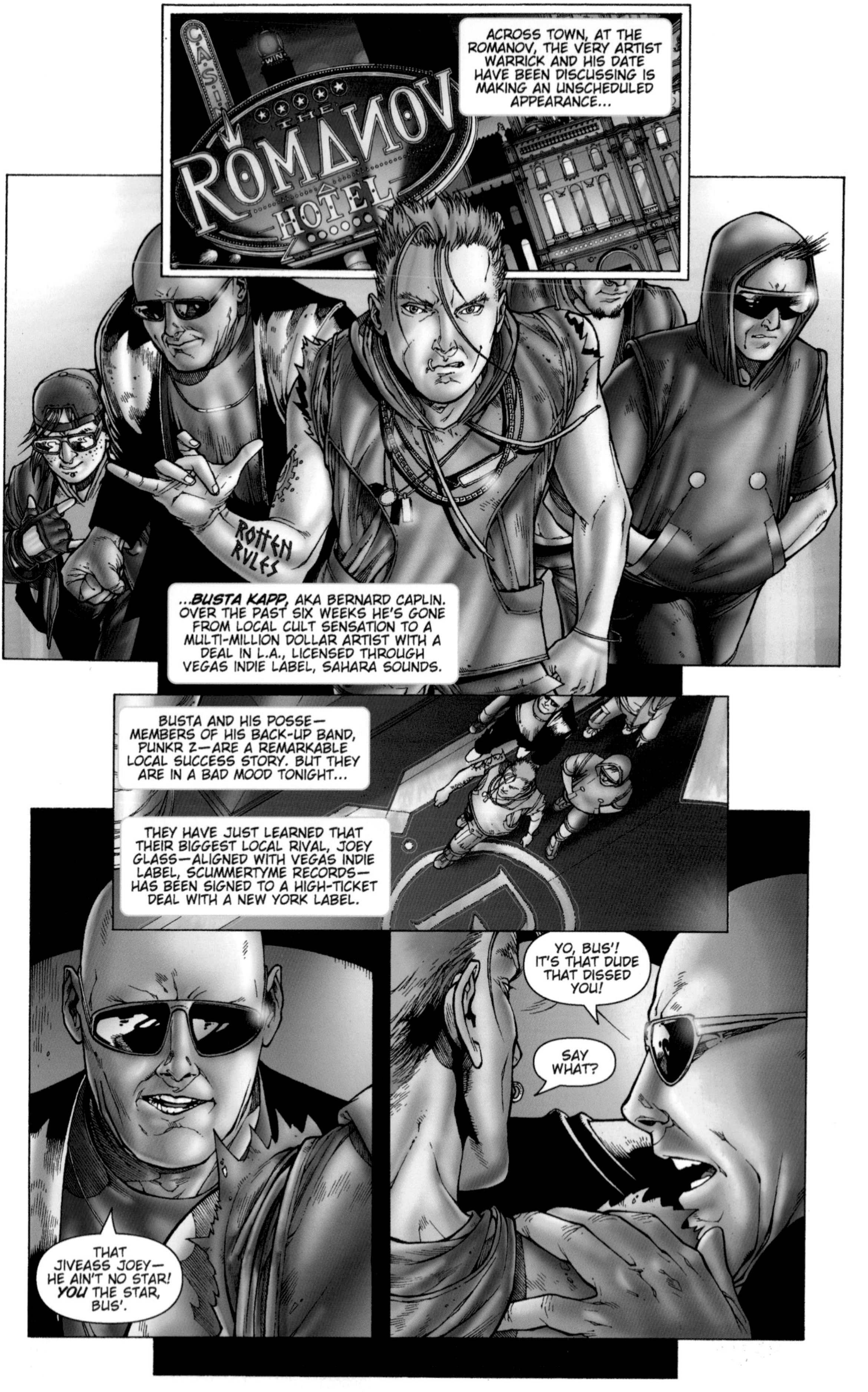

CASINO
WIN
THE ROMANOV HOTEL
ACROSS TOWN, AT THE ROMANOV, THE VERY ARTIST WARRICK AND HIS DATE HAVE BEEN DISCUSSING IS MAKING AN UNSCHEDULED APPEARANCE...
ROTTEN RULES
...BUSTA KAPP, AKA BERNARD CAPLIN. OVER THE PAST SIX WEEKS HE'S GONE FROM LOCAL CULT SENSATION TO A MULTI-MILLION DOLLAR ARTIST WITH A DEAL IN L.A., LICENSED THROUGH VEGAS INDIE LABEL, SAHARA SOUNDS.
BUSTA AND HIS POSSE—MEMBERS OF HIS BACK-UP BAND, PUNKR Z—ARE A REMARKABLE LOCAL SUCCESS STORY. BUT THEY ARE IN A BAD MOOD TONIGHT...
THEY HAVE JUST LEARNED THAT THEIR BIGGEST LOCAL RIVAL, JOEY GLASS—ALIGNED WITH VEGAS INDIE LABEL, SCUMMERTYME RECORDS—HAS BEEN SIGNED TO A HIGH-TICKET DEAL WITH A NEW YORK LABEL.
THAT JIVEASS JOEY—HE AIN'T NO STAR! ***YOU*** THE STAR, BUS'.
YO, BUS'! IT'S THAT DUDE THAT DISSED YOU!
SAY WHAT?

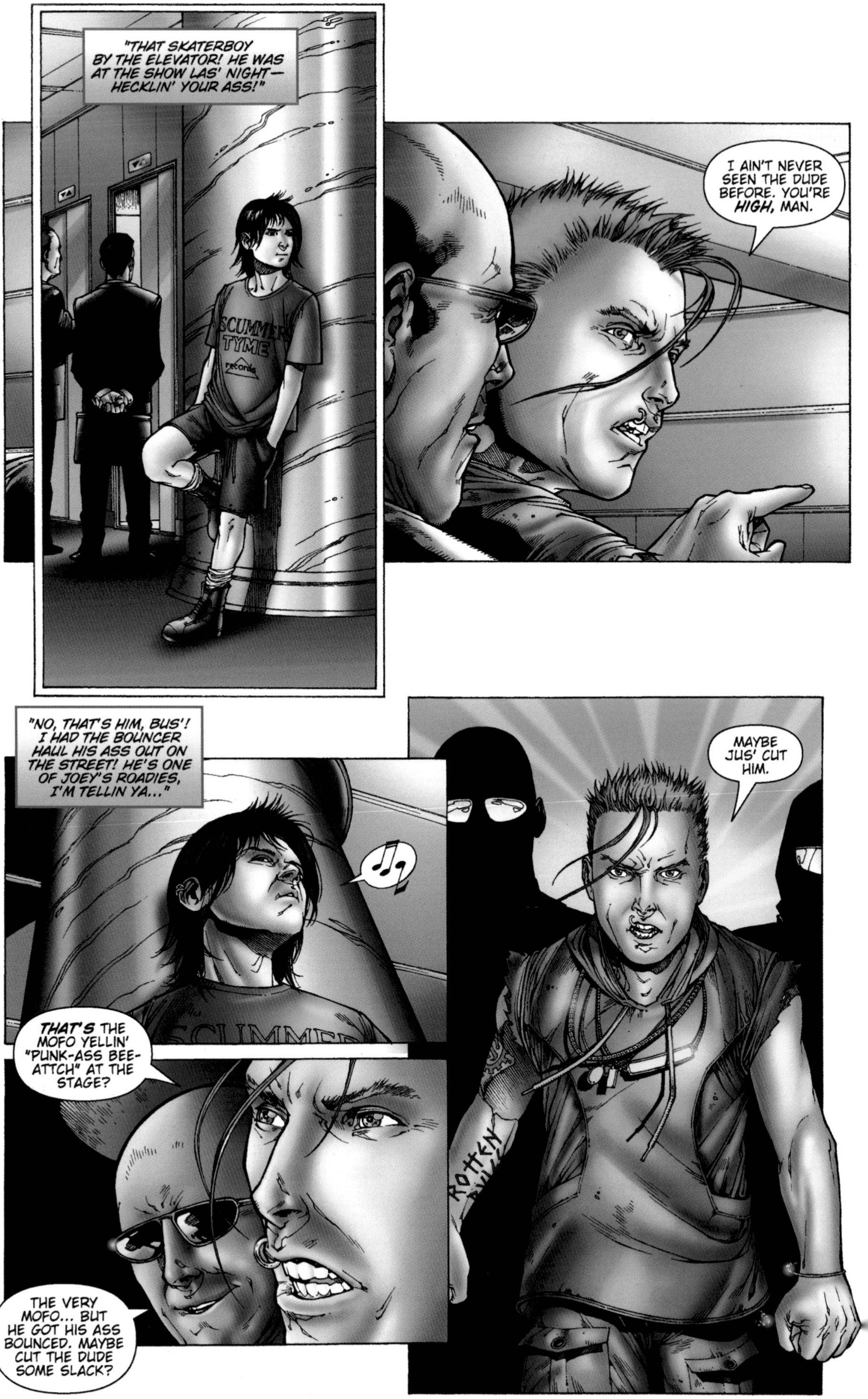
"THAT SKATERBOY BY THE ELEVATOR! HE WAS AT THE SHOW LAS' NIGHT— HECKLIN' YOUR ASS!"
SCUMMER TYME records
I AIN'T NEVER SEEN THE DUDE BEFORE. YOU'RE HIGH, MAN.
"NO, THAT'S HIM, BUS'! I HAD THE BOUNCER HAUL HIS ASS OUT ON THE STREET! HE'S ONE OF JOEY'S ROADIES, I'M TELLIN YA..."
THAT'S THE MOFO YELLIN' "PUNK-ASS BEE-ATTCH" AT THE STAGE?
THE VERY MOFO... BUT HE GOT HIS ASS BOUNCED. MAYBE CUT THE DUDE SOME SLACK?
MAYBE JUS' CUT HIM.

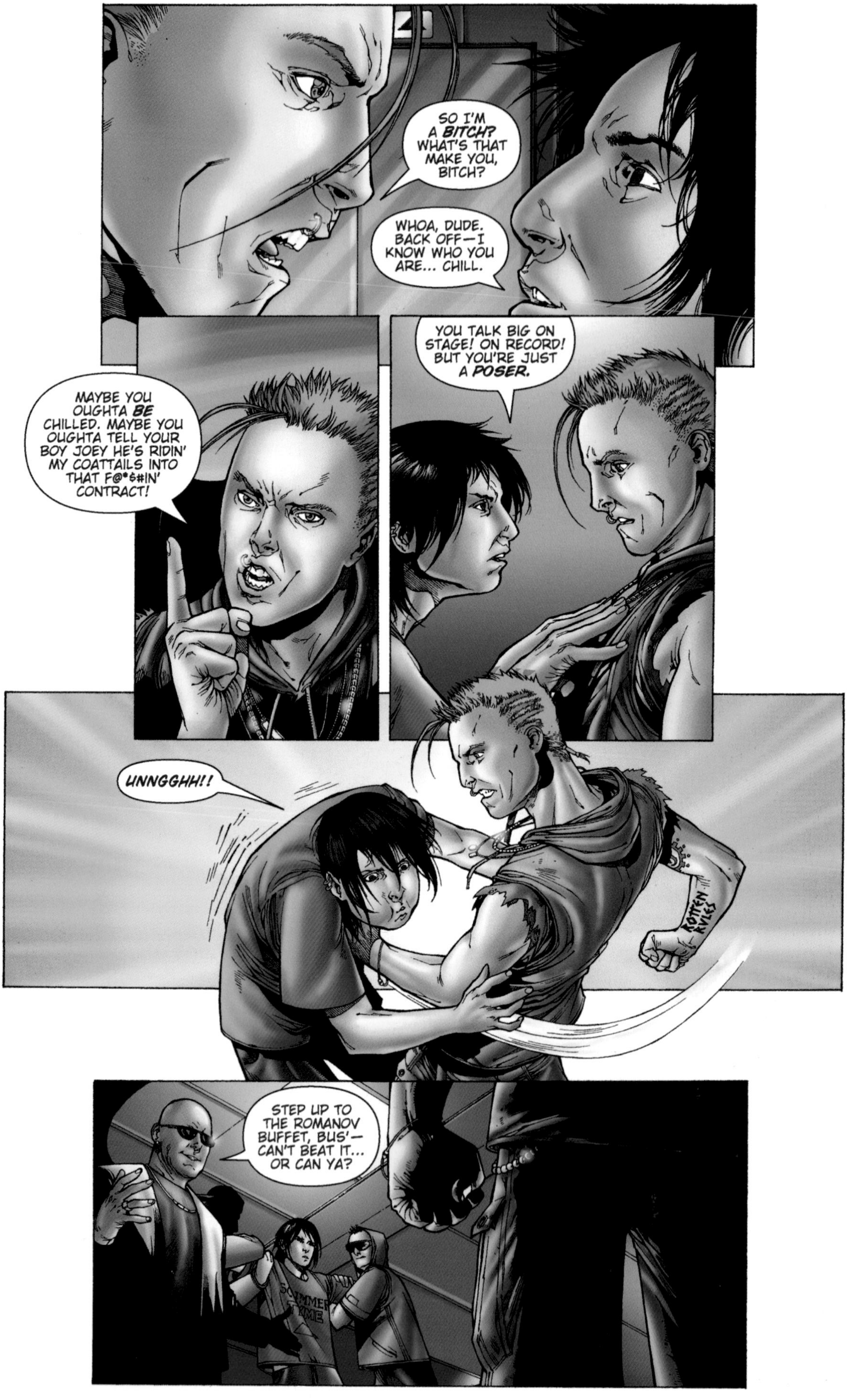
SO I'M A BITCH? WHAT'S THAT MAKE YOU, BITCH?
WHOA, DUDE. BACK OFF—I KNOW WHO YOU ARE... CHILL.
MAYBE YOU OUGHTA BE CHILLED. MAYBE YOU OUGHTA TELL YOUR BOY JOEY HE'S RIDIN' MY COATTAILS INTO THAT F@*$#IN' CONTRACT!
YOU TALK BIG ON STAGE! ON RECORD! BUT YOU'RE JUST A POSER.
UNNGGHH!!
ROTTEN RULES
STEP UP TO THE ROMANOV BUFFET, BUS'—CAN'T BEAT IT... OR CAN YA?

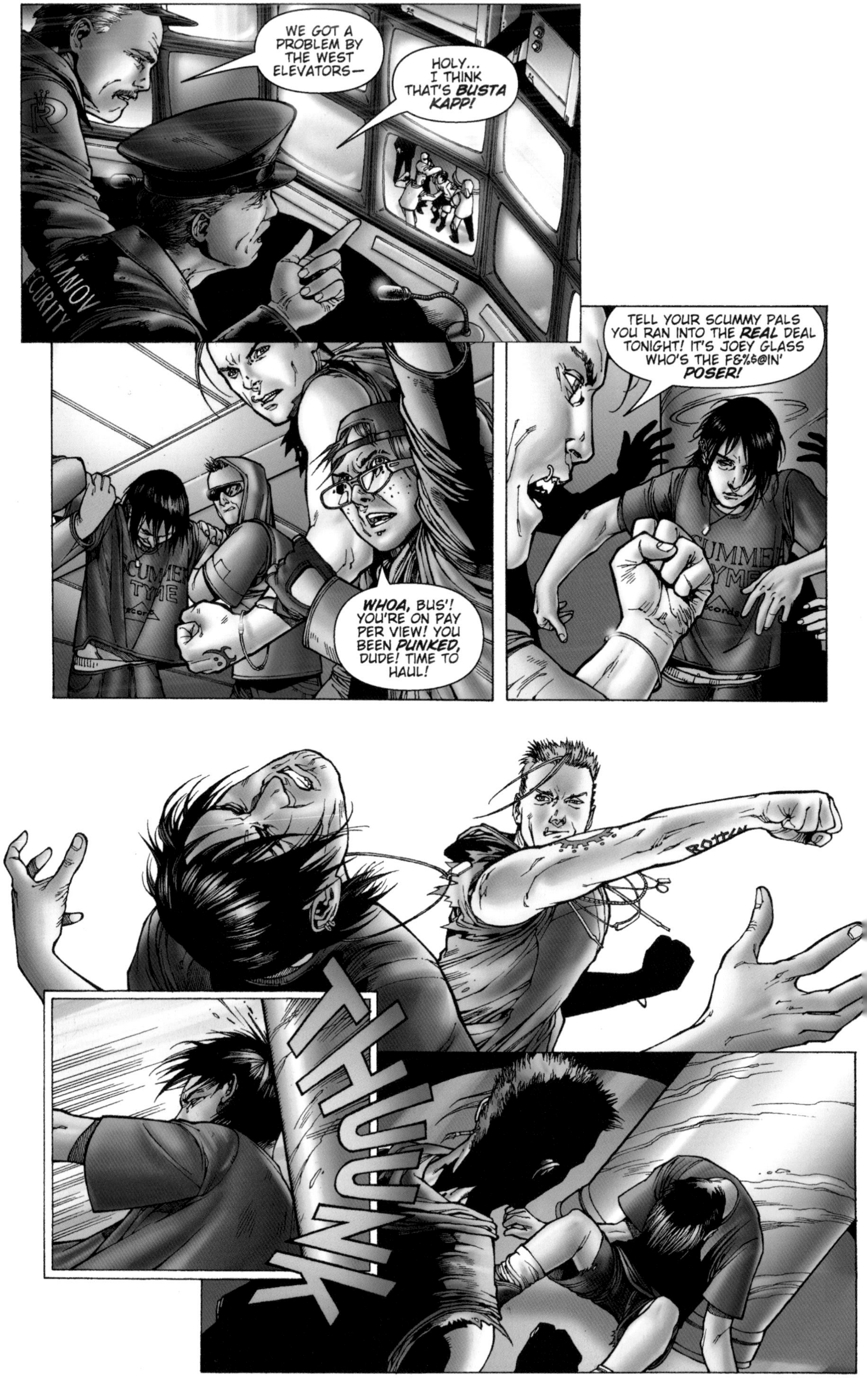
WE GOT A PROBLEM BY THE WEST ELEVATORS—
HOLY... I THINK THAT'S BUSTA KAPP!
ROMANOV SECURITY
WHOA, BUS'! YOU'RE ON PAY PER VIEW! YOU BEEN PUNKED, DUDE! TIME TO HAUL!
TELL YOUR SCUMMY PALS YOU RAN INTO THE REAL DEAL TONIGHT! IT'S JOEY GLASS WHO'S THE F&%$@IN' POSER!
THUNK

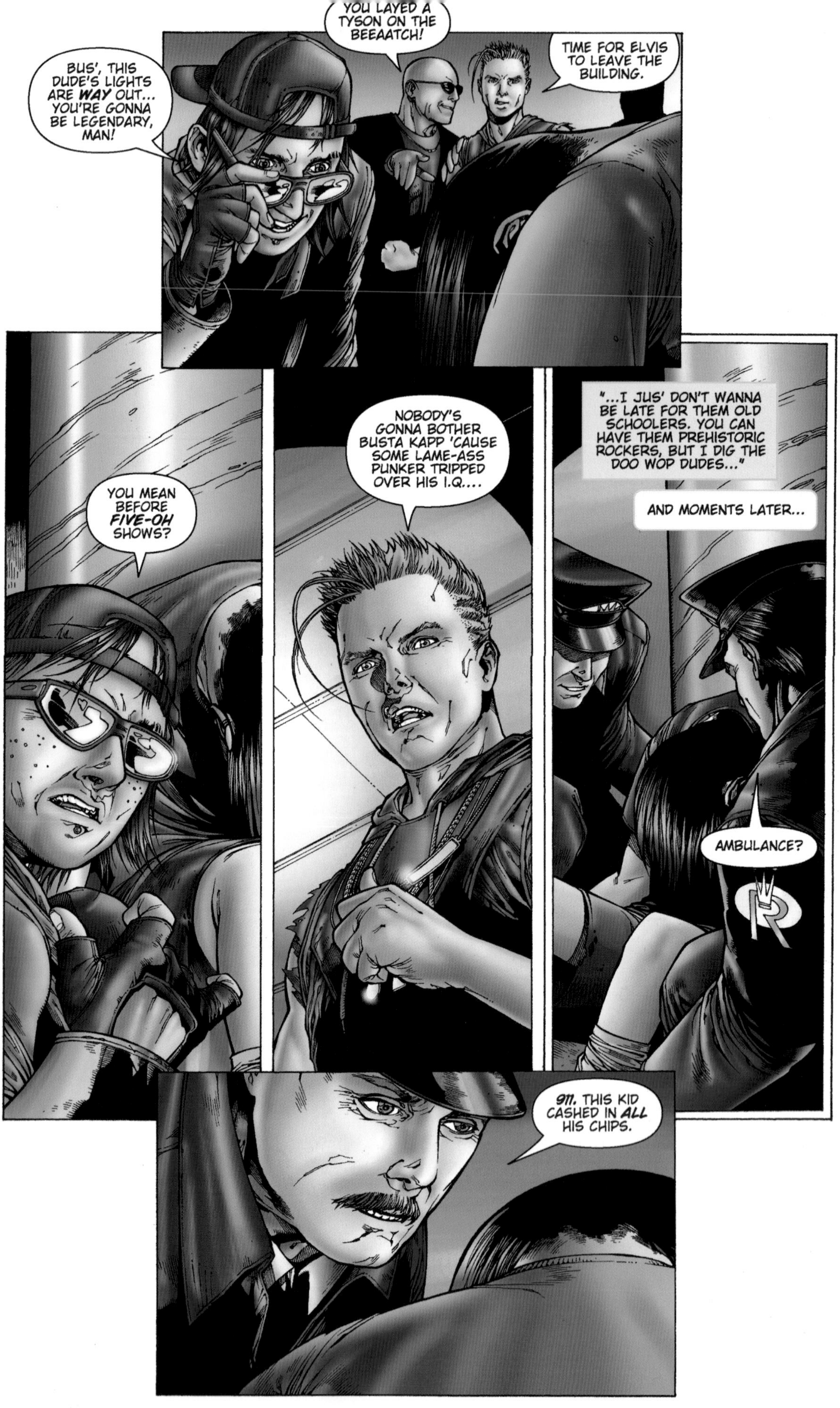
BUS', THIS DUDE'S LIGHTS ARE WAY OUT... YOU'RE GONNA BE LEGENDARY, MAN!
YOU LAYED A TYSON ON THE BEEAATCH!
TIME FOR ELVIS TO LEAVE THE BUILDING.
YOU MEAN BEFORE FIVE-OH SHOWS?
NOBODY'S GONNA BOTHER BUSTA KAPP 'CAUSE SOME LAME-ASS PUNKER TRIPPED OVER HIS I.Q....
"...I JUS' DON'T WANNA BE LATE FOR THEM OLD SCHOOLERS. YOU CAN HAVE THEM PREHISTORIC ROCKERS, BUT I DIG THE DOO WOP DUDES..."
AND MOMENTS LATER...
AMBULANCE?
911. THIS KID CASHED IN ALL HIS CHIPS.

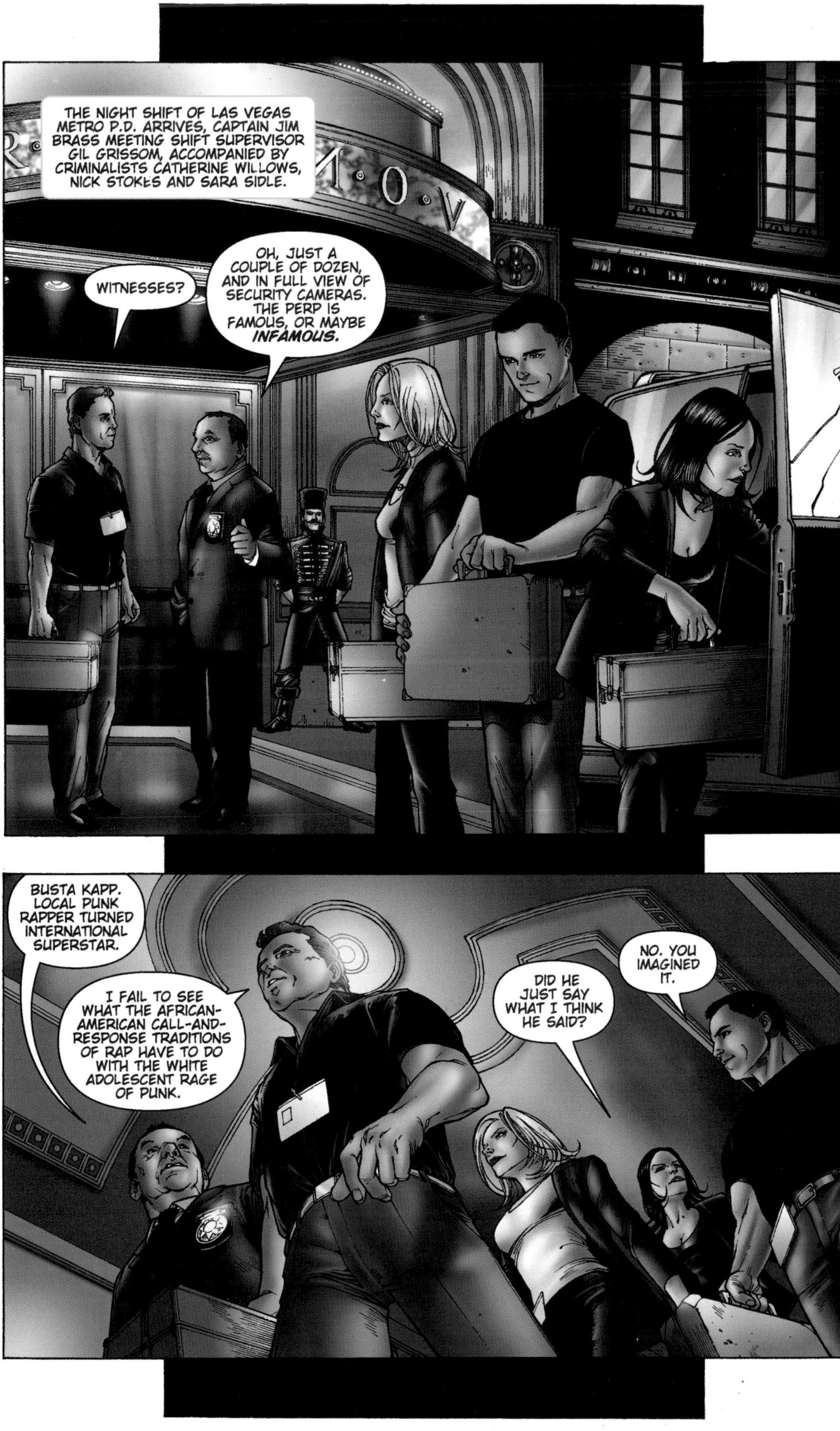
THE NIGHT SHIFT OF LAS VEGAS METRO P.D. ARRIVES, CAPTAIN JIM BRASS MEETING SHIFT SUPERVISOR GIL GRISSOM, ACCOMPANIED BY CRIMINALISTS CATHERINE WILLOWS, NICK STOKES AND SARA SIDLE.
WITNESSES?
OH, JUST A COUPLE OF DOZEN, AND IN FULL VIEW OF SECURITY CAMERAS. THE PERP IS FAMOUS, OR MAYBE *INFAMOUS.*
BUSTA KAPP. LOCAL PUNK RAPPER TURNED INTERNATIONAL SUPERSTAR.
I FAIL TO SEE WHAT THE AFRICAN-AMERICAN CALL-AND-RESPONSE TRADITIONS OF RAP HAVE TO DO WITH THE WHITE ADOLESCENT RAGE OF PUNK.
DID HE JUST SAY WHAT I THINK HE SAID?
NO. YOU IMAGINED IT.

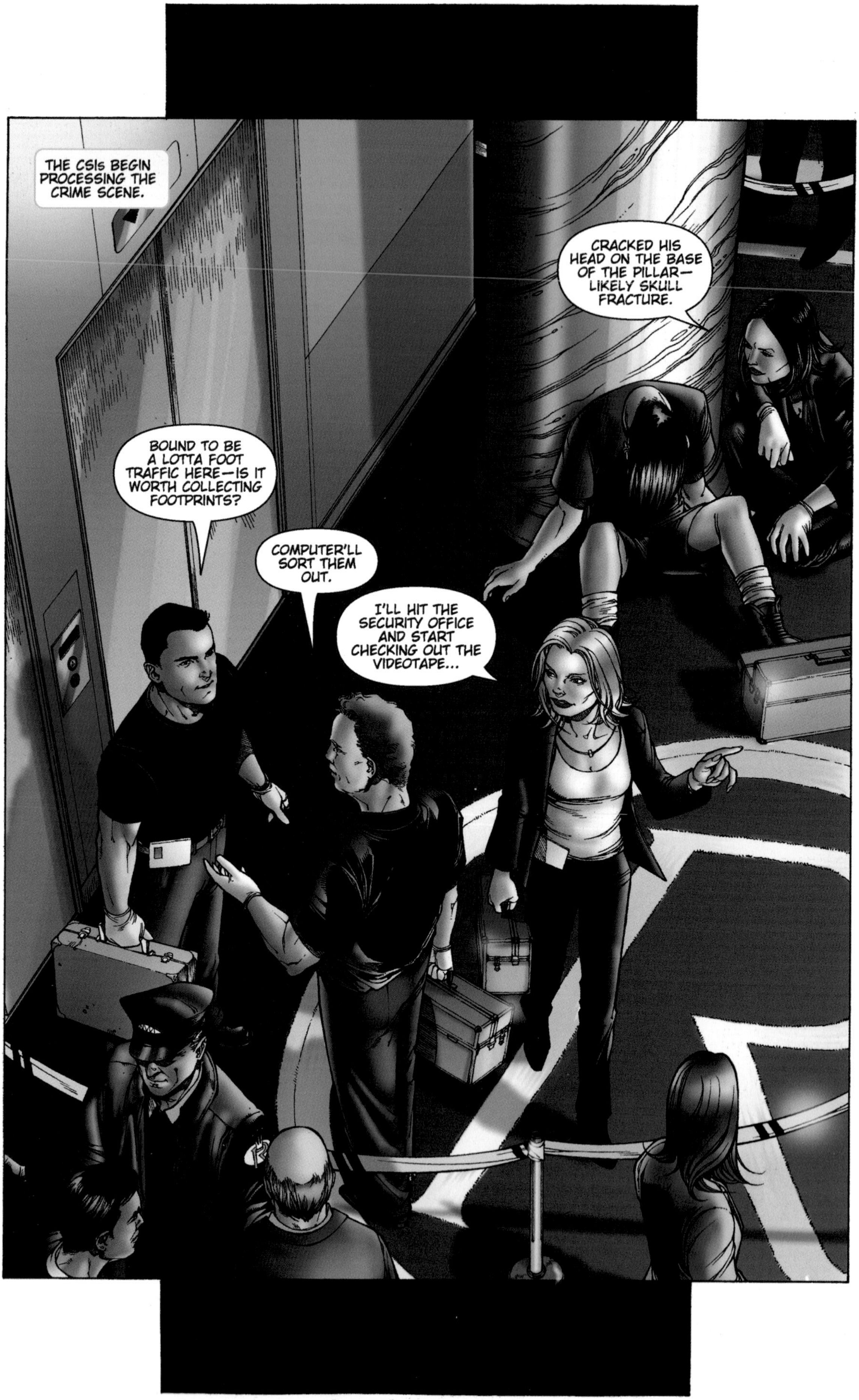
THE CSIs BEGIN PROCESSING THE CRIME SCENE.
CRACKED HIS HEAD ON THE BASE OF THE PILLAR—LIKELY SKULL FRACTURE.
BOUND TO BE A LOTTA FOOT TRAFFIC HERE—IS IT WORTH COLLECTING FOOTPRINTS?
COMPUTER'LL SORT THEM OUT.
I'LL HIT THE SECURITY OFFICE AND START CHECKING OUT THE VIDEOTAPE...

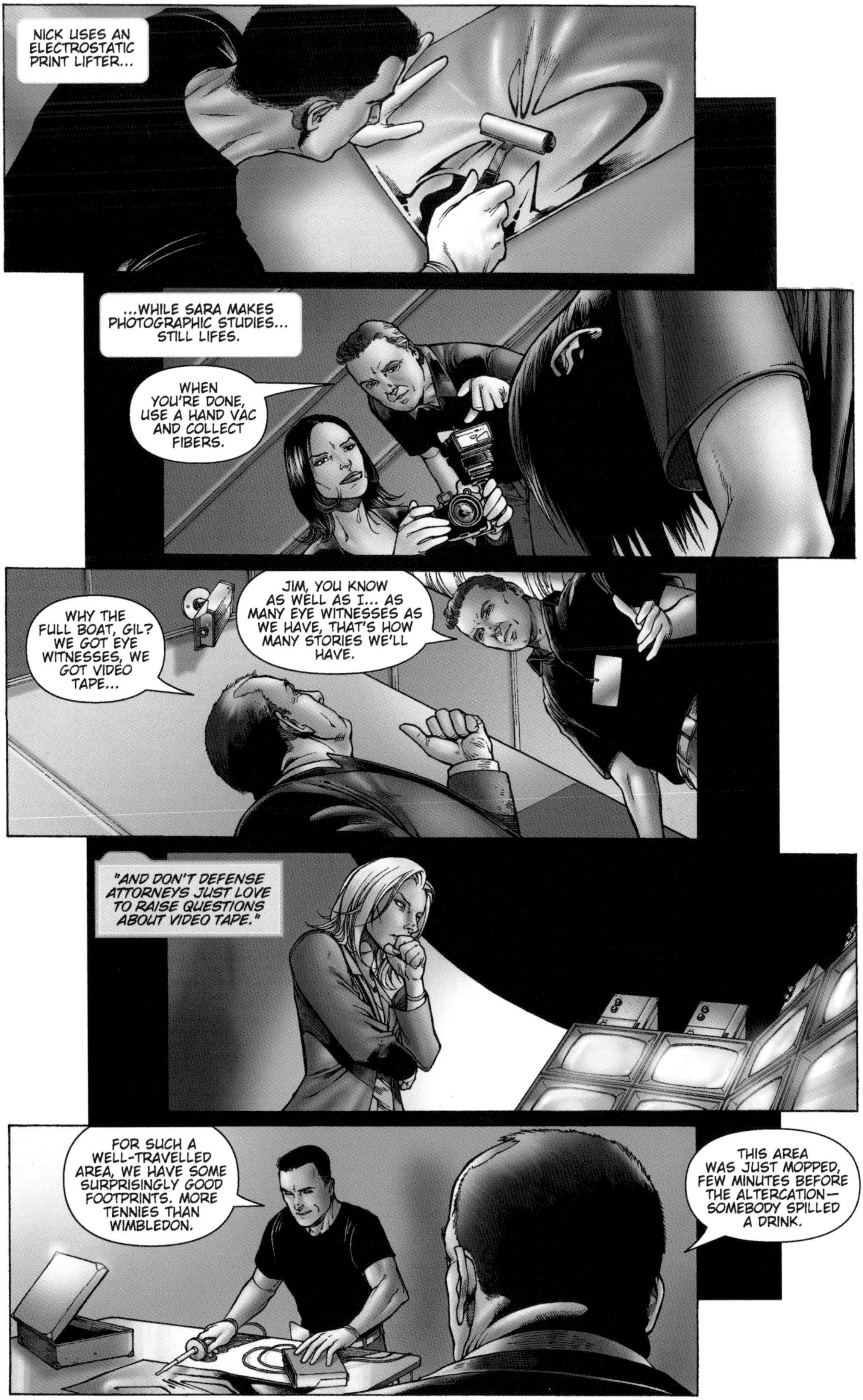
NICK USES AN ELECTROSTATIC PRINT LIFTER...
...WHILE SARA MAKES PHOTOGRAPHIC STUDIES... STILL LIFES.
WHEN YOU'RE DONE, USE A HAND VAC AND COLLECT FIBERS.
WHY THE FULL BOAT, GIL? WE GOT EYE WITNESSES, WE GOT VIDEO TAPE...
JIM, YOU KNOW AS WELL AS I... AS MANY EYE WITNESSES AS WE HAVE, THAT'S HOW MANY STORIES WE'LL HAVE.
"AND DON'T DEFENSE ATTORNEYS JUST LOVE TO RAISE QUESTIONS ABOUT VIDEO TAPE."
FOR SUCH A WELL-TRAVELLED AREA, WE HAVE SOME SURPRISINGLY GOOD FOOTPRINTS. MORE TENNIES THAN WIMBLEDON.
THIS AREA WAS JUST MOPPED, FEW MINUTES BEFORE THE ALTERCATION— SOMEBODY SPILLED A DRINK.

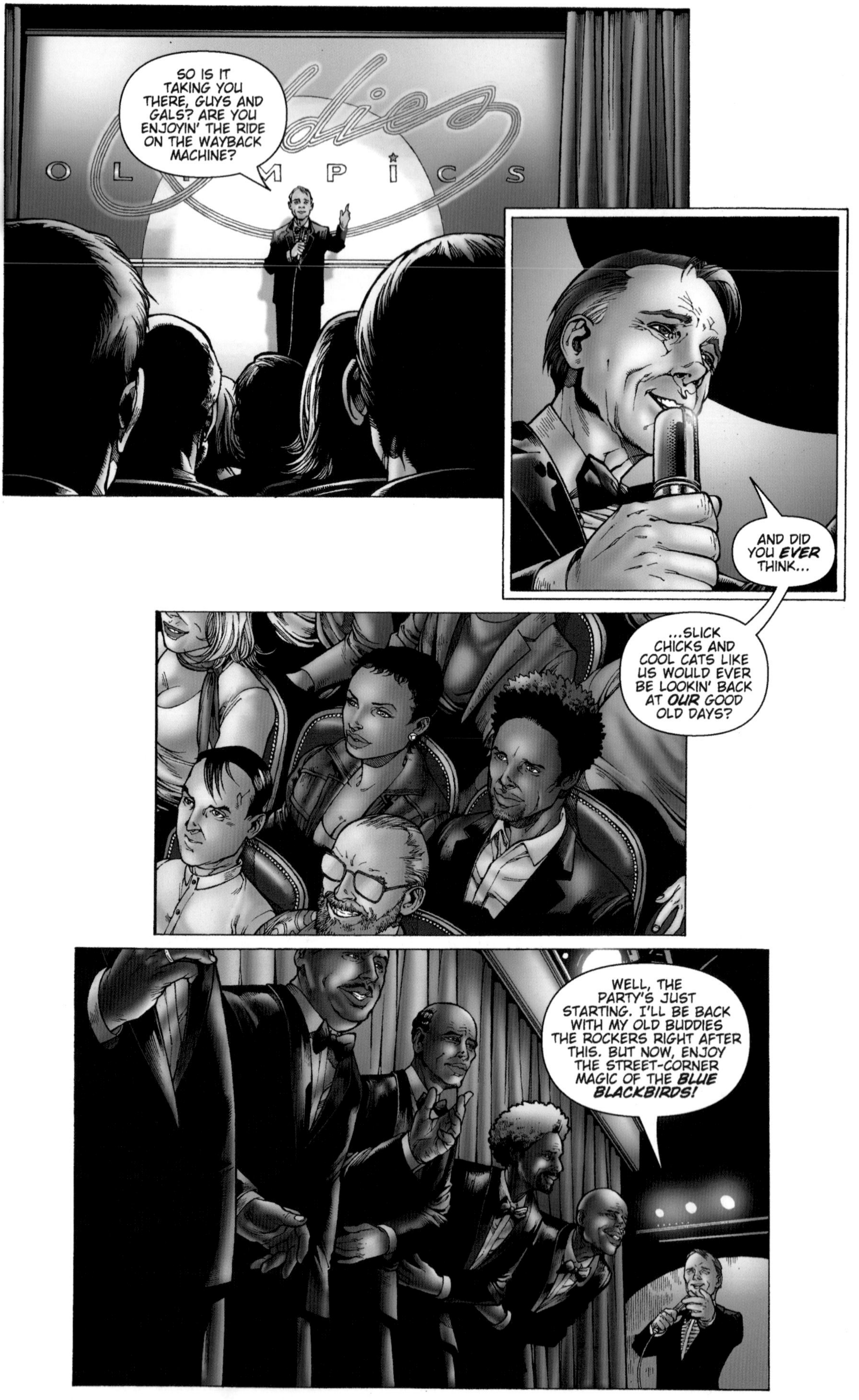
SO IS IT TAKING YOU THERE, GUYS AND GALS? ARE YOU ENJOYIN' THE RIDE ON THE WAYBACK MACHINE?
AND DID YOU **EVER** THINK...
...SLICK CHICKS AND COOL CATS LIKE US WOULD EVER BE LOOKIN' BACK AT **OUR** GOOD OLD DAYS?
WELL, THE PARTY'S JUST STARTING. I'LL BE BACK WITH MY OLD BUDDIES THE ROCKERS RIGHT AFTER THIS. BUT NOW, ENJOY THE STREET-CORNER MAGIC OF THE **BLUE BLACKBIRDS!**

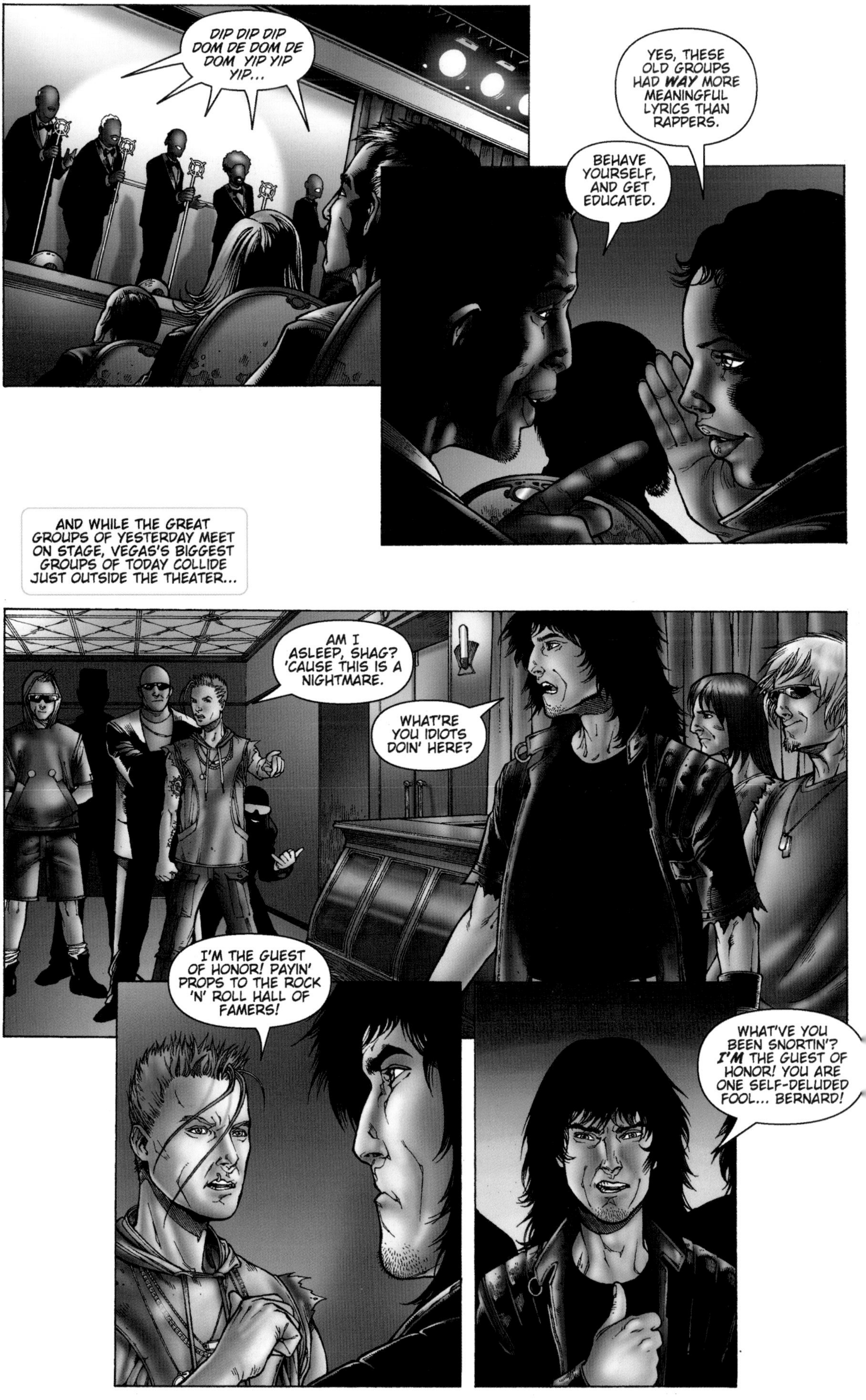
DIP DIP DIP DOM DE DOM DE DOM YIP YIP YIP...
YES, THESE OLD GROUPS HAD WAY MORE MEANINGFUL LYRICS THAN RAPPERS.
BEHAVE YOURSELF, AND GET EDUCATED.
AND WHILE THE GREAT GROUPS OF YESTERDAY MEET ON STAGE, VEGAS'S BIGGEST GROUPS OF TODAY COLLIDE JUST OUTSIDE THE THEATER...
AM I ASLEEP, SHAG? 'CAUSE THIS IS A NIGHTMARE.
WHAT'RE YOU IDIOTS DOIN' HERE?
I'M THE GUEST OF HONOR! PAYIN' PROPS TO THE ROCK 'N' ROLL HALL OF FAMERS!
WHAT'VE YOU BEEN SNORTIN'? I'M THE GUEST OF HONOR! YOU ARE ONE SELF-DELUDED FOOL... BERNARD!

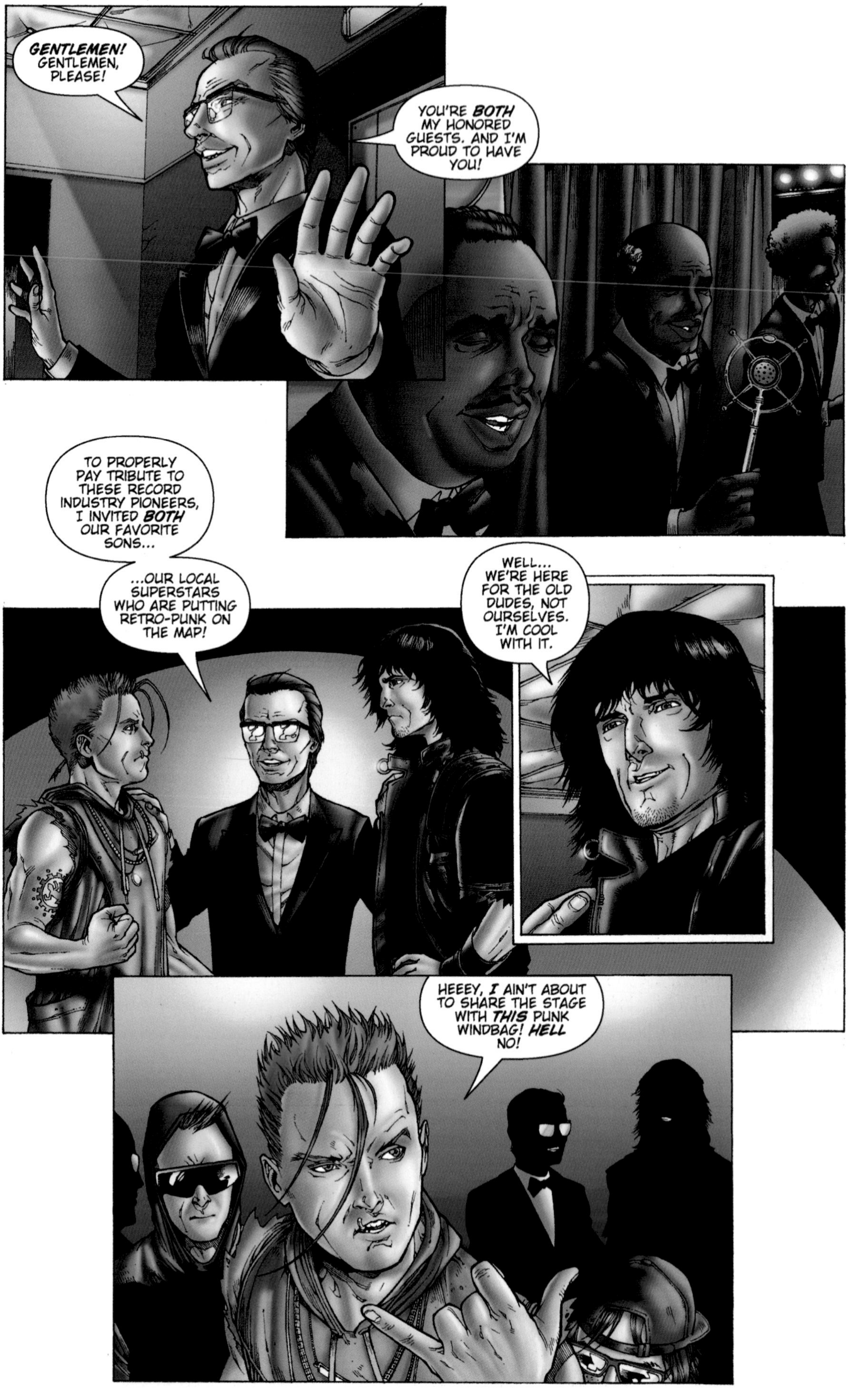
GENTLEMEN! GENTLEMEN, PLEASE!
YOU'RE BOTH MY HONORED GUESTS. AND I'M PROUD TO HAVE YOU!
TO PROPERLY PAY TRIBUTE TO THESE RECORD INDUSTRY PIONEERS, I INVITED BOTH OUR FAVORITE SONS...
...OUR LOCAL SUPERSTARS WHO ARE PUTTING RETRO-PUNK ON THE MAP!
WELL... WE'RE HERE FOR THE OLD DUDES, NOT OURSELVES. I'M COOL WITH IT.
HEEEY, I AIN'T ABOUT TO SHARE THE STAGE WITH THIS PUNK WINDBAG! HELL NO!

AND IN THE SECURITY CENTER OF THE ROMANOV, GIL GRISSOM, CATHERINE WILLOWS, AND CAPTAIN JIM BRASS ARE LOOKING AT VIDEOTAPES OF THE INCIDENT...

"NO DOUBT THAT BUSTA KAPP AND HIS 'POSSE' ARE EQUALLY CULPABLE."

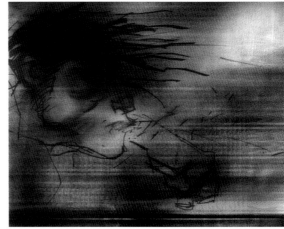

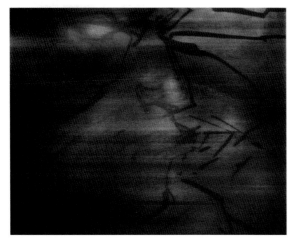

"ALSO NO DOUBT, JIM, THAT THE BLOW DIRECTLY CAUSING THE FATALITY WAS DELIVERED BY BUSTA KAPP."

"NONETHELESS, WE HAVE PLENTY TO DO IN THE LAB. BUT I WOULD AGREE WITH WHAT YOU IMPLY: WE HAVE A CLEAR-CUT SUSPECT AND SEVERAL ACCOMPLICES."

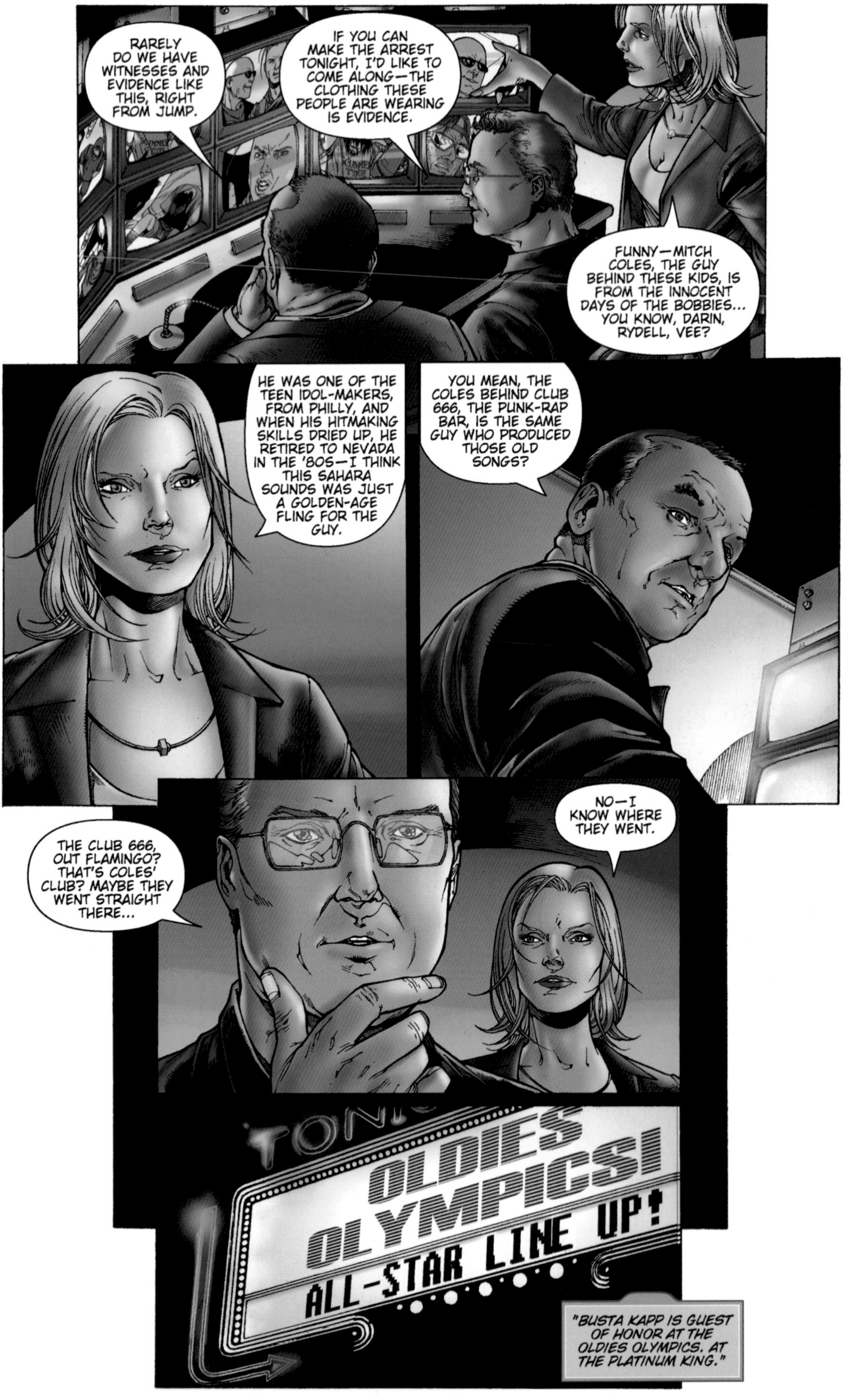
RARELY DO WE HAVE WITNESSES AND EVIDENCE LIKE THIS, RIGHT FROM JUMP.
IF YOU CAN MAKE THE ARREST TONIGHT, I'D LIKE TO COME ALONG—THE CLOTHING THESE PEOPLE ARE WEARING IS EVIDENCE.
FUNNY—MITCH COLES, THE GUY BEHIND THESE KIDS, IS FROM THE INNOCENT DAYS OF THE BOBBIES... YOU KNOW, DARIN, RYDELL, VEE?
HE WAS ONE OF THE TEEN IDOL-MAKERS, FROM PHILLY, AND WHEN HIS HITMAKING SKILLS DRIED UP, HE RETIRED TO NEVADA IN THE '80S—I THINK THIS SAHARA SOUNDS WAS JUST A GOLDEN-AGE FLING FOR THE GUY.
YOU MEAN, THE COLES BEHIND CLUB 666, THE PUNK-RAP BAR, IS THE SAME GUY WHO PRODUCED THOSE OLD SONGS?
THE CLUB 666, OUT FLAMINGO? THAT'S COLES' CLUB? MAYBE THEY WENT STRAIGHT THERE...
NO—I KNOW WHERE THEY WENT.
OLDIES OLYMPICS!
ALL-STAR LINE UP!
"BUSTA KAPP IS GUEST OF HONOR AT THE OLDIES OLYMPICS. AT THE PLATINUM KING."

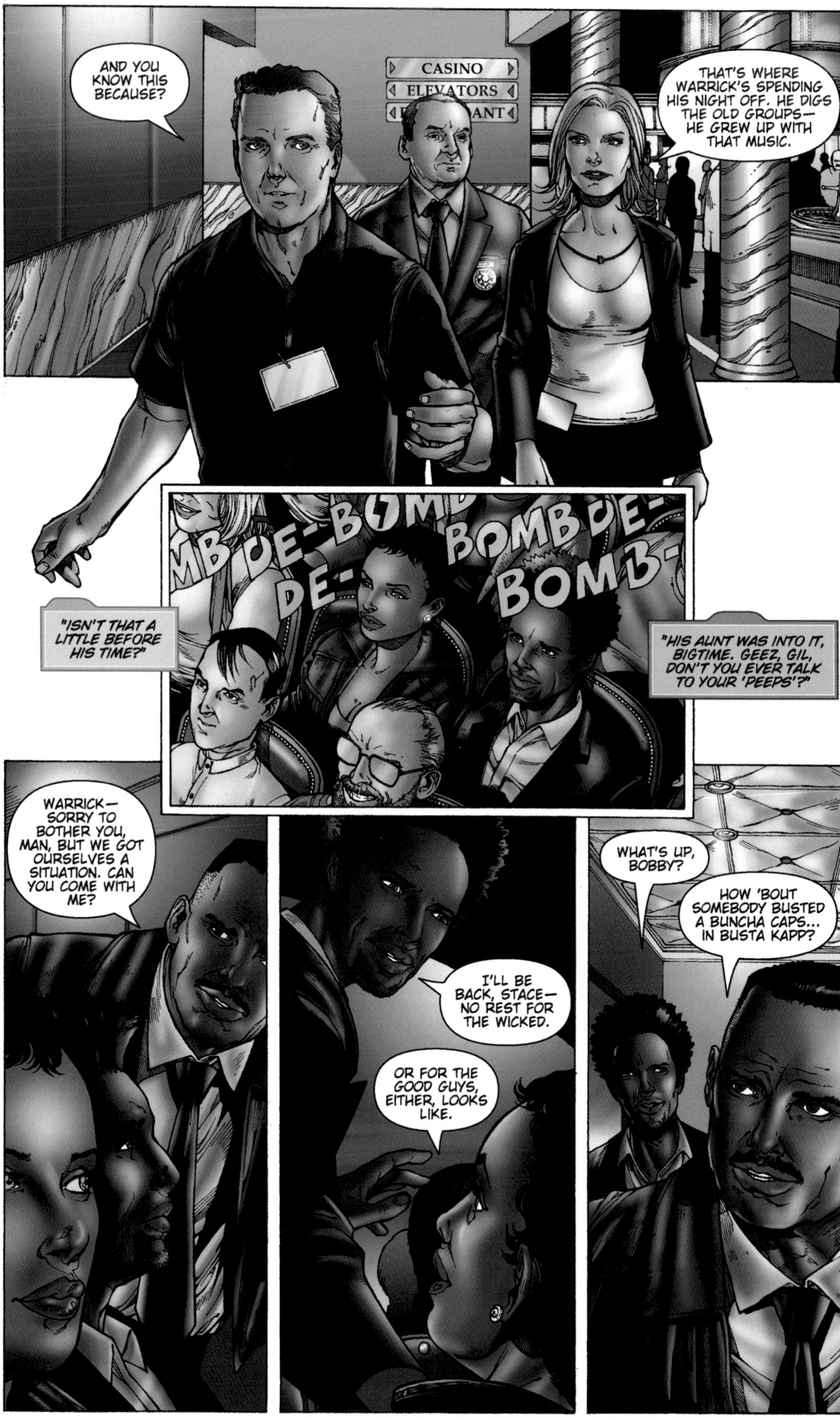
AND YOU KNOW THIS BECAUSE?
CASINO
ELEVATORS
THAT'S WHERE WARRICK'S SPENDING HIS NIGHT OFF. HE DIGS THE OLD GROUPS— HE GREW UP WITH THAT MUSIC.
"ISN'T THAT A LITTLE BEFORE HIS TIME?"
MB DE-BOMB DE- BOMB DE- BOMB-
"HIS AUNT WAS INTO IT, BIGTIME. GEEZ, GIL, DON'T YOU EVER TALK TO YOUR 'PEEPS'?"
WARRICK— SORRY TO BOTHER YOU, MAN, BUT WE GOT OURSELVES A SITUATION. CAN YOU COME WITH ME?
I'LL BE BACK, STACE— NO REST FOR THE WICKED.
OR FOR THE GOOD GUYS, EITHER, LOOKS LIKE.
WHAT'S UP, BOBBY?
HOW 'BOUT SOMEBODY BUSTED A BUNCHA CAPS... IN BUSTA KAPP?

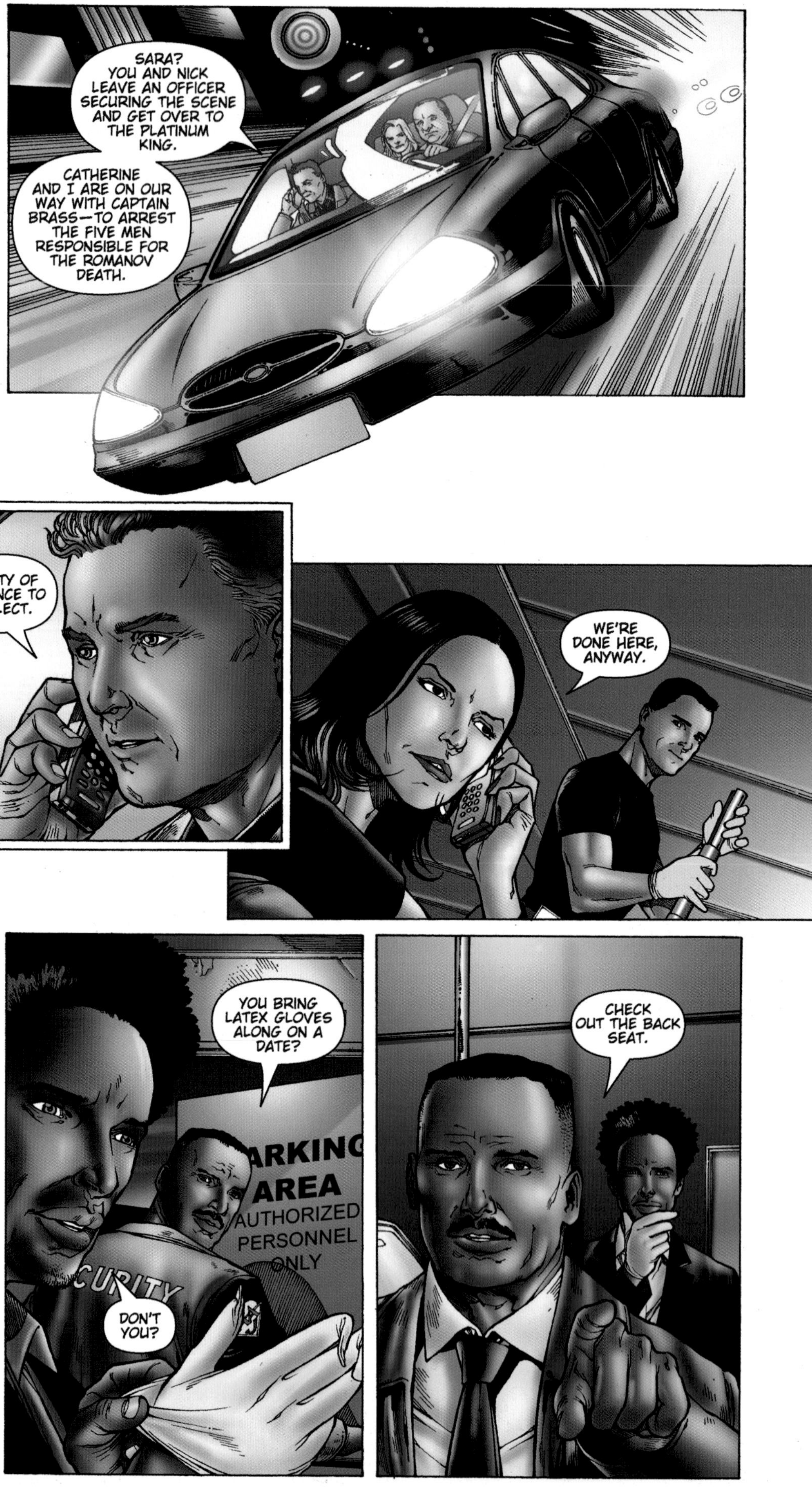
SARA? YOU AND NICK LEAVE AN OFFICER SECURING THE SCENE AND GET OVER TO THE PLATINUM KING.
CATHERINE AND I ARE ON OUR WAY WITH CAPTAIN BRASS—TO ARREST THE FIVE MEN RESPONSIBLE FOR THE ROMANOV DEATH.
PLENTY OF EVIDENCE TO COLLECT.
WE'RE DONE HERE, ANYWAY.
YOU BRING LATEX GLOVES ALONG ON A DATE?
ARKING AREA AUTHORIZED PERSONNEL ONLY
CURITY
DON'T YOU?
CHECK OUT THE BACK SEAT.

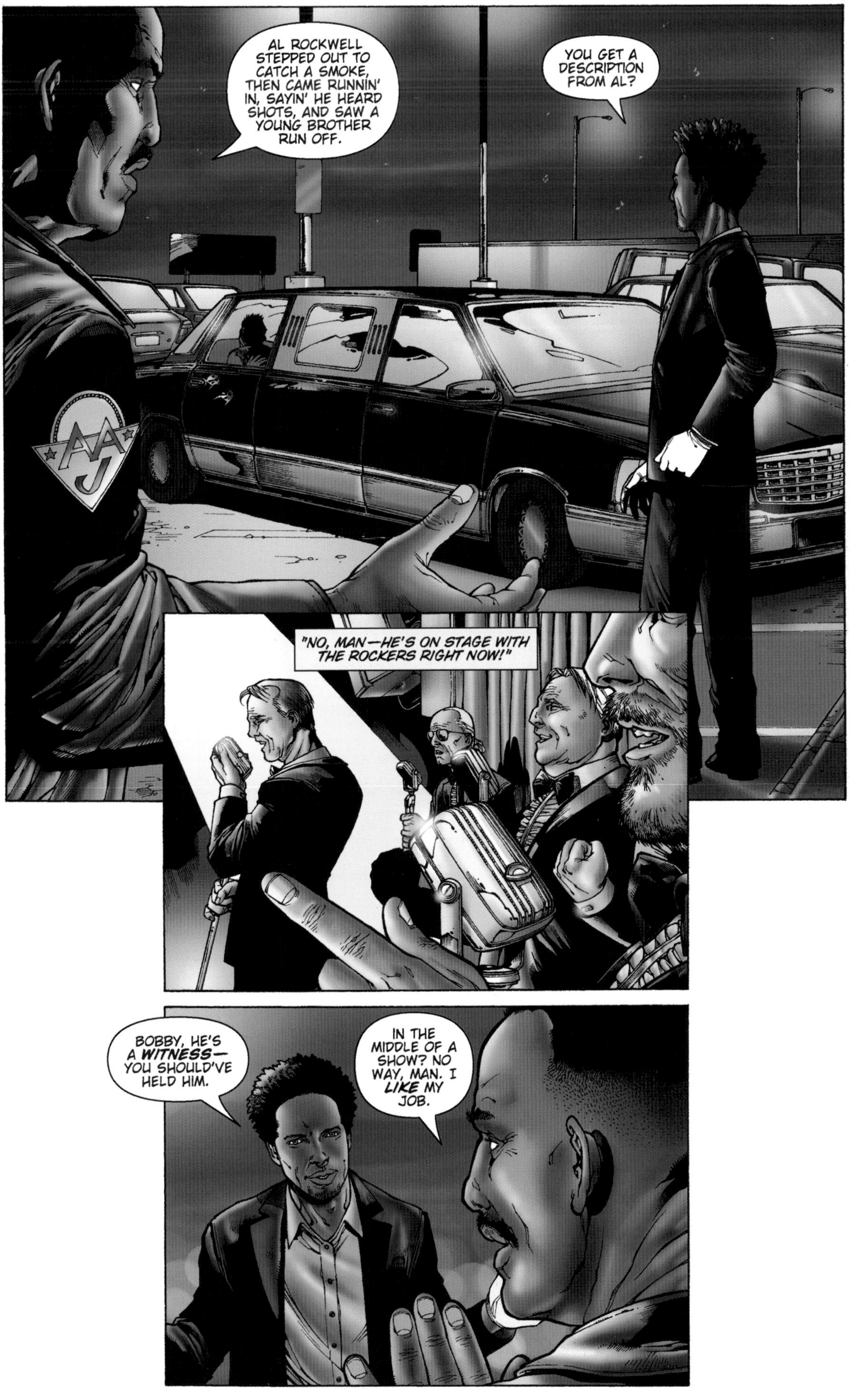
AL ROCKWELL STEPPED OUT TO CATCH A SMOKE, THEN CAME RUNNIN' IN, SAYIN' HE HEARD SHOTS, AND SAW A YOUNG BROTHER RUN OFF.
YOU GET A DESCRIPTION FROM AL?
"NO, MAN—HE'S ON STAGE WITH THE ROCKERS RIGHT NOW!"
BOBBY, HE'S A *WITNESS*—YOU SHOULD'VE HELD HIM.
IN THE MIDDLE OF A SHOW? NO WAY, MAN. I *LIKE* MY JOB.

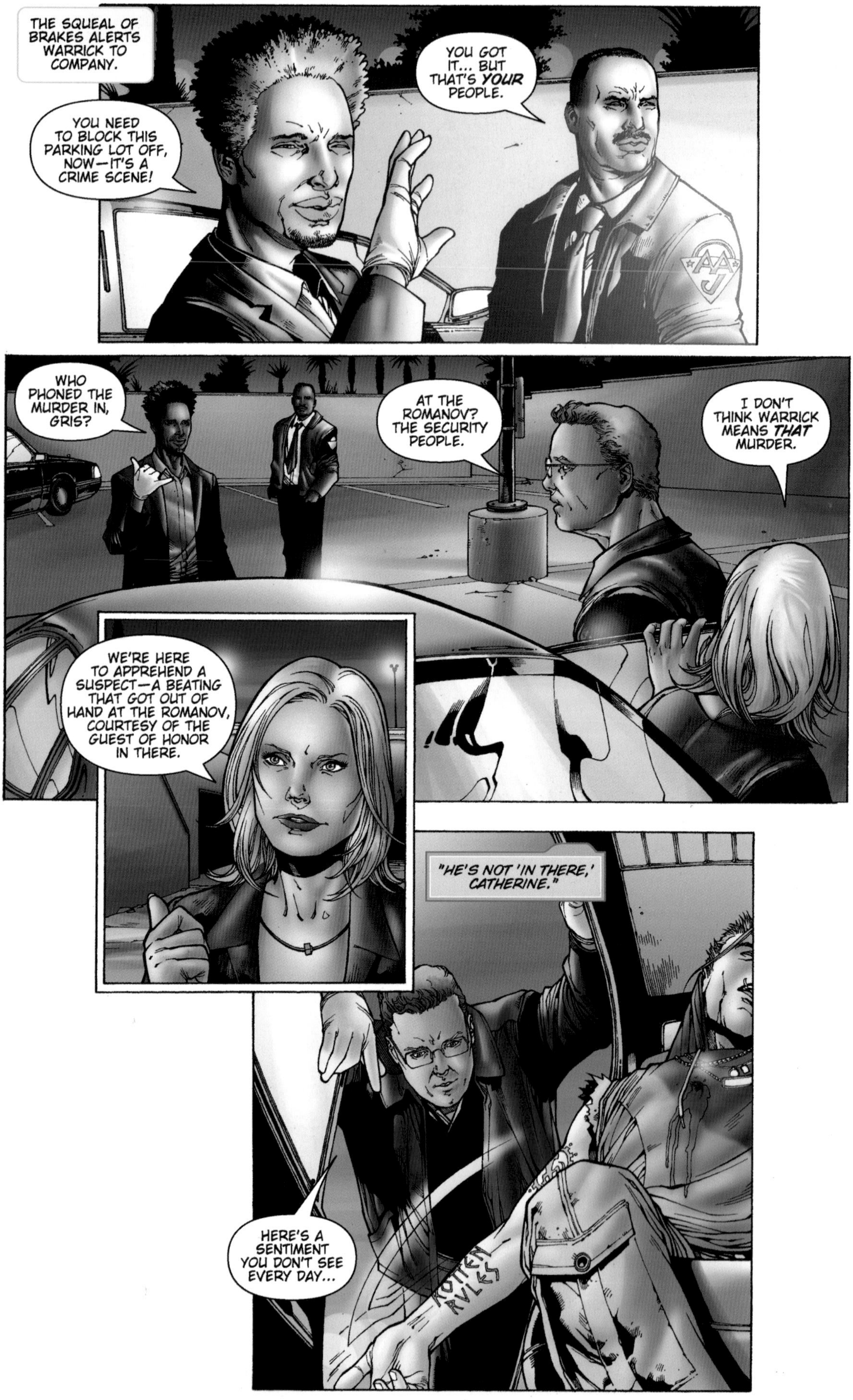
THE SQUEAL OF BRAKES ALERTS WARRICK TO COMPANY.
YOU NEED TO BLOCK THIS PARKING LOT OFF, NOW—IT'S A CRIME SCENE!
YOU GOT IT... BUT THAT'S *YOUR* PEOPLE.
WHO PHONED THE MURDER IN, GRIS?
AT THE ROMANOV? THE SECURITY PEOPLE.
I DON'T THINK WARRICK MEANS *THAT* MURDER.
WE'RE HERE TO APPREHEND A SUSPECT—A BEATING THAT GOT OUT OF HAND AT THE ROMANOV, COURTESY OF THE GUEST OF HONOR IN THERE.
"HE'S NOT 'IN THERE,' CATHERINE."
HERE'S A SENTIMENT YOU DON'T SEE EVERY DAY...
ROTTEN RULES

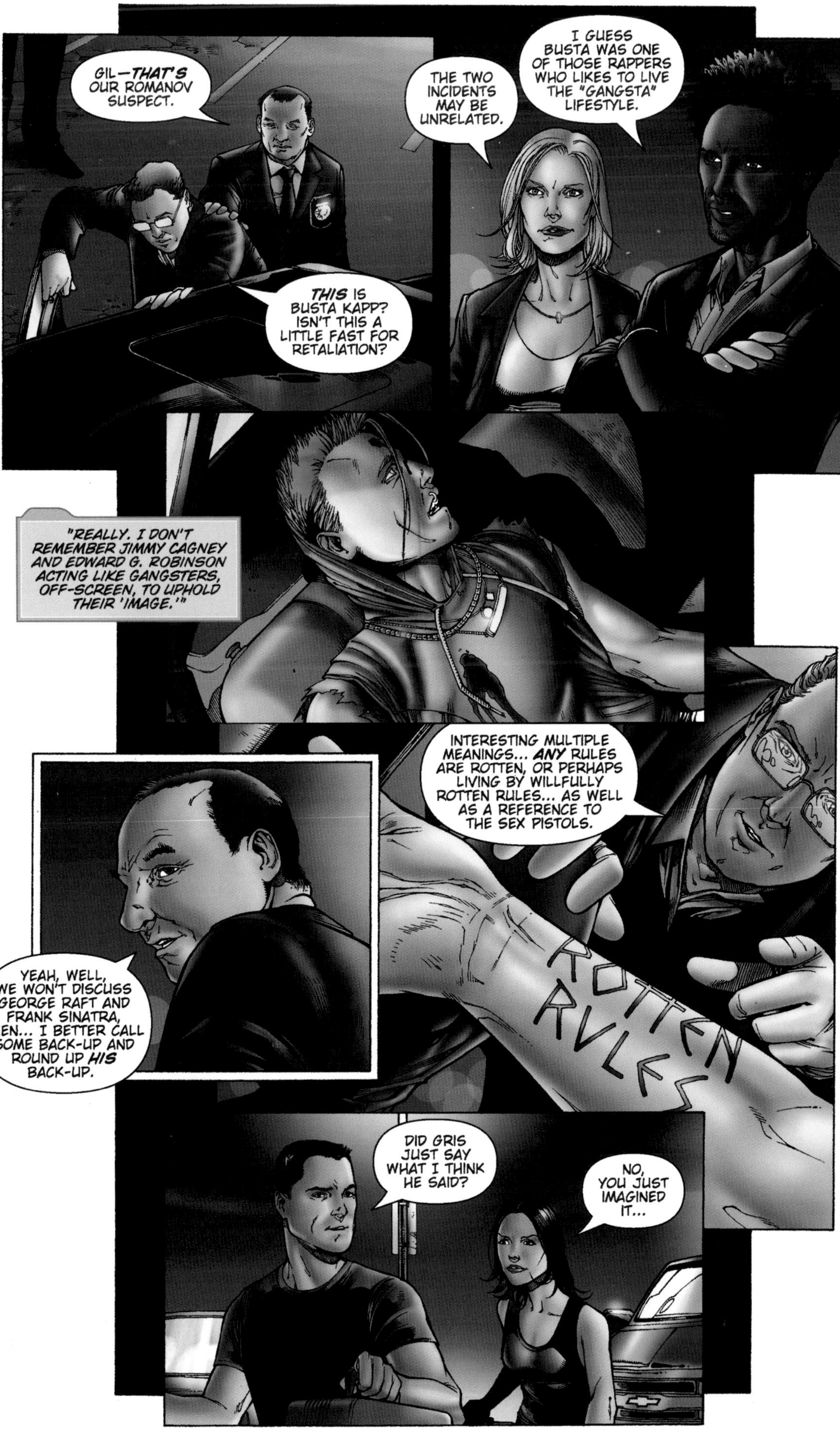
GIL—THAT'S OUR ROMANOV SUSPECT.
THIS IS BUSTA KAPP? ISN'T THIS A LITTLE FAST FOR RETALIATION?
THE TWO INCIDENTS MAY BE UNRELATED.
I GUESS BUSTA WAS ONE OF THOSE RAPPERS WHO LIKES TO LIVE THE "GANGSTA" LIFESTYLE.
"REALLY. I DON'T REMEMBER JIMMY CAGNEY AND EDWARD G. ROBINSON ACTING LIKE GANGSTERS, OFF-SCREEN, TO UPHOLD THEIR 'IMAGE.'"
INTERESTING MULTIPLE MEANINGS... ANY RULES ARE ROTTEN, OR PERHAPS LIVING BY WILLFULLY ROTTEN RULES... AS WELL AS A REFERENCE TO THE SEX PISTOLS.
ROTTEN RVLES
YEAH, WELL, WE WON'T DISCUSS GEORGE RAFT AND FRANK SINATRA, THEN... I BETTER CALL SOME BACK-UP AND ROUND UP HIS BACK-UP.
DID GRIS JUST SAY WHAT I THINK HE SAID?
NO, YOU JUST IMAGINED IT...

chapter two
# Crime Seen

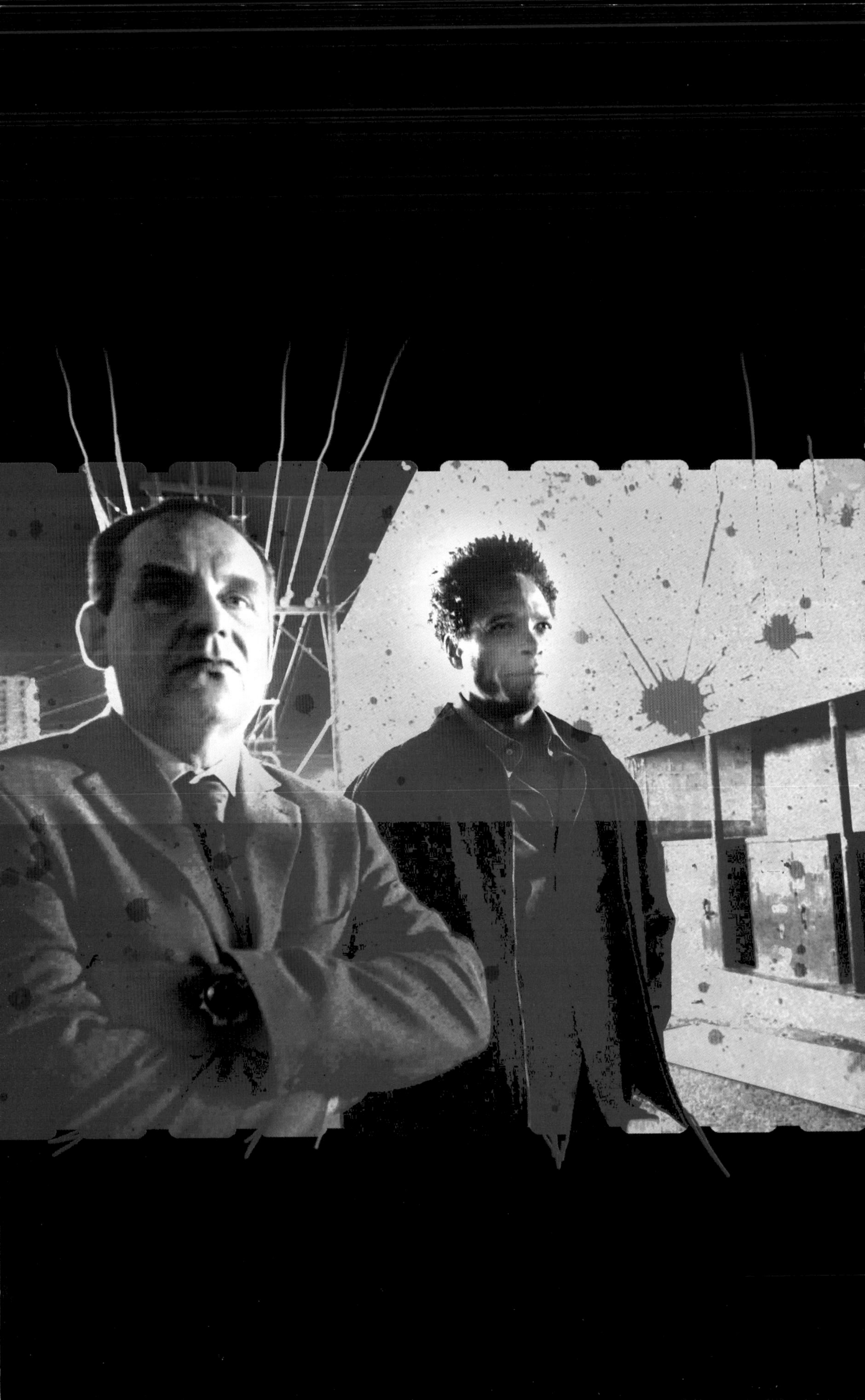

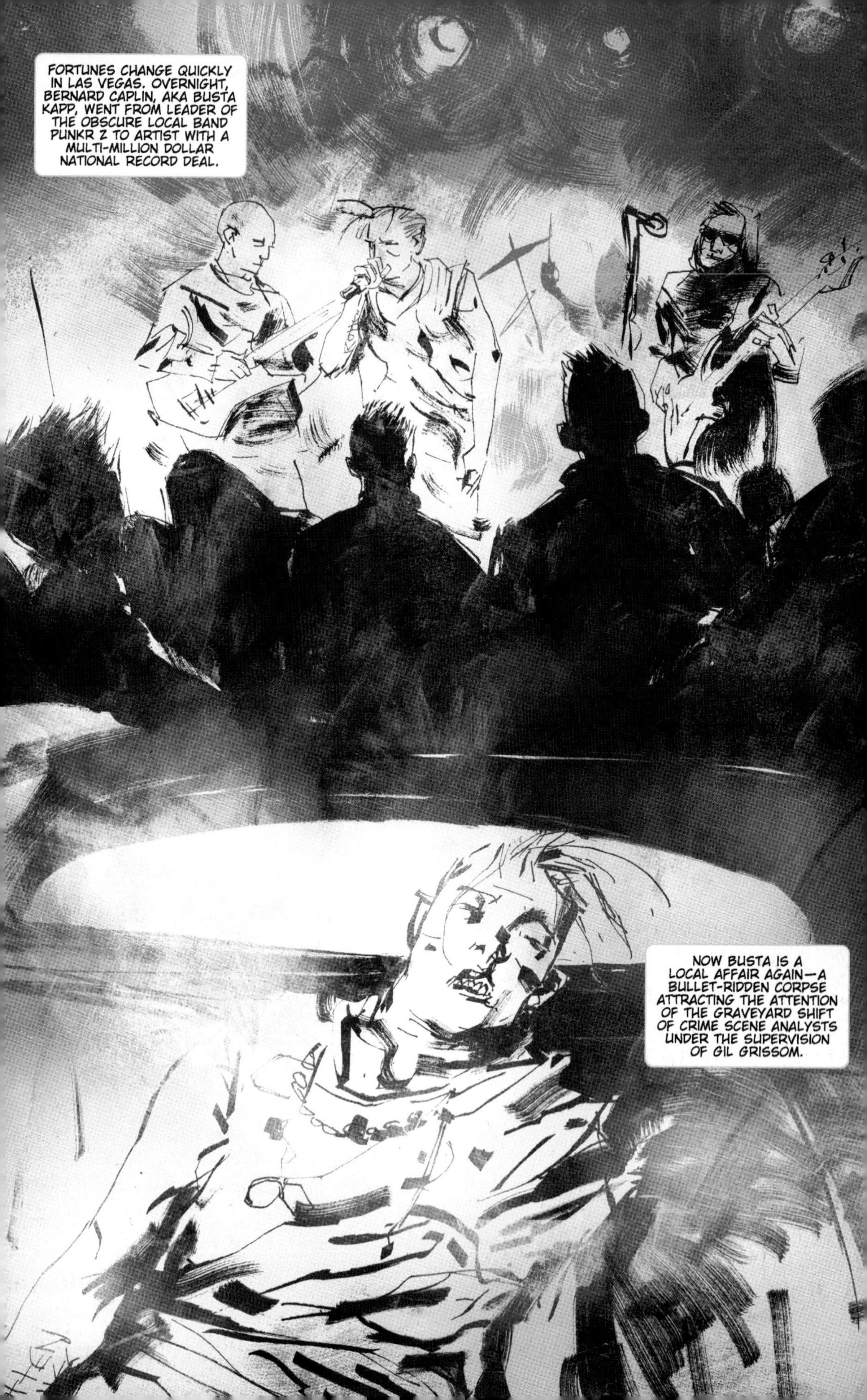
FORTUNES CHANGE QUICKLY IN LAS VEGAS. OVERNIGHT, BERNARD CAPLIN, AKA BUSTA KAPP, WENT FROM LEADER OF THE OBSCURE LOCAL BAND PUNKR Z TO ARTIST WITH A MULTI-MILLION DOLLAR NATIONAL RECORD DEAL.
NOW BUSTA IS A LOCAL AFFAIR AGAIN—A BULLET-RIDDEN CORPSE ATTRACTING THE ATTENTION OF THE GRAVEYARD SHIFT OF CRIME SCENE ANALYSTS UNDER THE SUPERVISION OF GIL GRISSOM.

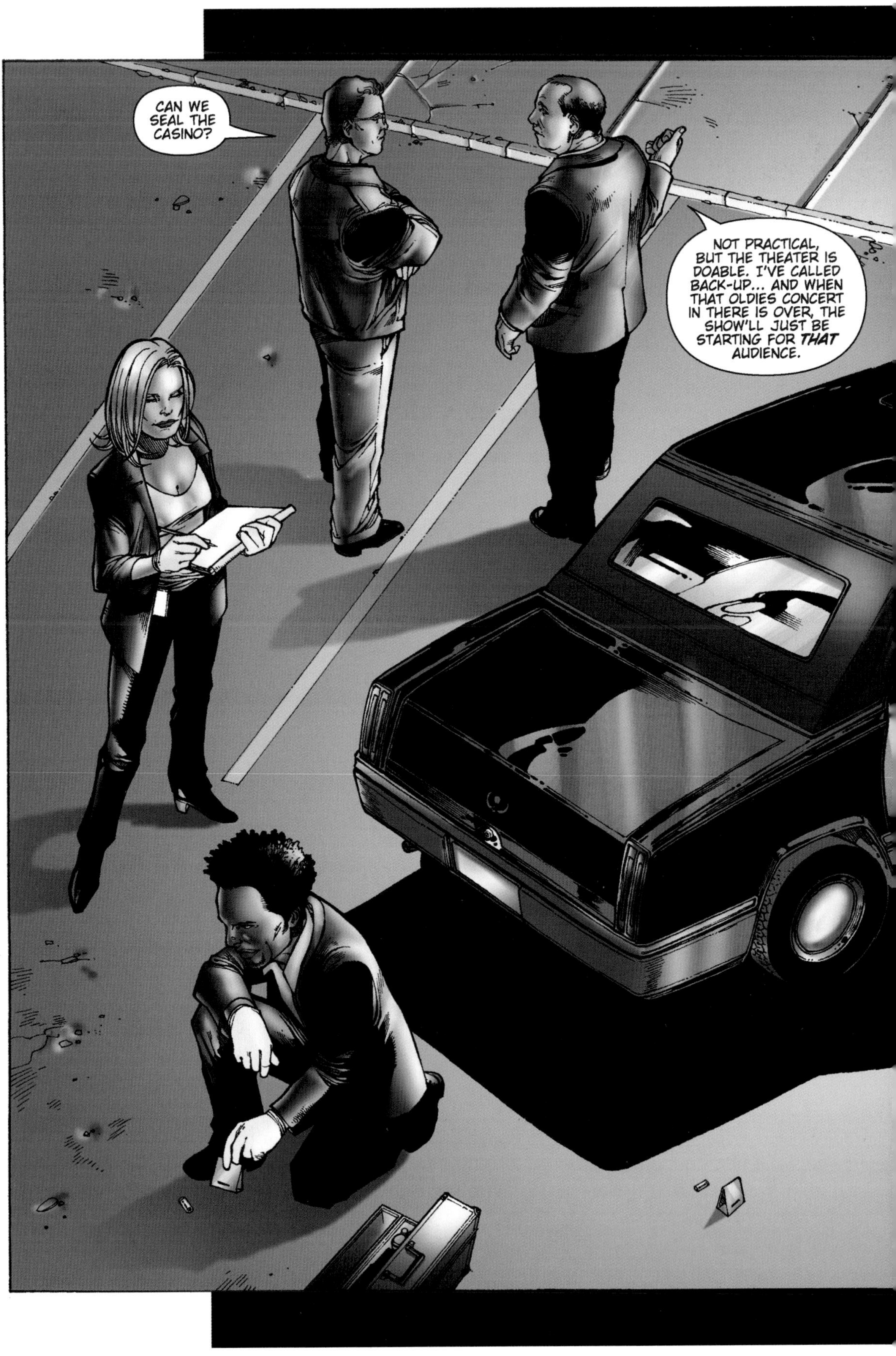
CAN WE SEAL THE CASINO?
NOT PRACTICAL, BUT THE THEATER IS DOABLE. I'VE CALLED BACK-UP... AND WHEN THAT OLDIES CONCERT IN THERE IS OVER, THE SHOW'LL JUST BE STARTING FOR *THAT* AUDIENCE.

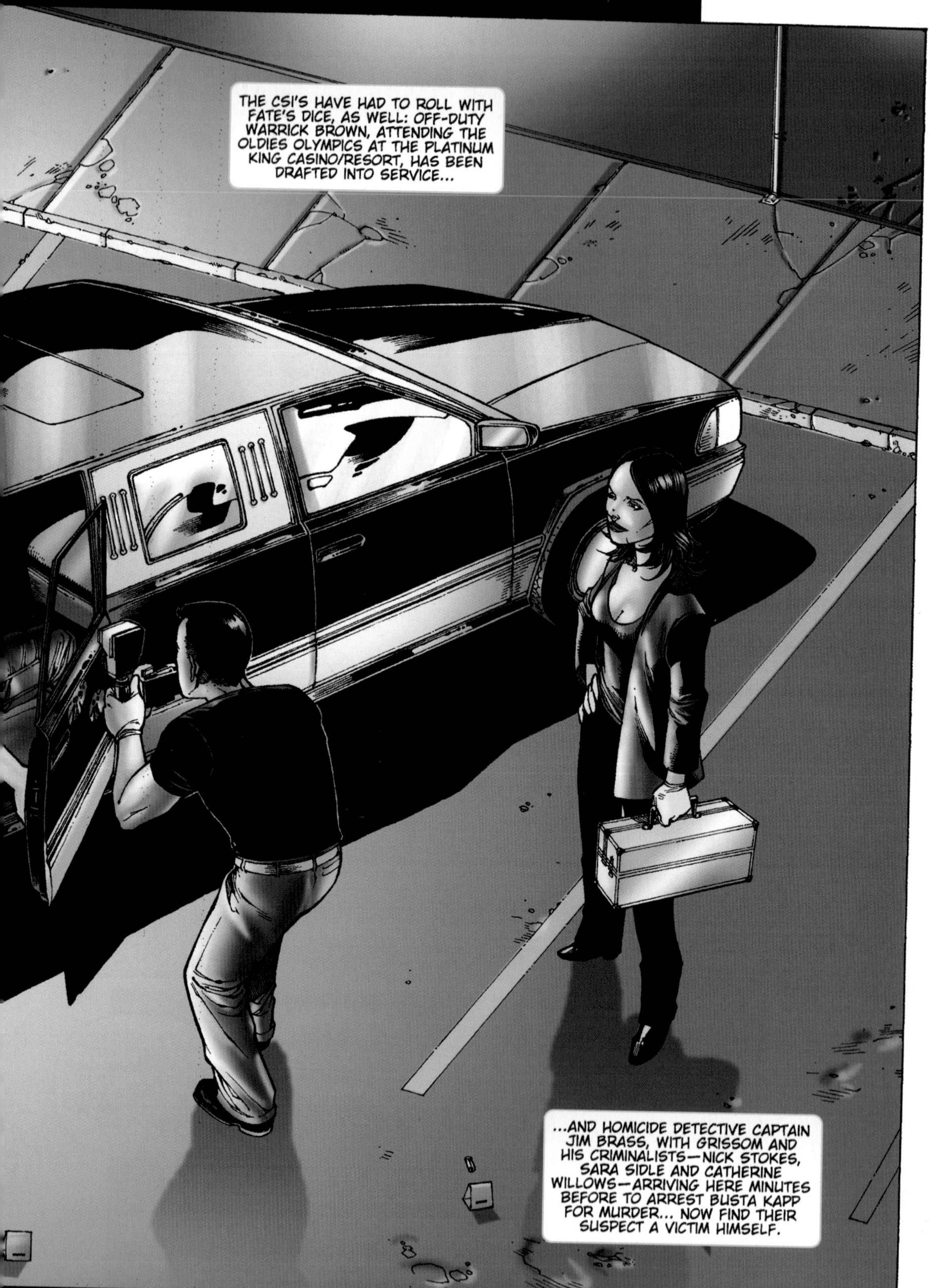
THE CSI'S HAVE HAD TO ROLL WITH FATE'S DICE, AS WELL: OFF-DUTY WARRICK BROWN, ATTENDING THE OLDIES OLYMPICS AT THE PLATINUM KING CASINO/RESORT, HAS BEEN DRAFTED INTO SERVICE...
...AND HOMICIDE DETECTIVE CAPTAIN JIM BRASS, WITH GRISSOM AND HIS CRIMINALISTS—NICK STOKES, SARA SIDLE AND CATHERINE WILLOWS—ARRIVING HERE MINUTES BEFORE TO ARREST BUSTA KAPP FOR MURDER... NOW FIND THEIR SUSPECT A VICTIM HIMSELF.

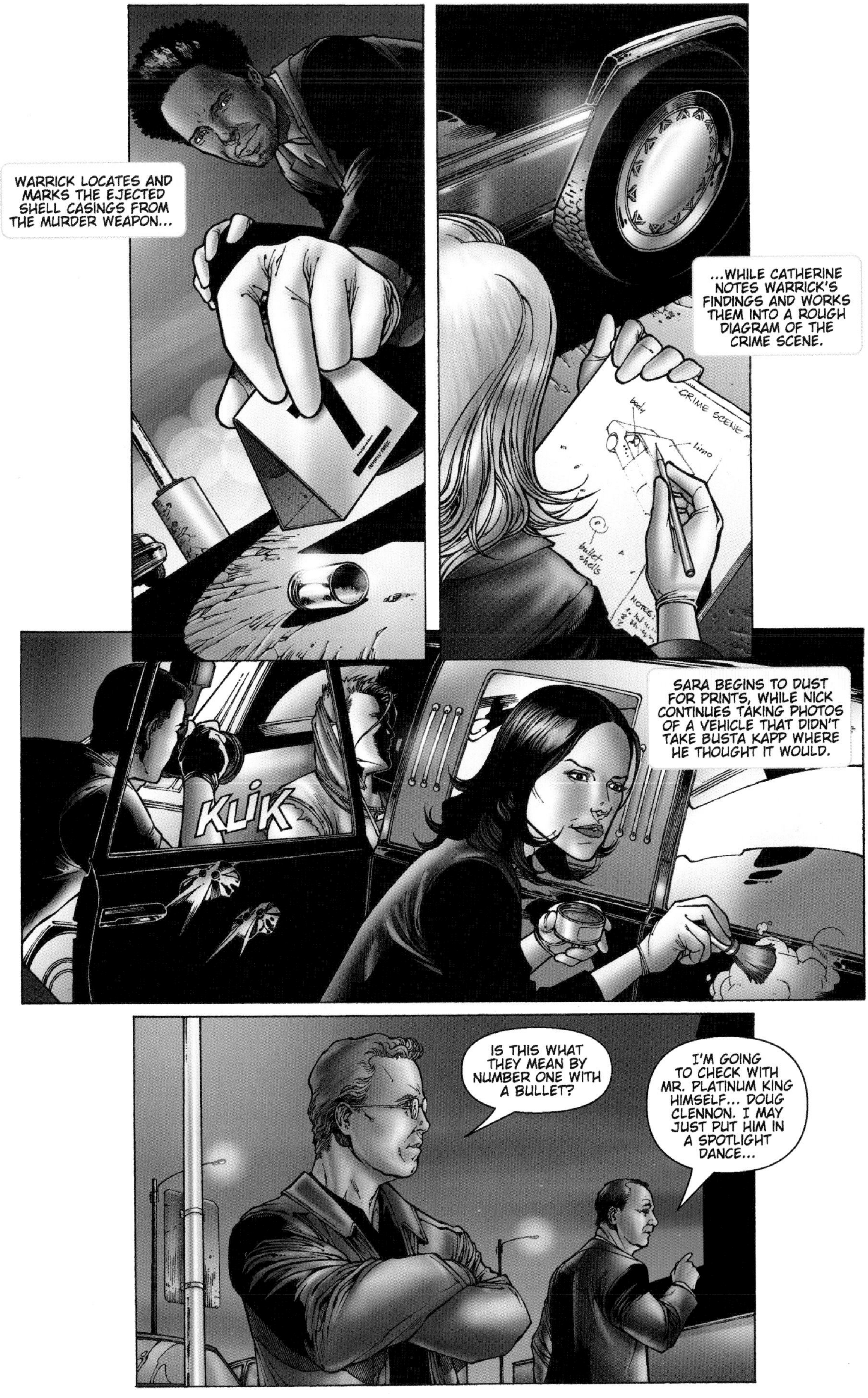
WARRICK LOCATES AND MARKS THE EJECTED SHELL CASINGS FROM THE MURDER WEAPON...
...WHILE CATHERINE NOTES WARRICK'S FINDINGS AND WORKS THEM INTO A ROUGH DIAGRAM OF THE CRIME SCENE.
CRIME SCENE
body
limo
bullet shells
SARA BEGINS TO DUST FOR PRINTS, WHILE NICK CONTINUES TAKING PHOTOS OF A VEHICLE THAT DIDN'T TAKE BUSTA KAPP WHERE HE THOUGHT IT WOULD.
KLIK
IS THIS WHAT THEY MEAN BY NUMBER ONE WITH A BULLET?
I'M GOING TO CHECK WITH MR. PLATINUM KING HIMSELF... DOUG CLENNON. I MAY JUST PUT HIM IN A SPOTLIGHT DANCE...

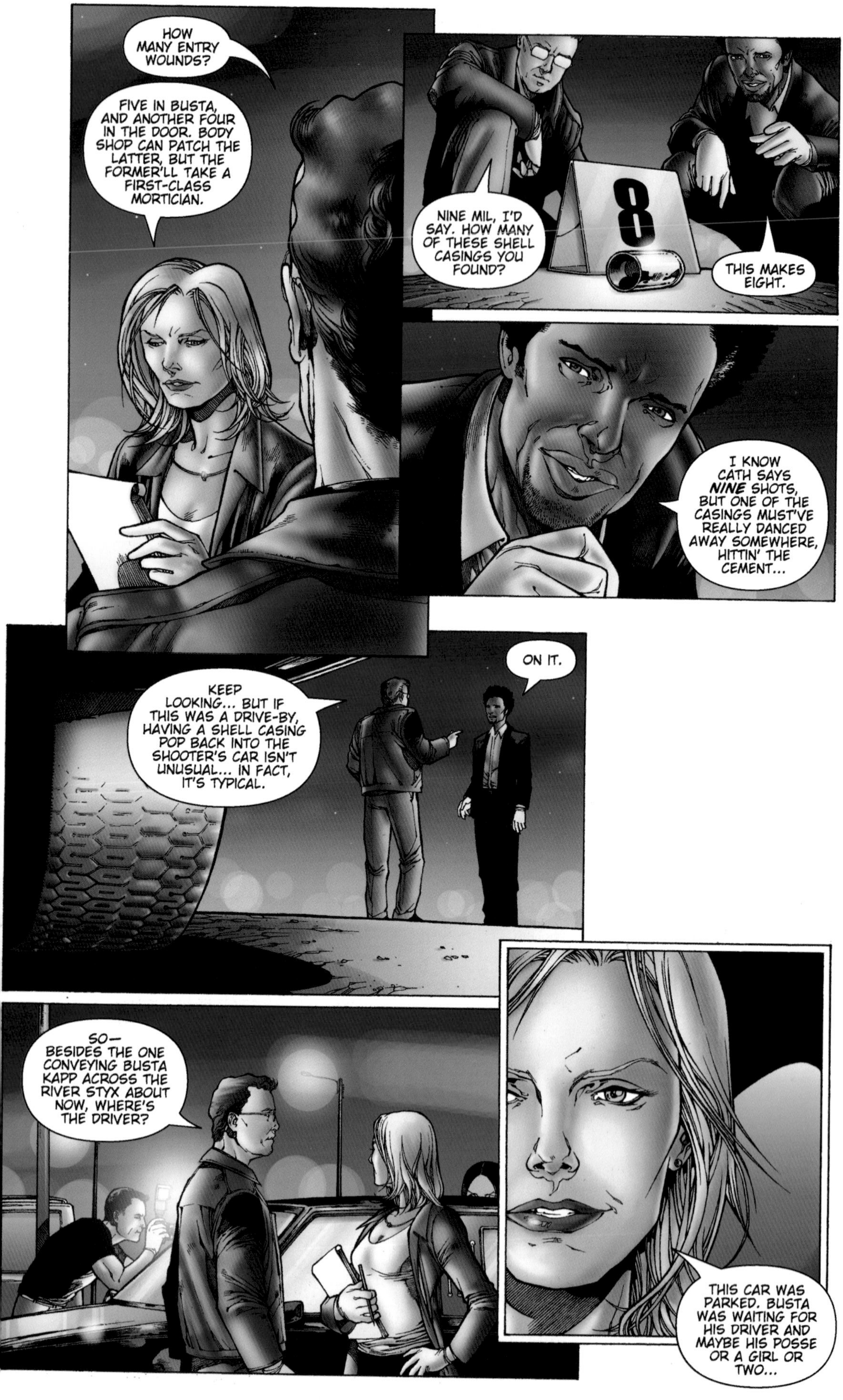
HOW MANY ENTRY WOUNDS?
FIVE IN BUSTA, AND ANOTHER FOUR IN THE DOOR. BODY SHOP CAN PATCH THE LATTER, BUT THE FORMER'LL TAKE A FIRST-CLASS MORTICIAN.
8
NINE MIL, I'D SAY. HOW MANY OF THESE SHELL CASINGS YOU FOUND?
THIS MAKES EIGHT.
I KNOW CATH SAYS *NINE* SHOTS, BUT ONE OF THE CASINGS MUST'VE REALLY DANCED AWAY SOMEWHERE, HITTIN' THE CEMENT...
KEEP LOOKING... BUT IF THIS WAS A DRIVE-BY, HAVING A SHELL CASING POP BACK INTO THE SHOOTER'S CAR ISN'T UNUSUAL... IN FACT, IT'S TYPICAL.
ON IT.
SO— BESIDES THE ONE CONVEYING BUSTA KAPP ACROSS THE RIVER STYX ABOUT NOW, WHERE'S THE DRIVER?
THIS CAR WAS PARKED. BUSTA WAS WAITING FOR HIS DRIVER AND MAYBE HIS POSSE OR A GIRL OR TWO...

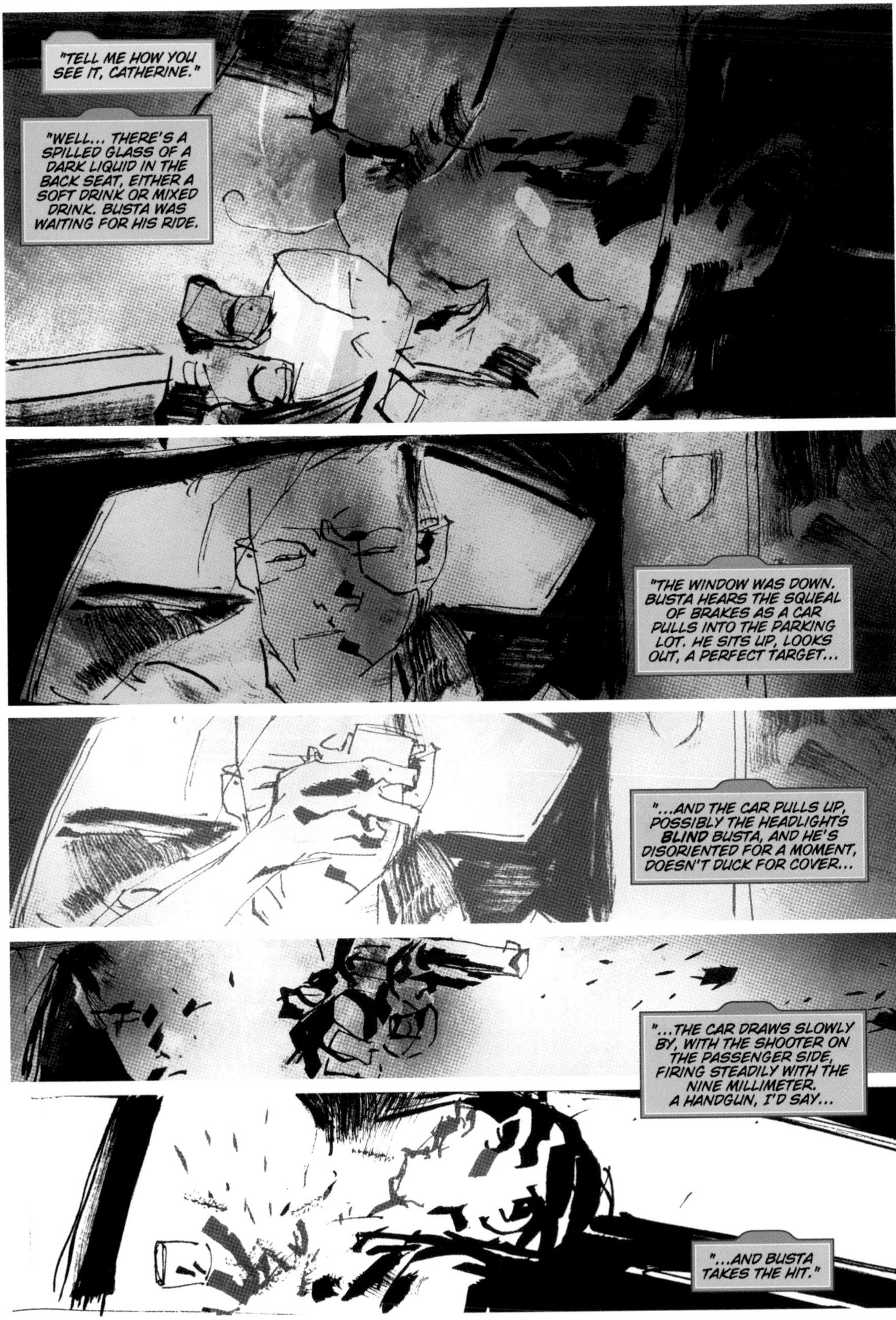
"TELL ME HOW YOU SEE IT, CATHERINE."
"WELL... THERE'S A SPILLED GLASS OF A DARK LIQUID IN THE BACK SEAT, EITHER A SOFT DRINK OR MIXED DRINK. BUSTA WAS WAITING FOR HIS RIDE.
"THE WINDOW WAS DOWN. BUSTA HEARS THE SQUEAL OF BRAKES AS A CAR PULLS INTO THE PARKING LOT. HE SITS UP, LOOKS OUT, A PERFECT TARGET...
"...AND THE CAR PULLS UP, POSSIBLY THE HEADLIGHTS BLIND BUSTA, AND HE'S DISORIENTED FOR A MOMENT, DOESN'T DUCK FOR COVER...
"...THE CAR DRAWS SLOWLY BY, WITH THE SHOOTER ON THE PASSENGER SIDE, FIRING STEADILY WITH THE NINE MILLIMETER. A HANDGUN, I'D SAY...
"...AND BUSTA TAKES THE HIT."

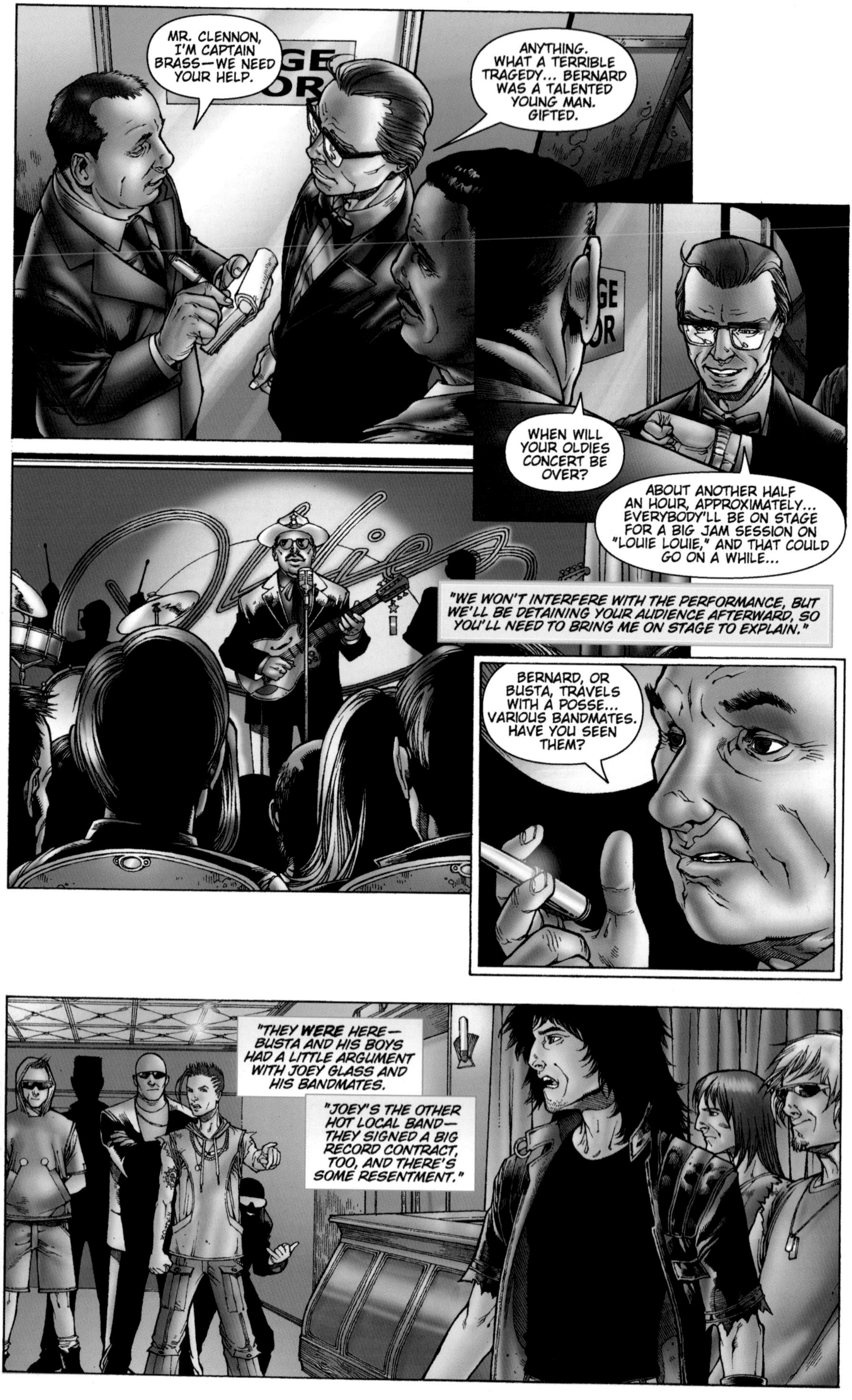
MR. CLENNON, I'M CAPTAIN BRASS—WE NEED YOUR HELP.
ANYTHING. WHAT A TERRIBLE TRAGEDY... BERNARD WAS A TALENTED YOUNG MAN. GIFTED.
WHEN WILL YOUR OLDIES CONCERT BE OVER?
ABOUT ANOTHER HALF AN HOUR, APPROXIMATELY... EVERYBODY'LL BE ON STAGE FOR A BIG JAM SESSION ON "LOUIE LOUIE," AND THAT COULD GO ON A WHILE...
"WE WON'T INTERFERE WITH THE PERFORMANCE, BUT WE'LL BE DETAINING YOUR AUDIENCE AFTERWARD, SO YOU'LL NEED TO BRING ME ON STAGE TO EXPLAIN."
BERNARD, OR BUSTA, TRAVELS WITH A POSSE... VARIOUS BANDMATES. HAVE YOU SEEN THEM?
"THEY WERE HERE—BUSTA AND HIS BOYS HAD A LITTLE ARGUMENT WITH JOEY GLASS AND HIS BANDMATES.
"JOEY'S THE OTHER HOT LOCAL BAND—THEY SIGNED A BIG RECORD CONTRACT, TOO, AND THERE'S SOME RESENTMENT."

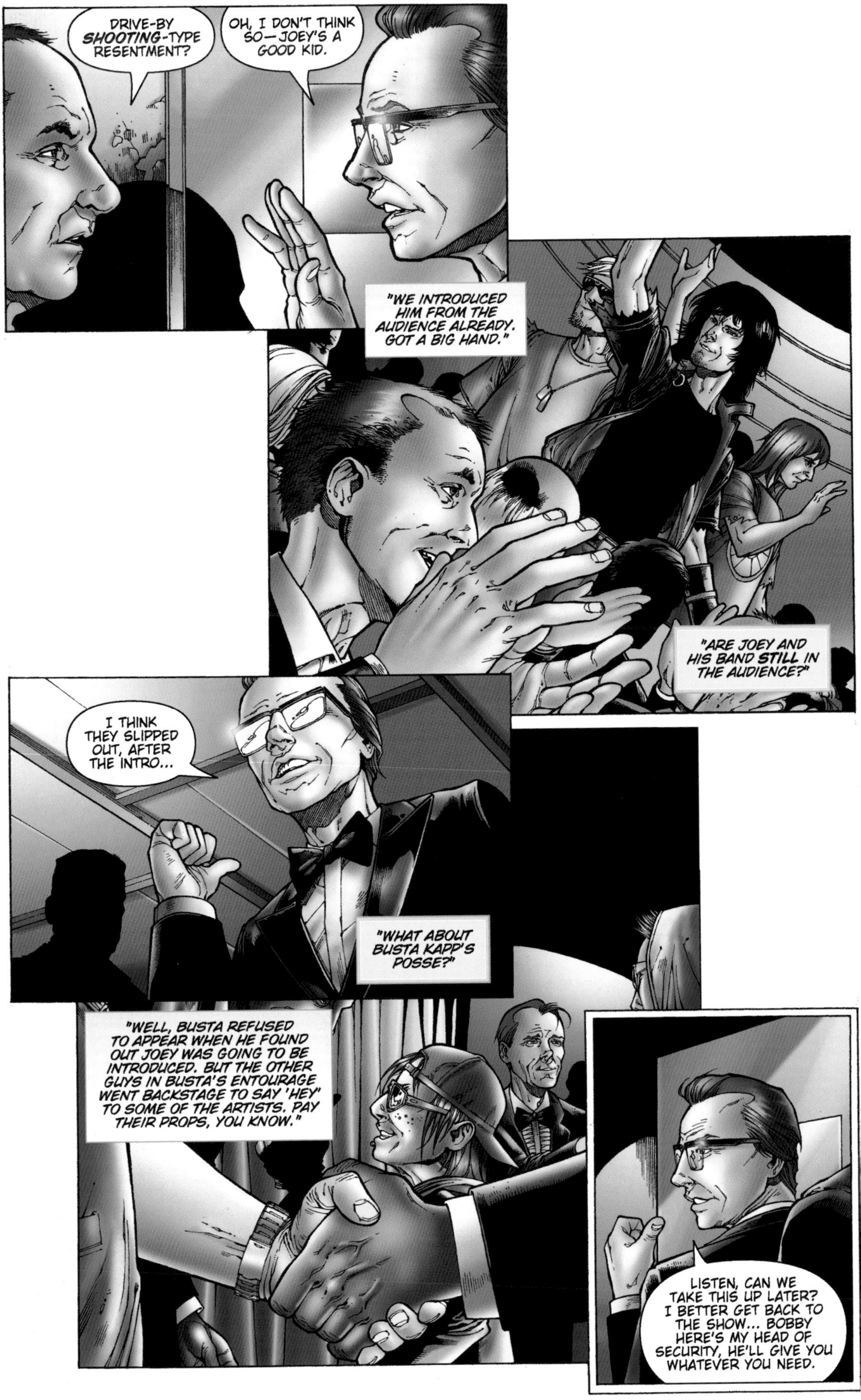
DRIVE-BY SHOOTING-TYPE RESENTMENT?
OH, I DON'T THINK SO—JOEY'S A GOOD KID.
"WE INTRODUCED HIM FROM THE AUDIENCE ALREADY. GOT A BIG HAND."
"ARE JOEY AND HIS BAND STILL IN THE AUDIENCE?"
I THINK THEY SLIPPED OUT, AFTER THE INTRO...
"WHAT ABOUT BUSTA KAPP'S POSSE?"
"WELL, BUSTA REFUSED TO APPEAR WHEN HE FOUND OUT JOEY WAS GOING TO BE INTRODUCED. BUT THE OTHER GUYS IN BUSTA'S ENTOURAGE WENT BACKSTAGE TO SAY 'HEY' TO SOME OF THE ARTISTS. PAY THEIR PROPS, YOU KNOW."
LISTEN, CAN WE TAKE THIS UP LATER? I BETTER GET BACK TO THE SHOW... BOBBY HERE'S MY HEAD OF SECURITY, HE'LL GIVE YOU WHATEVER YOU NEED.

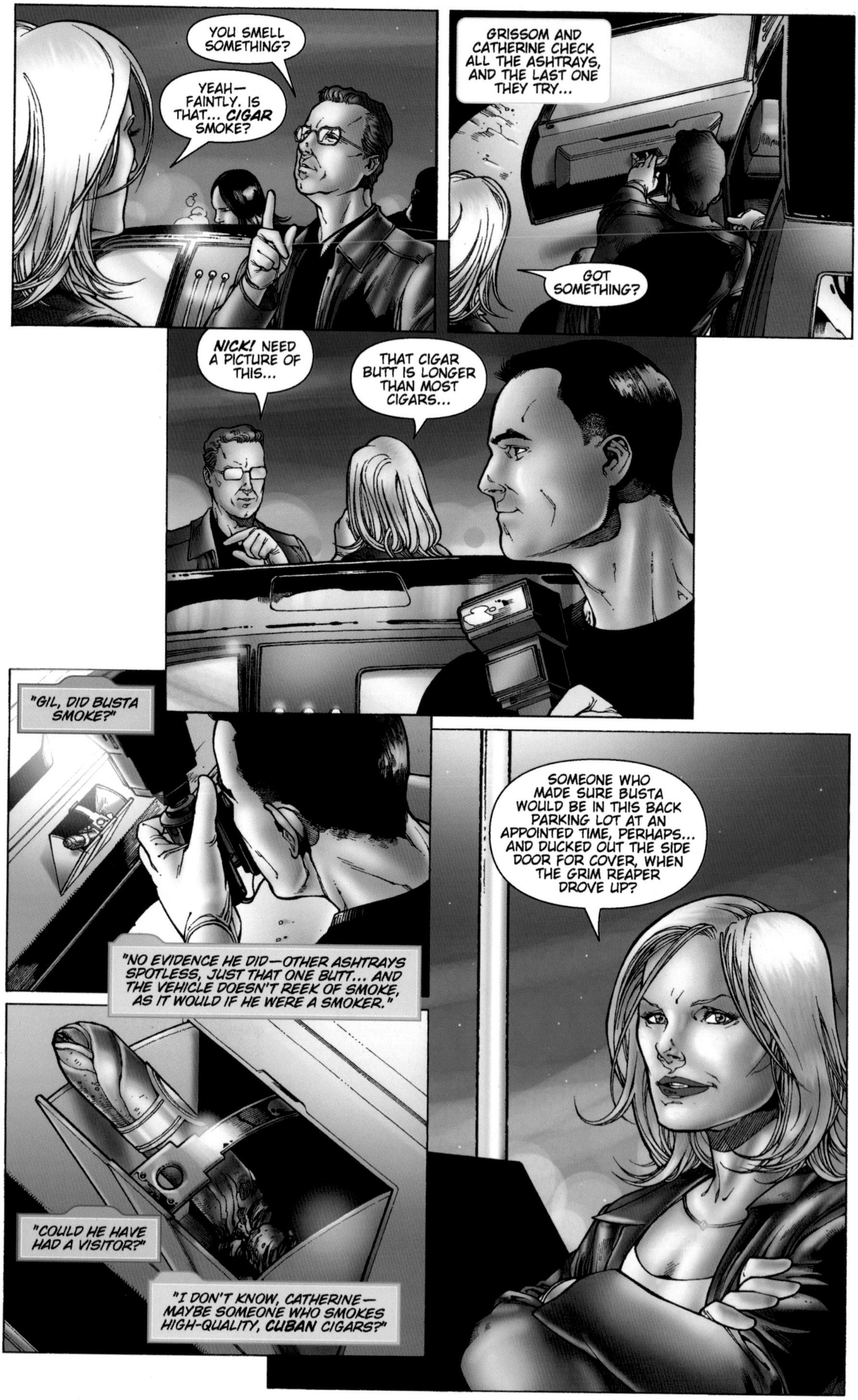
YOU SMELL SOMETHING?
YEAH— FAINTLY. IS THAT... CIGAR SMOKE?
GRISSOM AND CATHERINE CHECK ALL THE ASHTRAYS, AND THE LAST ONE THEY TRY...
GOT SOMETHING?
NICK! NEED A PICTURE OF THIS...
THAT CIGAR BUTT IS LONGER THAN MOST CIGARS...
"GIL, DID BUSTA SMOKE?"
"NO EVIDENCE HE DID—OTHER ASHTRAYS SPOTLESS, JUST THAT ONE BUTT... AND THE VEHICLE DOESN'T REEK OF SMOKE, AS IT WOULD IF HE WERE A SMOKER."
SOMEONE WHO MADE SURE BUSTA WOULD BE IN THIS BACK PARKING LOT AT AN APPOINTED TIME, PERHAPS... AND DUCKED OUT THE SIDE DOOR FOR COVER, WHEN THE GRIM REAPER DROVE UP?
"COULD HE HAVE HAD A VISITOR?"
"I DON'T KNOW, CATHERINE— MAYBE SOMEONE WHO SMOKES HIGH-QUALITY, CUBAN CIGARS?"

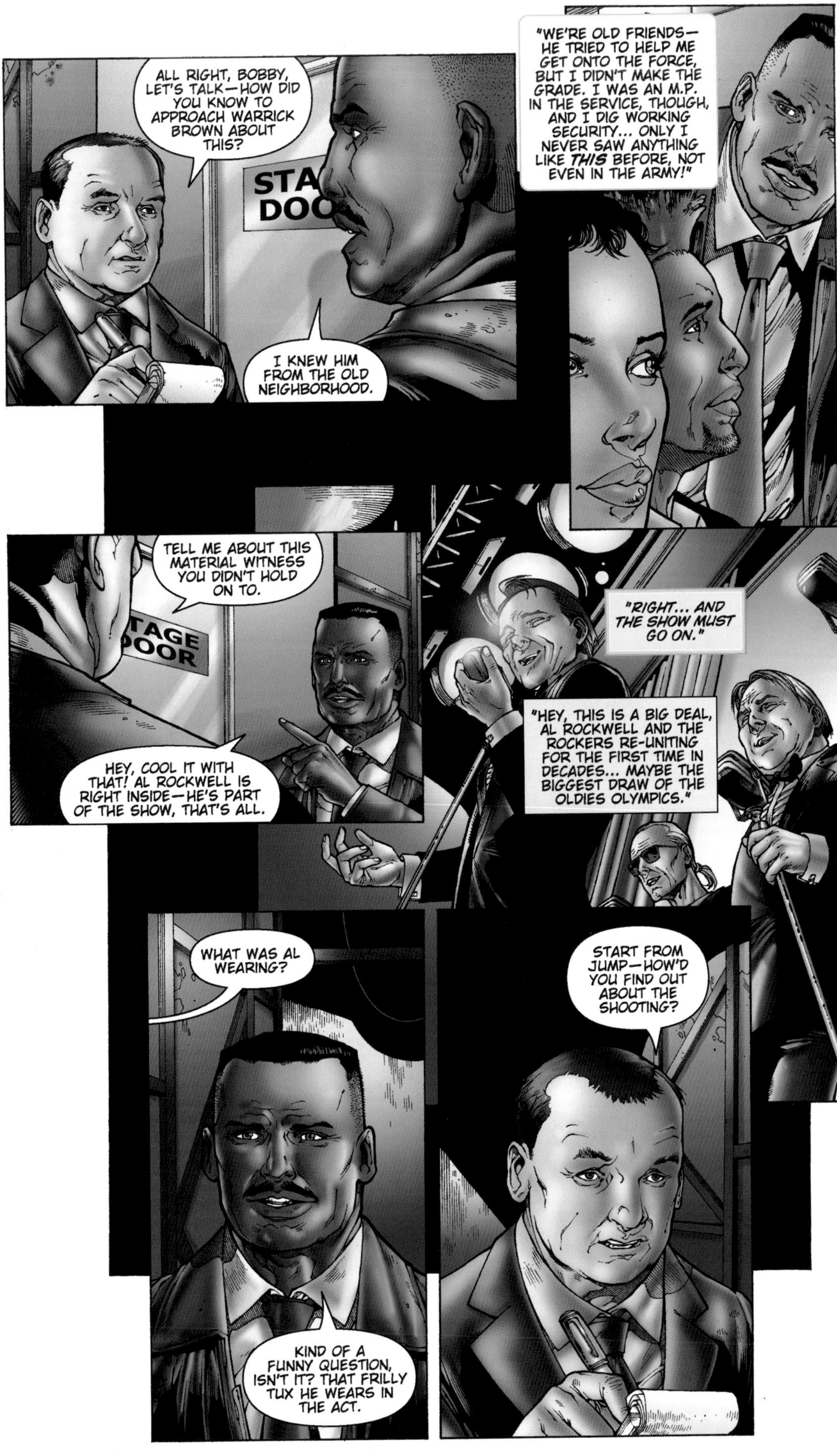
ALL RIGHT, BOBBY, LET'S TALK—HOW DID YOU KNOW TO APPROACH WARRICK BROWN ABOUT THIS?
STAGE DOOR
I KNEW HIM FROM THE OLD NEIGHBORHOOD.
"WE'RE OLD FRIENDS—HE TRIED TO HELP ME GET ONTO THE FORCE, BUT I DIDN'T MAKE THE GRADE. I WAS AN M.P. IN THE SERVICE, THOUGH, AND I DIG WORKING SECURITY... ONLY I NEVER SAW ANYTHING LIKE *THIS* BEFORE, NOT EVEN IN THE ARMY!"
TELL ME ABOUT THIS MATERIAL WITNESS YOU DIDN'T HOLD ON TO.
STAGE DOOR
HEY, COOL IT WITH THAT! AL ROCKWELL IS RIGHT INSIDE—HE'S PART OF THE SHOW, THAT'S ALL.
"RIGHT... AND THE SHOW MUST GO ON."
"HEY, THIS IS A BIG DEAL, AL ROCKWELL AND THE ROCKERS RE-UNITING FOR THE FIRST TIME IN DECADES... MAYBE THE BIGGEST DRAW OF THE OLDIES OLYMPICS."
WHAT WAS AL WEARING?
KIND OF A FUNNY QUESTION, ISN'T IT? THAT FRILLY TUX HE WEARS IN THE ACT.
START FROM JUMP—HOW'D YOU FIND OUT ABOUT THE SHOOTING?

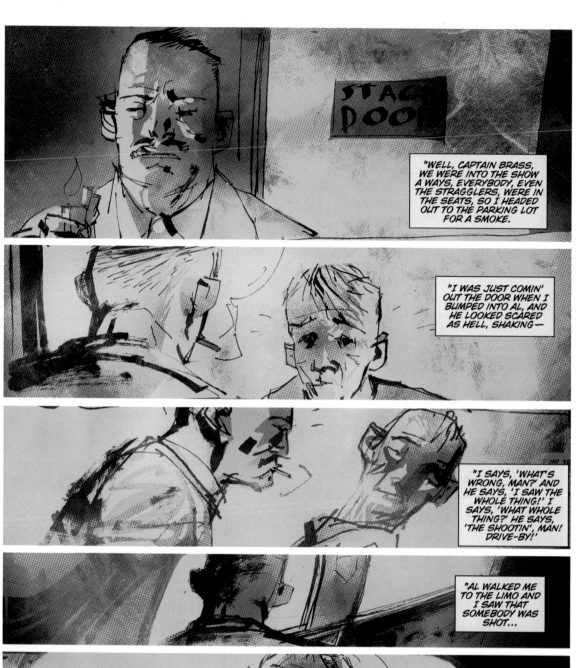

"WELL, CAPTAIN BRASS, WE WERE INTO THE SHOW A WAYS, EVERYBODY, EVEN THE STRAGGLERS, WERE IN THE SEATS, SO I HEADED OUT TO THE PARKING LOT FOR A SMOKE.

"I WAS JUST COMIN' OUT THE DOOR WHEN I BUMPED INTO AL, AND HE LOOKED SCARED AS HELL, SHAKING—

"I SAYS, 'WHAT'S WRONG, MAN?' AND HE SAYS, 'I SAW THE WHOLE THING!' I SAYS, 'WHAT WHOLE THING?' HE SAYS, 'THE SHOOTIN', MAN! DRIVE-BY!'

"AL WALKED ME TO THE LIMO AND I SAW THAT SOMEBODY WAS SHOT...

"I TOOK A CLOSER LOOK, AND SAW IT WAS BUSTA KAPP.

"AL SAYS, 'CALL THE COPS, CALL 911... BUT I GOTTA GET ON STAGE.' I DIDN'T ARGUE... YOU SAID IT YOURSELF, CAPTAIN: SHOW MUST GO ON."

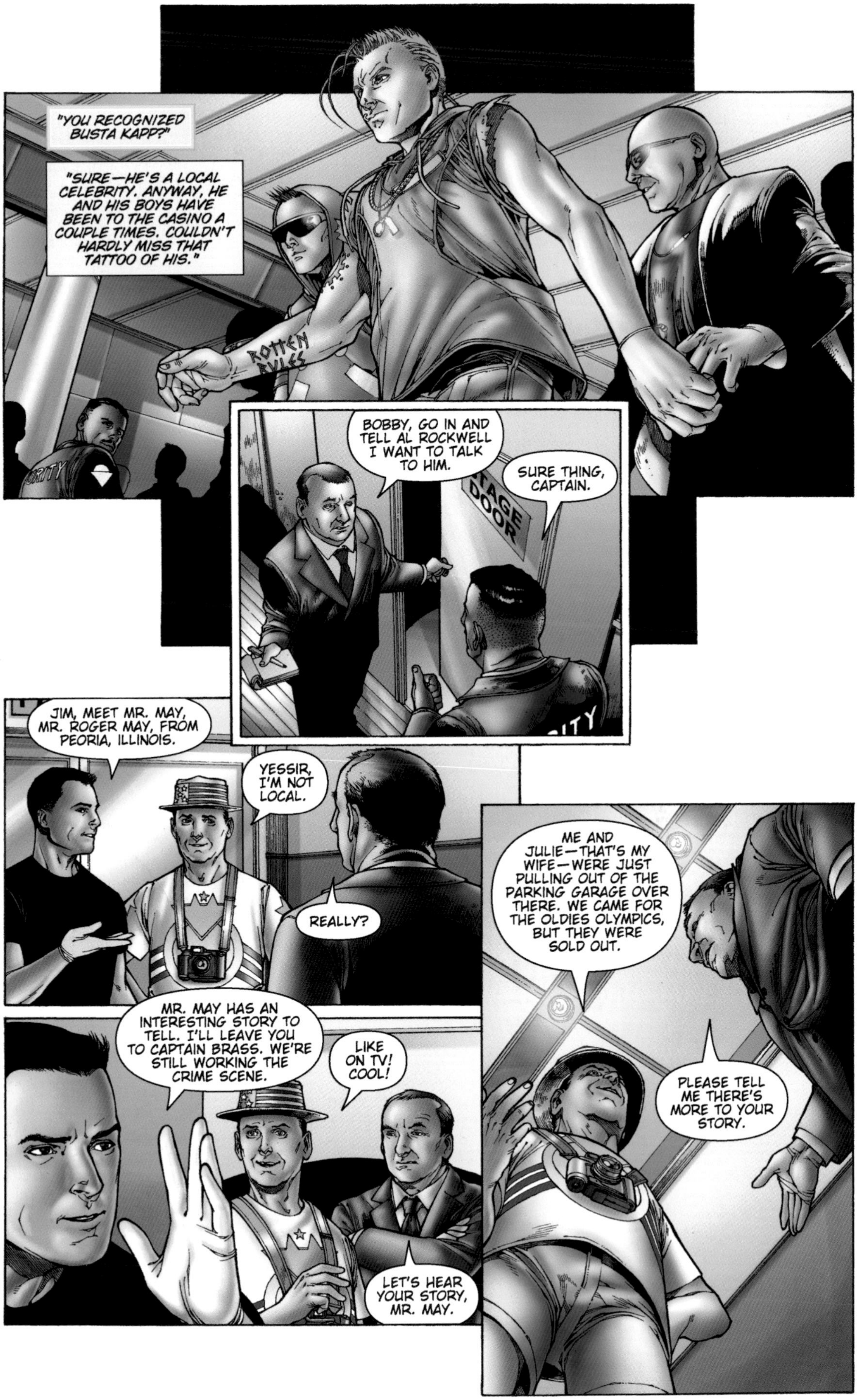
"YOU RECOGNIZED BUSTA KAPP?"
"SURE—HE'S A LOCAL CELEBRITY. ANYWAY, HE AND HIS BOYS HAVE BEEN TO THE CASINO A COUPLE TIMES. COULDN'T HARDLY MISS THAT TATTOO OF HIS."
ROTTEN RULES
BOBBY, GO IN AND TELL AL ROCKWELL I WANT TO TALK TO HIM.
SURE THING, CAPTAIN.
STAGE DOOR
JIM, MEET MR. MAY, MR. ROGER MAY, FROM PEORIA, ILLINOIS.
YESSIR, I'M NOT LOCAL.
REALLY?
MR. MAY HAS AN INTERESTING STORY TO TELL. I'LL LEAVE YOU TO CAPTAIN BRASS. WE'RE STILL WORKING THE CRIME SCENE.
LIKE ON TV! COOL!
LET'S HEAR YOUR STORY, MR. MAY.
ME AND JULIE—THAT'S MY WIFE—WERE JUST PULLING OUT OF THE PARKING GARAGE OVER THERE. WE CAME FOR THE OLDIES OLYMPICS, BUT THEY WERE SOLD OUT.
PLEASE TELL ME THERE'S MORE TO YOUR STORY.

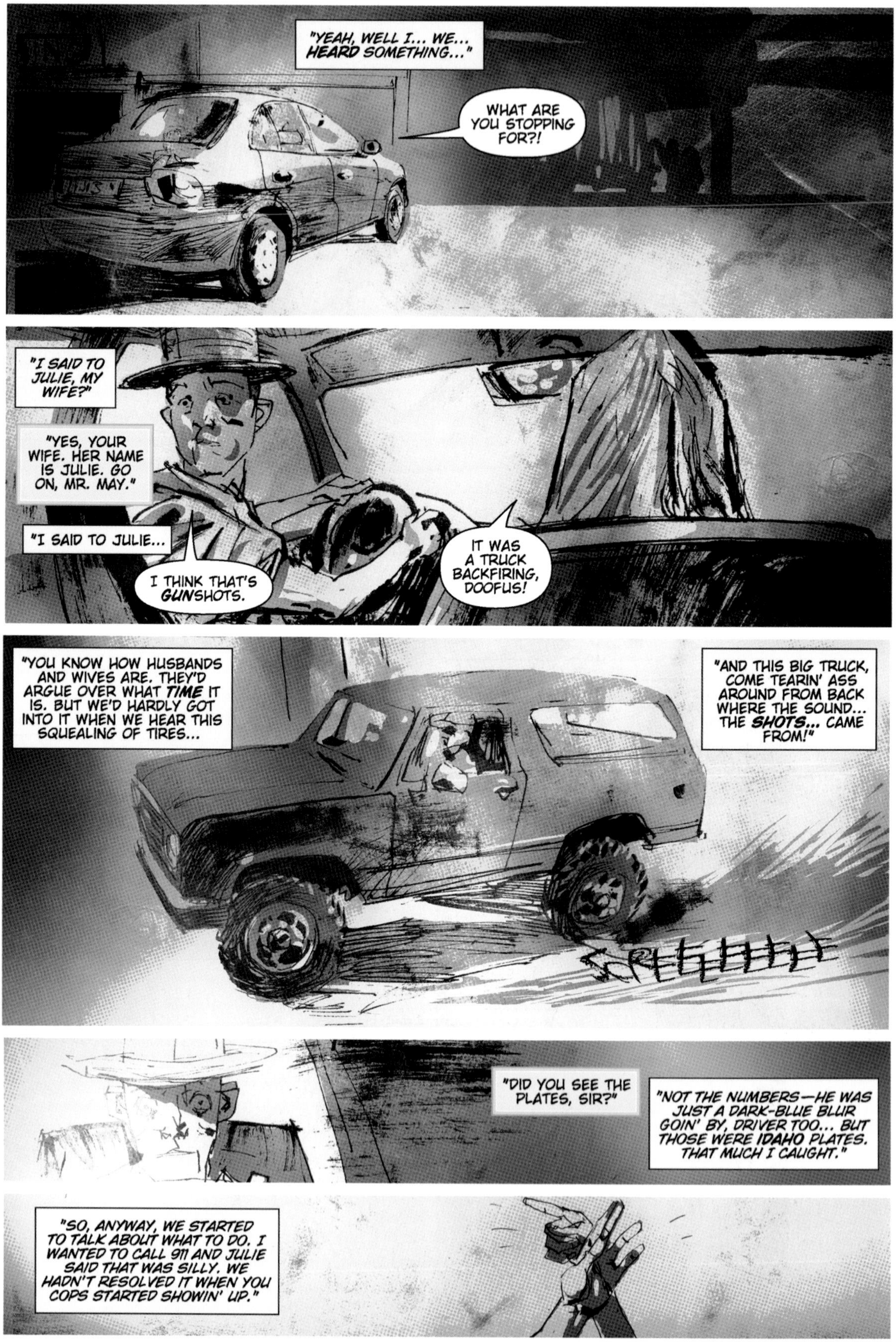
"YEAH, WELL I... WE... **HEARD** SOMETHING..."
WHAT ARE YOU STOPPING FOR?!
"I SAID TO JULIE, MY WIFE?"
"YES, YOUR WIFE. HER NAME IS JULIE. GO ON, MR. MAY."
"I SAID TO JULIE...
I THINK THAT'S **GUN**SHOTS.
IT WAS A TRUCK BACKFIRING, DOOFUS!
"YOU KNOW HOW HUSBANDS AND WIVES ARE. THEY'D ARGUE OVER WHAT **TIME** IT IS. BUT WE'D HARDLY GOT INTO IT WHEN WE HEAR THIS SQUEALING OF TIRES...
"AND THIS BIG TRUCK, COME TEARIN' ASS AROUND FROM BACK WHERE THE SOUND... THE **SHOTS...** CAME FROM!"
SCREEEEEEE
"DID YOU SEE THE PLATES, SIR?"
"NOT THE NUMBERS—HE WAS JUST A DARK-BLUE BLUR GOIN' BY, DRIVER TOO... BUT THOSE WERE **IDAHO** PLATES. THAT MUCH I CAUGHT."
"SO, ANYWAY, WE STARTED TO TALK ABOUT WHAT TO DO. I WANTED TO CALL 911 AND JULIE SAID THAT WAS SILLY. WE HADN'T RESOLVED IT WHEN YOU COPS STARTED SHOWIN' UP."

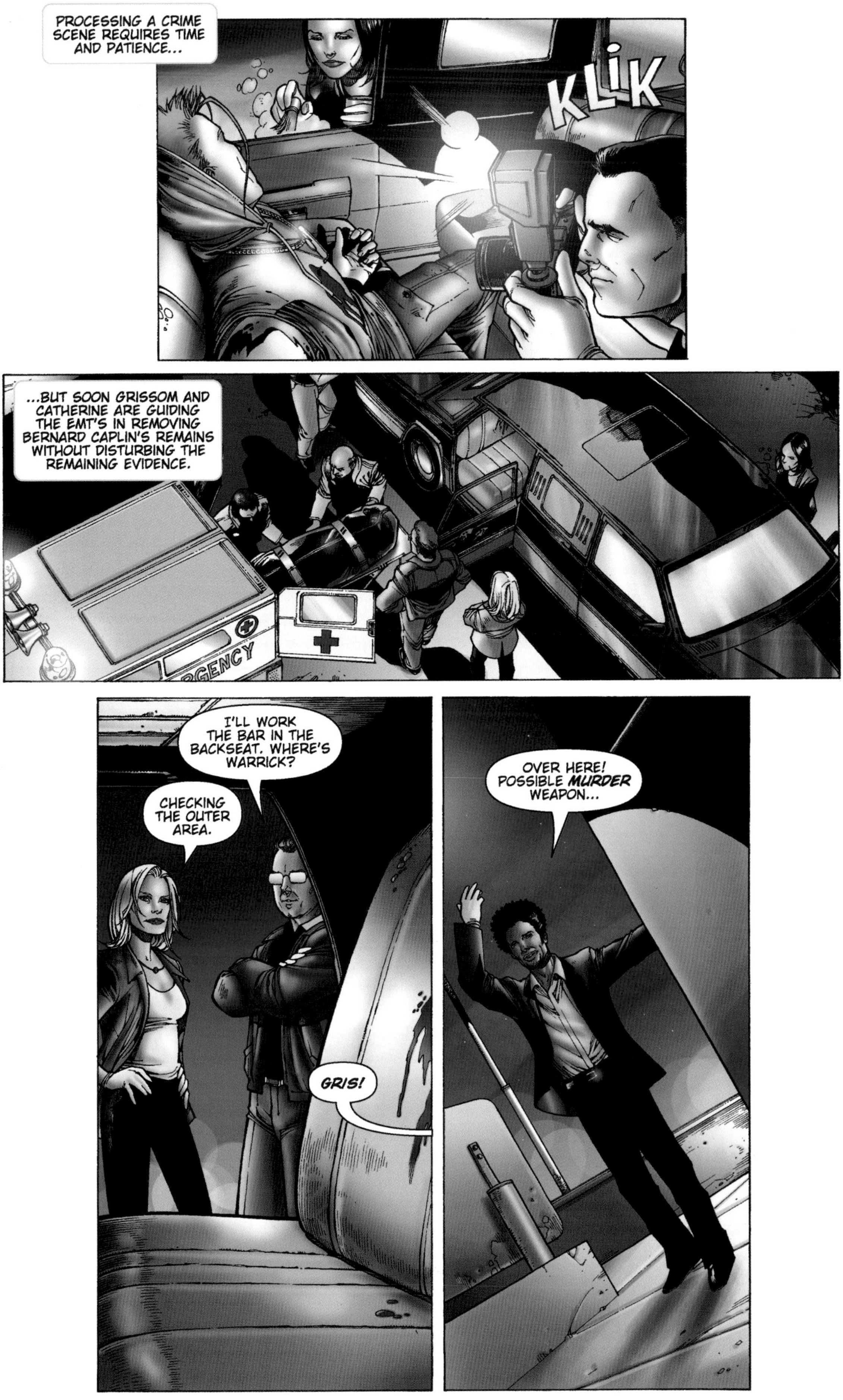
PROCESSING A CRIME SCENE REQUIRES TIME AND PATIENCE...
KLIK
...BUT SOON GRISSOM AND CATHERINE ARE GUIDING THE EMT'S IN REMOVING BERNARD CAPLIN'S REMAINS WITHOUT DISTURBING THE REMAINING EVIDENCE.
I'LL WORK THE BAR IN THE BACKSEAT. WHERE'S WARRICK?
CHECKING THE OUTER AREA.
GRIS!
OVER HERE! POSSIBLE MURDER WEAPON...

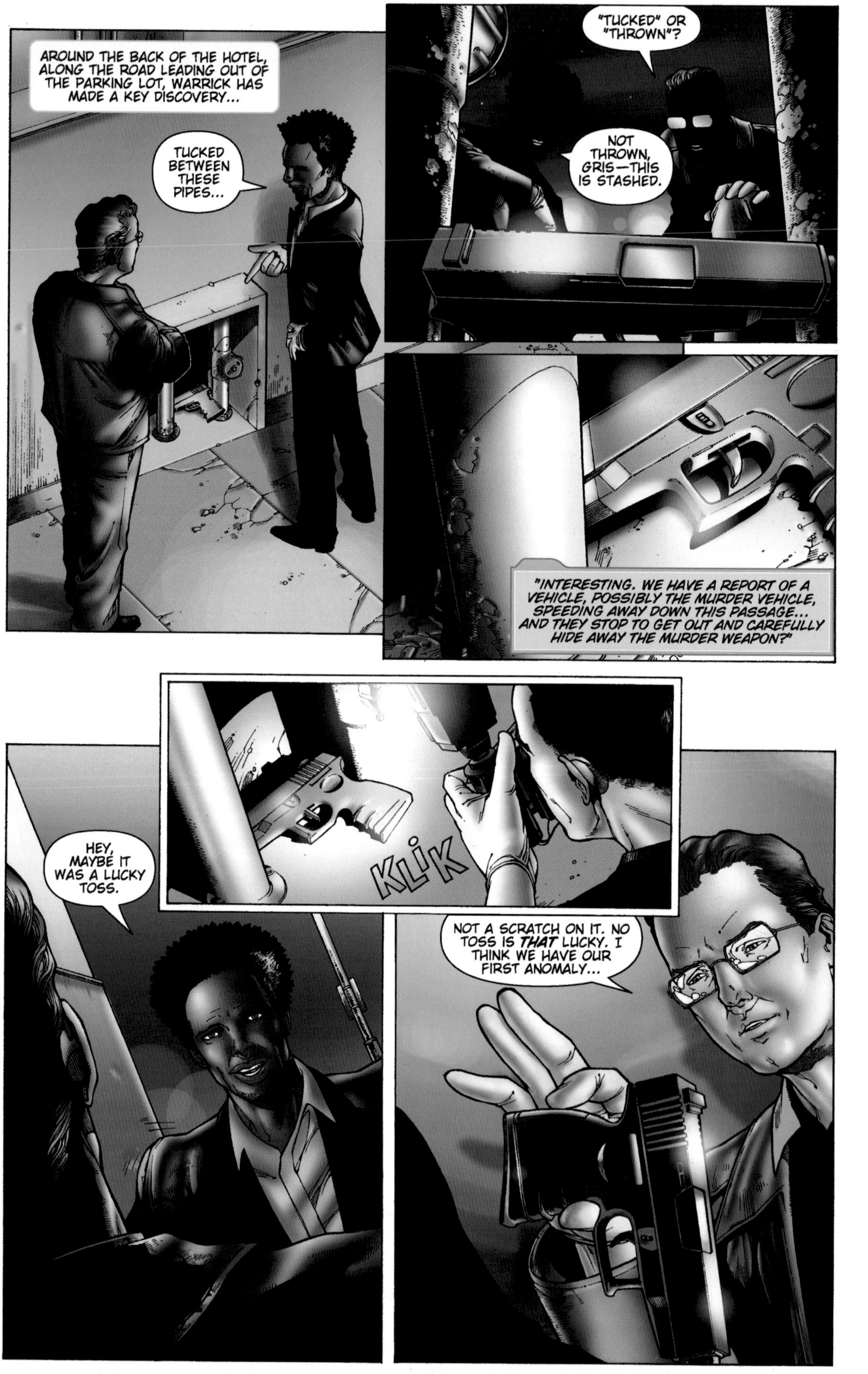
AROUND THE BACK OF THE HOTEL, ALONG THE ROAD LEADING OUT OF THE PARKING LOT, WARRICK HAS MADE A KEY DISCOVERY...
TUCKED BETWEEN THESE PIPES...
"TUCKED" OR "THROWN"?
NOT THROWN, GRIS—THIS IS STASHED.
"INTERESTING. WE HAVE A REPORT OF A VEHICLE, POSSIBLY THE MURDER VEHICLE, SPEEDING AWAY DOWN THIS PASSAGE... AND THEY STOP TO GET OUT AND CAREFULLY HIDE AWAY THE MURDER WEAPON?"
KLIK
HEY, MAYBE IT WAS A LUCKY TOSS.
NOT A SCRATCH ON IT. NO TOSS IS THAT LUCKY. I THINK WE HAVE OUR FIRST ANOMALY...

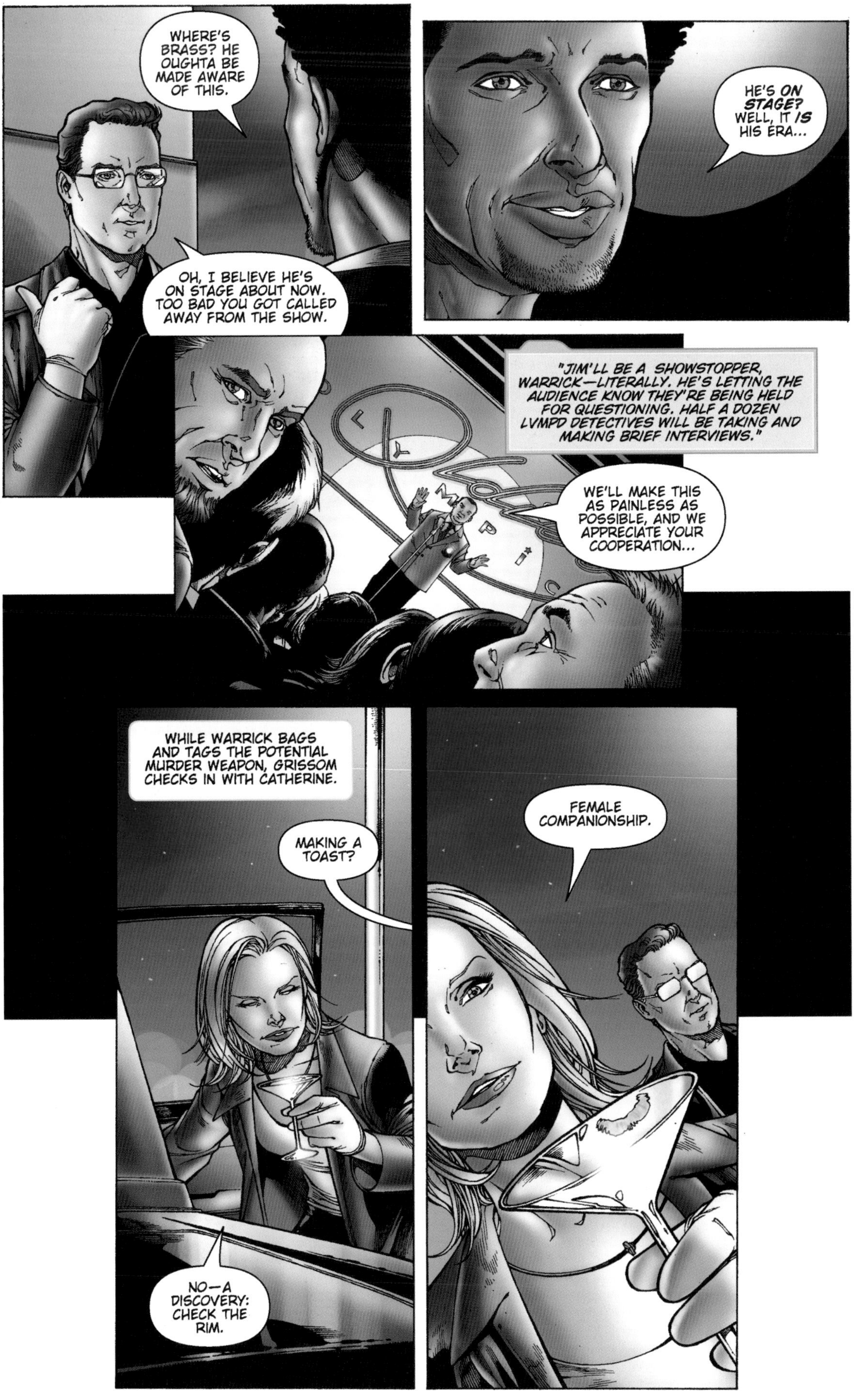
WHERE'S BRASS? HE OUGHTA BE MADE AWARE OF THIS.
OH, I BELIEVE HE'S ON STAGE ABOUT NOW. TOO BAD YOU GOT CALLED AWAY FROM THE SHOW.
HE'S ON STAGE? WELL, IT IS HIS ERA...
"JIM'LL BE A SHOWSTOPPER, WARRICK—LITERALLY. HE'S LETTING THE AUDIENCE KNOW THEY'RE BEING HELD FOR QUESTIONING. HALF A DOZEN LVMPD DETECTIVES WILL BE TAKING AND MAKING BRIEF INTERVIEWS."
WE'LL MAKE THIS AS PAINLESS AS POSSIBLE, AND WE APPRECIATE YOUR COOPERATION...
WHILE WARRICK BAGS AND TAGS THE POTENTIAL MURDER WEAPON, GRISSOM CHECKS IN WITH CATHERINE.
MAKING A TOAST?
NO—A DISCOVERY: CHECK THE RIM.
FEMALE COMPANIONSHIP.

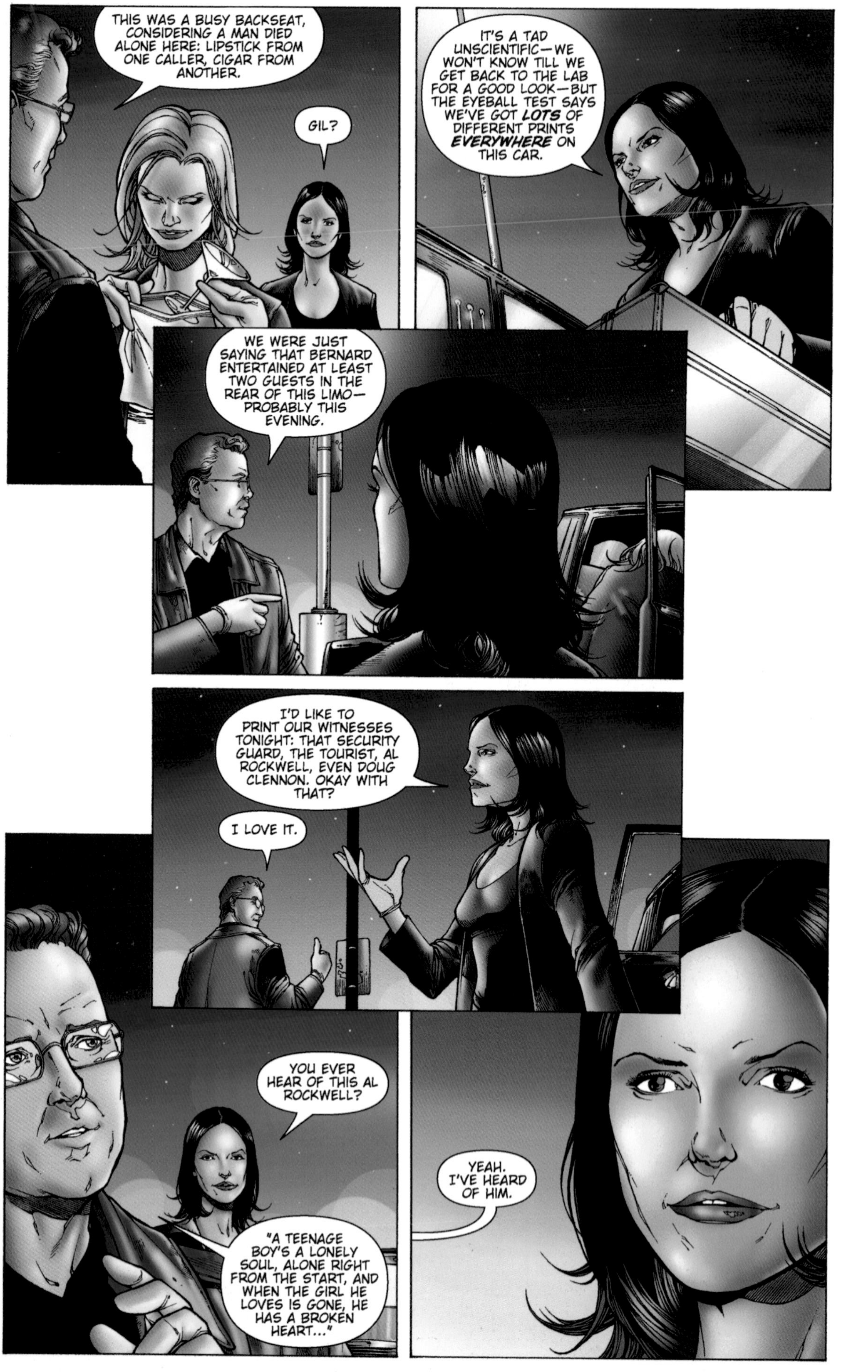
THIS WAS A BUSY BACKSEAT, CONSIDERING A MAN DIED ALONE HERE: LIPSTICK FROM ONE CALLER, CIGAR FROM ANOTHER.
GIL?
IT'S A TAD UNSCIENTIFIC—WE WON'T KNOW TILL WE GET BACK TO THE LAB FOR A GOOD LOOK—BUT THE EYEBALL TEST SAYS WE'VE GOT **LOTS** OF DIFFERENT PRINTS ***EVERYWHERE*** ON THIS CAR.
WE WERE JUST SAYING THAT BERNARD ENTERTAINED AT LEAST TWO GUESTS IN THE REAR OF THIS LIMO—PROBABLY THIS EVENING.
I'D LIKE TO PRINT OUR WITNESSES TONIGHT: THAT SECURITY GUARD, THE TOURIST, AL ROCKWELL, EVEN DOUG CLENNON. OKAY WITH THAT?
I LOVE IT.
YOU EVER HEAR OF THIS AL ROCKWELL?
"A TEENAGE BOY'S A LONELY SOUL, ALONE RIGHT FROM THE START, AND WHEN THE GIRL HE LOVES IS GONE, HE HAS A BROKEN HEART..."
YEAH. I'VE HEARD OF HIM.

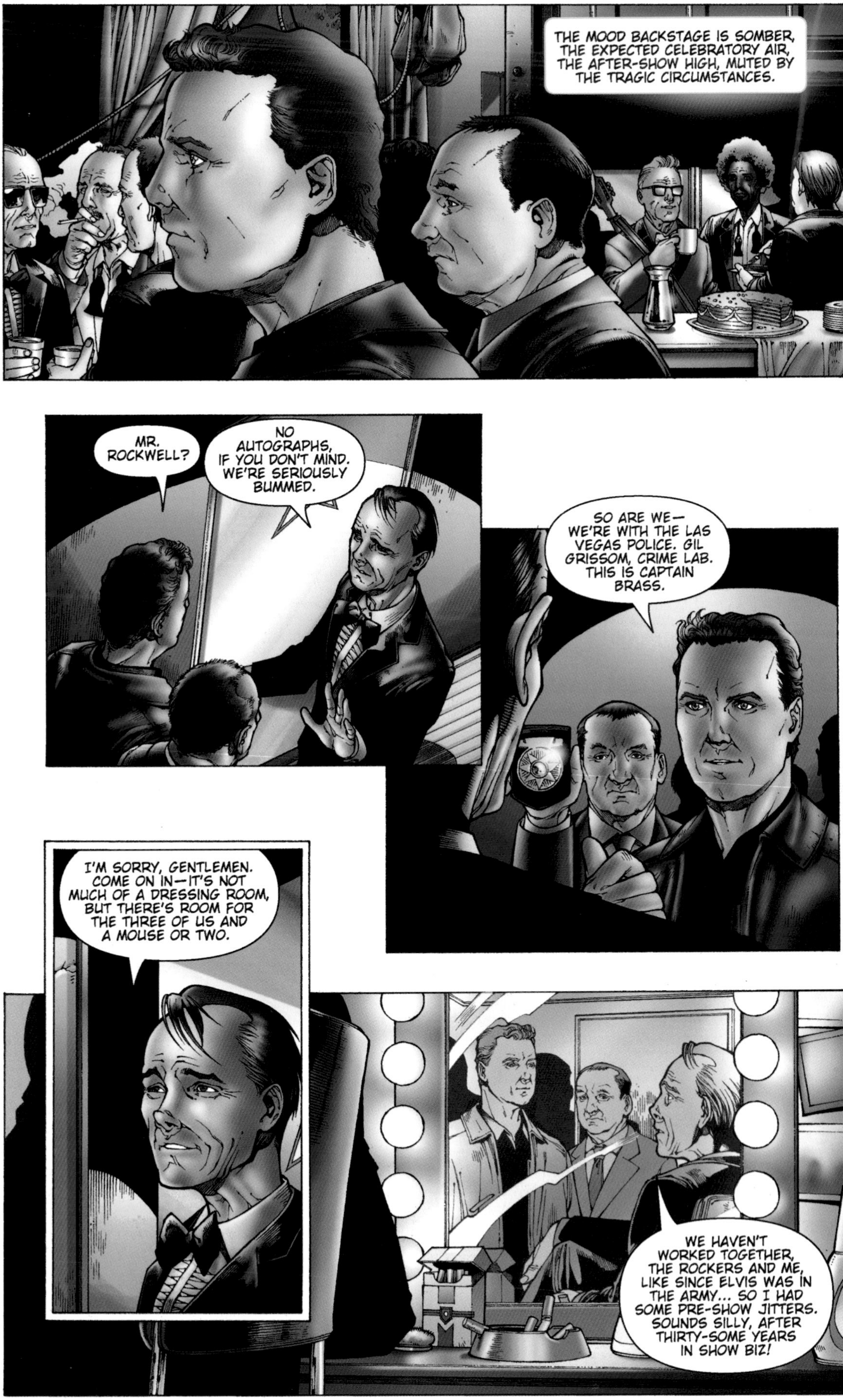
THE MOOD BACKSTAGE IS SOMBER, THE EXPECTED CELEBRATORY AIR, THE AFTER-SHOW HIGH, MUTED BY THE TRAGIC CIRCUMSTANCES.
MR. ROCKWELL?
NO AUTOGRAPHS, IF YOU DON'T MIND. WE'RE SERIOUSLY BUMMED.
SO ARE WE— WE'RE WITH THE LAS VEGAS POLICE. GIL GRISSOM, CRIME LAB. THIS IS CAPTAIN BRASS.
I'M SORRY, GENTLEMEN. COME ON IN—IT'S NOT MUCH OF A DRESSING ROOM, BUT THERE'S ROOM FOR THE THREE OF US AND A MOUSE OR TWO.
WE HAVEN'T WORKED TOGETHER, THE ROCKERS AND ME, LIKE SINCE ELVIS WAS IN THE ARMY... SO I HAD SOME PRE-SHOW JITTERS. SOUNDS SILLY, AFTER THIRTY-SOME YEARS IN SHOW BIZ!

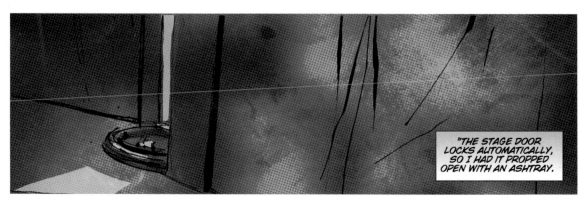

"THE STAGE DOOR LOCKS AUTOMATICALLY, SO I HAD IT PROPPED OPEN WITH AN ASHTRAY."

"THE LIMO WAS SITTING THERE — ENGINE WASN'T GOING OR ANYTHING. I HAD KIND OF A FRONT VIEW, SO THE TINTED WINDOW MEANT I COULDN'T TELL WHO WAS IN THE CAR OR ANYTHING.

"BUT I TURNED MY BACK TO THE CAR, 'CAUSE I WANTED MY OWN PRIVACY, GOIN' OVER LYRICS IN MY MIND... SOME OF THESE TUNES WE HAVEN'T DONE IN AGES! EMBARRASSING WHEN THE AUDIENCE KNOWS THE WORDS AND YOU DON'T.

"I GUESS I WAS CONSCIOUS OF A VEHICLE PULLING IN, BUT I DIDN'T TURN TO LOOK, NOT AT FIRST... TILL THERE WAS THIS POPPING SOUND, AND THEN MORE POPPING — KINDA LIKE FIRECRACKERS, FOURTH OF JULY.

"THE SHOOTING HAD STOPPED BY THE TIME I TURNED, BUT I SAW THIS KID HANGING OUT THE WINDOW OF A RED PICK-UP TRUCK, I THINK A CHEVY. HE WAS WHITE, SOMEWHERE BETWEEN SEVENTEEN AND TWENTY, A... SKATEBOARDER KINDA KID."

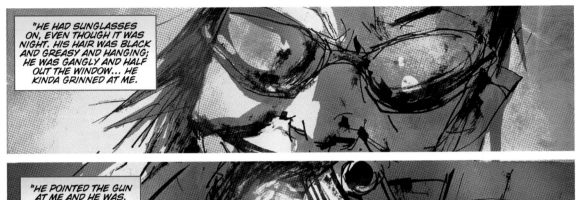

"HE HAD SUNGLASSES ON, EVEN THOUGH IT WAS NIGHT. HIS HAIR WAS BLACK AND GREASY AND HANGING; HE WAS GANGLY AND HALF OUT THE WINDOW... HE KINDA GRINNED AT ME.

"HE POINTED THE GUN AT ME AND HE WAS, LIKE, ON DRUGS OR SOMETHING. HE SAID...

BANG BANG, POPS. YOU'RE DEAD.

"WELL, I'M NOT ASHAMED TO SAY IT SCARED THE HELL OUT OF ME. KID MUST'VE PULLED AWAY THEN, BUT I WAS SCRAMBLING TO GET IN THE DOOR.

"AND IN MY HASTE, I KICKED THE DAMN ASHTRAY, AND LOCKED MYSELF OUT!

"THANK GOD THAT SECURITY GUARD, BOBBY WHAT'S-IT, CAME OUT ABOUT THEN, OR I MIGHTA GONE ON STAGE WISHIN' I'D WORN ADULT DIAPERS, IF YOU GET MY DRIFT."

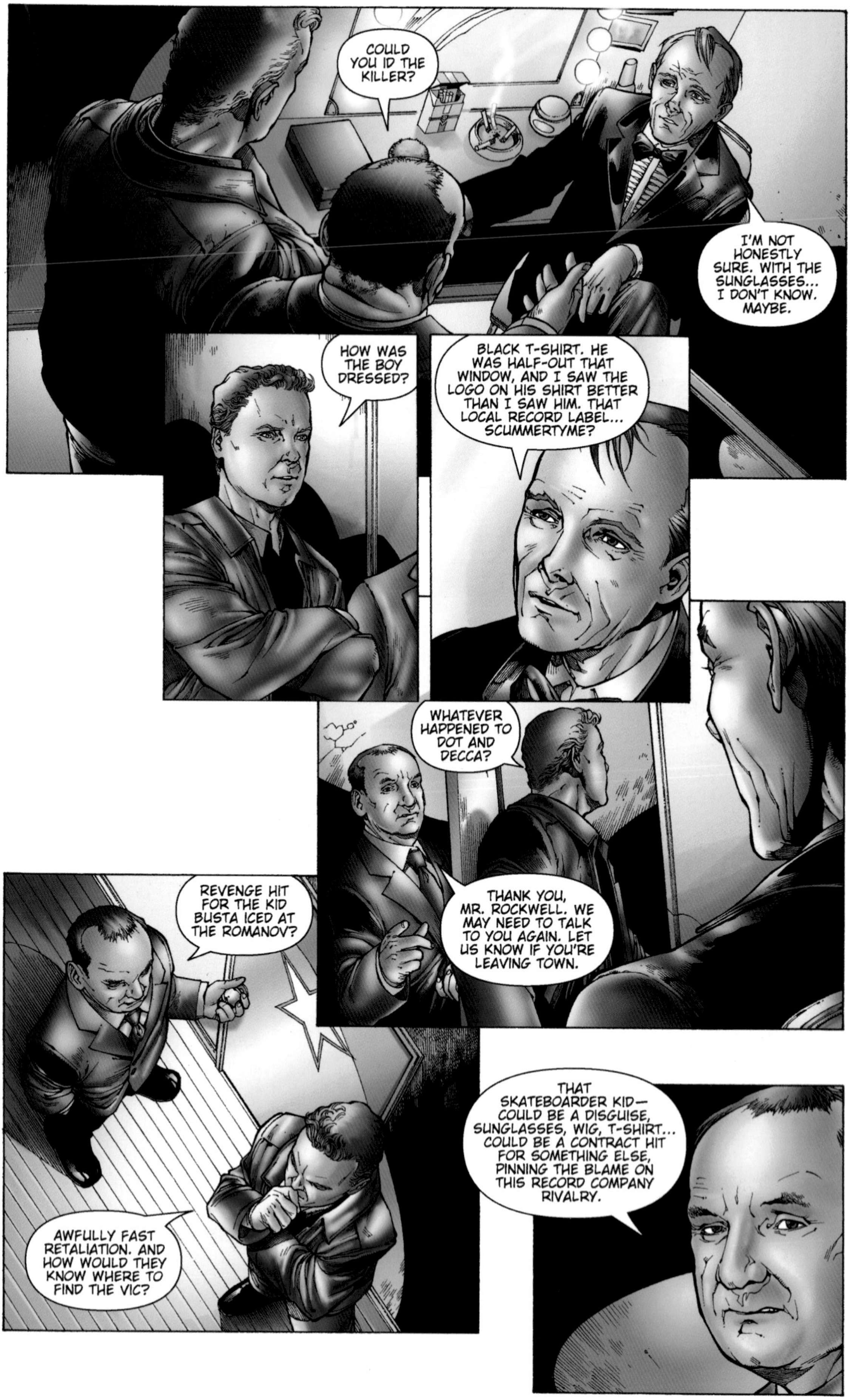
COULD YOU ID THE KILLER?
I'M NOT HONESTLY SURE. WITH THE SUNGLASSES... I DON'T KNOW. MAYBE.
HOW WAS THE BOY DRESSED?
BLACK T-SHIRT. HE WAS HALF-OUT THAT WINDOW, AND I SAW THE LOGO ON HIS SHIRT BETTER THAN I SAW HIM. THAT LOCAL RECORD LABEL... SCUMMERTYME?
WHATEVER HAPPENED TO DOT AND DECCA?
THANK YOU, MR. ROCKWELL. WE MAY NEED TO TALK TO YOU AGAIN. LET US KNOW IF YOU'RE LEAVING TOWN.
REVENGE HIT FOR THE KID BUSTA ICED AT THE ROMANOV?
AWFULLY FAST RETALIATION. AND HOW WOULD THEY KNOW WHERE TO FIND THE VIC?
THAT SKATEBOARDER KID— COULD BE A DISGUISE, SUNGLASSES, WIG, T-SHIRT... COULD BE A CONTRACT HIT FOR SOMETHING ELSE, PINNING THE BLAME ON THIS RECORD COMPANY RIVALRY.

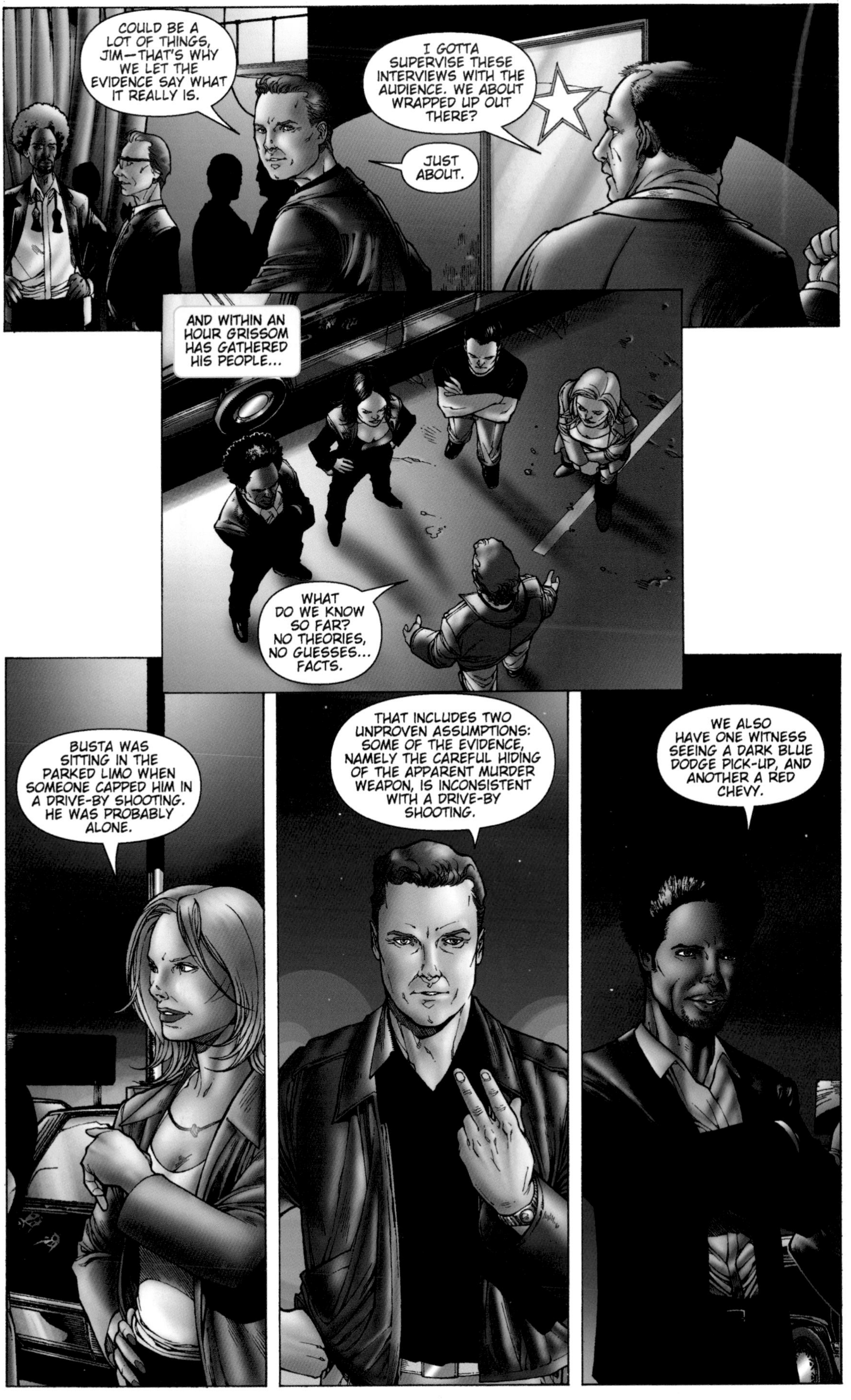
COULD BE A LOT OF THINGS, JIM—THAT'S WHY WE LET THE EVIDENCE SAY WHAT IT REALLY IS.
I GOTTA SUPERVISE THESE INTERVIEWS WITH THE AUDIENCE. WE ABOUT WRAPPED UP OUT THERE?
JUST ABOUT.
AND WITHIN AN HOUR GRISSOM HAS GATHERED HIS PEOPLE...
WHAT DO WE KNOW SO FAR? NO THEORIES, NO GUESSES... FACTS.
BUSTA WAS SITTING IN THE PARKED LIMO WHEN SOMEONE CAPPED HIM IN A DRIVE-BY SHOOTING. HE WAS PROBABLY ALONE.
THAT INCLUDES TWO UNPROVEN ASSUMPTIONS: SOME OF THE EVIDENCE, NAMELY THE CAREFUL HIDING OF THE APPARENT MURDER WEAPON, IS INCONSISTENT WITH A DRIVE-BY SHOOTING.
WE ALSO HAVE ONE WITNESS SEEING A DARK BLUE DODGE PICK-UP, AND ANOTHER A RED CHEVY.

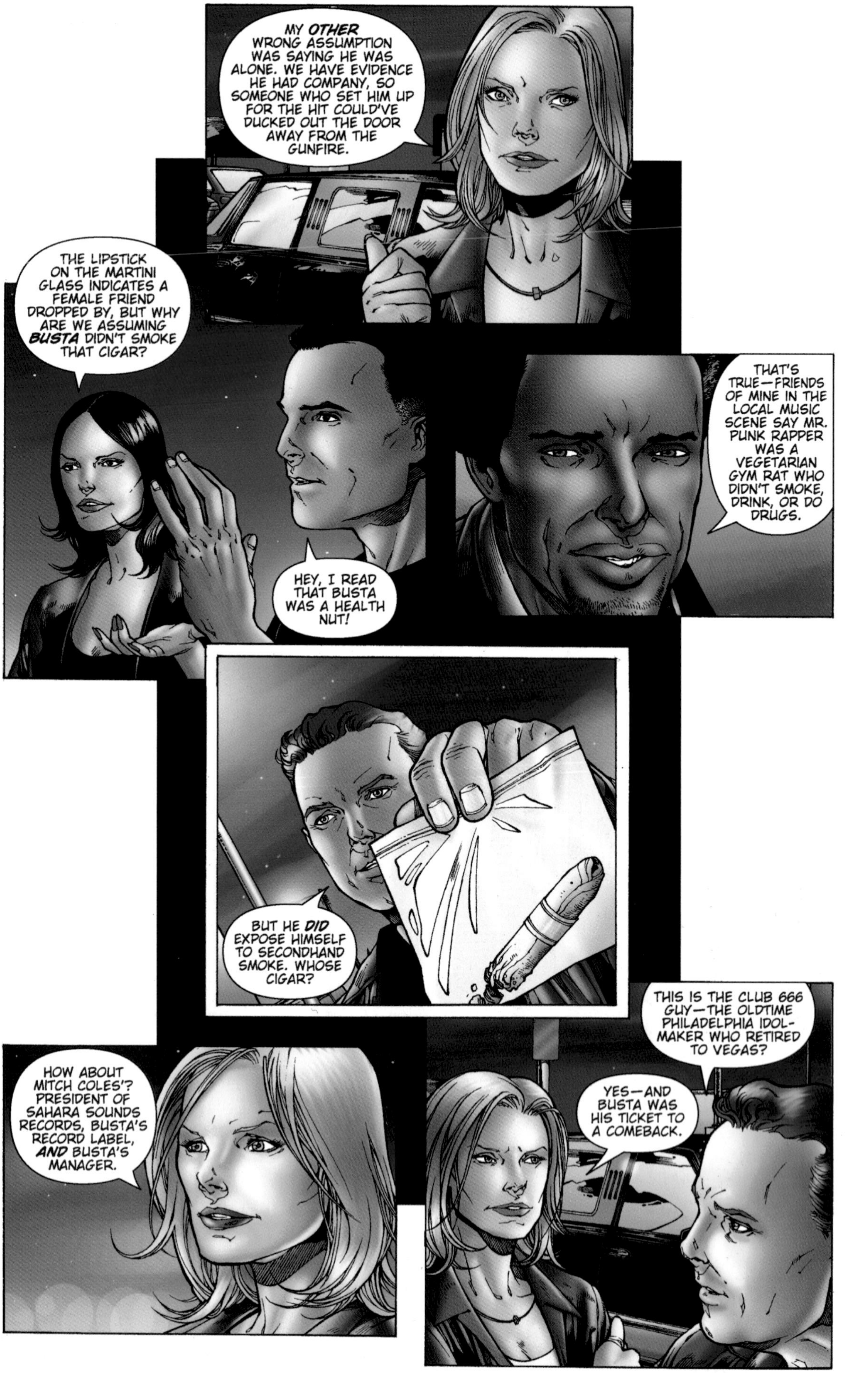
MY OTHER WRONG ASSUMPTION WAS SAYING HE WAS ALONE. WE HAVE EVIDENCE HE HAD COMPANY, SO SOMEONE WHO SET HIM UP FOR THE HIT COULD'VE DUCKED OUT THE DOOR AWAY FROM THE GUNFIRE.
THE LIPSTICK ON THE MARTINI GLASS INDICATES A FEMALE FRIEND DROPPED BY, BUT WHY ARE WE ASSUMING BUSTA DIDN'T SMOKE THAT CIGAR?
HEY, I READ THAT BUSTA WAS A HEALTH NUT!
THAT'S TRUE—FRIENDS OF MINE IN THE LOCAL MUSIC SCENE SAY MR. PUNK RAPPER WAS A VEGETARIAN GYM RAT WHO DIDN'T SMOKE, DRINK, OR DO DRUGS.
BUT HE DID EXPOSE HIMSELF TO SECONDHAND SMOKE. WHOSE CIGAR?
HOW ABOUT MITCH COLES'? PRESIDENT OF SAHARA SOUNDS RECORDS, BUSTA'S RECORD LABEL, AND BUSTA'S MANAGER.
THIS IS THE CLUB 666 GUY—THE OLDTIME PHILADELPHIA IDOL-MAKER WHO RETIRED TO VEGAS?
YES—AND BUSTA WAS HIS TICKET TO A COMEBACK.

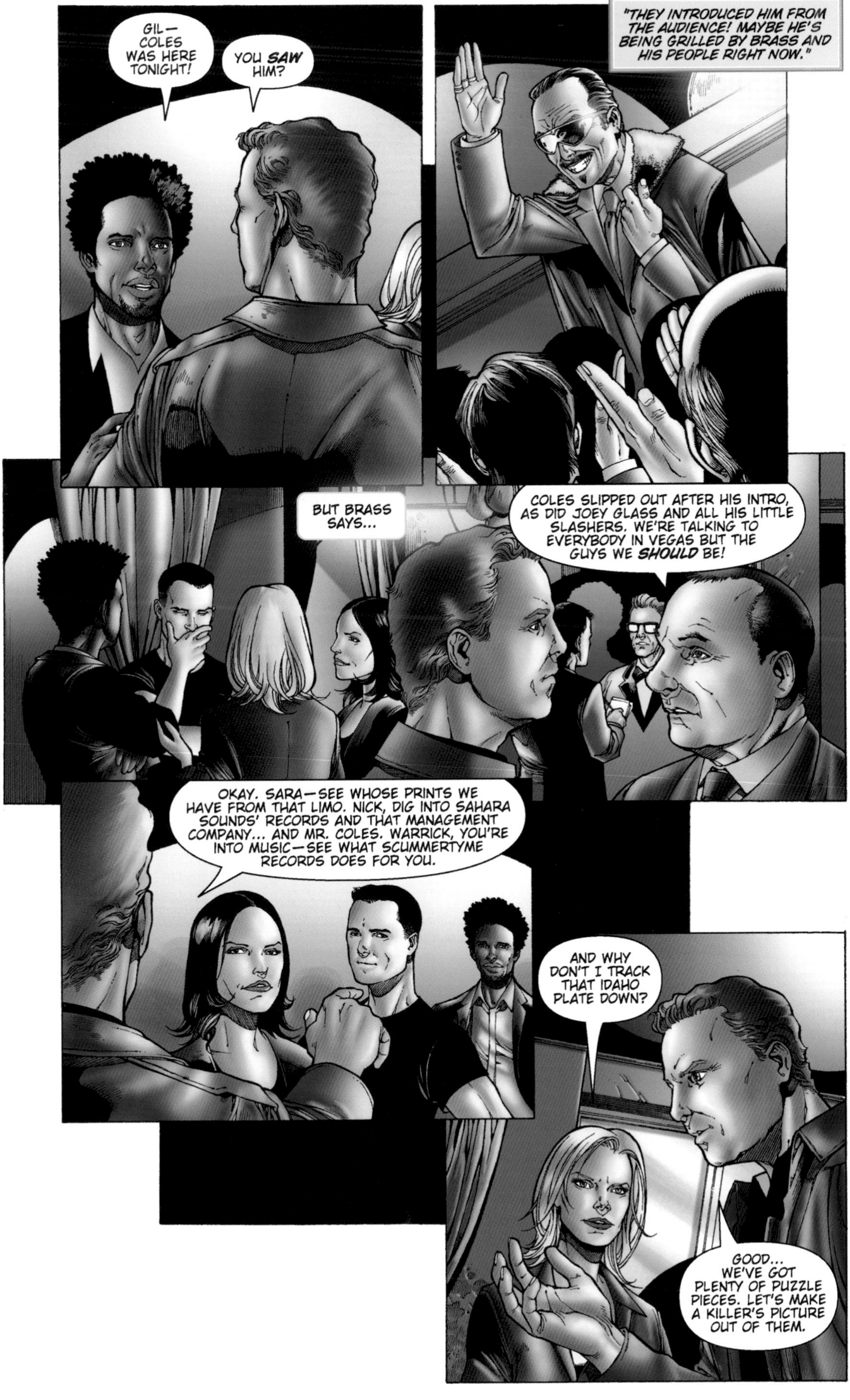
GIL—COLES WAS HERE TONIGHT!
YOU SAW HIM?
"THEY INTRODUCED HIM FROM THE AUDIENCE! MAYBE HE'S BEING GRILLED BY BRASS AND HIS PEOPLE RIGHT NOW."
BUT BRASS SAYS...
COLES SLIPPED OUT AFTER HIS INTRO, AS DID JOEY GLASS AND ALL HIS LITTLE SLASHERS. WE'RE TALKING TO EVERYBODY IN VEGAS BUT THE GUYS WE SHOULD BE!
OKAY. SARA—SEE WHOSE PRINTS WE HAVE FROM THAT LIMO. NICK, DIG INTO SAHARA SOUNDS' RECORDS AND THAT MANAGEMENT COMPANY... AND MR. COLES. WARRICK, YOU'RE INTO MUSIC—SEE WHAT SCUMMERTYME RECORDS DOES FOR YOU.
AND WHY DON'T I TRACK THAT IDAHO PLATE DOWN?
GOOD... WE'VE GOT PLENTY OF PUZZLE PIECES. LET'S MAKE A KILLER'S PICTURE OUT OF THEM.

# chapter three
# Lipstick On Your Collar

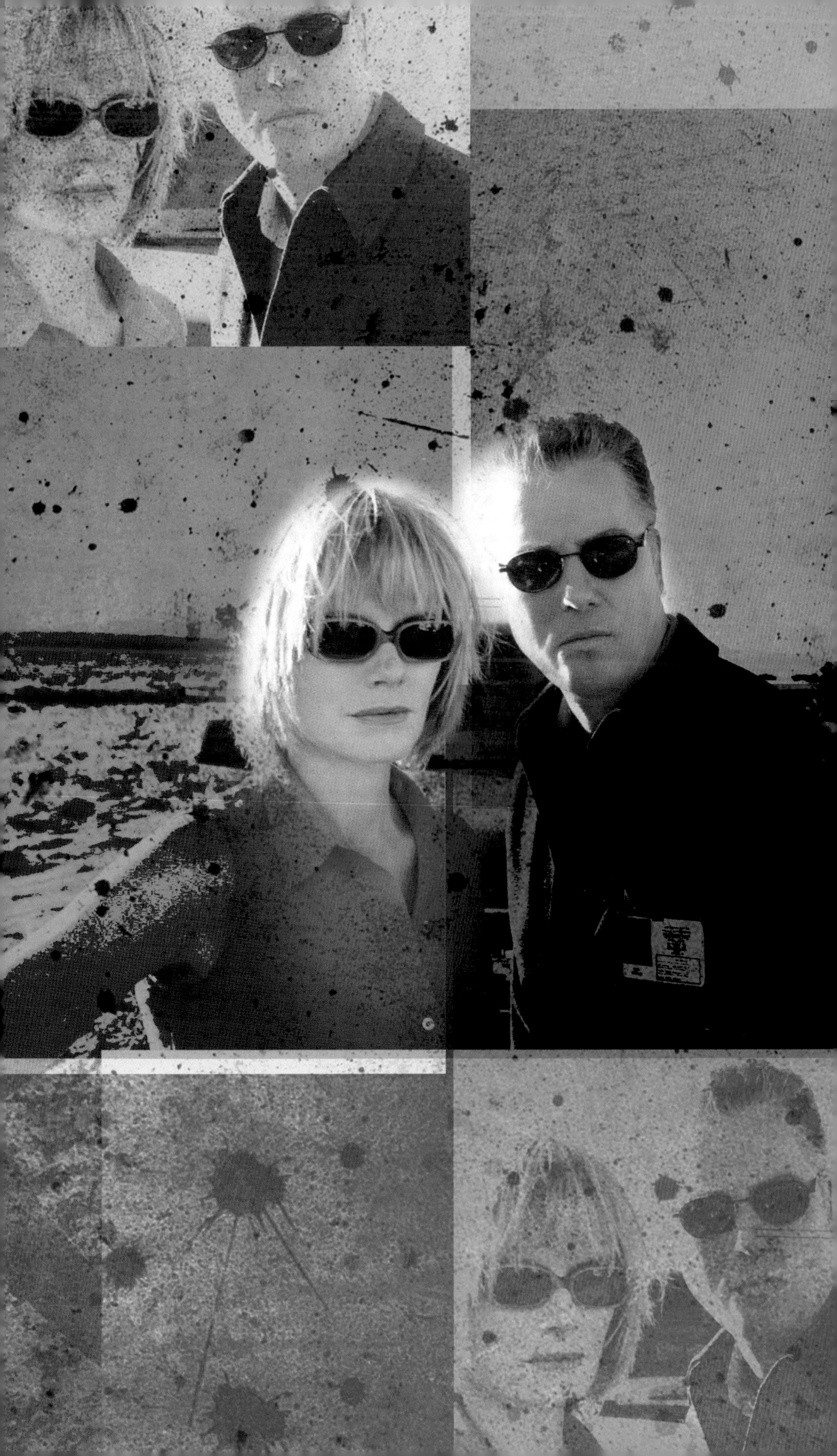

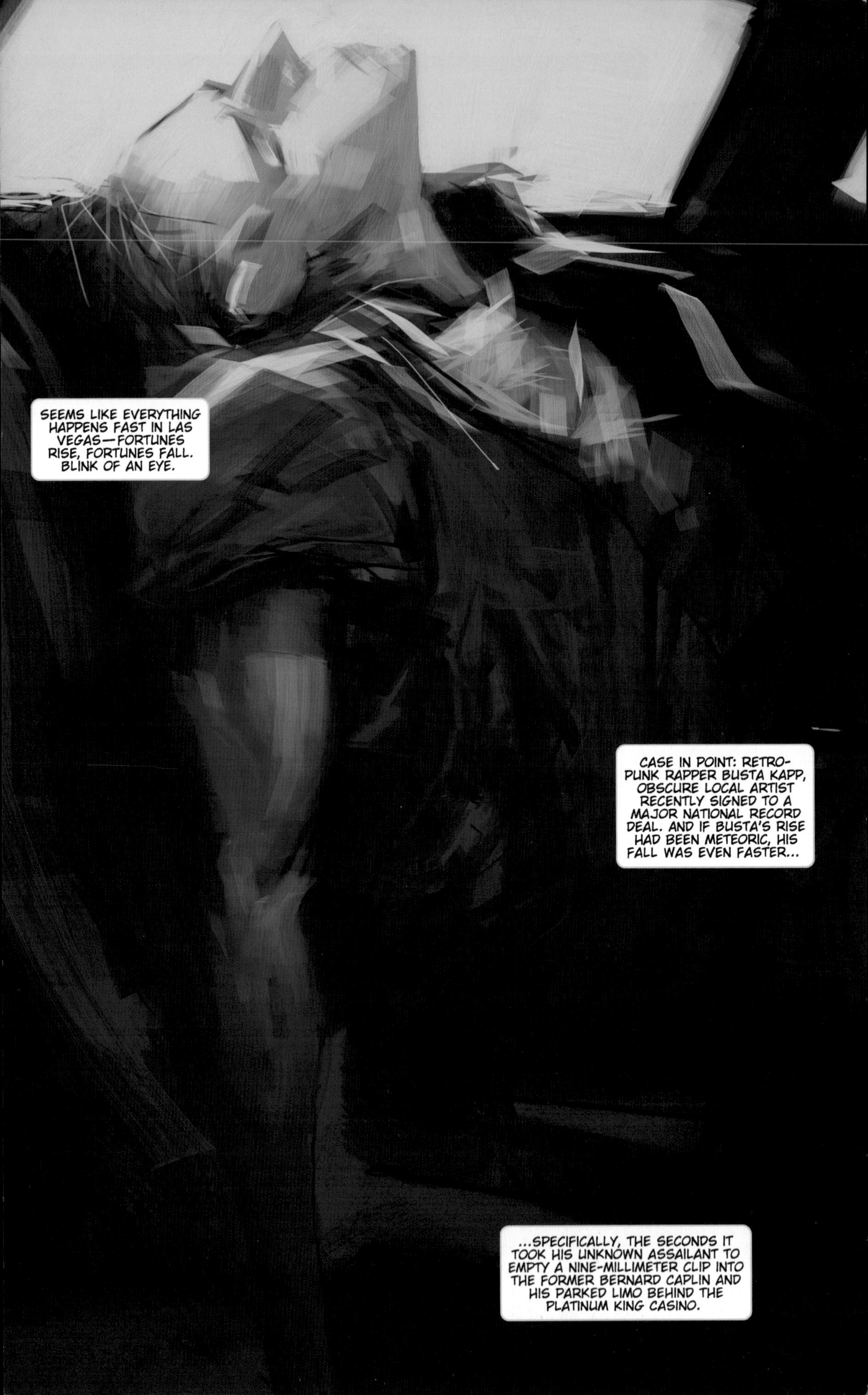
SEEMS LIKE EVERYTHING HAPPENS FAST IN LAS VEGAS—FORTUNES RISE, FORTUNES FALL. BLINK OF AN EYE.
CASE IN POINT: RETRO-PUNK RAPPER BUSTA KAPP, OBSCURE LOCAL ARTIST RECENTLY SIGNED TO A MAJOR NATIONAL RECORD DEAL. AND IF BUSTA'S RISE HAD BEEN METEORIC, HIS FALL WAS EVEN FASTER...
...SPECIFICALLY, THE SECONDS IT TOOK HIS UNKNOWN ASSAILANT TO EMPTY A NINE-MILLIMETER CLIP INTO THE FORMER BERNARD CAPLIN AND HIS PARKED LIMO BEHIND THE PLATINUM KING CASINO.

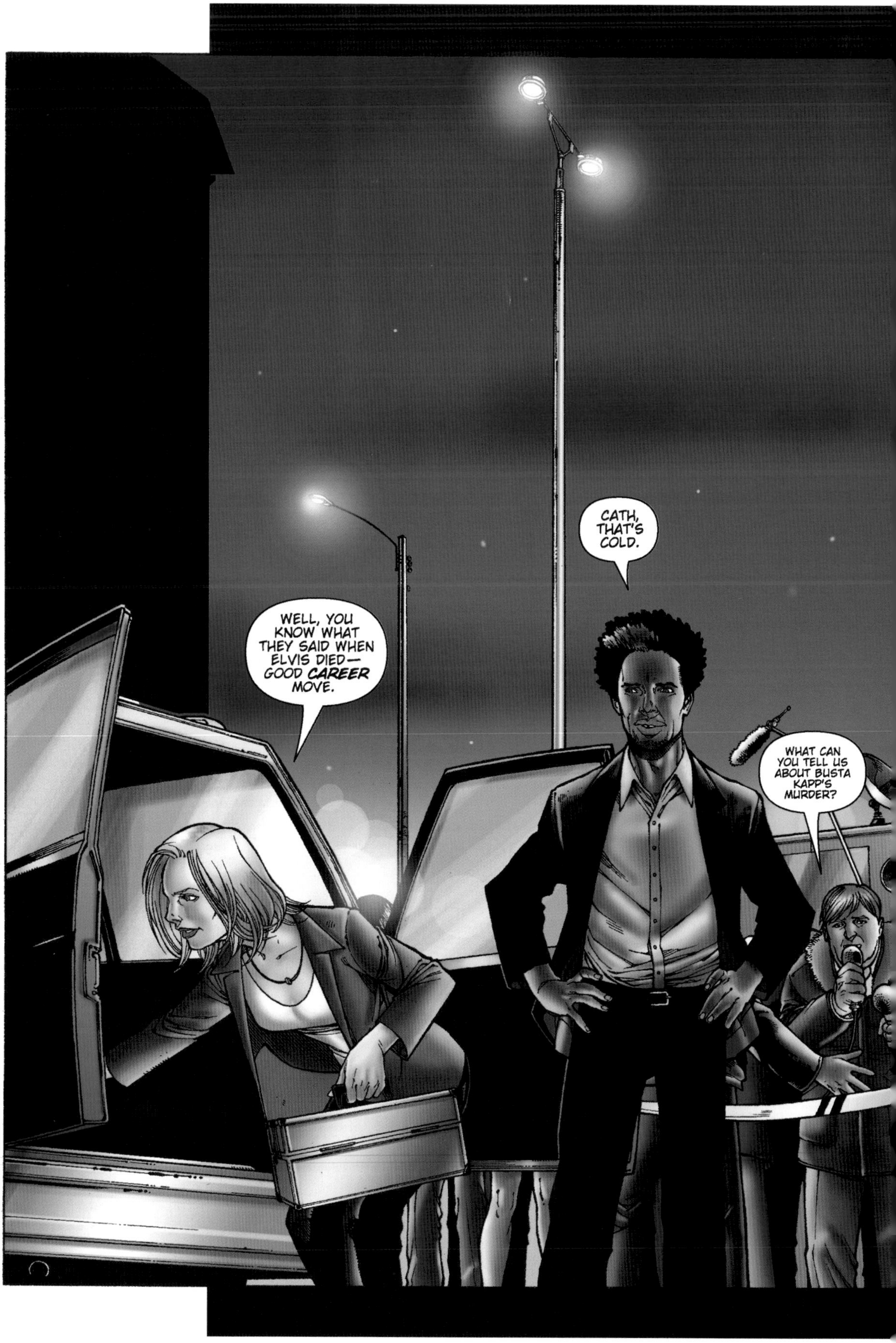
WELL, YOU KNOW WHAT THEY SAID WHEN ELVIS DIED—GOOD CAREER MOVE.
CATH, THAT'S COLD.
WHAT CAN YOU TELL US ABOUT BUSTA KAPP'S MURDER?

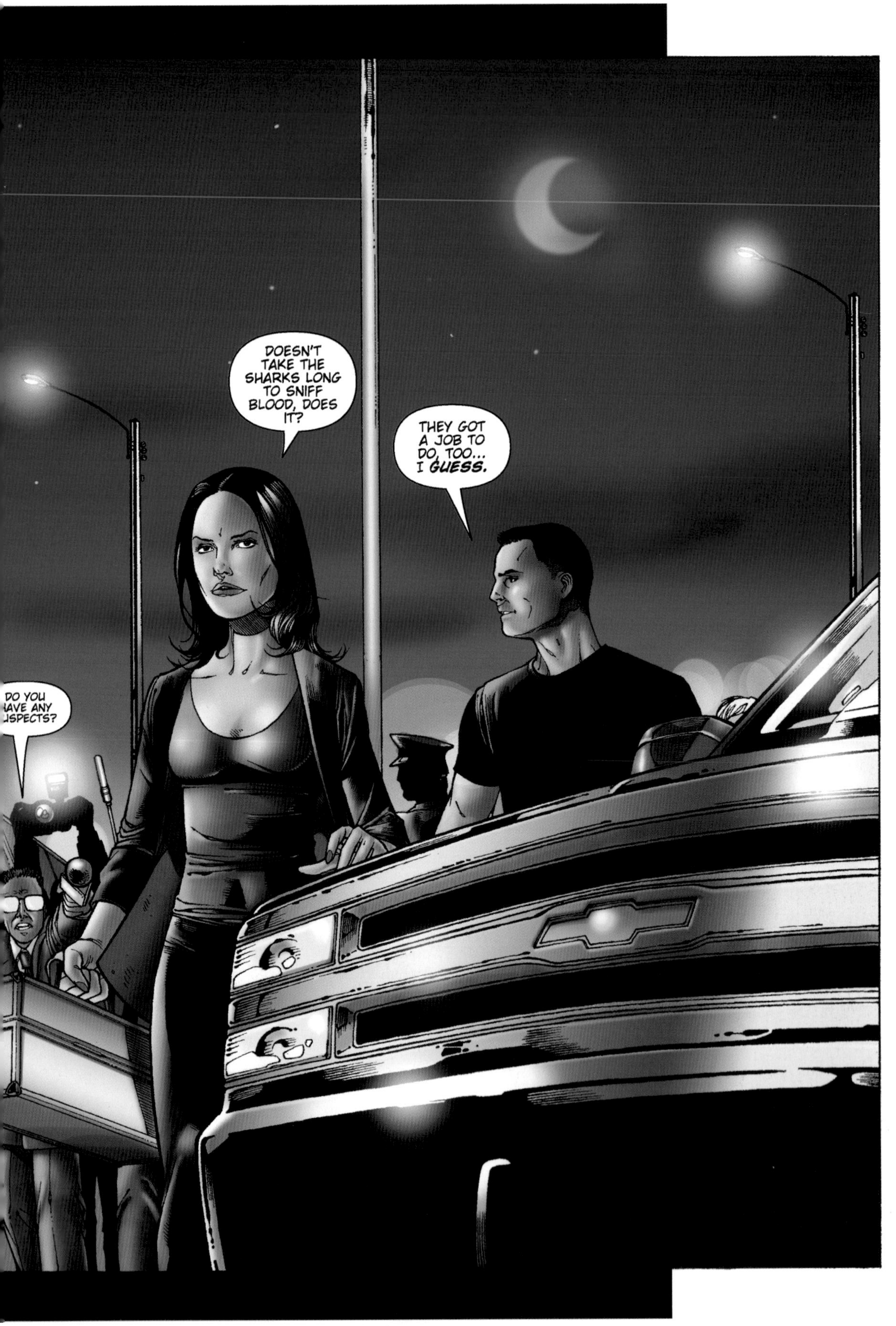
DO YOU AVE ANY ISPECTS?
DOESN'T TAKE THE SHARKS LONG TO SNIFF BLOOD, DOES IT?
THEY GOT A JOB TO DO, TOO... I **GUESS.**

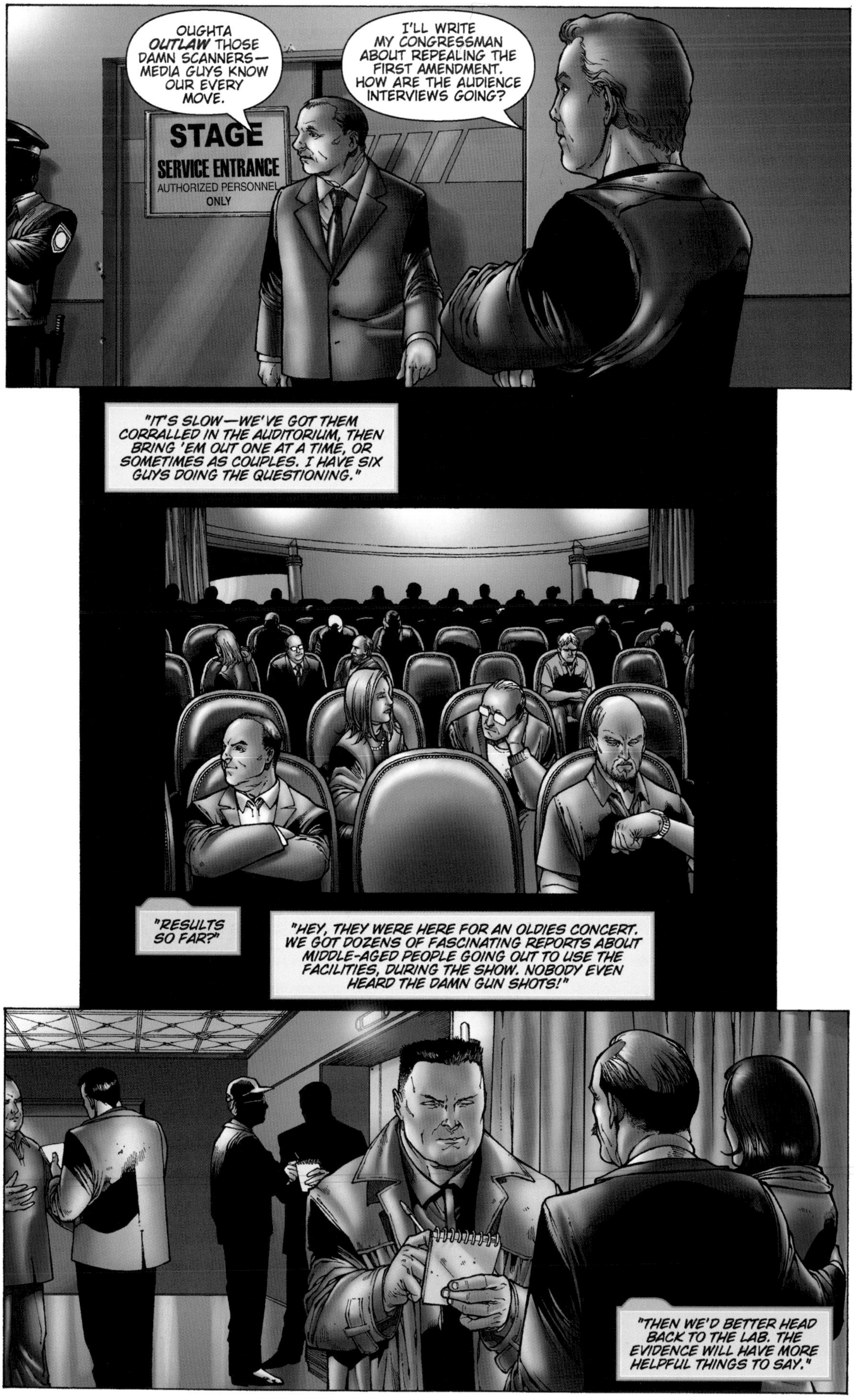
OUGHTA OUTLAW THOSE DAMN SCANNERS— MEDIA GUYS KNOW OUR EVERY MOVE.
I'LL WRITE MY CONGRESSMAN ABOUT REPEALING THE FIRST AMENDMENT. HOW ARE THE AUDIENCE INTERVIEWS GOING?
STAGE
SERVICE ENTRANCE
AUTHORIZED PERSONNEL ONLY
"IT'S SLOW—WE'VE GOT THEM CORRALLED IN THE AUDITORIUM, THEN BRING 'EM OUT ONE AT A TIME, OR SOMETIMES AS COUPLES. I HAVE SIX GUYS DOING THE QUESTIONING."
"RESULTS SO FAR?"
"HEY, THEY WERE HERE FOR AN OLDIES CONCERT. WE GOT DOZENS OF FASCINATING REPORTS ABOUT MIDDLE-AGED PEOPLE GOING OUT TO USE THE FACILITIES, DURING THE SHOW. NOBODY EVEN HEARD THE DAMN GUN SHOTS!"
"THEN WE'D BETTER HEAD BACK TO THE LAB. THE EVIDENCE WILL HAVE MORE HELPFUL THINGS TO SAY."

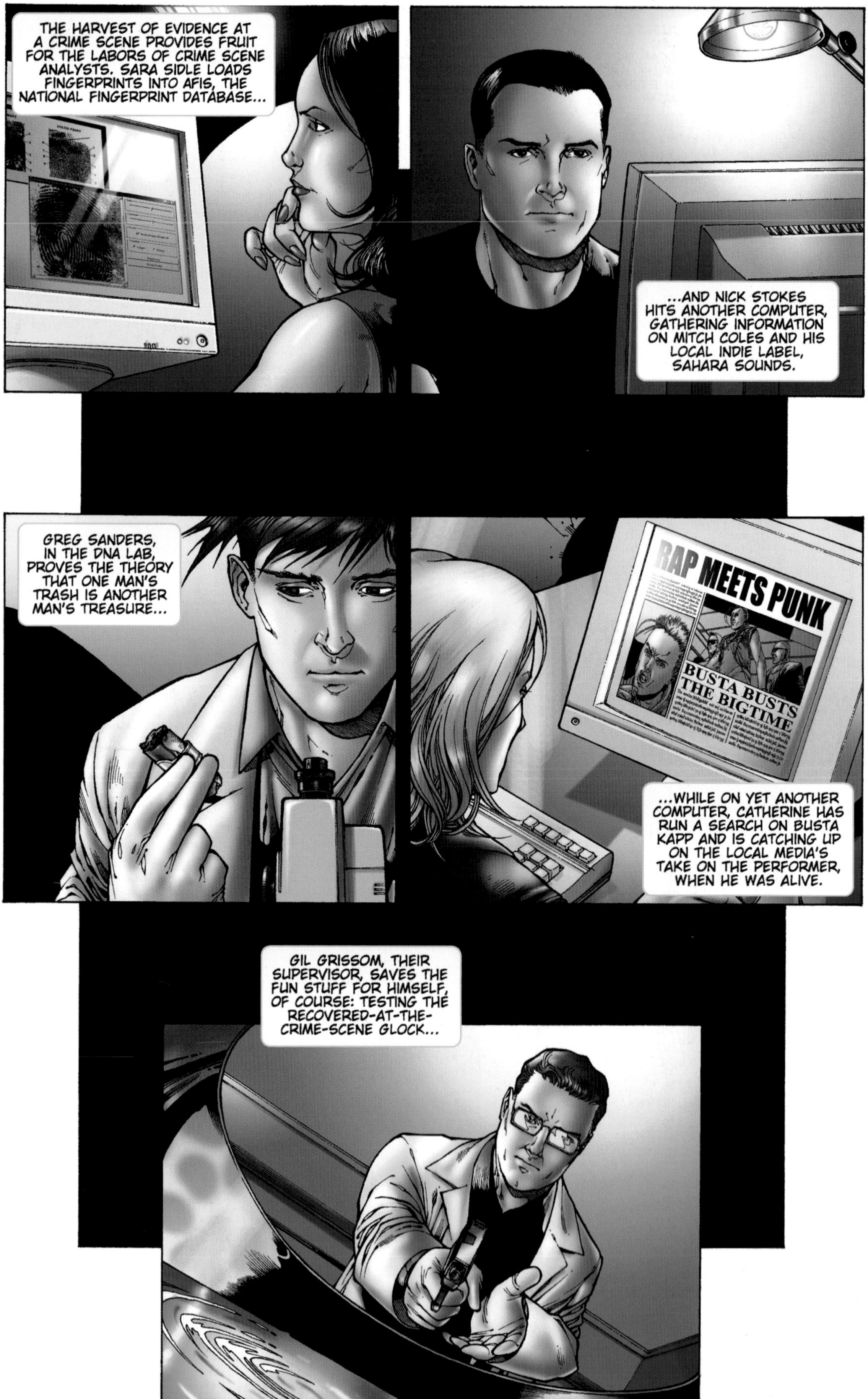
THE HARVEST OF EVIDENCE AT A CRIME SCENE PROVIDES FRUIT FOR THE LABORS OF CRIME SCENE ANALYSTS. SARA SIDLE LOADS FINGERPRINTS INTO AFIS, THE NATIONAL FINGERPRINT DATABASE...
...AND NICK STOKES HITS ANOTHER COMPUTER, GATHERING INFORMATION ON MITCH COLES AND HIS LOCAL INDIE LABEL, SAHARA SOUNDS.
GREG SANDERS, IN THE DNA LAB, PROVES THE THEORY THAT ONE MAN'S TRASH IS ANOTHER MAN'S TREASURE...
RAP MEETS PUNK
BUSTA BUSTS THE BIGTIME
...WHILE ON YET ANOTHER COMPUTER, CATHERINE HAS RUN A SEARCH ON BUSTA KAPP AND IS CATCHING UP ON THE LOCAL MEDIA'S TAKE ON THE PERFORMER, WHEN HE WAS ALIVE.
GIL GRISSOM, THEIR SUPERVISOR, SAVES THE FUN STUFF FOR HIMSELF, OF COURSE: TESTING THE RECOVERED-AT-THE-CRIME-SCENE GLOCK...

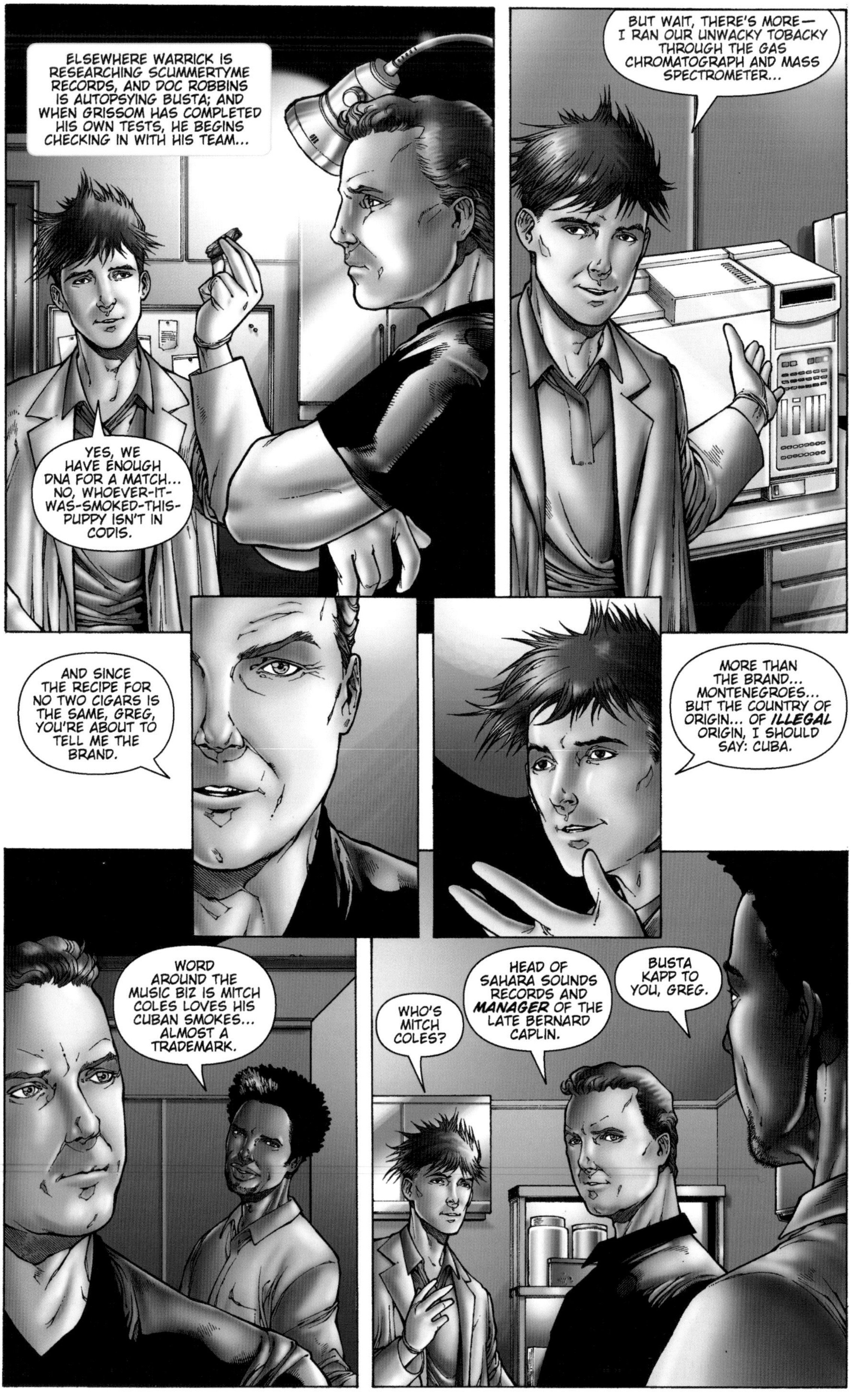
ELSEWHERE WARRICK IS RESEARCHING SCUMMERTYME RECORDS, AND DOC ROBBINS IS AUTOPSYING BUSTA; AND WHEN GRISSOM HAS COMPLETED HIS OWN TESTS, HE BEGINS CHECKING IN WITH HIS TEAM...
YES, WE HAVE ENOUGH DNA FOR A MATCH... NO, WHOEVER-IT-WAS-SMOKED-THIS-PUPPY ISN'T IN CODIS.
BUT WAIT, THERE'S MORE— I RAN OUR UNWACKY TOBACKY THROUGH THE GAS CHROMATOGRAPH AND MASS SPECTROMETER...
AND SINCE THE RECIPE FOR NO TWO CIGARS IS THE SAME, GREG, YOU'RE ABOUT TO TELL ME THE BRAND.
MORE THAN THE BRAND... MONTENEGROES... BUT THE COUNTRY OF ORIGIN... OF ILLEGAL ORIGIN, I SHOULD SAY: CUBA.
WORD AROUND THE MUSIC BIZ IS MITCH COLES LOVES HIS CUBAN SMOKES... ALMOST A TRADEMARK.
WHO'S MITCH COLES?
HEAD OF SAHARA SOUNDS RECORDS AND MANAGER OF THE LATE BERNARD CAPLIN.
BUSTA KAPP TO YOU, GREG.

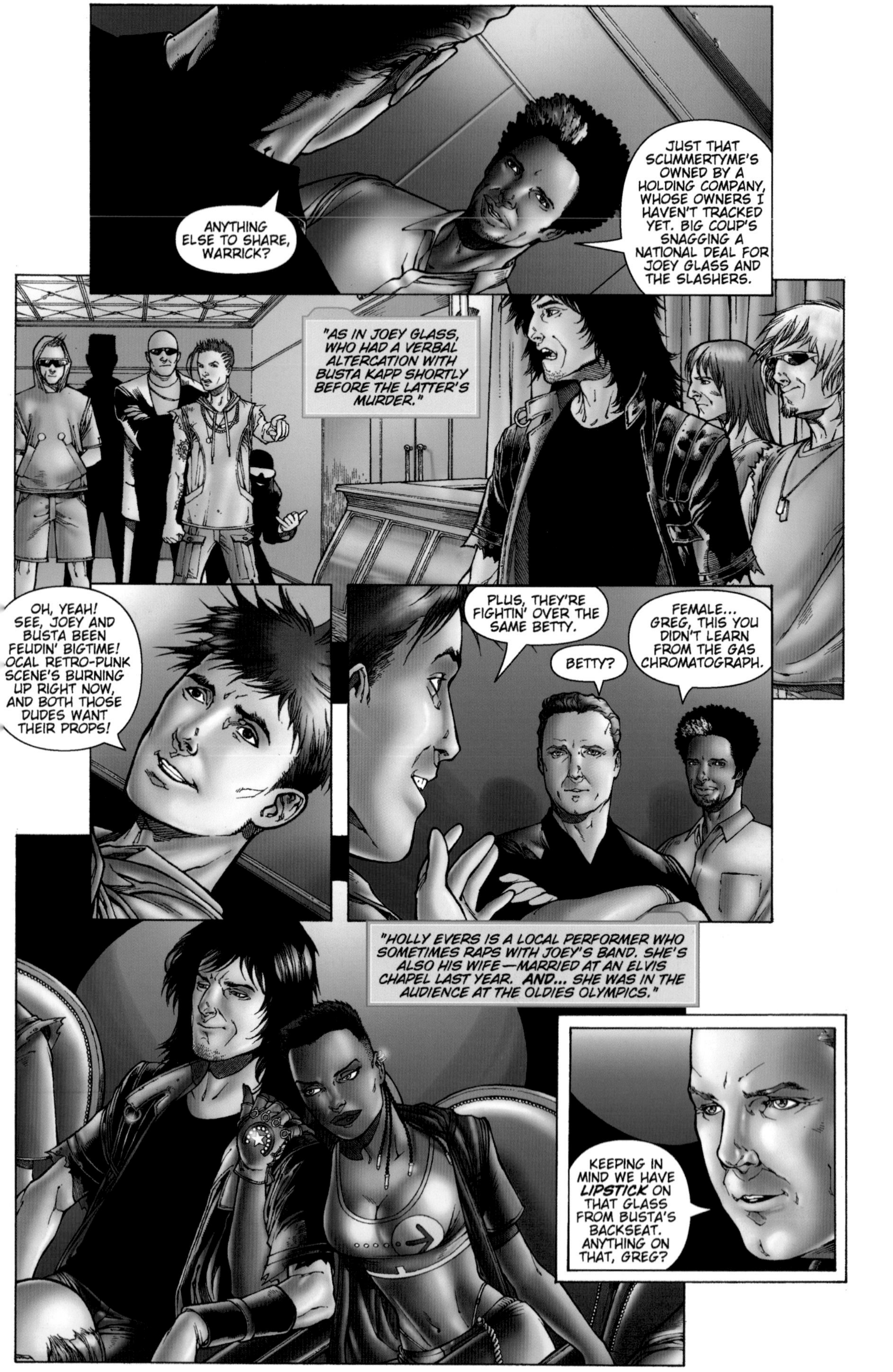
ANYTHING ELSE TO SHARE, WARRICK?
JUST THAT SCUMMERTYME'S OWNED BY A HOLDING COMPANY, WHOSE OWNERS I HAVEN'T TRACKED YET. BIG COUP'S SNAGGING A NATIONAL DEAL FOR JOEY GLASS AND THE SLASHERS.
"AS IN JOEY GLASS, WHO HAD A VERBAL ALTERCATION WITH BUSTA KAPP SHORTLY BEFORE THE LATTER'S MURDER."
OH, YEAH! SEE, JOEY AND BUSTA BEEN FEUDIN' BIGTIME! OCAL RETRO-PUNK SCENE'S BURNING UP RIGHT NOW, AND BOTH THOSE DUDES WANT THEIR PROPS!
PLUS, THEY'RE FIGHTIN' OVER THE SAME BETTY.
BETTY?
FEMALE... GREG, THIS YOU DIDN'T LEARN FROM THE GAS CHROMATOGRAPH.
"HOLLY EVERS IS A LOCAL PERFORMER WHO SOMETIMES RAPS WITH JOEY'S BAND. SHE'S ALSO HIS WIFE—MARRIED AT AN ELVIS CHAPEL LAST YEAR. AND... SHE WAS IN THE AUDIENCE AT THE OLDIES OLYMPICS."
KEEPING IN MIND WE HAVE LIPSTICK ON THAT GLASS FROM BUSTA'S BACKSEAT. ANYTHING ON THAT, GREG?

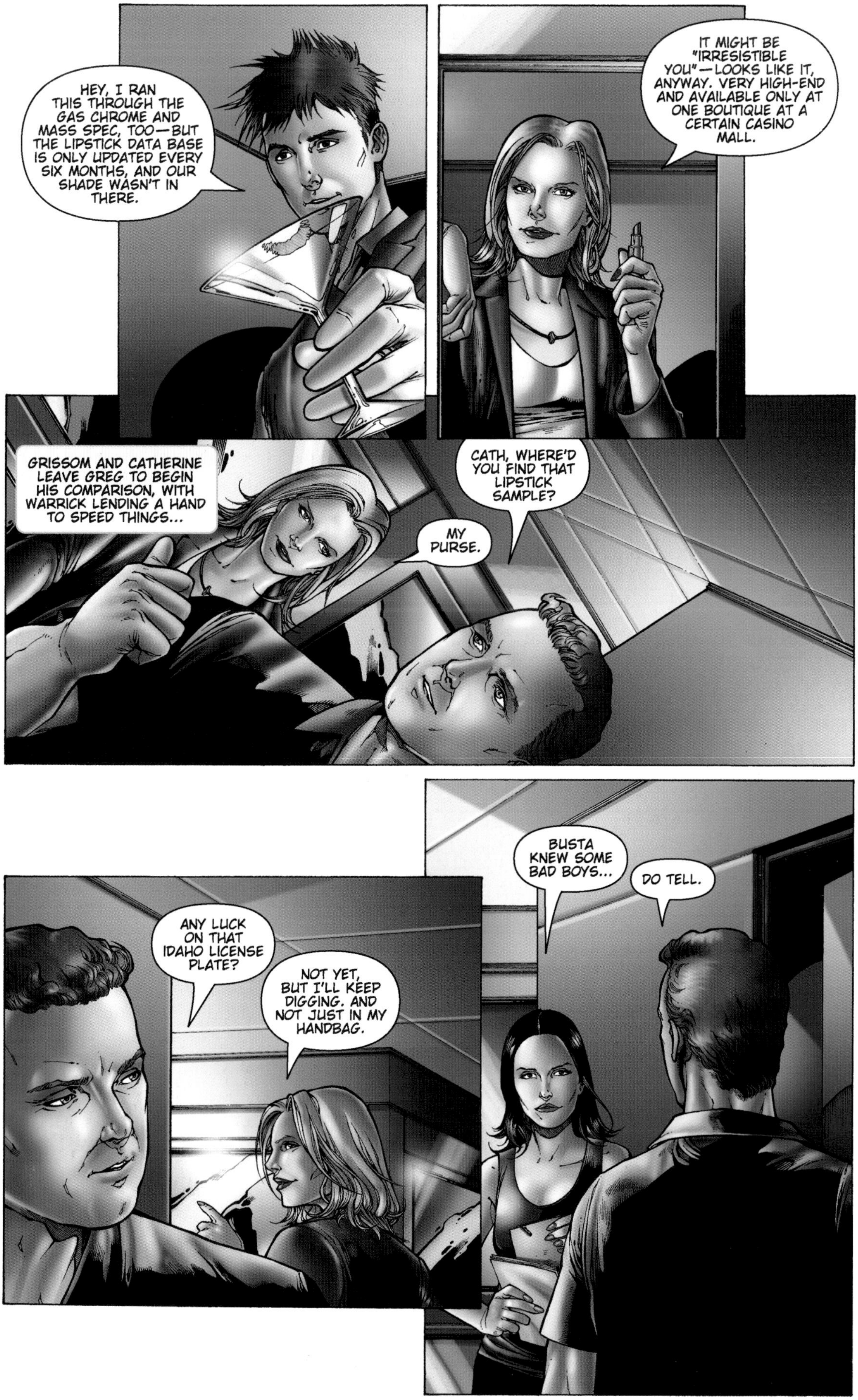
HEY, I RAN THIS THROUGH THE GAS CHROME AND MASS SPEC, TOO—BUT THE LIPSTICK DATA BASE IS ONLY UPDATED EVERY SIX MONTHS, AND OUR SHADE WASN'T IN THERE.
IT MIGHT BE "IRRESISTIBLE YOU"—LOOKS LIKE IT, ANYWAY. VERY HIGH-END AND AVAILABLE ONLY AT ONE BOUTIQUE AT A CERTAIN CASINO MALL.
GRISSOM AND CATHERINE LEAVE GREG TO BEGIN HIS COMPARISON, WITH WARRICK LENDING A HAND TO SPEED THINGS...
CATH, WHERE'D YOU FIND THAT LIPSTICK SAMPLE?
MY PURSE.
ANY LUCK ON THAT IDAHO LICENSE PLATE?
NOT YET, BUT I'LL KEEP DIGGING. AND NOT JUST IN MY HANDBAG.
BUSTA KNEW SOME BAD BOYS...
DO TELL.

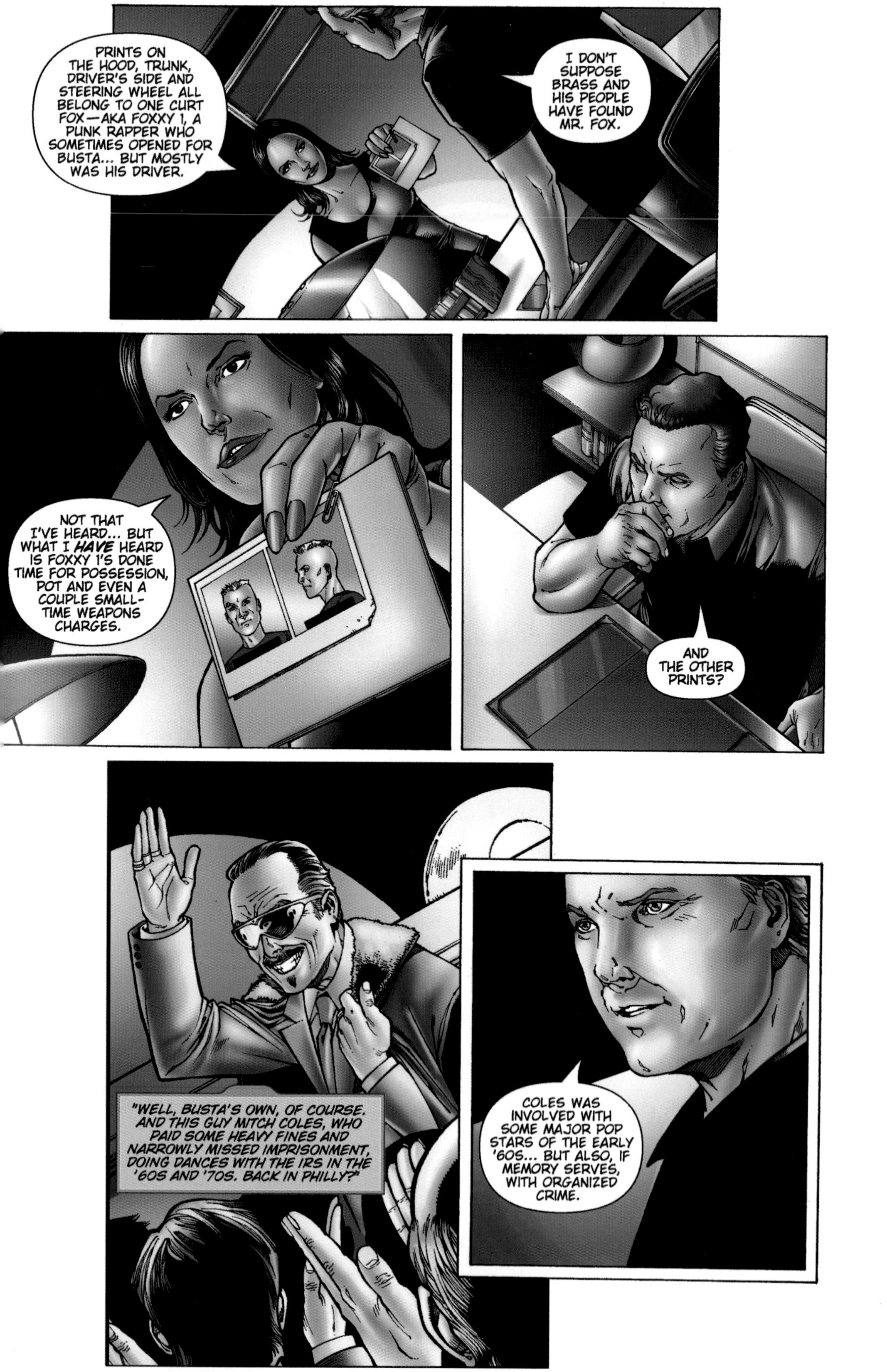
PRINTS ON THE HOOD, TRUNK, DRIVER'S SIDE AND STEERING WHEEL ALL BELONG TO ONE CURT FOX—AKA FOXXY 1, A PUNK RAPPER WHO SOMETIMES OPENED FOR BUSTA... BUT MOSTLY WAS HIS DRIVER.
I DON'T SUPPOSE BRASS AND HIS PEOPLE HAVE FOUND MR. FOX.
NOT THAT I'VE HEARD... BUT WHAT I *HAVE* HEARD IS FOXXY 1'S DONE TIME FOR POSSESSION, POT AND EVEN A COUPLE SMALL-TIME WEAPONS CHARGES.
AND THE OTHER PRINTS?
"WELL, BUSTA'S OWN, OF COURSE. AND THIS GUY MITCH COLES, WHO PAID SOME HEAVY FINES AND NARROWLY MISSED IMPRISONMENT, DOING DANCES WITH THE IRS IN THE '60S AND '70S. BACK IN PHILLY?"
COLES WAS INVOLVED WITH SOME MAJOR POP STARS OF THE EARLY '60S... BUT ALSO, IF MEMORY SERVES, WITH ORGANIZED CRIME.

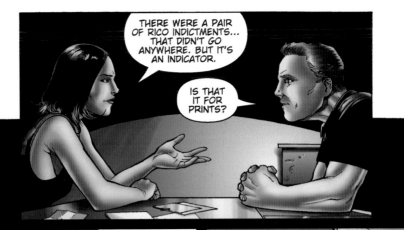

THERE WERE A PAIR OF RICO INDICTMENTS... THAT DIDN'T GO ANYWHERE. BUT IT'S AN INDICATOR.

IS THAT IT FOR PRINTS?

NO... A COUPLE OF SURPRISE GUESTS LEFT PRINTS ON AN OUTER CAR DOOR AND SIDE PANEL. FIRST, BUSTA'S FELLOW RAPPER AND CLOSE PERSONAL FRIEND... JOEY GLASS. AND ALSO A CERTAIN FEMALE...

HOPE EVERS.

WHAT ARE YOU, GRISSOM, PSYCHIC? HEY... THAT WASN'T A *GUESS* WAS IT? I'M TELLING!

TELLING ON THE TEACHER IS DANGEROUS.

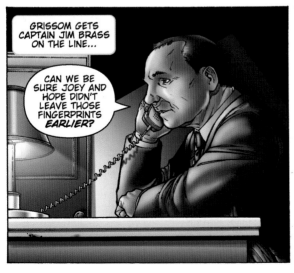

GRISSOM GETS CAPTAIN JIM BRASS ON THE LINE...

CAN WE BE SURE JOEY AND HOPE DIDN'T LEAVE THOSE FINGERPRINTS *EARLIER?*

NO WAY— NIGHT HE DIED. IN THIS CLIMATE, FINGERPRINTS ON THE OUTSIDE OF A CAR EVAPORATE QUICKLY, Y'KNOW.

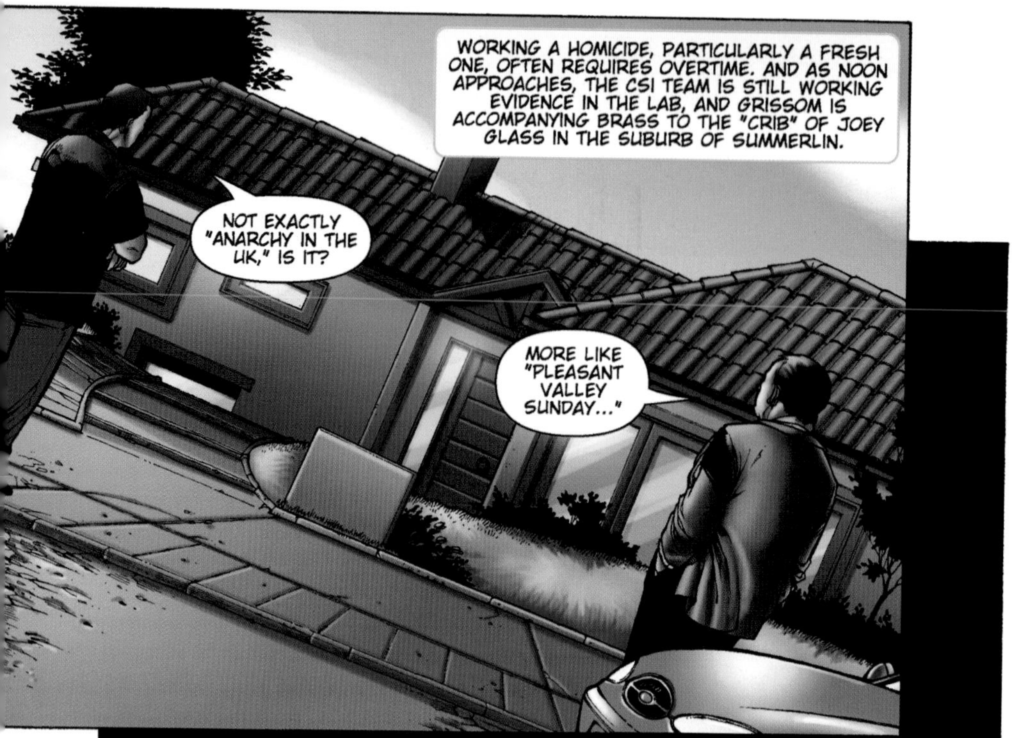
WORKING A HOMICIDE, PARTICULARLY A FRESH ONE, OFTEN REQUIRES OVERTIME. AND AS NOON APPROACHES, THE CSI TEAM IS STILL WORKING EVIDENCE IN THE LAB, AND GRISSOM IS ACCOMPANYING BRASS TO THE "CRIB" OF JOEY GLASS IN THE SUBURB OF SUMMERLIN.
NOT EXACTLY "ANARCHY IN THE UK," IS IT?
MORE LIKE "PLEASANT VALLEY SUNDAY..."

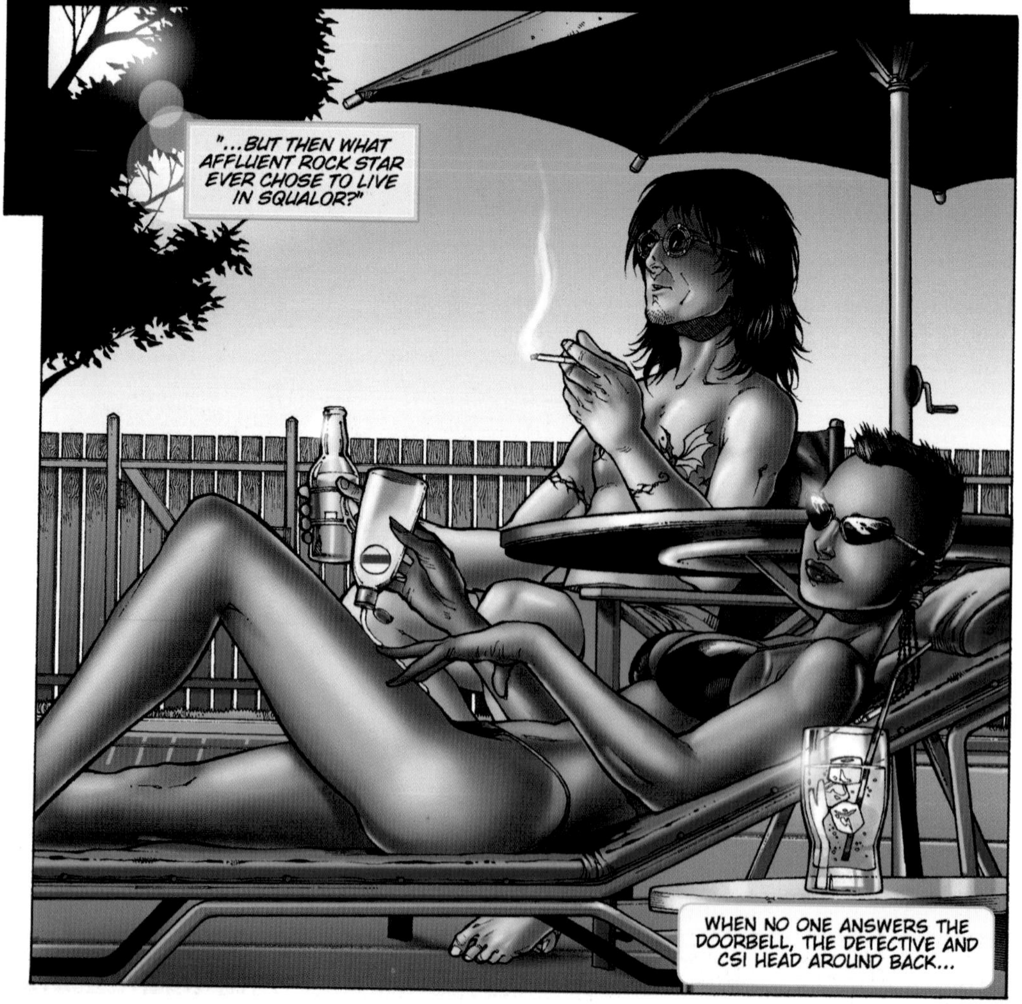
"...BUT THEN WHAT AFFLUENT ROCK STAR EVER CHOSE TO LIVE IN SQUALOR?"
WHEN NO ONE ANSWERS THE DOORBELL, THE DETECTIVE AND CSI HEAD AROUND BACK...

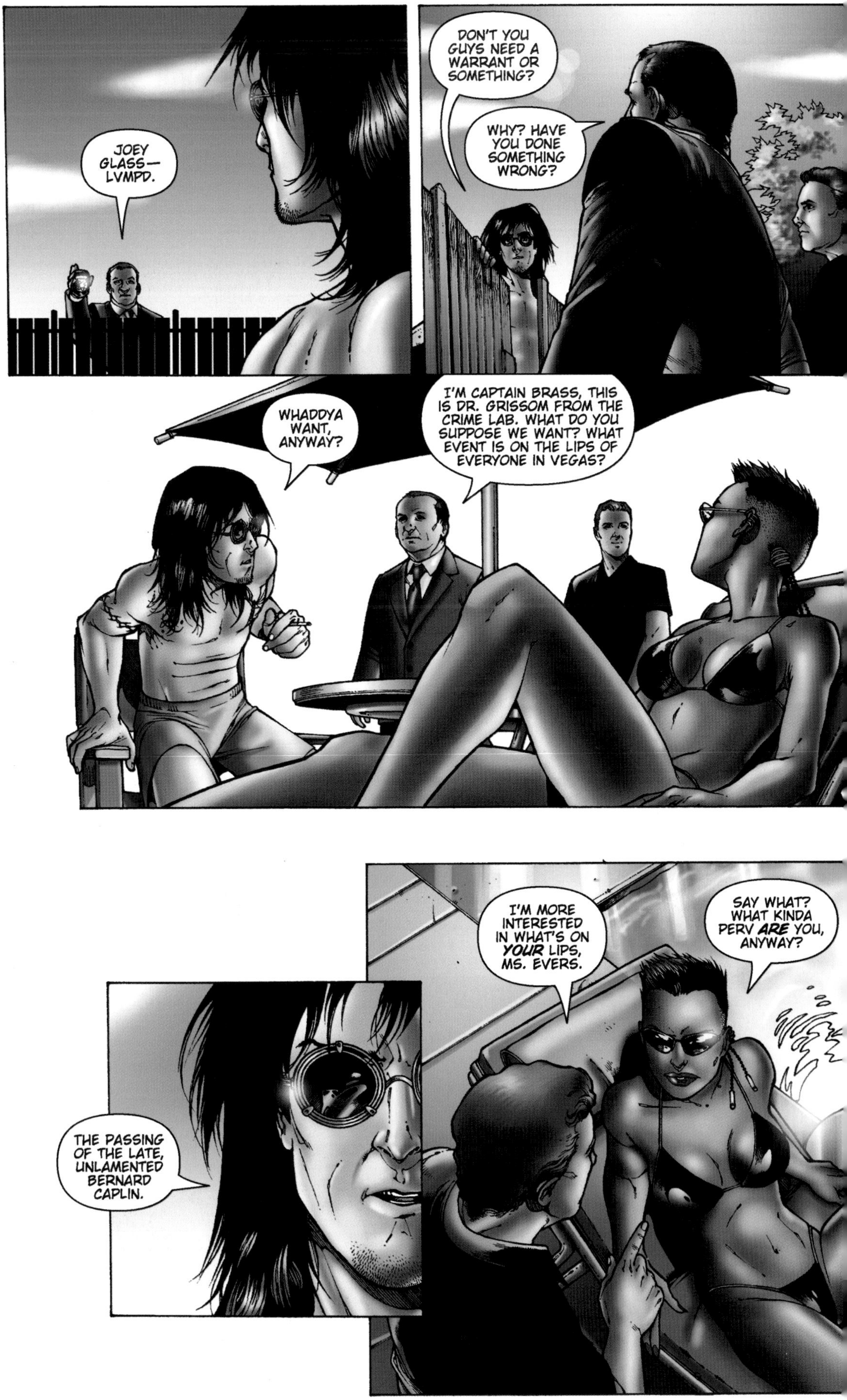
JOEY GLASS— LVMPD.
DON'T YOU GUYS NEED A WARRANT OR SOMETHING?
WHY? HAVE YOU DONE SOMETHING WRONG?
WHADDYA WANT, ANYWAY?
I'M CAPTAIN BRASS, THIS IS DR. GRISSOM FROM THE CRIME LAB. WHAT DO YOU SUPPOSE WE WANT? WHAT EVENT IS ON THE LIPS OF EVERYONE IN VEGAS?
THE PASSING OF THE LATE, UNLAMENTED BERNARD CAPLIN.
I'M MORE INTERESTED IN WHAT'S ON *YOUR* LIPS, MS. EVERS.
SAY WHAT? WHAT KINDA PERV *ARE* YOU, ANYWAY?

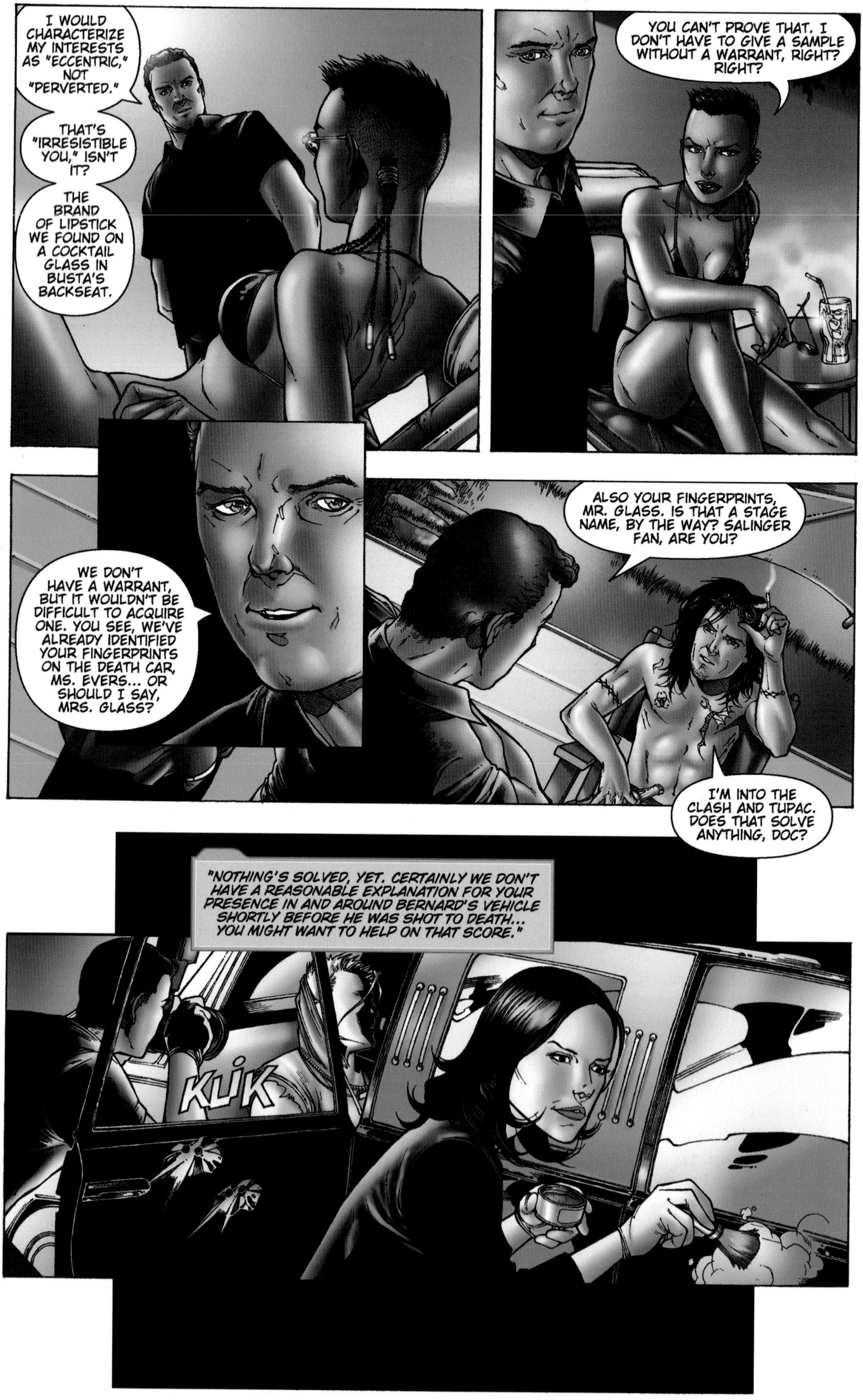
I WOULD CHARACTERIZE MY INTERESTS AS "ECCENTRIC," NOT "PERVERTED."
THAT'S "IRRESISTIBLE YOU," ISN'T IT?
THE BRAND OF LIPSTICK WE FOUND ON A COCKTAIL GLASS IN BUSTA'S BACKSEAT.
YOU CAN'T PROVE THAT. I DON'T HAVE TO GIVE A SAMPLE WITHOUT A WARRANT, RIGHT? RIGHT?
WE DON'T HAVE A WARRANT, BUT IT WOULDN'T BE DIFFICULT TO ACQUIRE ONE. YOU SEE, WE'VE ALREADY IDENTIFIED YOUR FINGERPRINTS ON THE DEATH CAR, MS. EVERS... OR SHOULD I SAY, MRS. GLASS?
ALSO YOUR FINGERPRINTS, MR. GLASS. IS THAT A STAGE NAME, BY THE WAY? SALINGER FAN, ARE YOU?
I'M INTO THE CLASH AND TUPAC. DOES THAT SOLVE ANYTHING, DOC?
"NOTHING'S SOLVED, YET. CERTAINLY WE DON'T HAVE A REASONABLE EXPLANATION FOR YOUR PRESENCE IN AND AROUND BERNARD'S VEHICLE SHORTLY BEFORE HE WAS SHOT TO DEATH... YOU MIGHT WANT TO HELP ON THAT SCORE."
KLIK

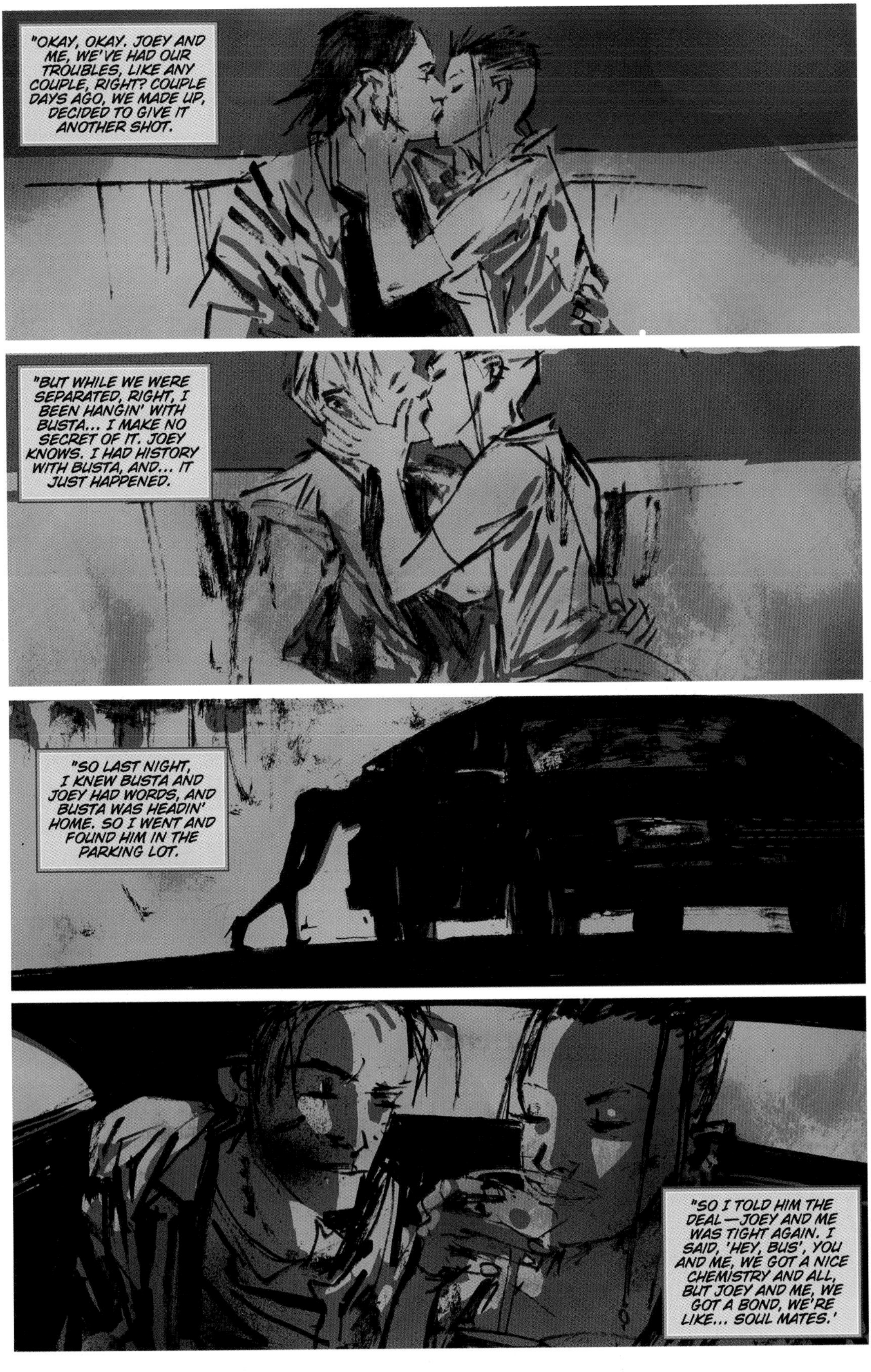
"OKAY, OKAY. JOEY AND ME, WE'VE HAD OUR TROUBLES, LIKE ANY COUPLE, RIGHT? COUPLE DAYS AGO, WE MADE UP, DECIDED TO GIVE IT ANOTHER SHOT.
"BUT WHILE WE WERE SEPARATED, RIGHT, I BEEN HANGIN' WITH BUSTA... I MAKE NO SECRET OF IT. JOEY KNOWS. I HAD HISTORY WITH BUSTA, AND... IT JUST HAPPENED.
"SO LAST NIGHT, I KNEW BUSTA AND JOEY HAD WORDS, AND BUSTA WAS HEADIN' HOME. SO I WENT AND FOUND HIM IN THE PARKING LOT.
"SO I TOLD HIM THE DEAL—JOEY AND ME WAS TIGHT AGAIN. I SAID, 'HEY, BUS', YOU AND ME, WE GOT A NICE CHEMISTRY AND ALL, BUT JOEY AND ME, WE GOT A BOND, WE'RE LIKE... SOUL MATES.'

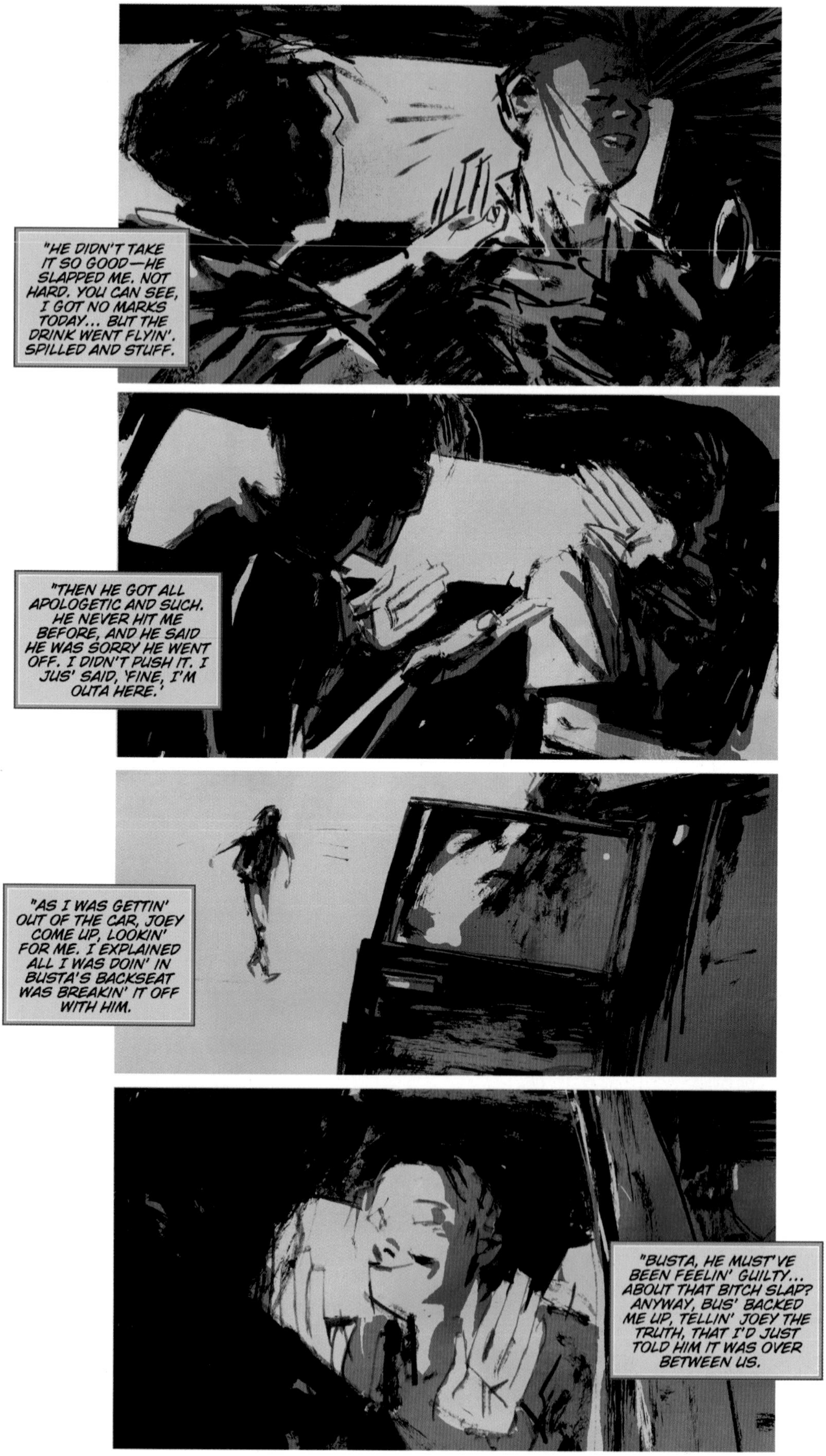
"HE DIDN'T TAKE IT SO GOOD—HE SLAPPED ME. NOT HARD. YOU CAN SEE, I GOT NO MARKS TODAY... BUT THE DRINK WENT FLYIN'. SPILLED AND STUFF.
"THEN HE GOT ALL APOLOGETIC AND SUCH. HE NEVER HIT ME BEFORE, AND HE SAID HE WAS SORRY HE WENT OFF. I DIDN'T PUSH IT. I JUS' SAID, 'FINE, I'M OUTA HERE.'
"AS I WAS GETTIN' OUT OF THE CAR, JOEY COME UP, LOOKIN' FOR ME. I EXPLAINED ALL I WAS DOIN' IN BUSTA'S BACKSEAT WAS BREAKIN' IT OFF WITH HIM.
"BUSTA, HE MUST'VE BEEN FEELIN' GUILTY... ABOUT THAT BITCH SLAP? ANYWAY, BUS' BACKED ME UP, TELLIN' JOEY THE TRUTH, THAT I'D JUST TOLD HIM IT WAS OVER BETWEEN US.

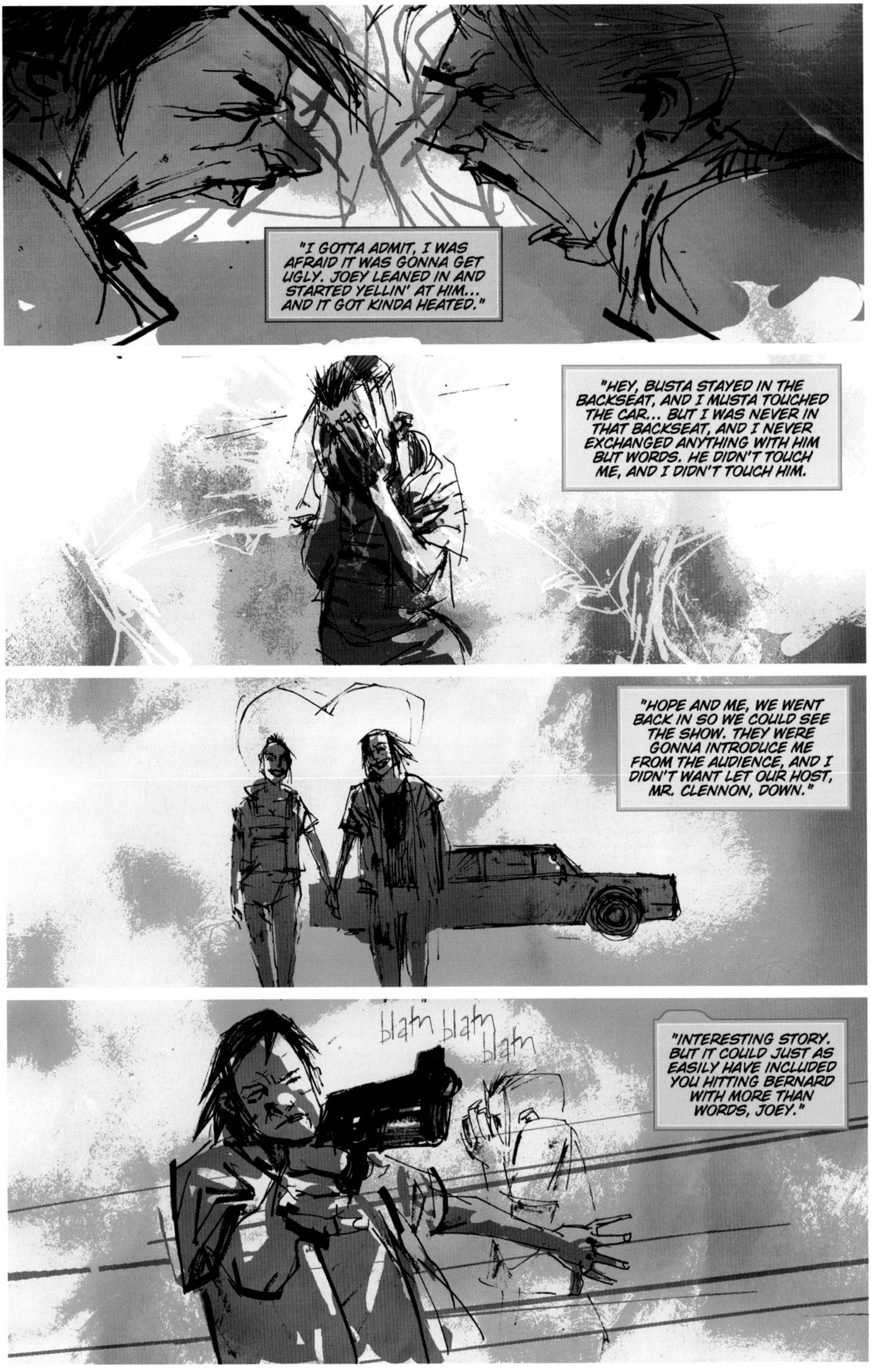
"I GOTTA ADMIT, I WAS AFRAID IT WAS GONNA GET UGLY. JOEY LEANED IN AND STARTED YELLIN' AT HIM... AND IT GOT KINDA HEATED."
"HEY, BUSTA STAYED IN THE BACKSEAT, AND I MUSTA TOUCHED THE CAR... BUT I WAS NEVER IN THAT BACKSEAT, AND I NEVER EXCHANGED ANYTHING WITH HIM BUT WORDS. HE DIDN'T TOUCH ME, AND I DIDN'T TOUCH HIM.
"HOPE AND ME, WE WENT BACK IN SO WE COULD SEE THE SHOW. THEY WERE GONNA INTRODUCE ME FROM THE AUDIENCE, AND I DIDN'T WANT LET OUR HOST, MR. CLENNON, DOWN."
blatn blatn blatn
"INTERESTING STORY. BUT IT COULD JUST AS EASILY HAVE INCLUDED YOU HITTING BERNARD WITH MORE THAN WORDS, JOEY."

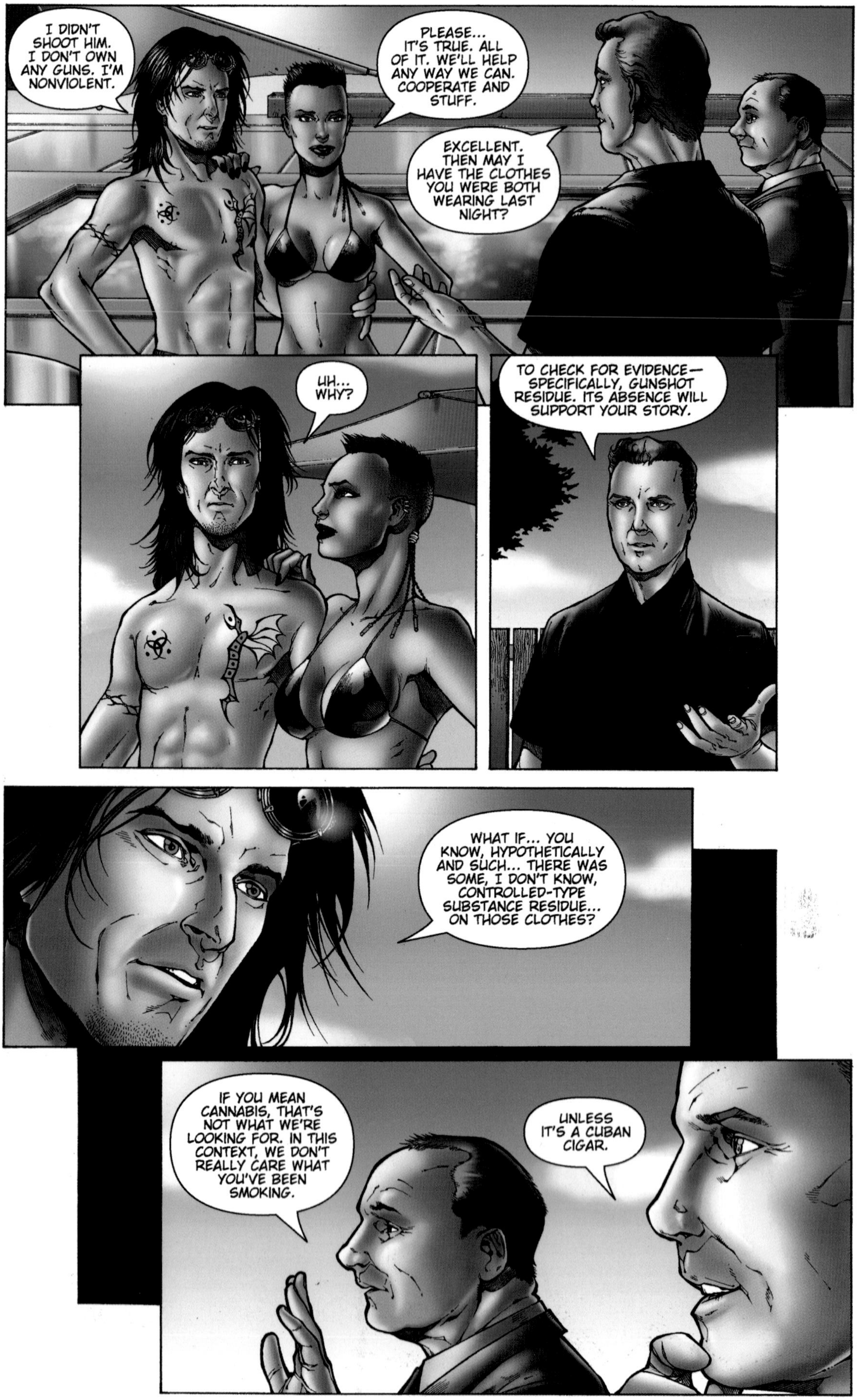
I DIDN'T SHOOT HIM. I DON'T OWN ANY GUNS. I'M NONVIOLENT.
PLEASE... IT'S TRUE. ALL OF IT. WE'LL HELP ANY WAY WE CAN. COOPERATE AND STUFF.
EXCELLENT. THEN MAY I HAVE THE CLOTHES YOU WERE BOTH WEARING LAST NIGHT?
UH... WHY?
TO CHECK FOR EVIDENCE— SPECIFICALLY, GUNSHOT RESIDUE. ITS ABSENCE WILL SUPPORT YOUR STORY.
WHAT IF... YOU KNOW, HYPOTHETICALLY AND SUCH... THERE WAS SOME, I DON'T KNOW, CONTROLLED-TYPE SUBSTANCE RESIDUE... ON THOSE CLOTHES?
IF YOU MEAN CANNABIS, THAT'S NOT WHAT WE'RE LOOKING FOR. IN THIS CONTEXT, WE DON'T REALLY CARE WHAT YOU'VE BEEN SMOKING.
UNLESS IT'S A CUBAN CIGAR.

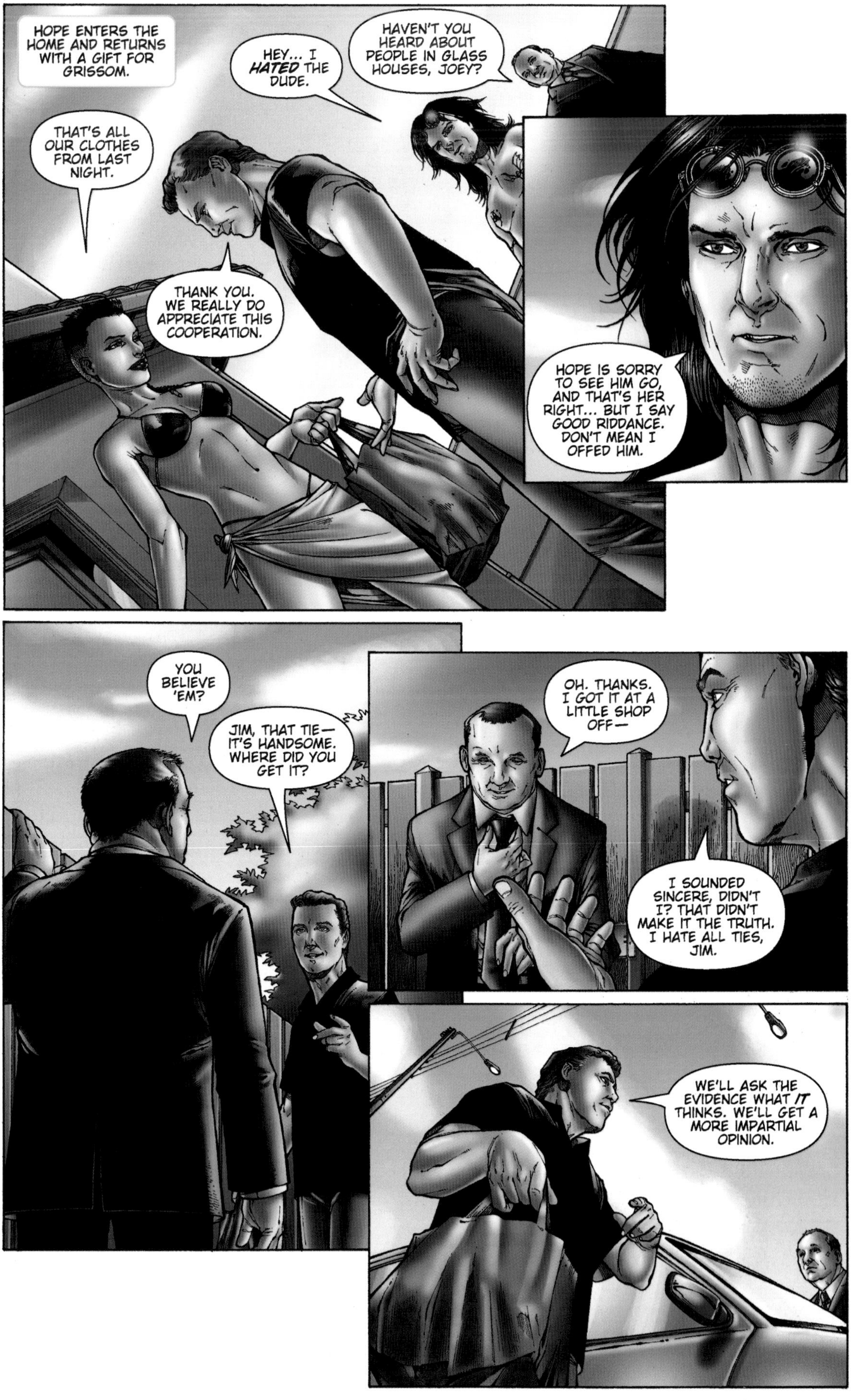
HOPE ENTERS THE HOME AND RETURNS WITH A GIFT FOR GRISSOM.
HEY... I *HATED* THE DUDE.
HAVEN'T YOU HEARD ABOUT PEOPLE IN GLASS HOUSES, JOEY?
THAT'S ALL OUR CLOTHES FROM LAST NIGHT.
THANK YOU. WE REALLY DO APPRECIATE THIS COOPERATION.
HOPE IS SORRY TO SEE HIM GO, AND THAT'S HER RIGHT... BUT I SAY GOOD RIDDANCE. DON'T MEAN I OFFED HIM.
YOU BELIEVE 'EM?
JIM, THAT TIE— IT'S HANDSOME. WHERE DID YOU GET IT?
OH. THANKS. I GOT IT AT A LITTLE SHOP OFF—
I SOUNDED SINCERE, DIDN'T I? THAT DIDN'T MAKE IT THE TRUTH. I HATE ALL TIES, JIM.
WE'LL ASK THE EVIDENCE WHAT *IT* THINKS. WE'LL GET A MORE IMPARTIAL OPINION.

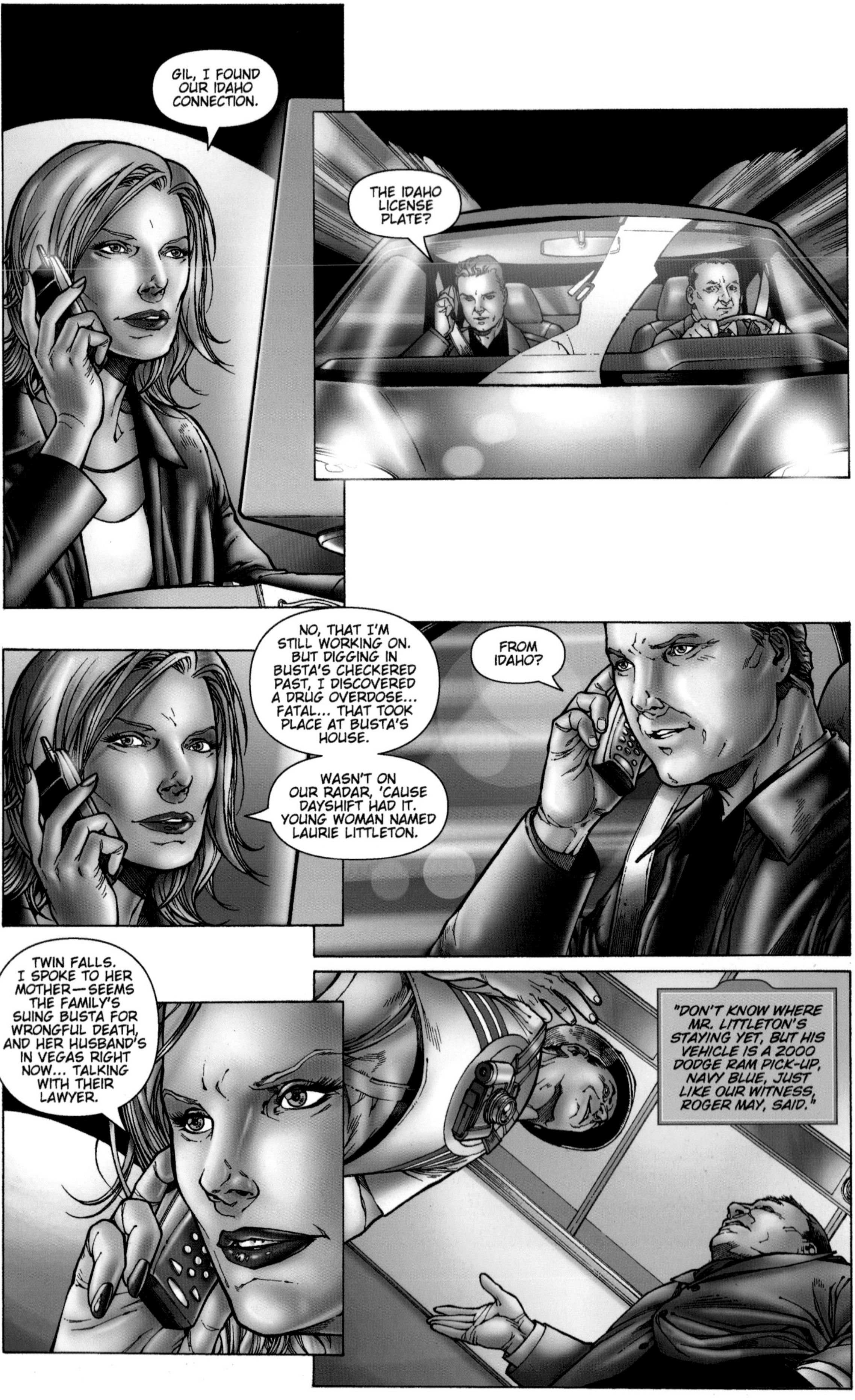
GIL, I FOUND OUR IDAHO CONNECTION.
THE IDAHO LICENSE PLATE?
NO, THAT I'M STILL WORKING ON. BUT DIGGING IN BUSTA'S CHECKERED PAST, I DISCOVERED A DRUG OVERDOSE... FATAL... THAT TOOK PLACE AT BUSTA'S HOUSE.
WASN'T ON OUR RADAR, 'CAUSE DAYSHIFT HAD IT. YOUNG WOMAN NAMED LAURIE LITTLETON.
FROM IDAHO?
TWIN FALLS. I SPOKE TO HER MOTHER—SEEMS THE FAMILY'S SUING BUSTA FOR WRONGFUL DEATH, AND HER HUSBAND'S IN VEGAS RIGHT NOW... TALKING WITH THEIR LAWYER.
"DON'T KNOW WHERE MR. LITTLETON'S STAYING YET, BUT HIS VEHICLE IS A 2000 DODGE RAM PICK-UP, NAVY BLUE, JUST LIKE OUR WITNESS, ROGER MAY, SAID."

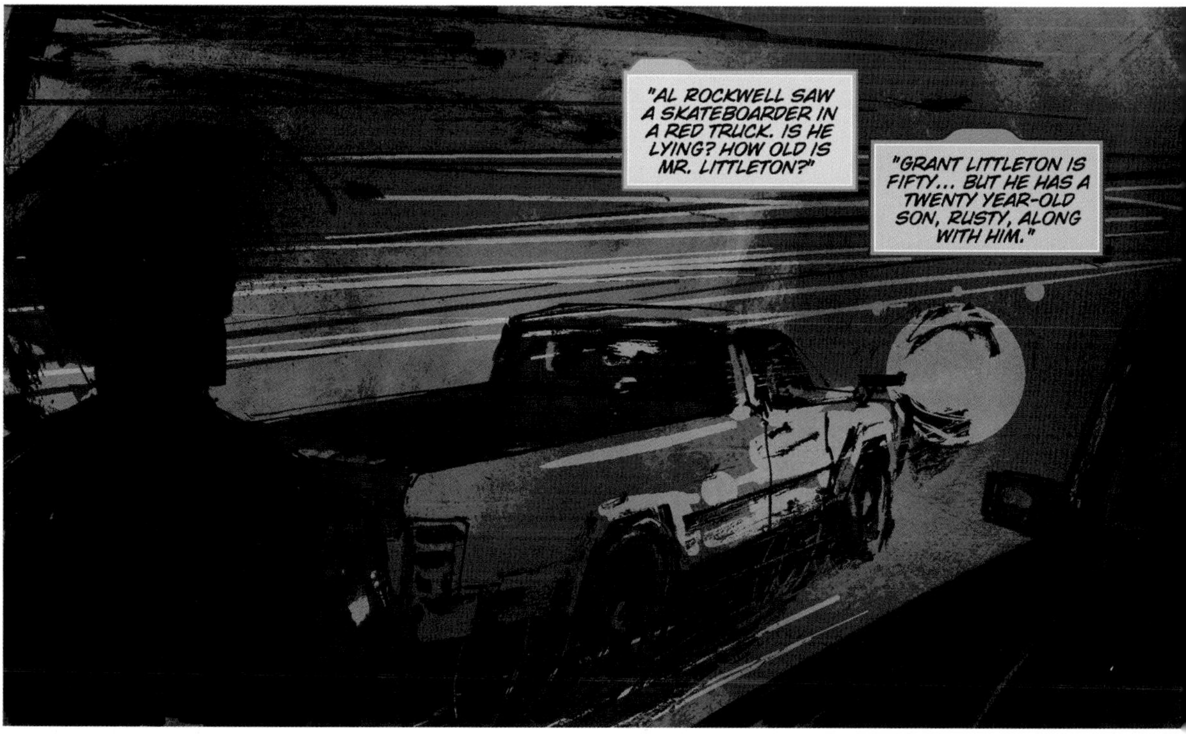
"AL ROCKWELL SAW A SKATEBOARDER IN A RED TRUCK. IS HE LYING? HOW OLD IS MR. LITTLETON?"
"GRANT LITTLETON IS FIFTY... BUT HE HAS A TWENTY YEAR-OLD SON, RUSTY, ALONG WITH HIM."

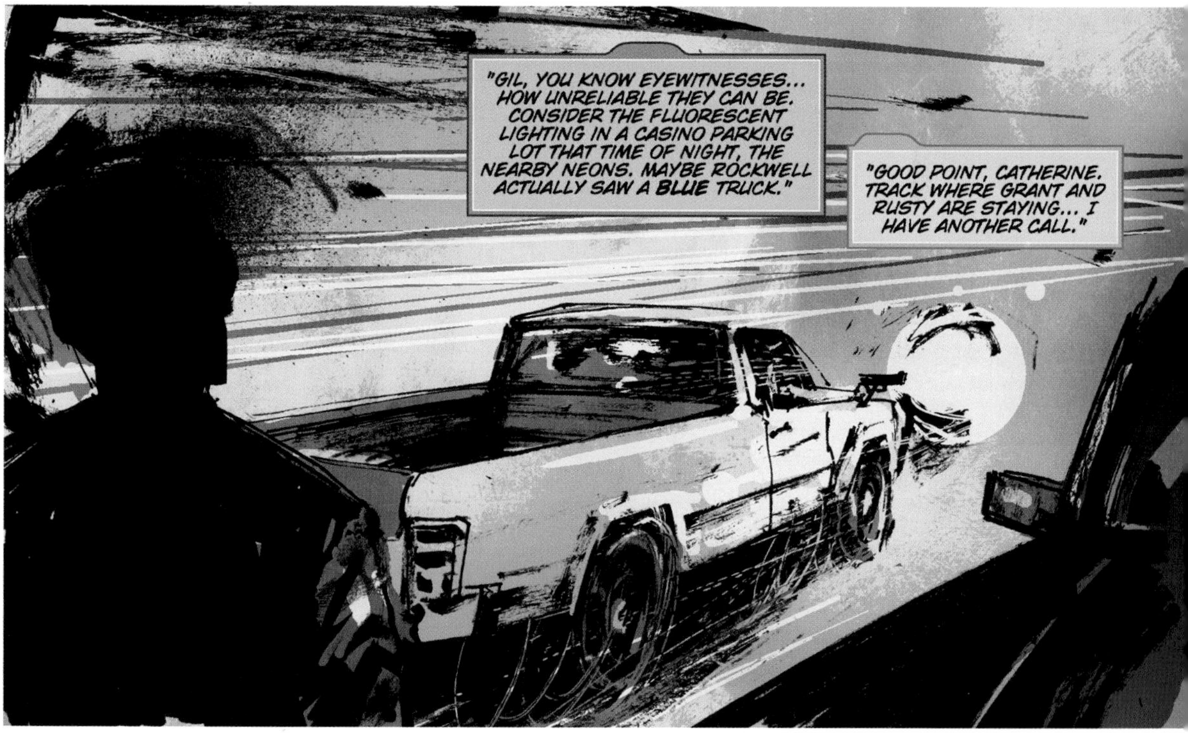
"GIL, YOU KNOW EYEWITNESSES... HOW UNRELIABLE THEY CAN BE. CONSIDER THE FLUORESCENT LIGHTING IN A CASINO PARKING LOT THAT TIME OF NIGHT, THE NEARBY NEONS. MAYBE ROCKWELL ACTUALLY SAW A **BLUE** TRUCK."
"GOOD POINT, CATHERINE. TRACK WHERE GRANT AND RUSTY ARE STAYING... I HAVE ANOTHER CALL."

IF MITCH COLES WAS STEALING FROM HIS CLIENT BERNARD CAPLIN, THEN WE HAVE A MURDER MOTIVE. IS THIS RUMOR OR FACT?

HEY, GRIS— WE NEED A WARRANT TO GO AFTER THE BOOKS AT SAHARA SOUNDS AND IDOL THREAT MANAGEMENT. I JUST SPOKE TO ONE OF BUSTA'S BANDMATES, WHO SAYS THERE ARE SERIOUS DISCREPANCIES.

"TWO DAYS AGO, BUSTA HIRED AN ACCOUNTANT TO DO AN INDEPENDENT AUDIT. OH, AND COLES HAS A GLOCK REGISTERED IN HIS NAME. THAT DOESN'T MAKE IT THE ONE WE FOUND, OF COURSE."

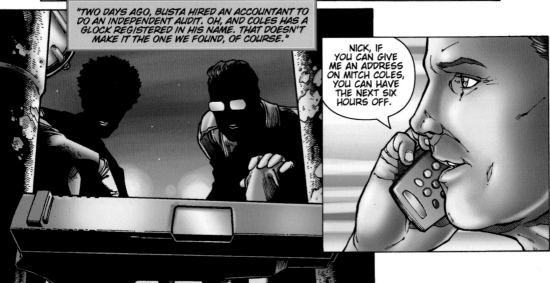

NICK, IF YOU CAN GIVE ME AN ADDRESS ON MITCH COLES, YOU CAN HAVE THE NEXT SIX HOURS OFF.

"I DON'T WANT 'EM OFF, GRIS. BUT I'LL TRADE YOU THE ADDRESS FOR ME MEETING YOU OUT THERE..."

"YOU DRIVE A HARD BARGAIN, NICK. DONE."

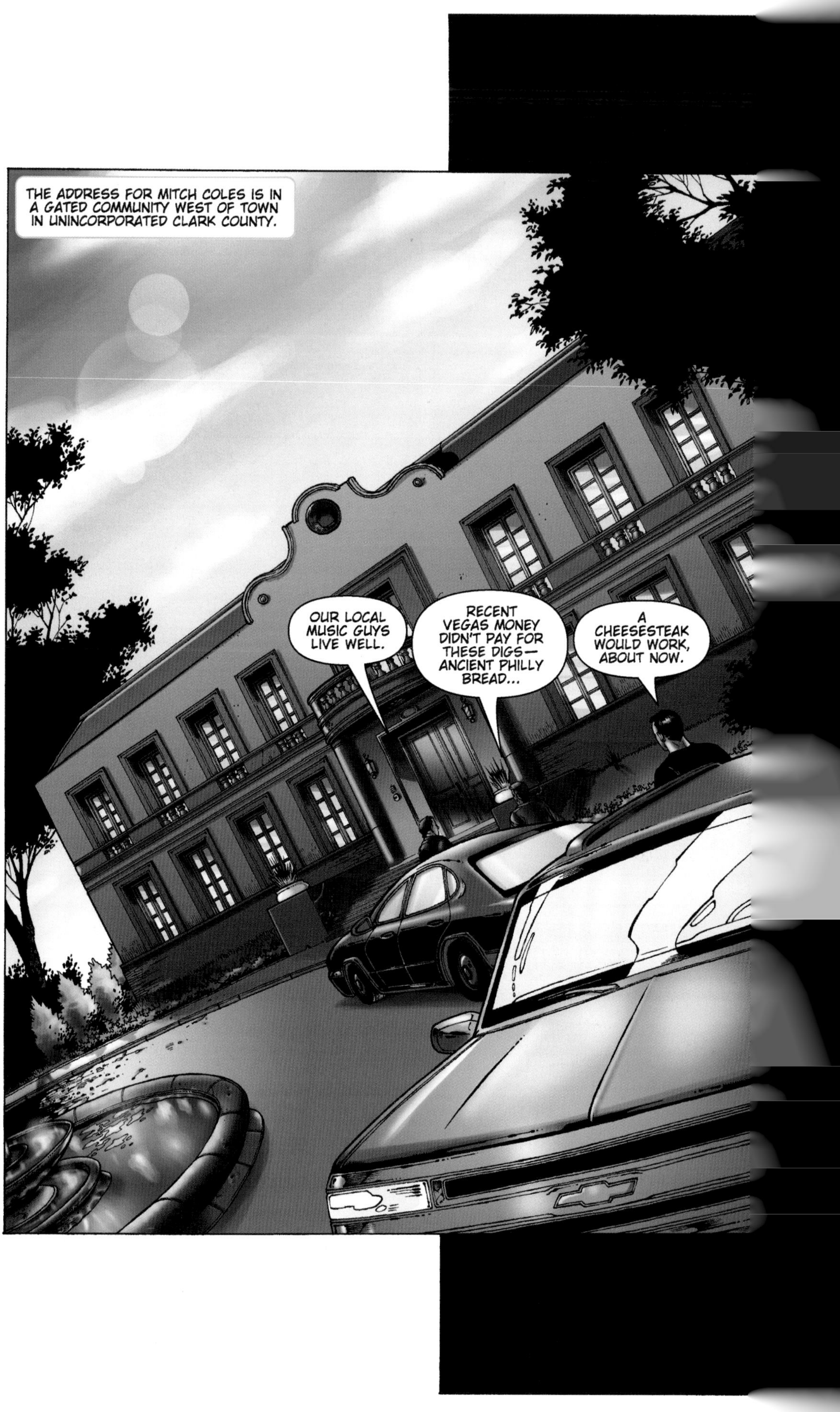
THE ADDRESS FOR MITCH COLES IS IN A GATED COMMUNITY WEST OF TOWN IN UNINCORPORATED CLARK COUNTY.
OUR LOCAL MUSIC GUYS LIVE WELL.
RECENT VEGAS MONEY DIDN'T PAY FOR THESE DIGS— ANCIENT PHILLY BREAD...
A CHEESESTEAK WOULD WORK, ABOUT NOW.

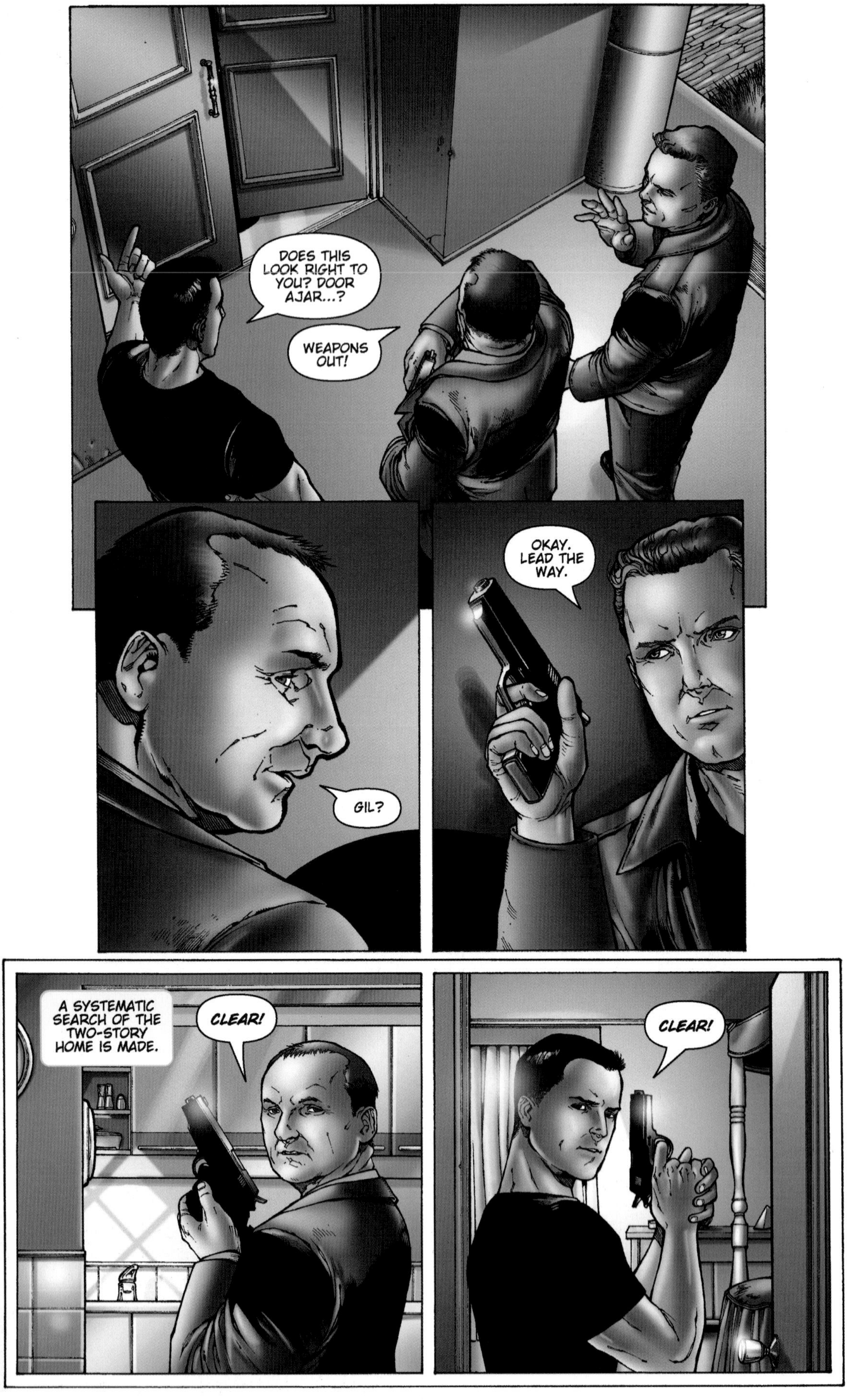
DOES THIS LOOK RIGHT TO YOU? DOOR AJAR...?
WEAPONS OUT!
GIL?
OKAY. LEAD THE WAY.
A SYSTEMATIC SEARCH OF THE TWO-STORY HOME IS MADE.
CLEAR!
CLEAR!

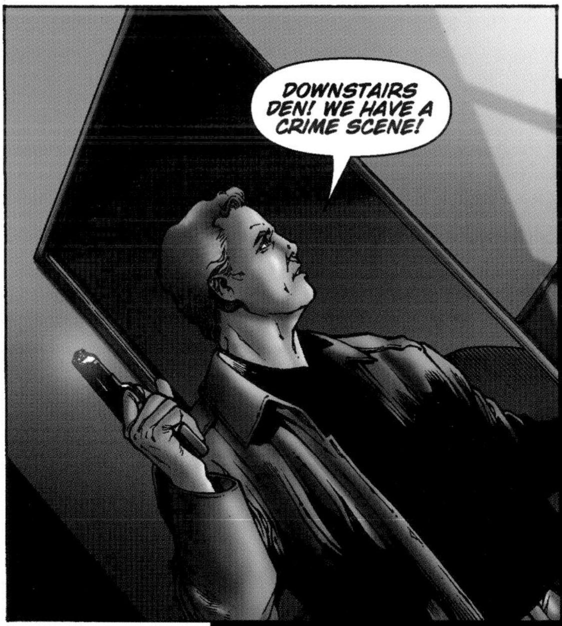
DOWNSTAIRS DEN! WE HAVE A CRIME SCENE!

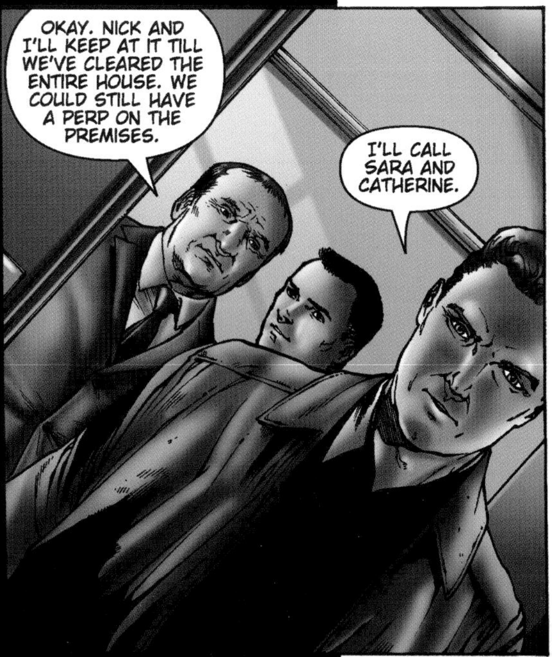
OKAY. NICK AND I'LL KEEP AT IT TILL WE'VE CLEARED THE ENTIRE HOUSE. WE COULD STILL HAVE A PERP ON THE PREMISES.
I'LL CALL SARA AND CATHERINE.

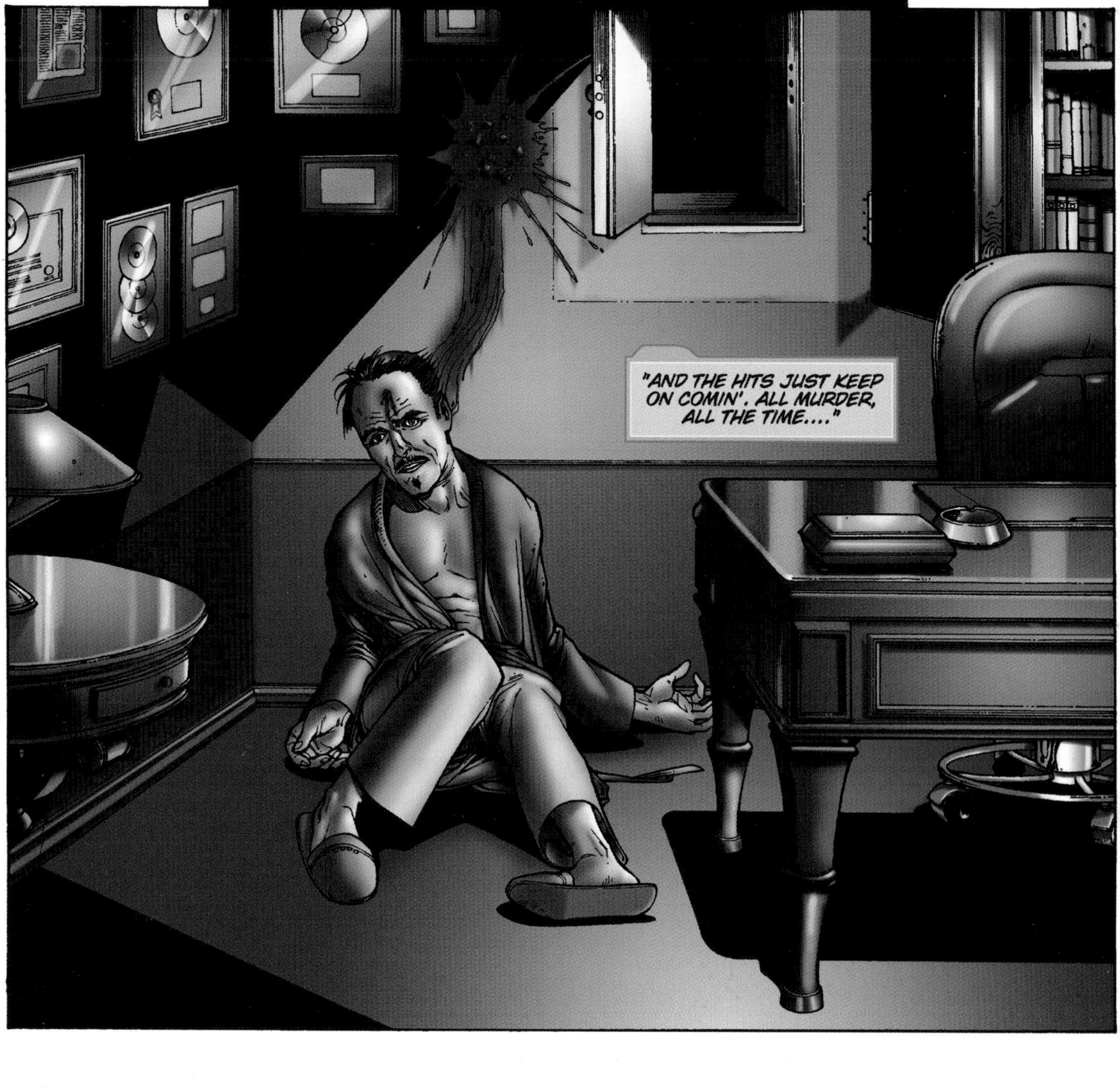
"AND THE HITS JUST KEEP ON COMIN'. ALL MURDER, ALL THE TIME...."

chapter four

# Gris Gone Wild

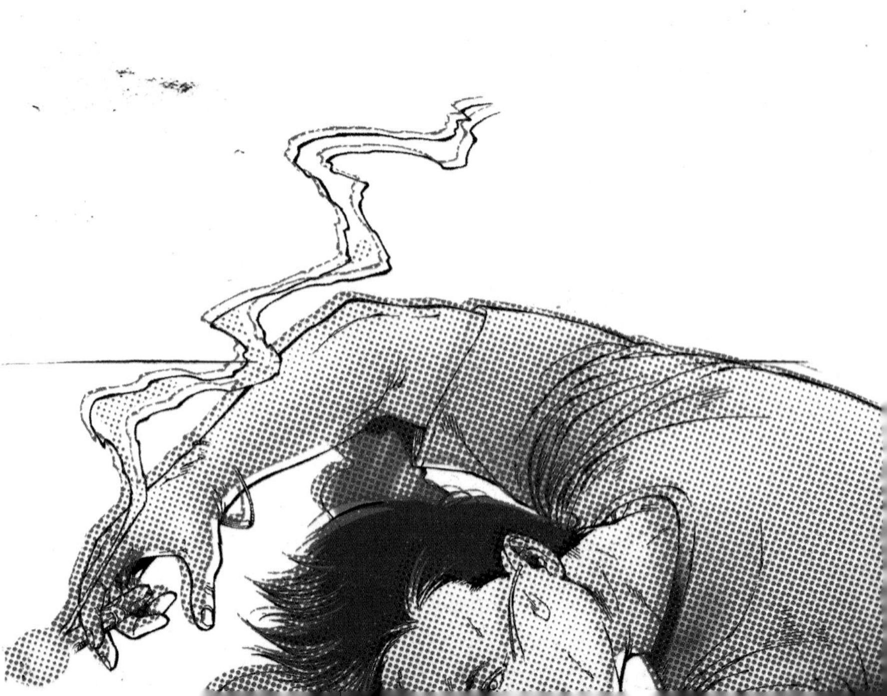

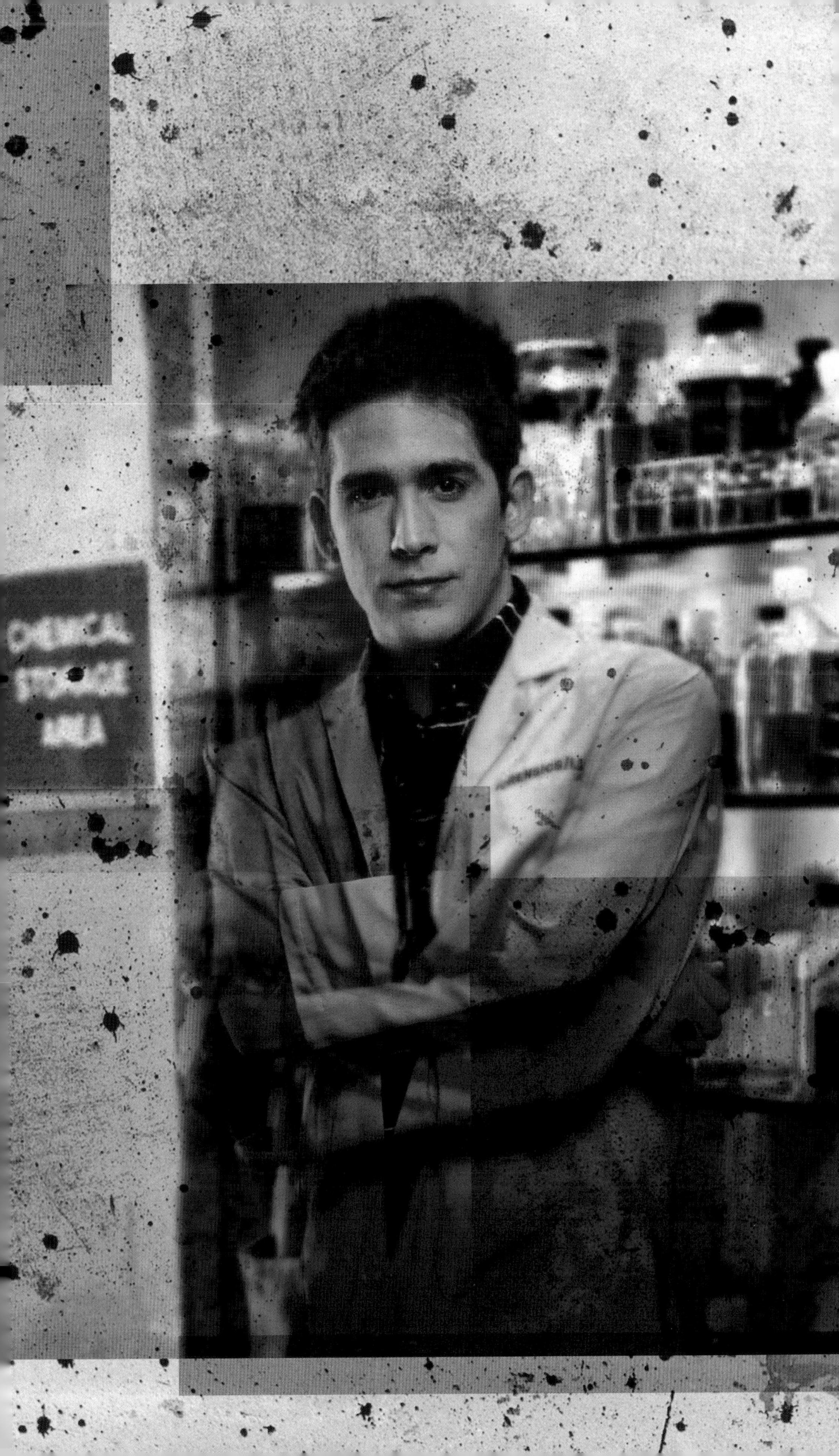

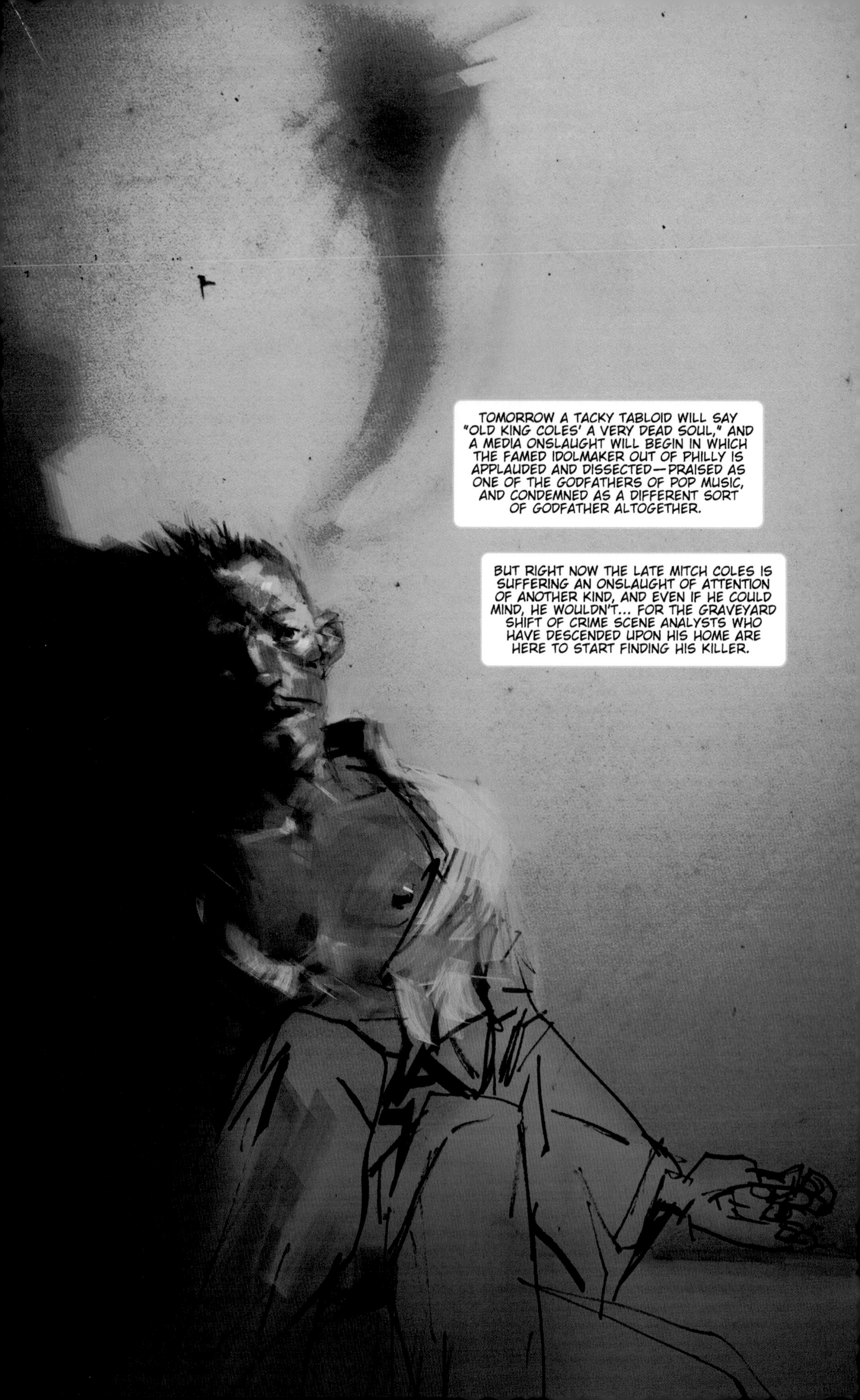
TOMORROW A TACKY TABLOID WILL SAY "OLD KING COLES' A VERY DEAD SOUL," AND A MEDIA ONSLAUGHT WILL BEGIN IN WHICH THE FAMED IDOLMAKER OUT OF PHILLY IS APPLAUDED AND DISSECTED—PRAISED AS ONE OF THE GODFATHERS OF POP MUSIC, AND CONDEMNED AS A DIFFERENT SORT OF GODFATHER ALTOGETHER.
BUT RIGHT NOW THE LATE MITCH COLES IS SUFFERING AN ONSLAUGHT OF ATTENTION OF ANOTHER KIND, AND EVEN IF HE COULD MIND, HE WOULDN'T... FOR THE GRAVEYARD SHIFT OF CRIME SCENE ANALYSTS WHO HAVE DESCENDED UPON HIS HOME ARE HERE TO START FINDING HIS KILLER.

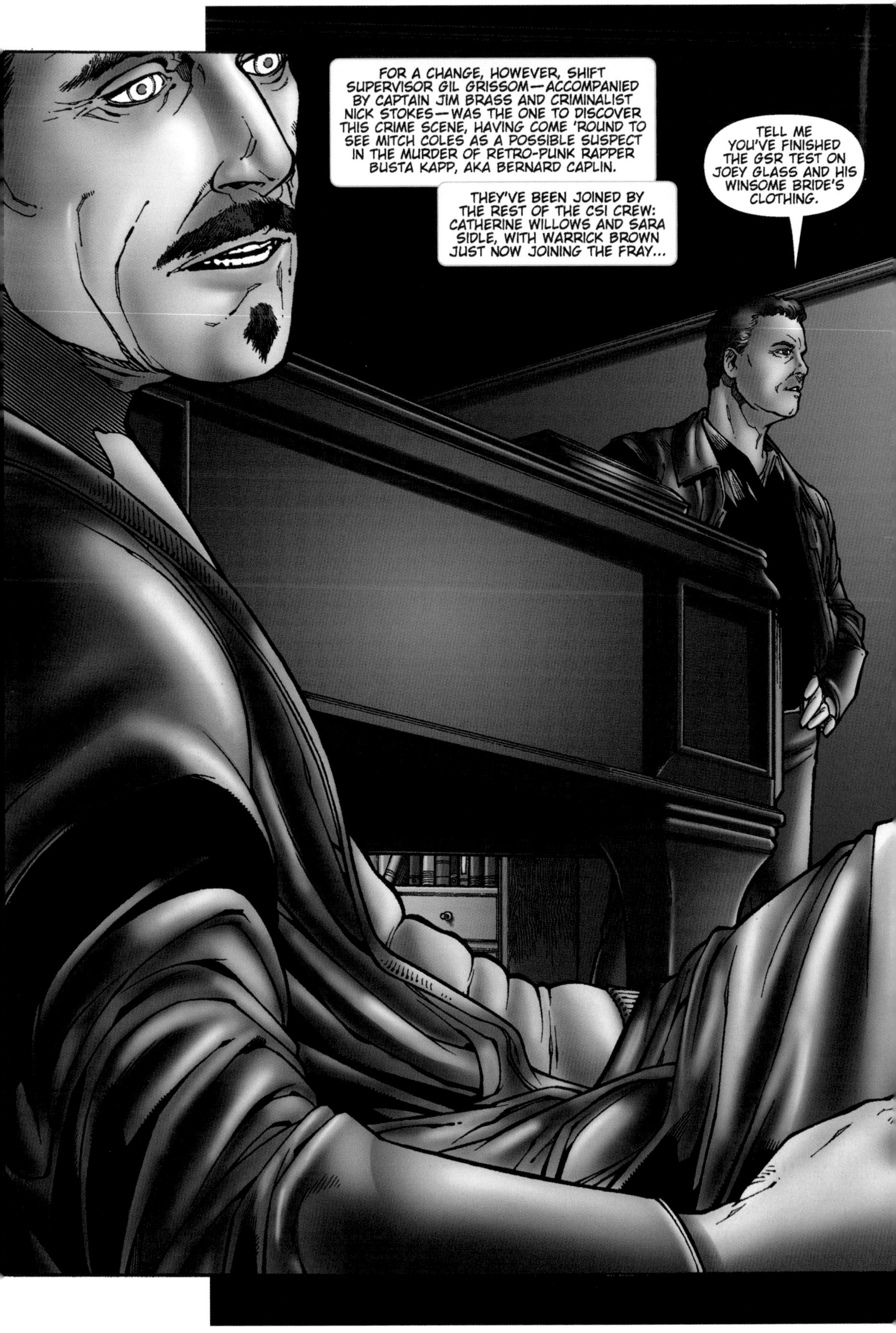
FOR A CHANGE, HOWEVER, SHIFT SUPERVISOR GIL GRISSOM—ACCOMPANIED BY CAPTAIN JIM BRASS AND CRIMINALIST NICK STOKES—WAS THE ONE TO DISCOVER THIS CRIME SCENE, HAVING COME 'ROUND TO SEE MITCH COLES AS A POSSIBLE SUSPECT IN THE MURDER OF RETRO-PUNK RAPPER BUSTA KAPP, AKA BERNARD CAPLIN.
THEY'VE BEEN JOINED BY THE REST OF THE CSI CREW: CATHERINE WILLOWS AND SARA SIDLE, WITH WARRICK BROWN JUST NOW JOINING THE FRAY...
TELL ME YOU'VE FINISHED THE GSR TEST ON JOEY GLASS AND HIS WINSOME BRIDE'S CLOTHING.

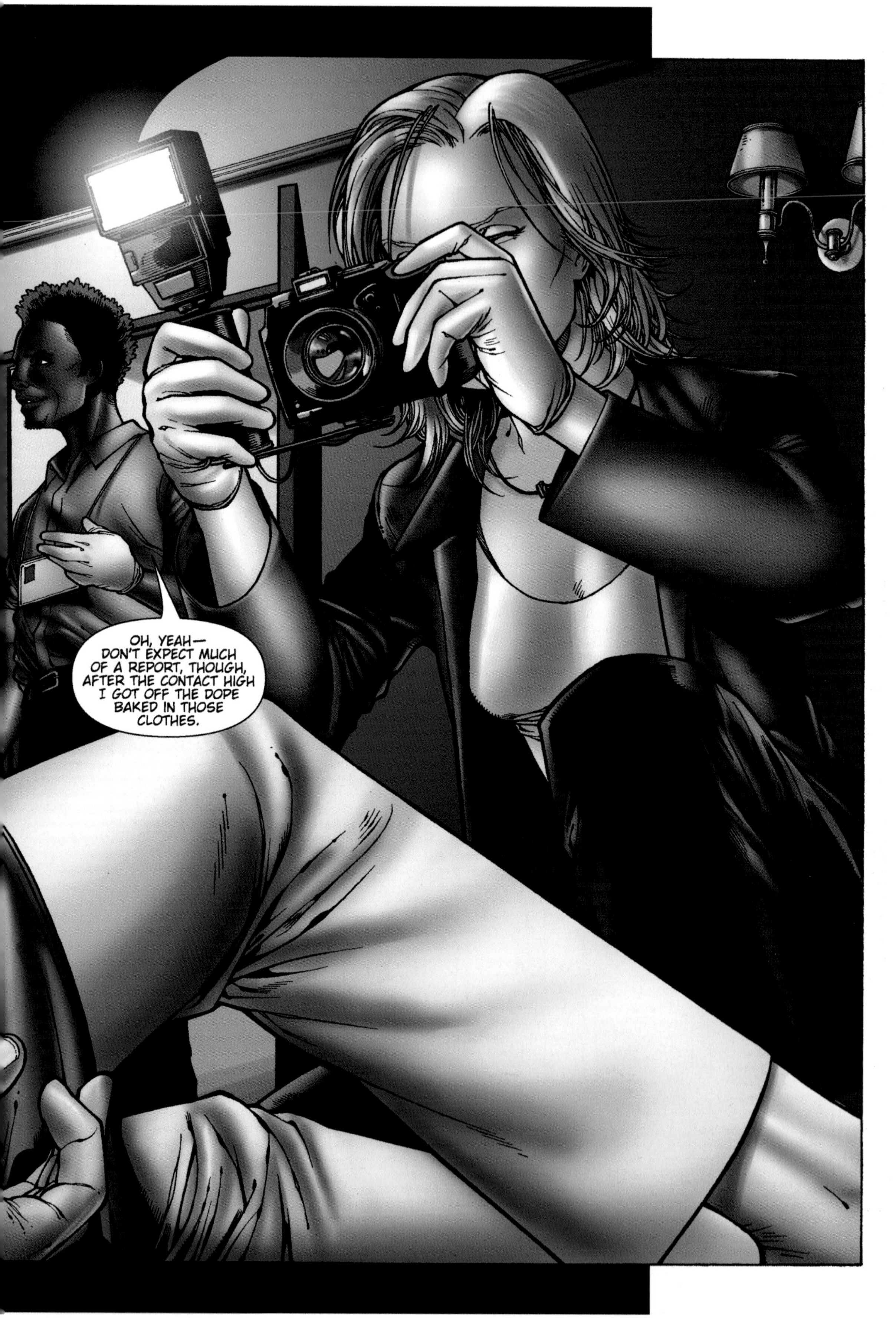
OH, YEAH— DON'T EXPECT MUCH OF A REPORT, THOUGH, AFTER THE CONTACT HIGH I GOT OFF THE DOPE BAKED IN THOSE CLOTHES.

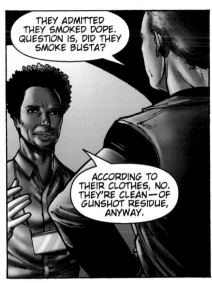

THEY ADMITTED THEY SMOKED DOPE. QUESTION IS, DID THEY SMOKE BUSTA?

ACCORDING TO THEIR CLOTHES, NO. THEY'RE CLEAN—OF GUNSHOT RESIDUE, ANYWAY.

CONFIRMED IT WAS THE CLOTHES THEY WORE AGAINST NEWS TEAM FOOTAGE. SO HOW DO YOU SEE THIS KILL GOING DOWN, GRIS?

"IT WOULD APPEAR MITCH COLES OPENED THE SAFE, POSSIBLY AT GUNPOINT; BUT HIS FACE WAS TURNED TO THE PERSON MAKING HIM DO SO...

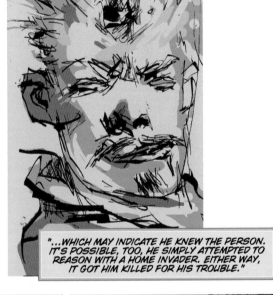

"...WHICH MAY INDICATE HE KNEW THE PERSON. IT'S POSSIBLE, TOO, HE SIMPLY ATTEMPTED TO REASON WITH A HOME INVADER. EITHER WAY, IT GOT HIM KILLED FOR HIS TROUBLE."

WORKS FOR ME. HEY, I GOT A LINE ON GRANT LITTLETON, FATHER OF THAT FEMALE OVERDOSE AT BUSTA'S CRIB. A LESTER DEAN CALLED AND SAID LITTLETON AND HIS SON ARE STAYING AT—

THE GOLD ARMADILLO!

LES'S AN OLD FRIEND. I WAS IN THE PROCESS OF LEAVING WORD WITH CONTACTS AT VARIOUS RESORTS WHEN YOU CALLED, GIL.

WHEN BRASS GETS BACK FROM HIS NEIGHBORHOOD CANVASS, MAYBE YOU TWO SHOULD DROP BY AND TALK TO YOUR OLD FRIEND AT THE ARMADILLO.

HEY, HAVIN' FRIENDS COMES IN HANDY... YOU SHOULD TRY IT.

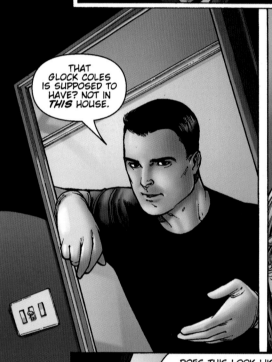

THAT GLOCK COLES IS SUPPOSED TO HAVE? NOT IN *THIS* HOUSE.

DID YOU TRY THE—

CIRCUIT BREAKER BOXES? YEAH. BEEN INSIDE EVERY VENT AND EVEN LESS GLAMOROUS PLACES. NO GLOCK.

DOES THIS LOOK LIKE A WORK BOOT TO YOU GUYS? 'CAUSE THE PRINTS WE MADE AT THE PLATINUM KING AND ROMANOV WERE A MIX OF TENNIES AND SMOOTH SOLES.

NICK, GO TALK TO THE GUARD AT THE GATE AND SEE IF ANY WORKMEN HAVE COME TO THE COLES HOUSE IN THE LAST 24.

TRY 'N' STOP ME.

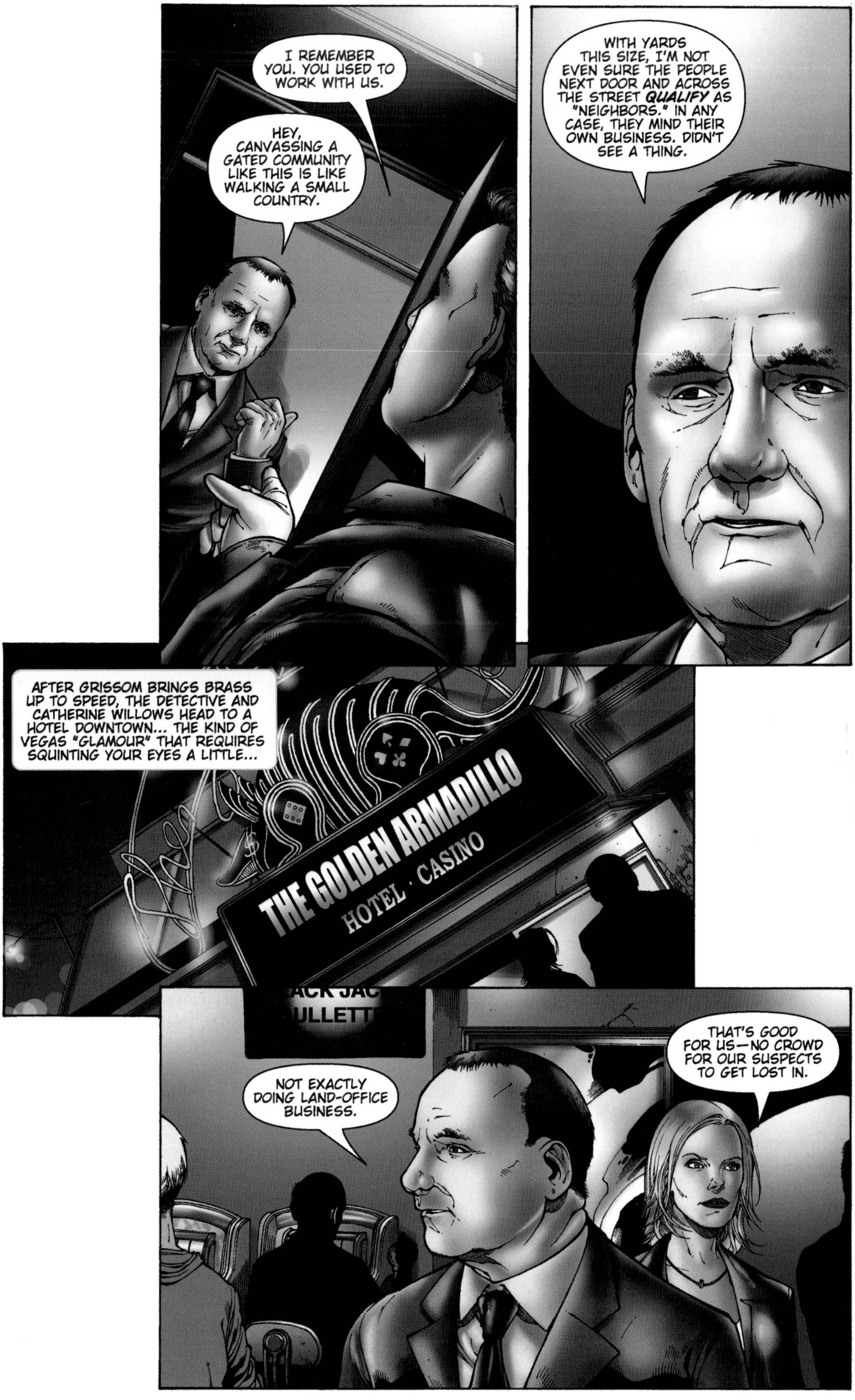
I REMEMBER YOU. YOU USED TO WORK WITH US.
HEY, CANVASSING A GATED COMMUNITY LIKE THIS IS LIKE WALKING A SMALL COUNTRY.
WITH YARDS THIS SIZE, I'M NOT EVEN SURE THE PEOPLE NEXT DOOR AND ACROSS THE STREET *QUALIFY* AS "NEIGHBORS." IN ANY CASE, THEY MIND THEIR OWN BUSINESS. DIDN'T SEE A THING.
AFTER GRISSOM BRINGS BRASS UP TO SPEED, THE DETECTIVE AND CATHERINE WILLOWS HEAD TO A HOTEL DOWNTOWN... THE KIND OF VEGAS "GLAMOUR" THAT REQUIRES SQUINTING YOUR EYES A LITTLE...
THE GOLDEN ARMADILLO
HOTEL · CASINO
NOT EXACTLY DOING LAND-OFFICE BUSINESS.
THAT'S GOOD FOR US—NO CROWD FOR OUR SUSPECTS TO GET LOST IN.

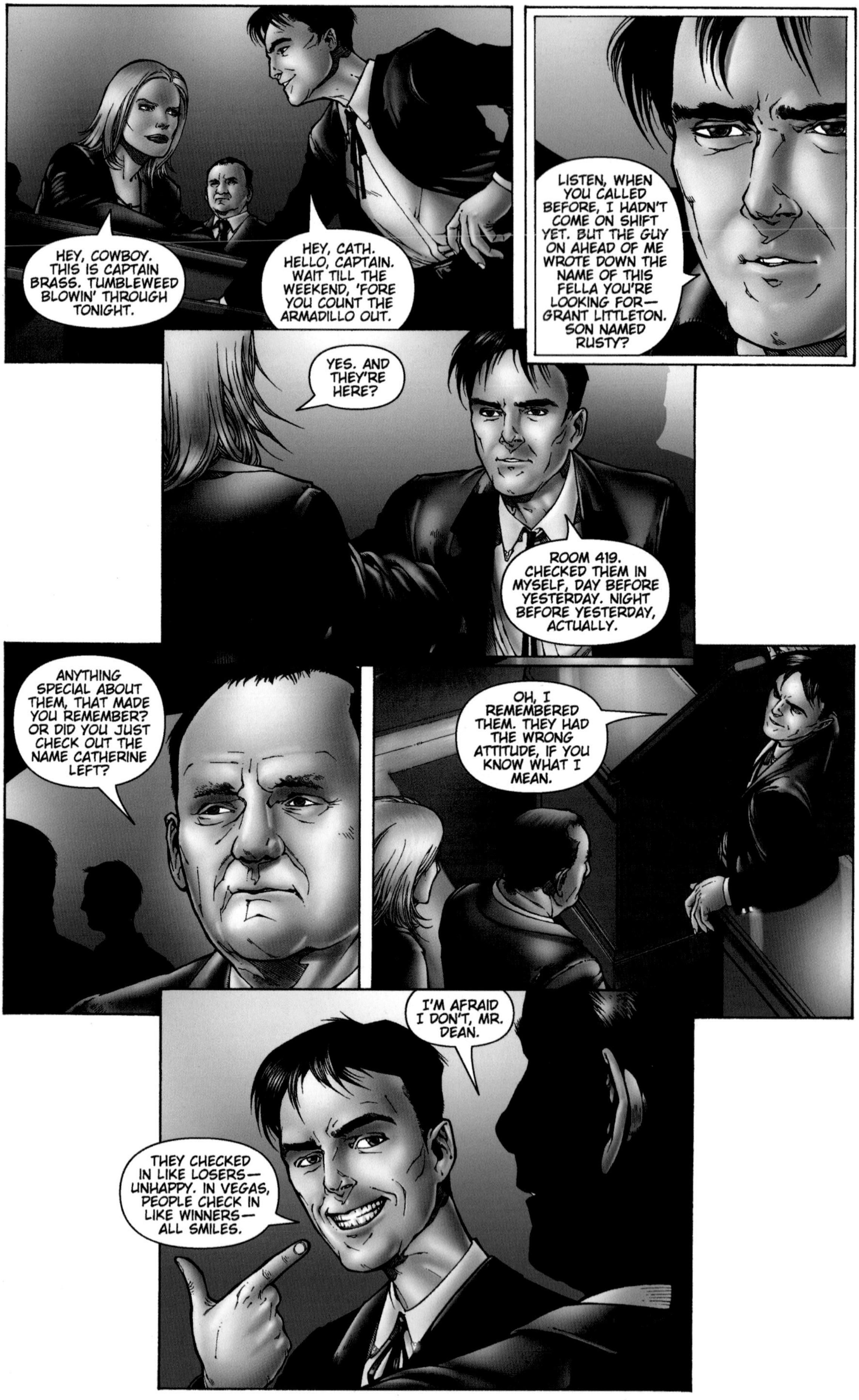
HEY, COWBOY. THIS IS CAPTAIN BRASS. TUMBLEWEED BLOWIN' THROUGH TONIGHT.
HEY, CATH. HELLO, CAPTAIN. WAIT TILL THE WEEKEND, 'FORE YOU COUNT THE ARMADILLO OUT.
LISTEN, WHEN YOU CALLED BEFORE, I HADN'T COME ON SHIFT YET. BUT THE GUY ON AHEAD OF ME WROTE DOWN THE NAME OF THIS FELLA YOU'RE LOOKING FOR—GRANT LITTLETON. SON NAMED RUSTY?
YES. AND THEY'RE HERE?
ROOM 419. CHECKED THEM IN MYSELF, DAY BEFORE YESTERDAY. NIGHT BEFORE YESTERDAY, ACTUALLY.
ANYTHING SPECIAL ABOUT THEM, THAT MADE YOU REMEMBER? OR DID YOU JUST CHECK OUT THE NAME CATHERINE LEFT?
OH, I REMEMBERED THEM. THEY HAD THE WRONG ATTITUDE, IF YOU KNOW WHAT I MEAN.
I'M AFRAID I DON'T, MR. DEAN.
THEY CHECKED IN LIKE LOSERS—UNHAPPY. IN VEGAS, PEOPLE CHECK IN LIKE WINNERS—ALL SMILES.

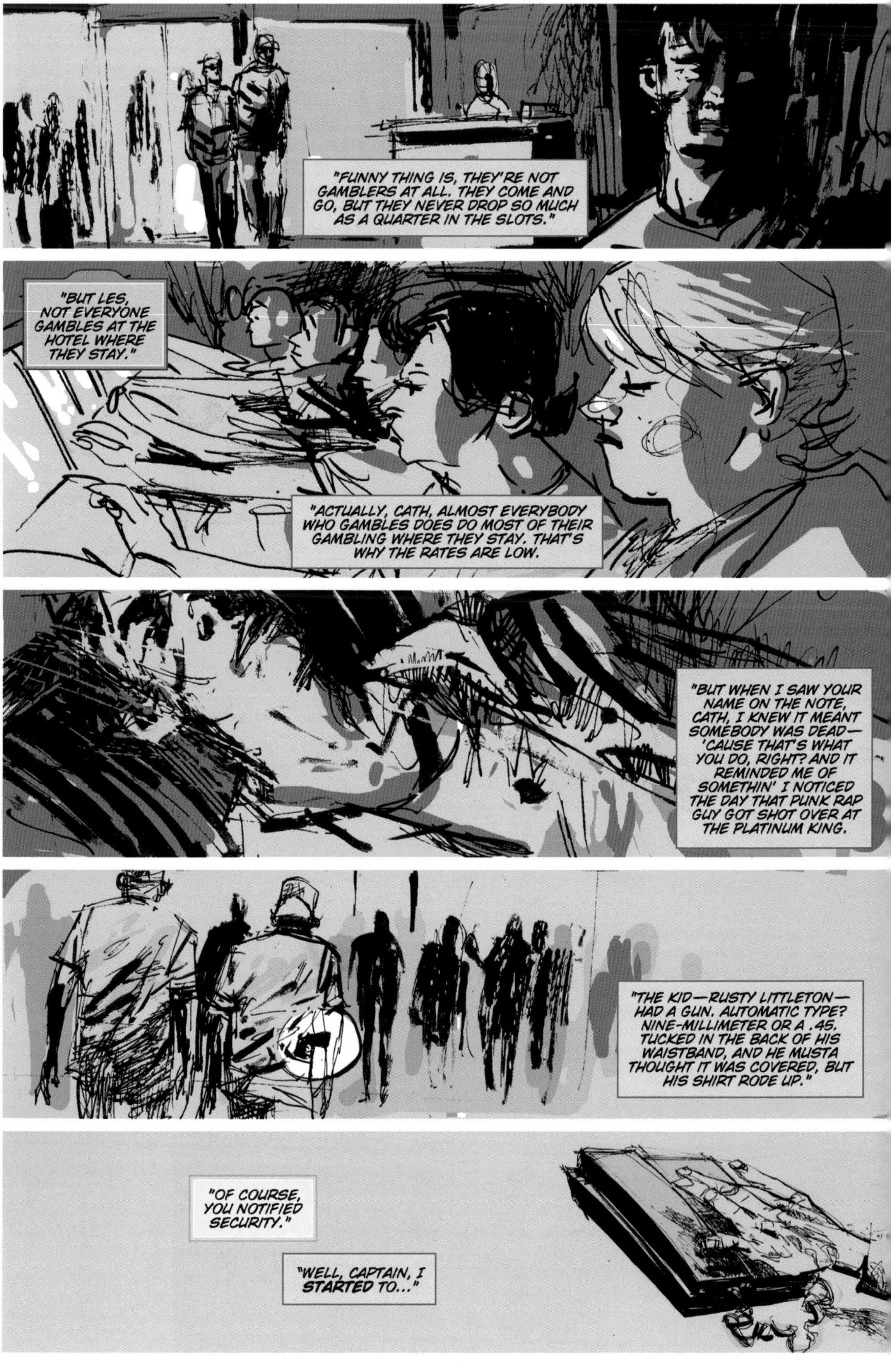
"FUNNY THING IS, THEY'RE NOT GAMBLERS AT ALL. THEY COME AND GO, BUT THEY NEVER DROP SO MUCH AS A QUARTER IN THE SLOTS."
"BUT LES, NOT EVERYONE GAMBLES AT THE HOTEL WHERE THEY STAY."
"ACTUALLY, CATH, ALMOST EVERYBODY WHO GAMBLES DOES DO MOST OF THEIR GAMBLING WHERE THEY STAY. THAT'S WHY THE RATES ARE LOW.
"BUT WHEN I SAW YOUR NAME ON THE NOTE, CATH, I KNEW IT MEANT SOMEBODY WAS DEAD—'CAUSE THAT'S WHAT YOU DO, RIGHT? AND IT REMINDED ME OF SOMETHIN' I NOTICED THE DAY THAT PUNK RAP GUY GOT SHOT OVER AT THE PLATINUM KING.
"THE KID—RUSTY LITTLETON—HAD A GUN. AUTOMATIC TYPE? NINE-MILLIMETER OR A .45. TUCKED IN THE BACK OF HIS WAISTBAND, AND HE MUSTA THOUGHT IT WAS COVERED, BUT HIS SHIRT RODE UP."
"OF COURSE, YOU NOTIFIED SECURITY."
"WELL, CAPTAIN, I STARTED TO..."

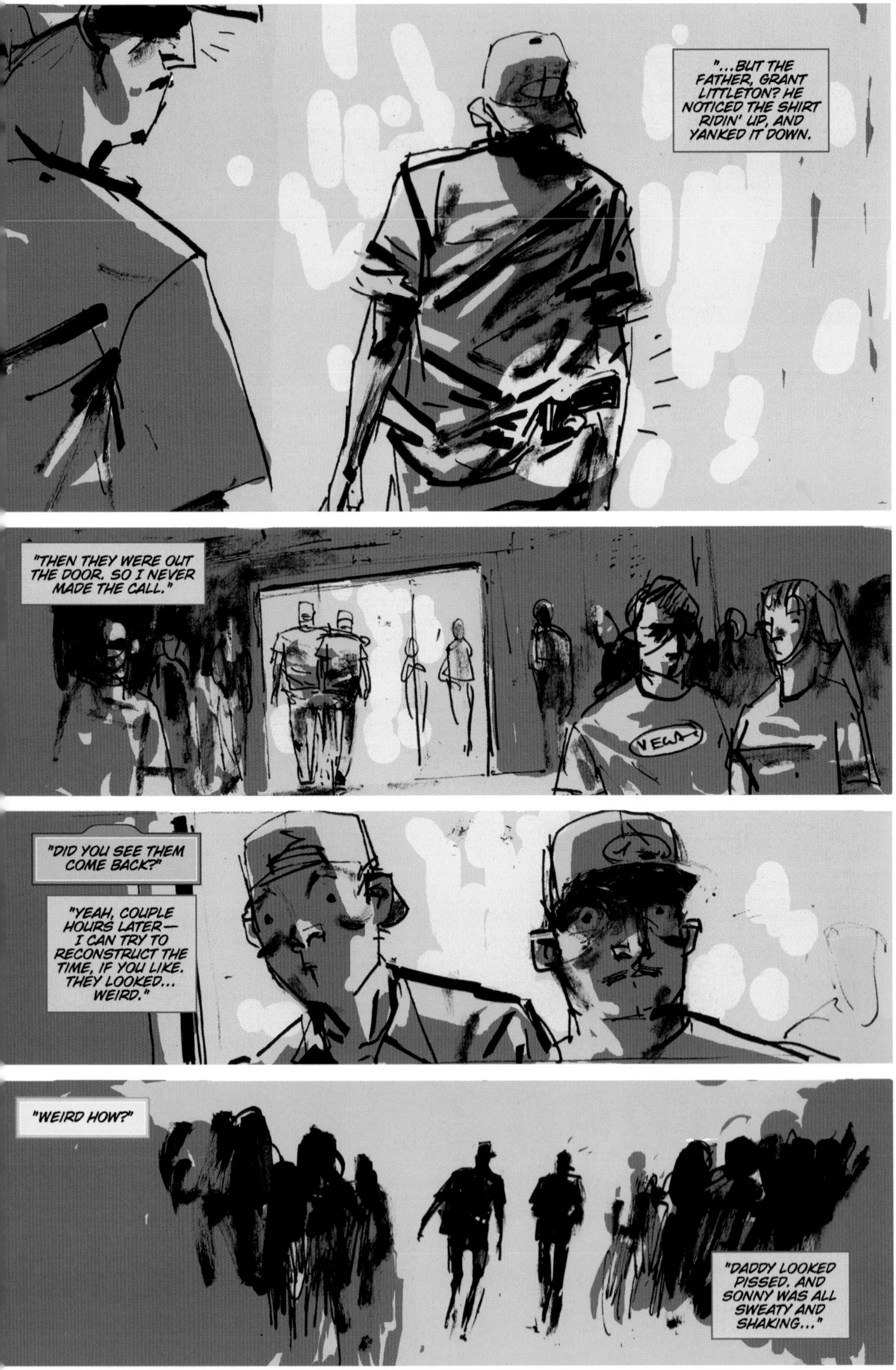
"...BUT THE FATHER, GRANT LITTLETON? HE NOTICED THE SHIRT RIDIN' UP, AND YANKED IT DOWN.
"THEN THEY WERE OUT THE DOOR. SO I NEVER MADE THE CALL."
"DID YOU SEE THEM COME BACK?"
"YEAH, COUPLE HOURS LATER— I CAN TRY TO RECONSTRUCT THE TIME, IF YOU LIKE. THEY LOOKED... WEIRD."
"WEIRD HOW?"
"DADDY LOOKED PISSED. AND SONNY WAS ALL SWEATY AND SHAKING..."

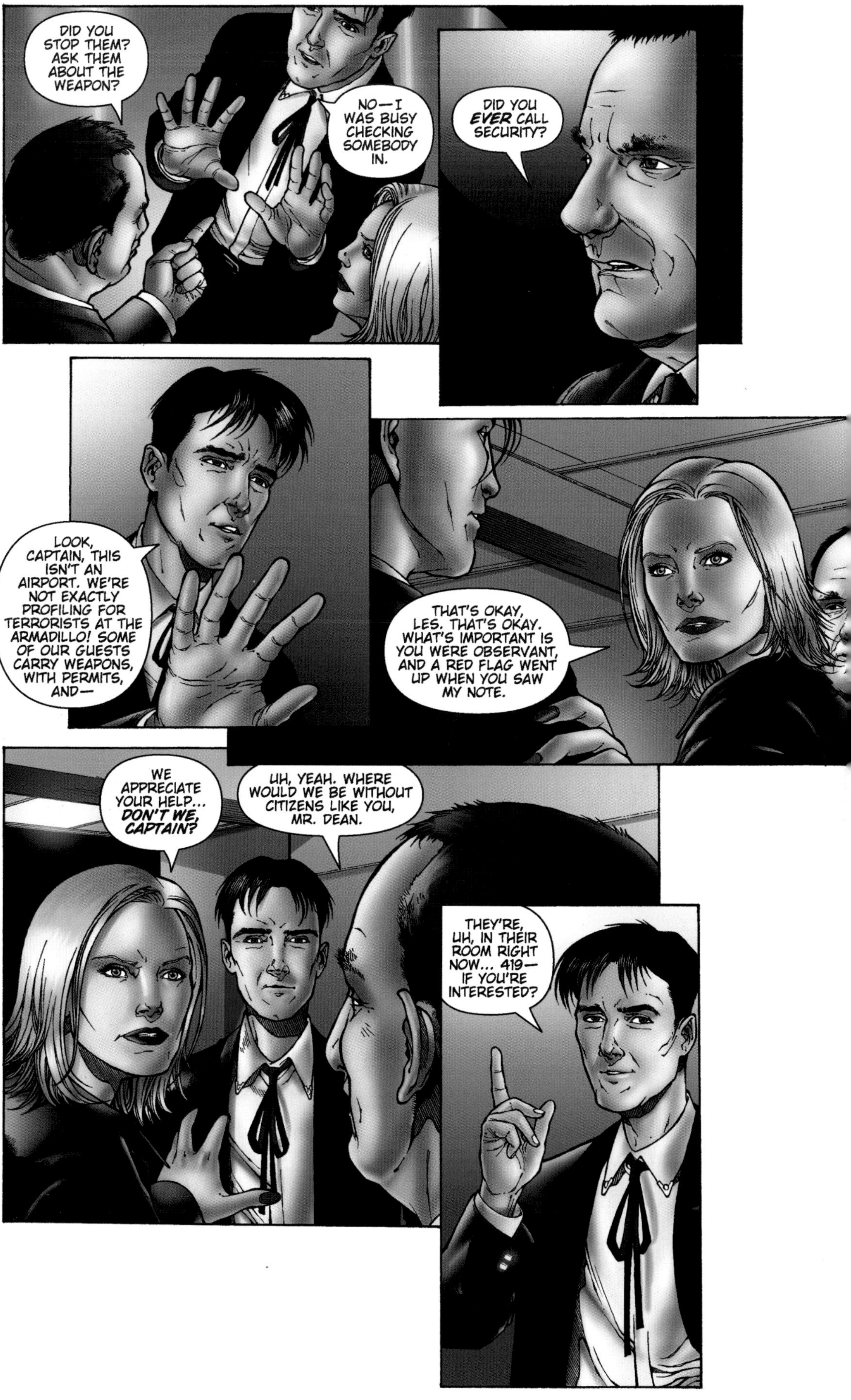
DID YOU STOP THEM? ASK THEM ABOUT THE WEAPON?
NO—I WAS BUSY CHECKING SOMEBODY IN.
DID YOU EVER CALL SECURITY?
LOOK, CAPTAIN, THIS ISN'T AN AIRPORT. WE'RE NOT EXACTLY PROFILING FOR TERRORISTS AT THE ARMADILLO! SOME OF OUR GUESTS CARRY WEAPONS, WITH PERMITS, AND—
THAT'S OKAY, LES. THAT'S OKAY. WHAT'S IMPORTANT IS YOU WERE OBSERVANT, AND A RED FLAG WENT UP WHEN YOU SAW MY NOTE.
WE APPRECIATE YOUR HELP... DON'T WE, CAPTAIN?
UH, YEAH. WHERE WOULD WE BE WITHOUT CITIZENS LIKE YOU, MR. DEAN.
THEY'RE, UH, IN THEIR ROOM RIGHT NOW... 419—IF YOU'RE INTERESTED?

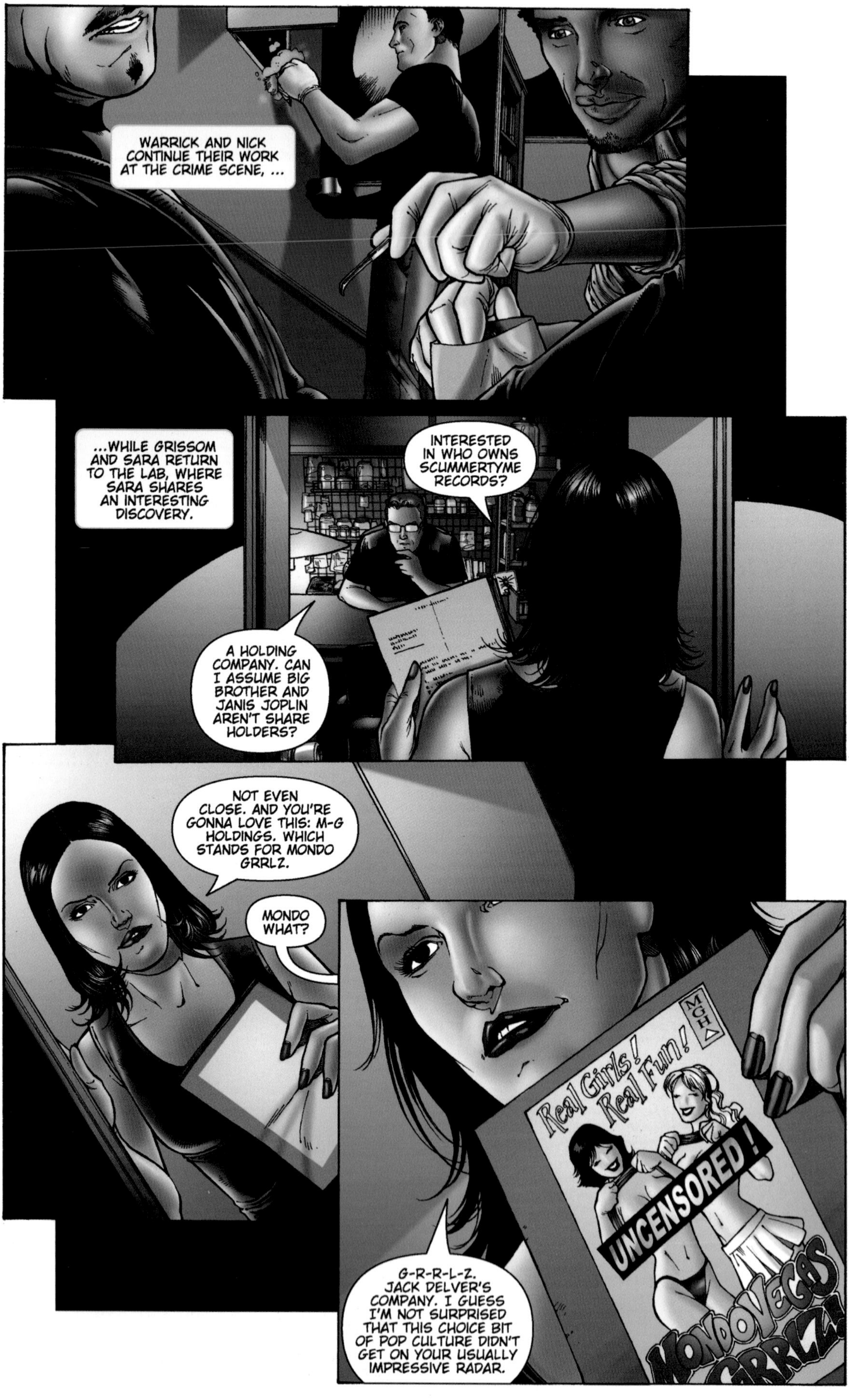
WARRICK AND NICK CONTINUE THEIR WORK AT THE CRIME SCENE, ...
...WHILE GRISSOM AND SARA RETURN TO THE LAB, WHERE SARA SHARES AN INTERESTING DISCOVERY.
INTERESTED IN WHO OWNS SCUMMERTYME RECORDS?
A HOLDING COMPANY. CAN I ASSUME BIG BROTHER AND JANIS JOPLIN AREN'T SHARE HOLDERS?
NOT EVEN CLOSE. AND YOU'RE GONNA LOVE THIS: M-G HOLDINGS. WHICH STANDS FOR MONDO GRRLZ.
MONDO WHAT?
G-R-R-L-Z. JACK DELVER'S COMPANY. I GUESS I'M NOT SURPRISED THAT THIS CHOICE BIT OF POP CULTURE DIDN'T GET ON YOUR USUALLY IMPRESSIVE RADAR.
MGH
Real Girls! Real Fun!
UNCENSORED!
MONDO VEGAS GRRLZ!

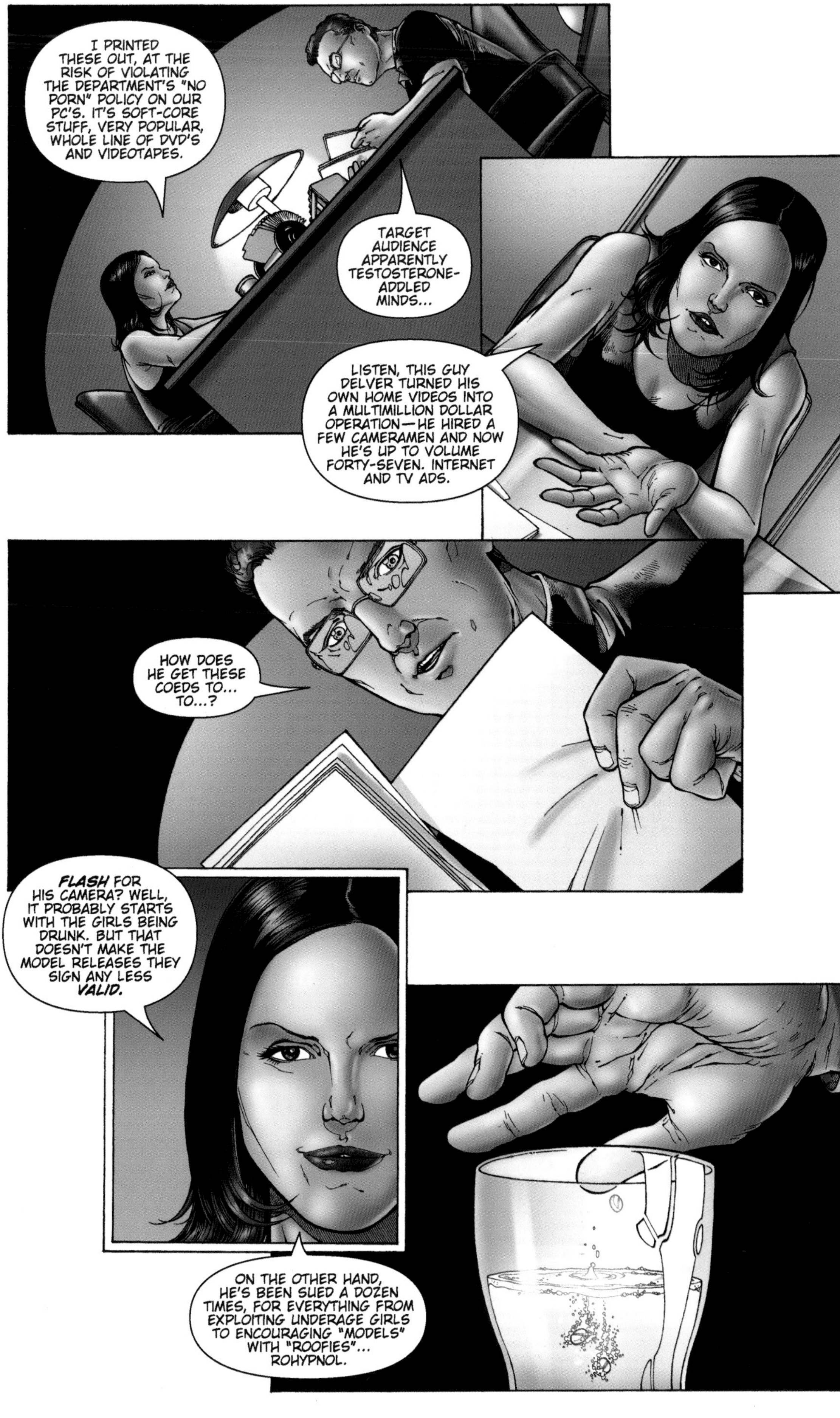
I PRINTED THESE OUT, AT THE RISK OF VIOLATING THE DEPARTMENT'S "NO PORN" POLICY ON OUR PC'S. IT'S SOFT-CORE STUFF, VERY POPULAR, WHOLE LINE OF DVD'S AND VIDEOTAPES.
TARGET AUDIENCE APPARENTLY TESTOSTERONE-ADDLED MINDS...
LISTEN, THIS GUY DELVER TURNED HIS OWN HOME VIDEOS INTO A MULTIMILLION DOLLAR OPERATION—HE HIRED A FEW CAMERAMEN AND NOW HE'S UP TO VOLUME FORTY-SEVEN. INTERNET AND TV ADS.
HOW DOES HE GET THESE COEDS TO... TO...?
FLASH FOR HIS CAMERA? WELL, IT PROBABLY STARTS WITH THE GIRLS BEING DRUNK. BUT THAT DOESN'T MAKE THE MODEL RELEASES THEY SIGN ANY LESS VALID.
ON THE OTHER HAND, HE'S BEEN SUED A DOZEN TIMES, FOR EVERYTHING FROM EXPLOITING UNDERAGE GIRLS TO ENCOURAGING "MODELS" WITH "ROOFIES"... ROHYPNOL.

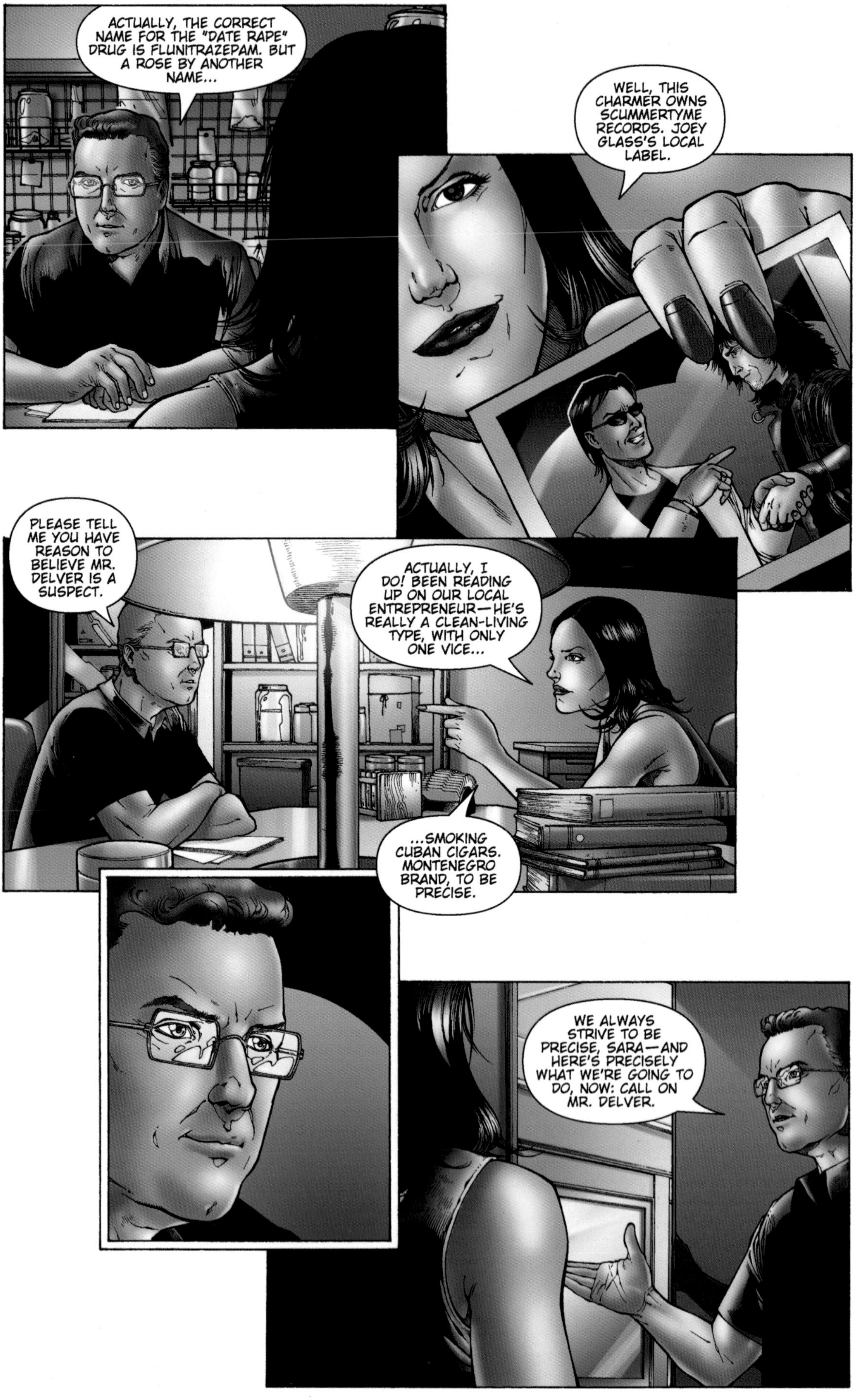
ACTUALLY, THE CORRECT NAME FOR THE "DATE RAPE" DRUG IS FLUNITRAZEPAM. BUT A ROSE BY ANOTHER NAME...
WELL, THIS CHARMER OWNS SCUMMERTYME RECORDS. JOEY GLASS'S LOCAL LABEL.
PLEASE TELL ME YOU HAVE REASON TO BELIEVE MR. DELVER IS A SUSPECT.
ACTUALLY, I DO! BEEN READING UP ON OUR LOCAL ENTREPRENEUR—HE'S REALLY A CLEAN-LIVING TYPE, WITH ONLY ONE VICE...
...SMOKING CUBAN CIGARS. MONTENEGRO BRAND, TO BE PRECISE.
WE ALWAYS STRIVE TO BE PRECISE, SARA—AND HERE'S PRECISELY WHAT WE'RE GOING TO DO, NOW: CALL ON MR. DELVER.

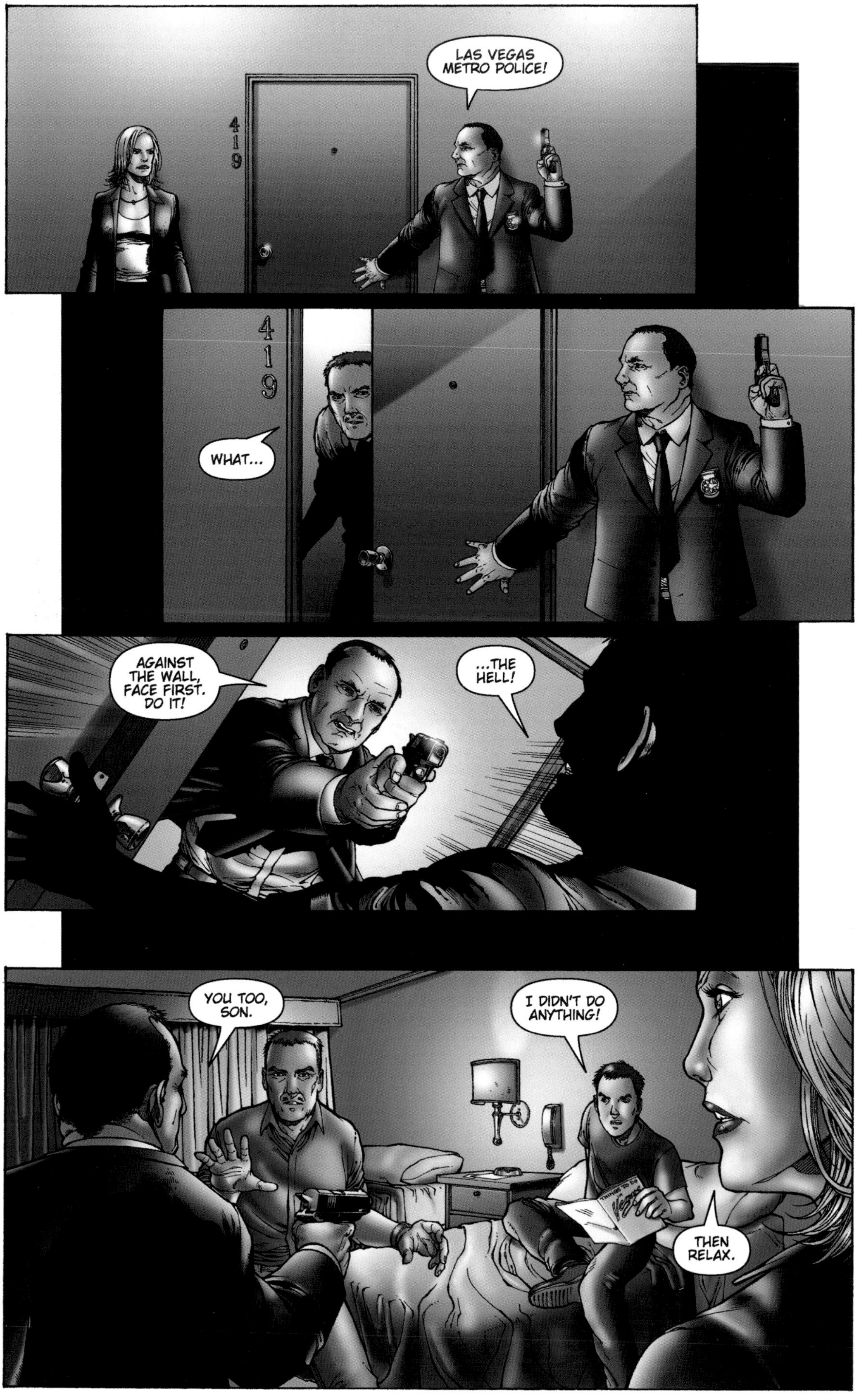
LAS VEGAS METRO POLICE!
WHAT...
AGAINST THE WALL, FACE FIRST. DO IT!
...THE HELL!
YOU TOO, SON.
I DIDN'T DO ANYTHING!
THEN RELAX.

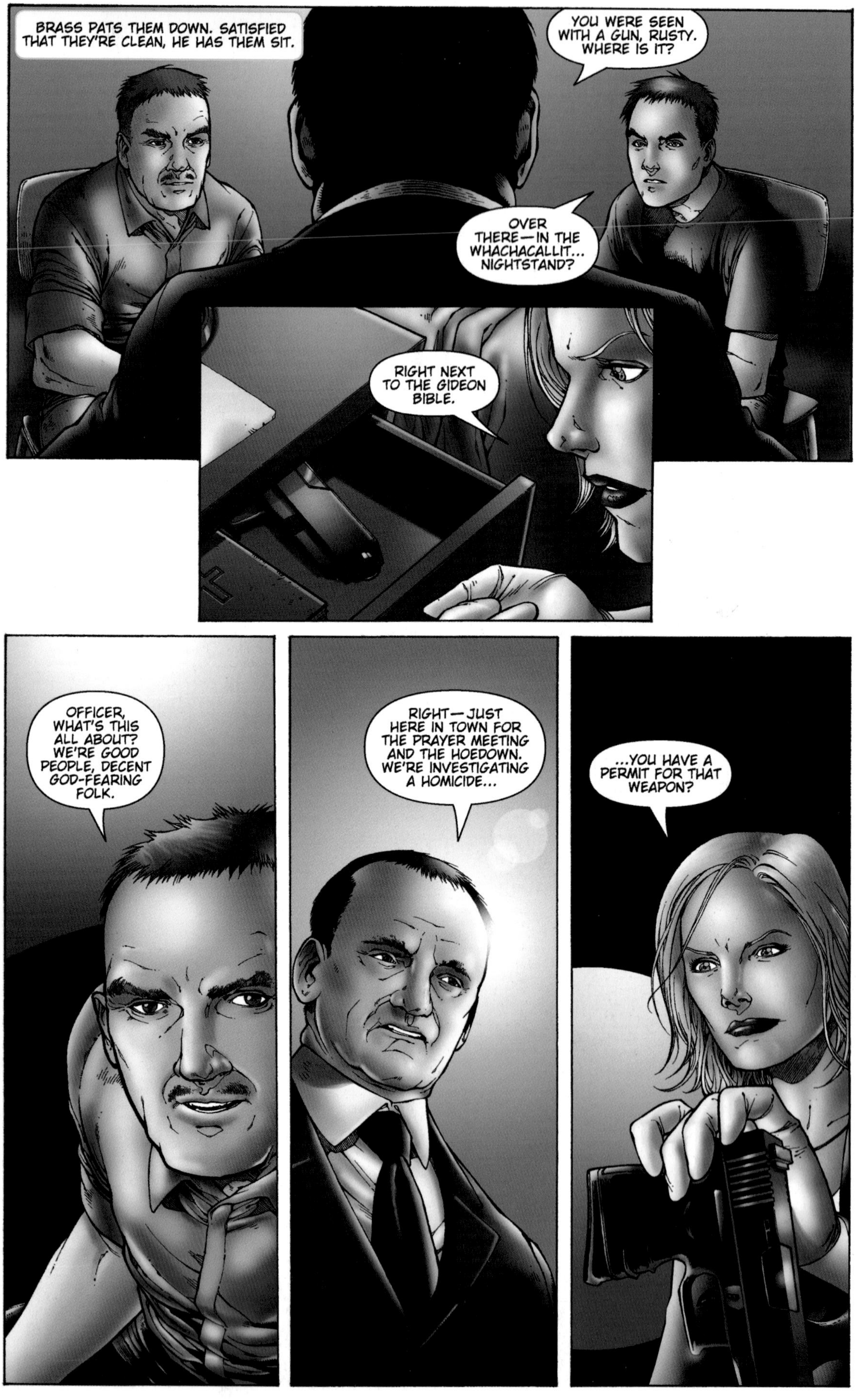
BRASS PATS THEM DOWN. SATISFIED THAT THEY'RE CLEAN, HE HAS THEM SIT.
YOU WERE SEEN WITH A GUN, RUSTY. WHERE IS IT?
OVER THERE—IN THE WHACHACALLIT... NIGHTSTAND?
RIGHT NEXT TO THE GIDEON BIBLE.
OFFICER, WHAT'S THIS ALL ABOUT? WE'RE GOOD PEOPLE, DECENT GOD-FEARING FOLK.
RIGHT—JUST HERE IN TOWN FOR THE PRAYER MEETING AND THE HOEDOWN. WE'RE INVESTIGATING A HOMICIDE...
...YOU HAVE A PERMIT FOR THAT WEAPON?

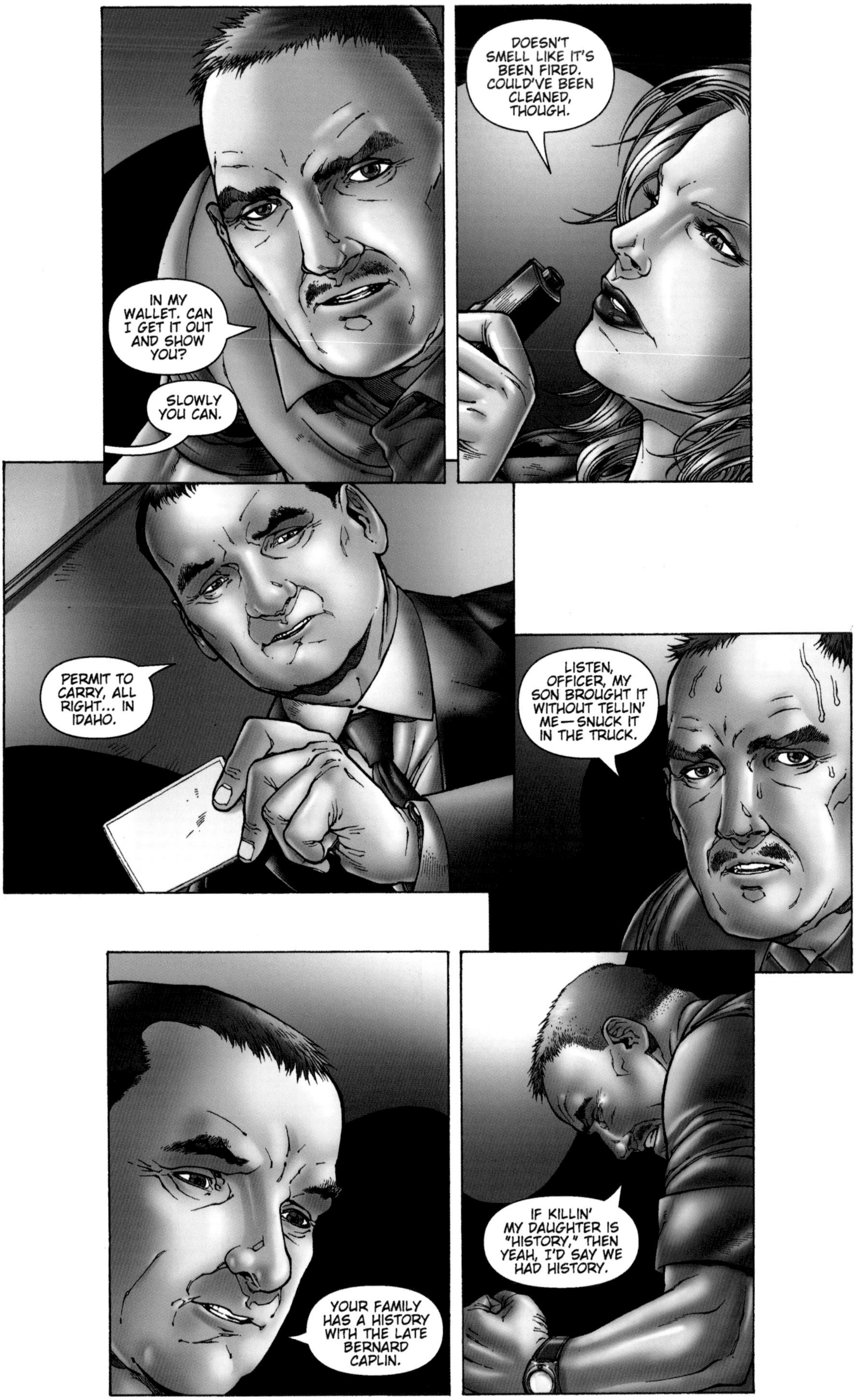
IN MY WALLET. CAN I GET IT OUT AND SHOW YOU?
SLOWLY YOU CAN.
DOESN'T SMELL LIKE IT'S BEEN FIRED. COULD'VE BEEN CLEANED, THOUGH.
PERMIT TO CARRY, ALL RIGHT... IN IDAHO.
LISTEN, OFFICER, MY SON BROUGHT IT WITHOUT TELLIN' ME—SNUCK IT IN THE TRUCK.
YOUR FAMILY HAS A HISTORY WITH THE LATE BERNARD CAPLIN.
IF KILLIN' MY DAUGHTER IS "HISTORY," THEN YEAH, I'D SAY WE HAD HISTORY.

BUSTA KAPP WAS A NO-GOOD DRUG ADDICT PERVERT SON-OF...

BOY HAS A BIT OF TROUBLE CONTROLLIN' HISSELF.

OH, I DON'T KNOW. FOR A MINUTE THERE, SORT OF SOUNDED LIKE HE MIGHT MAKE A PRETTY DECENT PUNK RAPPER HIMSELF.

THE S-O-B HAD IT COMIN'!

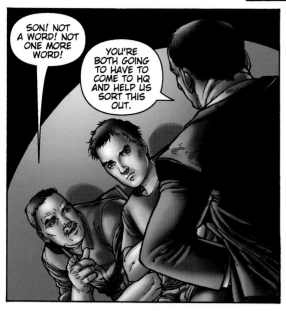

SON! NOT A WORD! NOT ONE MORE WORD!

YOU'RE BOTH GOING TO HAVE TO COME TO HQ AND HELP US SORT THIS OUT.

WHERE WERE YOU TWO WHEN THE SHOOTING AT THE PLATINUM KING TOOK PLACE?

"I WAS WITH MY LAWYER. MARVIN SANDRED, LOCAL MAN. THREE OF US WERE SITTIN', AT ONE OF THESE OUTDOOR CAFÉS, HAVIN' DINNER AND TALKIN' OVER THE LAWSUIT."

"THAT WAS WHEN THIS LIMO DROVE RIGHT PAST US, AND RUSTY NOTICED THE LICENSE PLATE— ONE OF THOSE PERSONALIZED ONES? BUSTA!"

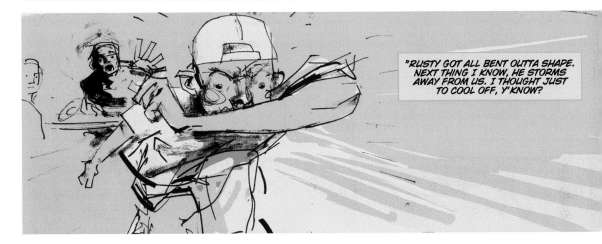

"RUSTY GOT ALL BENT OUTTA SHAPE. NEXT THING I KNOW, HE STORMS AWAY FROM US. I THOUGHT JUST TO COOL OFF, Y'KNOW?"

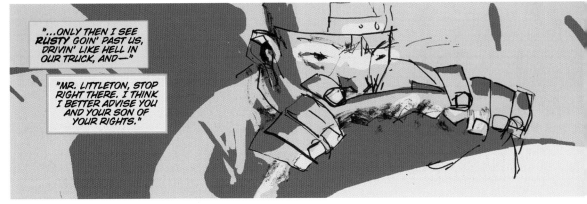

"...ONLY THEN I SEE RUSTY GOIN' PAST US, DRIVIN' LIKE HELL IN OUR TRUCK, AND—"

"MR. LITTLETON, STOP RIGHT THERE. I THINK I BETTER ADVISE YOU AND YOUR SON OF YOUR RIGHTS."

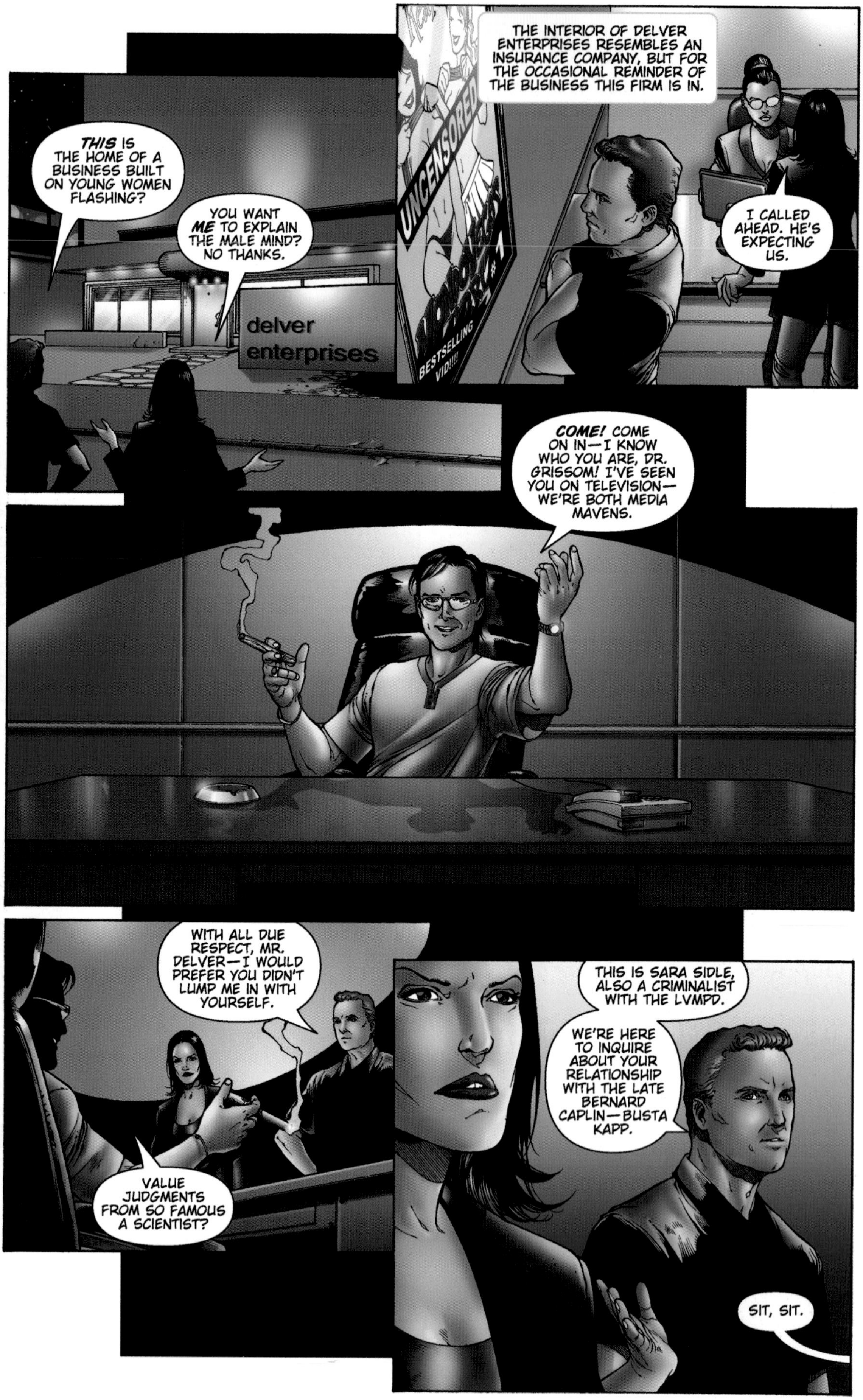
THIS IS THE HOME OF A BUSINESS BUILT ON YOUNG WOMEN FLASHING?
YOU WANT ME TO EXPLAIN THE MALE MIND? NO THANKS.
delver enterprises
THE INTERIOR OF DELVER ENTERPRISES RESEMBLES AN INSURANCE COMPANY, BUT FOR THE OCCASIONAL REMINDER OF THE BUSINESS THIS FIRM IS IN.
UNCENSORED
BESTSELLING VID!!!!
I CALLED AHEAD. HE'S EXPECTING US.
COME! COME ON IN—I KNOW WHO YOU ARE, DR. GRISSOM! I'VE SEEN YOU ON TELEVISION—WE'RE BOTH MEDIA MAVENS.
WITH ALL DUE RESPECT, MR. DELVER—I WOULD PREFER YOU DIDN'T LUMP ME IN WITH YOURSELF.
VALUE JUDGMENTS FROM SO FAMOUS A SCIENTIST?
THIS IS SARA SIDLE, ALSO A CRIMINALIST WITH THE LVMPD.
WE'RE HERE TO INQUIRE ABOUT YOUR RELATIONSHIP WITH THE LATE BERNARD CAPLIN—BUSTA KAPP.
SIT, SIT.

UH, MS. SIDLE. HERE'S MY CARD. WE'RE DOING A VIDEO ON PUBLIC SERVANTS, AND—

MR. DELVER— YOU'RE ABOUT TO SEE ME GET VERY UNSCIENTIFIC. WE'RE BUSY PEOPLE, AS I'M SURE YOU ARE. ANSWER MY QUESTION, PLEASE.

NO OFFENSE MEANT TO EITHER OF YOU. BUSTA WAS A FORMER SCUMMERTYME EMPLOYEE. HE WAS UNDER CONTRACT TO US.

I THOUGHT BUSTA WAS UNDER CONTRACT TO SAHARA SOUNDS?

HE CLAIMED WE BREACHED HIS CONTRACT—WHICH, OF COURSE, WE DIDN'T— AND HE SIGNED WITH SAHARA SOUNDS, WHEN HE STILL OWED US AN ALBUM.

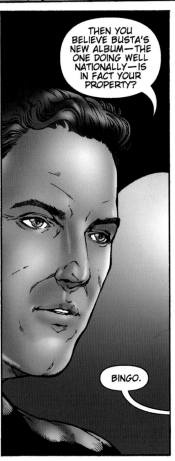

THEN YOU BELIEVE BUSTA'S NEW ALBUM—THE ONE DOING WELL NATIONALLY—IS IN FACT YOUR PROPERTY?

BINGO.

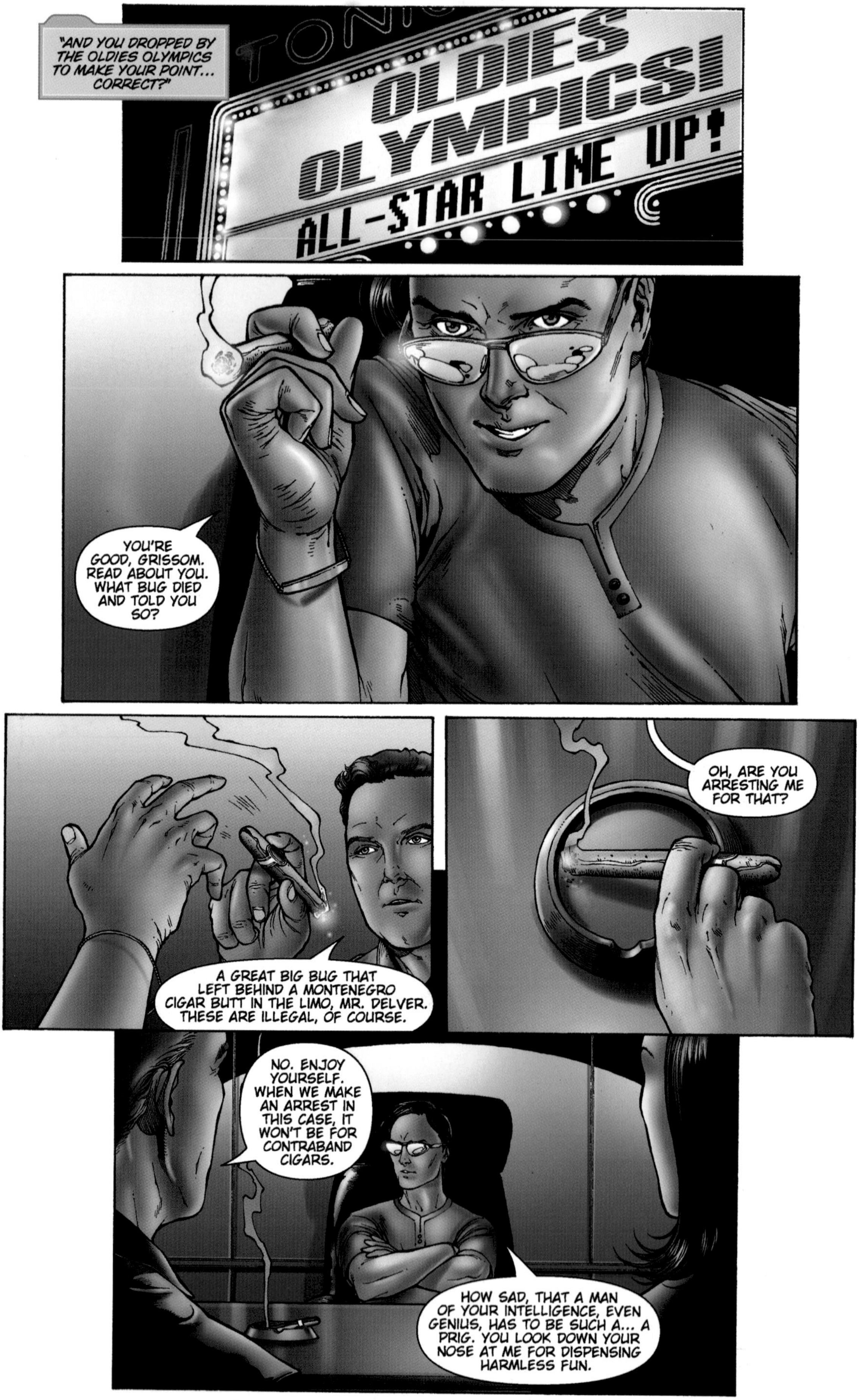
"AND YOU DROPPED BY THE OLDIES OLYMPICS TO MAKE YOUR POINT... CORRECT?"
OLDIES OLYMPICS!
ALL-STAR LINE UP!
YOU'RE GOOD, GRISSOM. READ ABOUT YOU. WHAT BUG DIED AND TOLD YOU SO?
A GREAT BIG BUG THAT LEFT BEHIND A MONTENEGRO CIGAR BUTT IN THE LIMO, MR. DELVER. THESE ARE ILLEGAL, OF COURSE.
OH, ARE YOU ARRESTING ME FOR THAT?
NO. ENJOY YOURSELF. WHEN WE MAKE AN ARREST IN THIS CASE, IT WON'T BE FOR CONTRABAND CIGARS.
HOW SAD, THAT A MAN OF YOUR INTELLIGENCE, EVEN GENIUS, HAS TO BE SUCH A... A PRIG. YOU LOOK DOWN YOUR NOSE AT ME FOR DISPENSING HARMLESS FUN.

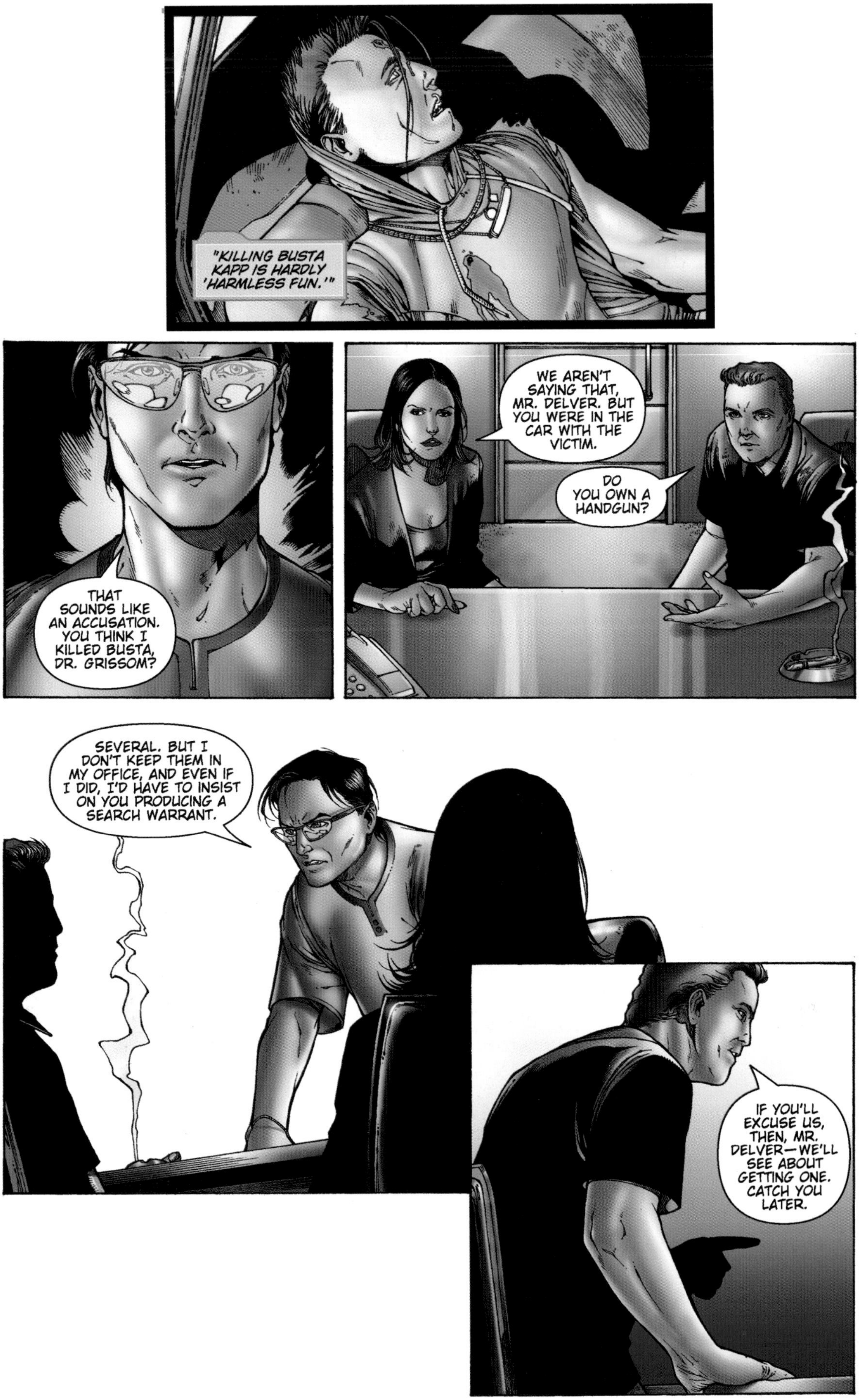
"KILLING BUSTA KAPP IS HARDLY 'HARMLESS FUN.'"
THAT SOUNDS LIKE AN ACCUSATION. YOU THINK I KILLED BUSTA, DR. GRISSOM?
WE AREN'T SAYING THAT, MR. DELVER. BUT YOU WERE IN THE CAR WITH THE VICTIM.
DO YOU OWN A HANDGUN?
SEVERAL. BUT I DON'T KEEP THEM IN MY OFFICE, AND EVEN IF I DID, I'D HAVE TO INSIST ON YOU PRODUCING A SEARCH WARRANT.
IF YOU'LL EXCUSE US, THEN, MR. DELVER—WE'LL SEE ABOUT GETTING ONE. CATCH YOU LATER.

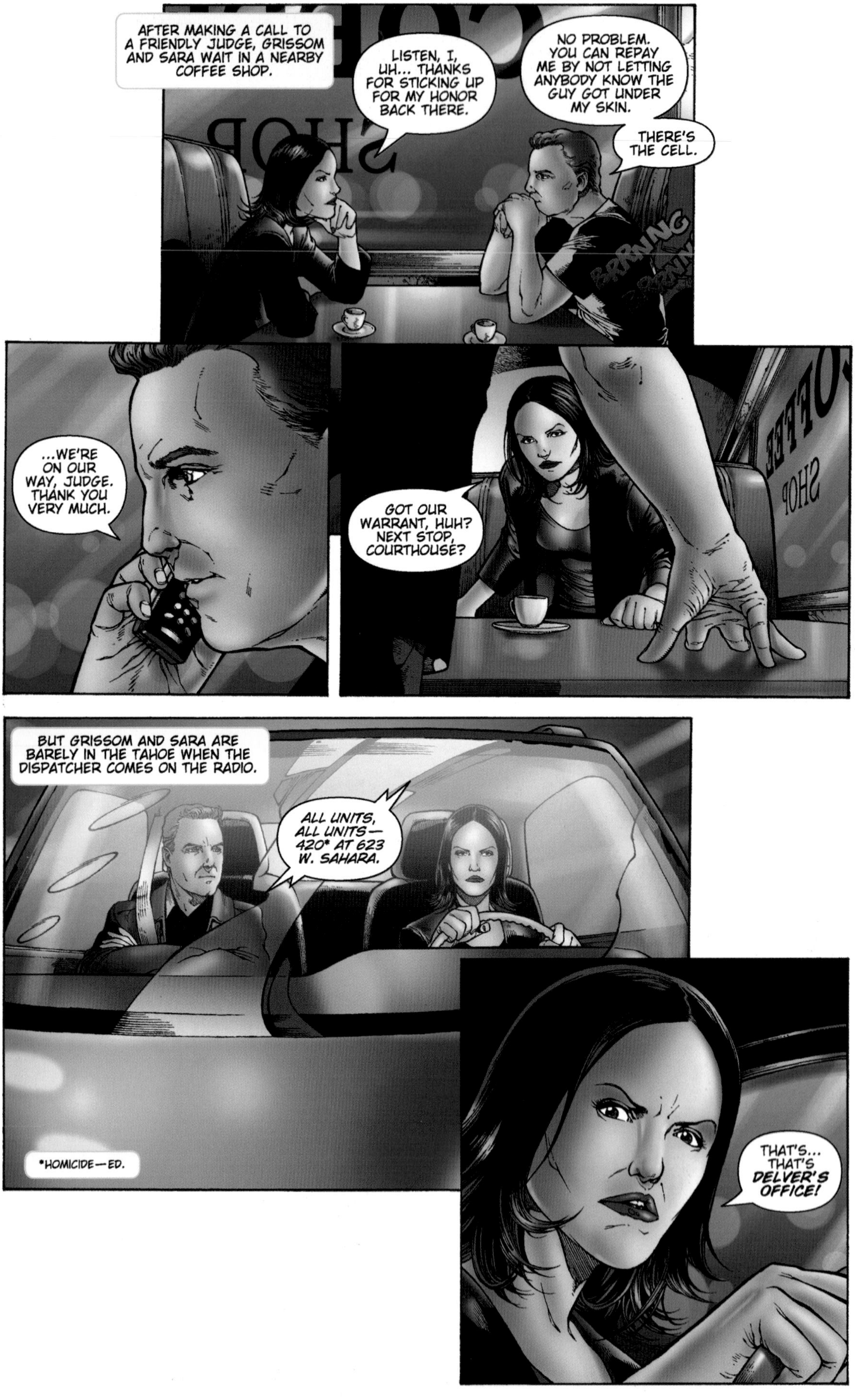
AFTER MAKING A CALL TO A FRIENDLY JUDGE, GRISSOM AND SARA WAIT IN A NEARBY COFFEE SHOP.
LISTEN, I, UH... THANKS FOR STICKING UP FOR MY HONOR BACK THERE.
NO PROBLEM. YOU CAN REPAY ME BY NOT LETTING ANYBODY KNOW THE GUY GOT UNDER MY SKIN.
THERE'S THE CELL.
BRRRING
...WE'RE ON OUR WAY, JUDGE. THANK YOU VERY MUCH.
GOT OUR WARRANT, HUH? NEXT STOP, COURTHOUSE?
BUT GRISSOM AND SARA ARE BARELY IN THE TAHOE WHEN THE DISPATCHER COMES ON THE RADIO.
ALL UNITS, ALL UNITS—420* AT 623 W. SAHARA.
*HOMICIDE—ED.
THAT'S... THAT'S DELVER'S OFFICE!

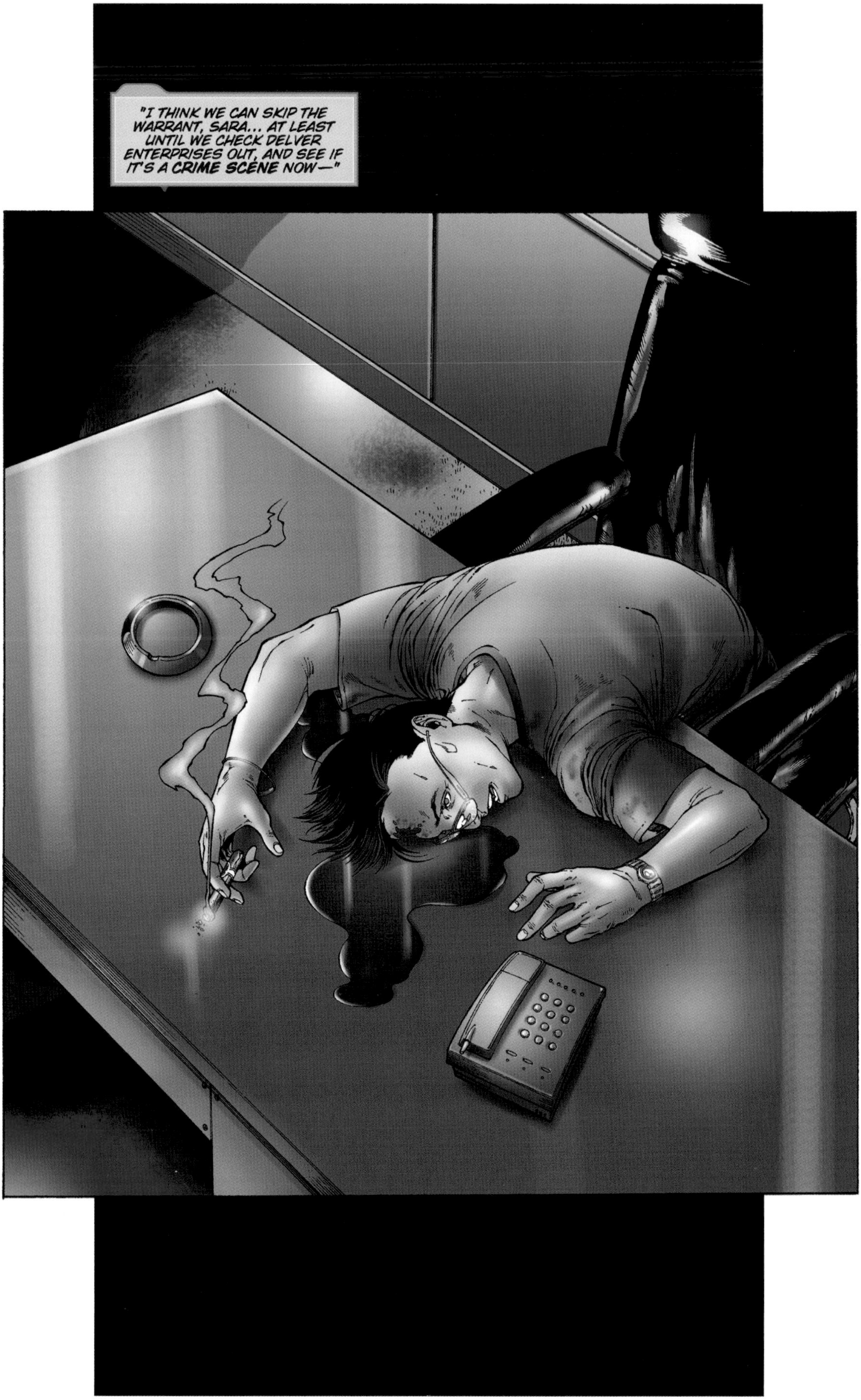
"I THINK WE CAN SKIP THE WARRANT, SARA... AT LEAST UNTIL WE CHECK DELVER ENTERPRISES OUT, AND SEE IF IT'S A CRIME SCENE NOW—"

# chapter five
# Rap Up

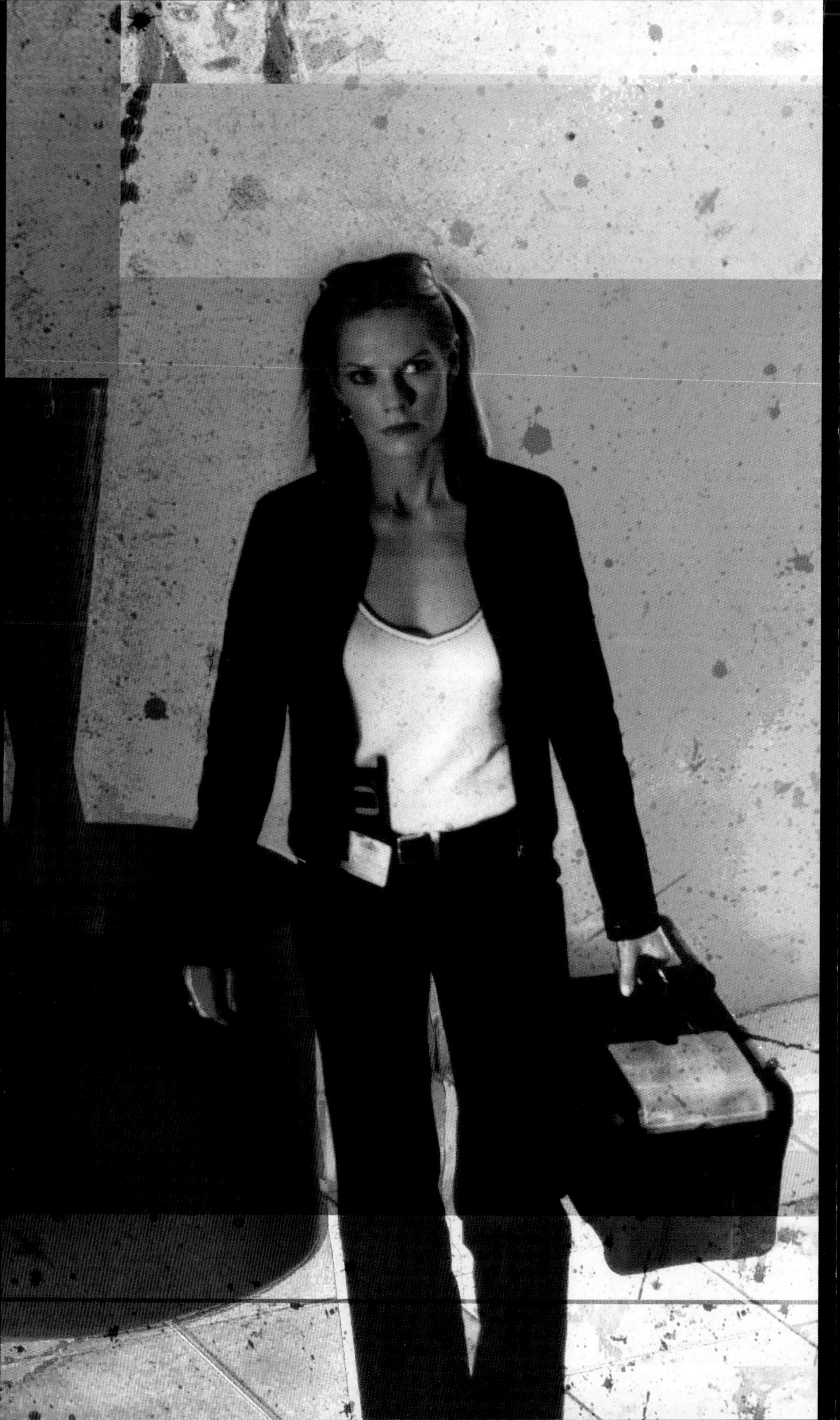

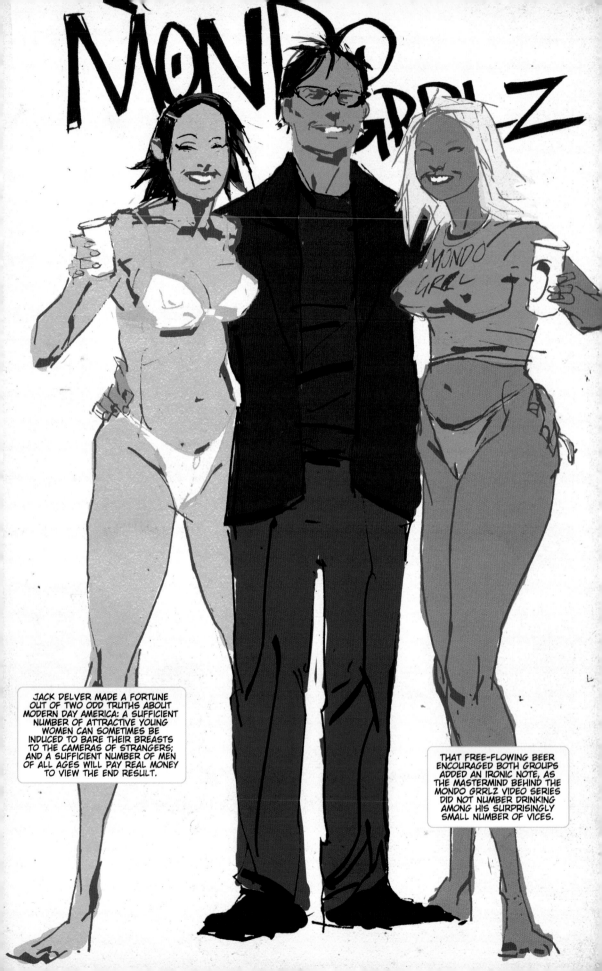

JACK DELVER MADE A FORTUNE
OUT OF TWO ODD TRUTHS ABOUT
MODERN DAY AMERICA: A SUFFICIENT
NUMBER OF ATTRACTIVE YOUNG
WOMEN CAN SOMETIMES BE
INDUCED TO BARE THEIR BREASTS
TO THE CAMERAS OF STRANGERS;
AND A SUFFICIENT NUMBER OF MEN
OF ALL AGES WILL PAY REAL MONEY
TO VIEW THE END RESULT.

THAT FREE-FLOWING BEER
ENCOURAGED BOTH GROUPS
ADDED AN IRONIC NOTE, AS
THE MASTERMIND BEHIND THE
MONDO GRRLZ VIDEO SERIES
DID NOT NUMBER DRINKING
AMONG HIS SURPRISINGLY
SMALL NUMBER OF VICES.

WHETHER JACK DELVER'S SOFTCORE PORN WAS GOOD CLEAN FUN OR BAD DIRTY EXPLOITATION IS NOT THE QUESTION GIL GRISSOM AND HIS TEAM OF CSI'S ARE PAID TO ANSWER. THE PERTINENT QUESTION NOW—WHO DECIDED THIS MULTIMILLIONAIRE-BEFORE-AGE-THIRTY WOULD NOT EVER *REACH* AGE THIRTY?

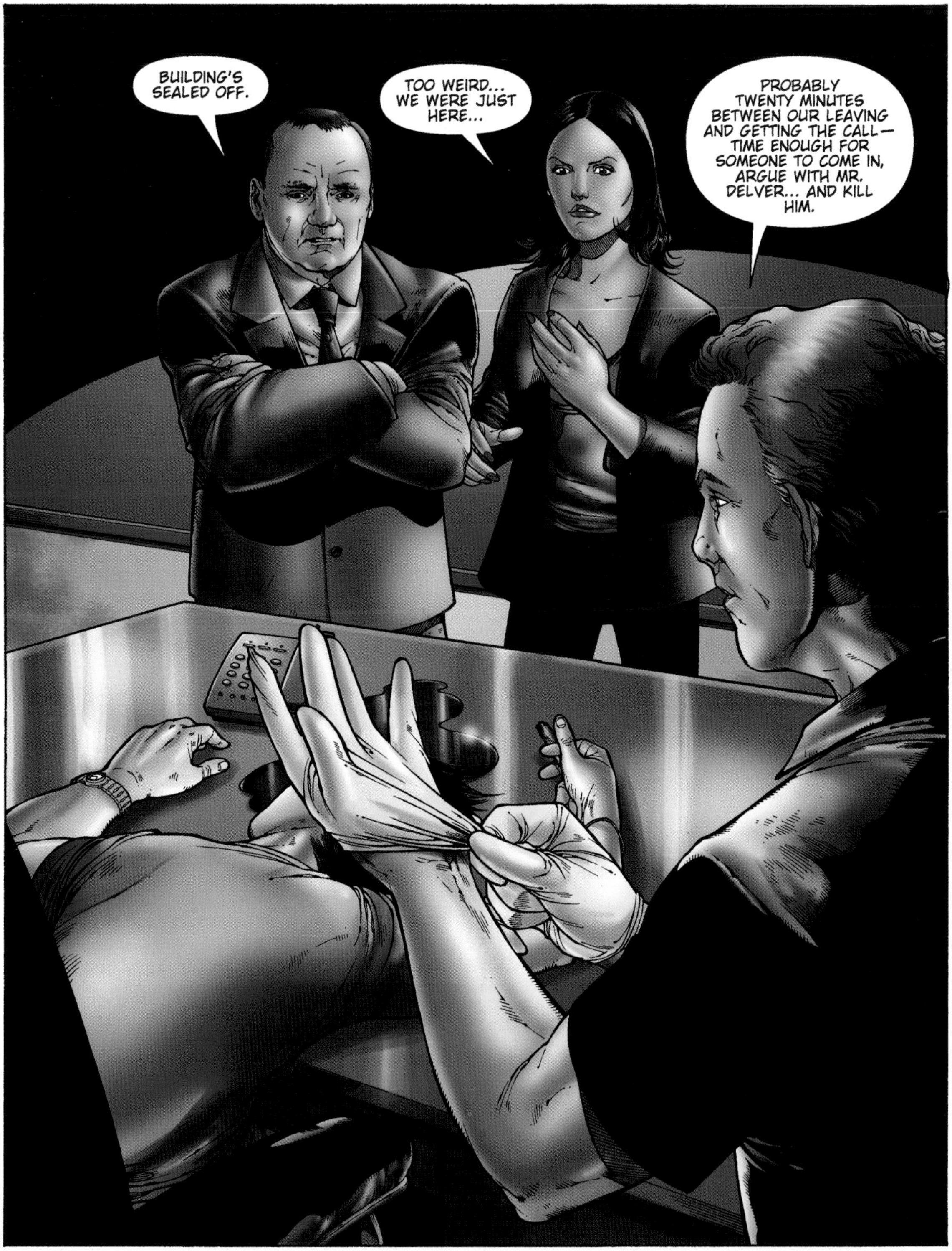

BUILDING'S SEALED OFF.
TOO WEIRD... WE WERE JUST HERE...
PROBABLY TWENTY MINUTES BETWEEN OUR LEAVING AND GETTING THE CALL— TIME ENOUGH FOR SOMEONE TO COME IN, ARGUE WITH MR. DELVER... AND KILL HIM.

...WHILE THE CSI's WORK THE CRIME SCENE.

IRONIC, ISN'T IT?

HOW SO?

BRASS QUESTIONS THE STAFF, STARTING WITH THE RECEPTIONIST/SECRETARY...

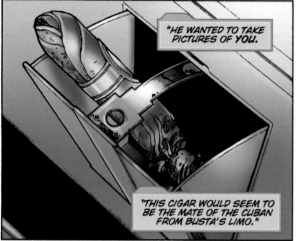

"HE WANTED TO TAKE PICTURES OF *YOU*.

"THIS CIGAR WOULD SEEM TO BE THE MATE OF THE CUBAN FROM BUSTA'S LIMO."

AND BY THE TIME SARA HAS MOVED ON TO USING THE ELECTROSTATIC PRINT LIFTER, IN SEARCH OF FOOTPRINTS...

...BRASS HAS RETURNED WITH AN UPDATE.

IT'S A SMALL STAFF— SECRETARY AND A BULLPEN OF THREE WHO DEAL WITH DISTRIBUTORS ON THE PHONE.

THE QUANTITY OF WITNESSES ISN'T AS IMPORTANT AS QUALITY—DID ANY OF THEM *SEE* ANYTHING?

NO—YOU SHOULD PARDON THE EXPRESSION, THEY WERE OUT TO LUNCH. SAME GROUP GOES TOGETHER EVERY DAY. NOBODY ON THE PHONES, JUST AN ANSWERING MACHINE.

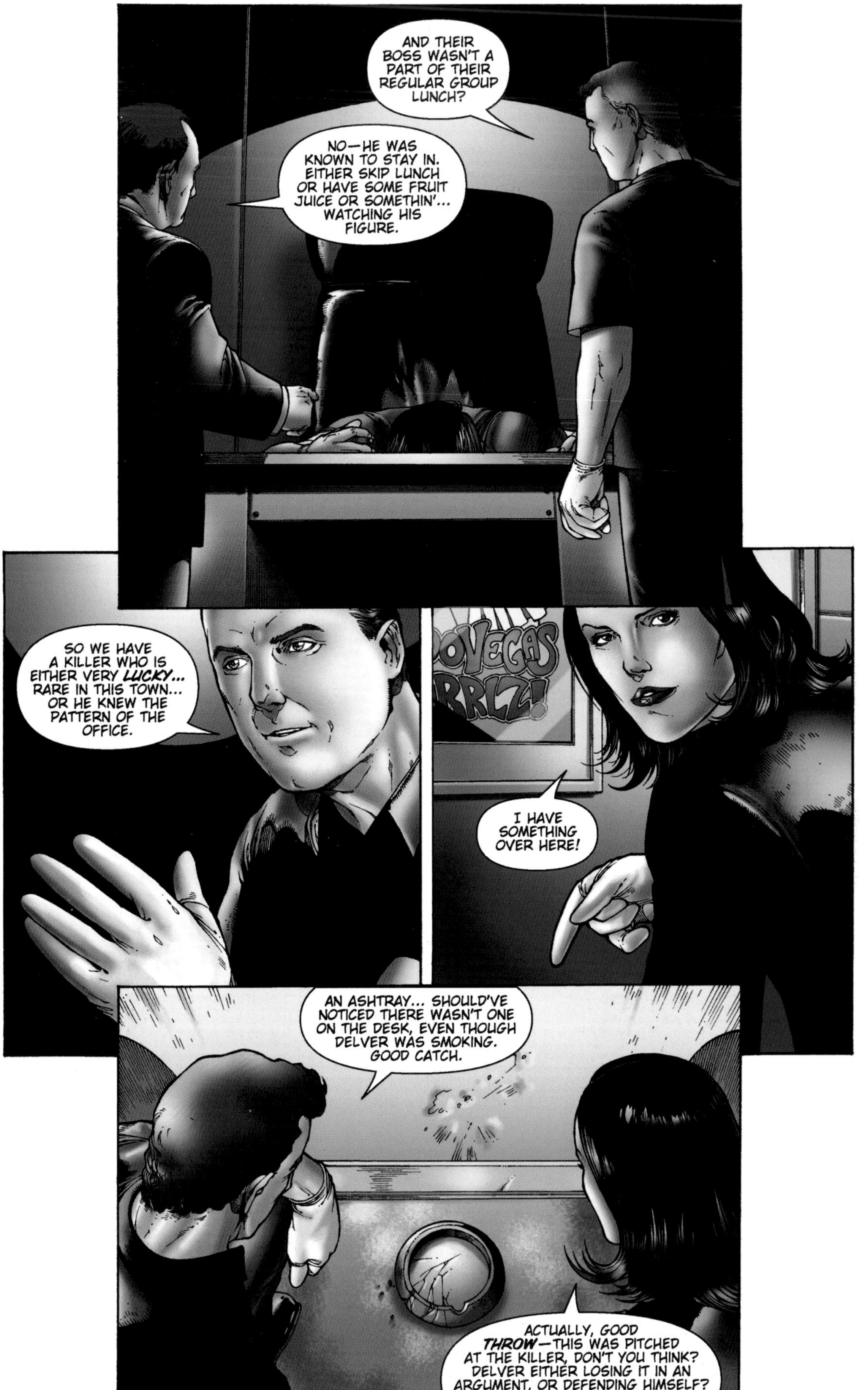
AND THEIR BOSS WASN'T A PART OF THEIR REGULAR GROUP LUNCH?
NO—HE WAS KNOWN TO STAY IN. EITHER SKIP LUNCH OR HAVE SOME FRUIT JUICE OR SOMETHIN'... WATCHING HIS FIGURE.
SO WE HAVE A KILLER WHO IS EITHER VERY LUCKY... RARE IN THIS TOWN... OR HE KNEW THE PATTERN OF THE OFFICE.
I HAVE SOMETHING OVER HERE!
AN ASHTRAY... SHOULD'VE NOTICED THERE WASN'T ONE ON THE DESK, EVEN THOUGH DELVER WAS SMOKING. GOOD CATCH.
ACTUALLY, GOOD THROW—THIS WAS PITCHED AT THE KILLER, DON'T YOU THINK? DELVER EITHER LOSING IT IN AN ARGUMENT, OR DEFENDING HIMSELF?

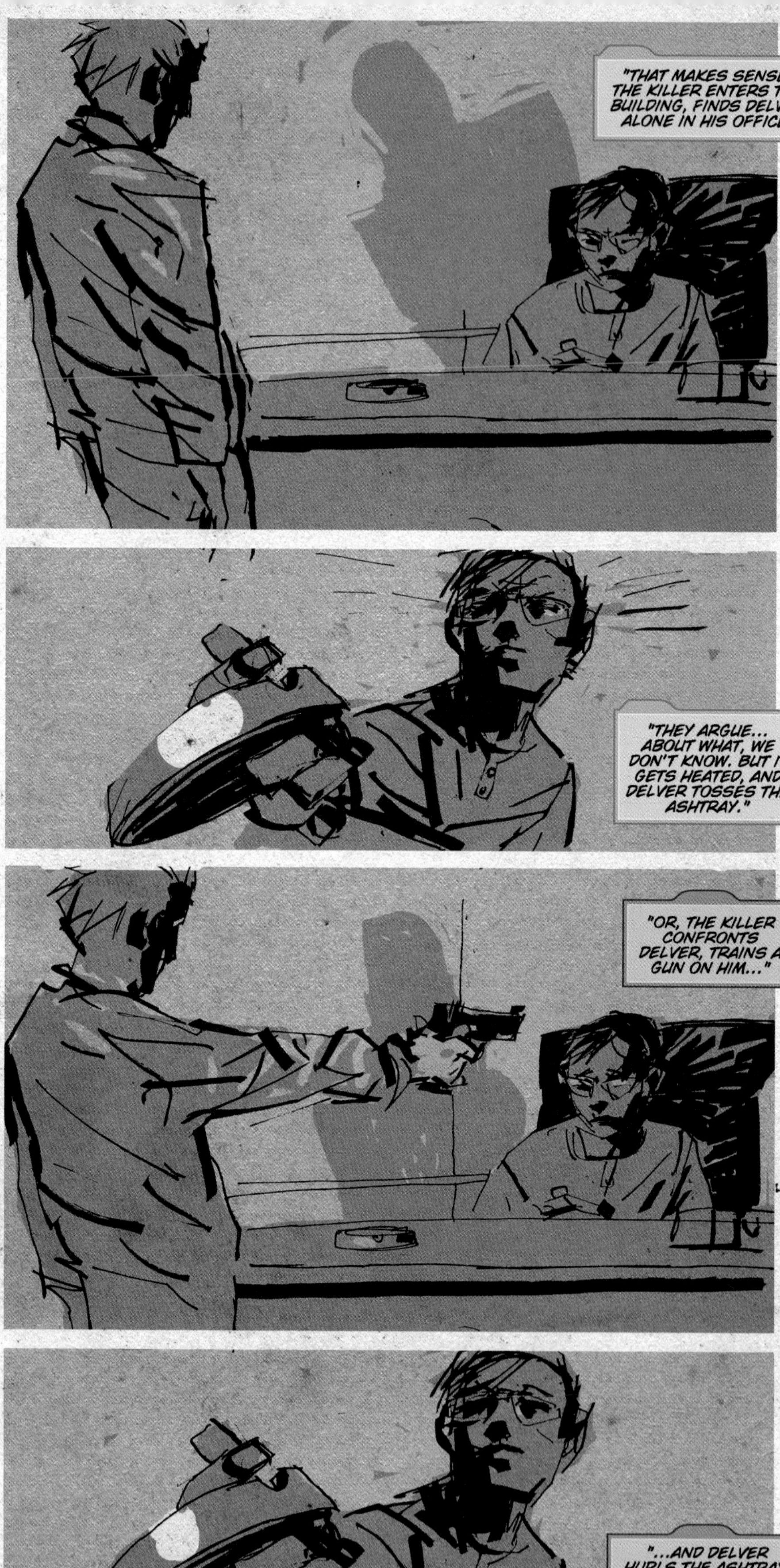
"THAT MAKES SENSE. THE KILLER ENTERS THE BUILDING, FINDS DELVER ALONE IN HIS OFFICE.
"THEY ARGUE... ABOUT WHAT, WE DON'T KNOW. BUT IT GETS HEATED, AND DELVER TOSSES THE ASHTRAY."
"OR, THE KILLER CONFRONTS DELVER, TRAINS A GUN ON HIM..."
"...AND DELVER HURLS THE ASHTRAY, IN SELF-DEFENSE!"

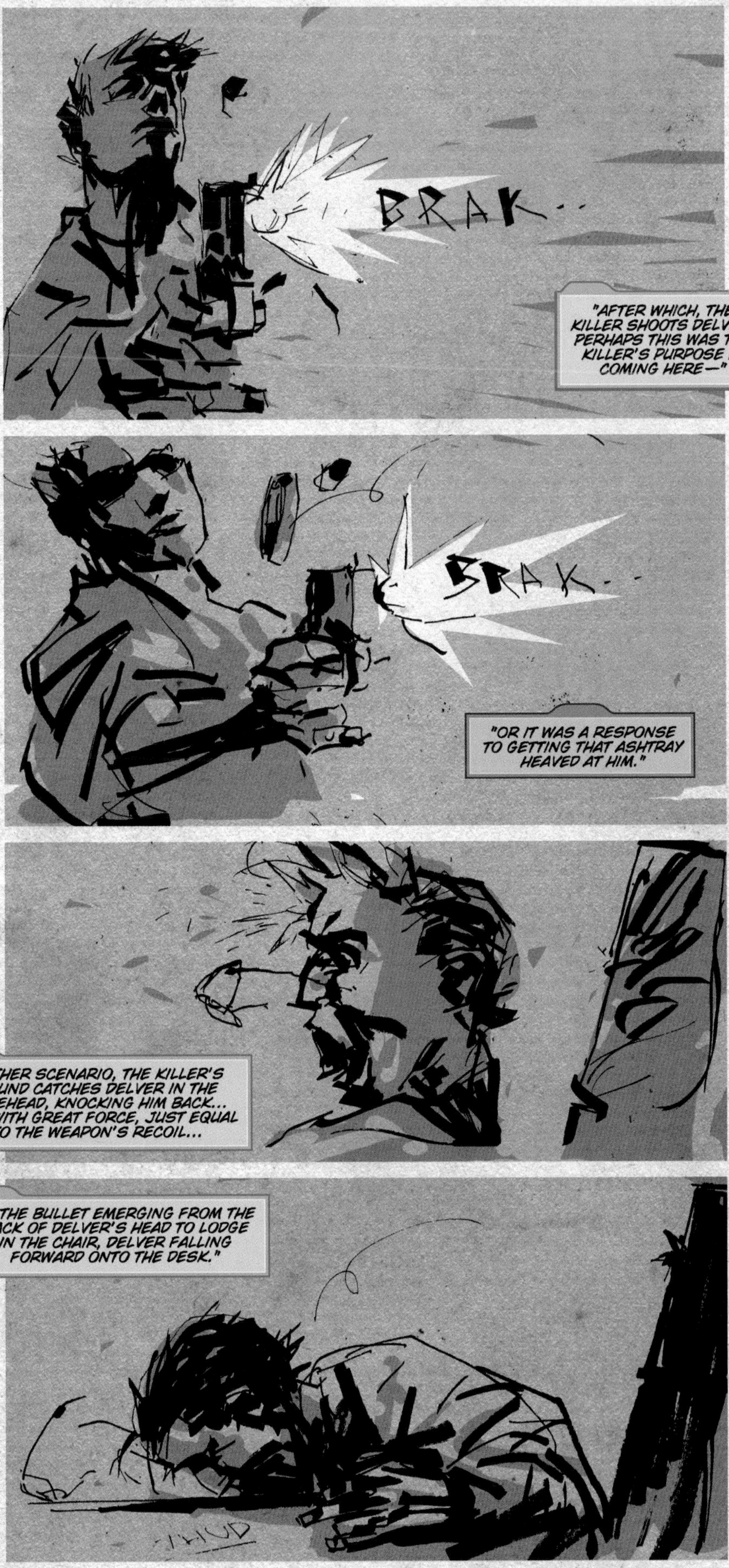
BRAK..
"AFTER WHICH, THE KILLER SHOOTS DELVER. PERHAPS THIS WAS THE KILLER'S PURPOSE IN COMING HERE—"
BRAK..
"OR IT WAS A RESPONSE TO GETTING THAT ASHTRAY HEAVED AT HIM."
"EITHER SCENARIO, THE KILLER'S ROUND CATCHES DELVER IN THE FOREHEAD, KNOCKING HIM BACK... NOT WITH GREAT FORCE, JUST EQUAL TO THE WEAPON'S RECOIL...
"...THE BULLET EMERGING FROM THE BACK OF DELVER'S HEAD TO LODGE IN THE CHAIR, DELVER FALLING FORWARD ONTO THE DESK."
THUD

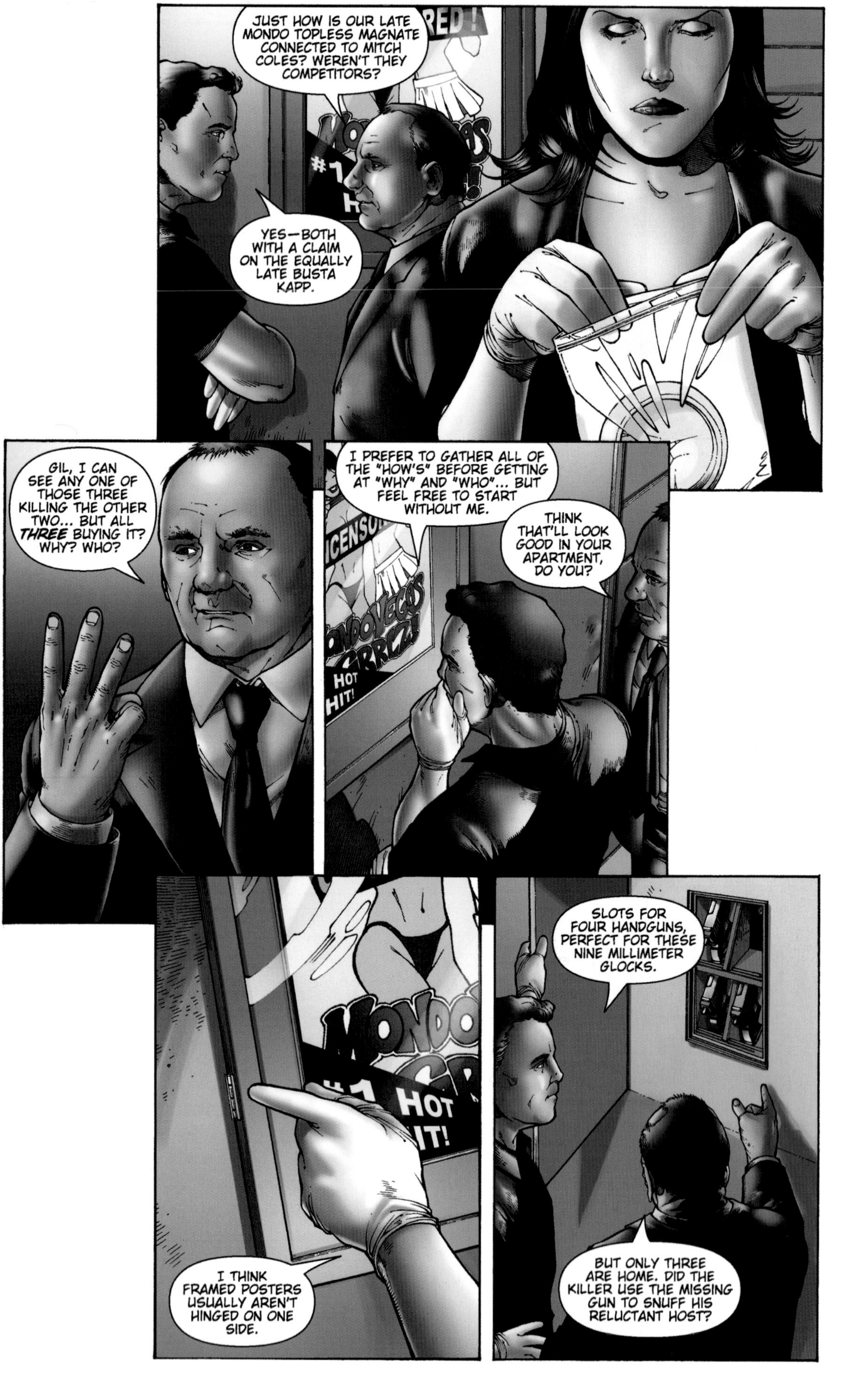
JUST HOW IS OUR LATE MONDO TOPLESS MAGNATE CONNECTED TO MITCH COLES? WEREN'T THEY COMPETITORS?
YES—BOTH WITH A CLAIM ON THE EQUALLY LATE BUSTA KAPP.
GIL, I CAN SEE ANY ONE OF THOSE THREE KILLING THE OTHER TWO... BUT ALL THREE BUYING IT? WHY? WHO?
I PREFER TO GATHER ALL OF THE "HOW'S" BEFORE GETTING AT "WHY" AND "WHO"... BUT FEEL FREE TO START WITHOUT ME.
THINK THAT'LL LOOK GOOD IN YOUR APARTMENT, DO YOU?
I THINK FRAMED POSTERS USUALLY AREN'T HINGED ON ONE SIDE.
SLOTS FOR FOUR HANDGUNS, PERFECT FOR THESE NINE MILLIMETER GLOCKS.
BUT ONLY THREE ARE HOME. DID THE KILLER USE THE MISSING GUN TO SNUFF HIS RELUCTANT HOST?

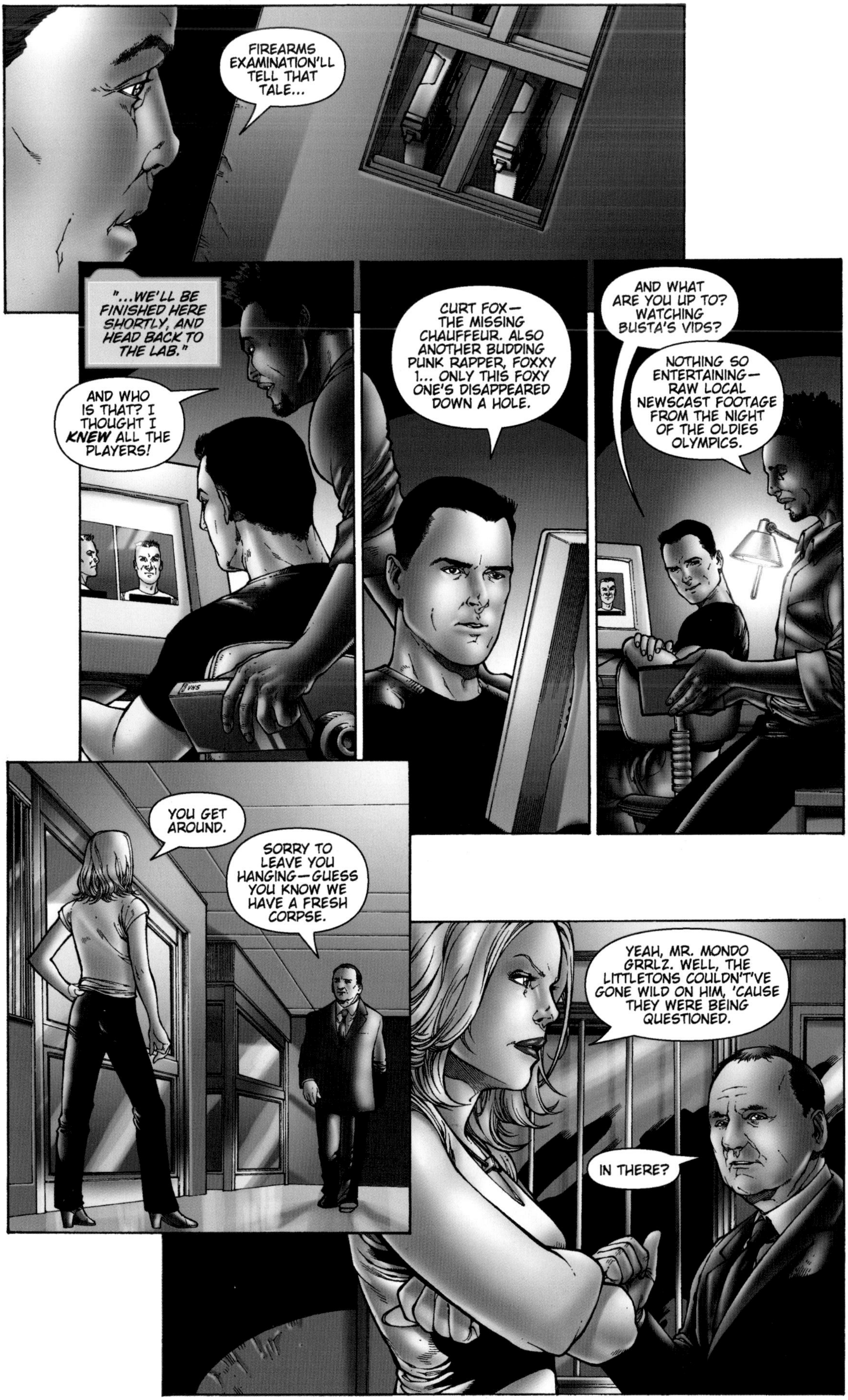
FIREARMS EXAMINATION'LL TELL THAT TALE...
"...WE'LL BE FINISHED HERE SHORTLY, AND HEAD BACK TO THE LAB."
AND WHO IS THAT? I THOUGHT I *KNEW* ALL THE PLAYERS!
CURT FOX—THE MISSING CHAUFFEUR. ALSO ANOTHER BUDDING PUNK RAPPER, FOXXY 1... ONLY THIS FOXY ONE'S DISAPPEARED DOWN A HOLE.
AND WHAT ARE YOU UP TO? WATCHING BUSTA'S VIDS?
NOTHING SO ENTERTAINING—RAW LOCAL NEWSCAST FOOTAGE FROM THE NIGHT OF THE OLDIES OLYMPICS.
YOU GET AROUND.
SORRY TO LEAVE YOU HANGING—GUESS YOU KNOW WE HAVE A FRESH CORPSE.
YEAH, MR. MONDO GRRLZ. WELL, THE LITTLETONS COULDN'T'VE GONE WILD ON HIM, 'CAUSE THEY WERE BEING QUESTIONED.
IN THERE?

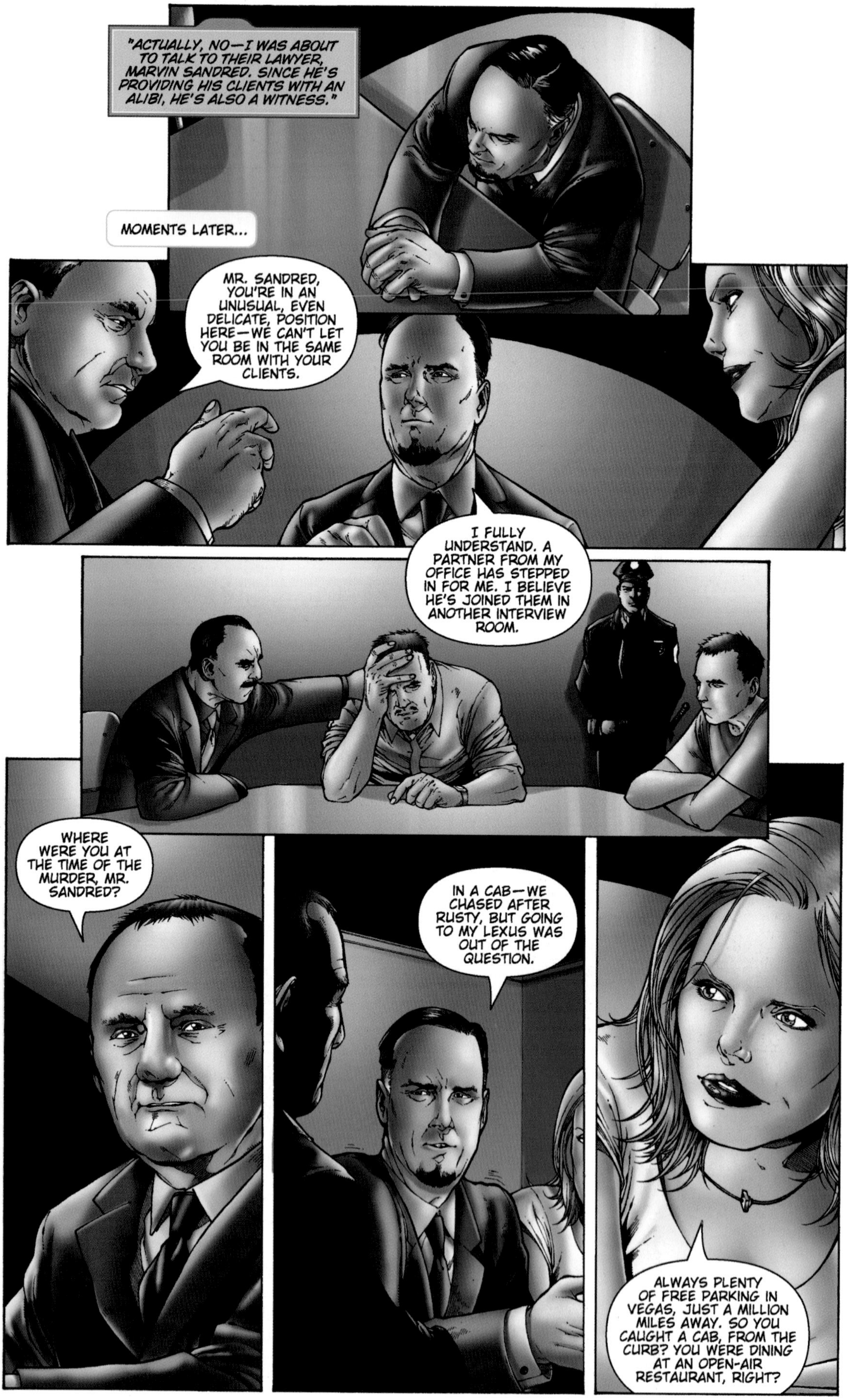
"ACTUALLY, NO—I WAS ABOUT TO TALK TO THEIR LAWYER, MARVIN SANDRED. SINCE HE'S PROVIDING HIS CLIENTS WITH AN ALIBI, HE'S ALSO A WITNESS."
MOMENTS LATER...
MR. SANDRED, YOU'RE IN AN UNUSUAL, EVEN DELICATE, POSITION HERE—WE CAN'T LET YOU BE IN THE SAME ROOM WITH YOUR CLIENTS.
I FULLY UNDERSTAND. A PARTNER FROM MY OFFICE HAS STEPPED IN FOR ME. I BELIEVE HE'S JOINED THEM IN ANOTHER INTERVIEW ROOM.
WHERE WERE YOU AT THE TIME OF THE MURDER, MR. SANDRED?
IN A CAB—WE CHASED AFTER RUSTY, BUT GOING TO MY LEXUS WAS OUT OF THE QUESTION.
ALWAYS PLENTY OF FREE PARKING IN VEGAS, JUST A MILLION MILES AWAY. SO YOU CAUGHT A CAB, FROM THE CURB? YOU WERE DINING AT AN OPEN-AIR RESTAURANT, RIGHT?

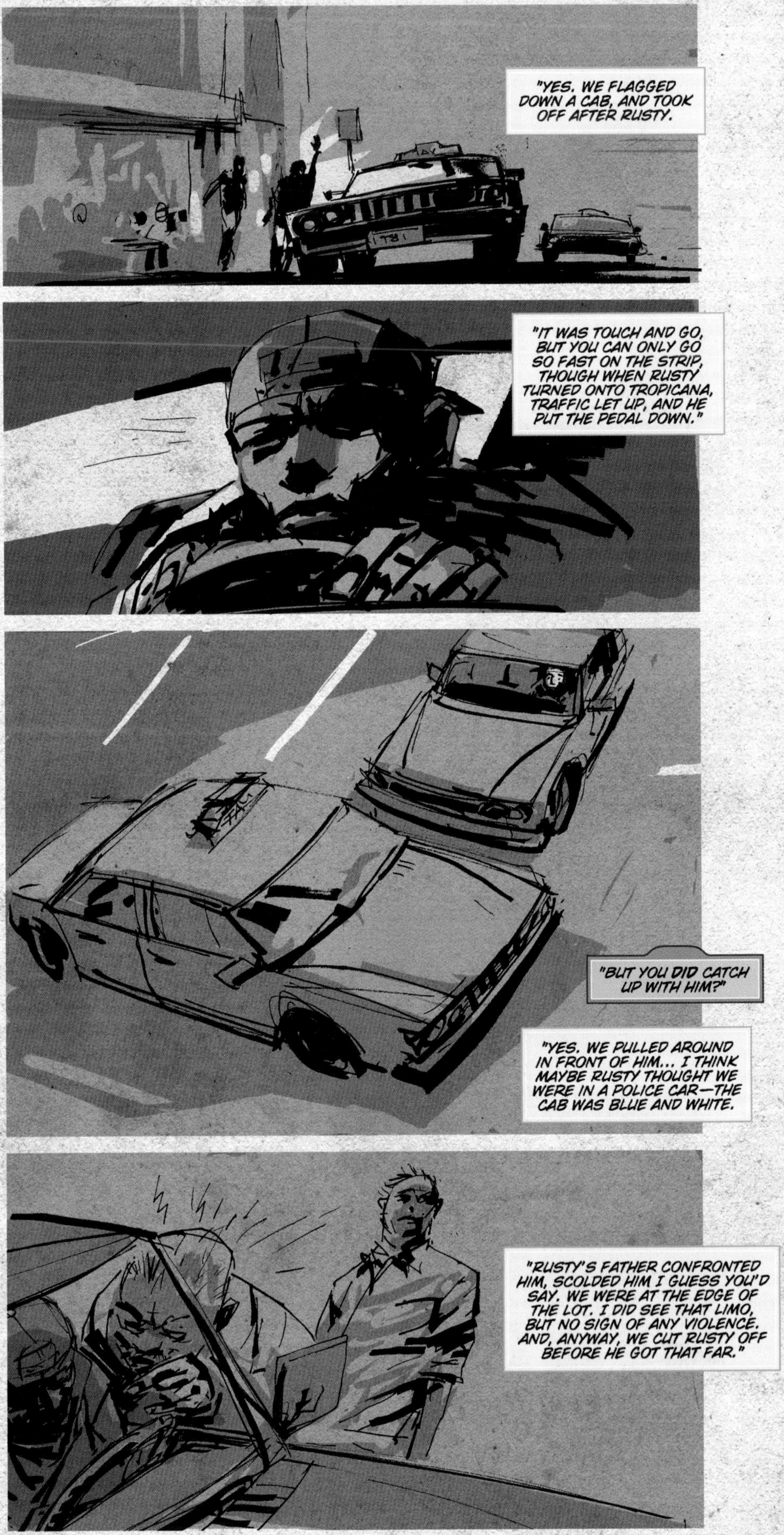
"YES. WE FLAGGED DOWN A CAB, AND TOOK OFF AFTER RUSTY.
"IT WAS TOUCH AND GO, BUT YOU CAN ONLY GO SO FAST ON THE STRIP, THOUGH WHEN RUSTY TURNED ONTO TROPICANA, TRAFFIC LET UP, AND HE PUT THE PEDAL DOWN."
"BUT YOU DID CATCH UP WITH HIM?"
"YES. WE PULLED AROUND IN FRONT OF HIM... I THINK MAYBE RUSTY THOUGHT WE WERE IN A POLICE CAR—THE CAB WAS BLUE AND WHITE.
"RUSTY'S FATHER CONFRONTED HIM, SCOLDED HIM I GUESS YOU'D SAY. WE WERE AT THE EDGE OF THE LOT. I DID SEE THAT LIMO, BUT NO SIGN OF ANY VIOLENCE. AND, ANYWAY, WE CUT RUSTY OFF BEFORE HE GOT THAT FAR."

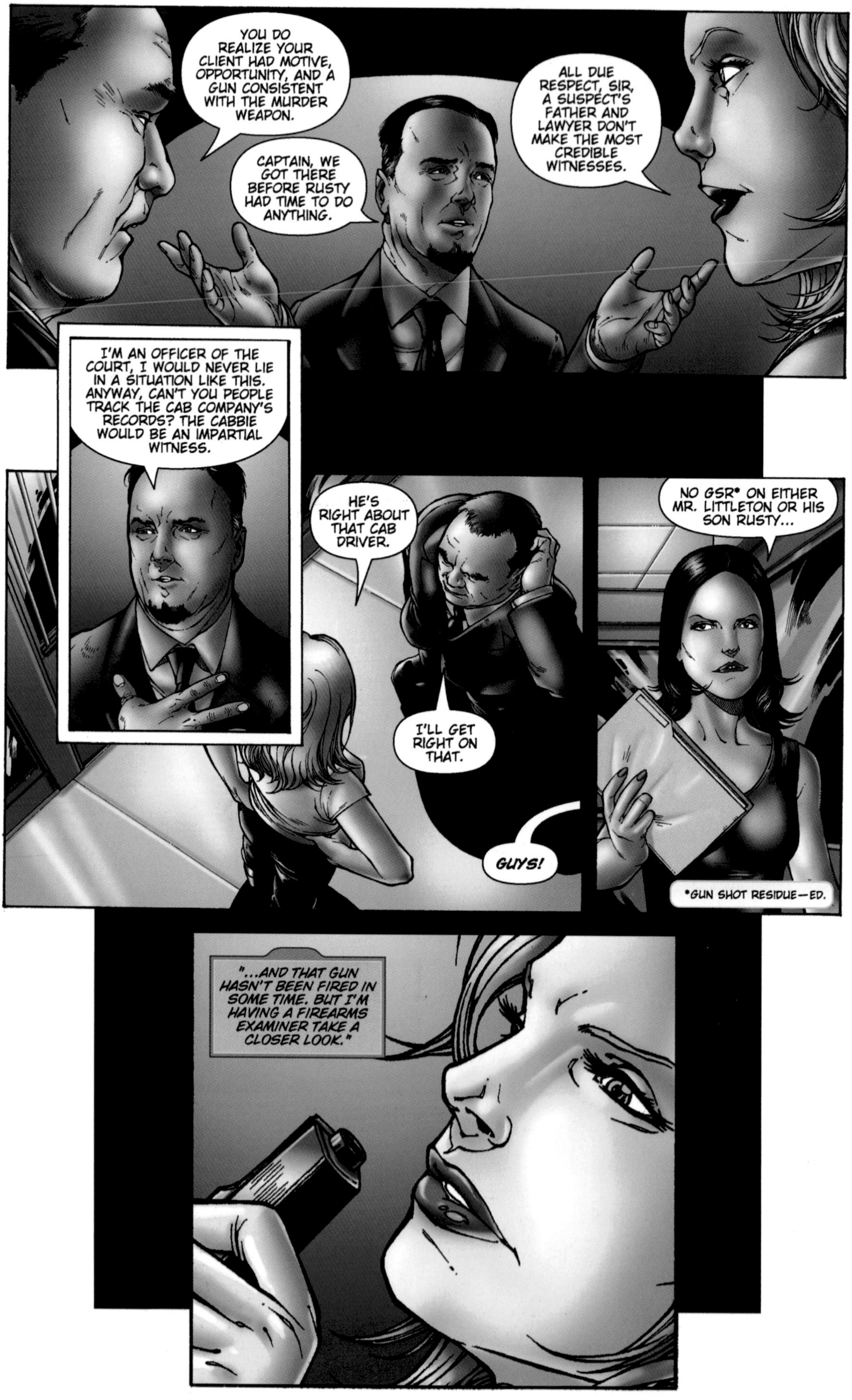
YOU DO REALIZE YOUR CLIENT HAD MOTIVE, OPPORTUNITY, AND A GUN CONSISTENT WITH THE MURDER WEAPON.
CAPTAIN, WE GOT THERE BEFORE RUSTY HAD TIME TO DO ANYTHING.
ALL DUE RESPECT, SIR, A SUSPECT'S FATHER AND LAWYER DON'T MAKE THE MOST CREDIBLE WITNESSES.
I'M AN OFFICER OF THE COURT, I WOULD NEVER LIE IN A SITUATION LIKE THIS. ANYWAY, CAN'T YOU PEOPLE TRACK THE CAB COMPANY'S RECORDS? THE CABBIE WOULD BE AN IMPARTIAL WITNESS.
HE'S RIGHT ABOUT THAT CAB DRIVER.
I'LL GET RIGHT ON THAT.
GUYS!
NO GSR* ON EITHER MR. LITTLETON OR HIS SON RUSTY...
*GUN SHOT RESIDUE—ED.
"...AND THAT GUN HASN'T BEEN FIRED IN SOME TIME. BUT I'M HAVING A FIREARMS EXAMINER TAKE A CLOSER LOOK."

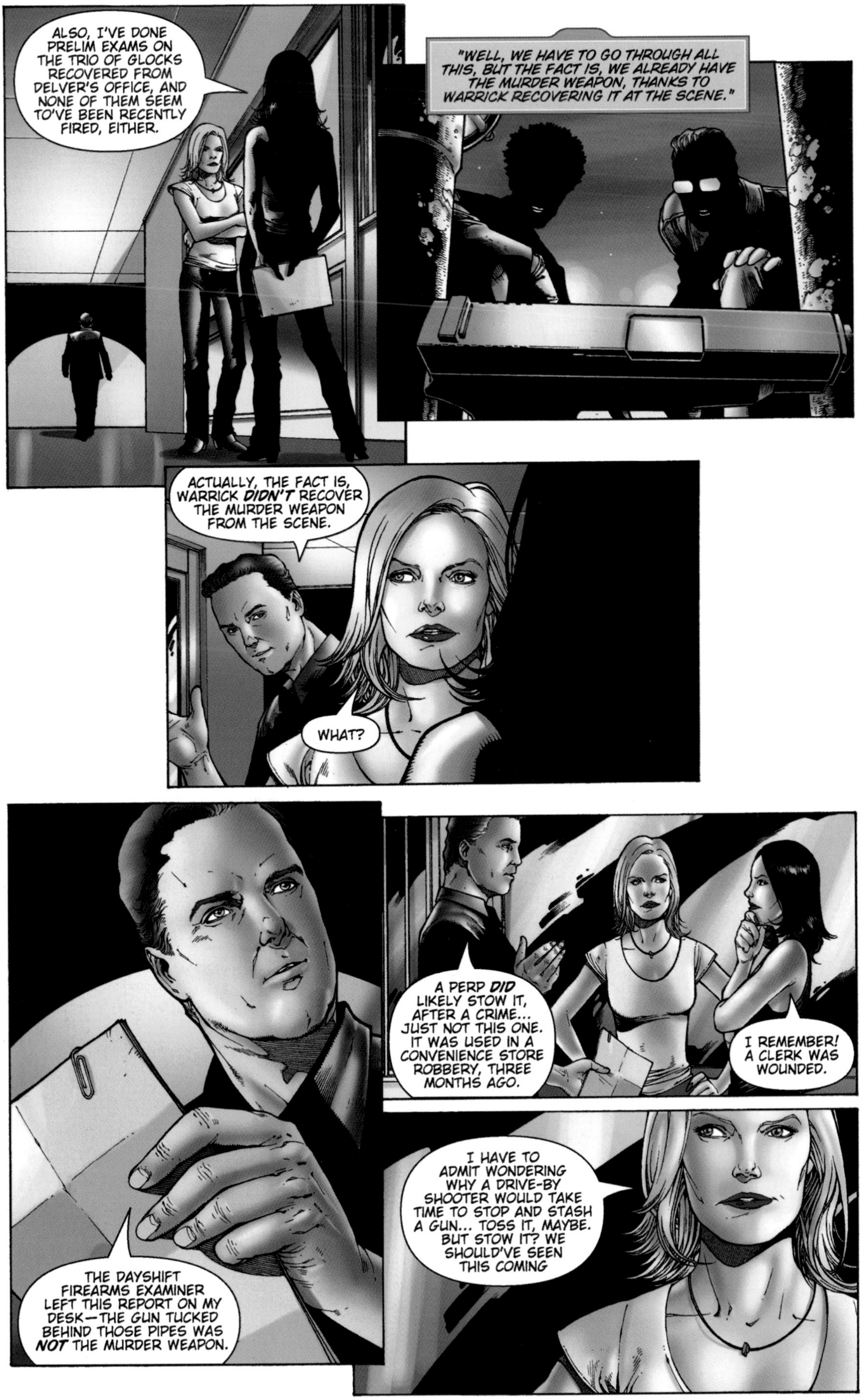
ALSO, I'VE DONE PRELIM EXAMS ON THE TRIO OF GLOCKS RECOVERED FROM DELVER'S OFFICE, AND NONE OF THEM SEEM TO'VE BEEN RECENTLY FIRED, EITHER.
"WELL, WE HAVE TO GO THROUGH ALL THIS, BUT THE FACT IS, WE ALREADY HAVE THE MURDER WEAPON, THANKS TO WARRICK RECOVERING IT AT THE SCENE."
ACTUALLY, THE FACT IS, WARRICK *DIDN'T* RECOVER THE MURDER WEAPON FROM THE SCENE.
WHAT?
THE DAYSHIFT FIREARMS EXAMINER LEFT THIS REPORT ON MY DESK—THE GUN TUCKED BEHIND THOSE PIPES WAS *NOT* THE MURDER WEAPON.
A PERP *DID* LIKELY STOW IT, AFTER A CRIME... JUST NOT THIS ONE. IT WAS USED IN A CONVENIENCE STORE ROBBERY, THREE MONTHS AGO.
I REMEMBER! A CLERK WAS WOUNDED.
I HAVE TO ADMIT WONDERING WHY A DRIVE-BY SHOOTER WOULD TAKE TIME TO STOP AND STASH A GUN... TOSS IT, MAYBE. BUT STOW IT? WE SHOULD'VE SEEN THIS COMING

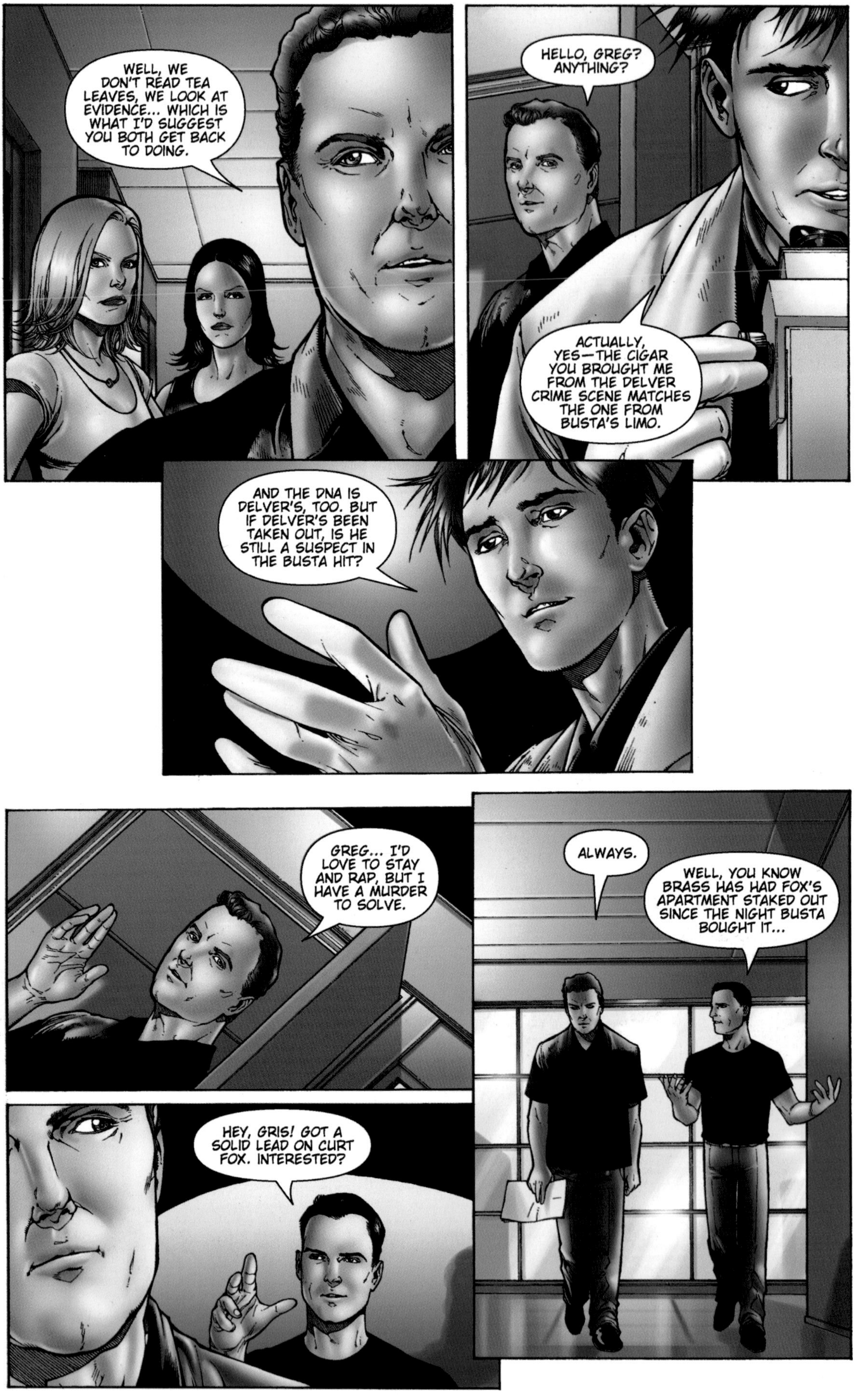
WELL, WE DON'T READ TEA LEAVES, WE LOOK AT EVIDENCE... WHICH IS WHAT I'D SUGGEST YOU BOTH GET BACK TO DOING.
HELLO, GREG? ANYTHING?
ACTUALLY, YES—THE CIGAR YOU BROUGHT ME FROM THE DELVER CRIME SCENE MATCHES THE ONE FROM BUSTA'S LIMO.
AND THE DNA IS DELVER'S, TOO. BUT IF DELVER'S BEEN TAKEN OUT, IS HE STILL A SUSPECT IN THE BUSTA HIT?
GREG... I'D LOVE TO STAY AND RAP, BUT I HAVE A MURDER TO SOLVE.
HEY, GRIS! GOT A SOLID LEAD ON CURT FOX. INTERESTED?
ALWAYS.
WELL, YOU KNOW BRASS HAS HAD FOX'S APARTMENT STAKED OUT SINCE THE NIGHT BUSTA BOUGHT IT...

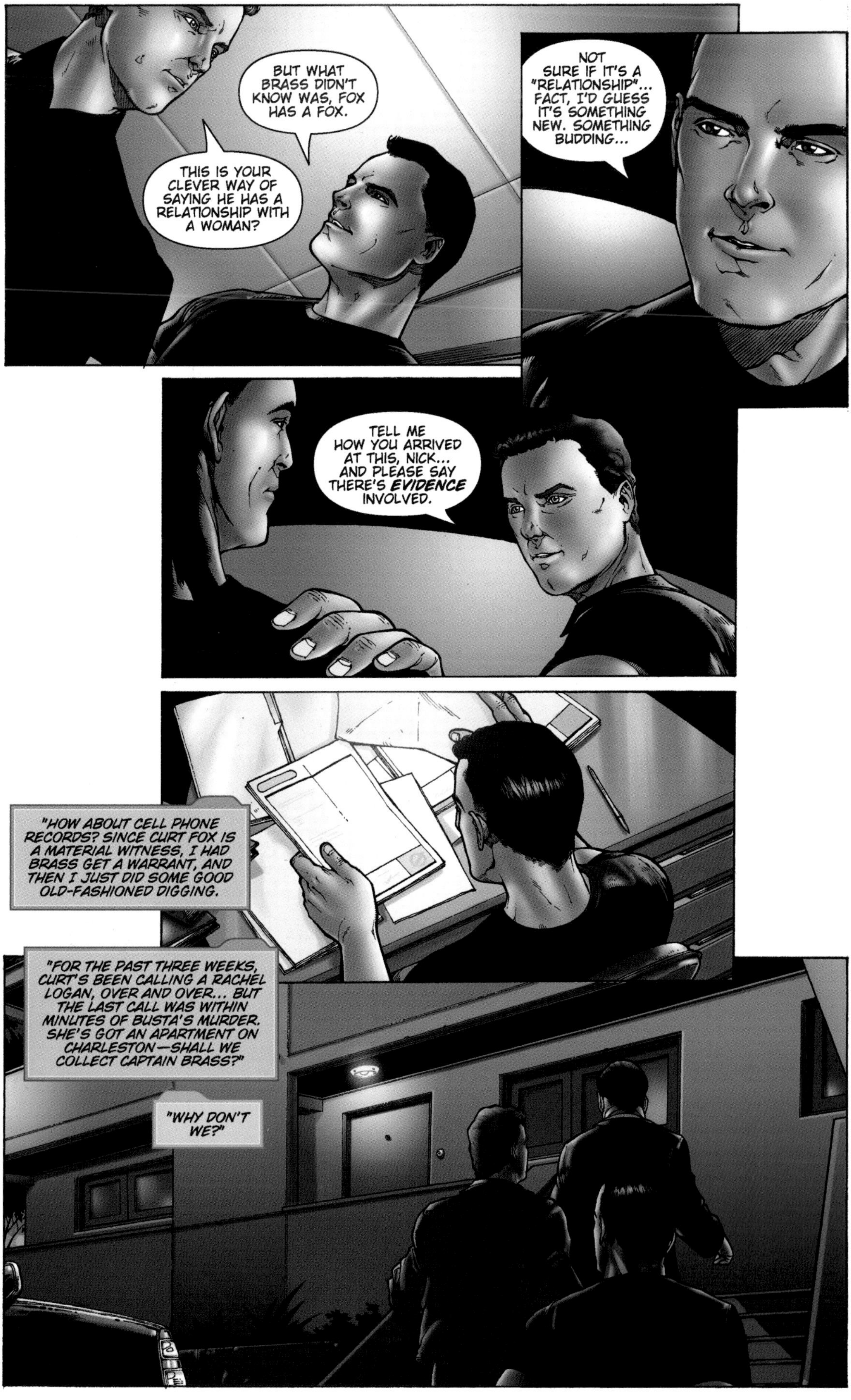
BUT WHAT BRASS DIDN'T KNOW WAS, FOX HAS A FOX.
THIS IS YOUR CLEVER WAY OF SAYING HE HAS A RELATIONSHIP WITH A WOMAN?
NOT SURE IF IT'S A "RELATIONSHIP"... FACT, I'D GUESS IT'S SOMETHING NEW. SOMETHING BUDDING...
TELL ME HOW YOU ARRIVED AT THIS, NICK... AND PLEASE SAY THERE'S *EVIDENCE* INVOLVED.
"HOW ABOUT CELL PHONE RECORDS? SINCE CURT FOX IS A MATERIAL WITNESS, I HAD BRASS GET A WARRANT, AND THEN I JUST DID SOME GOOD OLD-FASHIONED DIGGING.
"FOR THE PAST THREE WEEKS, CURT'S BEEN CALLING A RACHEL LOGAN, OVER AND OVER... BUT THE LAST CALL WAS WITHIN MINUTES OF BUSTA'S MURDER. SHE'S GOT AN APARTMENT ON CHARLESTON—SHALL WE COLLECT CAPTAIN BRASS?"
"WHY DON'T WE?"

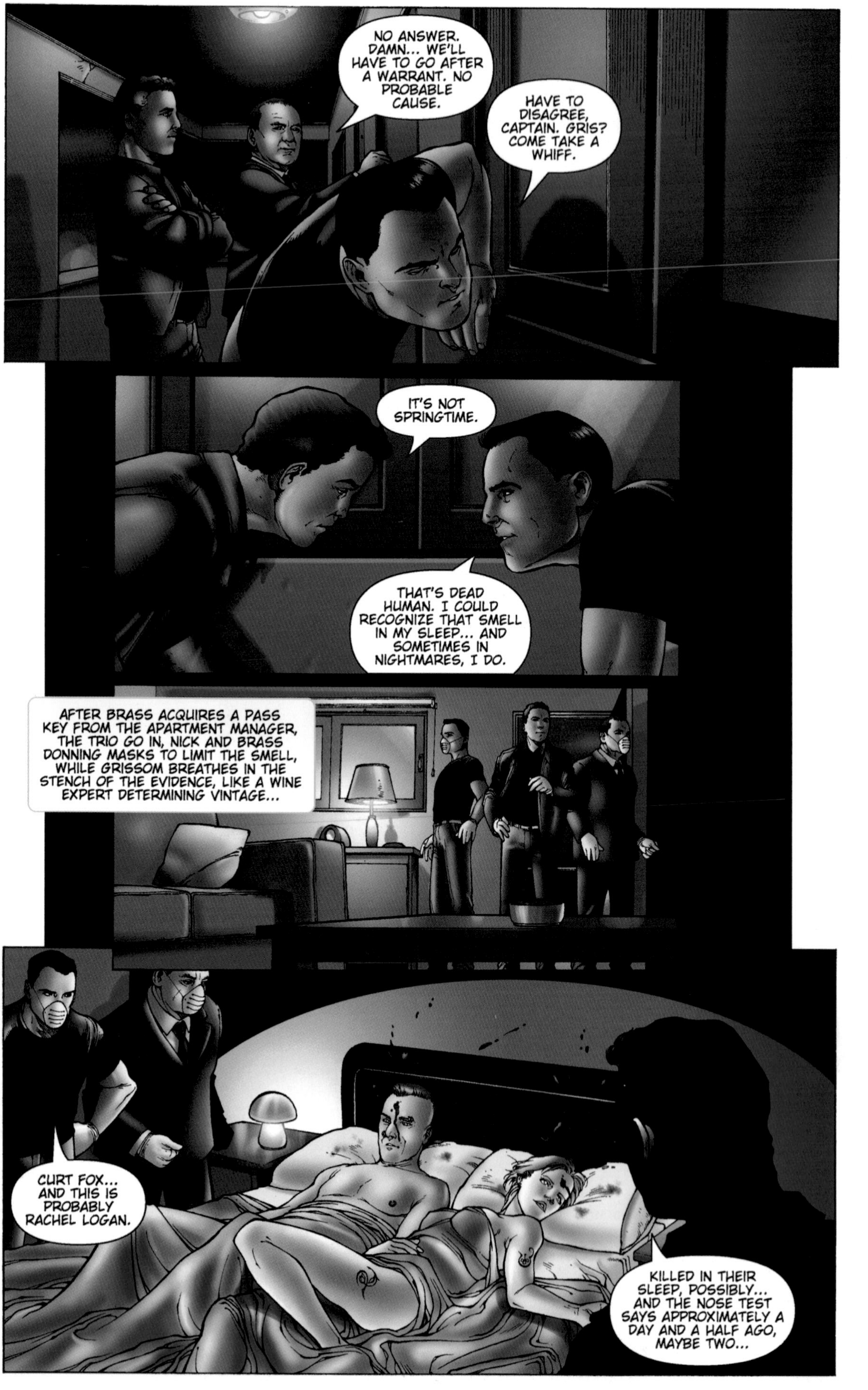
NO ANSWER. DAMN... WE'LL HAVE TO GO AFTER A WARRANT. NO PROBABLE CAUSE.
HAVE TO DISAGREE, CAPTAIN. GRIS? COME TAKE A WHIFF.
IT'S NOT SPRINGTIME.
THAT'S DEAD HUMAN. I COULD RECOGNIZE THAT SMELL IN MY SLEEP... AND SOMETIMES IN NIGHTMARES, I DO.
AFTER BRASS ACQUIRES A PASS KEY FROM THE APARTMENT MANAGER, THE TRIO GO IN, NICK AND BRASS DONNING MASKS TO LIMIT THE SMELL, WHILE GRISSOM BREATHES IN THE STENCH OF THE EVIDENCE, LIKE A WINE EXPERT DETERMINING VINTAGE...
CURT FOX... AND THIS IS PROBABLY RACHEL LOGAN.
KILLED IN THEIR SLEEP, POSSIBLY... AND THE NOSE TEST SAYS APPROXIMATELY A DAY AND A HALF AGO, MAYBE TWO...

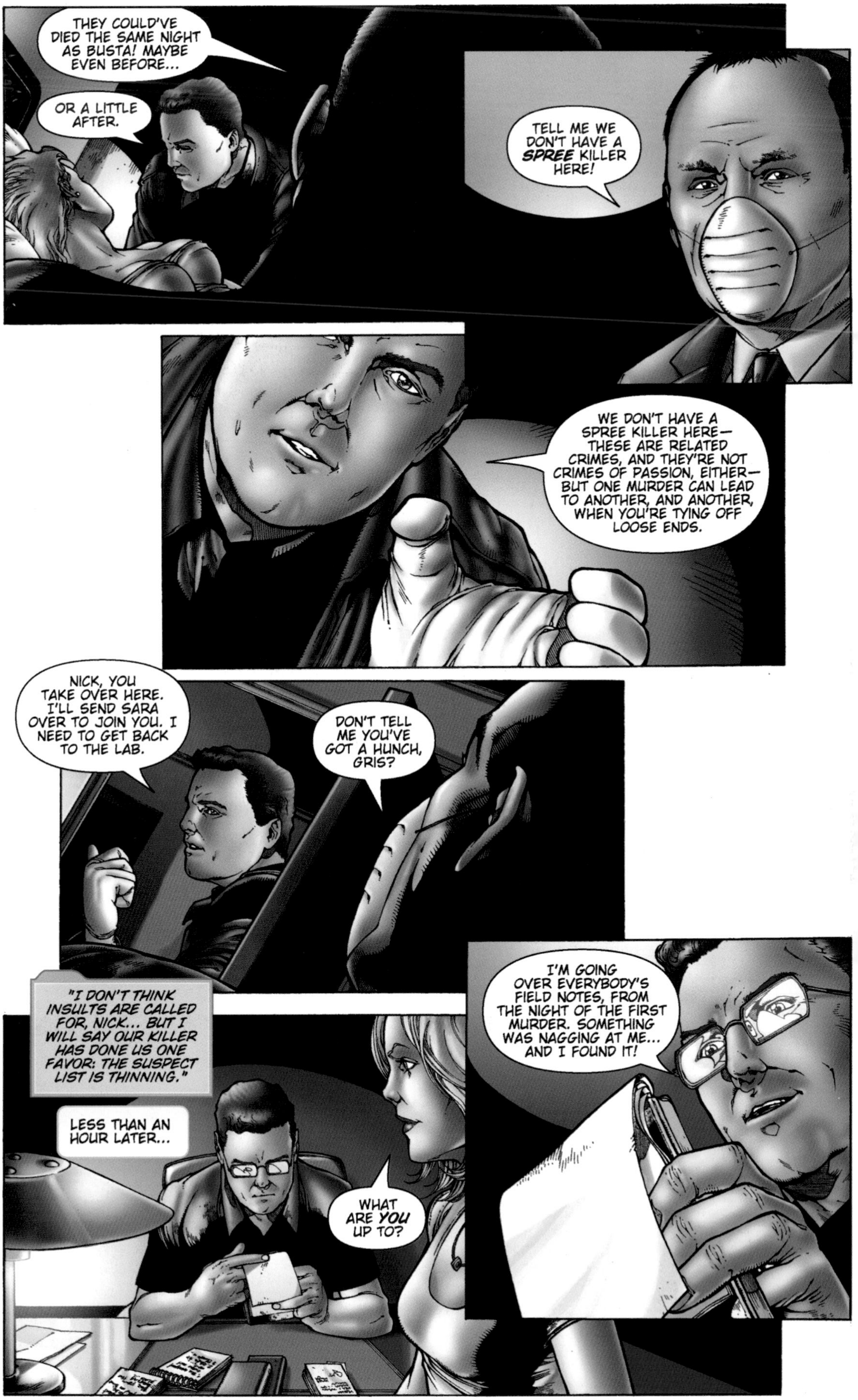

THEY COULD'VE DIED THE SAME NIGHT AS BUSTA! MAYBE EVEN BEFORE...
OR A LITTLE AFTER.
TELL ME WE DON'T HAVE A SPREE KILLER HERE!
WE DON'T HAVE A SPREE KILLER HERE— THESE ARE RELATED CRIMES, AND THEY'RE NOT CRIMES OF PASSION, EITHER— BUT ONE MURDER CAN LEAD TO ANOTHER, AND ANOTHER, WHEN YOU'RE TYING OFF LOOSE ENDS.
NICK, YOU TAKE OVER HERE. I'LL SEND SARA OVER TO JOIN YOU. I NEED TO GET BACK TO THE LAB.
DON'T TELL ME YOU'VE GOT A HUNCH, GRIS?
"I DON'T THINK INSULTS ARE CALLED FOR, NICK... BUT I WILL SAY OUR KILLER HAS DONE US ONE FAVOR: THE SUSPECT LIST IS THINNING."
LESS THAN AN HOUR LATER...
WHAT ARE YOU UP TO?
I'M GOING OVER EVERYBODY'S FIELD NOTES, FROM THE NIGHT OF THE FIRST MURDER. SOMETHING WAS NAGGING AT ME... AND I FOUND IT!

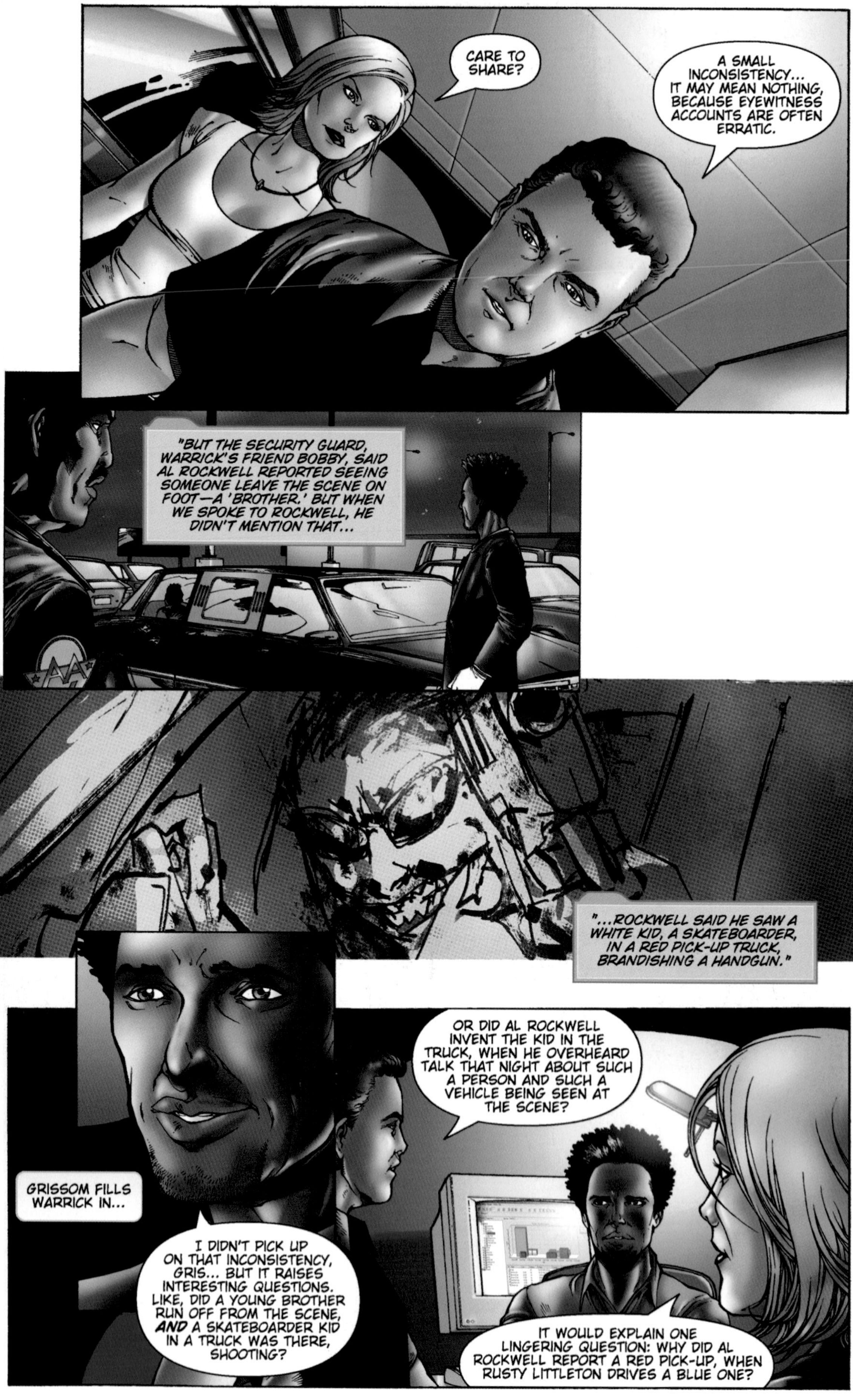
CARE TO SHARE?
A SMALL INCONSISTENCY... IT MAY MEAN NOTHING, BECAUSE EYEWITNESS ACCOUNTS ARE OFTEN ERRATIC.
"BUT THE SECURITY GUARD, WARRICK'S FRIEND BOBBY, SAID AL ROCKWELL REPORTED SEEING SOMEONE LEAVE THE SCENE ON FOOT—A 'BROTHER.' BUT WHEN WE SPOKE TO ROCKWELL, HE DIDN'T MENTION THAT...
"...ROCKWELL SAID HE SAW A WHITE KID, A SKATEBOARDER, IN A RED PICK-UP TRUCK, BRANDISHING A HANDGUN."
GRISSOM FILLS WARRICK IN...
OR DID AL ROCKWELL INVENT THE KID IN THE TRUCK, WHEN HE OVERHEARD TALK THAT NIGHT ABOUT SUCH A PERSON AND SUCH A VEHICLE BEING SEEN AT THE SCENE?
I DIDN'T PICK UP ON THAT INCONSISTENCY, GRIS... BUT IT RAISES INTERESTING QUESTIONS. LIKE, DID A YOUNG BROTHER RUN OFF FROM THE SCENE, AND A SKATEBOARDER KID IN A TRUCK WAS THERE, SHOOTING?
IT WOULD EXPLAIN ONE LINGERING QUESTION: WHY DID AL ROCKWELL REPORT A RED PICK-UP, WHEN RUSTY LITTLETON DRIVES A BLUE ONE?

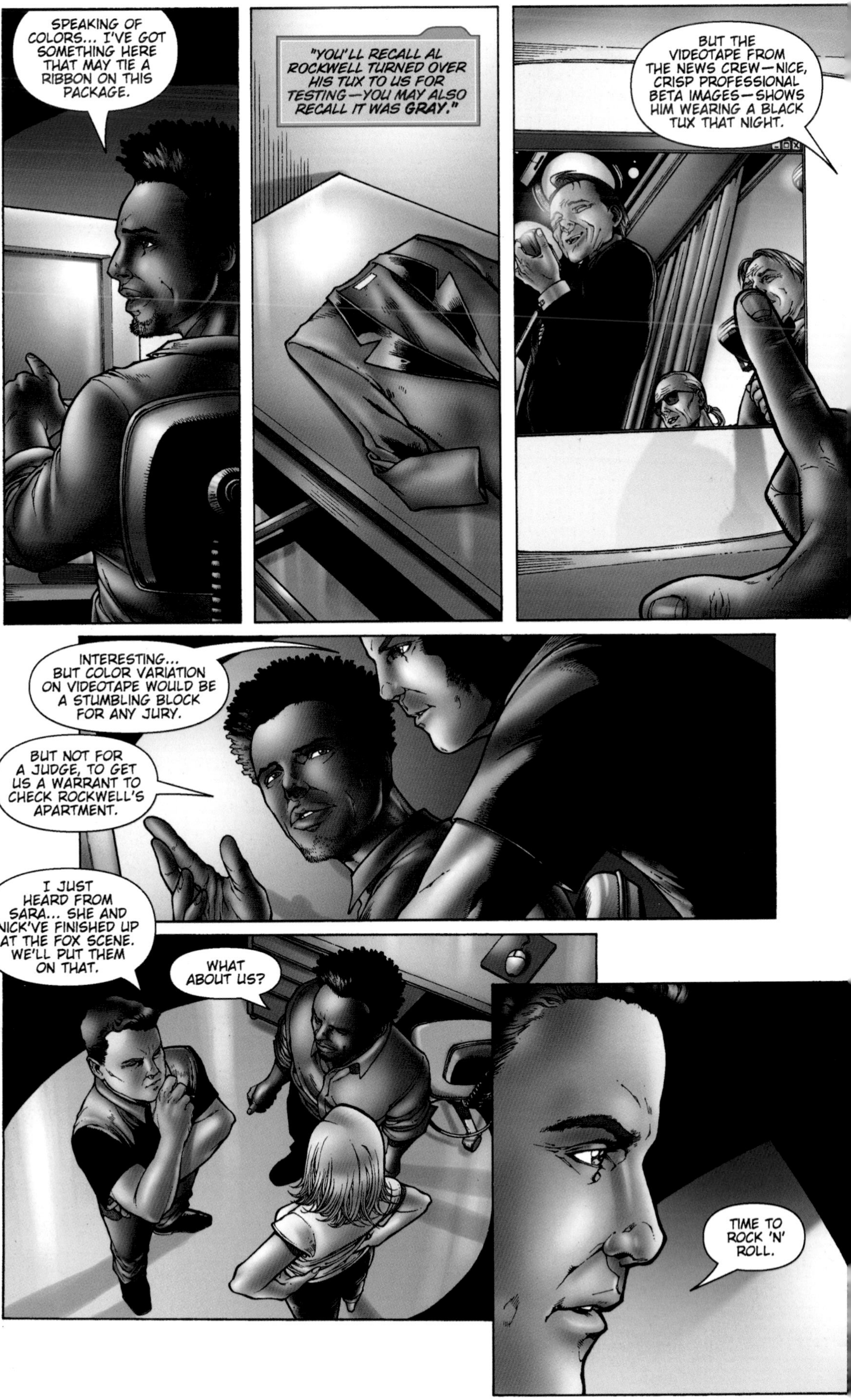

SPEAKING OF COLORS... I'VE GOT SOMETHING HERE THAT MAY TIE A RIBBON ON THIS PACKAGE.
"YOU'LL RECALL AL ROCKWELL TURNED OVER HIS TUX TO US FOR TESTING—YOU MAY ALSO RECALL IT WAS GRAY."
BUT THE VIDEOTAPE FROM THE NEWS CREW—NICE, CRISP PROFESSIONAL BETA IMAGES—SHOWS HIM WEARING A BLACK TUX THAT NIGHT.
INTERESTING... BUT COLOR VARIATION ON VIDEOTAPE WOULD BE A STUMBLING BLOCK FOR ANY JURY.
BUT NOT FOR A JUDGE, TO GET US A WARRANT TO CHECK ROCKWELL'S APARTMENT.
I JUST HEARD FROM SARA... SHE AND NICK'VE FINISHED UP AT THE FOX SCENE. WE'LL PUT THEM ON THAT.
WHAT ABOUT US?
TIME TO ROCK 'N' ROLL.

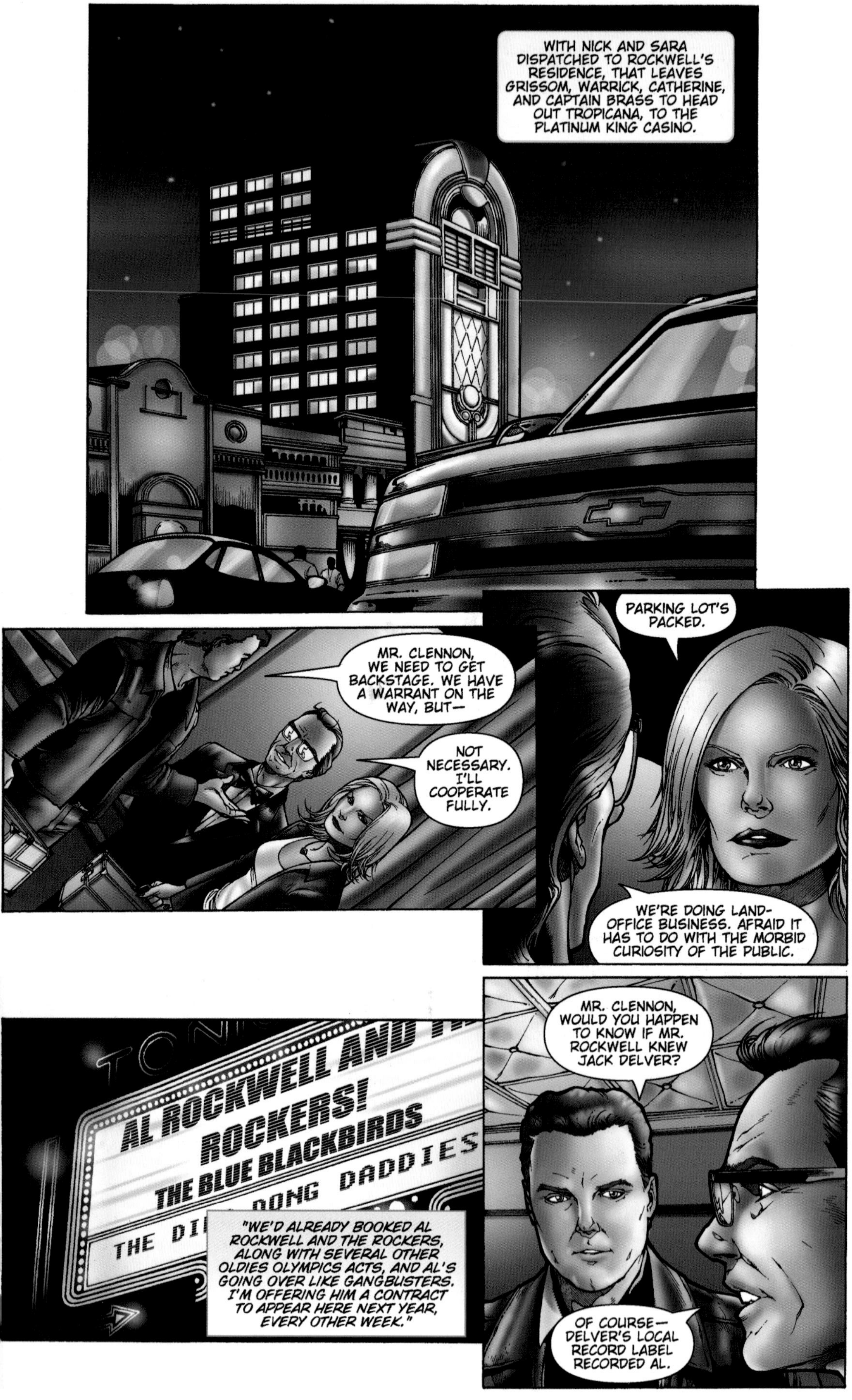
WITH NICK AND SARA DISPATCHED TO ROCKWELL'S RESIDENCE, THAT LEAVES GRISSOM, WARRICK, CATHERINE, AND CAPTAIN BRASS TO HEAD OUT TROPICANA, TO THE PLATINUM KING CASINO.
PARKING LOT'S PACKED.
WE'RE DOING LAND-OFFICE BUSINESS. AFRAID IT HAS TO DO WITH THE MORBID CURIOSITY OF THE PUBLIC.
MR. CLENNON, WE NEED TO GET BACKSTAGE. WE HAVE A WARRANT ON THE WAY, BUT—
NOT NECESSARY. I'LL COOPERATE FULLY.
AL ROCKWELL AND
ROCKERS!
THE BLUE BLACKBIRDS
DONG DADDIES
"WE'D ALREADY BOOKED AL ROCKWELL AND THE ROCKERS, ALONG WITH SEVERAL OTHER OLDIES OLYMPICS ACTS, AND AL'S GOING OVER LIKE GANGBUSTERS. I'M OFFERING HIM A CONTRACT TO APPEAR HERE NEXT YEAR, EVERY OTHER WEEK."
MR. CLENNON, WOULD YOU HAPPEN TO KNOW IF MR. ROCKWELL KNEW JACK DELVER?
OF COURSE—DELVER'S LOCAL RECORD LABEL RECORDED AL.

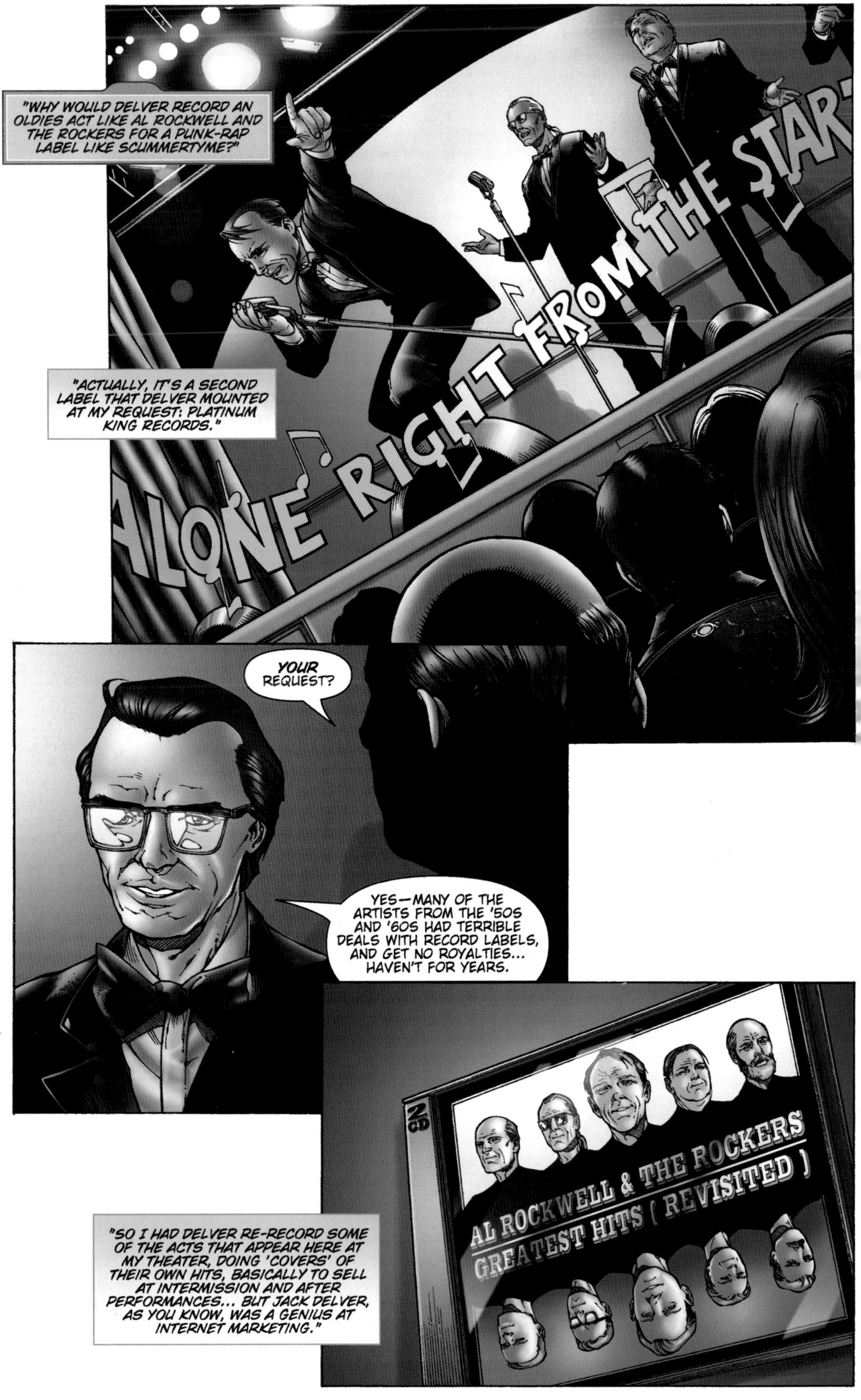
"WHY WOULD DELVER RECORD AN OLDIES ACT LIKE AL ROCKWELL AND THE ROCKERS FOR A PUNK-RAP LABEL LIKE SCUMMERTYME?"
"ACTUALLY, IT'S A SECOND LABEL THAT DELVER MOUNTED AT MY REQUEST: PLATINUM KING RECORDS."
ALONE RIGHT FROM THE STAR
*YOUR* REQUEST?
YES—MANY OF THE ARTISTS FROM THE '50S AND '60S HAD TERRIBLE DEALS WITH RECORD LABELS, AND GET NO ROYALTIES... HAVEN'T FOR YEARS.
2 CD
AL ROCKWELL & THE ROCKERS
GREATEST HITS ( REVISITED )
"SO I HAD DELVER RE-RECORD SOME OF THE ACTS THAT APPEAR HERE AT MY THEATER, DOING 'COVERS' OF THEIR OWN HITS, BASICALLY TO SELL AT INTERMISSION AND AFTER PERFORMANCES... BUT JACK DELVER, AS YOU KNOW, WAS A GENIUS AT INTERNET MARKETING."

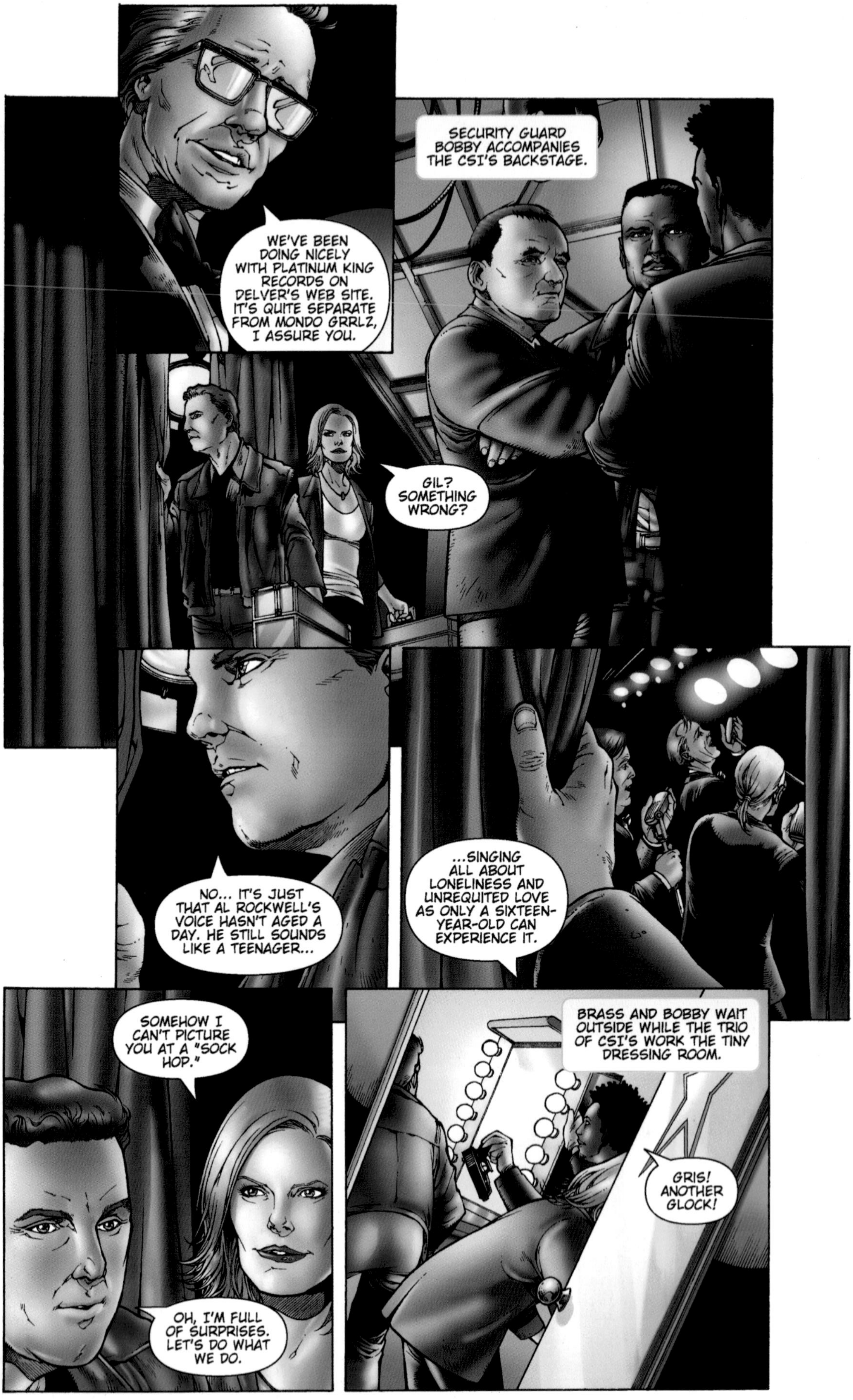
WE'VE BEEN DOING NICELY WITH PLATINUM KING RECORDS ON DELVER'S WEB SITE. IT'S QUITE SEPARATE FROM MONDO GRRLZ, I ASSURE YOU.
SECURITY GUARD BOBBY ACCOMPANIES THE CSI'S BACKSTAGE.
GIL? SOMETHING WRONG?
NO... IT'S JUST THAT AL ROCKWELL'S VOICE HASN'T AGED A DAY. HE STILL SOUNDS LIKE A TEENAGER...
...SINGING ALL ABOUT LONELINESS AND UNREQUITED LOVE AS ONLY A SIXTEEN-YEAR-OLD CAN EXPERIENCE IT.
SOMEHOW I CAN'T PICTURE YOU AT A "SOCK HOP."
OH, I'M FULL OF SURPRISES. LET'S DO WHAT WE DO.
BRASS AND BOBBY WAIT OUTSIDE WHILE THE TRIO OF CSI'S WORK THE TINY DRESSING ROOM.
GRIS! ANOTHER GLOCK!

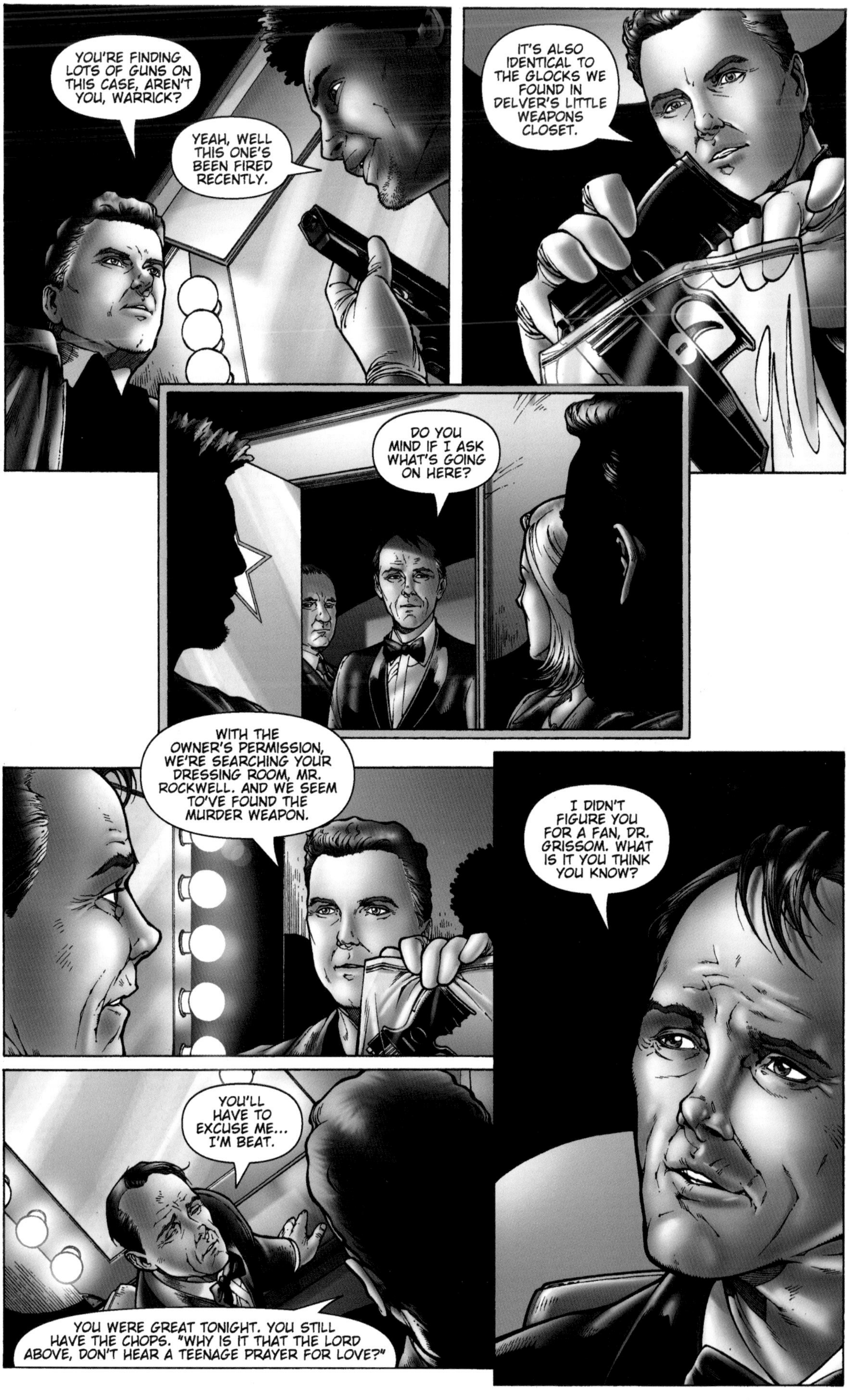
YOU'RE FINDING LOTS OF GUNS ON THIS CASE, AREN'T YOU, WARRICK?
YEAH, WELL THIS ONE'S BEEN FIRED RECENTLY.
IT'S ALSO IDENTICAL TO THE GLOCKS WE FOUND IN DELVER'S LITTLE WEAPONS CLOSET.
DO YOU MIND IF I ASK WHAT'S GOING ON HERE?
WITH THE OWNER'S PERMISSION, WE'RE SEARCHING YOUR DRESSING ROOM, MR. ROCKWELL. AND WE SEEM TO'VE FOUND THE MURDER WEAPON.
I DIDN'T FIGURE YOU FOR A FAN, DR. GRISSOM. WHAT IS IT YOU THINK YOU KNOW?
YOU'LL HAVE TO EXCUSE ME... I'M BEAT.
YOU WERE GREAT TONIGHT. YOU STILL HAVE THE CHOPS. "WHY IS IT THAT THE LORD ABOVE, DON'T HEAR A TEENAGE PRAYER FOR LOVE?"

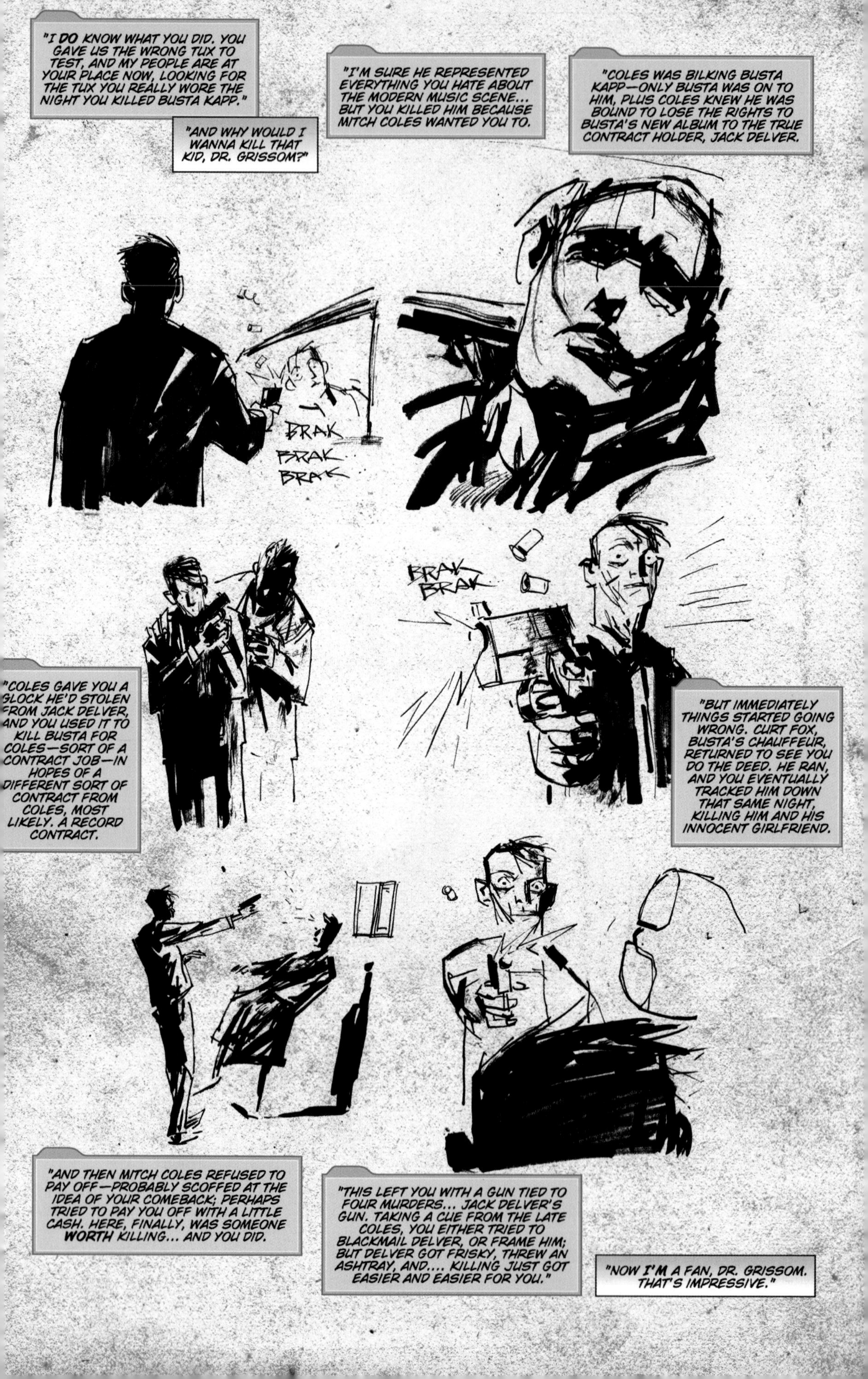
"I DO KNOW WHAT YOU DID. YOU GAVE US THE WRONG TUX TO TEST, AND MY PEOPLE ARE AT YOUR PLACE NOW, LOOKING FOR THE TUX YOU REALLY WORE THE NIGHT YOU KILLED BUSTA KAPP."
"AND WHY WOULD I WANNA KILL THAT KID, DR. GRISSOM?"
"I'M SURE HE REPRESENTED EVERYTHING YOU HATE ABOUT THE MODERN MUSIC SCENE... BUT YOU KILLED HIM BECAUSE MITCH COLES WANTED YOU TO.
"COLES WAS BILKING BUSTA KAPP—ONLY BUSTA WAS ON TO HIM, PLUS COLES KNEW HE WAS BOUND TO LOSE THE RIGHTS TO BUSTA'S NEW ALBUM TO THE TRUE CONTRACT HOLDER, JACK DELVER.
BRAK BRAK BRAK
BRAK BRAK
"COLES GAVE YOU A GLOCK HE'D STOLEN FROM JACK DELVER, AND YOU USED IT TO KILL BUSTA FOR COLES—SORT OF A CONTRACT JOB—IN HOPES OF A DIFFERENT SORT OF CONTRACT FROM COLES, MOST LIKELY. A RECORD CONTRACT.
"BUT IMMEDIATELY THINGS STARTED GOING WRONG. CURT FOX, BUSTA'S CHAUFFEUR, RETURNED TO SEE YOU DO THE DEED. HE RAN, AND YOU EVENTUALLY TRACKED HIM DOWN THAT SAME NIGHT, KILLING HIM AND HIS INNOCENT GIRLFRIEND.
"AND THEN MITCH COLES REFUSED TO PAY OFF—PROBABLY SCOFFED AT THE IDEA OF YOUR COMEBACK; PERHAPS TRIED TO PAY YOU OFF WITH A LITTLE CASH. HERE, FINALLY, WAS SOMEONE WORTH KILLING... AND YOU DID.
"THIS LEFT YOU WITH A GUN TIED TO FOUR MURDERS... JACK DELVER'S GUN. TAKING A CUE FROM THE LATE COLES, YOU EITHER TRIED TO BLACKMAIL DELVER, OR FRAME HIM; BUT DELVER GOT FRISKY, THREW AN ASHTRAY, AND.... KILLING JUST GOT EASIER AND EASIER FOR YOU."
"NOW I'M A FAN, DR. GRISSOM. THAT'S IMPRESSIVE."

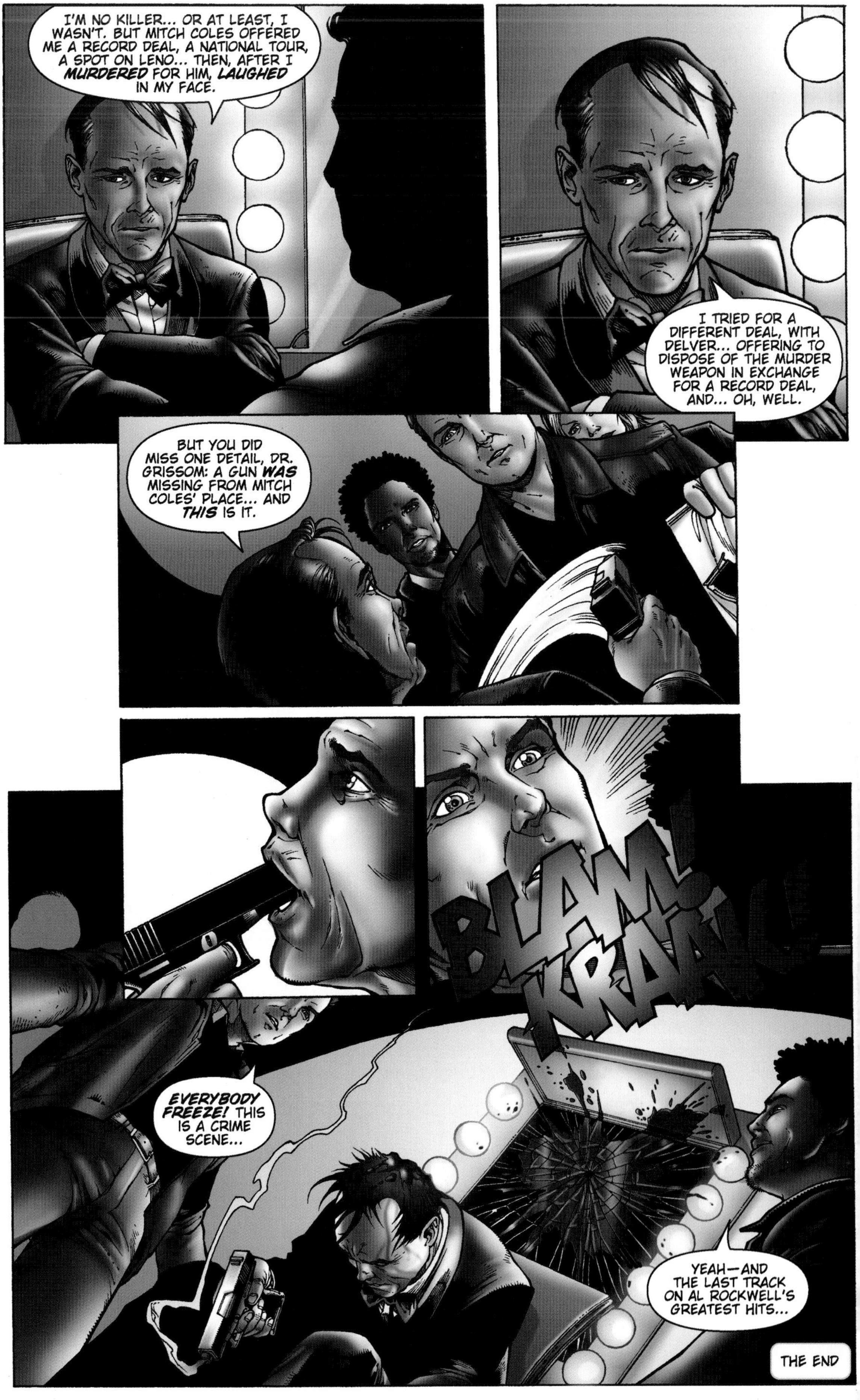
I'M NO KILLER... OR AT LEAST, I WASN'T. BUT MITCH COLES OFFERED ME A RECORD DEAL, A NATIONAL TOUR, A SPOT ON LENO... THEN, AFTER I MURDERED FOR HIM, LAUGHED IN MY FACE.
I TRIED FOR A DIFFERENT DEAL, WITH DELVER... OFFERING TO DISPOSE OF THE MURDER WEAPON IN EXCHANGE FOR A RECORD DEAL, AND... OH, WELL.
BUT YOU DID MISS ONE DETAIL, DR. GRISSOM: A GUN WAS MISSING FROM MITCH COLES' PLACE... AND THIS IS IT.
BLAM!
KRAAK!
EVERYBODY FREEZE! THIS IS A CRIME SCENE...
YEAH—AND THE LAST TRACK ON AL ROCKWELL'S GREATEST HITS...
THE END

# Catherine Willows Speaks!

## An Interview with **Marg Helgenberger**

rg Helgenberger as Catherine Willows.

**You have had quite a varied career in both film and television. Do you prefer television over film, or vice-versa, and why?**

I enjoy the pace of and creative collaborations of series television, but not the hours or length of season. Also, just the fact that I've done a series before, and I always found it to be such a creative process between the writers and the actors, just an on-going sort of throwing back of ideas and throwing out ideas and going with it. It's exciting, actually, you know. Because you say, "How about that? All right, commit". And then you do it, and it's really fun. I actually find it's sometimes a lot more fun than doing movies because you don't have time to think, you know, or sit in your trailer. As for films, it's all about the material, director and cast.

**You've played roles in so many different genres — soap opera, medical drama, sci-fi, etc. Did you bring parts of previous roles into creating your Catherine Willows character?**

I always try to infuse 'spunk' into all my roles. I am the first to admit that there is a pattern to my parts. I play all sorts of law enforcement types. I either play cops or criminals — I'm either on the right side of the law or on the wrong side. I gravitate toward edgier material because it suits my nature. I find it fascinating to play. I'm just that kind of person.

**Is this part more physical than other roles you've had in the past?**

We're not cops, we are criminologists, and so we do all the stuff that is kind of painstaking. We are collecting fibres, saliva samples, prints and so forth. You have to be excruciatingly careful with what you are collecting because it can all be thrown out if you screw up. There are obviously times when my character is going to be in jeopardy and I'm going to have to make fast decisions. I love energetic kinds of acting — anything where you can put action behind the words. It is more fun to watch and it is more fun to play.

**What about your own personality? Is any part of Marg Helgenberger reflected in your portrayal of Catherine Willows, or are you completely different?**

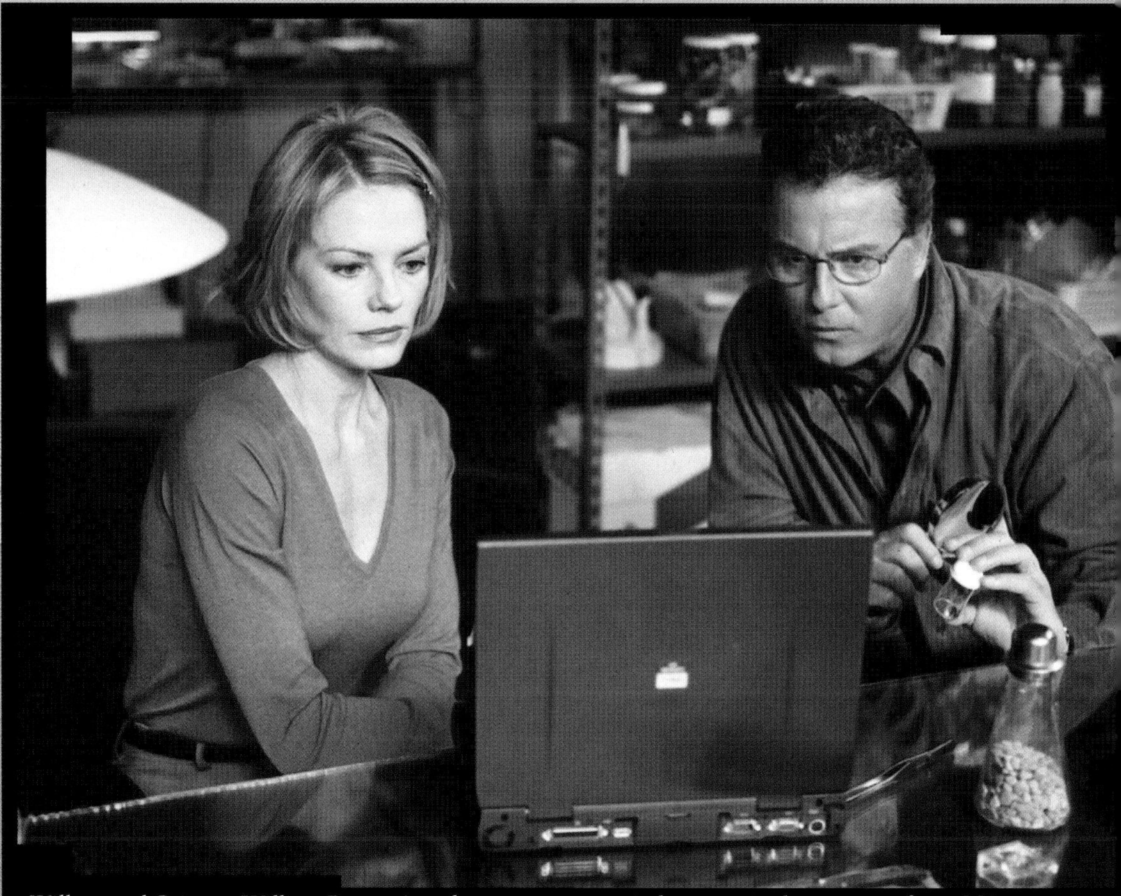

*Willows and Grissom (William Petersen) at the computer — a vital weapon in the armoury of any CSI.*

I couldn't play a role for 10 months of the year and not use aspects of my personality, commitment, determination, sense of fun and logic.

***How would you characterise the relationship between Grissom and Willows? Catherine's seniority and experience seem to put her on a virtually equal footing with Gil.***

The relationship between Grissom and Willows complements each other. It is like Yin and Yang.

***What about the show's 'gross factor'? Is it hard to deal with some of the more grisly aspects of homicide you encounter on the show?***

Well, sometimes the gruesomeness of the crime gets to me, because you're thinking about the victim's last few minutes. But as for the corpses and stuff, no, it doesn't because we know it's prosthesis and we know it's fake. I do have a lot of empathy for the actors playing the corpses because they've got to endure hours of prosthetic make-up and then lie on a slab with nothing on, and not breathe while we're shooting the scene. That's where my empathy lies.

***Have you had a chance to go out in the field with an actual CSI? Is there an actual person that your character is based on?***

Catherine Willows is loosely based on Las Vegas criminalist Yolanda McClery, and I've tagged along

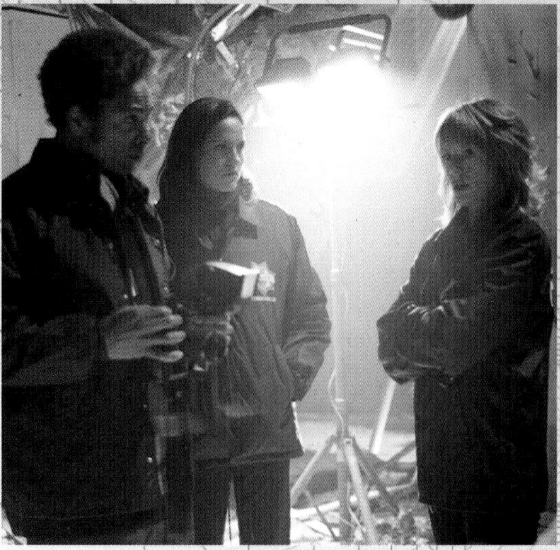

*Lights! Camera! Action! Willows with Warrick (Gary Dourdan) and Sara (Jorja Fox).*

with her a few times. She told me she works the night shift because, since it gets so hot in Vegas, when you go out to a crime scene and a body has been there for God knows how long… well, you get the idea. Apparently the heat makes it, like, 5,000 times worse.

***Much has been made on the show of Catherine's exotic dancer past. Do you feel that this real-life experience gives her an edge over more traditional, scientifically trained and sheltered compatriots when it comes to cracking cases?***
I feel that Catherine's former career helps in understanding human nature and pathology.

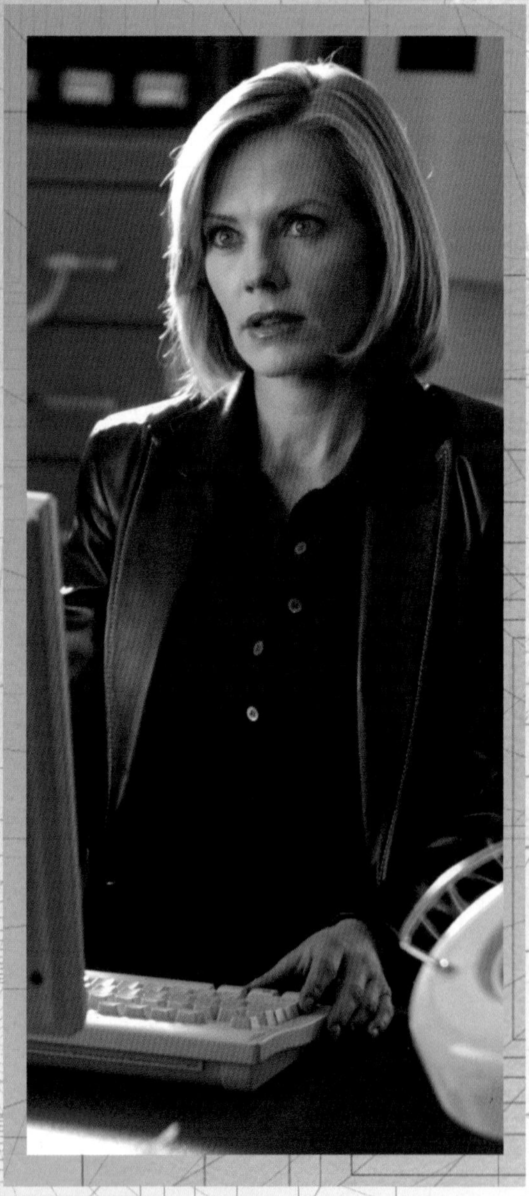

*"Are you sure this is a QWERTY keyboard?"*

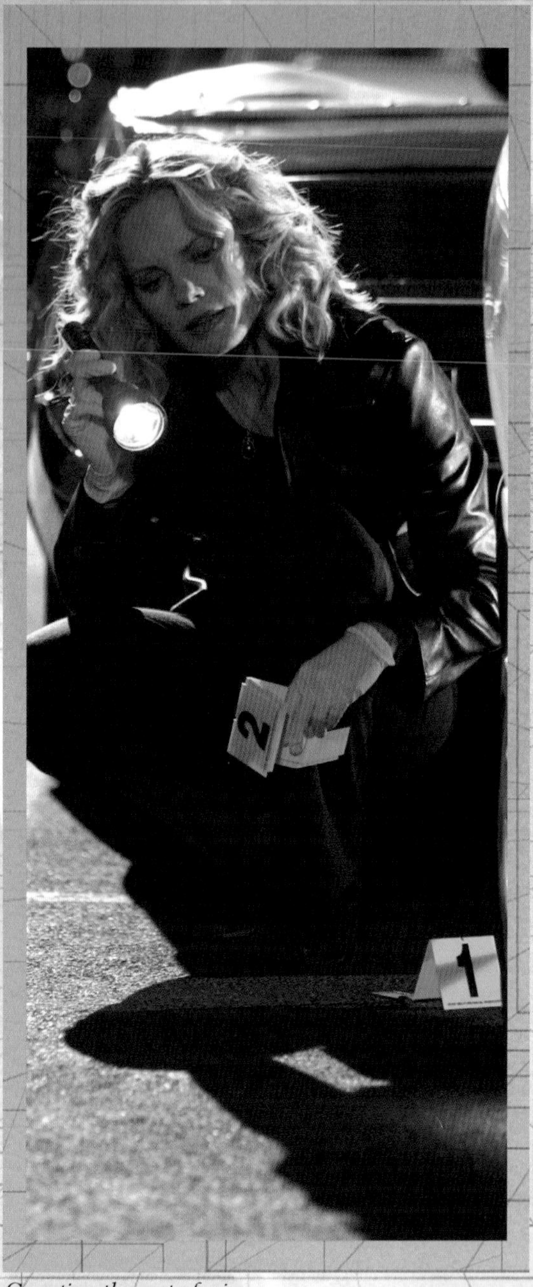

2
1


*Counting the cost of crime…*

***Another big difference between Catherine and the others is that her home life is more defined. We've met her controlling ex-husband, Eddie, as well as her daughter. Would you like to see this side of Willows' personality explored more in the future?***
I'm always interested in exploring Catherine's single motherhood. I feel an affinity for people who have been through hardships but are able to keep going. My mother is a breast cancer survivor yet has always looked on the bright side of life. I find that kind of person fascinating to play.

# Warrick Brown Speaks!

An Interview with **Gary Dourdan**

Gary Dourdan began his acting career at an early age when he enrolled in a prestigious inner city programme in Philadelphia called 'Freedom Theater'. Born and raised in Philadelphia, Dourdan expanded on his theatre roots and began making weekly trips to New York City for auditions and music lessons. Before long, Dourdan relocated to New York where his career escalated to numerous roles in off-Broadway plays.

Dourdan's career break came when he was cast in *The Cosby Show* spin-off series, *A Different World*, as the con artist Shazza. Television appearances that followed include *The Good Fight*, the HBO miniseries *Laurel Avenue*, and a lead role in Dick Wolf's series *Swift Justice*.

Shortly thereafter, Dourdan landed his first major role as the character Yates in *Playing God*, opposite David Duchovny and Angelina Jolie. The same year (1997), Dourdan appeared with Winona Ryder and Sigourney Weaver in *Alien: Resurrection*. Other notable credits include *Scarred City*, *New Jersey Turnpikes* and *Impostor*.

*Warrick Brown played by Gary Dourdan.*

**Warrick Brown was born and raised in Las Vegas, but Gary Dourdan wasn't. What do you think of Las Vegas when you visit now, for location shooting (or just for fun)? Do you share Warrick's love of the game?**
No, I don't play games.

**Warrick has pushed his luck with Gil Grissom on more than one occasion, and probably should have been fired. Somehow, though, he always gets another chance. What do you think it is that Gil sees in Warrick that gives him such faith?**
He is the best at what he does.

*Warrick Brown and Nick Stokes (George Eads): the Dynamic Duo.*

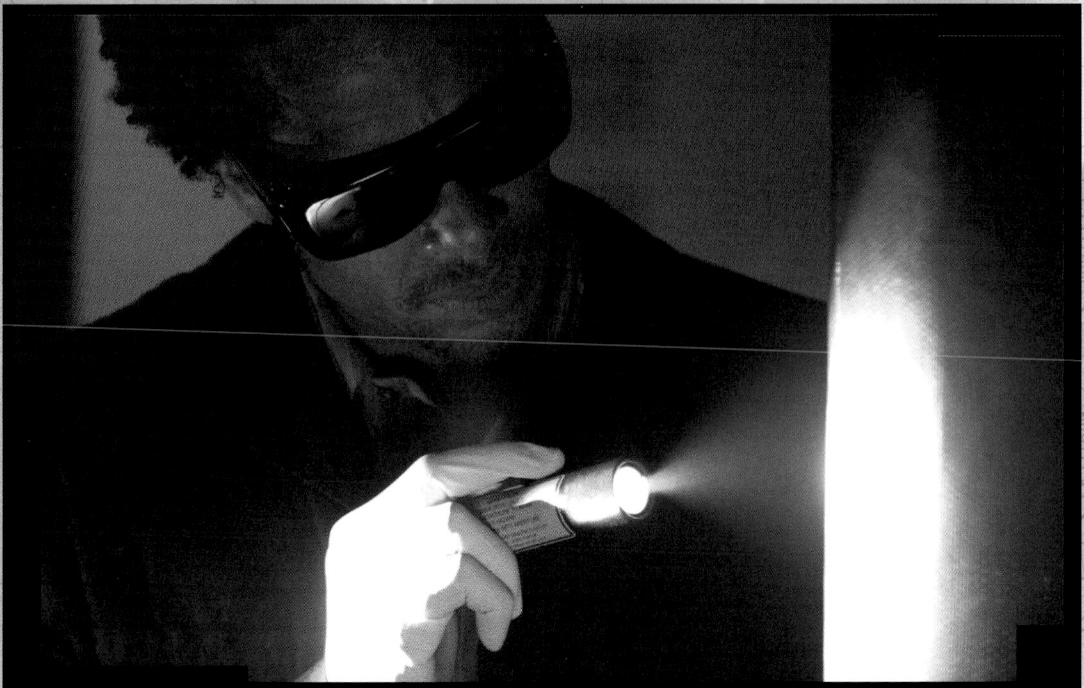
*Warrick at work. Shades by Bono.*

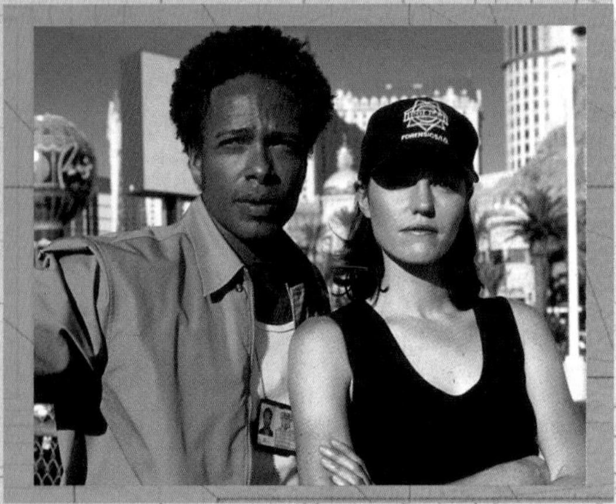
*The graveyard shift finally get to catch some rays...*

***How much of Gary Dourdan do we see in Warrick Brown? We assume that you're not quite as interested in working with dead bodies as Warrick is, but there are other aspects of him — he's a very social person in lots of ways and he seems to know people everywhere in the city, he loves music — that you might share.***
I love music. I know cool people in the city and I'm a pretty social person like Warrick.

***The CSIs on the show often have to reconstruct a crime from what seems to be a the slimmest of clues. As an actor, do you ever feel like you're doing the same thing — building a character with a complete life from just words on paper?***
Yes.

***You've portrayed Malcolm X in a movie, among many other roles. What do you see as the differences between creating a character like Warrick from essentially whole cloth, and playing a real person?***
I have freedom to create from nothing at *CSI*.

***Does the nature of the material you work with on CSI — the detailed crime scenes and graphic visuals that give the show much of its power — ever get to you?***
NO.

***We don't often get much detail about the early lives of the CSIs but in 'Random Acts of Violence' we learned quite a bit about Warrick's past. How do you let what you know about his background inform the choices you make in playing the character's day-to-day life?***
Warrick is the 'street smart' cop and his past guides his wisdom.

***What's your favourite aspect of the show?***
Warrick Brown's gambling habits.

# Sara Sidle Speaks!

An Interview with **Jorja Fox**

*Sara Sidle has a BSc. in Physics from Harvard. Why do you think she turned away from theoretical physics to the very applied science of Crime Scene Investigation?*

I think Sara thrives on the rush. I think she's very result orientated and impatient. Working in the CSI environment allows her to solve scientific issues on a daily basis. I'm almost certain there is a skeleton or two in her closet that drives her to work for some kind of justice. I could see her though, in her older days, working on some quantum theory in a lab somewhere.

*Does portraying someone with such a specific and technical background pose any particular problems to you as an actor?*

Yeah, it gives me an inferiority complex. I've never felt so simple-minded as I have playing a genius. There's always a desire to play characters convincingly and in that area I'm acting more than usual.

*What about the material — decomposed bodies, strange diseases and violent death? Do you ever have trouble dealing with it?*

Usually at the beginning and end of the season. In the beginning I have to get into that mind set again, which takes a few weeks. I'm a little more vulnerable to it. At the end of the season, I'm tired from it all and usually looking forward to taking a break from it. I have so much fun at work, even on the crime scene days and the coroner days, but I'd be lying if I didn't say that it wears on you. The gore, on the other hand, as you know, I never get over.

*You've had regular gigs on three of TV's most highly acclaimed series — ER, The West Wing and CSI. We've heard that you have an interest in politics, which would explain The West Wing, but was there anything which particularly drew you to CSI?*

The pilot script put me in a trance. There was just 'something about it'. Indefinable. I had been a fan

*Sara smiles. Sara Sidle played by Jorja Fox.*

*Sara's work often takes her beyond what's visible to the naked eye. Here, she employs an ultraviolet torch.*

of Petersen and Helgenberger's. And I liked Carol and Ann a lot, but, honestly, it seemed like a risk, and an adventurous one, so I leapt. The idea seemed fresh and different and a little nuts.

**You also do theatre work — how would you compare acting on TV's number one show to acting on stage?**

Stage is a thrill because it's live, it's in your face, and you know right away if an audience is enjoying it or not. There's that energy when you get a bunch of people in a room that doesn't happen much and is almost alchemical. Making a TV show is similar in that you get a bunch of people in a room and everybody focuses on one specific detail of a story for a period of time and then moves on to the next detail. I'm still amazed that 100 people ever do anything together at the same time, forget about 23 shows and 9 months' worth of stories. Being number one is fleeting, momentary and one of the best highs I've ever had. I wish everyone would get a chance to experience that. It's so rare, and, honestly, magical. It just doesn't happen. The odds are so stacked against it… and it's a complete and utter mystery. If people knew how to do it, everyone would be.

**You've also written plays and music — any interest in writing a CSI episode? Or comic book?**

I'd love to write an episode… Comic books I know nothing about. I wasn't allowed to read them as a kid. Maybe after some research.

*Gil Grissom (William Petersen), Sara and Nick Stokes (George Eads) shed light on another murder scene.*

# Doc Robbins Speaks!

## An Interview with **Robert David Hall**

**You're not a doctor but you play one on TV. Do people ever ask you for medical advice?**
No one has asked me for medical advice, but when I'm on the street sometimes fans call me 'Doc'. In fact, Anthony Zuiker — the show's creator — even calls me 'Doc'!

**Have you learned enough from the show to dispense any medical advice?**
Yes. If you want to live a very long life, stay away from coroners as long as you can.

**As Chief Medical Officer in Las Vegas, Doctor Al Robbins has a very demanding job. What similarities do you see in your work, as far as how much preparation is needed?**
Because we have professionals on the set to make sure what we're doing is as realistic as possible, I'm always aware of the proper way to hold instruments or how a procedure should be done. The similarities between acting like a coroner and actually being a coroner is like anything else in life: preparation is the key to success.

**What type of person does one have to be to handle the duties of a coroner?**
A person with a strong stomach.

**Do all the technical aspects of your role pose any problems to you as an actor?**
The technical aspects mean that when the camera is on me, I have to be a bit like Fred Astaire. I've got to know my lines, the procedures I need to perform — and here's the Fred Astaire part — I've got to make it look natural and graceful. Like I've done the procedure and said all of the long medical words hundreds of times.

**What attracted you to CSI?**
What attracted me to CSI is probably what attracts millions of viewers all over the world: intrigue, mystery, good stories and interesting characters.

*Robert David Hall as Doc Robbins.*

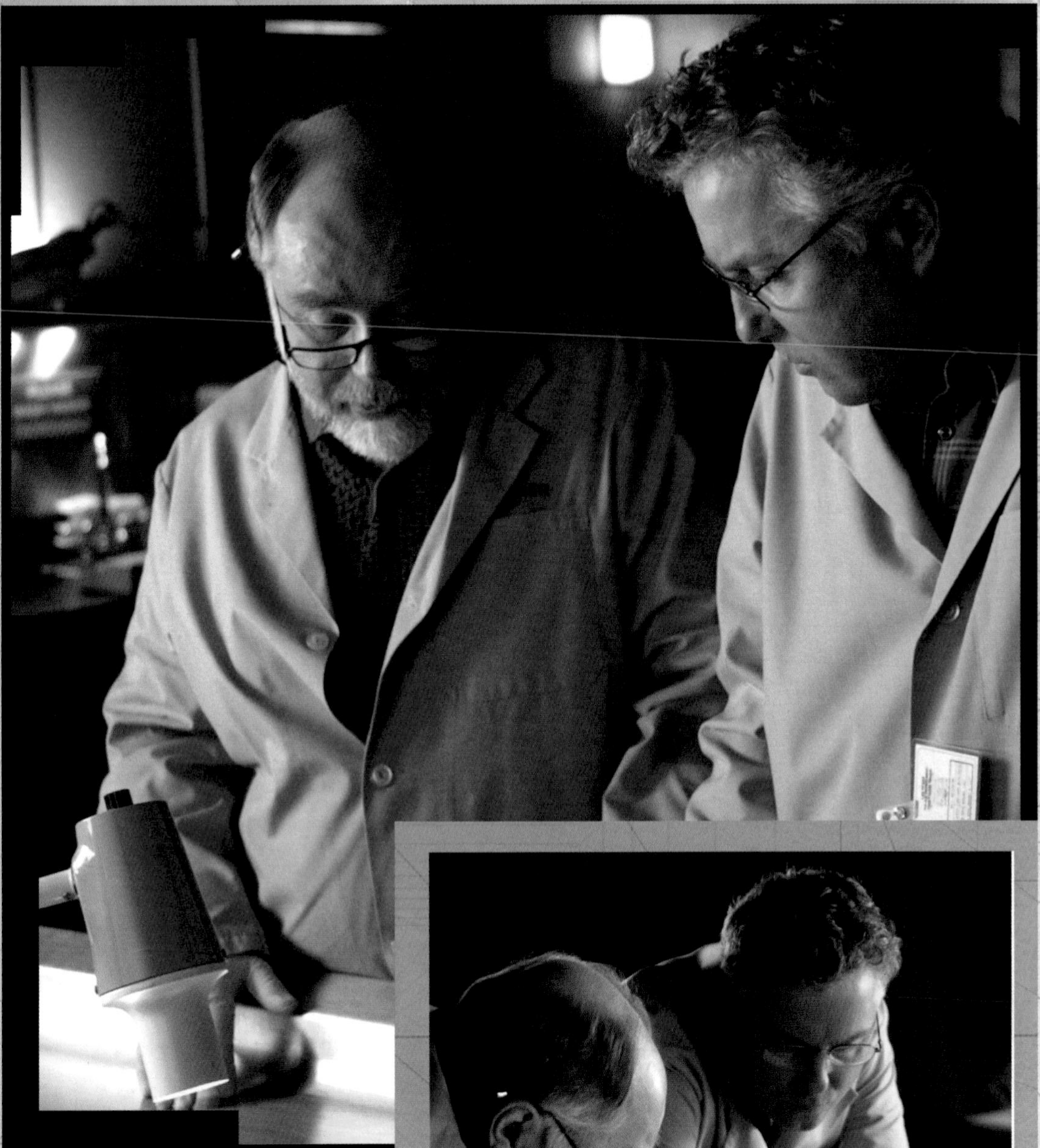

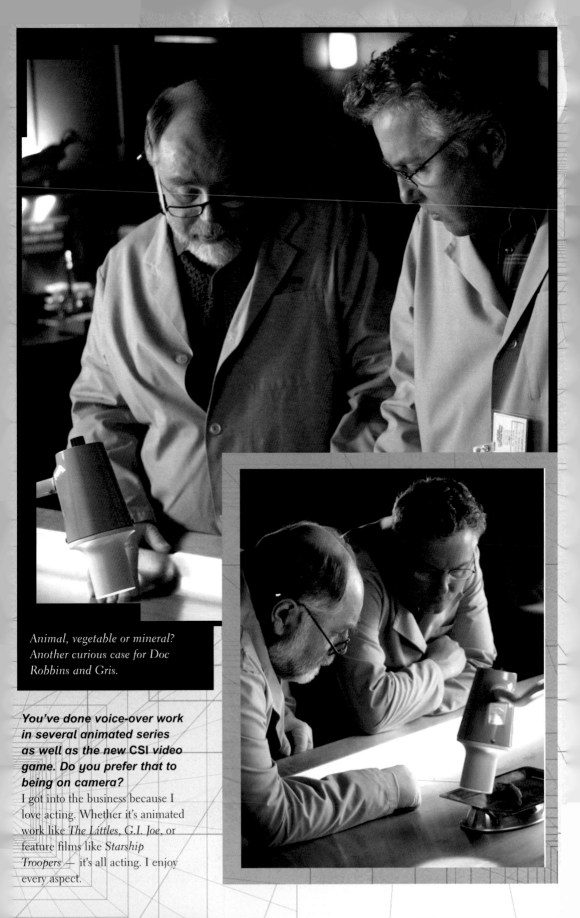

*Animal, vegetable or mineral? Another curious case for Doc Robbins and Gris.*

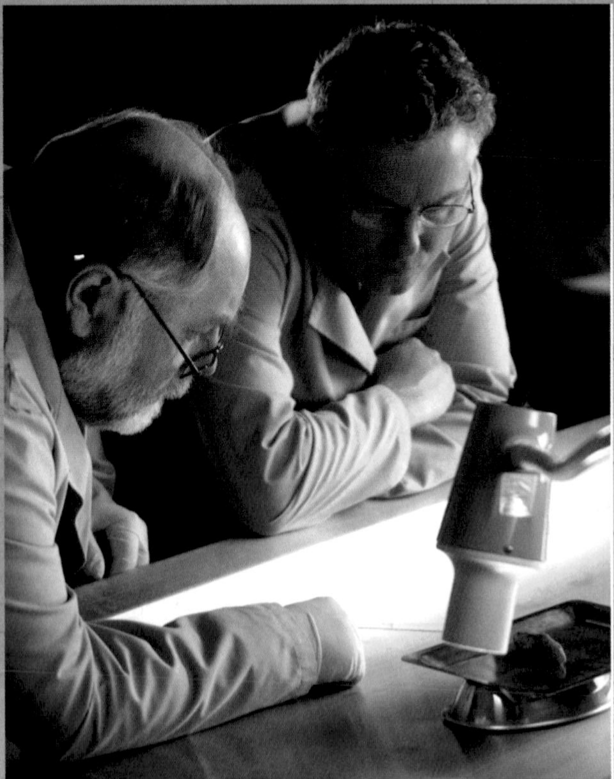

***You've done voice-over work in several animated series as well as the new CSI video game. Do you prefer that to being on camera?***

I got into the business because I love acting. Whether it's animated work like *The Littles*, *G.I. Joe*, or feature films like *Starship Troopers* — it's all acting. I enjoy every aspect.

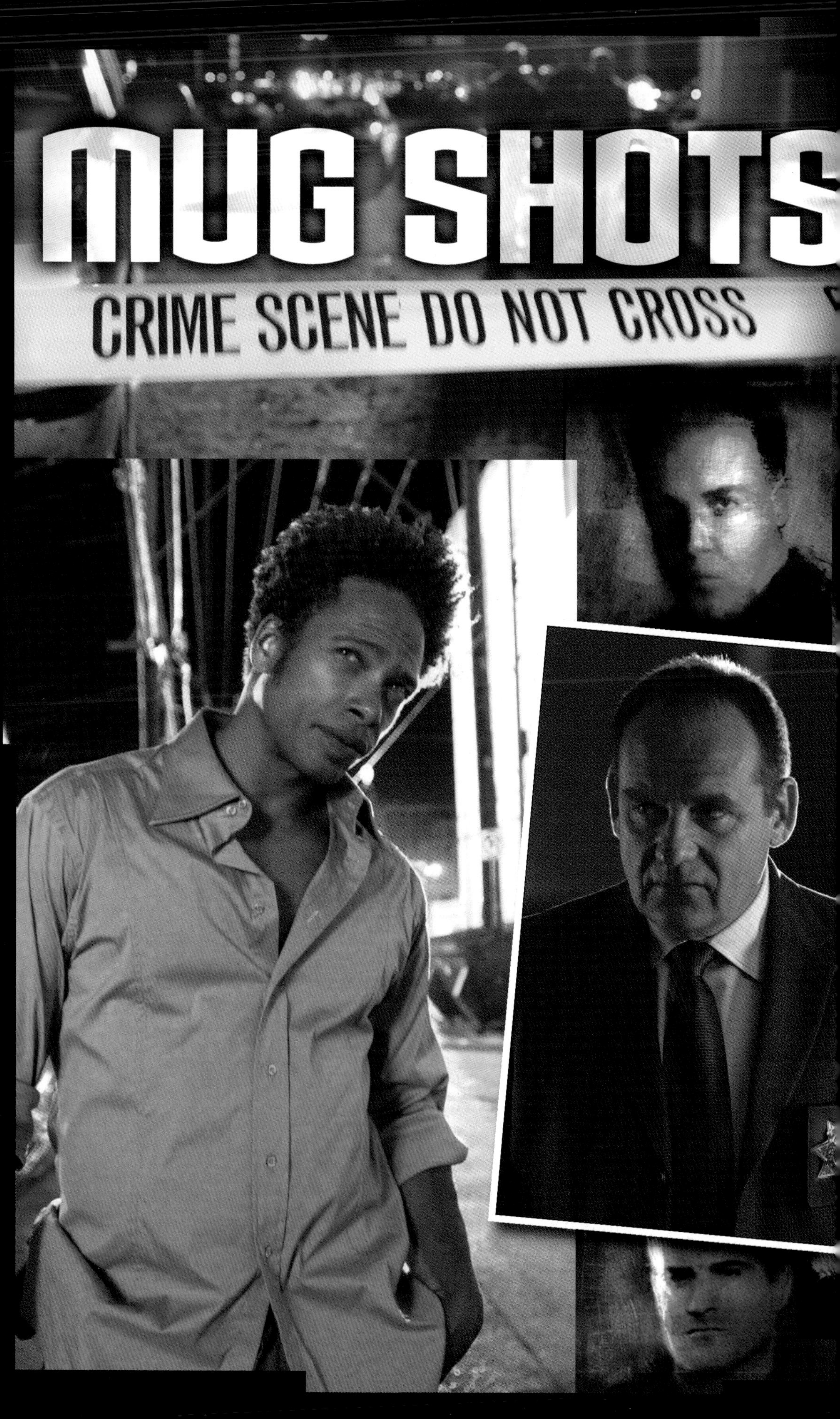
MUG SHOTS
CRIME SCENE DO NOT CROSS

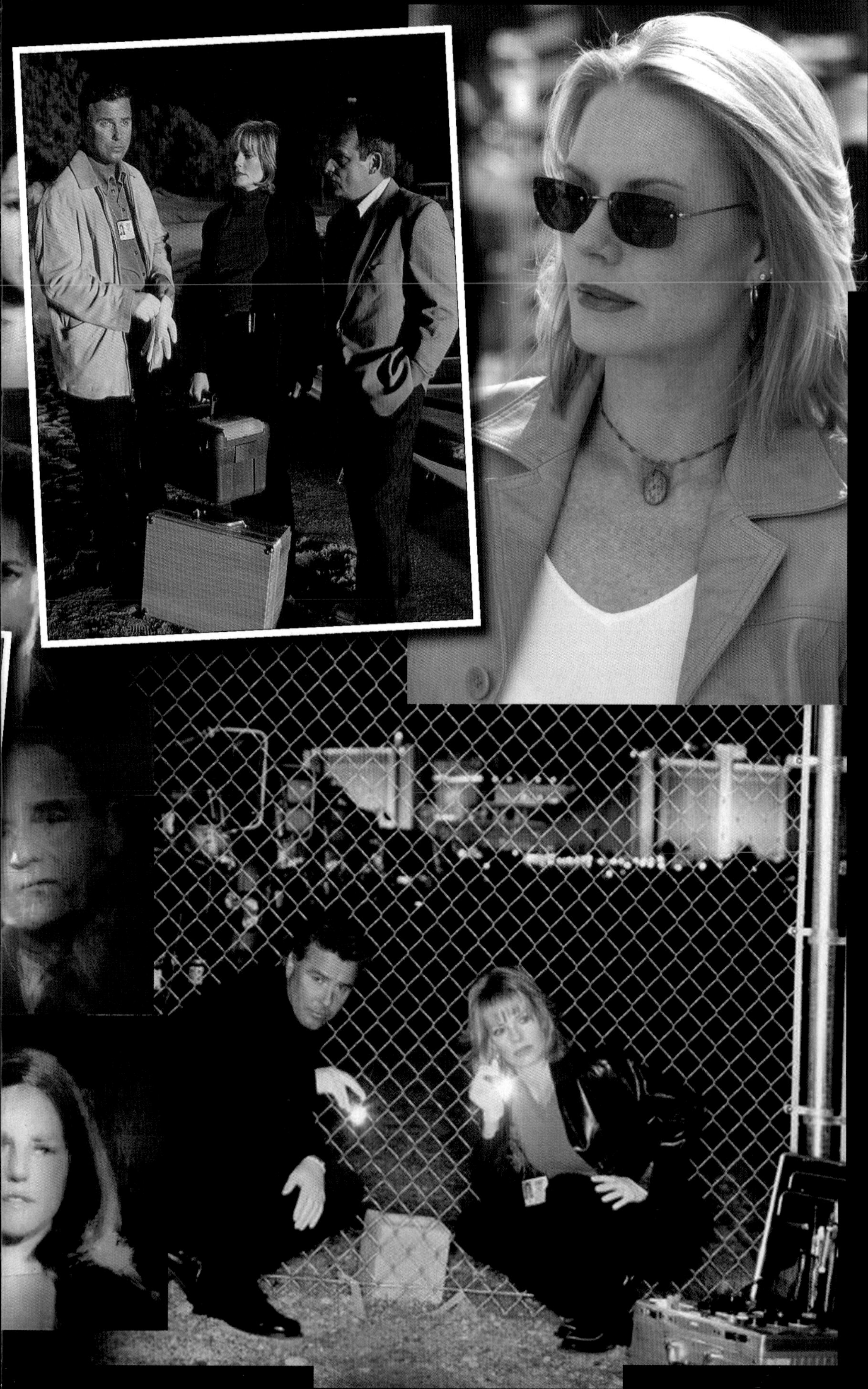

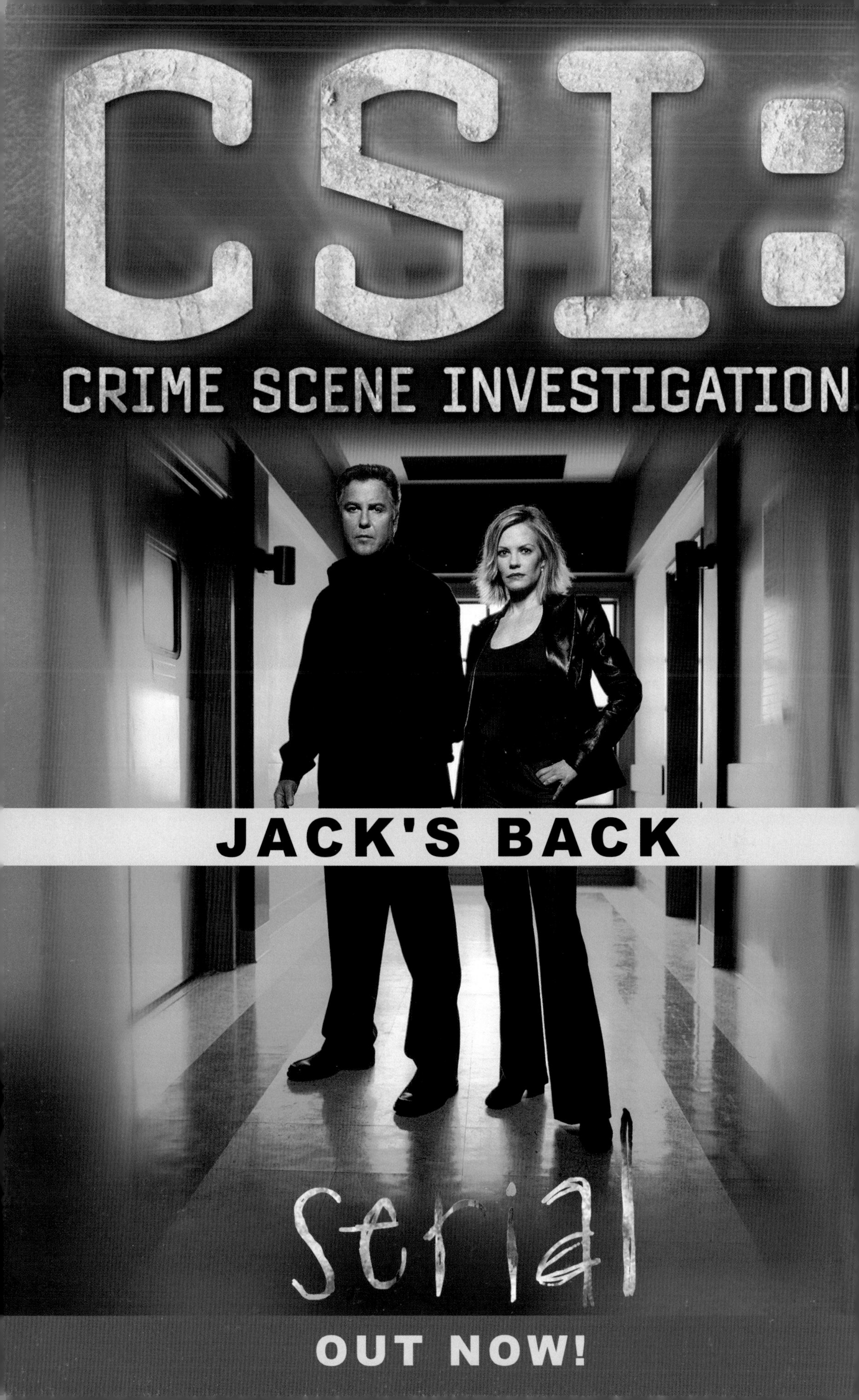
CSI:
CRIME SCENE INVESTIGATION
JACK'S BACK
serial
OUT NOW!

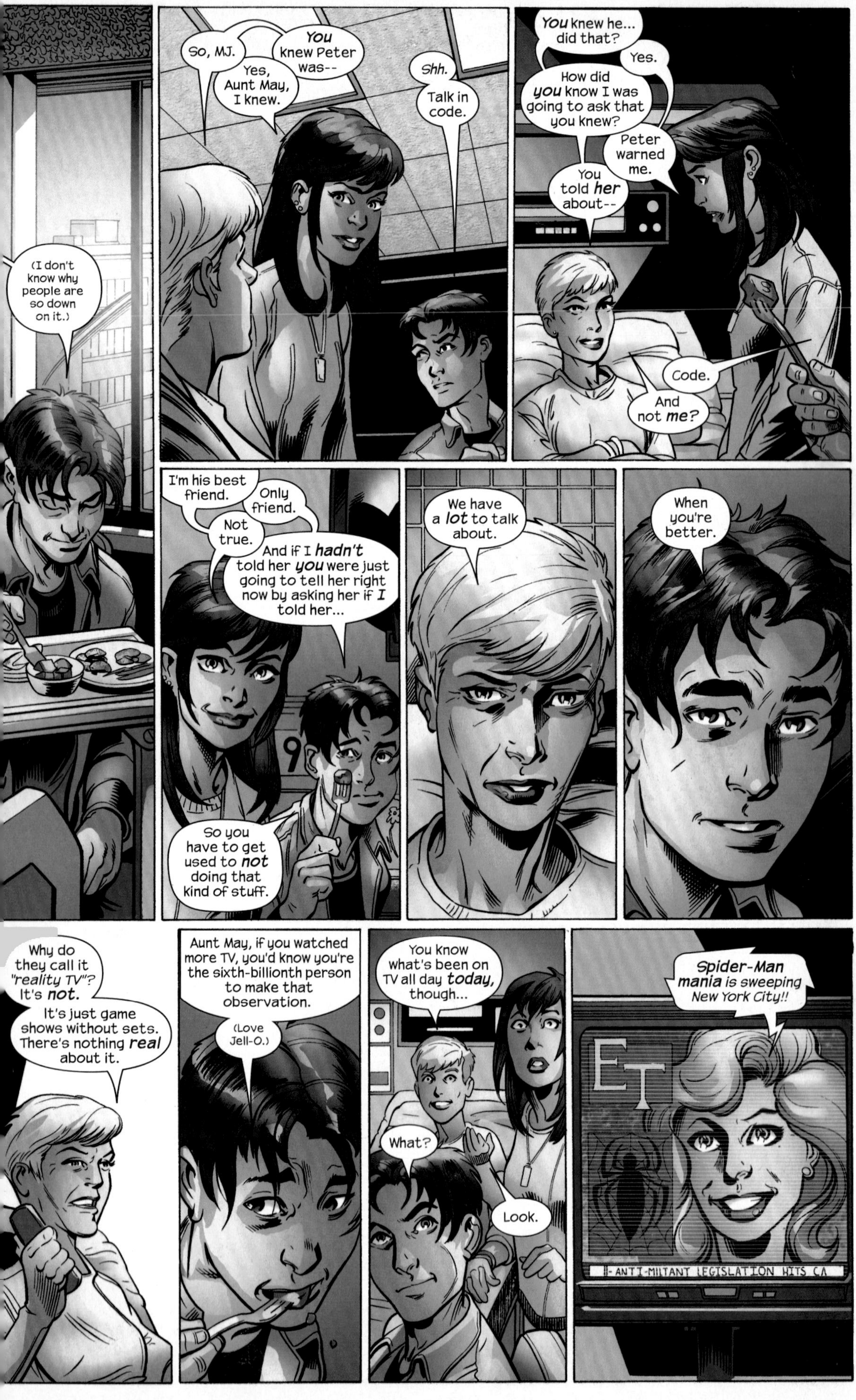

So, MJ.
You knew Peter was--
Yes, Aunt May, I knew.
Shh.
Talk in code.
You knew he... did that?
Yes.
How did you know I was going to ask that you knew?
Peter warned me.
You told her about--
Code.
And not me?
(I don't know why people are so down on it.)
I'm his best friend.
Only friend.
Not true.
And if I hadn't told her you were just going to tell her right now by asking her if I told her...
So you have to get used to not doing that kind of stuff.
We have a lot to talk about.
When you're better.
Why do they call it "reality TV"? It's not.
It's just game shows without sets. There's nothing real about it.
Aunt May, if you watched more TV, you'd know you're the sixth-billionth person to make that observation.
(Love Jell-O.)
You know what's been on TV all day today, though...
What?
Look.
Spider-Man mania is sweeping New York City!!
ET
ANTI-MUTANT LEGISLATION HITS CA

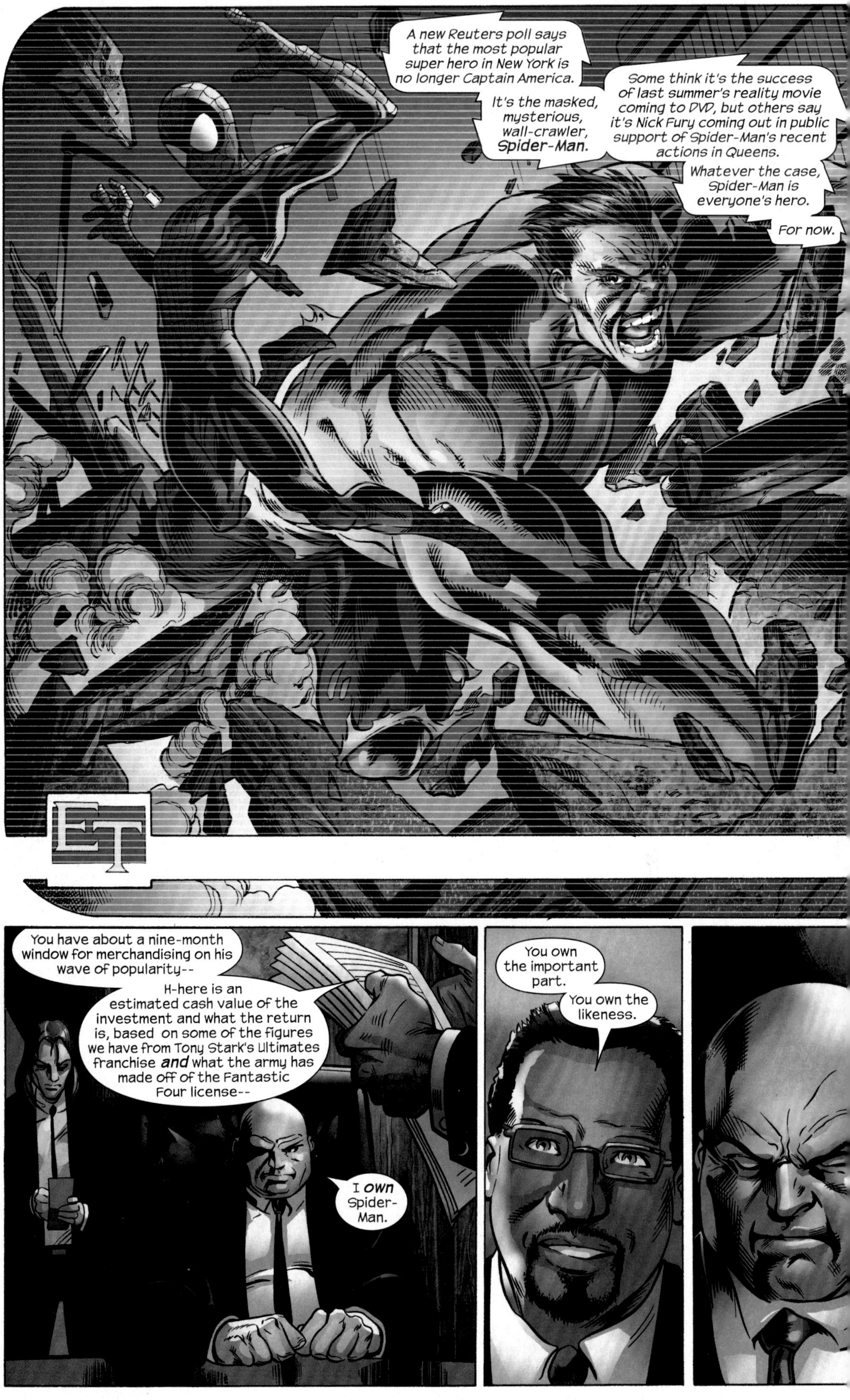
A new Reuters poll says that the most popular super hero in New York is no longer Captain America.
It's the masked, mysterious, wall-crawler, Spider-Man.
Some think it's the success of last summer's reality movie coming to DVD, but others say it's Nick Fury coming out in public support of Spider-Man's recent actions in Queens.
Whatever the case, Spider-Man is everyone's hero.
For now.
ET
You have about a nine-month window for merchandising on his wave of popularity--
H-here is an estimated cash value of the investment and what the return is, based on some of the figures we have from Tony Stark's Ultimates franchise and what the army has made off of the Fantastic Four license--
I own Spider-Man.
You own the important part.
You own the likeness.

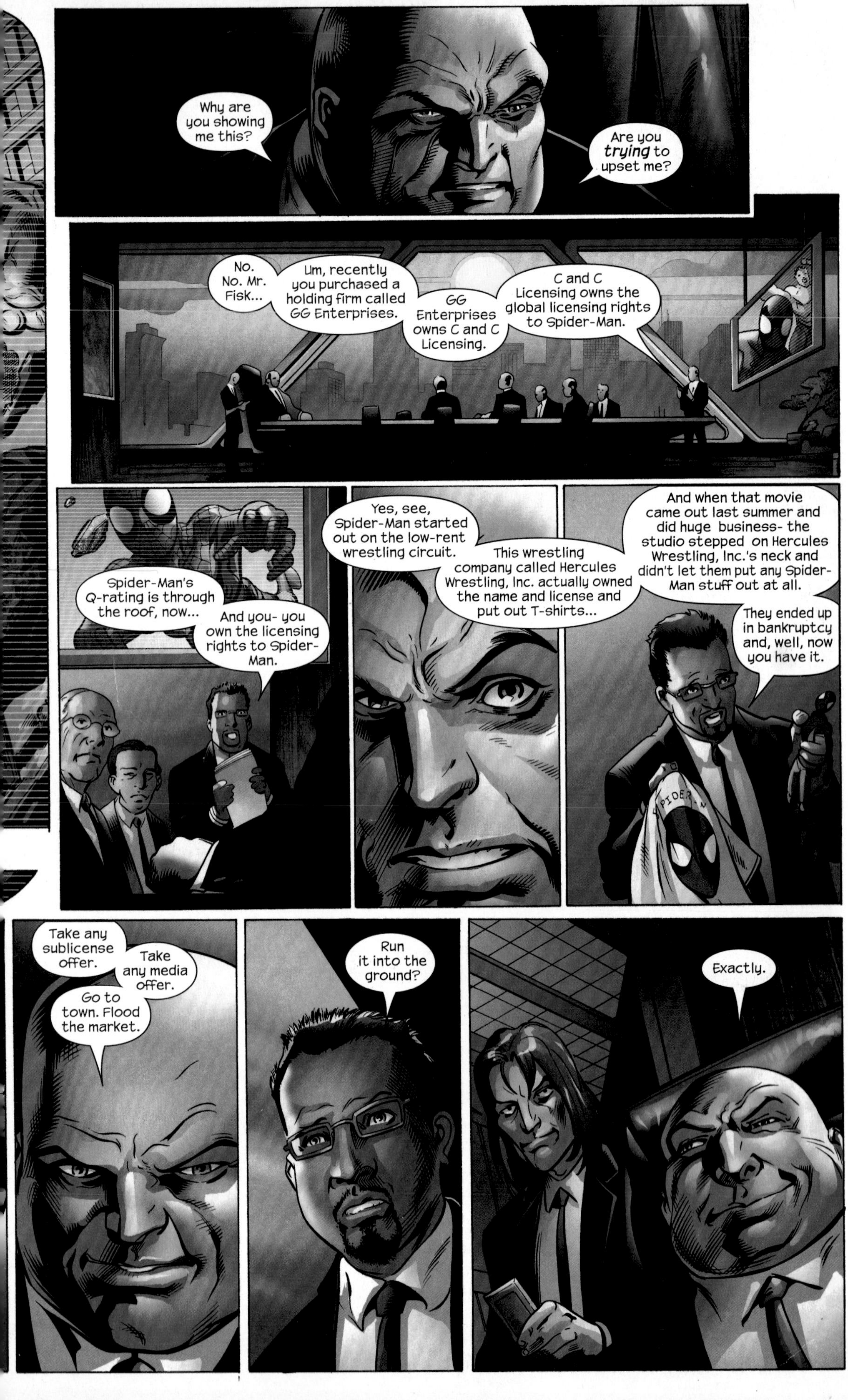
Why are you showing me this?
Are you *trying* to upset me?
No. No. Mr. Fisk...
Um, recently you purchased a holding firm called GG Enterprises.
GG Enterprises owns C and C Licensing.
C and C Licensing owns the global licensing rights to Spider-Man.
Spider-Man's Q-rating is through the roof, now...
And you- you own the licensing rights to Spider-Man.
Yes, see, Spider-Man started out on the low-rent wrestling circuit.
This wrestling company called Hercules Wrestling, Inc. actually owned the name and license and put out T-shirts...
And when that movie came out last summer and did huge business- the studio stepped on Hercules Wrestling, Inc.'s neck and didn't let them put any Spider-Man stuff out at all.
They ended up in bankruptcy and, well, now you have it.
Take any sublicense offer.
Take any media offer.
Go to town. Flood the market.
Run it into the ground?
Exactly.

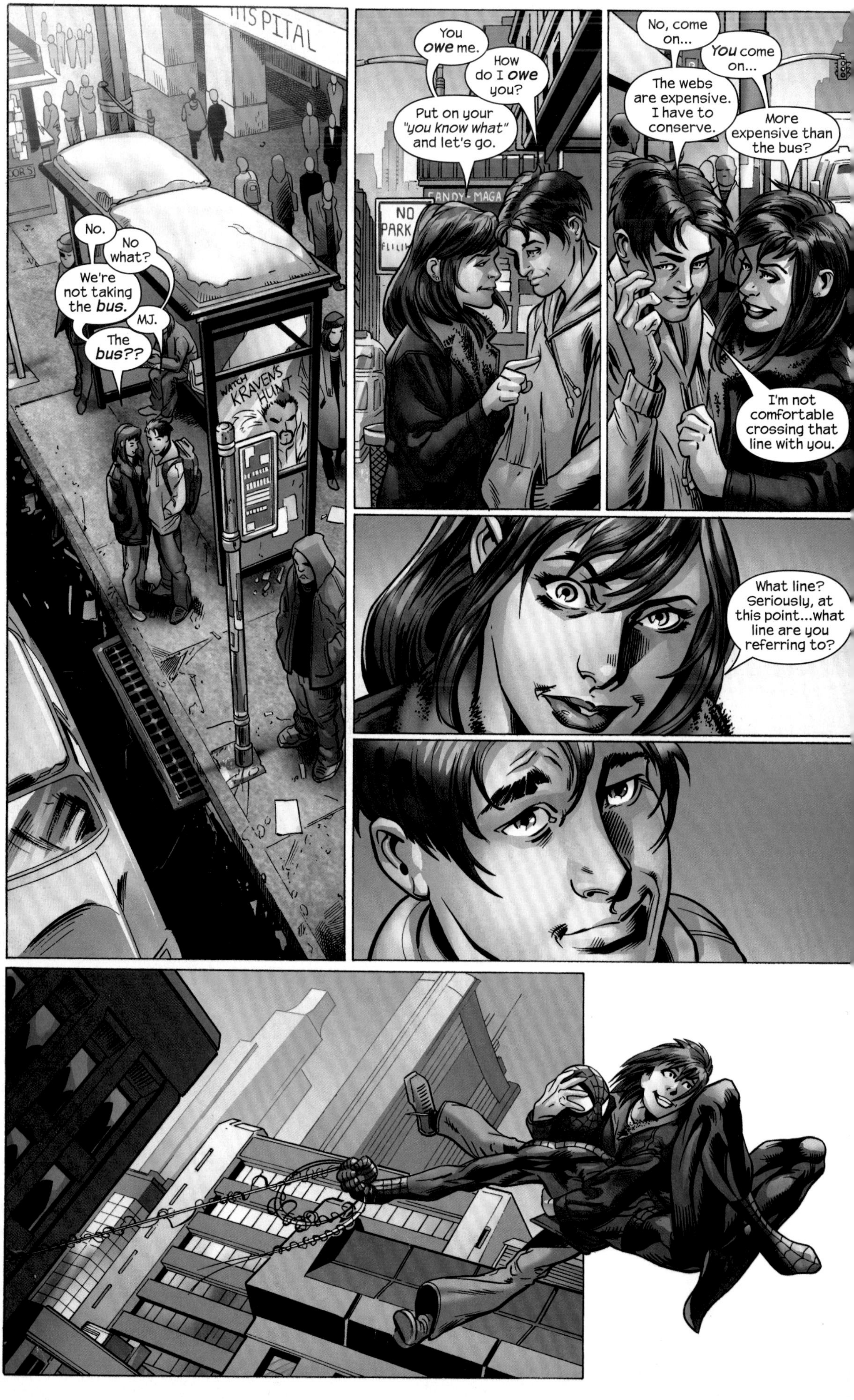
HOSPITAL
No.
No what?
We're not taking the bus.
MJ.
The bus??
WATCH KRAVEN'S HUNT
You owe me.
How do I owe you?
Put on your "you know what" and let's go.
NO PARK
No, come on...
You come on...
The webs are expensive. I have to conserve.
More expensive than the bus?
I'm not comfortable crossing that line with you.
What line? Seriously, at this point...what line are you referring to?

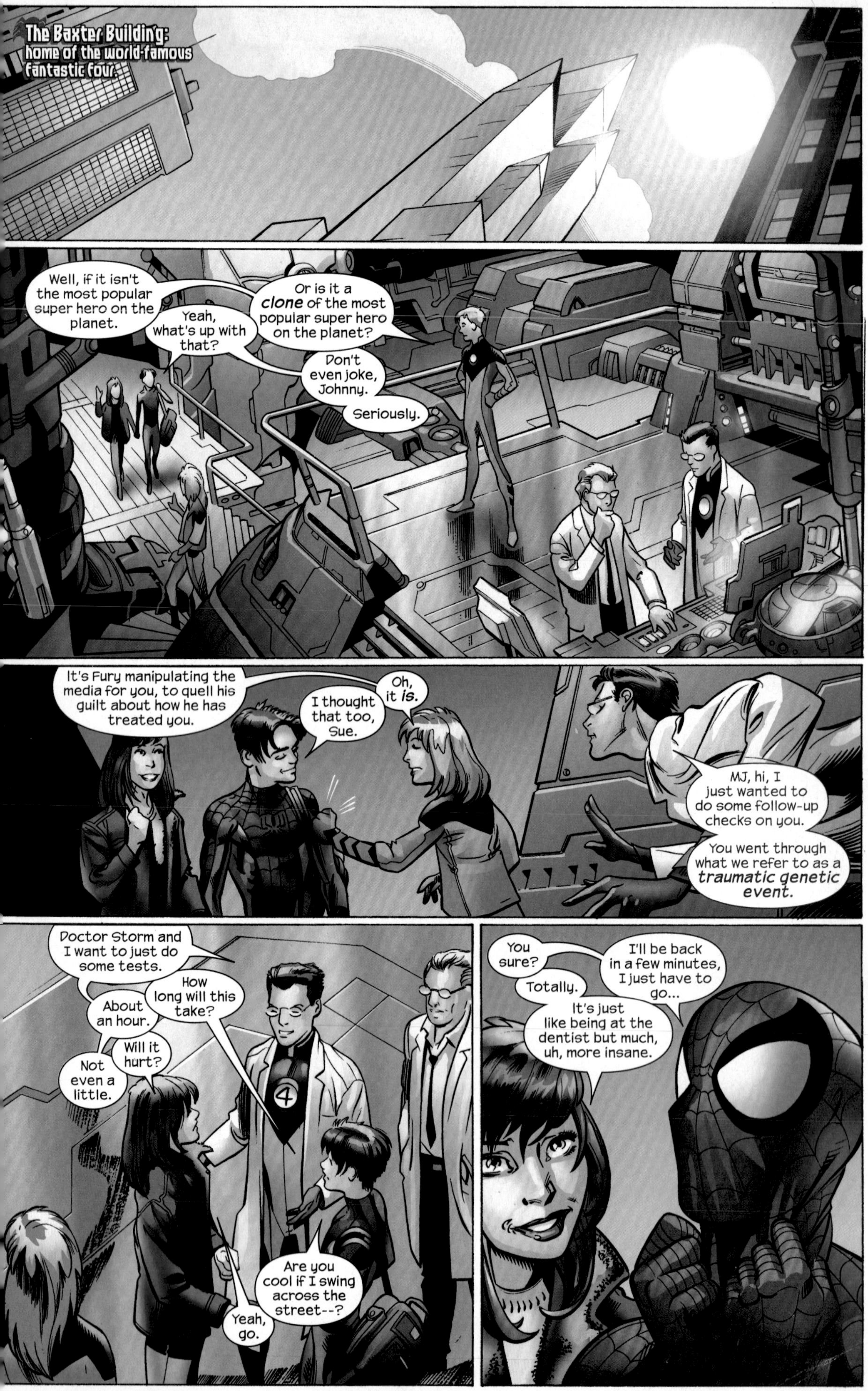
The Baxter Building: home of the world-famous Fantastic Four.
Well, if it isn't the most popular super hero on the planet.
Yeah, what's up with that?
Or is it a *clone* of the most popular super hero on the planet?
Don't even joke, Johnny.
Seriously.
It's Fury manipulating the media for you, to quell his guilt about how he has treated you.
I thought that too, Sue.
Oh, it *is.*
MJ, hi, I just wanted to do some follow-up checks on you.
You went through what we refer to as a *traumatic genetic event.*
Doctor Storm and I want to just do some tests.
How long will this take?
About an hour.
Will it hurt?
Not even a little.
Are you cool if I swing across the street--?
Yeah, go.
You sure?
I'll be back in a few minutes, I just have to go...
Totally.
It's just like being at the dentist but much, uh, more insane.

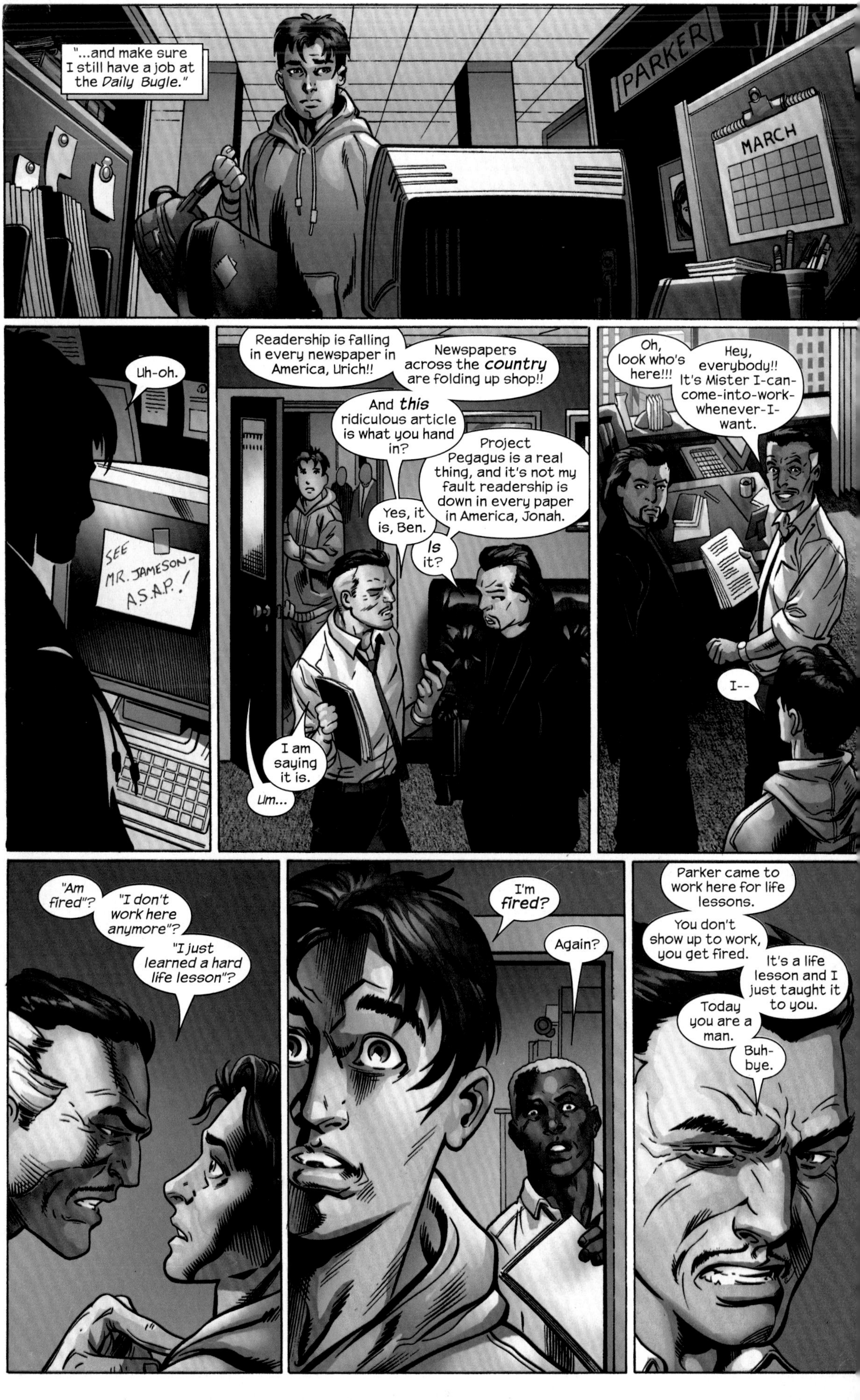
"...and make sure I still have a job at the Daily Bugle."
PARKER
MARCH
Uh-oh.
SEE MR. JAMESON-A.S.A.P.!
Readership is falling in every newspaper in America, Urich!!
Newspapers across the country are folding up shop!!
And this ridiculous article is what you hand in?
Project Pegagus is a real thing, and it's not my fault readership is down in every paper in America, Jonah.
Yes, it is, Ben.
Is it?
I am saying it is.
Um...
Oh, look who's here!!!
Hey, everybody!! It's Mister I-can-come-into-work-whenever-I-want.
I--
"Am fired"?
"I don't work here anymore"?
"I just learned a hard life lesson"?
I'm fired?
Again?
Parker came to work here for life lessons.
You don't show up to work, you get fired.
It's a life lesson and I just taught it to you.
Today you are a man.
Buh-bye.

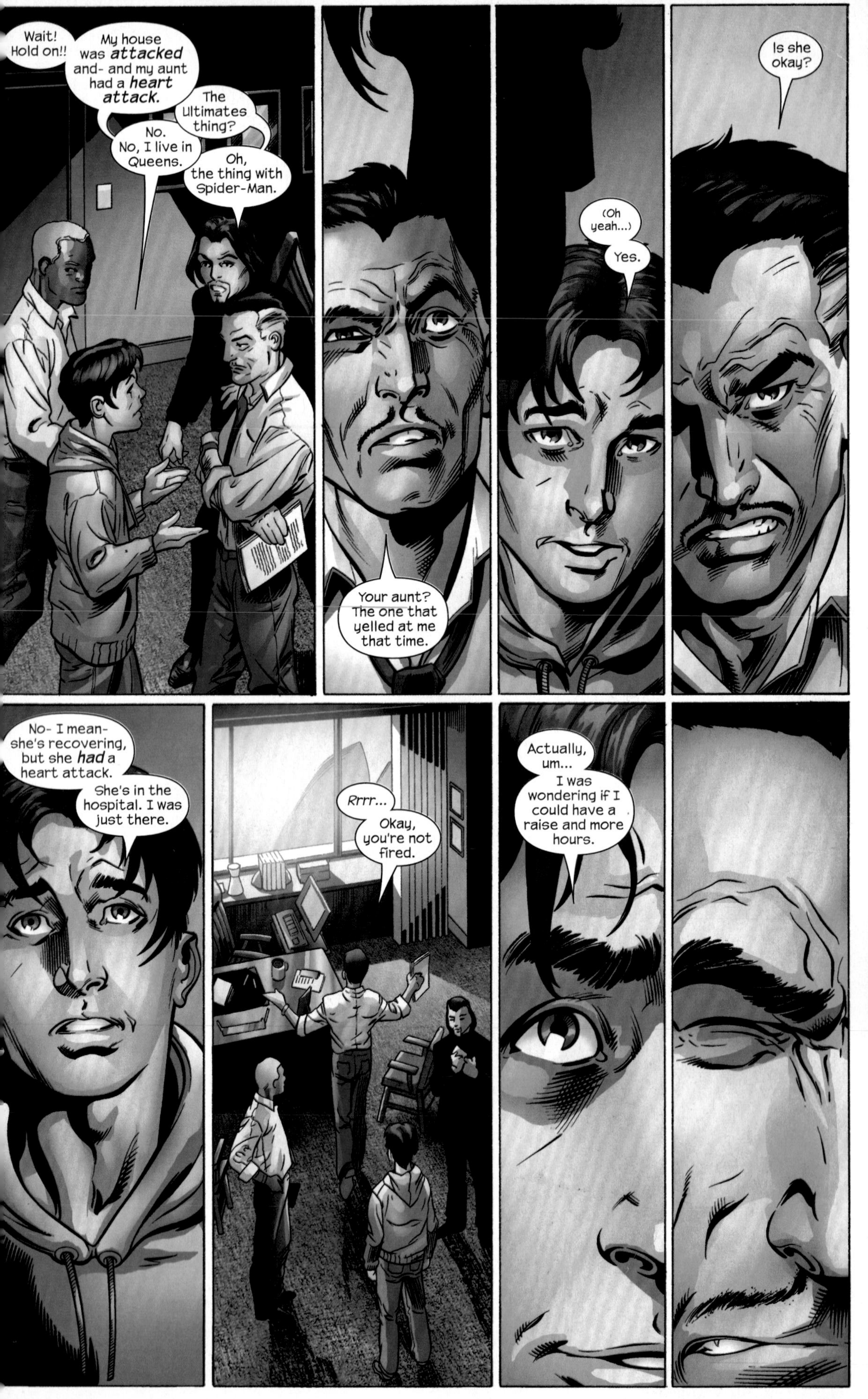
Wait! Hold on!!
My house was *attacked* and- and my aunt had a *heart attack.*
The Ultimates thing?
No. No, I live in Queens.
Oh, the thing with Spider-Man.
Your aunt? The one that yelled at me that time.
(Oh yeah...)
Yes.
Is she okay?
No- I mean- she's recovering, but she *had* a heart attack.
She's in the hospital. I was just there.
*Rrrr...*
Okay, you're not fired.
Actually, um...
I was wondering if I could have a raise and more hours.

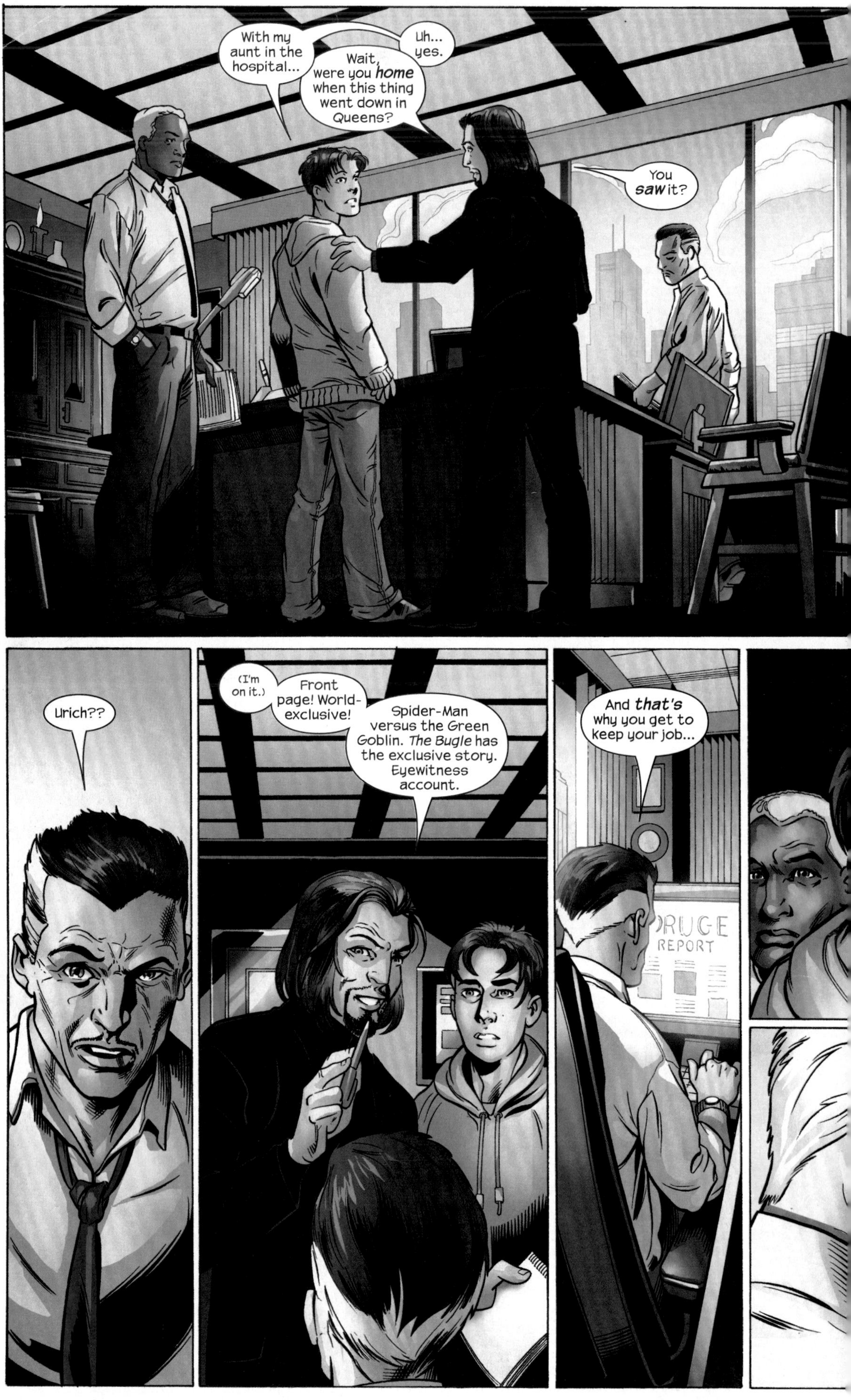
With my aunt in the hospital...
Uh... yes.
Wait, were you home when this thing went down in Queens?
You saw it?
Urich??
(I'm on it.)
Front page! World-exclusive!
Spider-Man versus the Green Goblin. The Bugle has the exclusive story. Eyewitness account.
And that's why you get to keep your job...
DRUGE REPORT

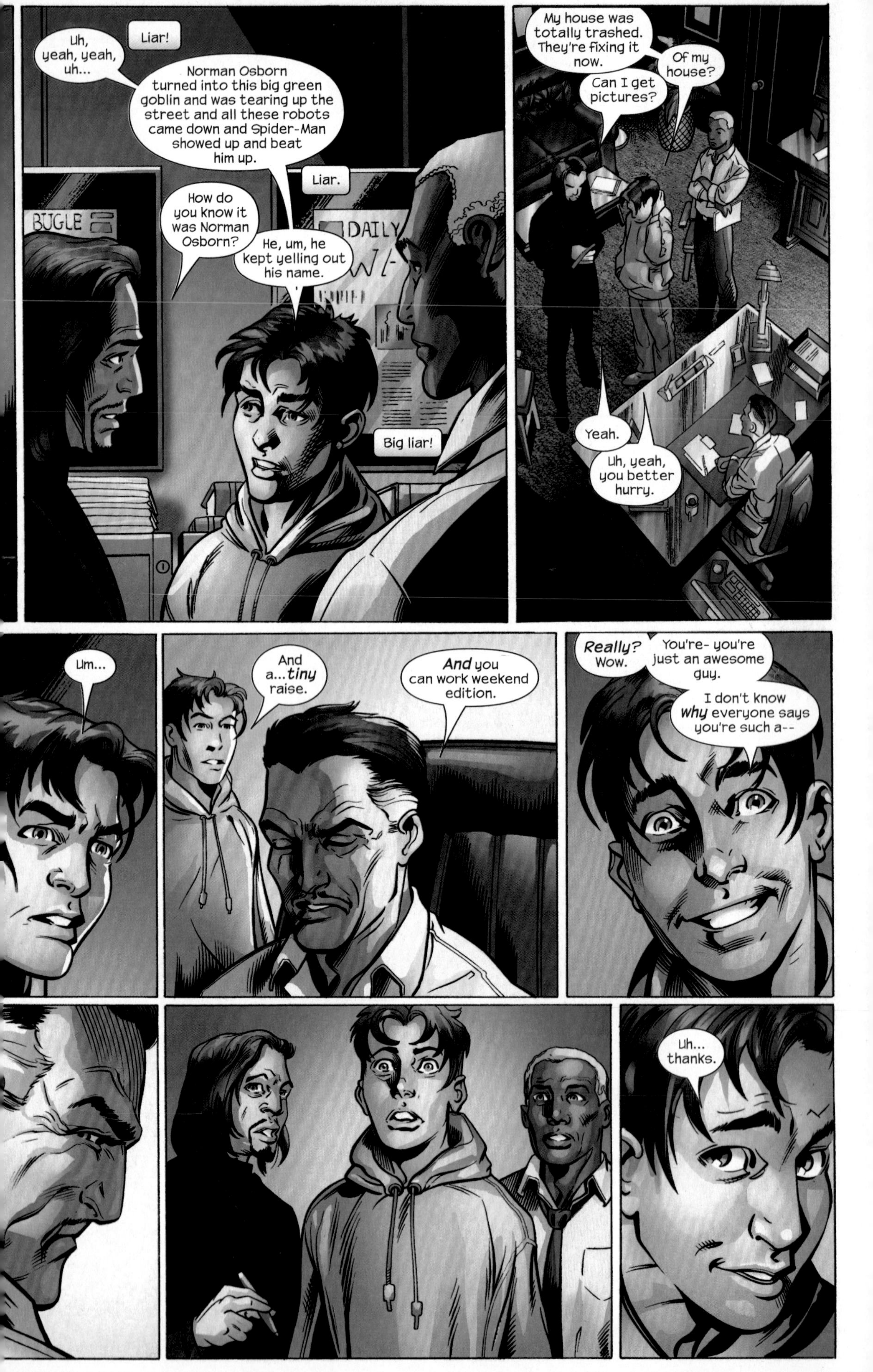

Uh, yeah, yeah, uh...
Liar!
Norman Osborn turned into this big green goblin and was tearing up the street and all these robots came down and Spider-Man showed up and beat him up.
Liar.
How do you know it was Norman Osborn?
He, um, he kept yelling out his name.
Big liar!
BUGLE
DAILY
My house was totally trashed. They're fixing it now.
Of my house?
Can I get pictures?
Yeah.
Uh, yeah, you better hurry.
Um...
And a...*tiny* raise.
*And* you can work weekend edition.
*Really?* Wow.
You're- you're just an awesome guy.
I don't know *why* everyone says you're such a--
Uh... thanks.

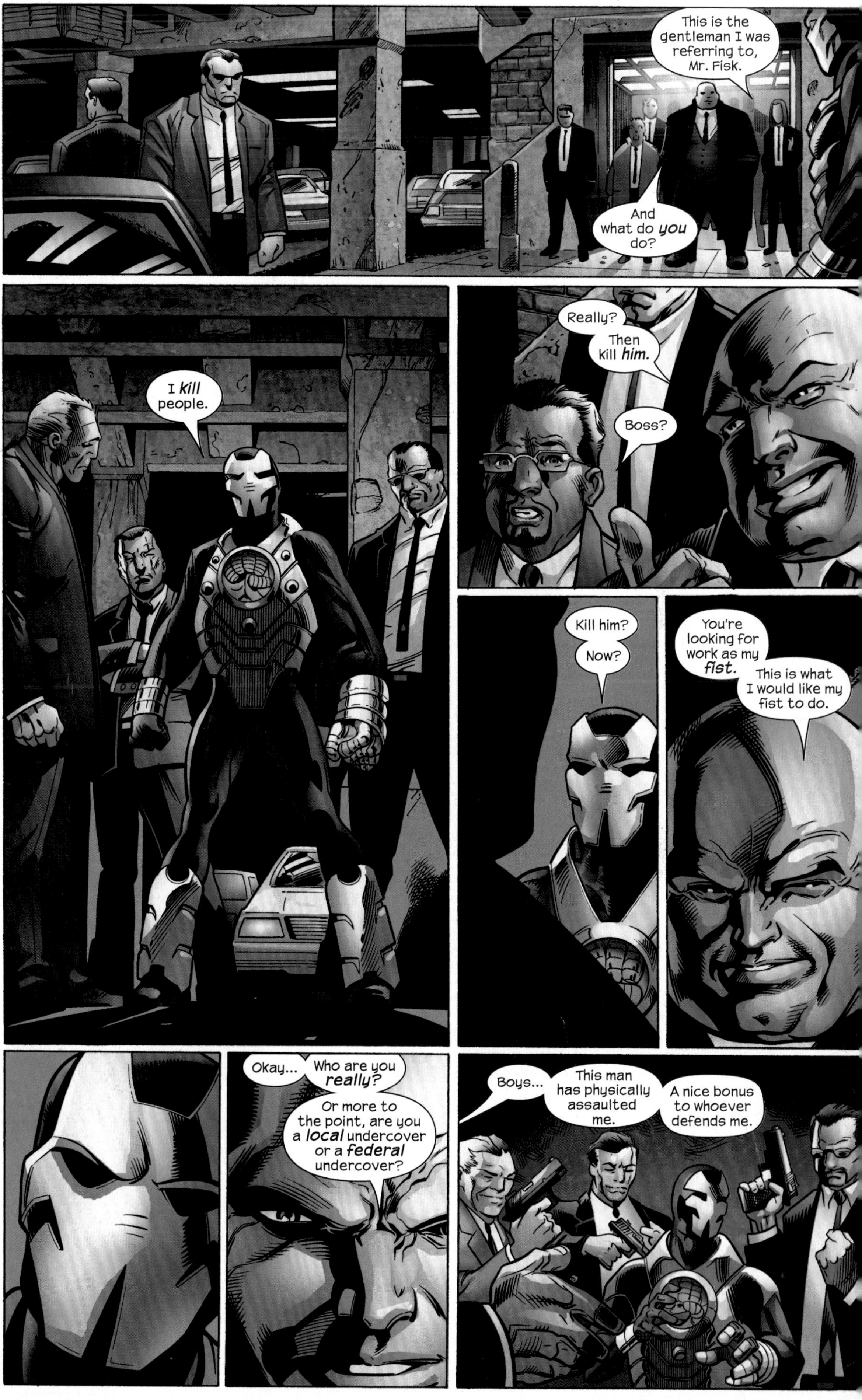
This is the gentleman I was referring to, Mr. Fisk.
And what do *you* do?
I *kill* people.
Really?
Then kill *him.*
Boss?
Kill him?
Now?
You're looking for work as my *fist.*
This is what I would like my fist to do.
Okay...
Who are you *really?*
Or more to the point, are you a *local* undercover or a *federal* undercover?
Boys...
This man has physically assaulted me.
A nice bonus to whoever defends me.

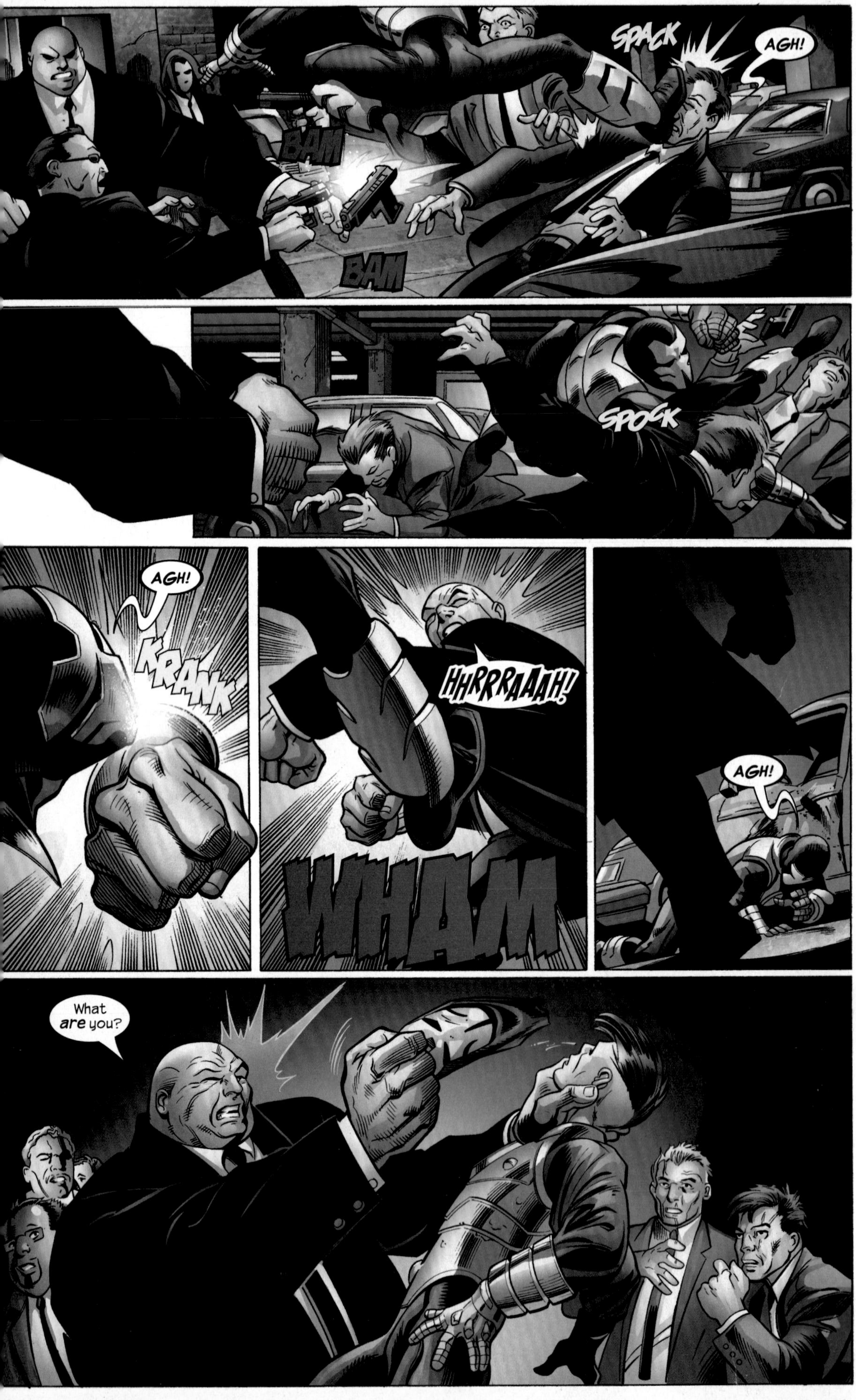
SPACK
AGH!
BAM
BAM
SPOCK
AGH!
KRANK
HHRRRAAAH!
WHAM
AGH!
What are you?

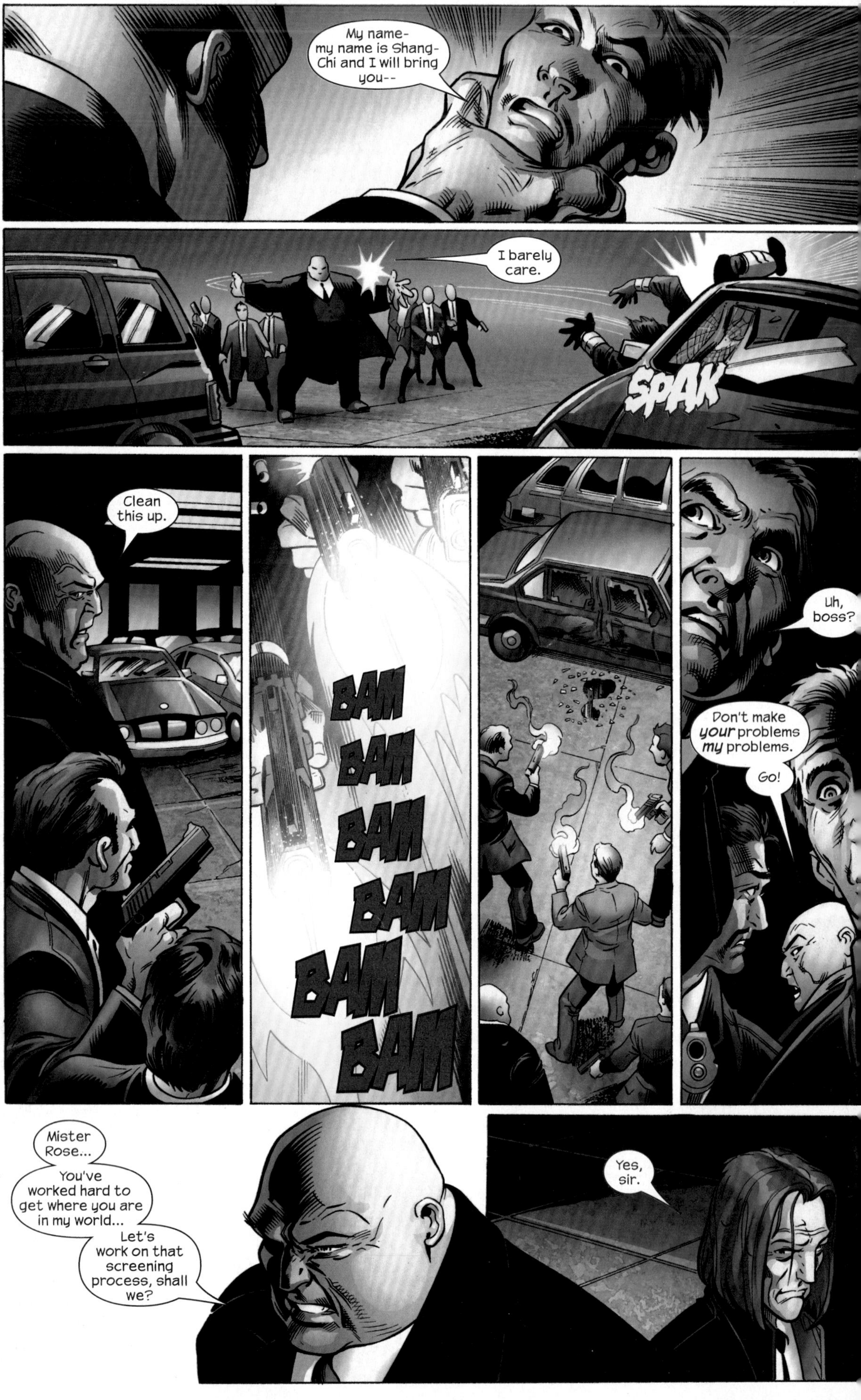

My name- my name is Shang-Chi and I will bring you--
I barely care.
SPAK
Clean this up.
BAM
BAM
BAM
BAM
BAM
BAM
Uh, boss?
Don't make *your* problems *my* problems.
Go!
Mister Rose...
You've worked hard to get where you are in my world...
Let's work on that screening process, shall we?
Yes, sir.

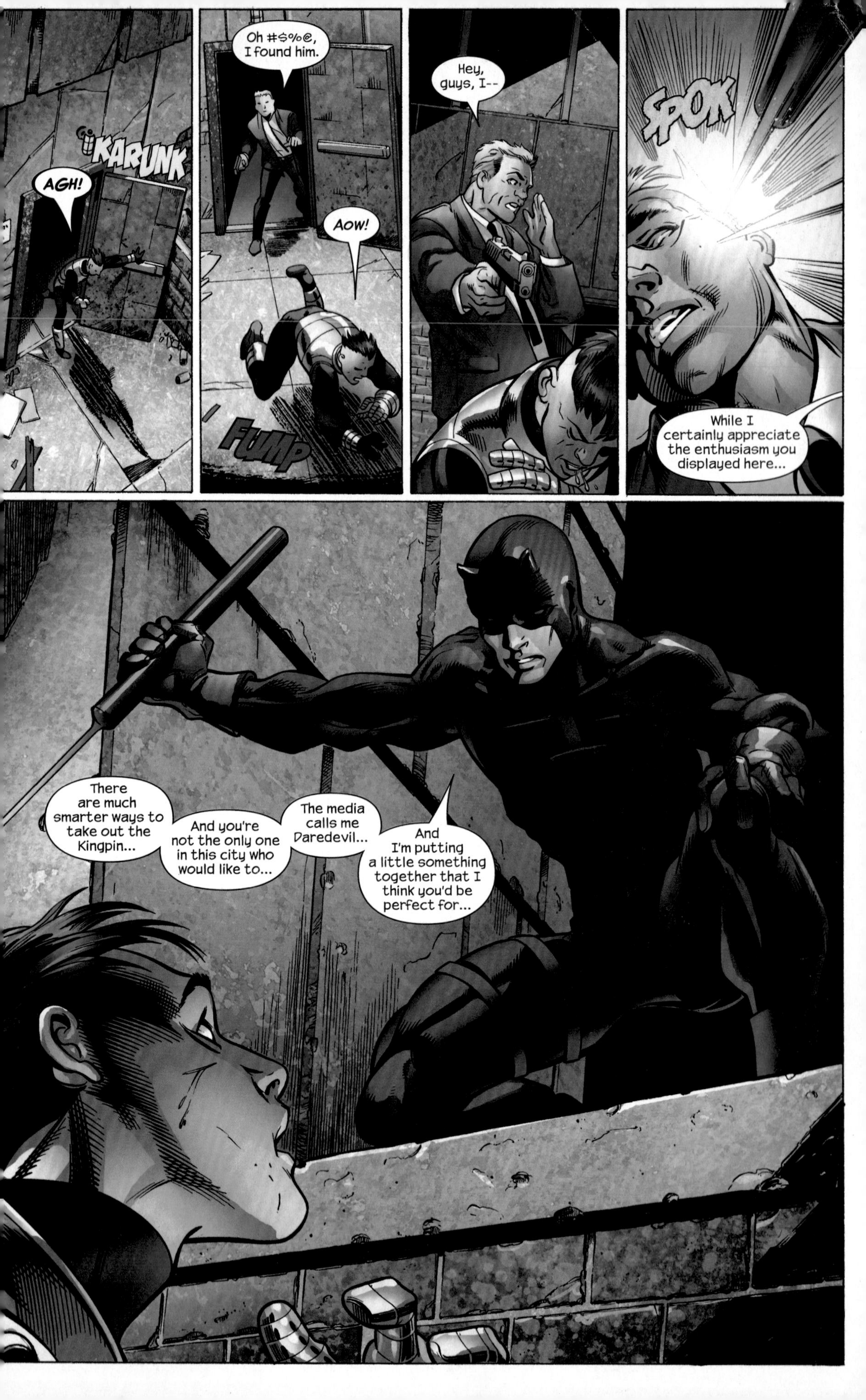
KARUNK
AGH!
Oh #$%@, I found him.
AOW!
FUMP
Hey, guys, I--
SPOK
While I certainly appreciate the enthusiasm you displayed here...
There are much smarter ways to take out the Kingpin...
And you're not the only one in this city who would like to...
The media calls me Daredevil...
And I'm putting a little something together that I think you'd be perfect for...

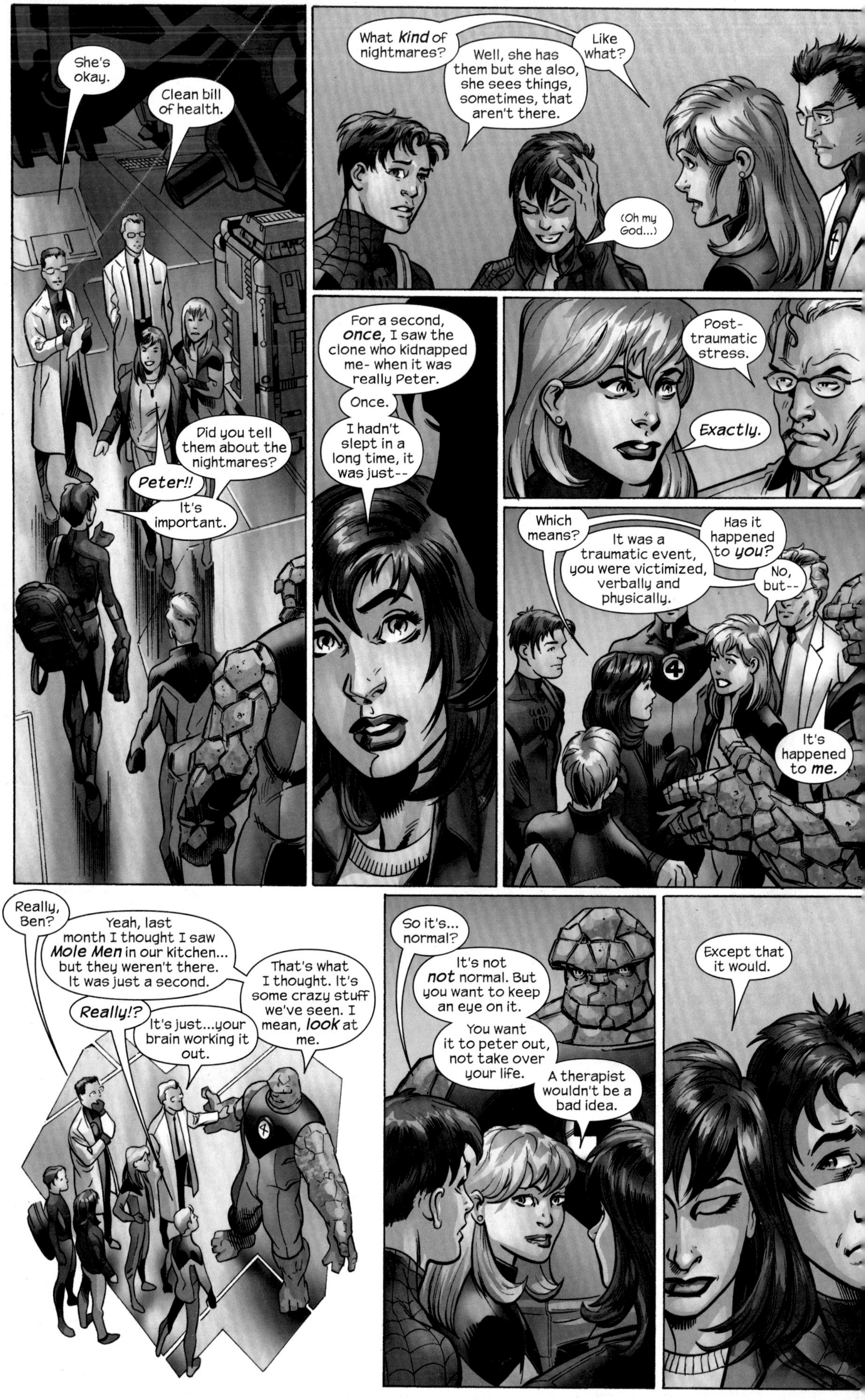
She's okay.
Clean bill of health.
Did you tell them about the nightmares?
Peter!!
It's important.
What *kind* of nightmares?
Like what?
Well, she has them but she also, she sees things, sometimes, that aren't there.
(Oh my God...)
For a second, *once,* I saw the clone who kidnapped me- when it was really Peter.
Once.
I hadn't slept in a long time, it was just--
Post-traumatic stress.
*Exactly.*
Which means?
It was a traumatic event, you were victimized, verbally and physically.
Has it happened to *you?*
No, but--
It's happened to *me.*
Really, Ben?
Yeah, last month I thought I saw *Mole Men* in our kitchen... but they weren't there. It was just a second.
That's what I thought. It's some crazy stuff we've seen. I mean, *look* at me.
*Really!?*
It's just...your brain working it out.
So it's... normal?
It's not *not* normal. But you want to keep an eye on it.
You want it to peter out, not take over your life.
A therapist wouldn't be a bad idea.
Except that it would.

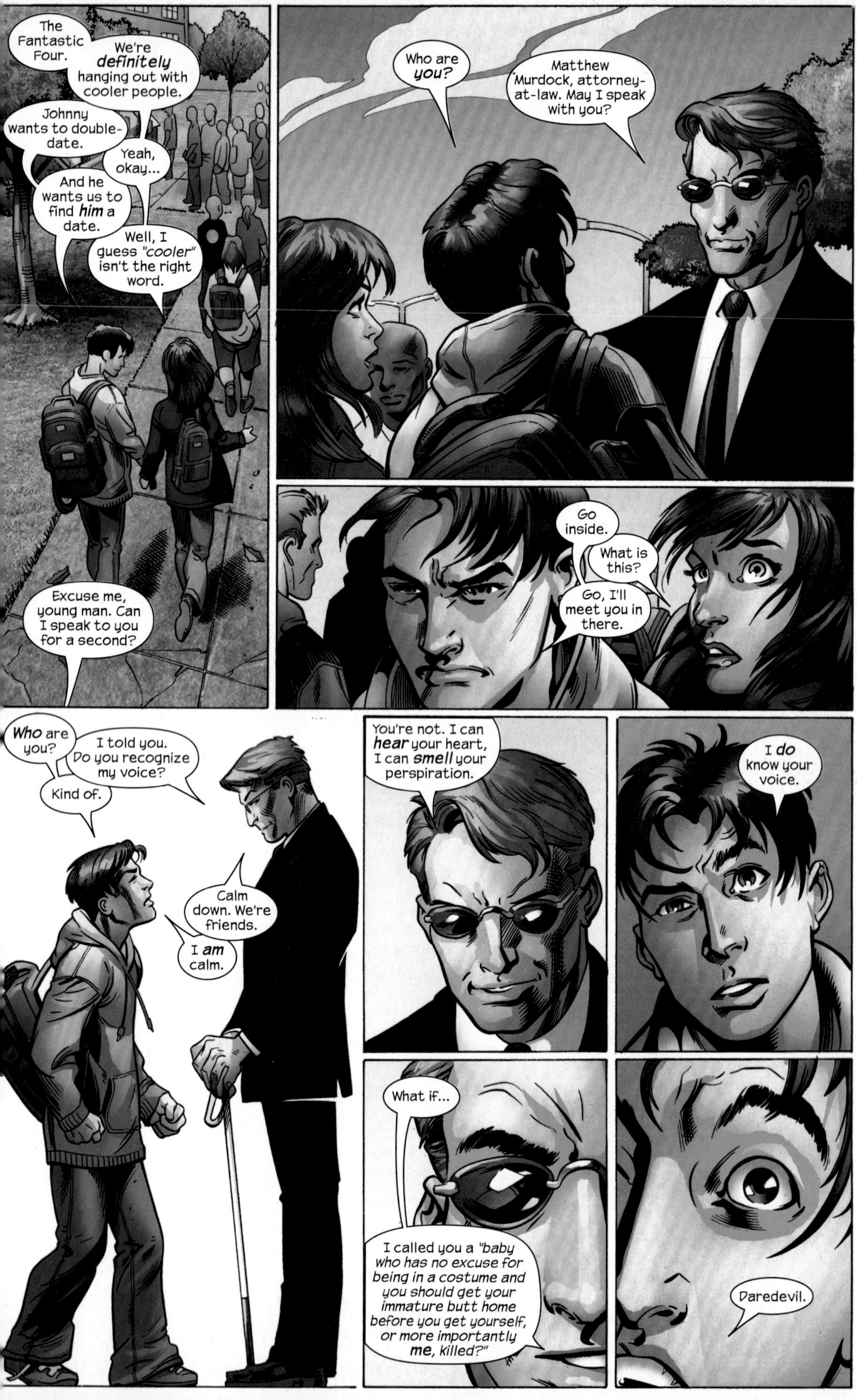
The Fantastic Four.
We're *definitely* hanging out with cooler people.
Johnny wants to double-date.
Yeah, okay...
And he wants us to find *him* a date.
Well, I guess *"cooler"* isn't the right word.
Excuse me, young man. Can I speak to you for a second?
Who are *you?*
Matthew Murdock, attorney-at-law. May I speak with you?
Go inside.
What is this?
Go, I'll meet you in there.
*Who* are you?
I told you. Do you recognize my voice?
Kind of.
Calm down. We're friends.
I *am* calm.
You're not. I can *hear* your heart, I can *smell* your perspiration.
I *do* know your voice.
What if...
*I called you a "baby who has no excuse for being in a costume and you should get your immature butt home before you get yourself, or more importantly* ***me****, killed?"*
Daredevil.

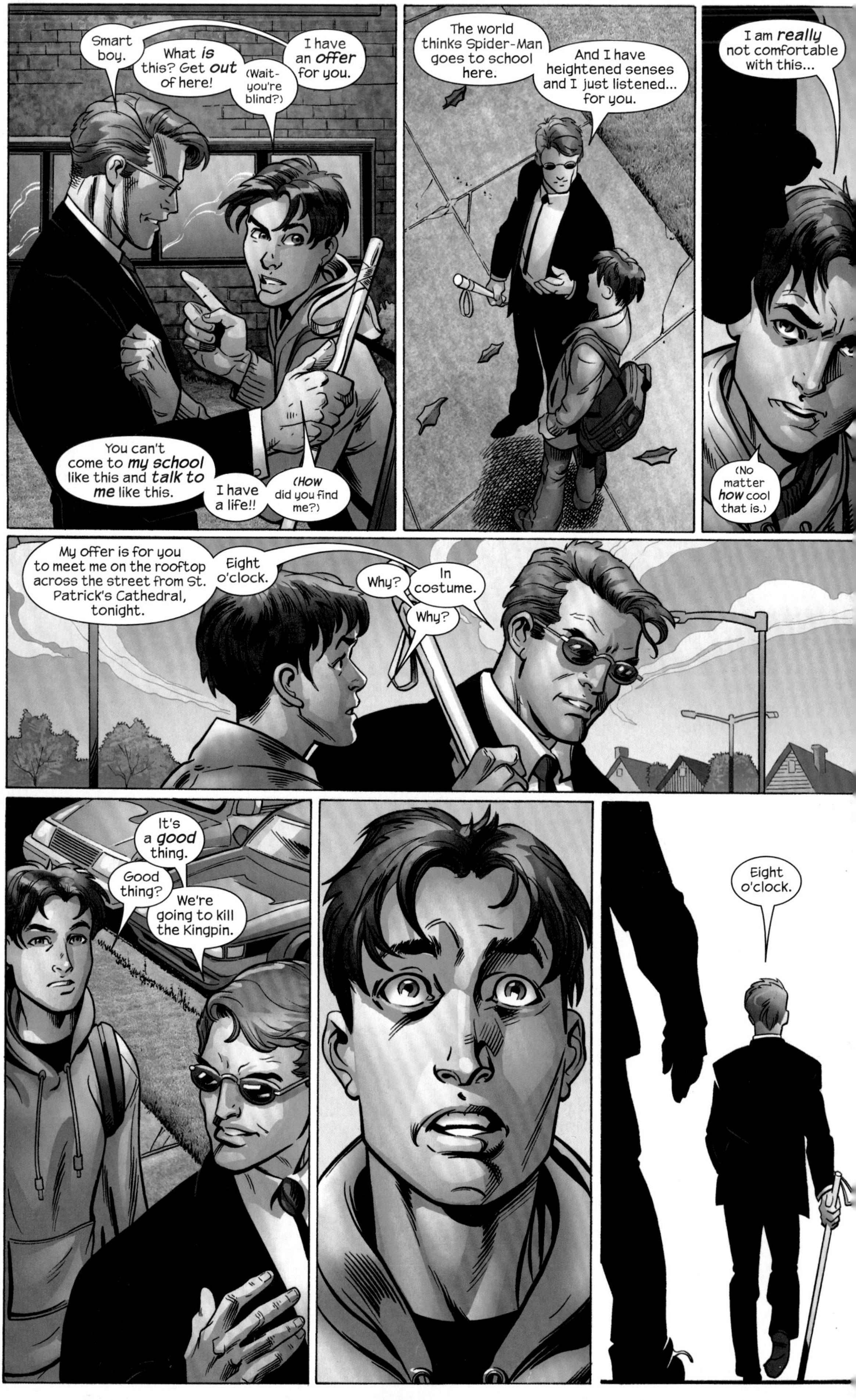
Smart boy.
What is this? Get out of here!
I have an offer for you.
(Wait- you're blind?)
You can't come to my school like this and talk to me like this.
I have a life!!
(How did you find me?)
The world thinks Spider-Man goes to school here.
And I have heightened senses and I just listened... for you.
I am really not comfortable with this...
(No matter how cool that is.)
My offer is for you to meet me on the rooftop across the street from St. Patrick's Cathedral, tonight.
Eight o'clock.
Why?
In costume.
Why?
It's a good thing.
Good thing?
We're going to kill the Kingpin.
Eight o'clock.

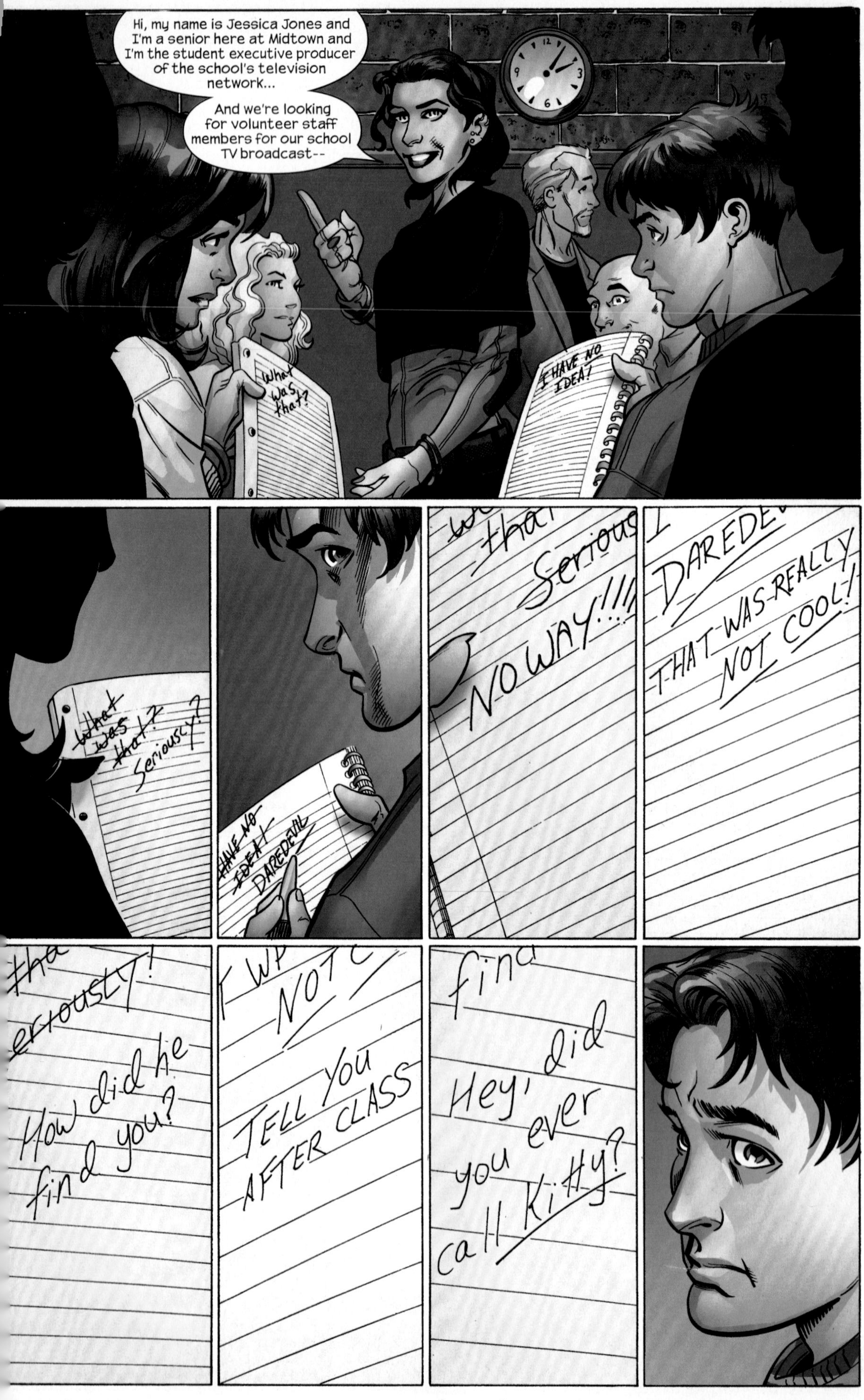

Hi, my name is Jessica Jones and I'm a senior here at Midtown and I'm the student executive producer of the school's television network...
And we're looking for volunteer staff members for our school TV broadcast--
What was that?
I HAVE NO IDEA!
Seriously?
DAREDEVIL
NO WAY!!!!
THAT WAS REALLY NOT COOL!
How did he find you?
TELL YOU AFTER CLASS
Hey, did you ever call Kitty?

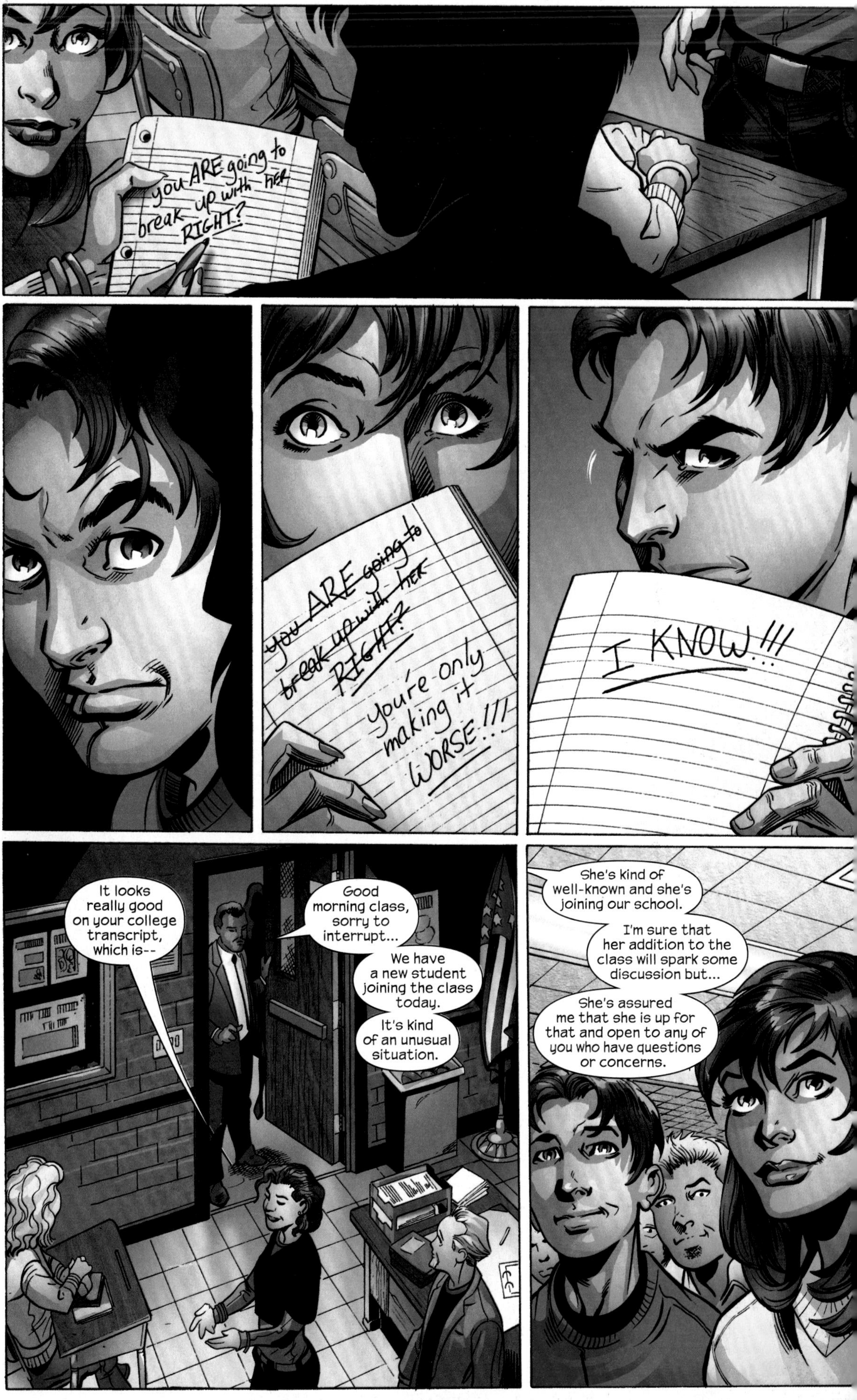
you ARE going to break up with her RIGHT?
you ARE going to break up with her RIGHT?
you're only making it WORSE!!!
I KNOW!!!
It looks really good on your college transcript, which is--
Good morning class, sorry to interrupt...
We have a new student joining the class today.
It's kind of an unusual situation.
She's kind of well-known and she's joining our school.
I'm sure that her addition to the class will spark some discussion but...
She's assured me that she is up for that and open to any of you who have questions or concerns.

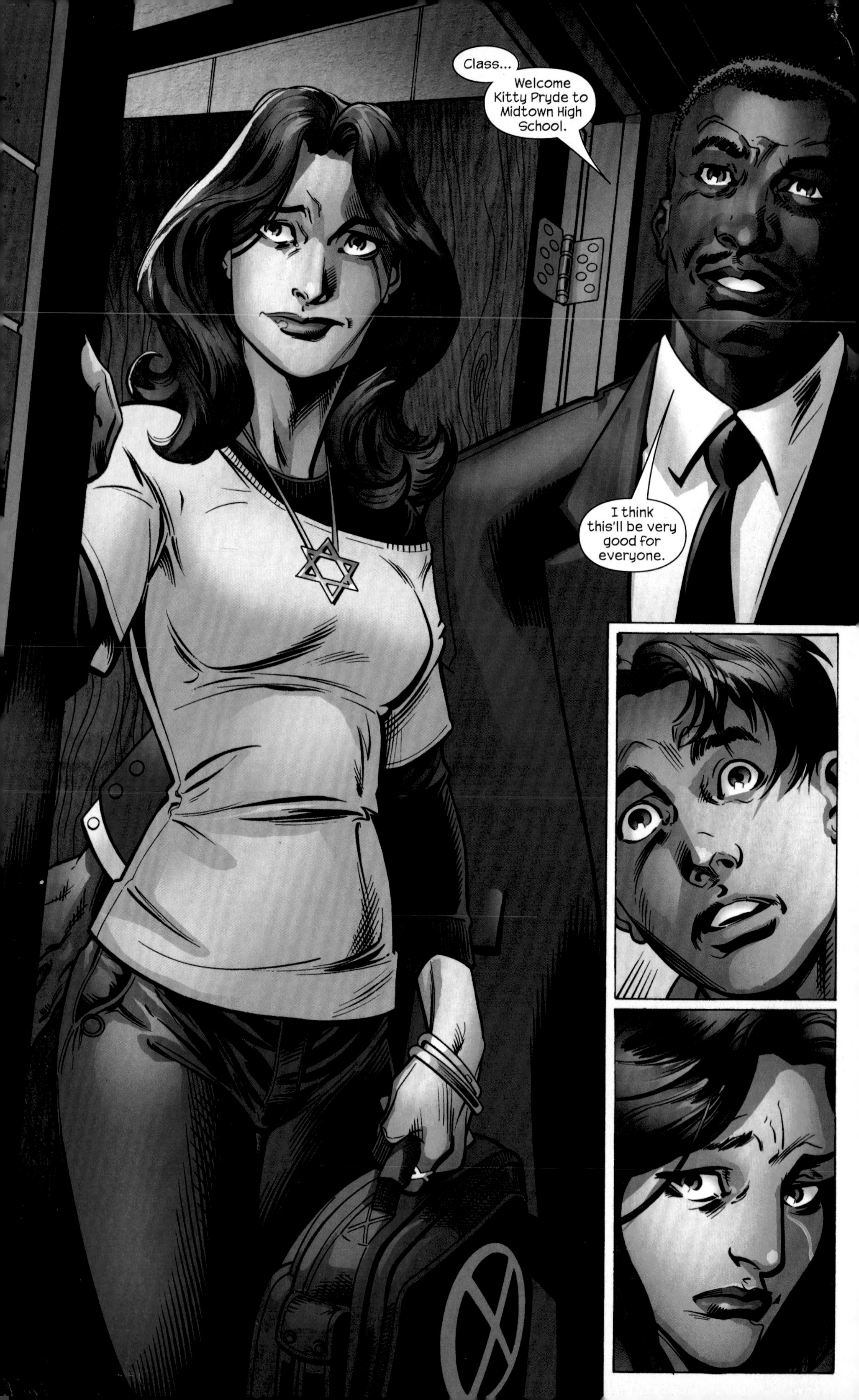
Class...
Welcome Kitty Pryde to Midtown High School.
I think this'll be very good for everyone.

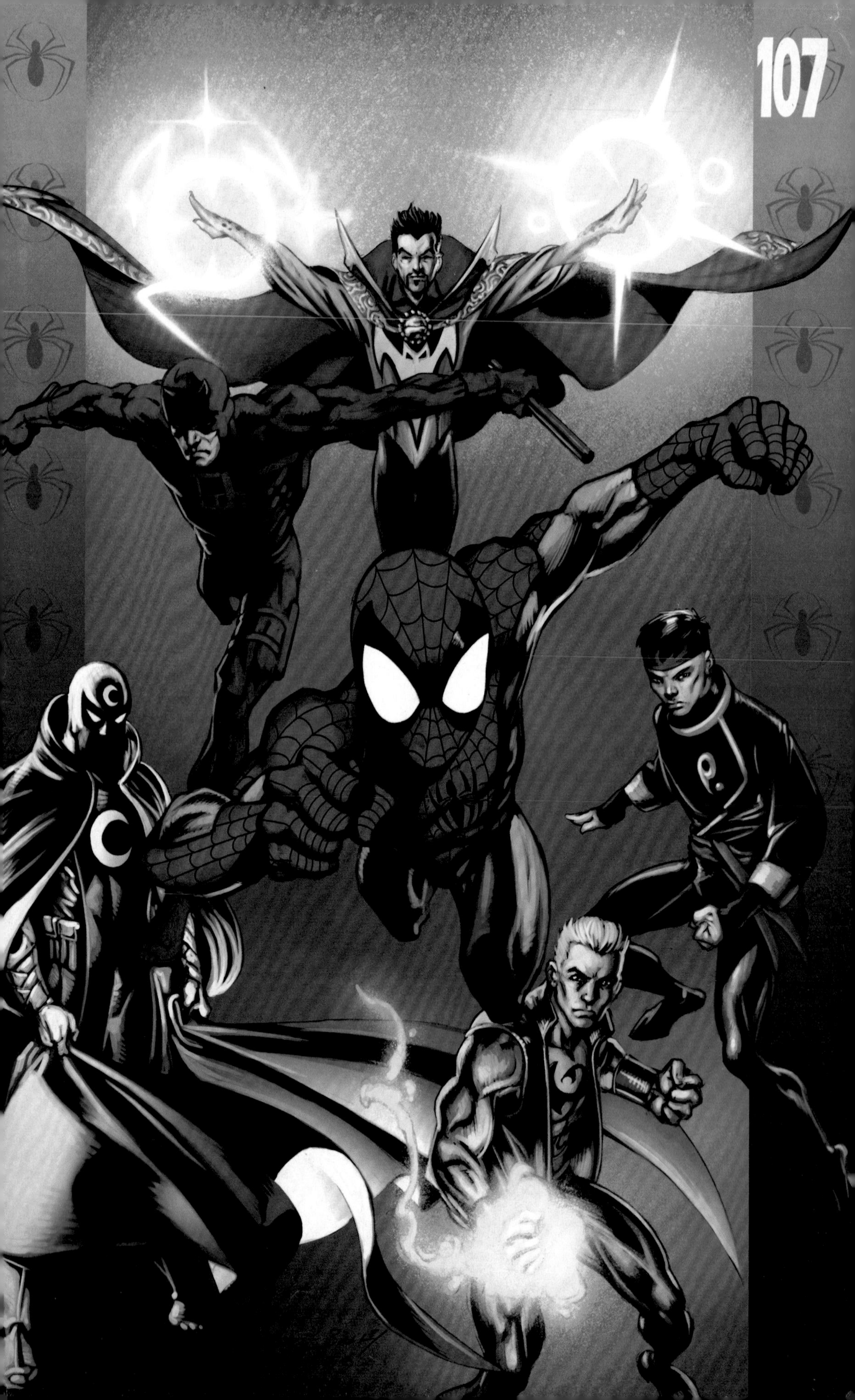
107

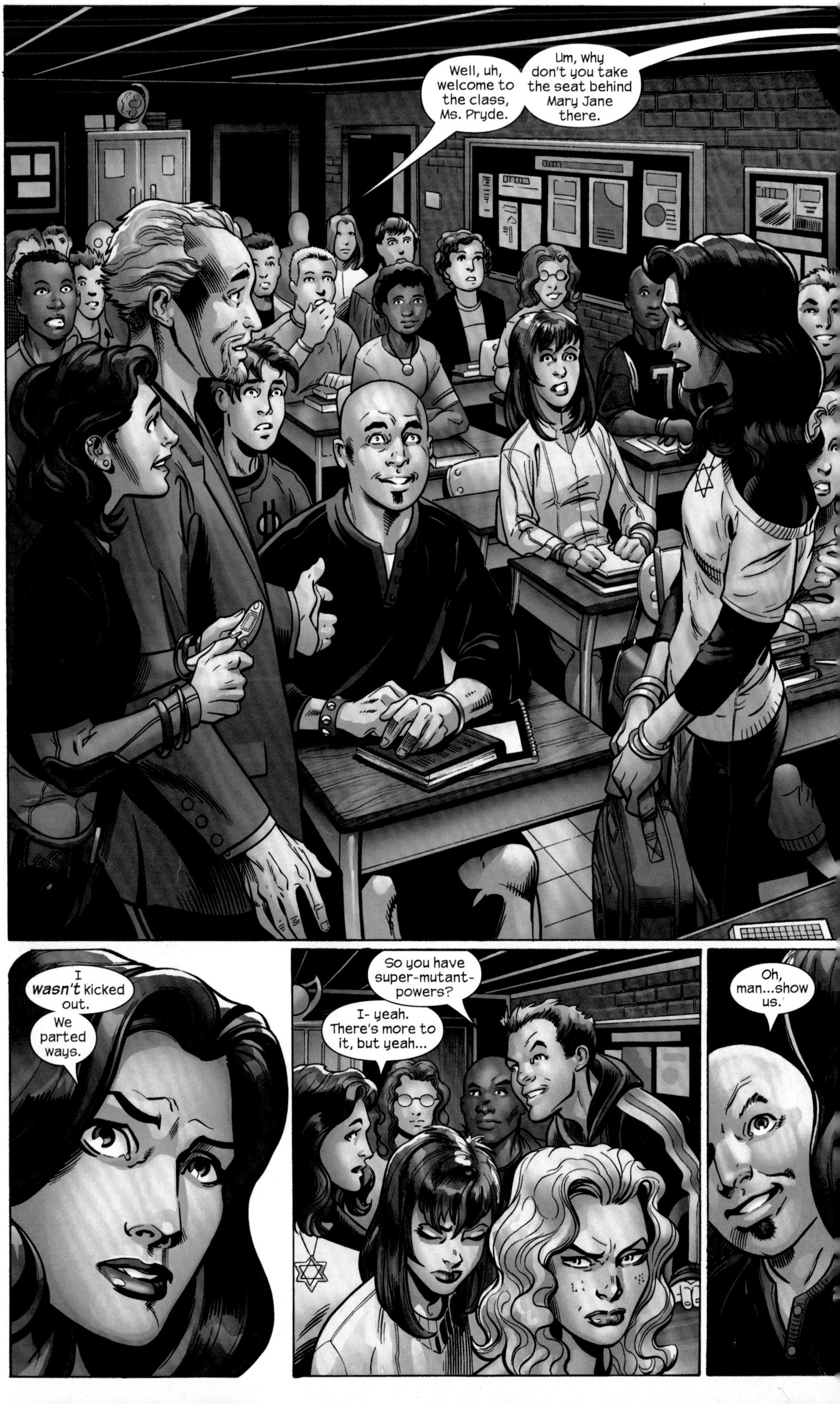
Well, uh, welcome to the class, Ms. Pryde.
Um, why don't you take the seat behind Mary Jane there.
I *wasn't* kicked out.
We parted ways.
So you have super-mutant-powers?
I- yeah. There's more to it, but yeah...
Oh, man...show us.

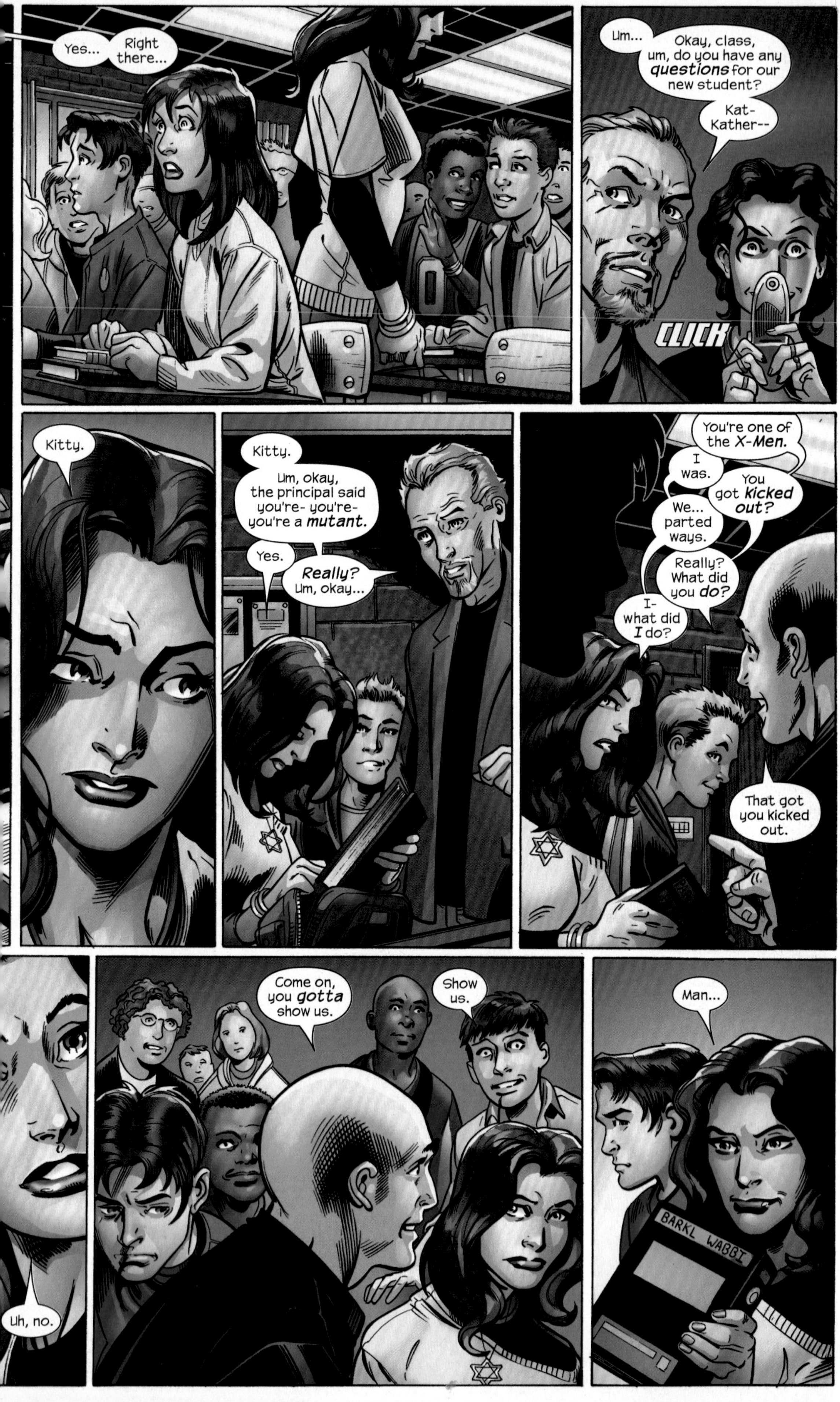
Yes...
Right there...
Um...
Okay, class, um, do you have any questions for our new student?
Kat- Kather--
CLICK
Kitty.
Kitty.
Um, okay, the principal said you're- you're- you're a mutant.
Yes.
Really? Um, okay...
You're one of the X-Men.
I was.
You got kicked out?
We... parted ways.
Really? What did you do?
I- what did I do?
That got you kicked out.
Come on, you gotta show us.
Show us.
Uh, no.
Man...
BARKL WABBI

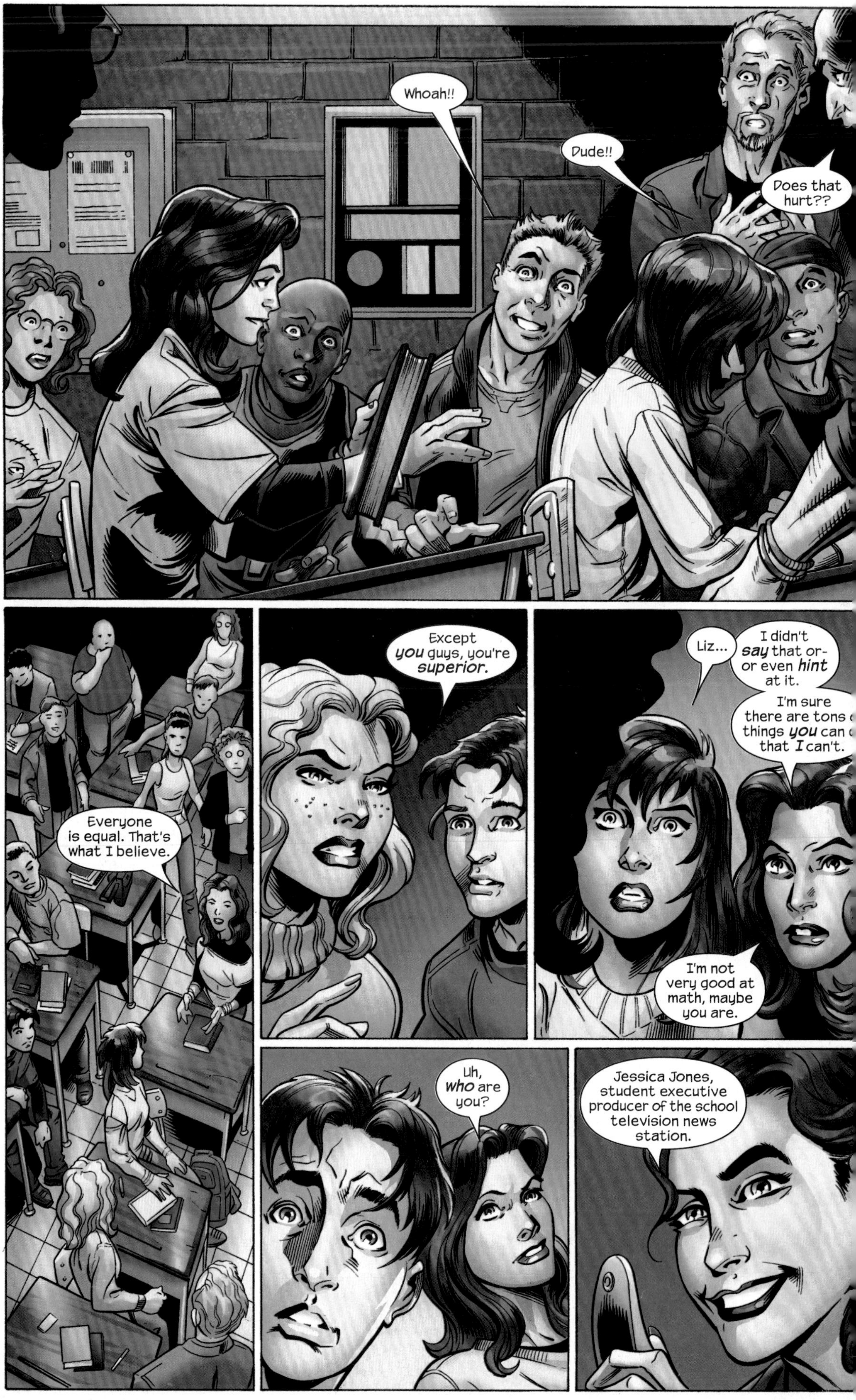

Whoah!!
Dude!!
Does that hurt??
Everyone is equal. That's what I believe.
Except *you* guys, you're *superior.*
Liz...
I didn't *say* that or- or even *hint* at it.
I'm sure there are tons things *you* can that *I* can't.
I'm not very good at math, maybe you are.
Uh, *who* are you?
Jessica Jones, student executive producer of the school television news station.

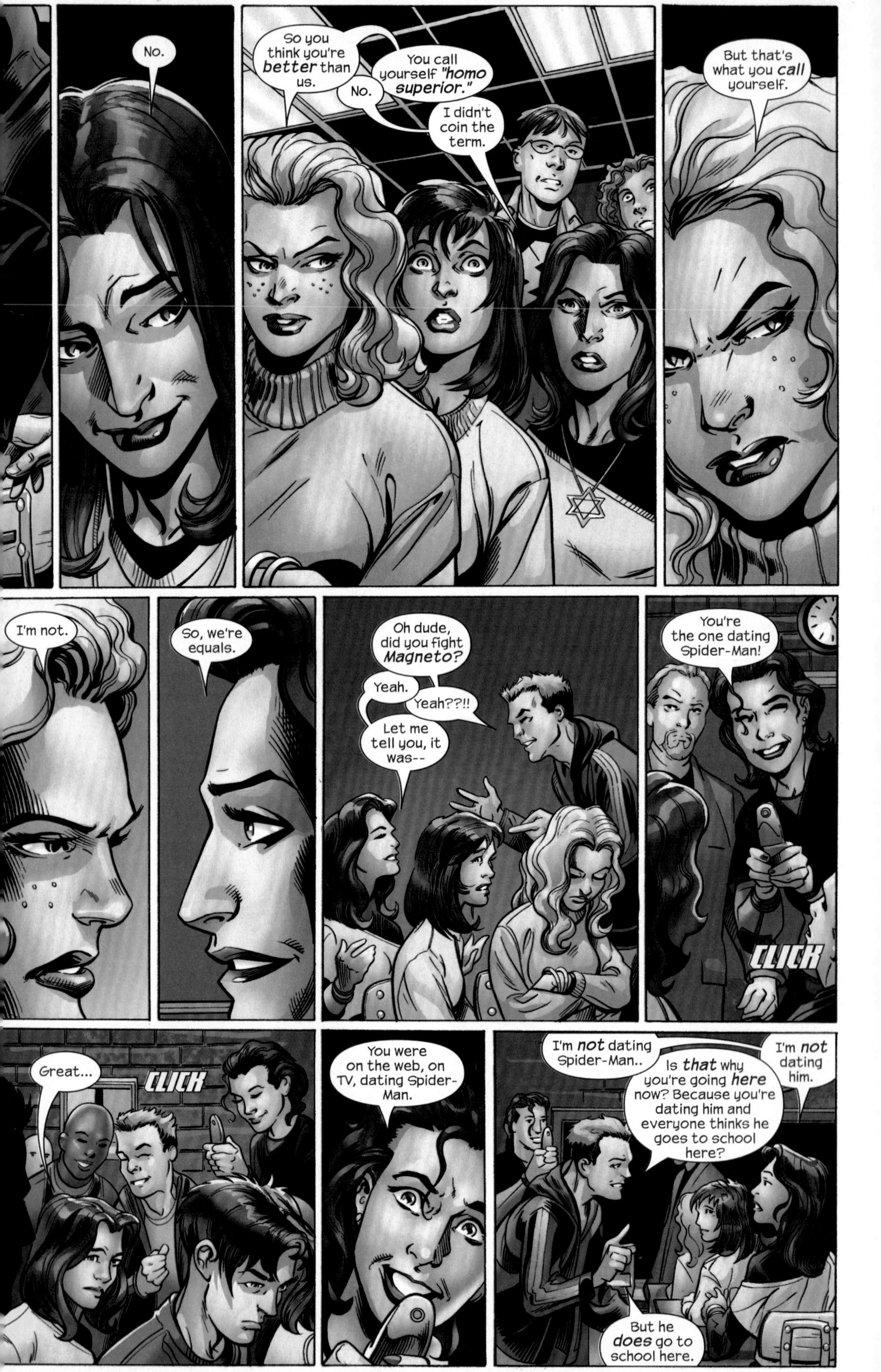
No.
So you think you're better than us.
You call yourself "homo superior."
No.
I didn't coin the term.
But that's what you call yourself.
I'm not.
So, we're equals.
Oh dude, did you fight Magneto?
Yeah.
Yeah??!!
Let me tell you, it was--
You're the one dating Spider-Man!
CLICK
Great...
CLICK
You were on the web, on TV, dating Spider-Man.
I'm not dating Spider-Man..
Is that why you're going here now? Because you're dating him and everyone thinks he goes to school here?
I'm not dating him.
But he does go to school here.

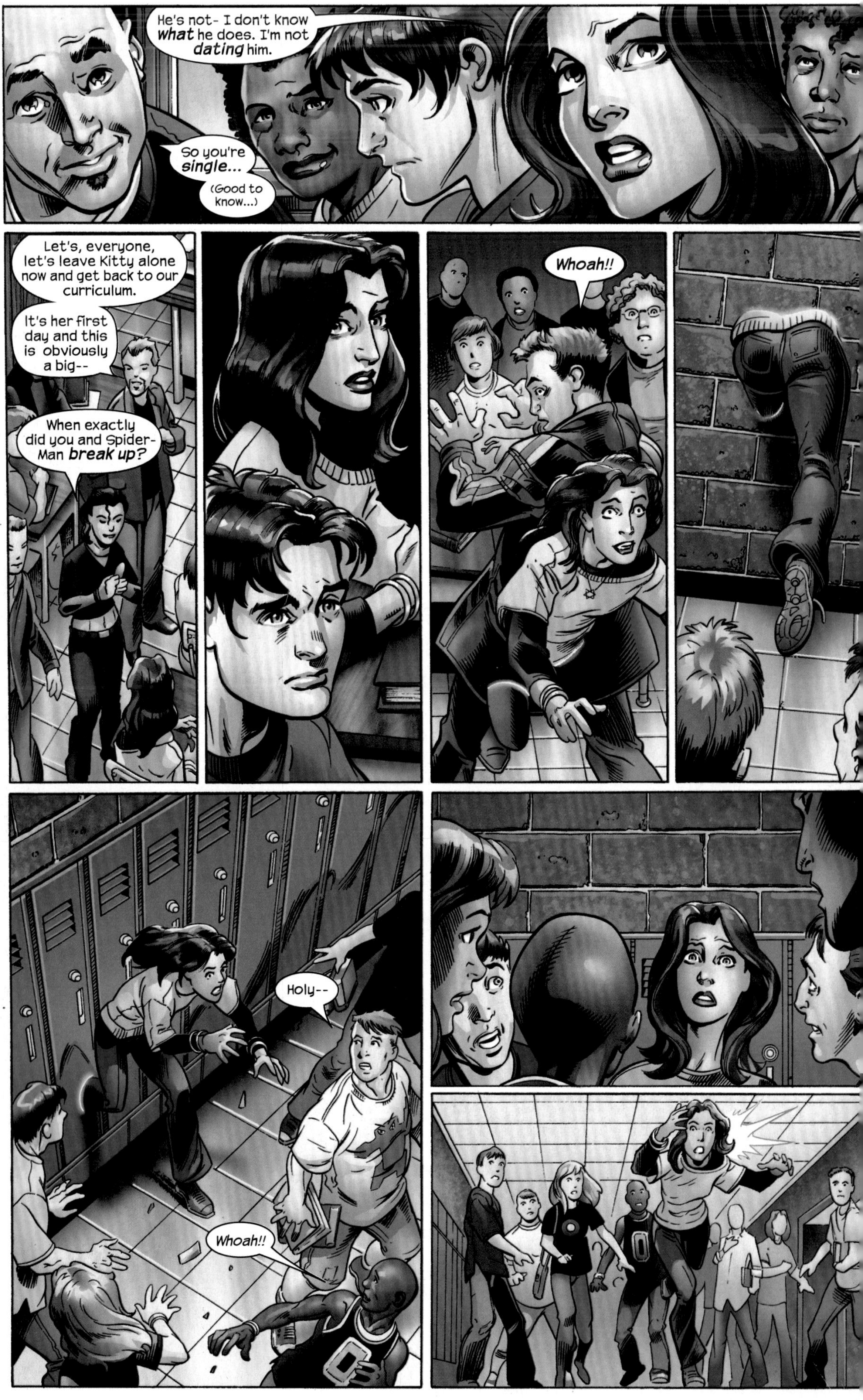
He's not- I don't know *what* he does. I'm not *dating* him.
So you're *single*...
(Good to know...)
Let's, everyone, let's leave Kitty alone now and get back to our curriculum.
It's her first day and this is obviously a big--
When exactly did you and Spider-Man *break up?*
*Whoah!!*
Holy--
*Whoah!!*

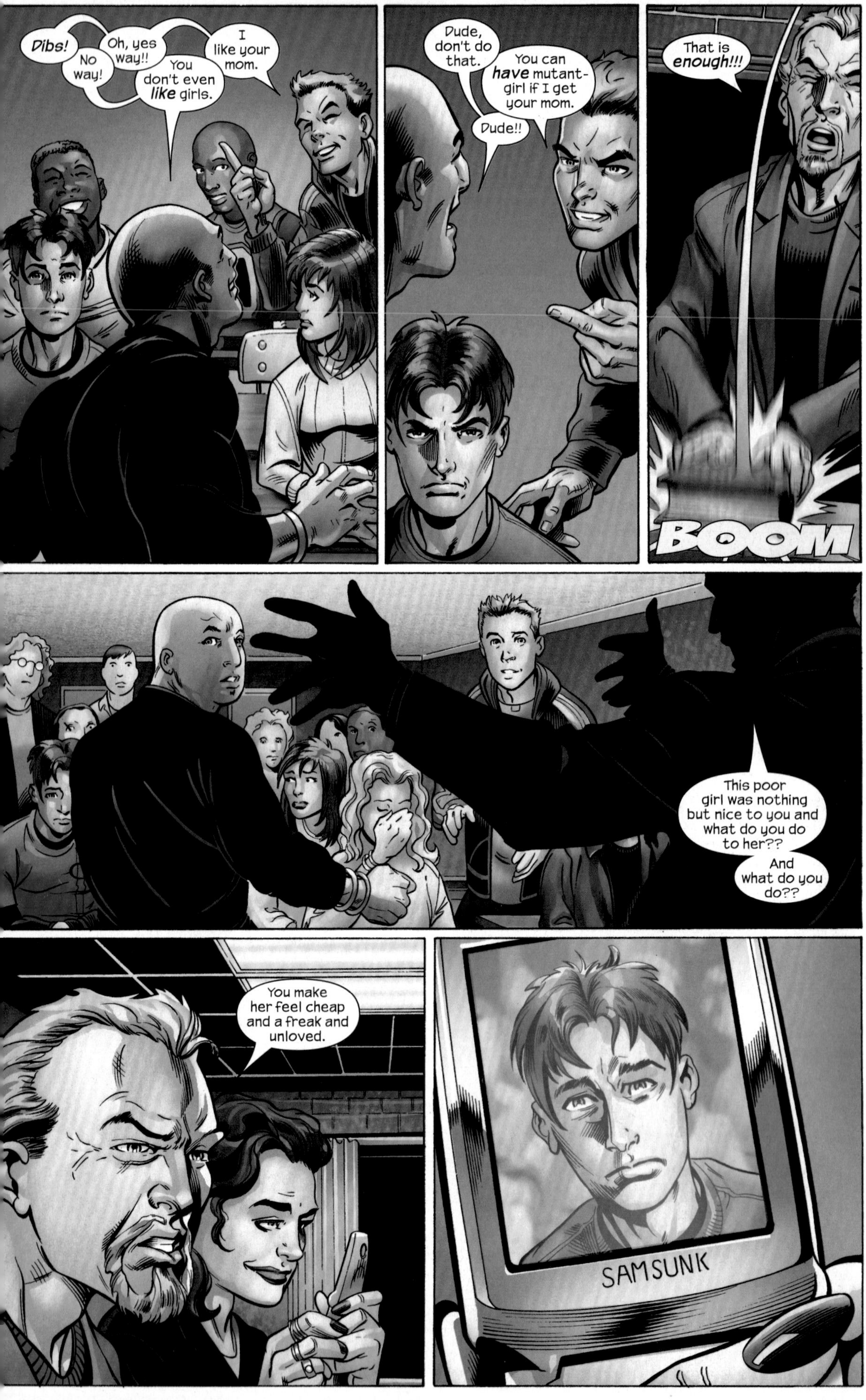
Dibs!
No way!
Oh, yes way!!
You don't even like girls.
I like your mom.
Dude, don't do that.
You can have mutant-girl if I get your mom.
Dude!!
That is enough!!!
BOOM
This poor girl was nothing but nice to you and what do you do to her??
And what do you do??
You make her feel cheap and a freak and unloved.
SAMSUNK

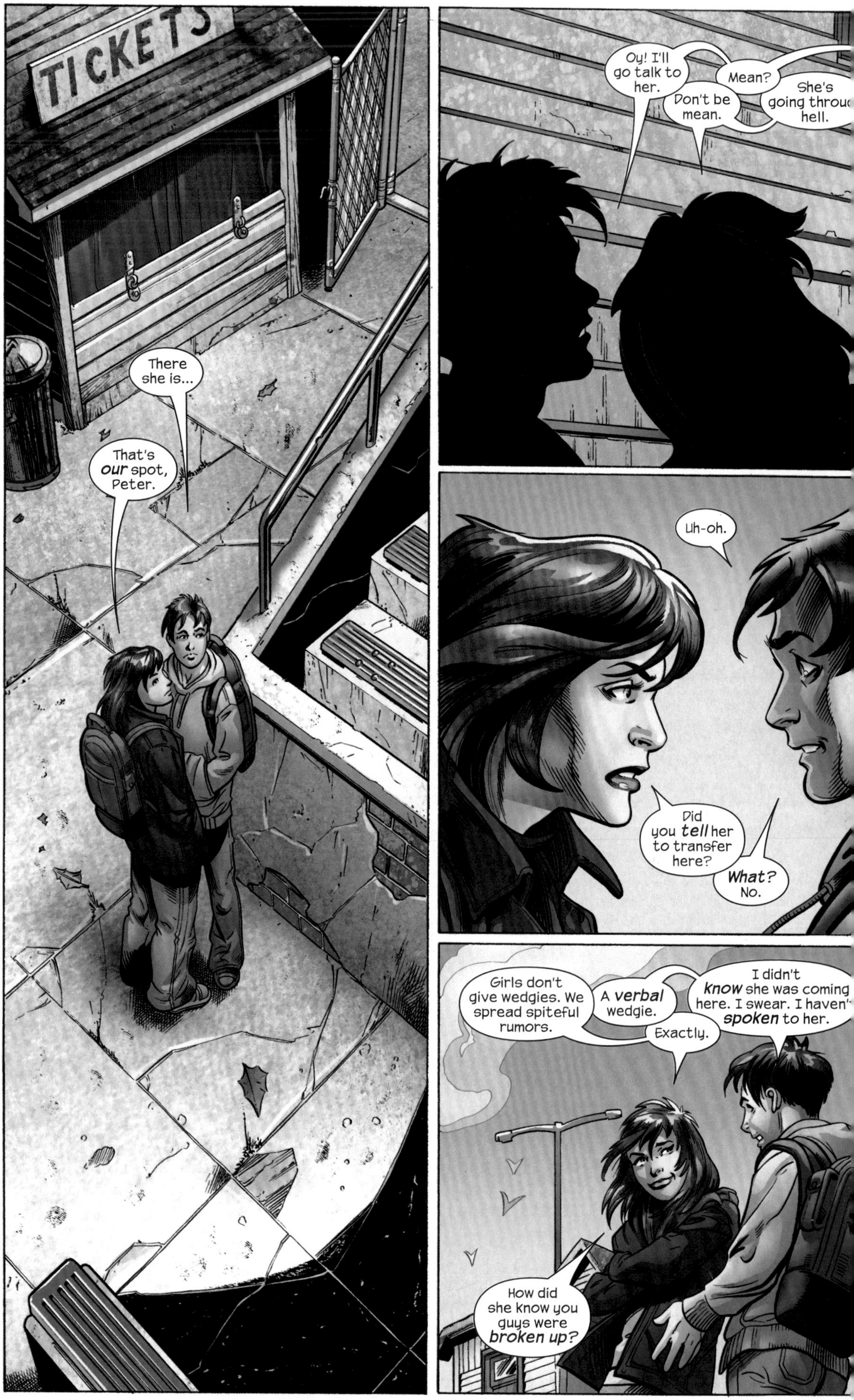
TICKETS
There she is...
That's our spot, Peter.
Oy! I'll go talk to her.
Don't be mean.
Mean?
She's going throu hell.
Uh-oh.
Did you tell her to transfer here?
What? No.
Girls don't give wedgies. We spread spiteful rumors.
A verbal wedgie.
Exactly.
I didn't know she was coming here. I swear. I haven't spoken to her.
How did she know you guys were broken up?

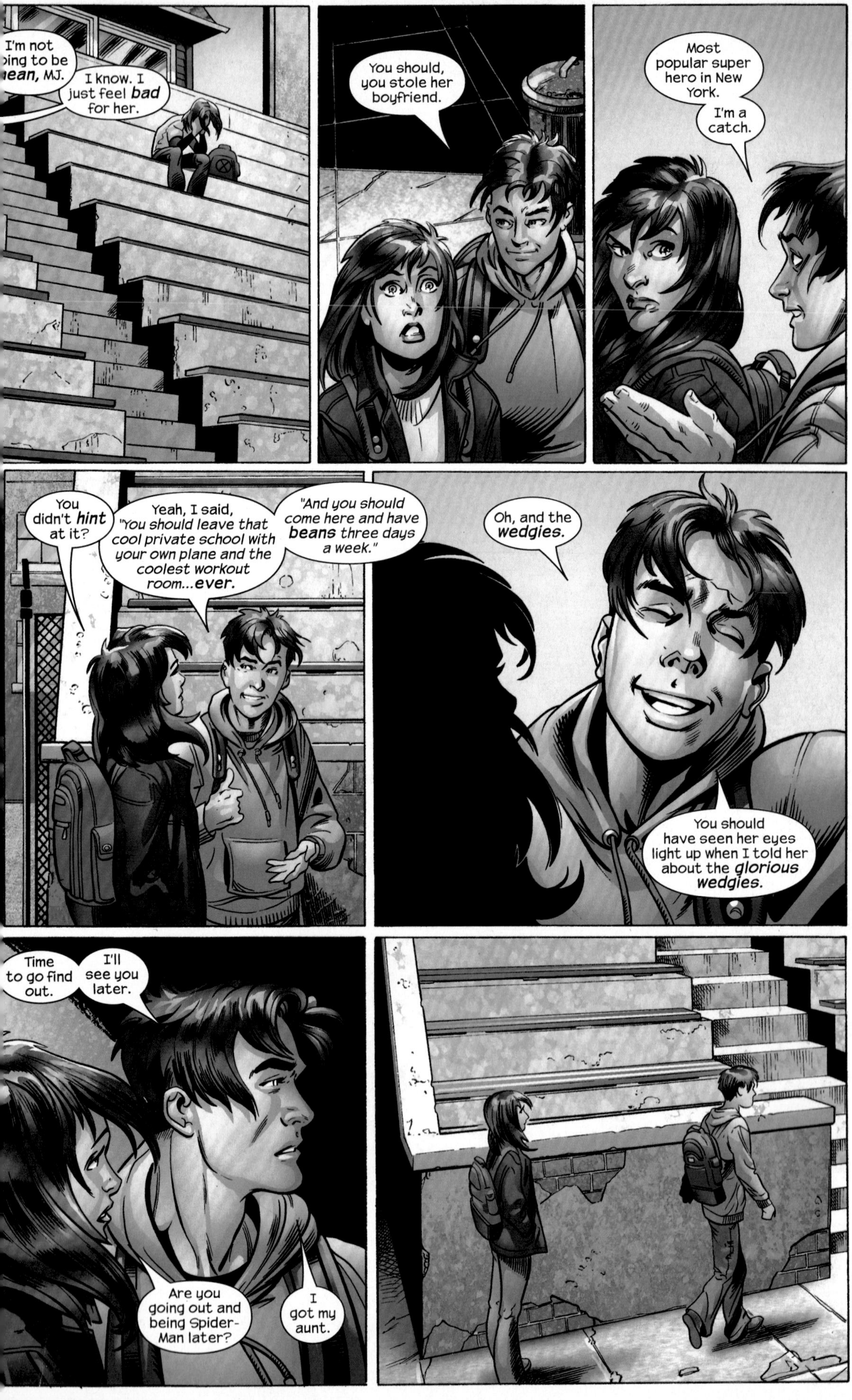
I'm not
oing to be
ean, MJ.
I know. I just feel bad for her.
You should, you stole her boyfriend.
Most popular super hero in New York.
I'm a catch.
You didn't hint at it?
Yeah, I said, "You should leave that cool private school with your own plane and the coolest workout room...ever.
"And you should come here and have beans three days a week."
Oh, and the wedgies.
You should have seen her eyes light up when I told her about the glorious wedgies.
Time to go find out.
I'll see you later.
Are you going out and being Spider-Man later?
I got my aunt.

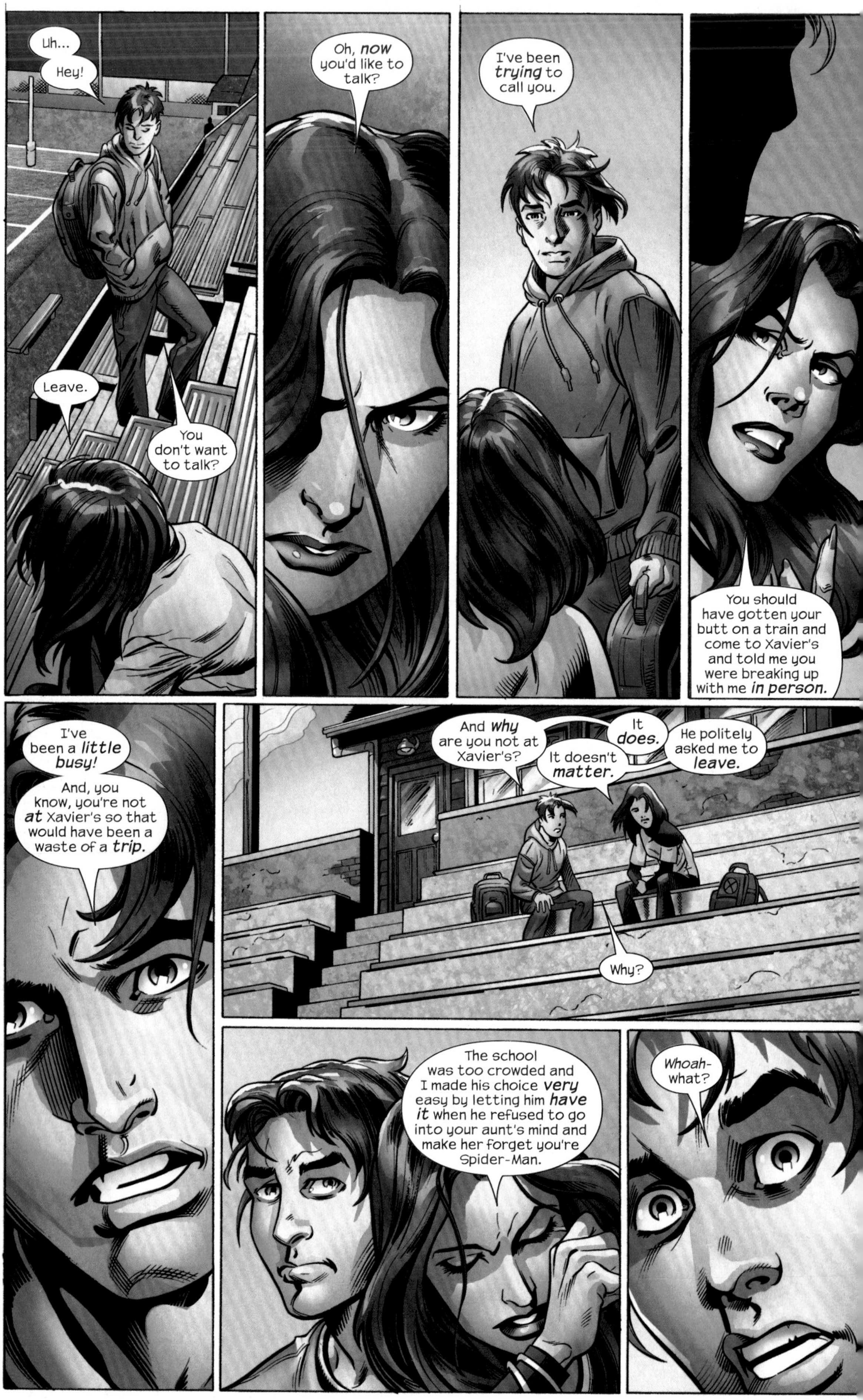
Uh...
Hey!
Leave.
You don't want to talk?
Oh, *now* you'd like to talk?
I've been *trying* to call you.
You should have gotten your butt on a train and come to Xavier's and told me you were breaking up with me *in person.*
I've been a *little busy!*
And, you know, you're not *at* Xavier's so that would have been a waste of a *trip.*
And *why* are you not at Xavier's?
It doesn't *matter.*
It *does.*
He politely asked me to *leave.*
Why?
The school was too crowded and I made his choice *very* easy by letting him *have it* when he refused to go into your aunt's mind and make her forget you're Spider-Man.
Whoah-what?

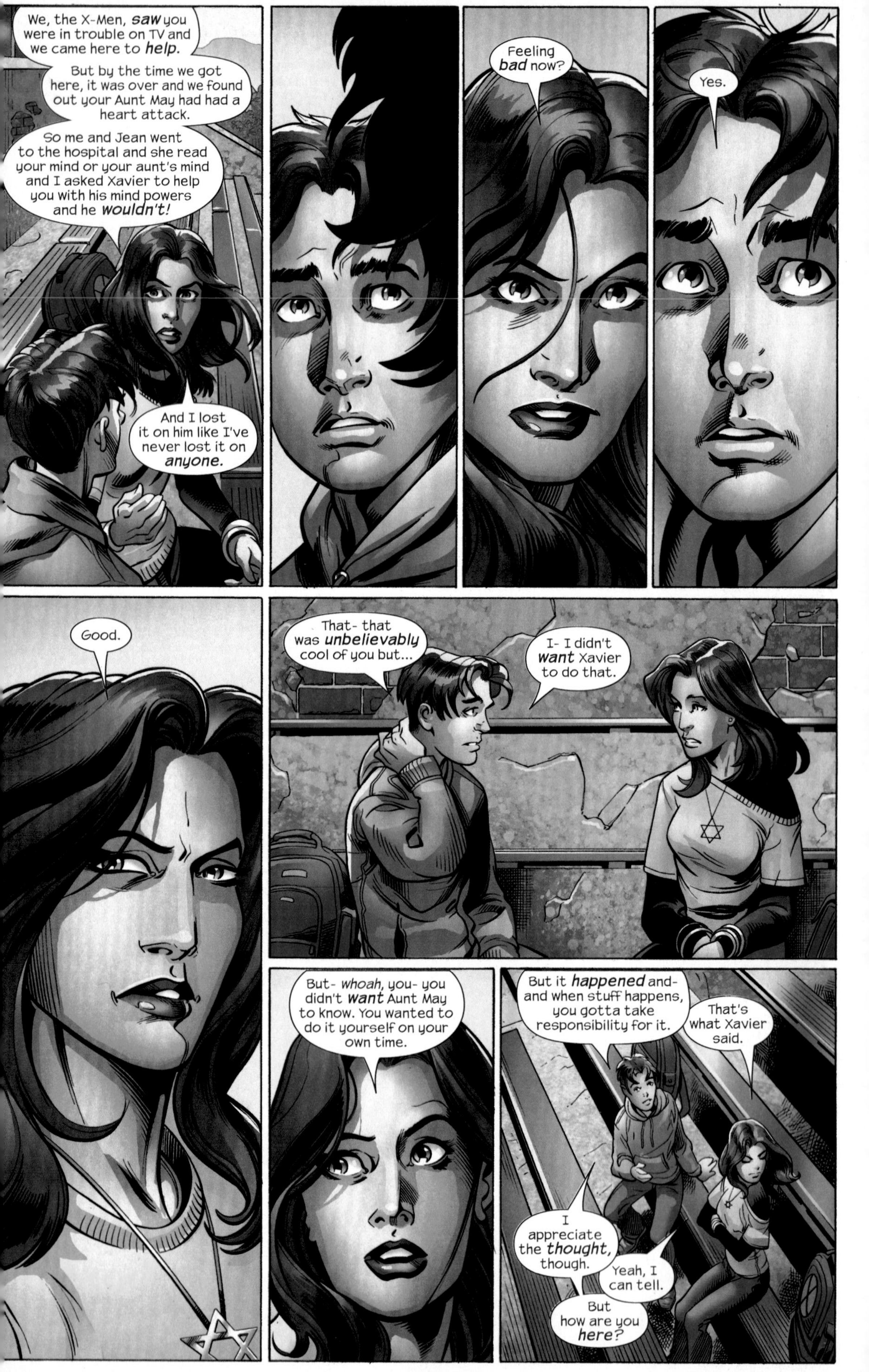

We, the X-Men, *saw* you were in trouble on TV and we came here to *help.*
But by the time we got here, it was over and we found out your Aunt May had had a heart attack.
So me and Jean went to the hospital and she read your mind or your aunt's mind and I asked Xavier to help you with his mind powers and he *wouldn't!*
And I lost it on him like I've never lost it on *anyone.*
Feeling *bad* now?
Yes.
Good.
That- that was *unbelievably* cool of you but...
I- I didn't *want* Xavier to do that.
But- *whoah,* you- you didn't *want* Aunt May to know. You wanted to do it yourself on your own time.
But it *happened* and- and when stuff happens, you gotta take responsibility for it.
That's what Xavier said.
I appreciate the *thought,* though.
Yeah, I can tell.
But how are you *here?*

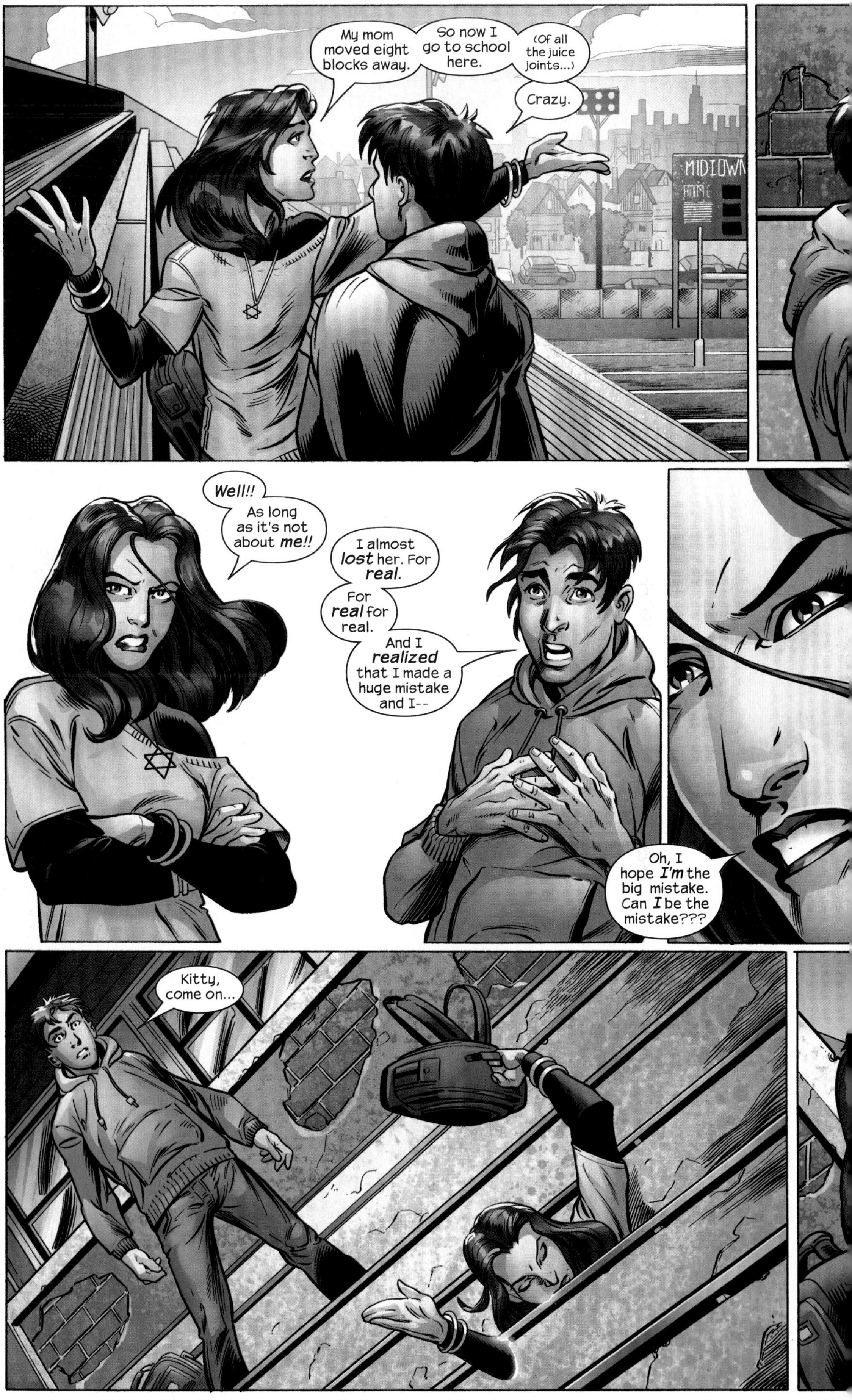
My mom moved eight blocks away.
So now I go to school here.
(Of all the juice joints...)
Crazy.
MIDTOWN
HOME
Well!!
As long as it's not about *me!!*
I almost *lost* her. For *real*.
For *real* for real.
And I *realized* that I made a huge mistake and I--
Oh, I hope *I'm* the big mistake. Can *I* be the mistake???
Kitty, come on...

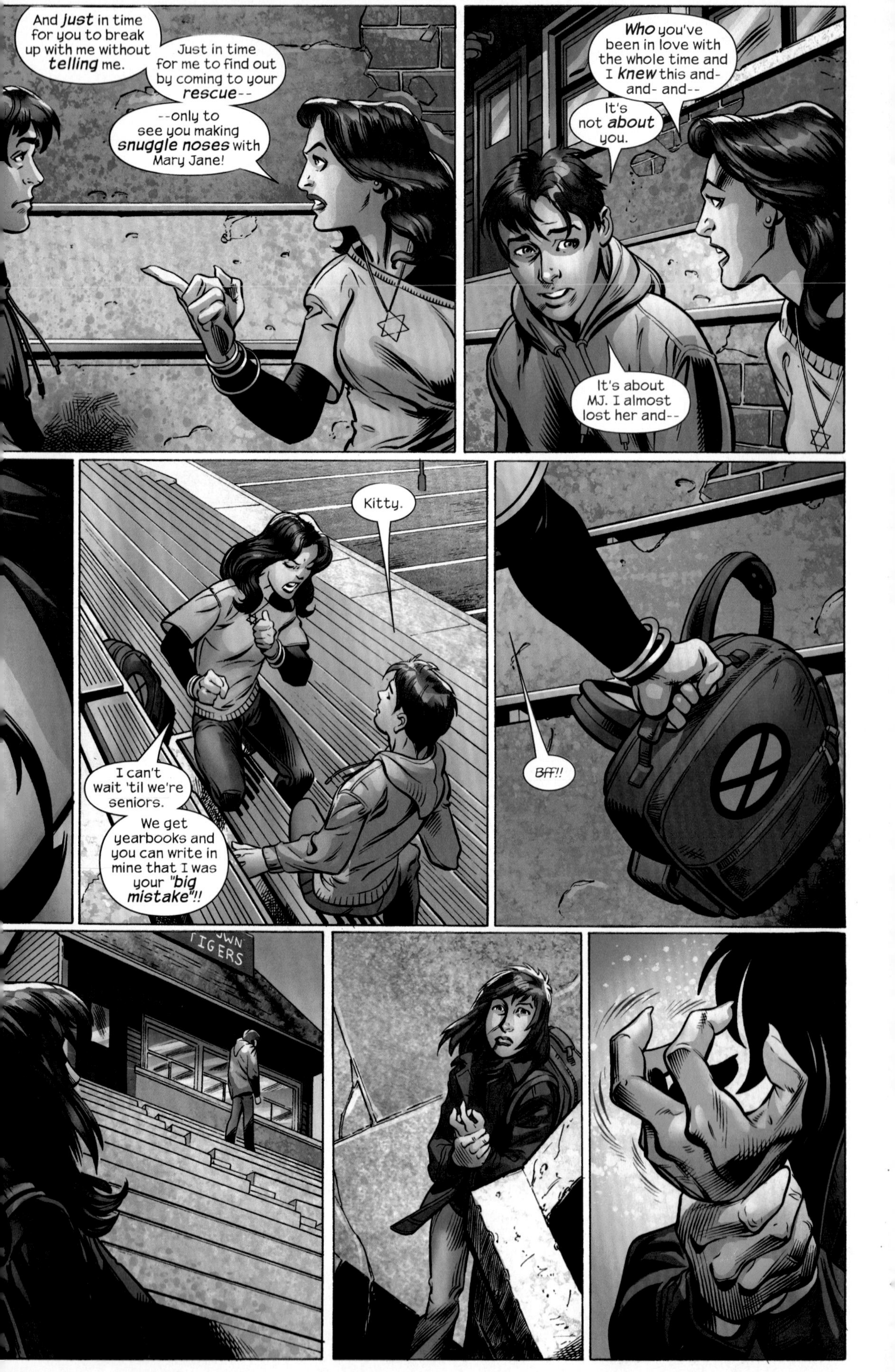
And just in time for you to break up with me without telling me.
Just in time for me to find out by coming to your rescue--
--only to see you making snuggle noses with Mary Jane!
Who you've been in love with the whole time and I knew this and- and- and--
It's not about you.
It's about MJ. I almost lost her and--
Kitty.
I can't wait 'til we're seniors.
We get yearbooks and you can write in mine that I was your "big mistake"!!
BFF!!
TIGERS

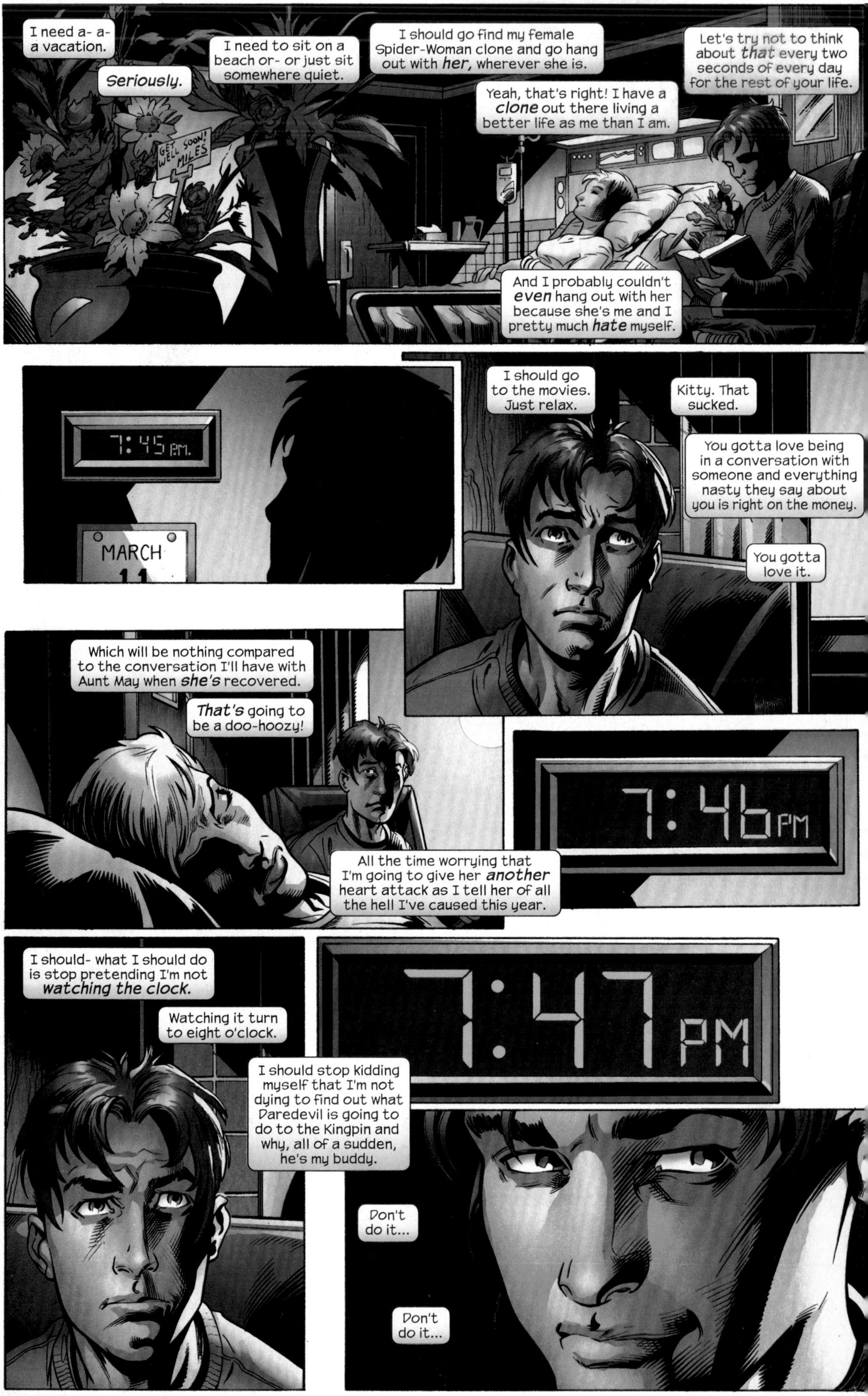
I need a- a-
a vacation.
Seriously.
I need to sit on a beach or- or just sit somewhere quiet.
I should go find my female Spider-Woman clone and go hang out with her, wherever she is.
Yeah, that's right! I have a clone out there living a better life as me than I am.
Let's try not to think about that every two seconds of every day for the rest of your life.
And I probably couldn't even hang out with her because she's me and I pretty much hate myself.
GET WELL SOON! MILES
7:45 P.M.
MARCH
I should go to the movies. Just relax.
Kitty. That sucked.
You gotta love being in a conversation with someone and everything nasty they say about you is right on the money.
You gotta love it.
Which will be nothing compared to the conversation I'll have with Aunt May when she's recovered.
That's going to be a doo-hoozy!
7:46 PM
All the time worrying that I'm going to give her another heart attack as I tell her of all the hell I've caused this year.
I should- what I should do is stop pretending I'm not watching the clock.
Watching it turn to eight o'clock.
7:47 PM
I should stop kidding myself that I'm not dying to find out what Daredevil is going to do to the Kingpin and why, all of a sudden, he's my buddy.
Don't do it...
Don't do it...

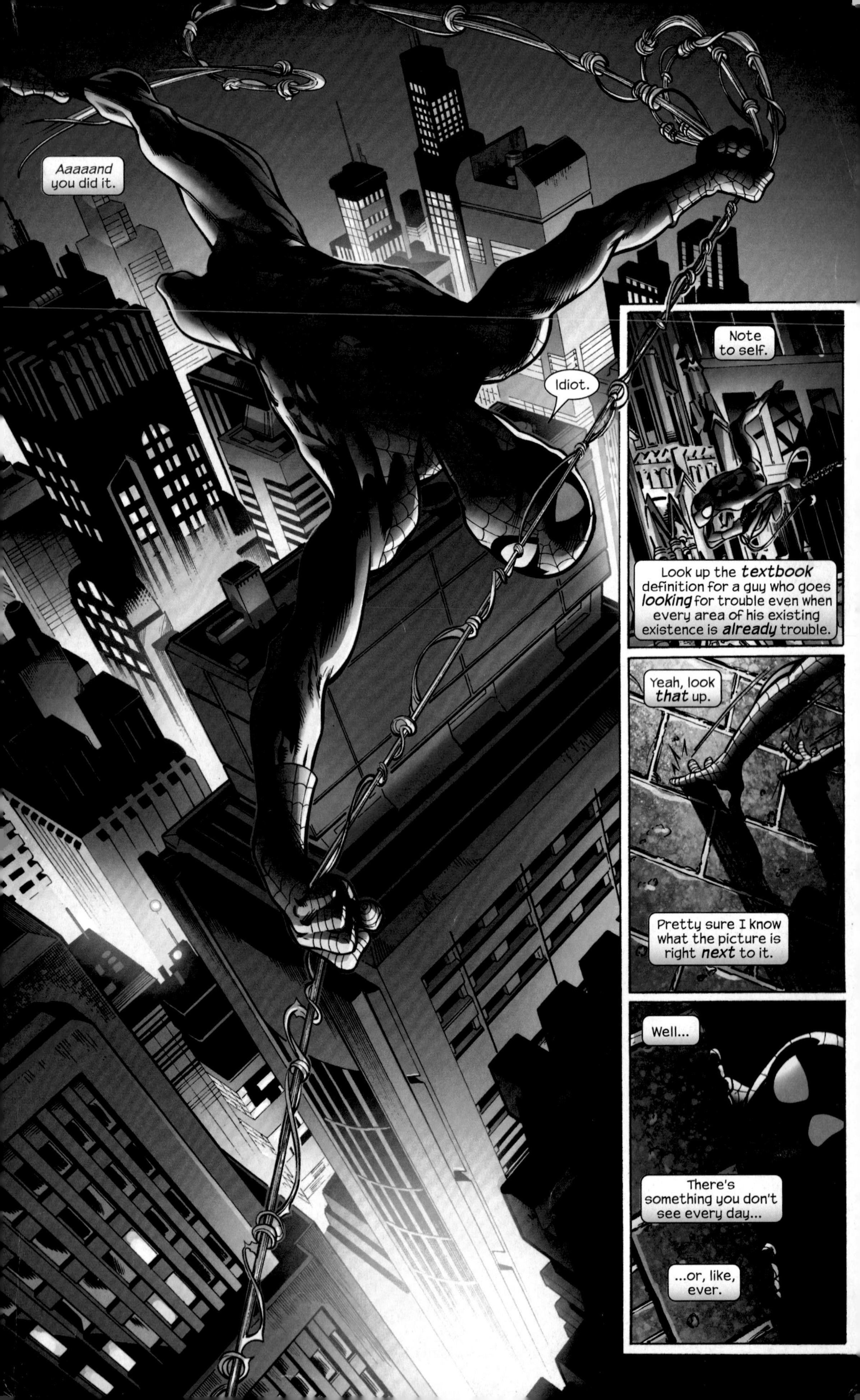
Aaaaand you did it.
Idiot.
Note to self.
Look up the *textbook* definition for a guy who goes *looking* for trouble even when every area of his existing existence is *already* trouble.
Yeah, look *that* up.
Pretty sure I know what the picture is right *next* to it.
Well...
There's something you don't see every day...
...or, like, ever.

A rooftop full of crazy people!

A rooftop full of people I've never had *anything* but nightmare run-ins with in the past...

Hmmm...

That's Doctor Strange, magician. Guy's on TV more than he sleeps.

Iron Fist. Don't know anything about him other than, you know, his iron fist and he hangs out with...

Shang-Chi. Master of Kung Fu. That guy's pretty cool, actually.

Oh, and there's Moon Knight, who I'm pretty sure is genuinely crazy.

And I'm not just making that presumption based on the costume.

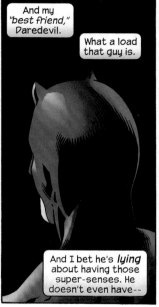

And my *"best friend,"* Daredevil.

What a load that guy is.

And I bet he's *lying* about having those super-senses. He doesn't even have--

Okay, he *has* super-senses.

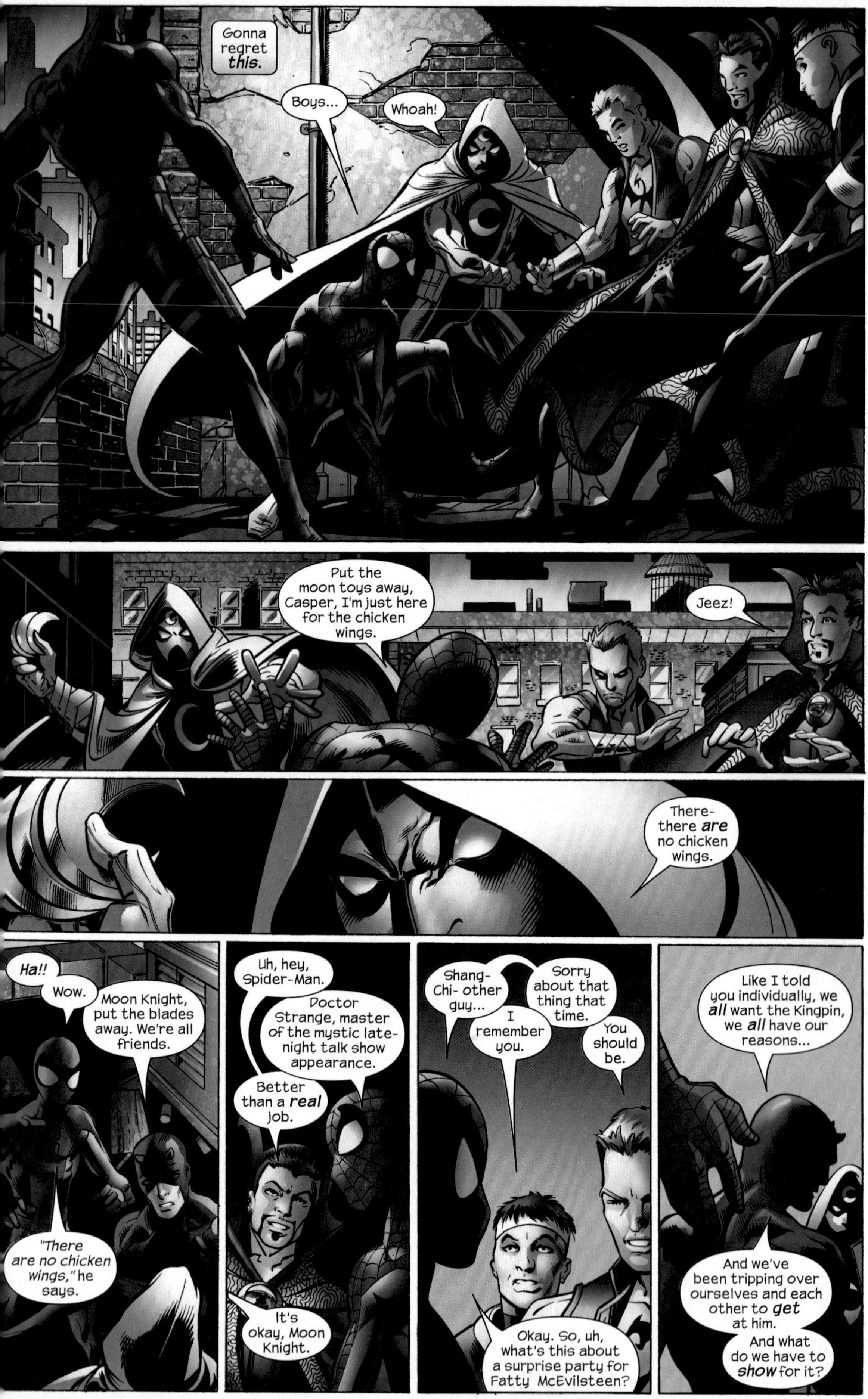
Gonna regret this.
Boys...
Whoah!
Put the moon toys away, Casper, I'm just here for the chicken wings.
Jeez!
There- there are no chicken wings.
Ha!!
Wow.
Moon Knight, put the blades away. We're all friends.
"There are no chicken wings," he says.
Uh, hey, Spider-Man.
Doctor Strange, master of the mystic late-night talk show appearance.
Better than a real job.
It's okay, Moon Knight.
Shang-Chi- other guy...
Sorry about that thing that time.
I remember you.
You should be.
Okay. So, uh, what's this about a surprise party for Fatty McEvilsteen?
Like I told you individually, we all want the Kingpin, we all have our reasons...
And we've been tripping over ourselves and each other to get at him.
And what do we have to show for it?

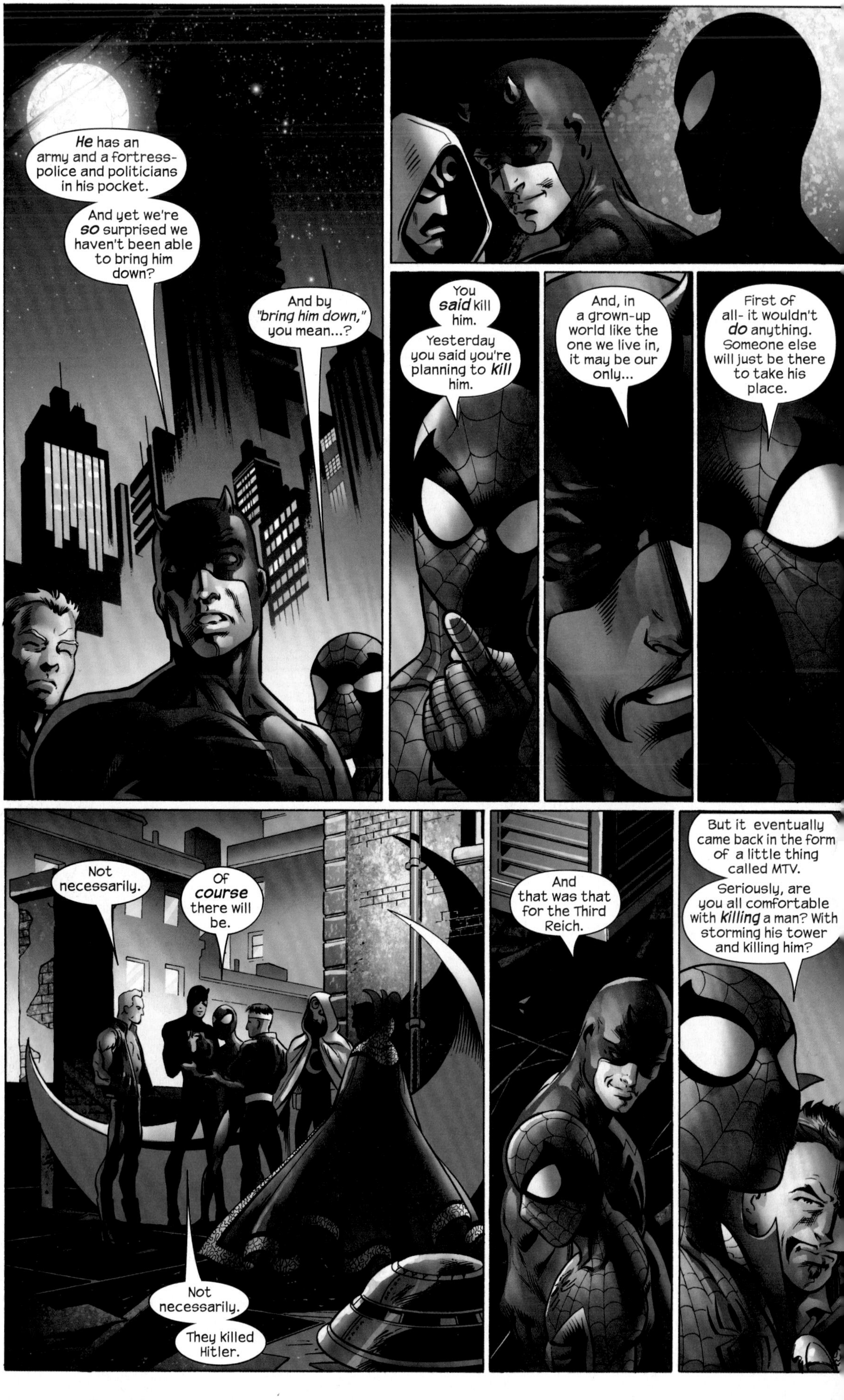
He has an army and a fortress-police and politicians in his pocket.
And yet we're SO surprised we haven't been able to bring him down?
And by "bring him down," you mean...?
You said kill him.
Yesterday you said you're planning to kill him.
And, in a grown-up world like the one we live in, it may be our only...
First of all- it wouldn't do anything. Someone else will just be there to take his place.
Not necessarily.
Of course there will be.
Not necessarily.
They killed Hitler.
And that was that for the Third Reich.
But it eventually came back in the form of a little thing called MTV.
Seriously, are you all comfortable with killing a man? With storming his tower and killing him?

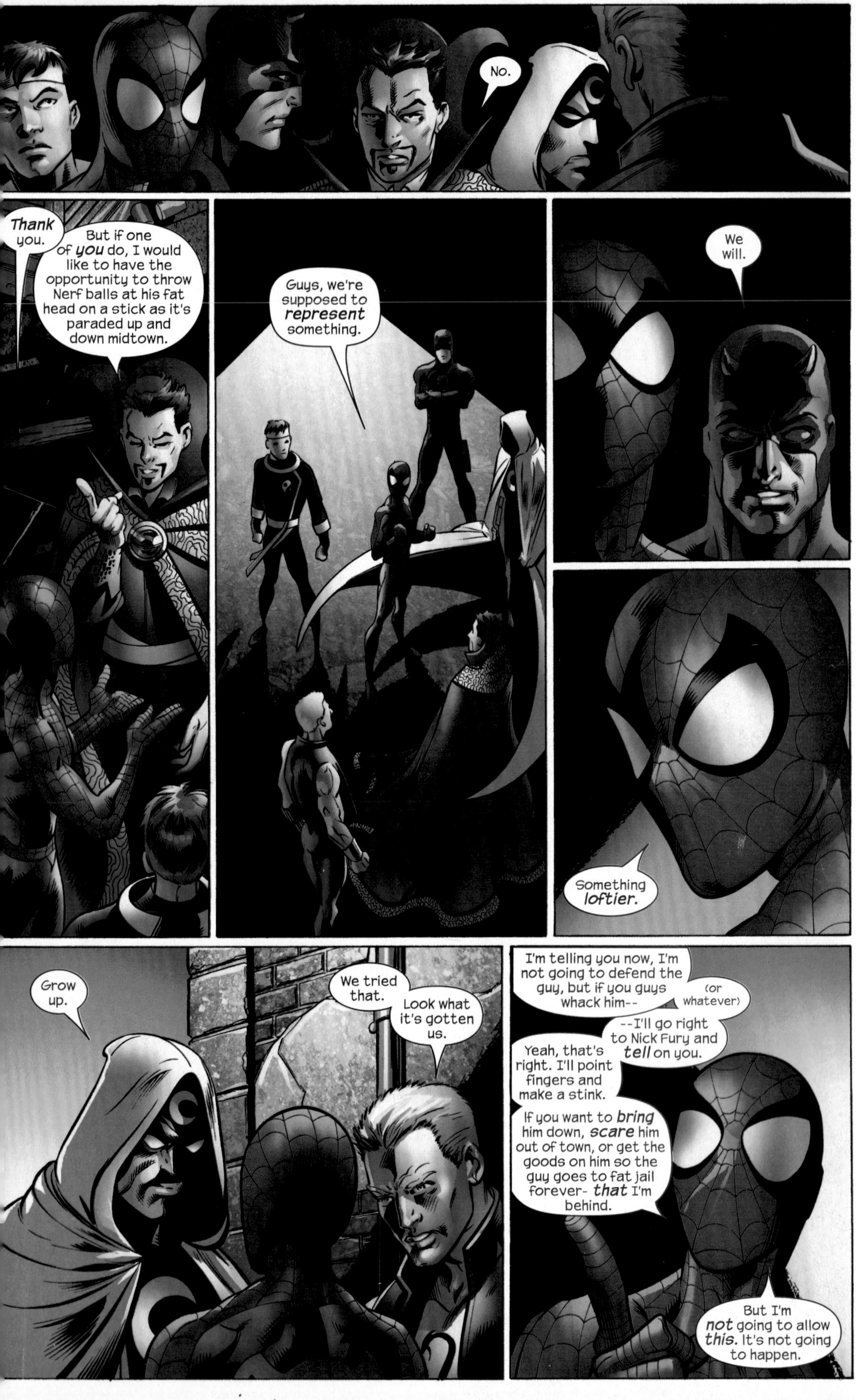
No.
Thank you.
But if one of you do, I would like to have the opportunity to throw Nerf balls at his fat head on a stick as it's paraded up and down midtown.
Guys, we're supposed to represent something.
We will.
Something loftier.
Grow up.
We tried that.
Look what it's gotten us.
I'm telling you now, I'm not going to defend the guy, but if you guys whack him--
(or whatever)
--I'll go right to Nick Fury and tell on you.
Yeah, that's right. I'll point fingers and make a stink.
If you want to bring him down, scare him out of town, or get the goods on him so the guy goes to fat jail forever- that I'm behind.
But I'm not going to allow this. It's not going to happen.

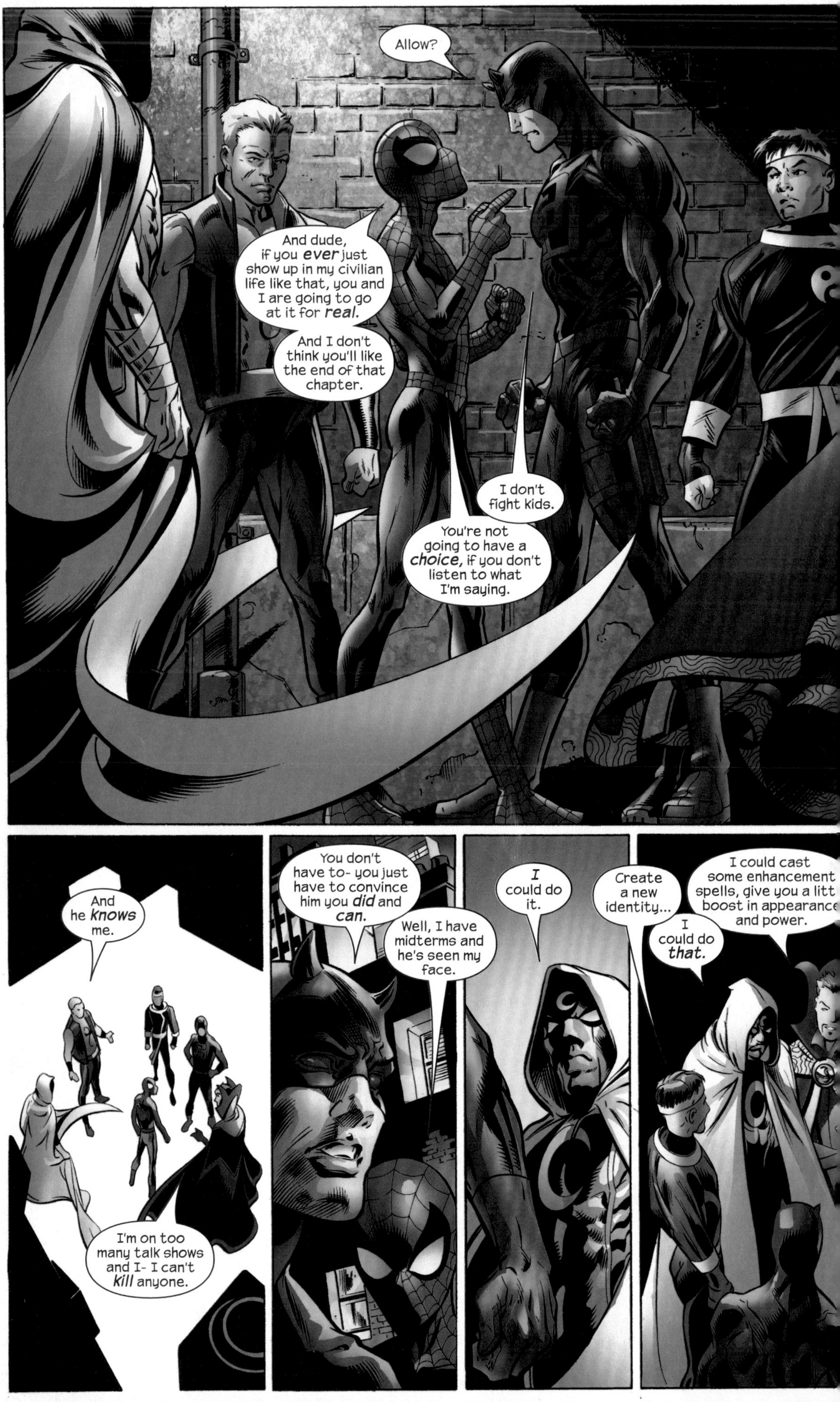
Allow?
And dude, if you *ever* just show up in my civilian life like that, you and I are going to go at it for *real.*
And I don't think you'll like the end of that chapter.
I don't fight kids.
You're not going to have a *choice,* if you don't listen to what I'm saying.
And he *knows* me.
I'm on too many talk shows and I- I can't *kill* anyone.
You don't have to- you just have to convince him you *did* and *can.*
Well, I have midterms and he's seen my face.
*I* could do it.
Create a new identity...
I could cast some enhancement spells, give you a litt boost in appearance and power.
I could do *that.*

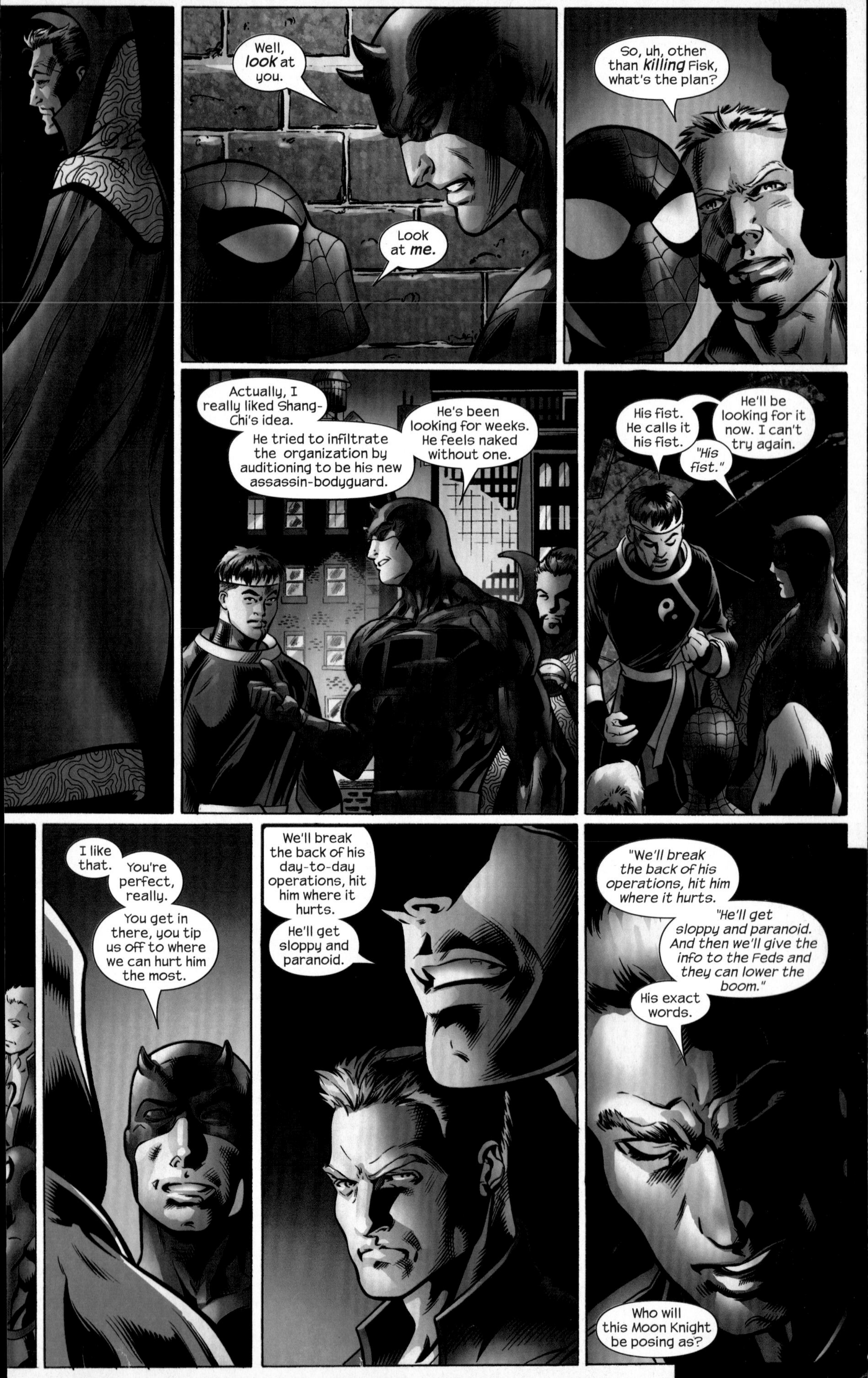
Well, look at you.
Look at me.
So, uh, other than killing Fisk, what's the plan?
Actually, I really liked Shang-Chi's idea.
He tried to infiltrate the organization by auditioning to be his new assassin-bodyguard.
He's been looking for weeks. He feels naked without one.
His fist. He calls it his fist.
He'll be looking for it now. I can't try again.
"His fist."
I like that.
You're perfect, really.
You get in there, you tip us off to where we can hurt him the most.
We'll break the back of his day-to-day operations, hit him where it hurts.
He'll get sloppy and paranoid.
"We'll break the back of his operations, hit him where it hurts.
"He'll get sloppy and paranoid. And then we'll give the info to the Feds and they can lower the boom."
His exact words.
Who will this Moon Knight be posing as?

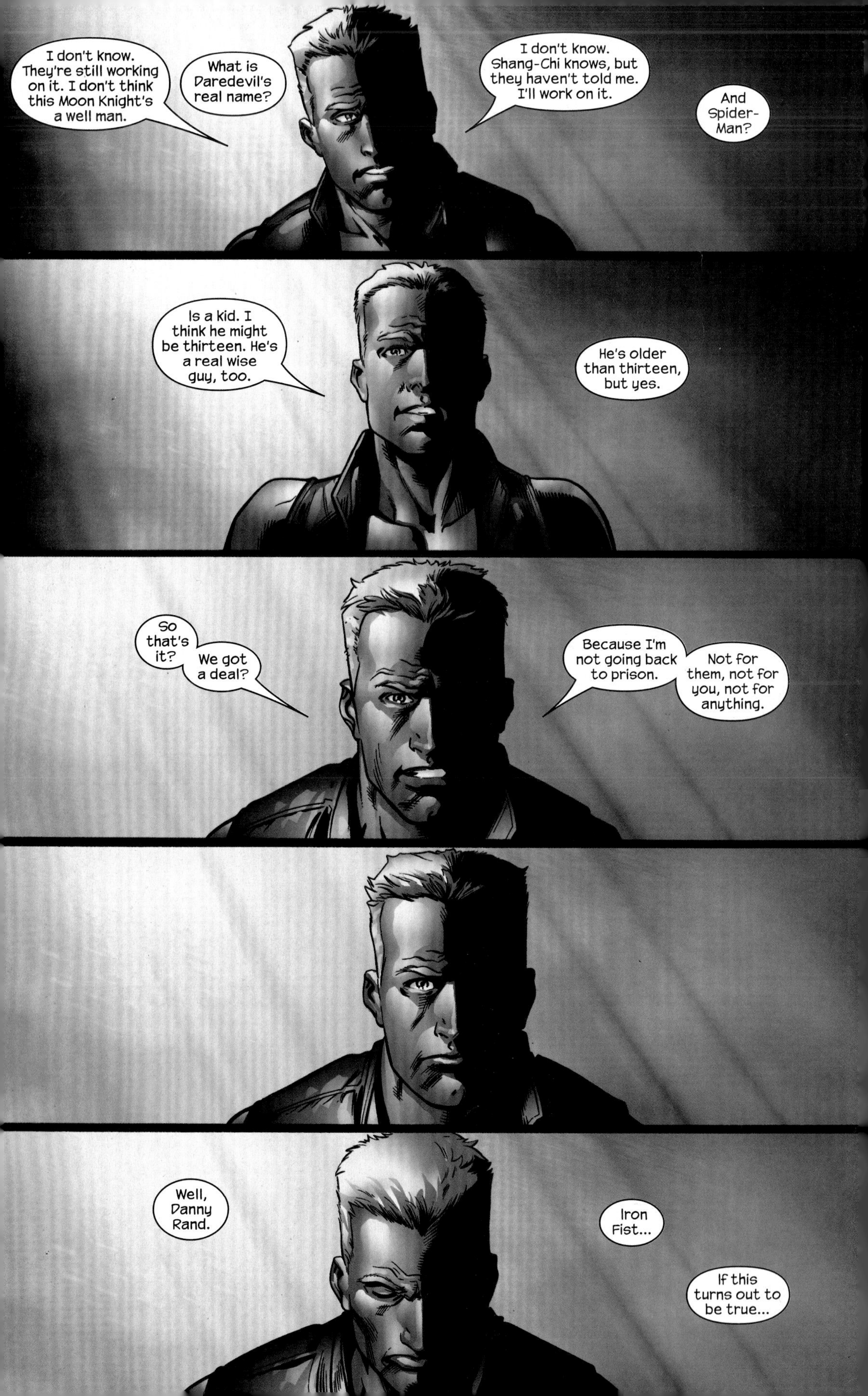
I don't know. They're still working on it. I don't think this Moon Knight's a well man.
What is Daredevil's real name?
I don't know. Shang-Chi knows, but they haven't told me. I'll work on it.
And Spider-Man?
Is a kid. I think he might be thirteen. He's a real wise guy, too.
He's older than thirteen, but yes.
So that's it?
We got a deal?
Because I'm not going back to prison.
Not for them, not for you, not for anything.
Well, Danny Rand.
Iron Fist...
If this turns out to be true...

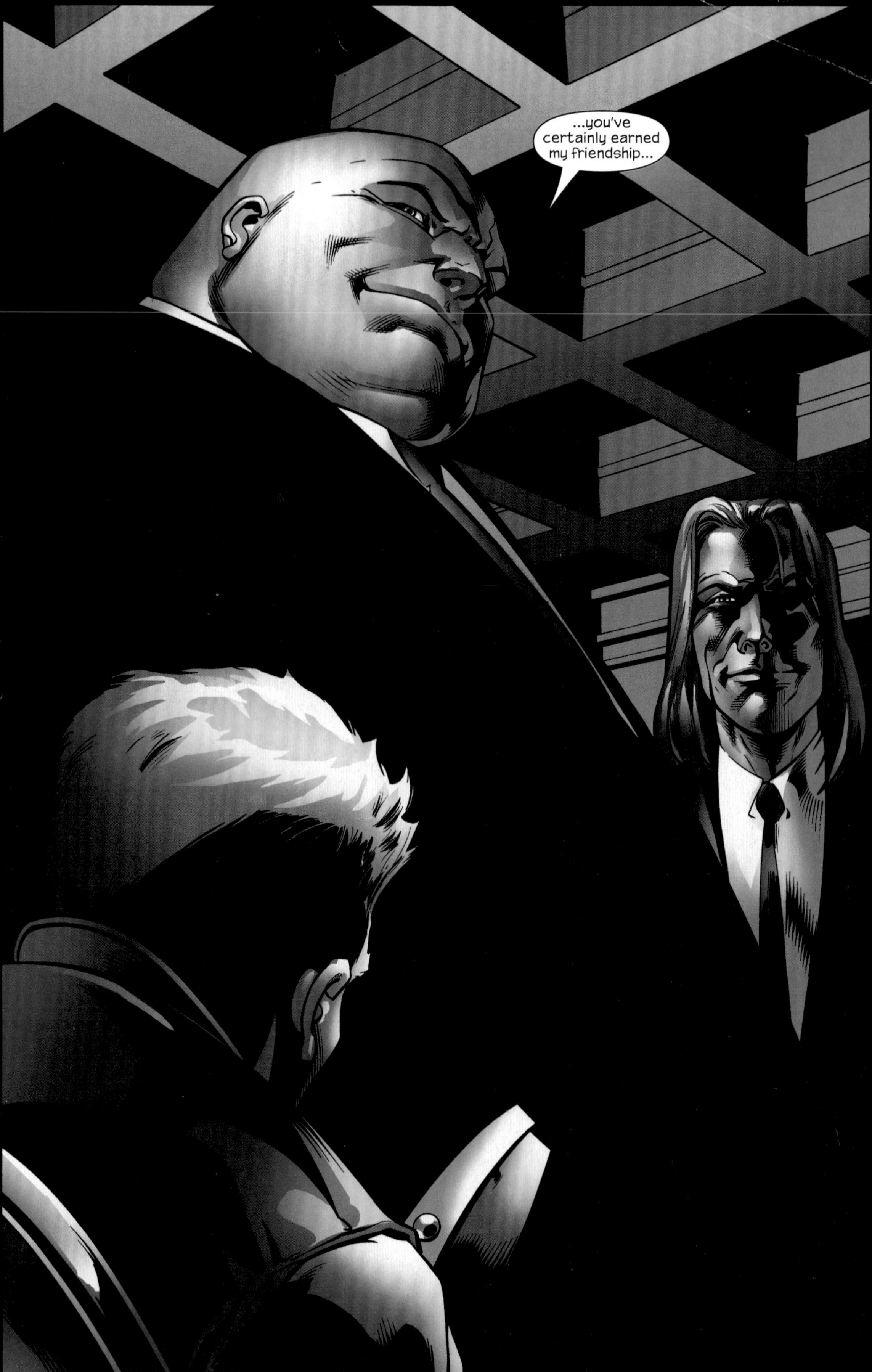
...you've certainly earned my friendship...

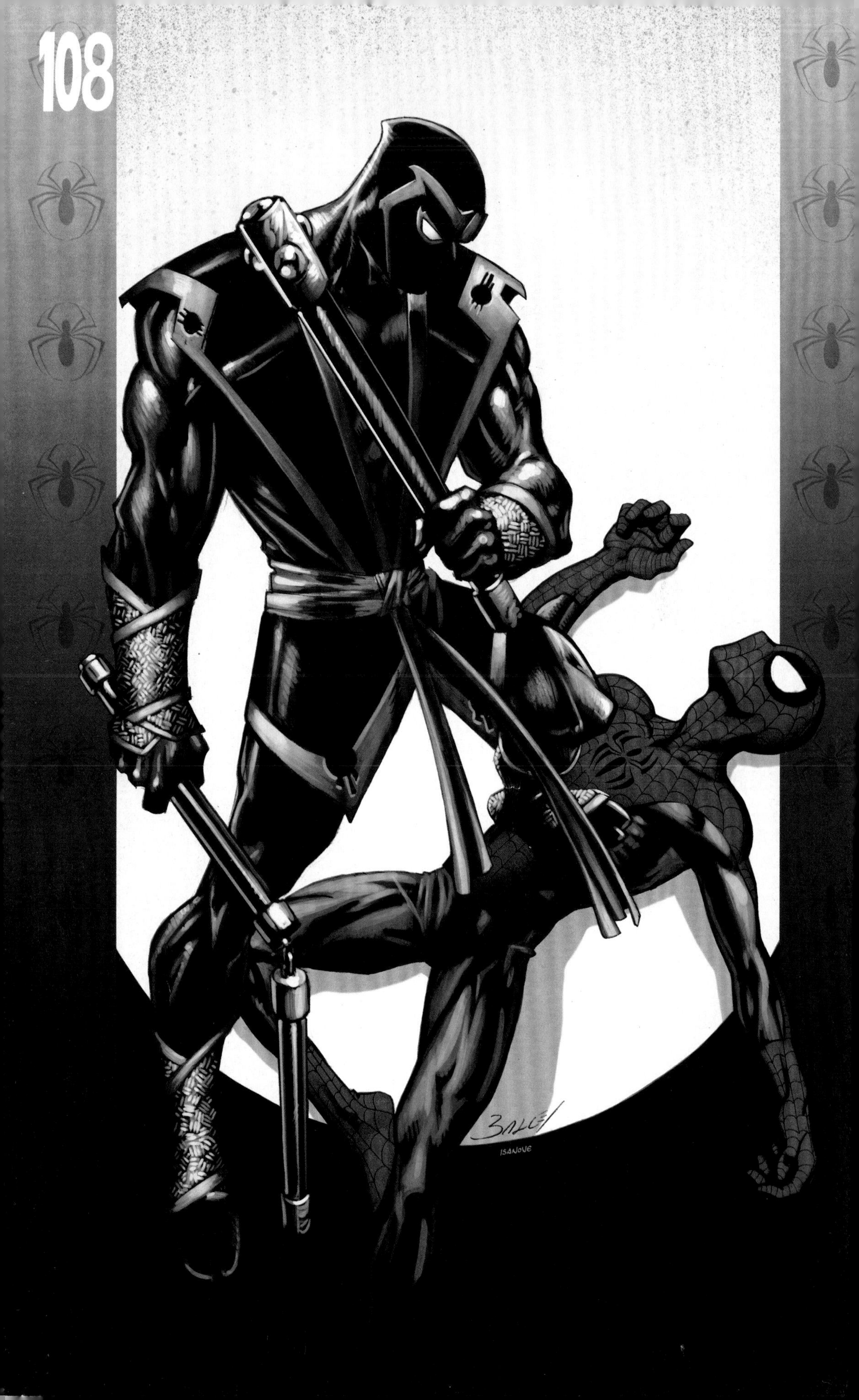
108

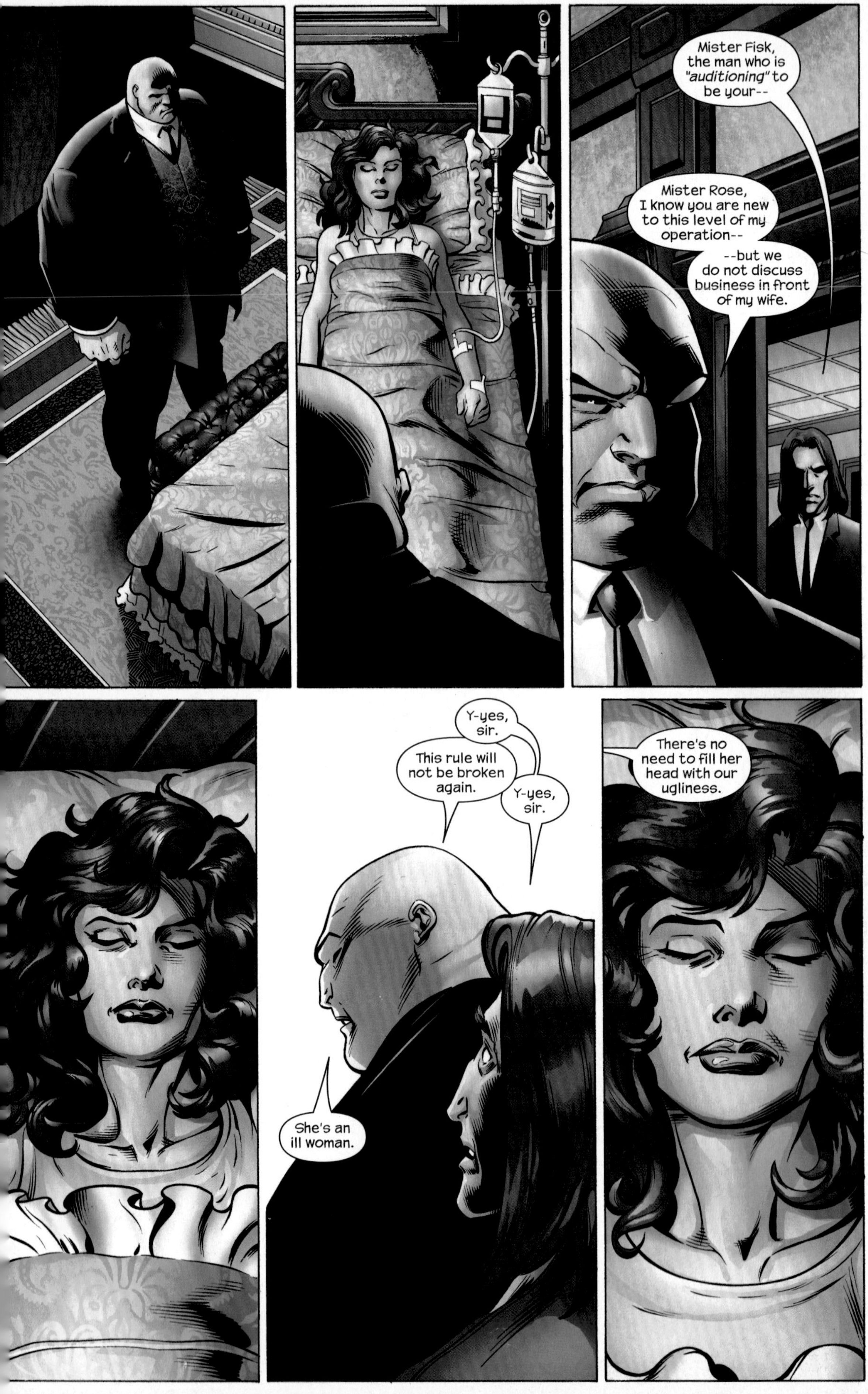
Mister Fisk, the man who is "auditioning" to be your--
Mister Rose, I know you are new to this level of my operation--
--but we do not discuss business in front of my wife.
This rule will not be broken again.
Y-yes, sir.
Y-yes, sir.
She's an ill woman.
There's no need to fill her head with our ugliness.

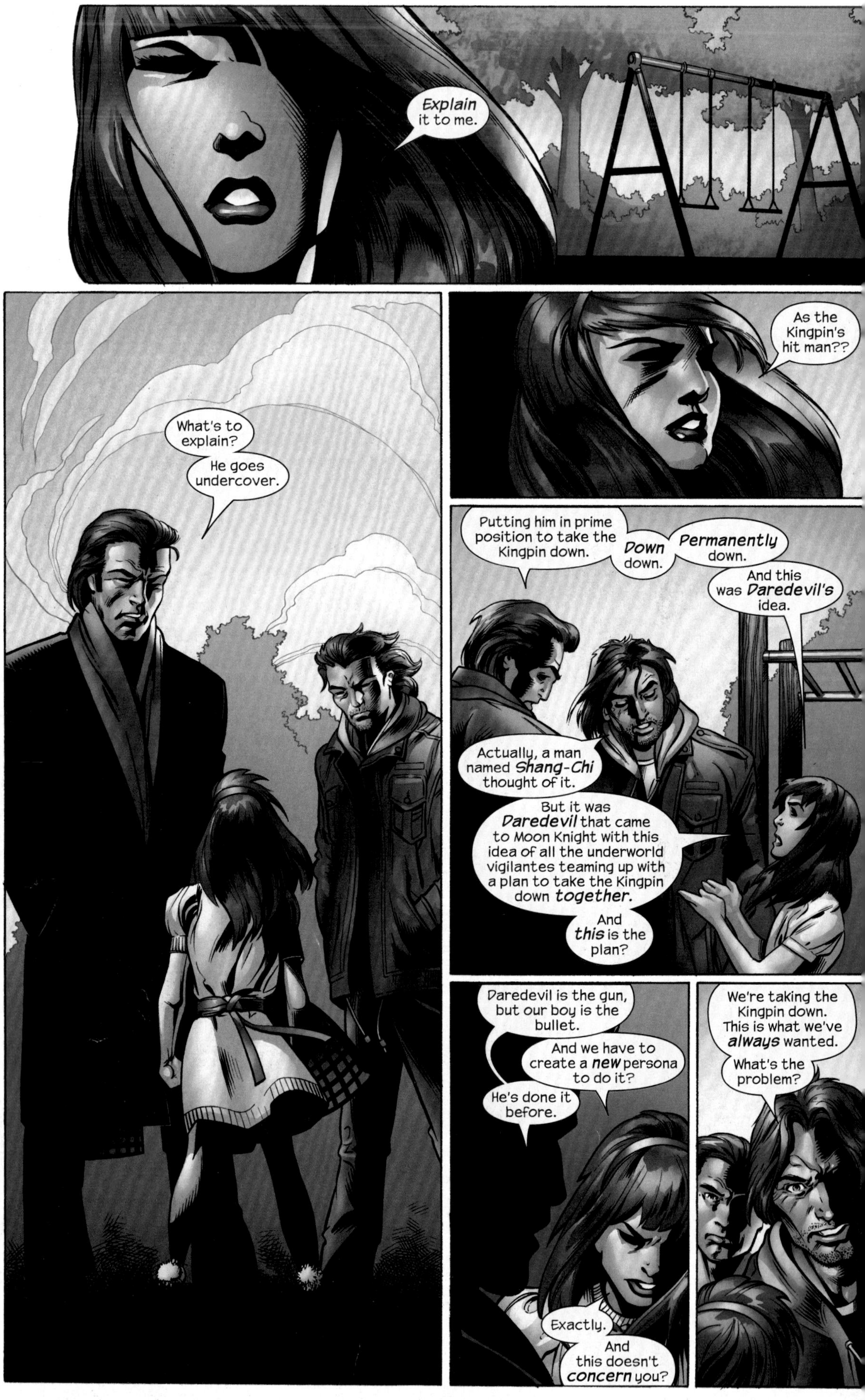
Explain it to me.
What's to explain?
He goes undercover.
As the Kingpin's hit man??
Putting him in prime position to take the Kingpin down.
Down down.
Permanently down.
And this was Daredevil's idea.
Actually, a man named Shang-Chi thought of it.
But it was Daredevil that came to Moon Knight with this idea of all the underworld vigilantes teaming up with a plan to take the Kingpin down together.
And this is the plan?
Daredevil is the gun, but our boy is the bullet.
And we have to create a new persona to do it?
He's done it before.
Exactly.
And this doesn't concern you?
We're taking the Kingpin down. This is what we've always wanted.
What's the problem?

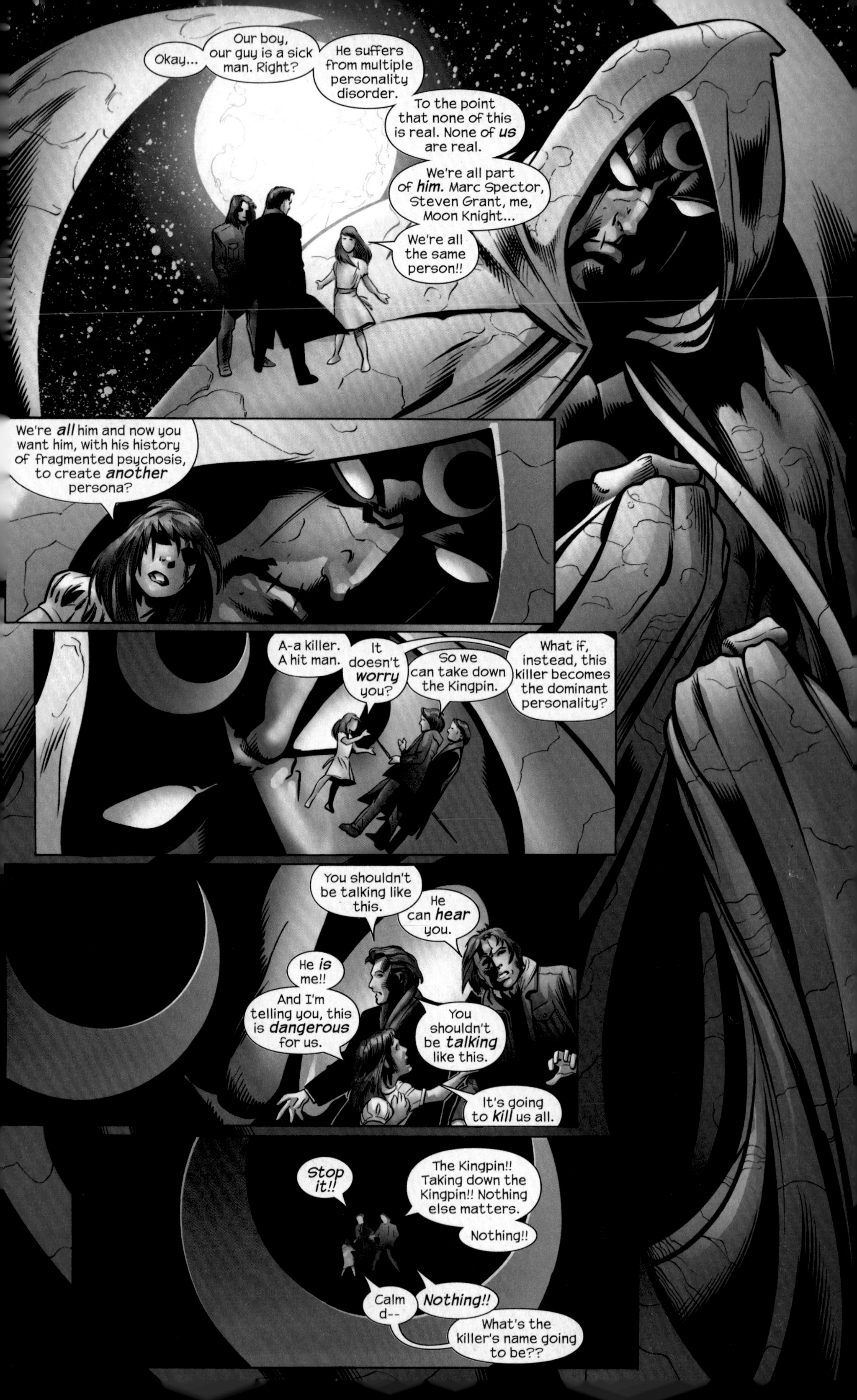
Okay...
Our boy, our guy is a sick man. Right?
He suffers from multiple personality disorder.
To the point that none of this is real. None of *us* are real.
We're all part of *him.* Marc Spector, Steven Grant, me, Moon Knight...
We're all the same person!!
We're *all* him and now you want him, with his history of fragmented psychosis, to create *another* persona?
A-a killer. A hit man.
It doesn't *worry* you?
So we can take down the Kingpin.
What if, instead, this killer becomes the dominant personality?
You shouldn't be talking like this.
He can *hear* you.
He *is* me!!
And I'm telling you, this is *dangerous* for us.
You shouldn't be *talking* like this.
It's going to *kill* us all.
*Stop it!!*
The Kingpin!! Taking down the Kingpin!! Nothing else matters.
Nothing!!
Calm d--
*Nothing!!*
What's the killer's name going to be??

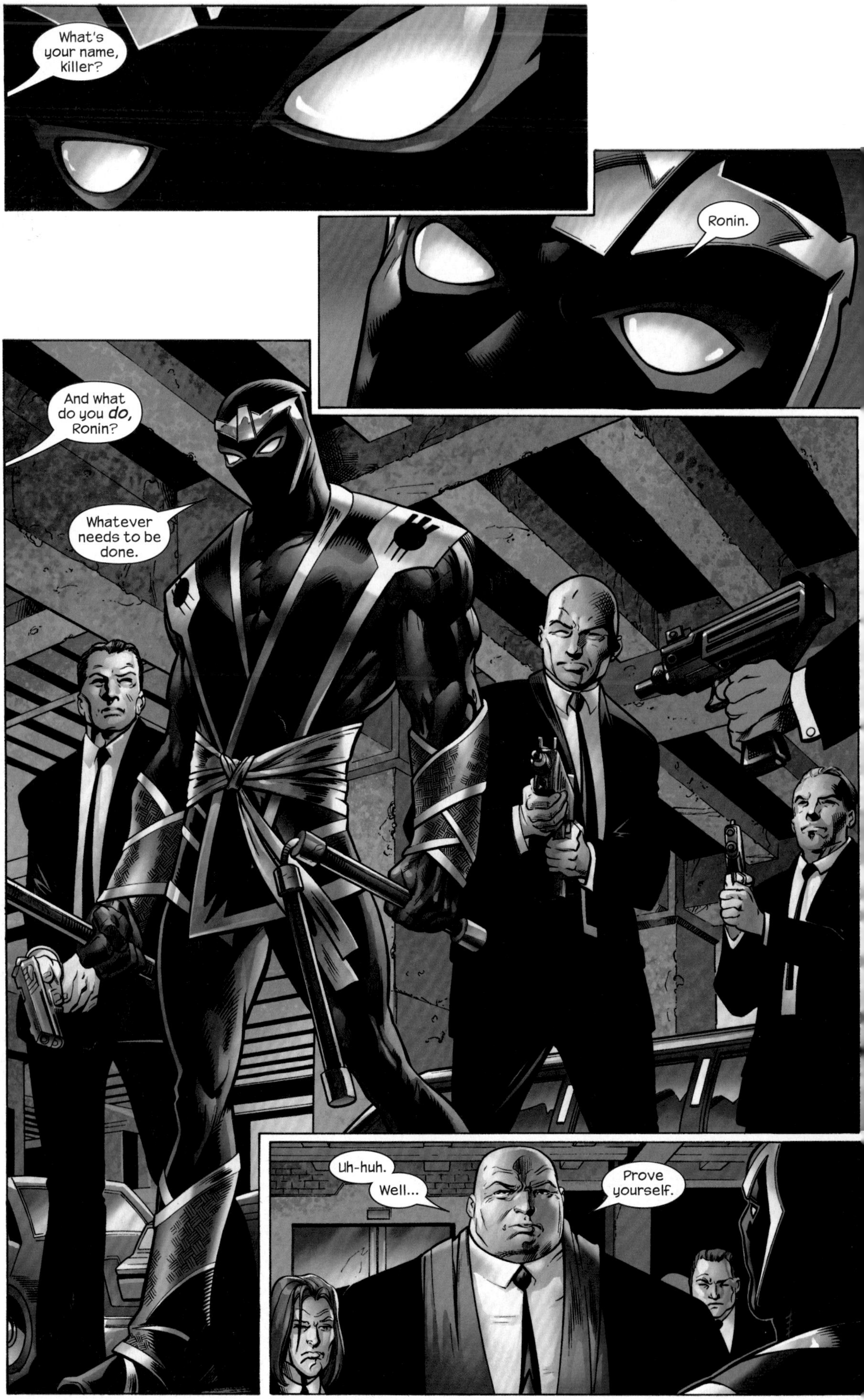
What's your name, killer?
Ronin.
And what do you *do,* Ronin?
Whatever needs to be done.
Uh-huh.
Well...
Prove yourself.

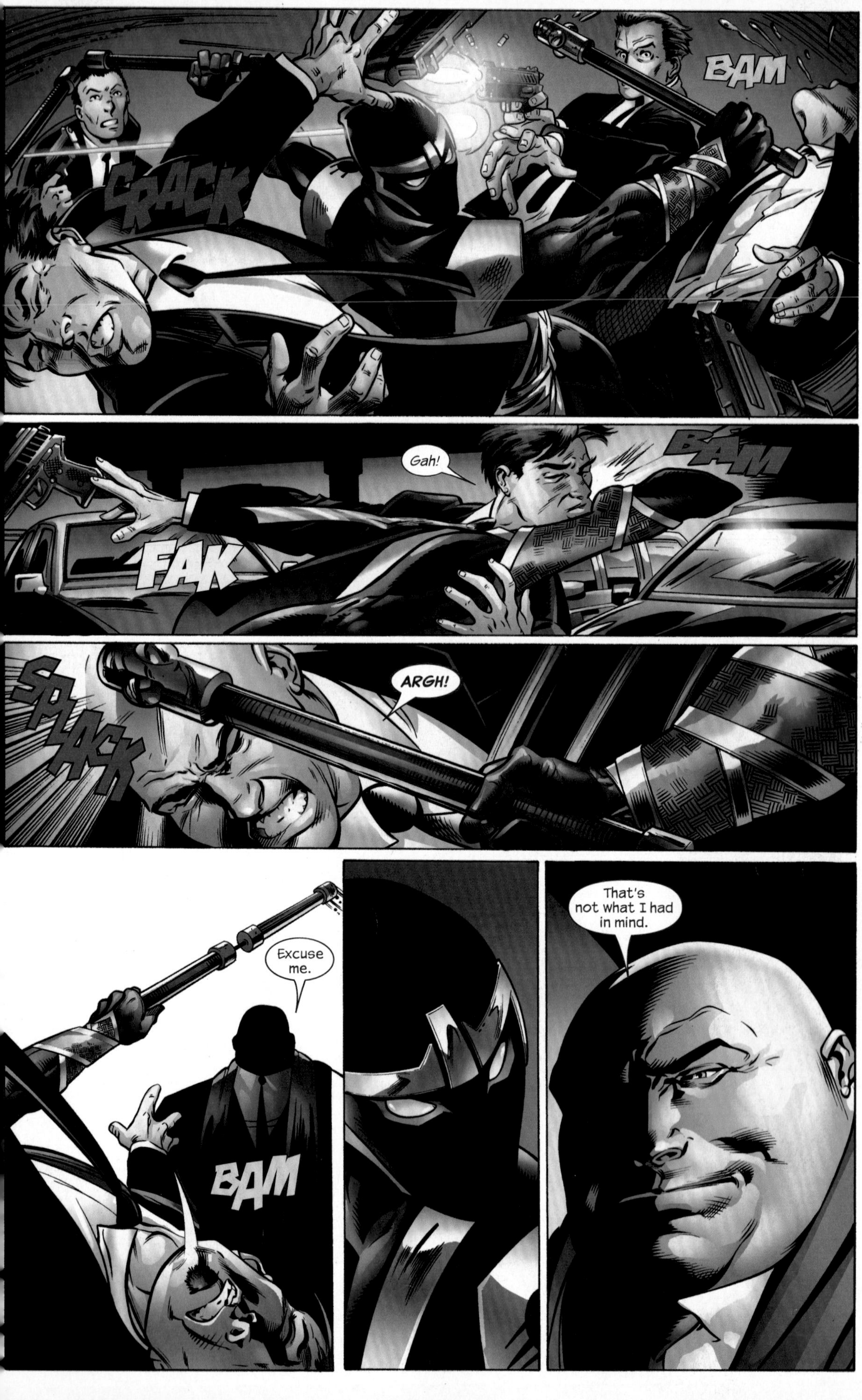
CRACK
BAM
Gah!
BAM
FAK
SPLACK
ARGH!
Excuse me.
BAM
That's not what I had in mind.

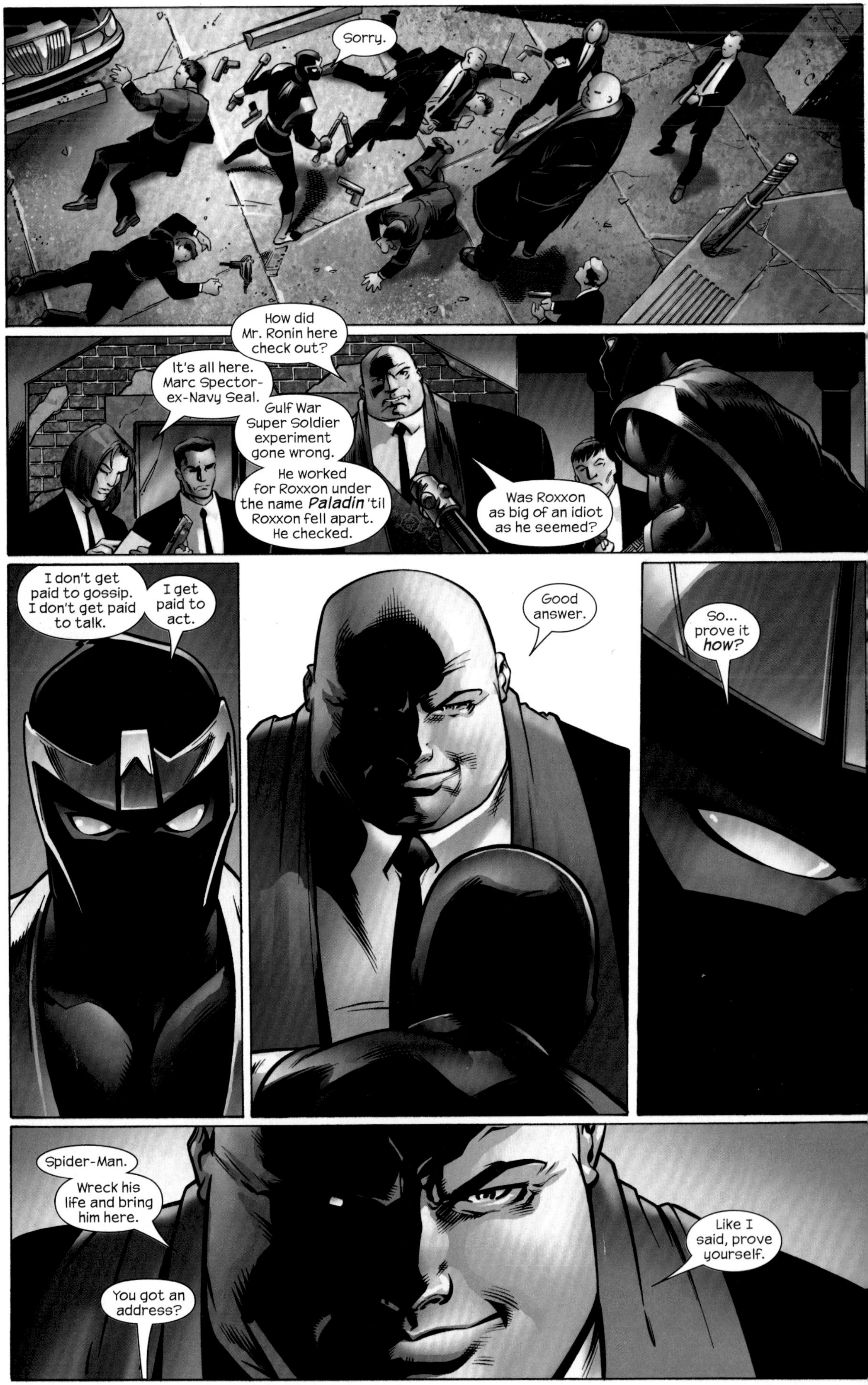
Sorry.
How did Mr. Ronin here check out?
It's all here. Marc Spector- ex-Navy Seal.
Gulf War Super Soldier experiment gone wrong.
He worked for Roxxon under the name *Paladin* 'til Roxxon fell apart. He checked.
Was Roxxon as big of an idiot as he seemed?
I don't get paid to gossip. I don't get paid to talk.
I get paid to act.
Good answer.
So... prove it *how?*
Spider-Man.
Wreck his life and bring him here.
You got an address?
Like I said, prove yourself.

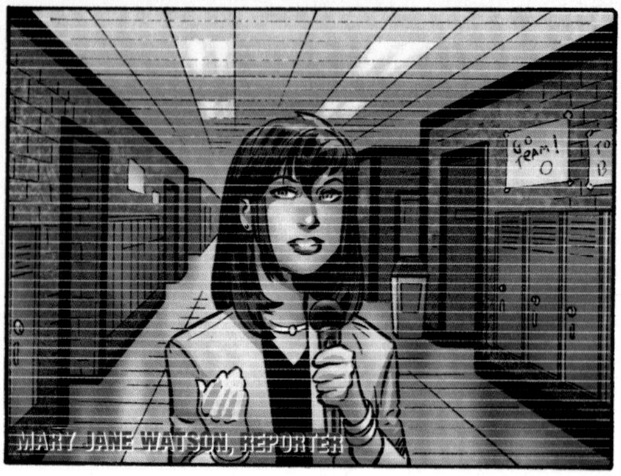
MARY JANE WATSON, REPORTER

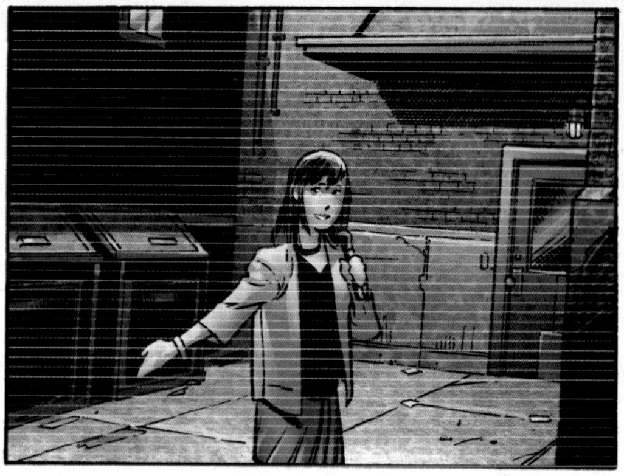

Spider-Man.

Every day the name echoes through the halls of Midtown High School.

The theory that this controversial costumed figure *may* either go to school here, or is on *faculty,* does not go away.

Just two weeks ago, in this very alley...

Fred Thompson, a sophomore here at Midtown High School, was kidnapped by mystery assailants who mistakenly took him for Spider-Man.

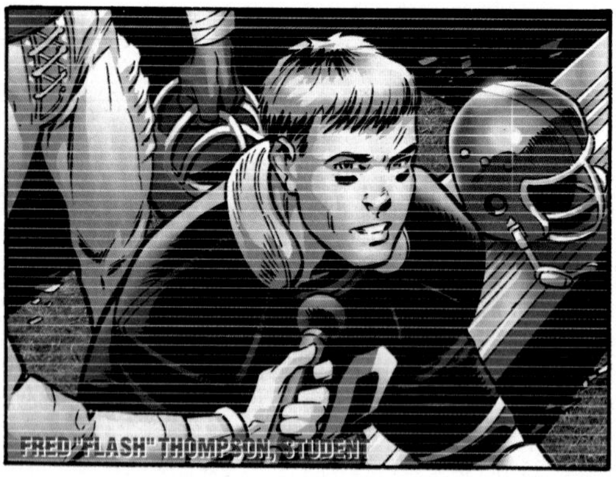
FRED "FLASH" THOMPSON, STUDEN

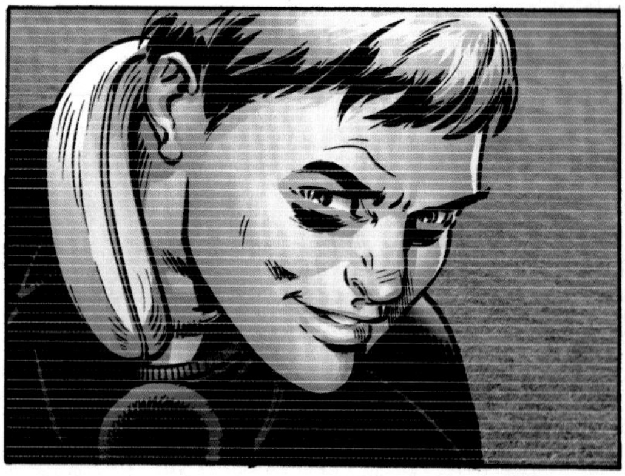

I'm kinda sick of *talking* about it.

I mean, I'm just happy to be alive.

They did this poll thing on the Internet... half the world thinks I'm Spider-Man, anyhow.

I might as well be.

But you still claim that you're not...

Duh. If I *was* Spider-Man, why the hell would I be sitting in school all day?

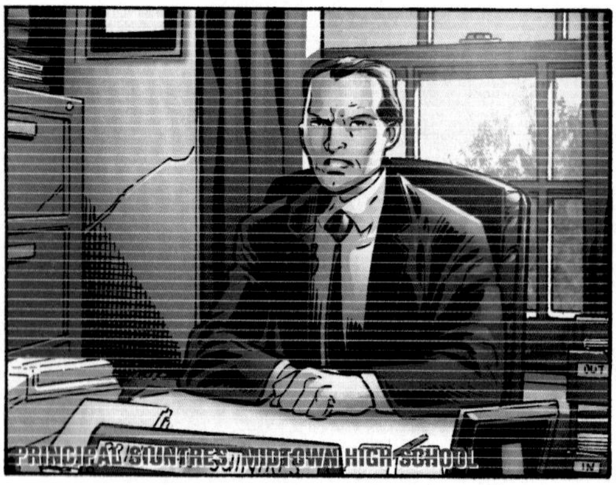
PRINCIPAL SIUNTRES, MIDTOWN HIGH SCHOOL

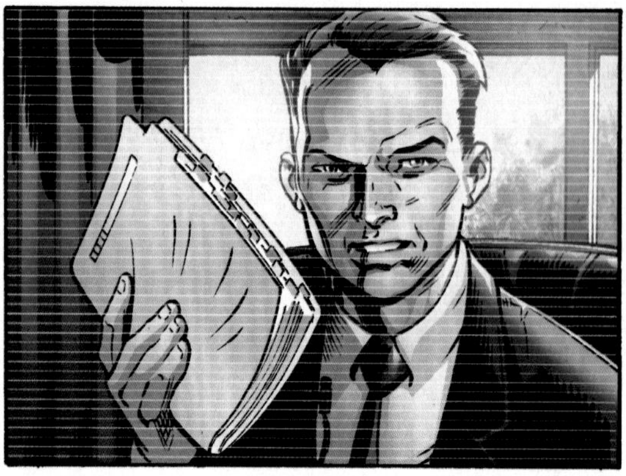

I asked Principal Siuntres *his* feelings on the growing Spider-Man controversy.

I don't *know* if Spider-Man is one of the students, but we're pretty *sure* that he is not one of the faculty.

We have done a *thorough* investigation of all *faculty* members and school employees...

And *no one* who works *here* matches his physical type.

The problem is- really, it doesn't *matter* if Spider-Man goes here or not, and I'll tell you why...

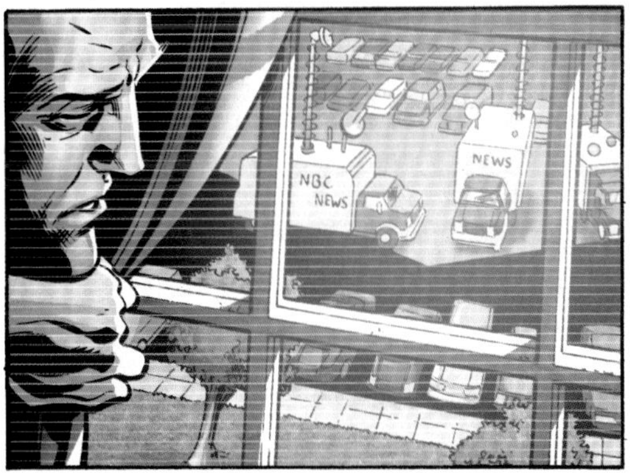
NBC NEWS
NEWS

So far most of the damage to this institution has come from the local and national media who keep *reporting* this story based on nothing but rumors!

They reported it with no facts.

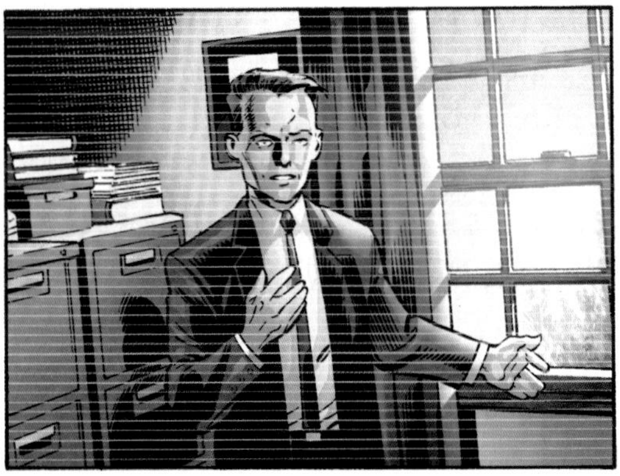

Flash Thompson was abducted by people who *thought* Spider-Man goes to school here.

It doesn't make it a *fact.*

A fact is when we catch him in the hall and *unmask* him.

Right now it's a *rumor.*

But there they are- they camp out in our parking lot, they distract and harass our students...

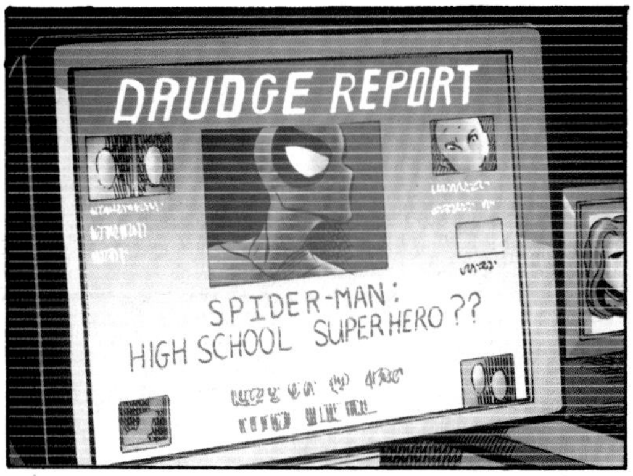
DRUDGE REPORT
SPIDER-MAN:
HIGH SCHOOL SUPERHERO??

And they'll keep *doing* it until someone gets *hurt!!*

And *then* they'll report *that* and pretend like they didn't have anything to *do* with it.

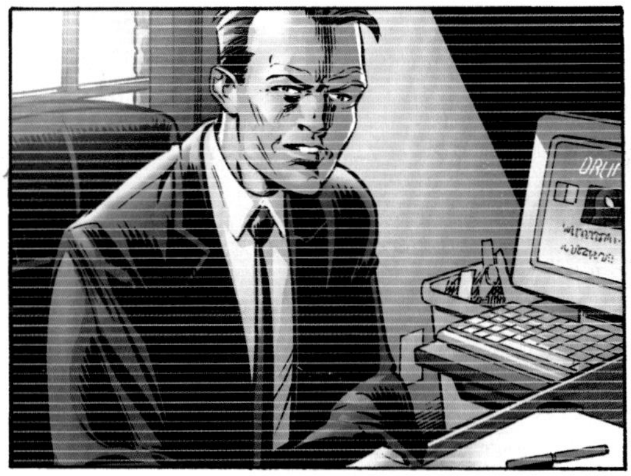

I worry about the students and families of this school *every day* and we take this Spider-Man situation very seriously.

It cost my predecessor his job.

But the truth is, I'd be proud to know Spider-Man went to school here.

He once saved my mother from an out-of-control bus.

Is that *true?*

Yes, it is.

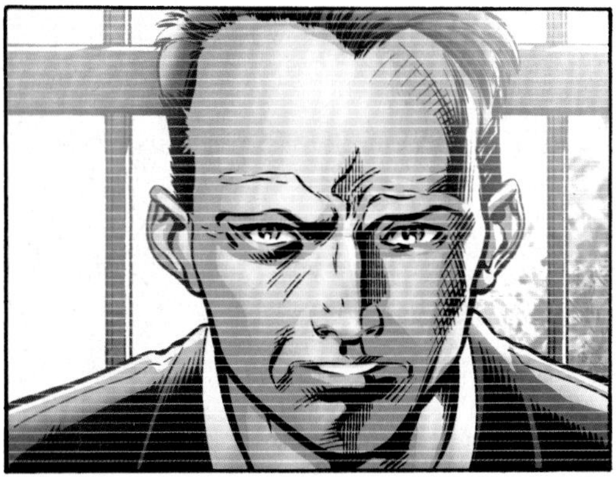

So if Spider-Man *does* go to this school and he is *watching* this...

...keep doing what you're doing.

The world desperately needs good people. And I'd be proud to hear that our school helped produce someone like you.

But I can't have chaos in my halls and I can't have children put in harm's way.

Keep it off school grounds.

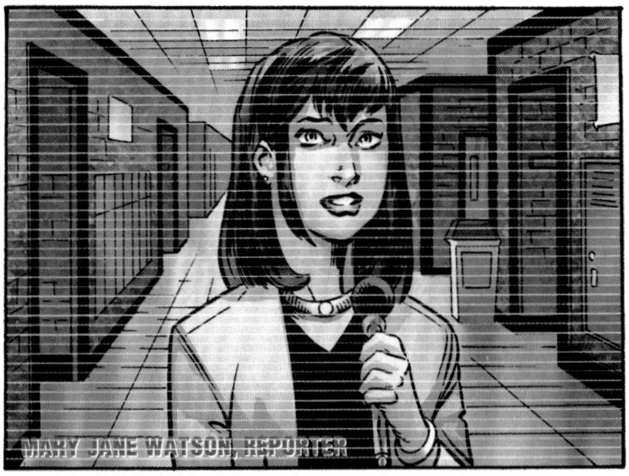
MARY JANE WATSON, REPORTER

For the Midtown High School News Channel Project...

This is Mary Jane Watson reporting.

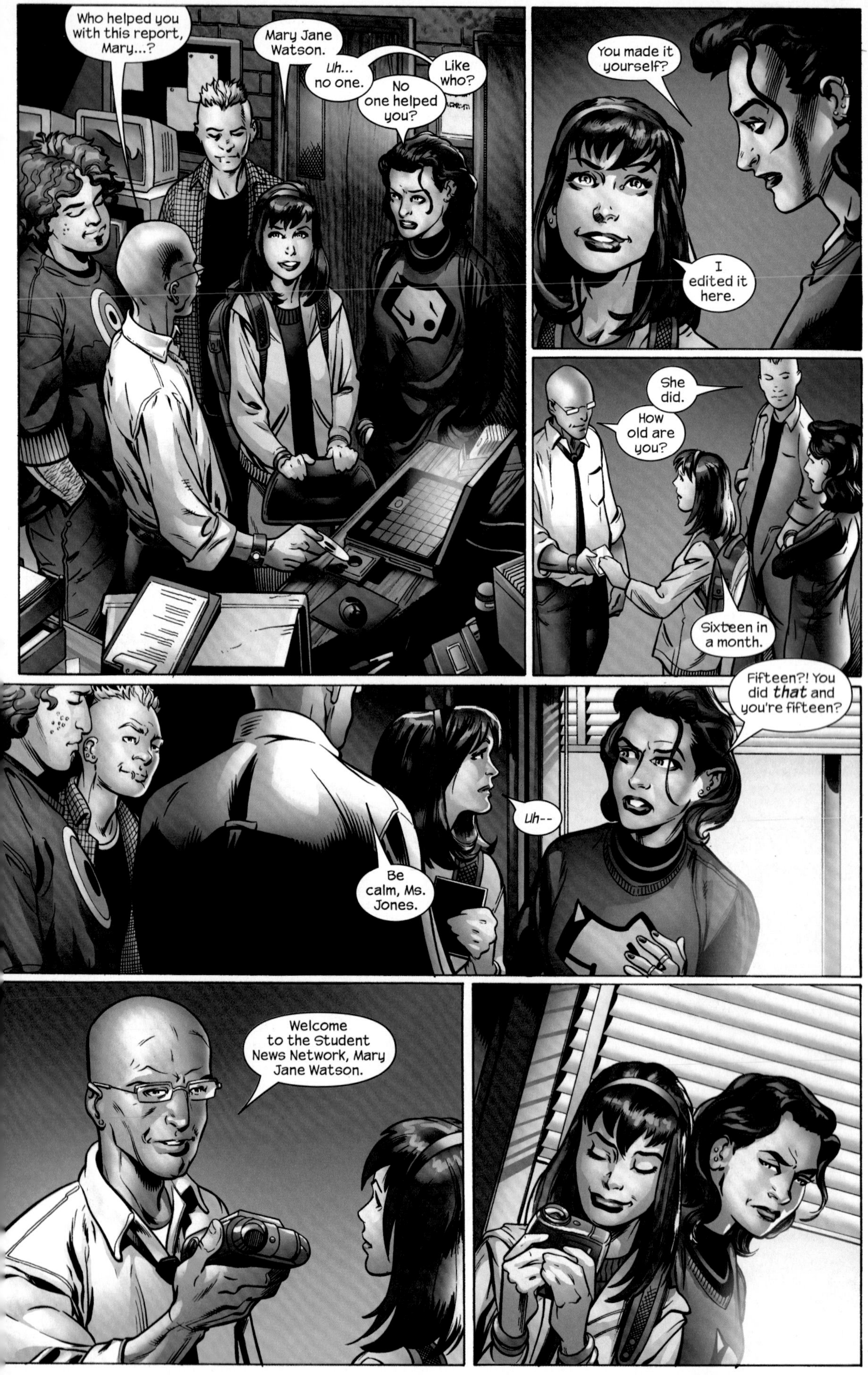
Who helped you with this report, Mary...?
Mary Jane Watson.
Like who?
Uh... no one.
No one helped you?
You made it yourself?
I edited it here.
She did.
How old are you?
Sixteen in a month.
Fifteen?! You did *that* and you're fifteen?
Uh--
Be calm, Ms. Jones.
Welcome to the Student News Network, Mary Jane Watson.

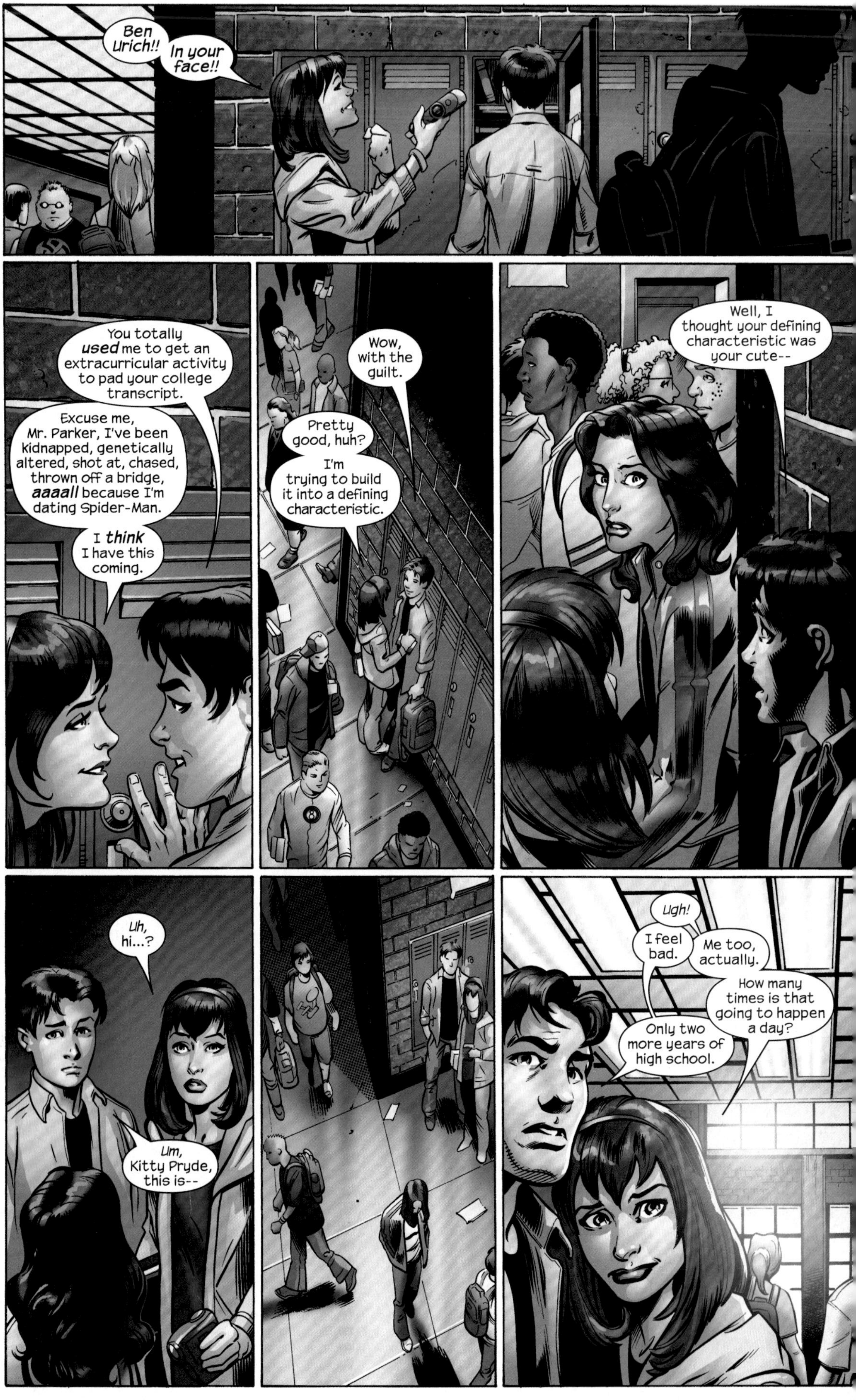
Ben Urich!!
In your face!!
You totally used me to get an extracurricular activity to pad your college transcript.
Excuse me, Mr. Parker, I've been kidnapped, genetically altered, shot at, chased, thrown off a bridge, aaaall because I'm dating Spider-Man.
I think I have this coming.
Wow, with the guilt.
Pretty good, huh?
I'm trying to build it into a defining characteristic.
Well, I thought your defining characteristic was your cute--
Uh, hi...?
Um, Kitty Pryde, this is--
Ugh!
I feel bad.
Me too, actually.
How many times is that going to happen a day?
Only two more years of high school.

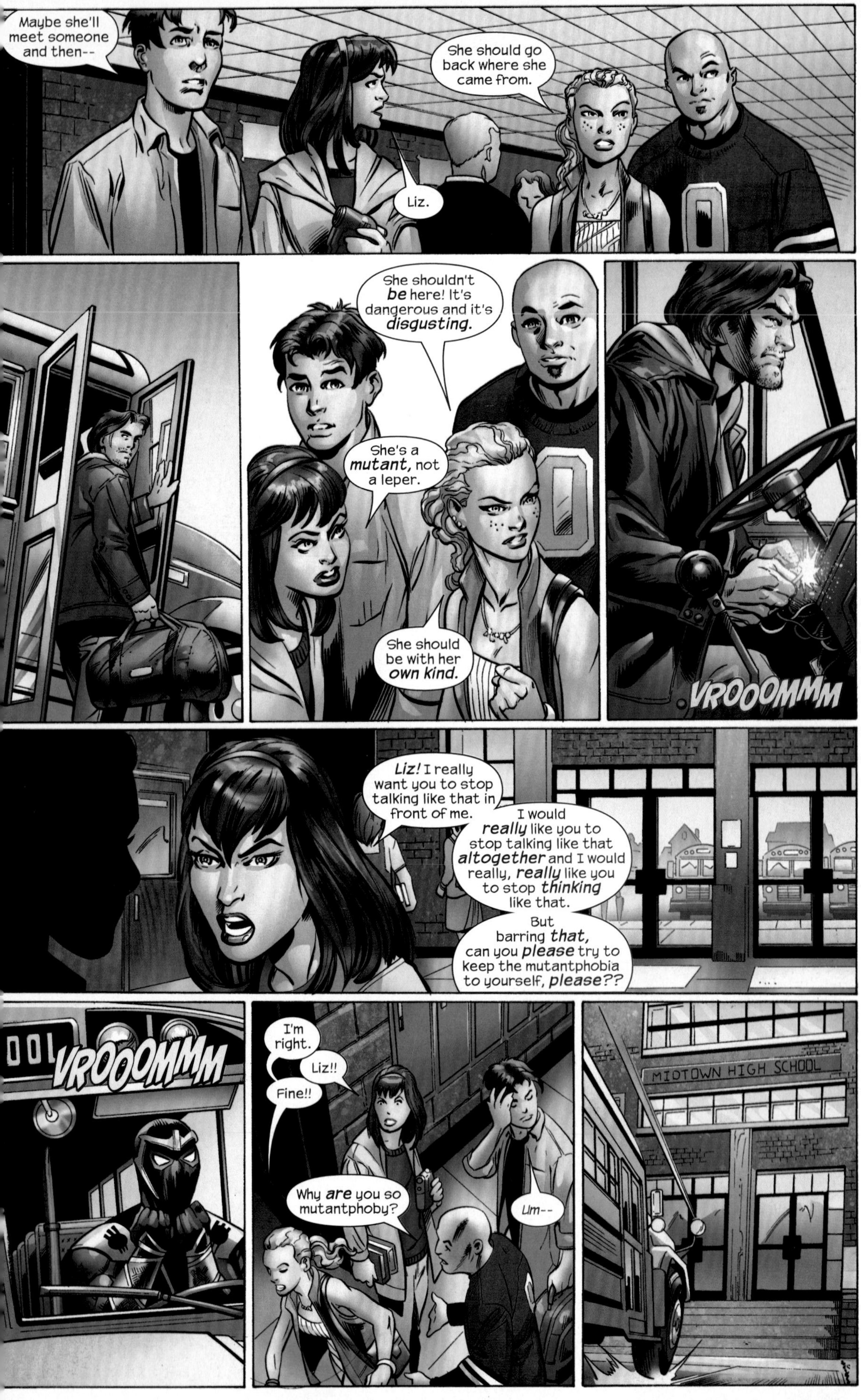
Maybe she'll meet someone and then--
She should go back where she came from.
Liz.
She shouldn't *be* here! It's dangerous and it's *disgusting.*
She's a *mutant,* not a leper.
She should be with her *own kind.*
VROOOMMM
*Liz!* I really want you to stop talking like that in front of me.
I would *really* like you to stop talking like that *altogether* and I would really, *really* like you to stop *thinking* like that.
But barring *that,* can you *please* try to keep the mutantphobia to yourself, *please??*
...
VROOOMMM
I'm right.
Liz!!
Fine!!
Why *are* you so mutantphoby?
Um--
MIDTOWN HIGH SCHOOL

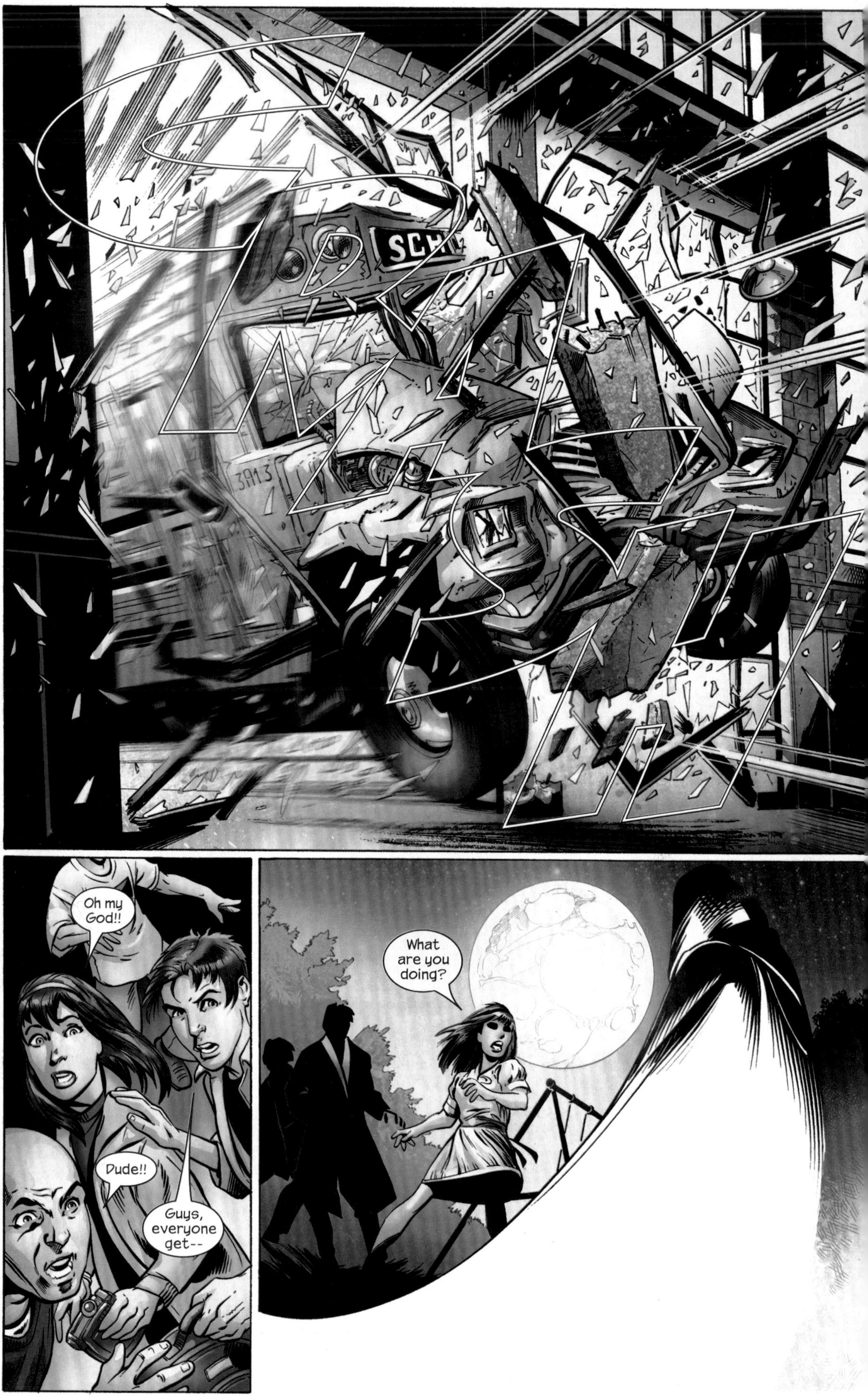
Oh my God!!
Dude!!
Guys, everyone get--
What are you doing?

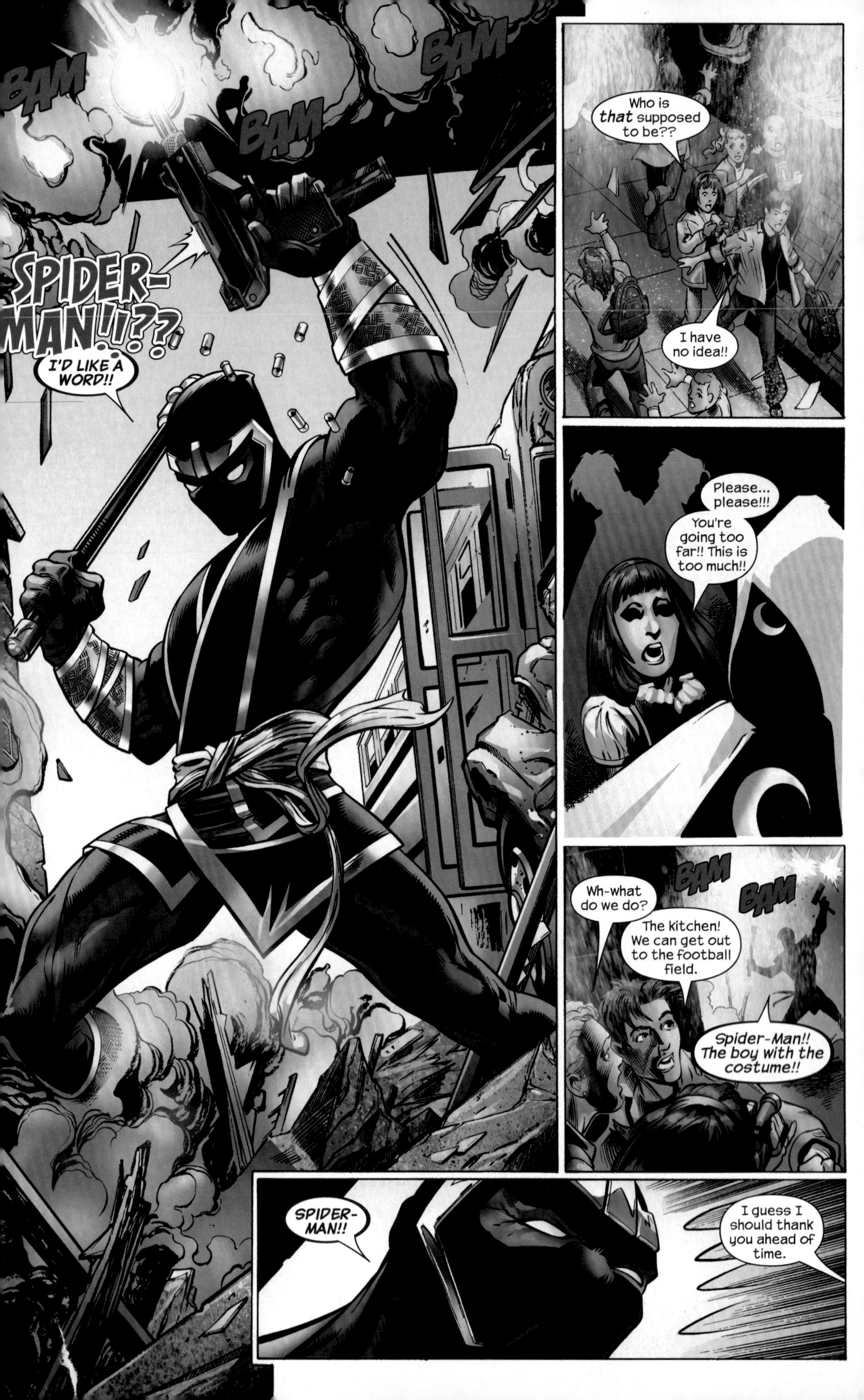
BAM
BAM
BAM
SPIDER-MAN!!??
I'D LIKE A WORD!!
Who is that supposed to be??
I have no idea!!
Please... please!!!
You're going too far!! This is too much!!
BAM
BAM
Wh-what do we do?
The kitchen! We can get out to the football field.
Spider-Man!! The boy with the costume!!
SPIDER-MAN!!
I guess I should thank you ahead of time.

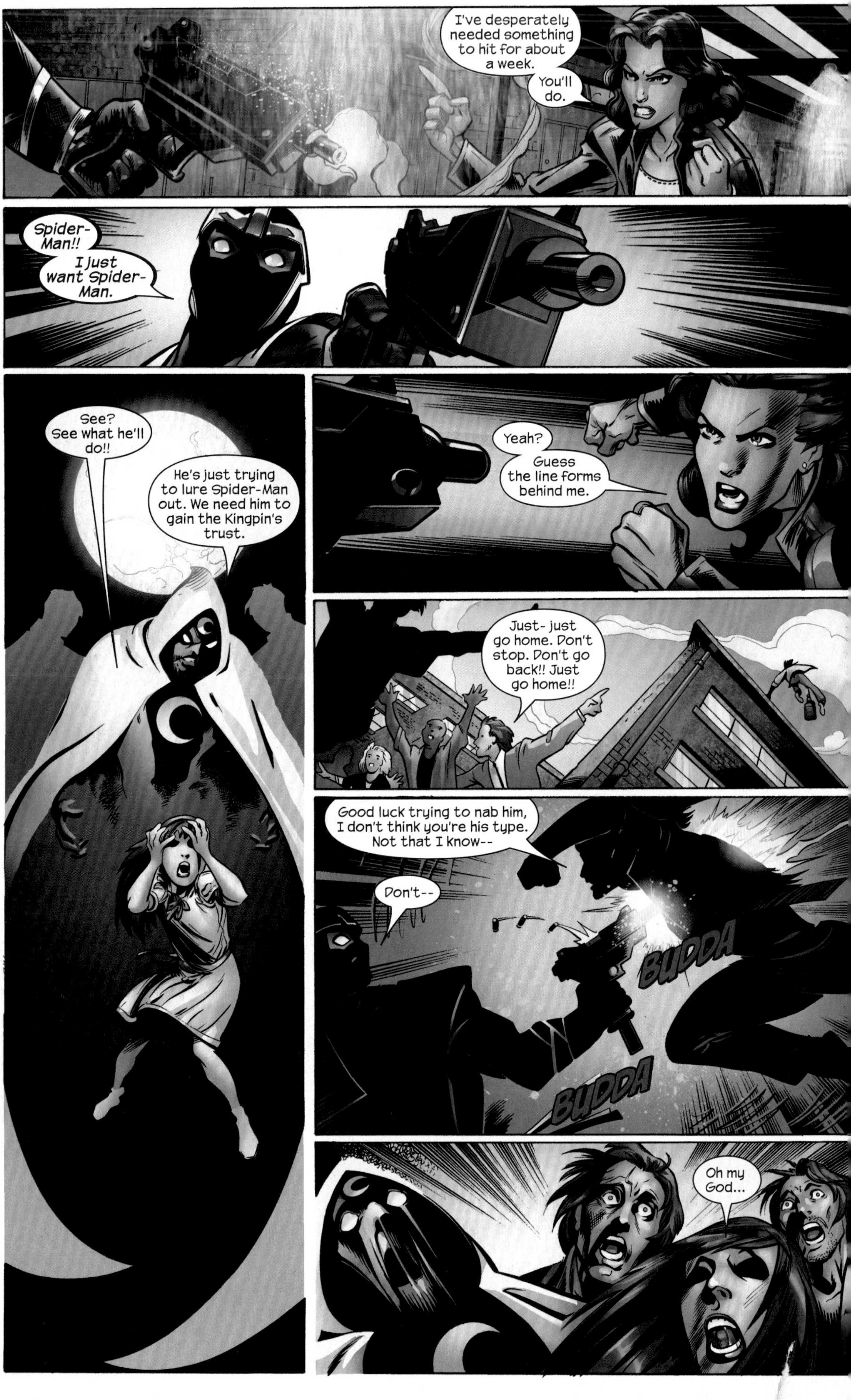

I've desperately needed something to hit for about a week.
You'll do.
Spider-Man!!
I just want Spider-Man.
See? See what he'll do!!
He's just trying to lure Spider-Man out. We need him to gain the Kingpin's trust.
Yeah?
Guess the line forms behind me.
Just- just go home. Don't stop. Don't go back!! Just go home!!
Good luck trying to nab him, I don't think you're his type. Not that I know--
Don't--
BUDDA
BUDDA
Oh my God...

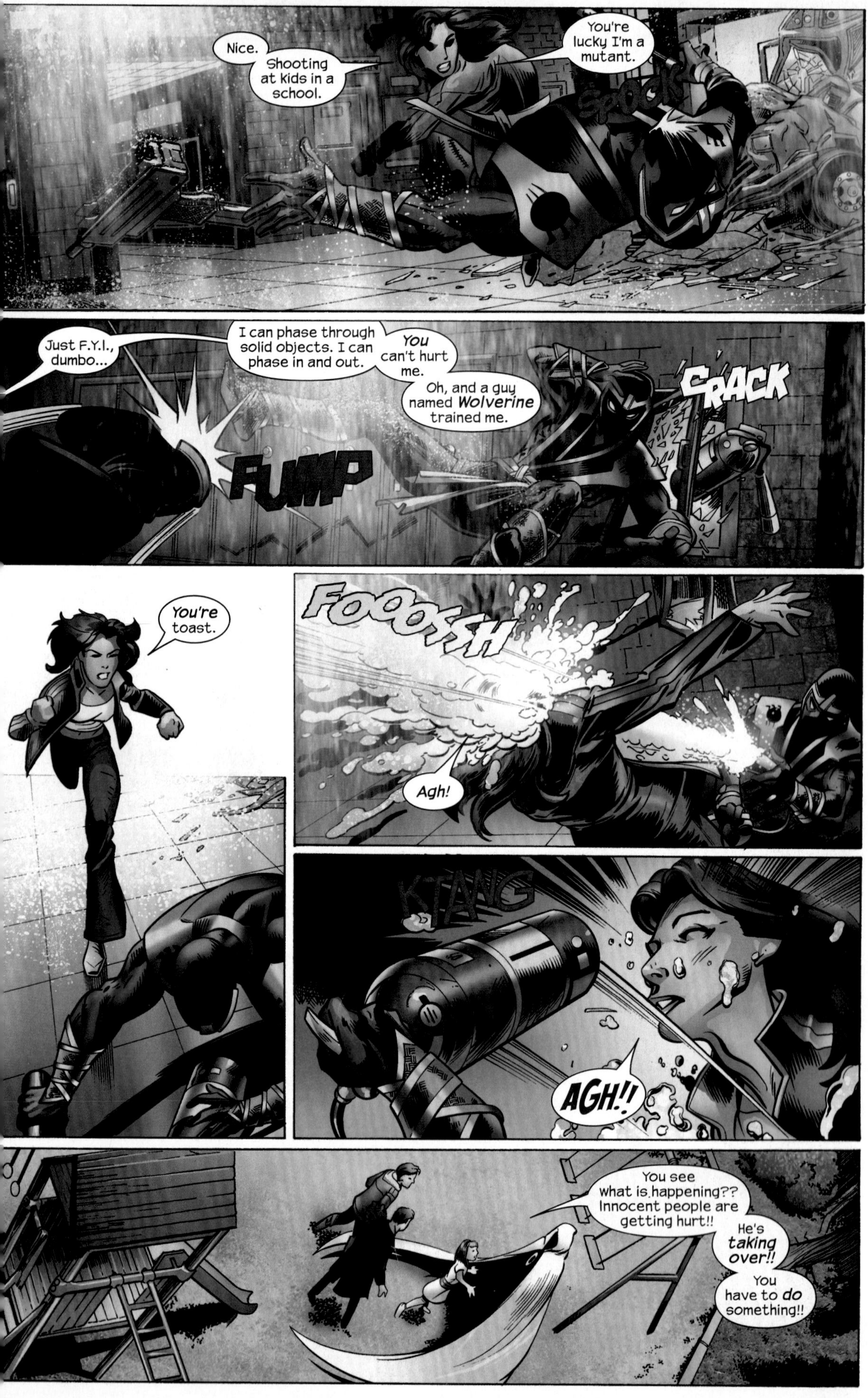

Nice. Shooting at kids in a school.
You're lucky I'm a mutant.
SPOCK
Just F.Y.I., dumbo...
I can phase through solid objects. I can phase in and out.
You can't hurt me.
Oh, and a guy named Wolverine trained me.
CRACK
FUMP
You're toast.
FOOOSH
Agh!
KTANG
AGH!!
You see what is happening?? Innocent people are getting hurt!!
He's taking over!!
You have to do something!!

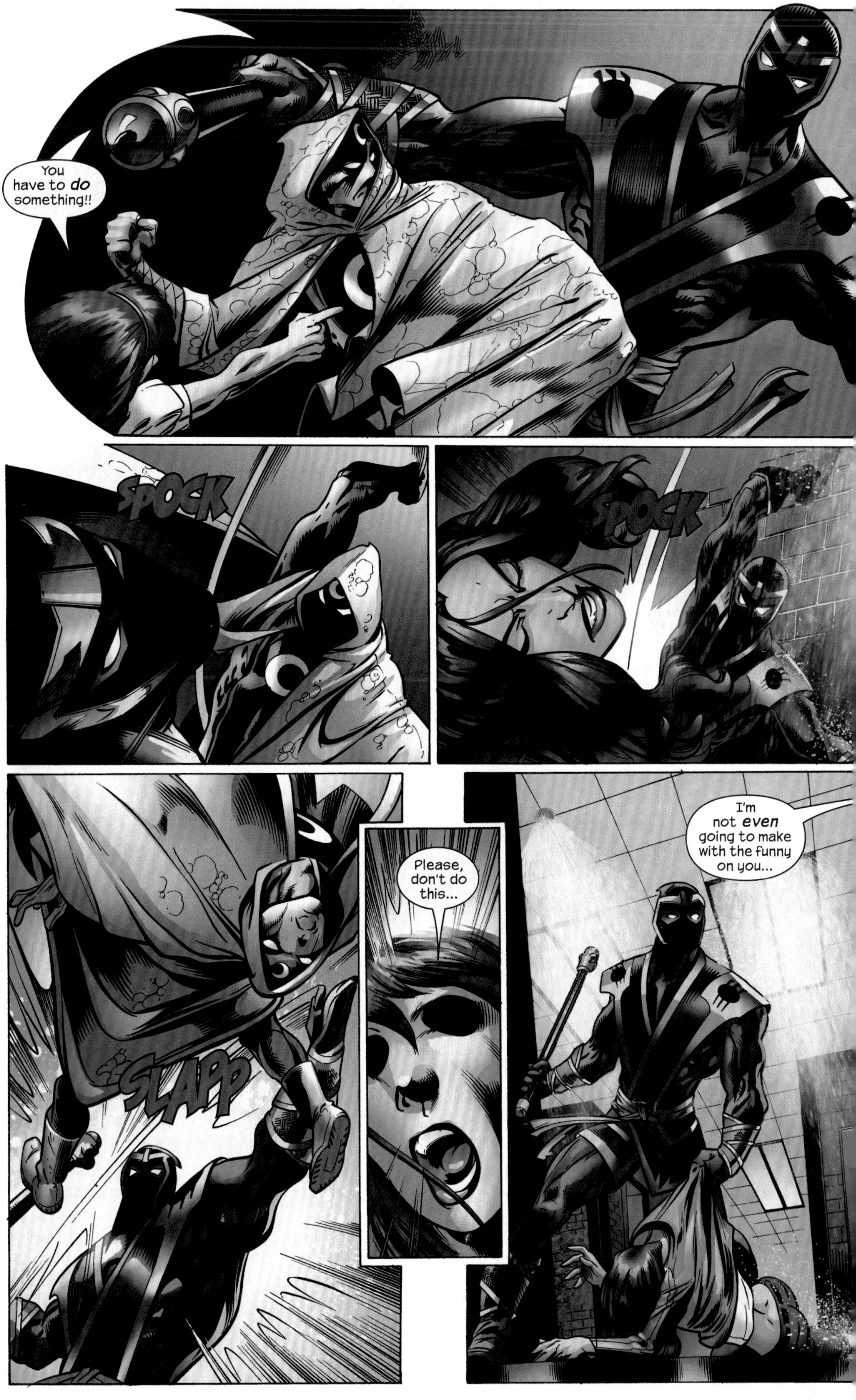
You have to do something!!
SPOCK
SPOCK
SLAPP
Please, don't do this...
I'm not even going to make with the funny on you...

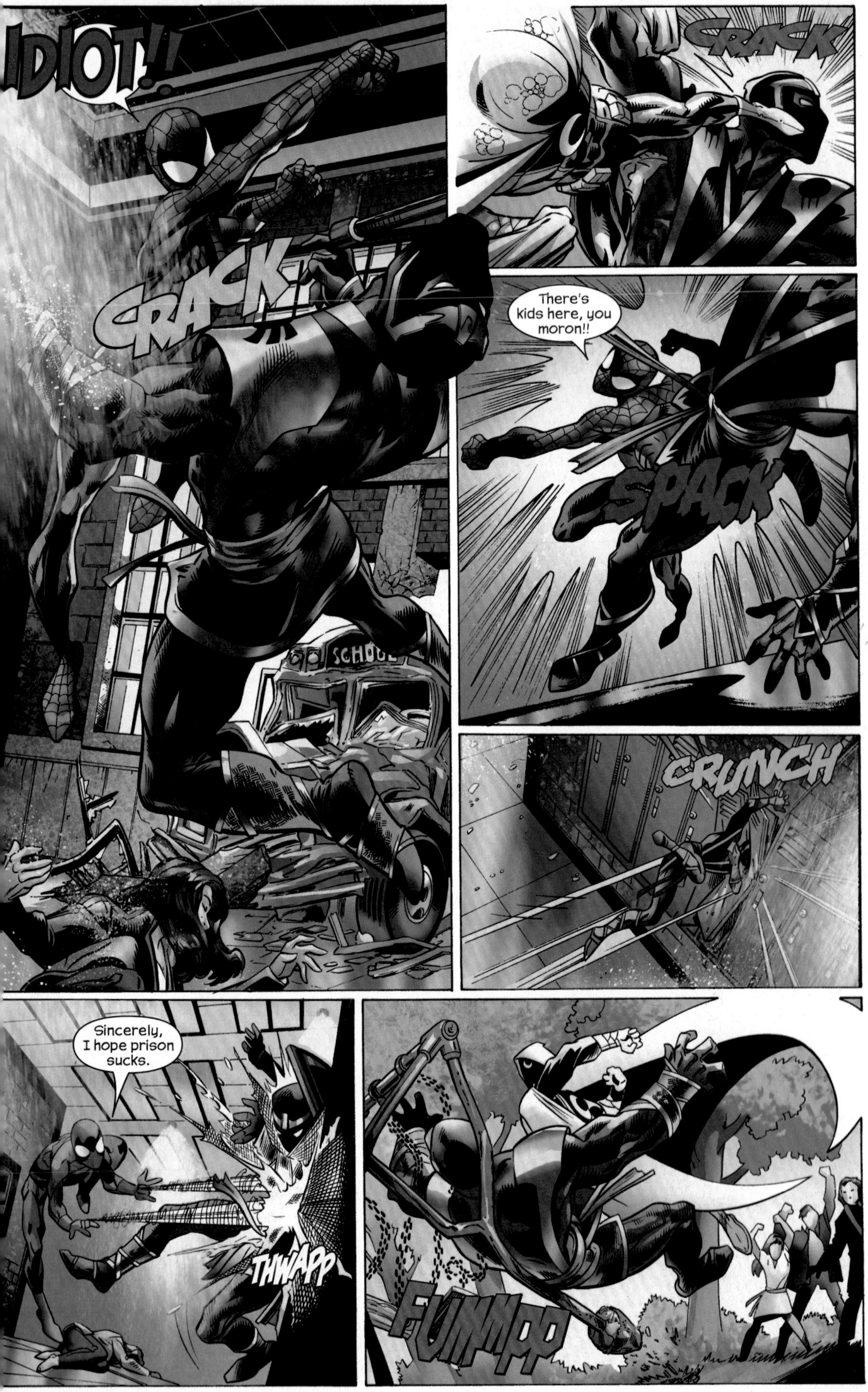
IDIOT!!
CRACK
CRACK
There's kids here, you moron!!
SPACK
CRUNCH
Sincerely, I hope prison sucks.
THWAPP
FUMMPP

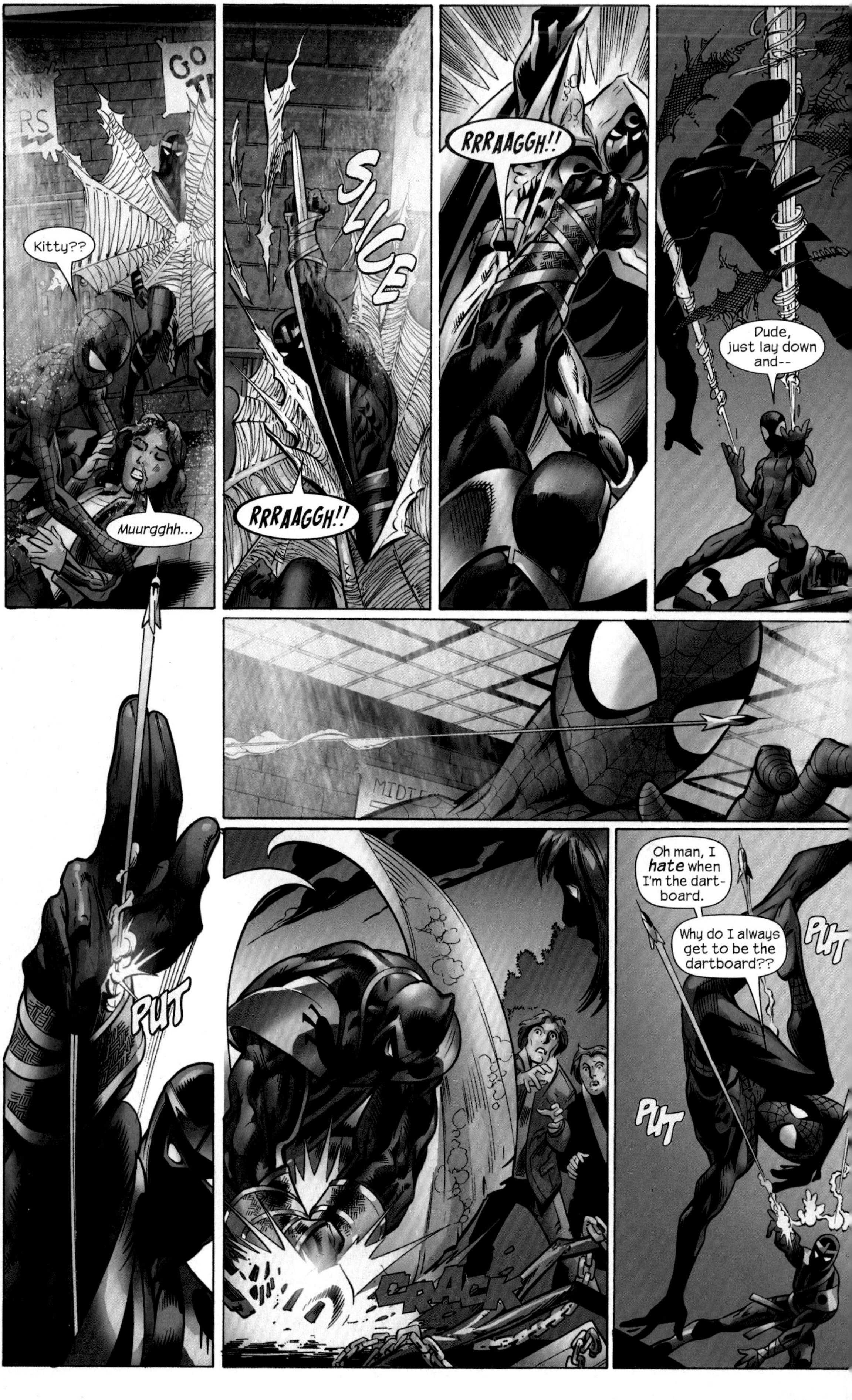
GO
Kitty??
Muurgghh...
SLICE
RRRAAGGH!!
RRRAAGGH!!
Dude, just lay down and--
PUT
Oh man, I hate when I'm the dart-board.
Why do I always get to be the dartboard??
PUT
PUT
CRACK

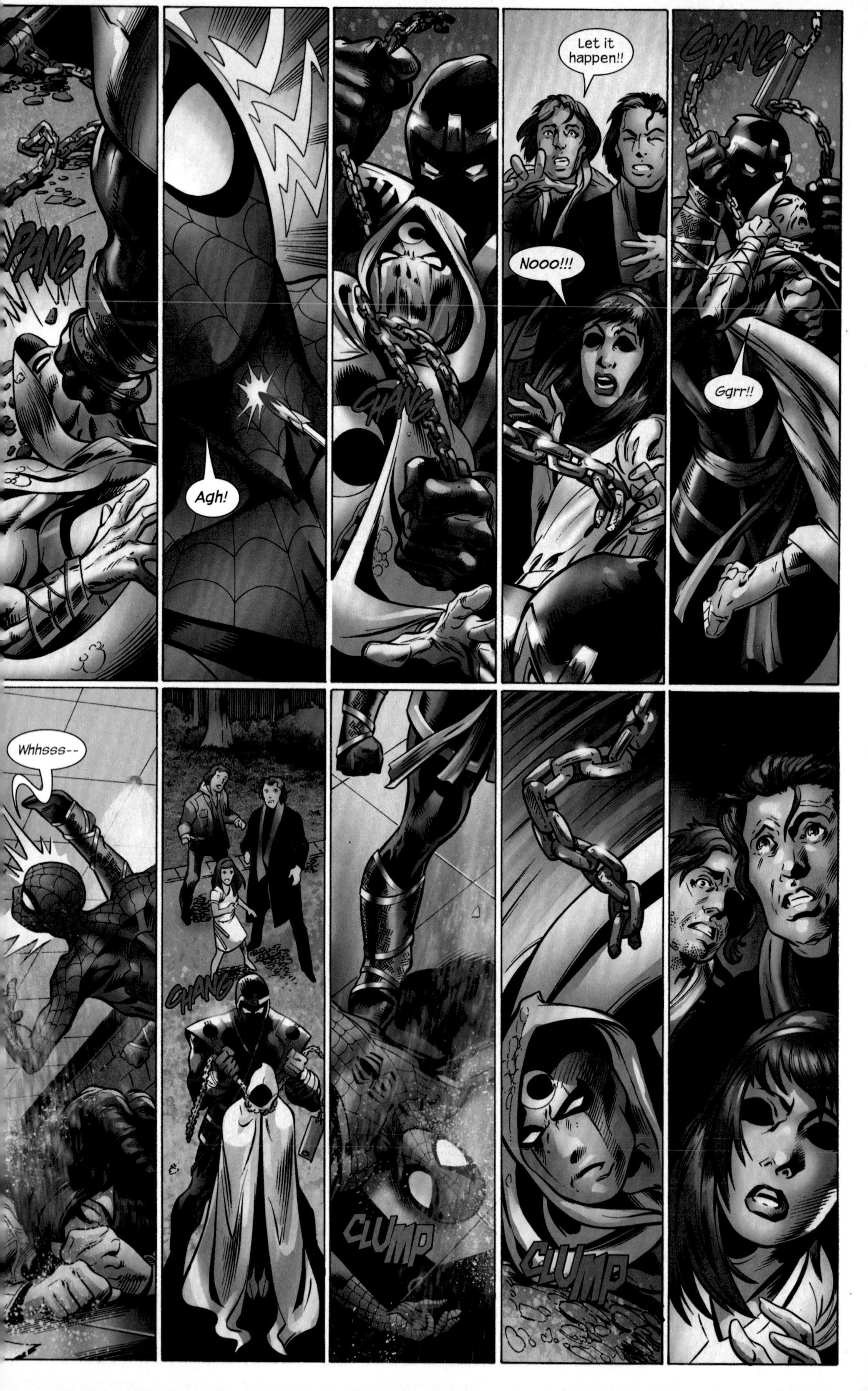
PANG
Agh!
CHANG
Let it happen!!
Nooo!!!
CHANG
Ggrr!!
Whhsss--
CHANG
CLUMP
CLUMP

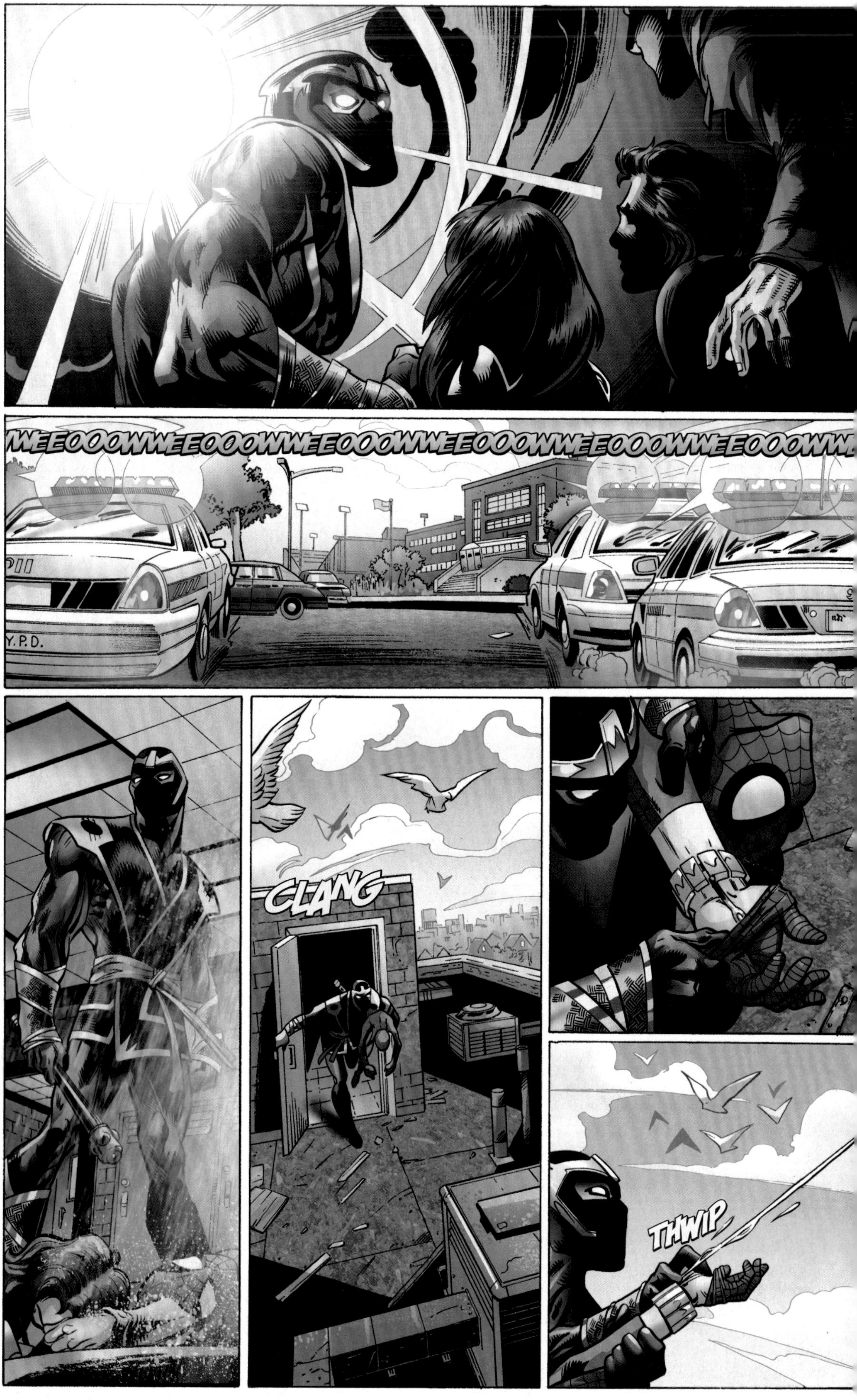
WEEOOOWWEEOOOWWEEOOOWWEEOOOWWEEOOOWWEEOOOWW
CLANG
THWIP

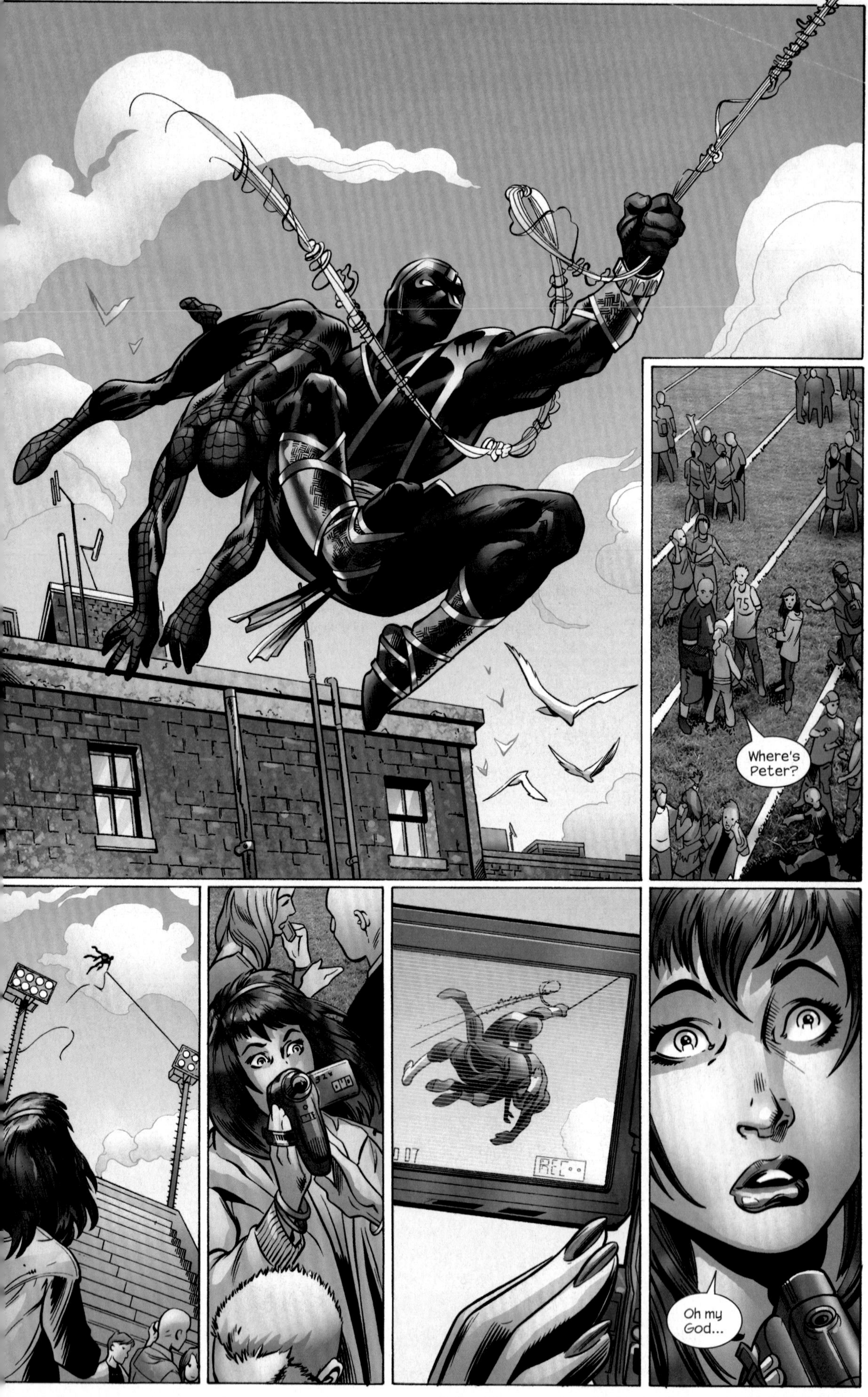
Where's Peter?
REC
Oh my God...

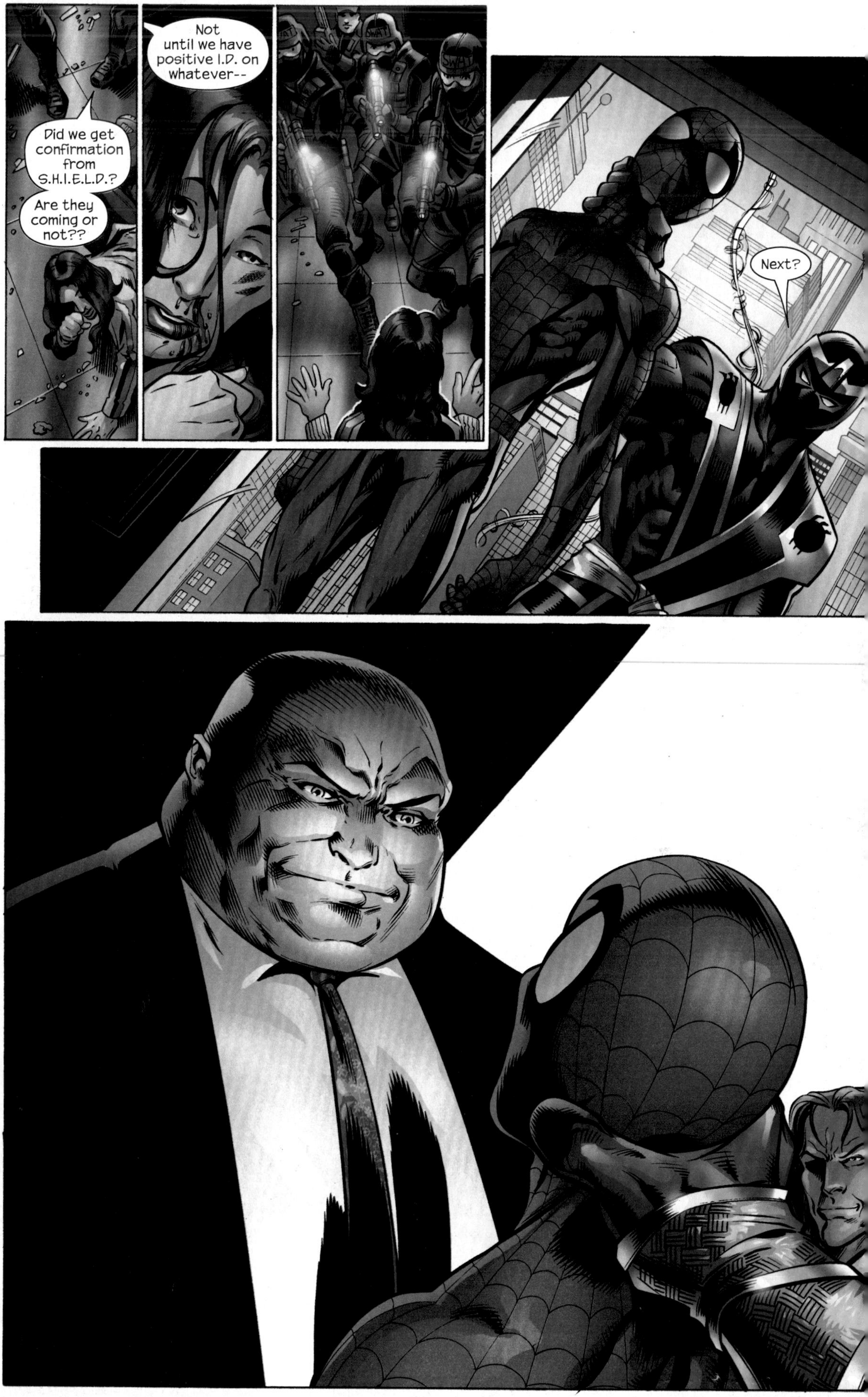

Did we get confirmation from S.H.I.E.L.D.?
Are they coming or not??
Not until we have positive I.D. on whatever--
Next?

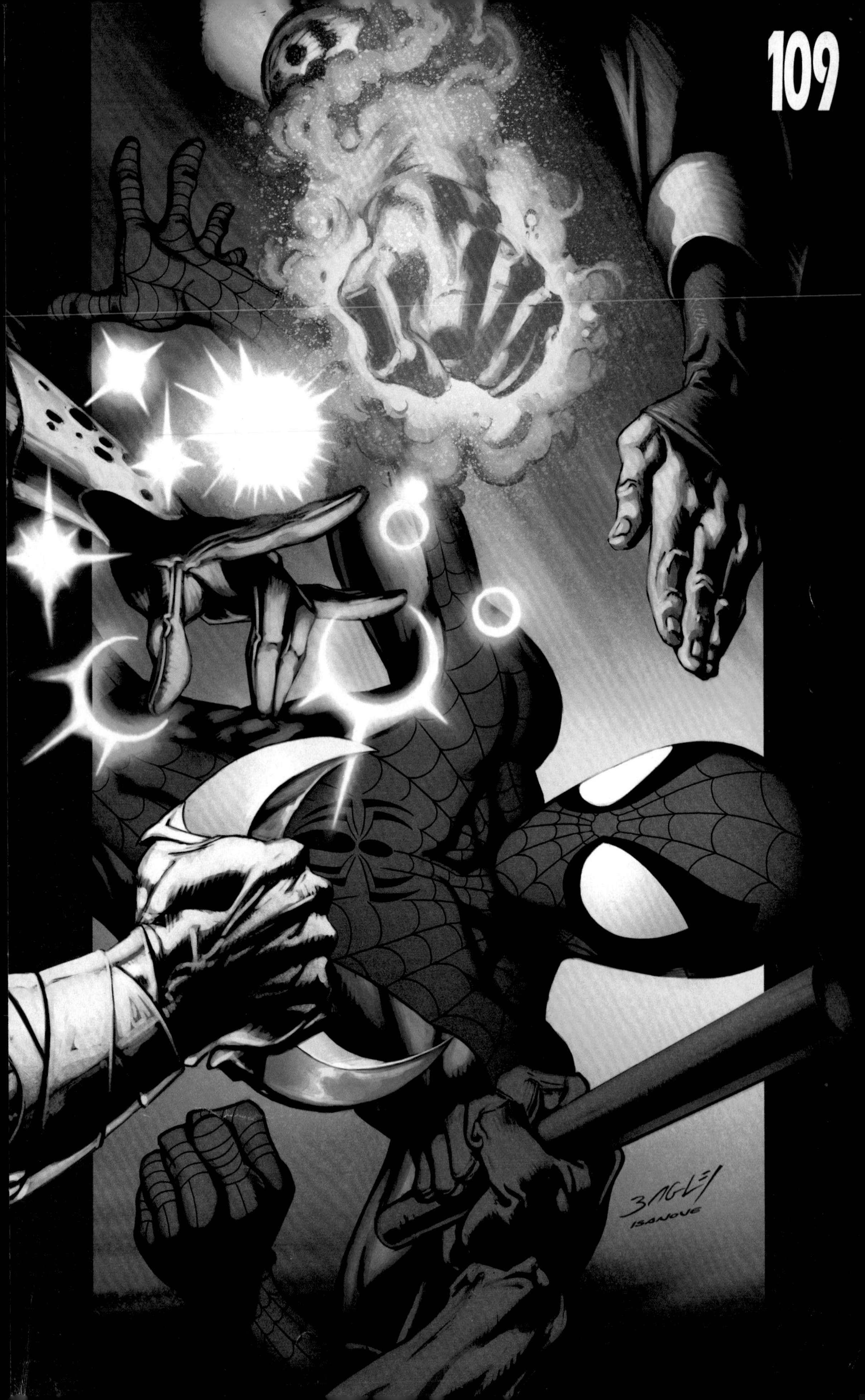
109

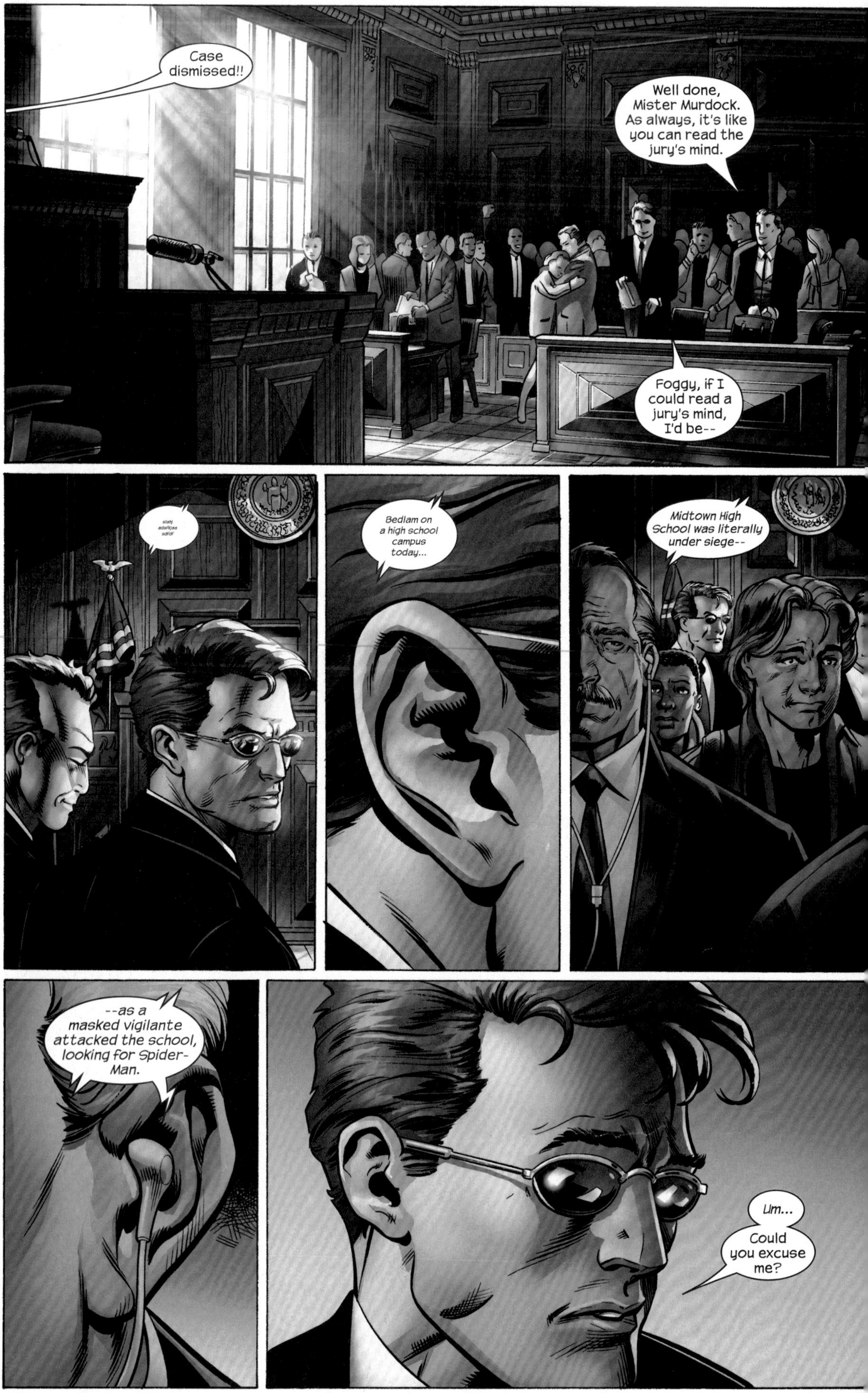
Case dismissed!!
Well done, Mister Murdock. As always, it's like you can read the jury's mind.
Foggy, if I could read a jury's mind, I'd be--
Bedlam on a high school campus today...
Midtown High School was literally under siege--
--as a masked vigilante attacked the school, looking for Spider-Man.
Um... Could you excuse me?

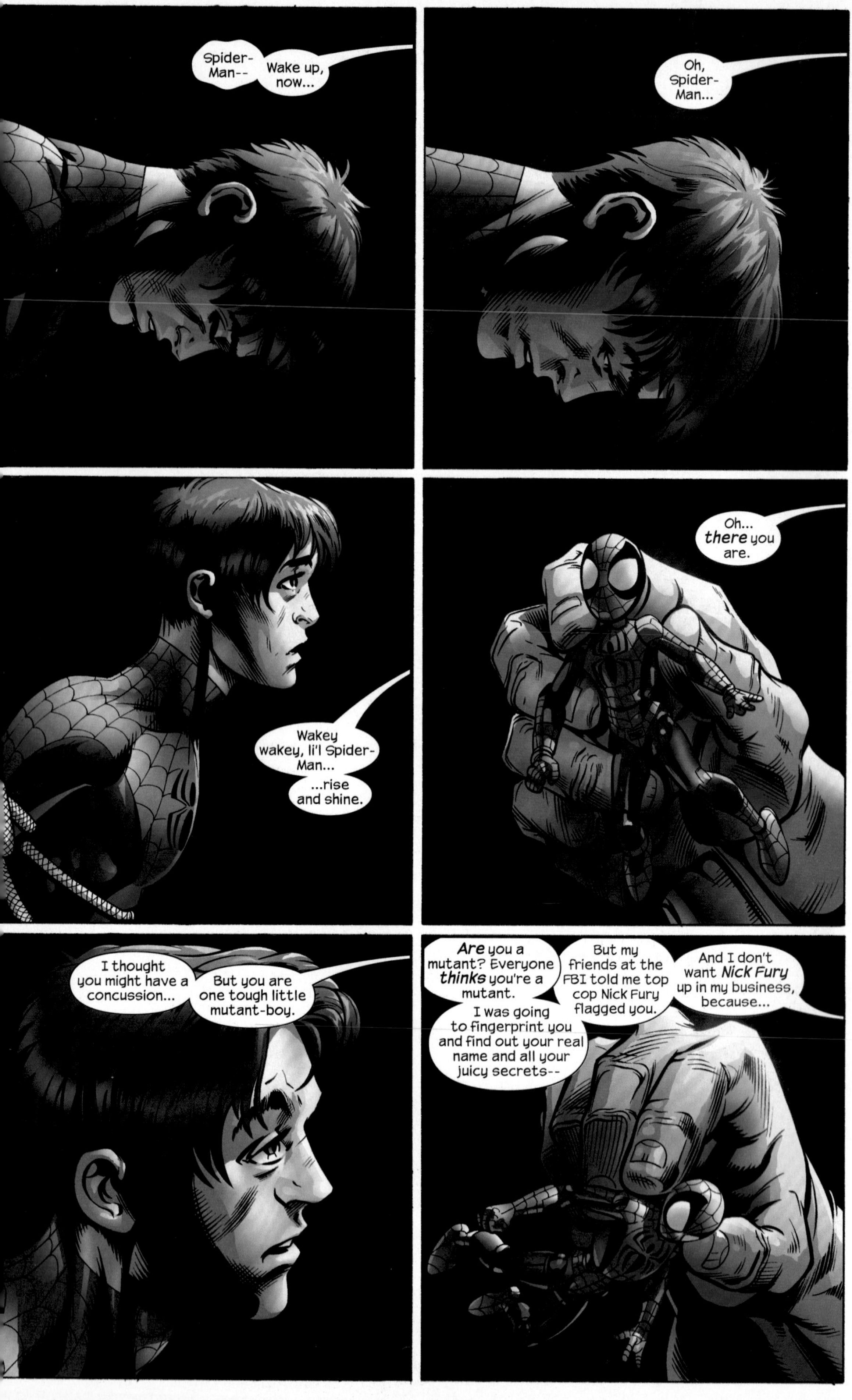
Spider-Man--
Wake up, now...
Oh, Spider-Man...
Wakey wakey, li'l Spider-Man...
...rise and shine.
Oh... *there* you are.
I thought you might have a concussion...
But you are one tough little mutant-boy.
*Are* you a mutant? Everyone *thinks* you're a mutant.
I was going to fingerprint you and find out your real name and all your juicy secrets--
But my friends at the FBI told me top cop Nick Fury flagged you.
And I don't want *Nick Fury* up in my business, because...

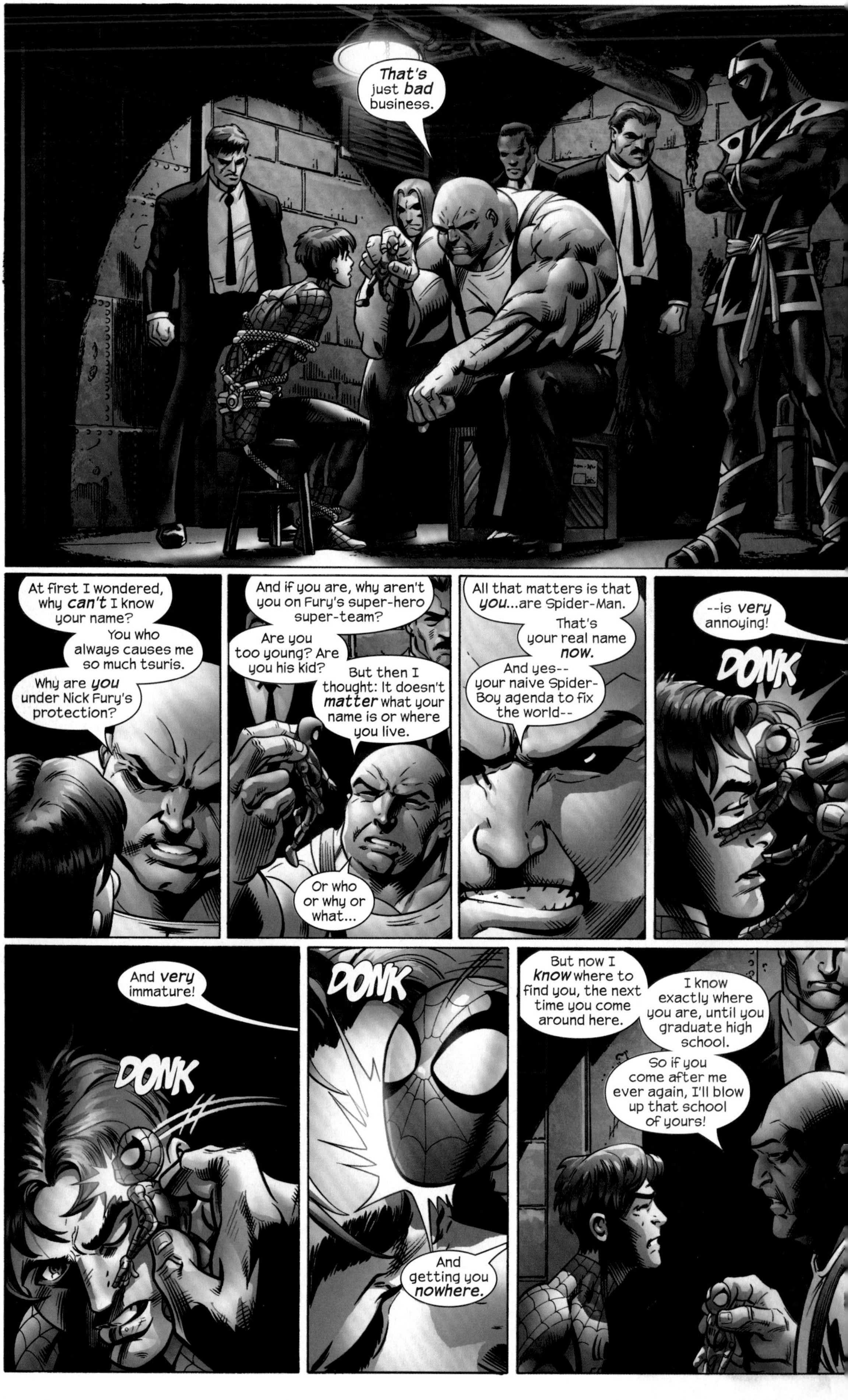
That's just bad business.
At first I wondered, why can't I know your name?
You who always causes me so much tsuris.
Why are you under Nick Fury's protection?
And if you are, why aren't you on Fury's super-hero super-team?
Are you too young? Are you his kid?
But then I thought: It doesn't matter what your name is or where you live.
Or who or why or what...
All that matters is that you...are Spider-Man.
That's your real name now.
And yes--your naive Spider-Boy agenda to fix the world--
--is very annoying!
DONK
And very immature!
DONK
DONK
And getting you nowhere.
But now I know where to find you, the next time you come around here.
I know exactly where you are, until you graduate high school.
So if you come after me ever again, I'll blow up that school of yours!

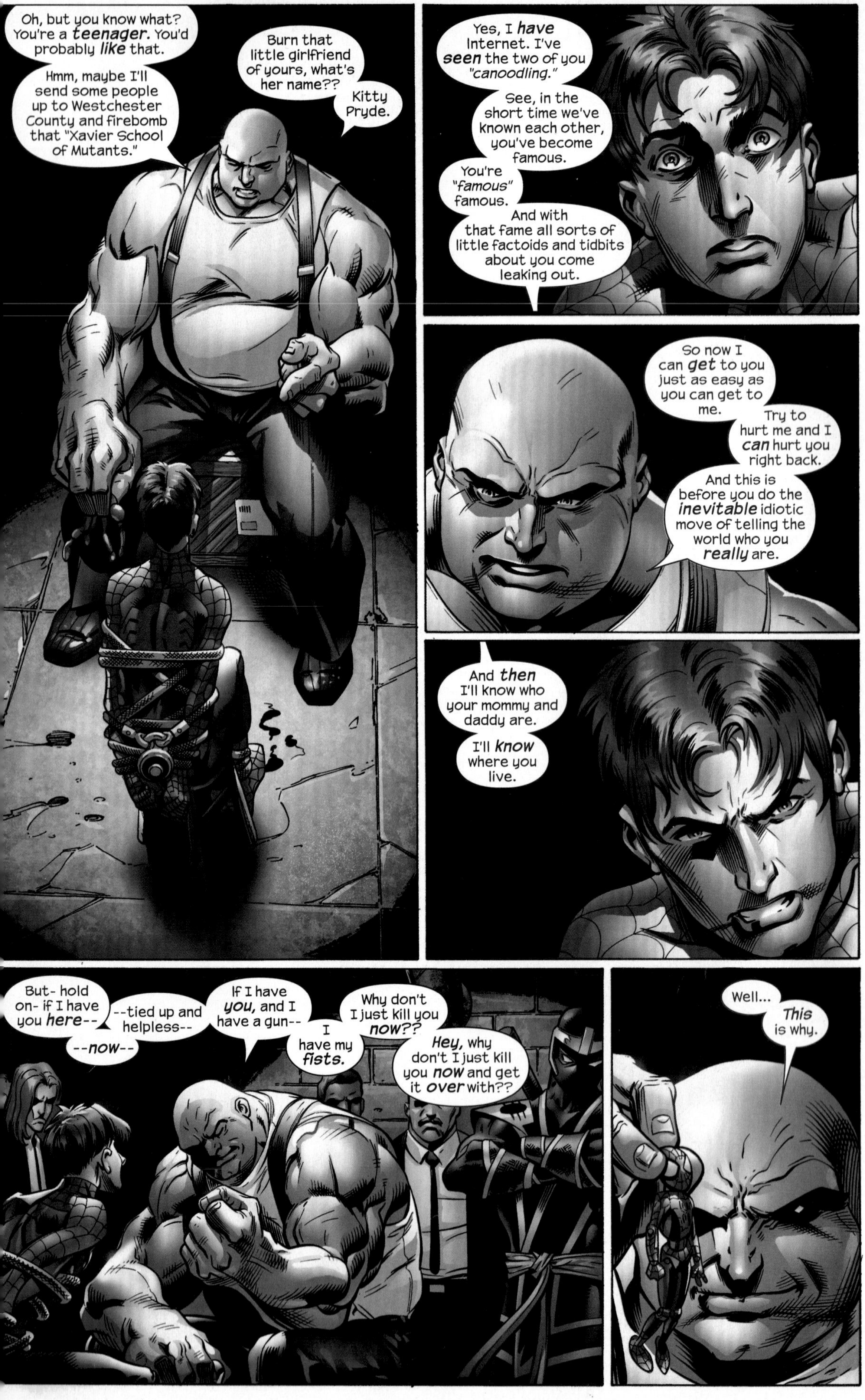
Oh, but you know what? You're a teenager. You'd probably like that.
Hmm, maybe I'll send some people up to Westchester County and firebomb that "Xavier School of Mutants."
Burn that little girlfriend of yours, what's her name??
Kitty Pryde.
Yes, I have Internet. I've seen the two of you "canoodling."
See, in the short time we've known each other, you've become famous.
You're "famous" famous.
And with that fame all sorts of little factoids and tidbits about you come leaking out.
So now I can get to you just as easy as you can get to me.
Try to hurt me and I can hurt you right back.
And this is before you do the inevitable idiotic move of telling the world who you really are.
And then I'll know who your mommy and daddy are.
I'll know where you live.
But- hold on- if I have you here--
--now--
--tied up and helpless--
If I have you, and I have a gun--
I have my fists.
Why don't I just kill you now??
Hey, why don't I just kill you now and get it over with??
Well...
This is why.

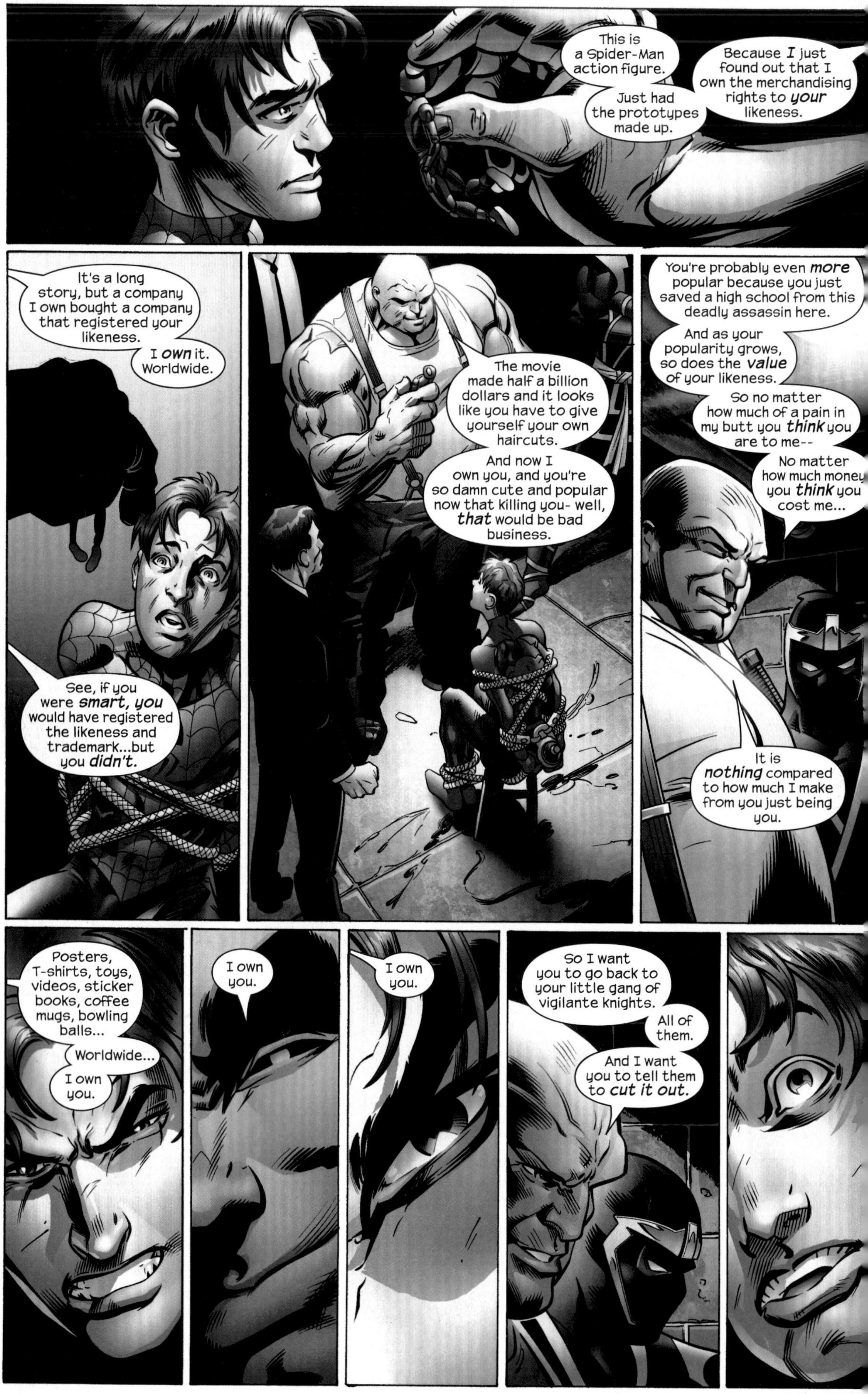
This is a Spider-Man action figure.
Just had the prototypes made up.
Because I just found out that I own the merchandising rights to your likeness.
It's a long story, but a company I own bought a company that registered your likeness.
I own it. Worldwide.
See, if you were smart, you would have registered the likeness and trademark...but you didn't.
The movie made half a billion dollars and it looks like you have to give yourself your own haircuts.
And now I own you, and you're so damn cute and popular now that killing you- well, that would be bad business.
You're probably even more popular because you just saved a high school from this deadly assassin here.
And as your popularity grows, so does the value of your likeness.
So no matter how much of a pain in my butt you think you are to me--
No matter how much money you think you cost me...
It is nothing compared to how much I make from you just being you.
Posters, T-shirts, toys, videos, sticker books, coffee mugs, bowling balls...
Worldwide...
I own you.
I own you.
I own you.
So I want you to go back to your little gang of vigilante knights.
All of them.
And I want you to tell them to cut it out.

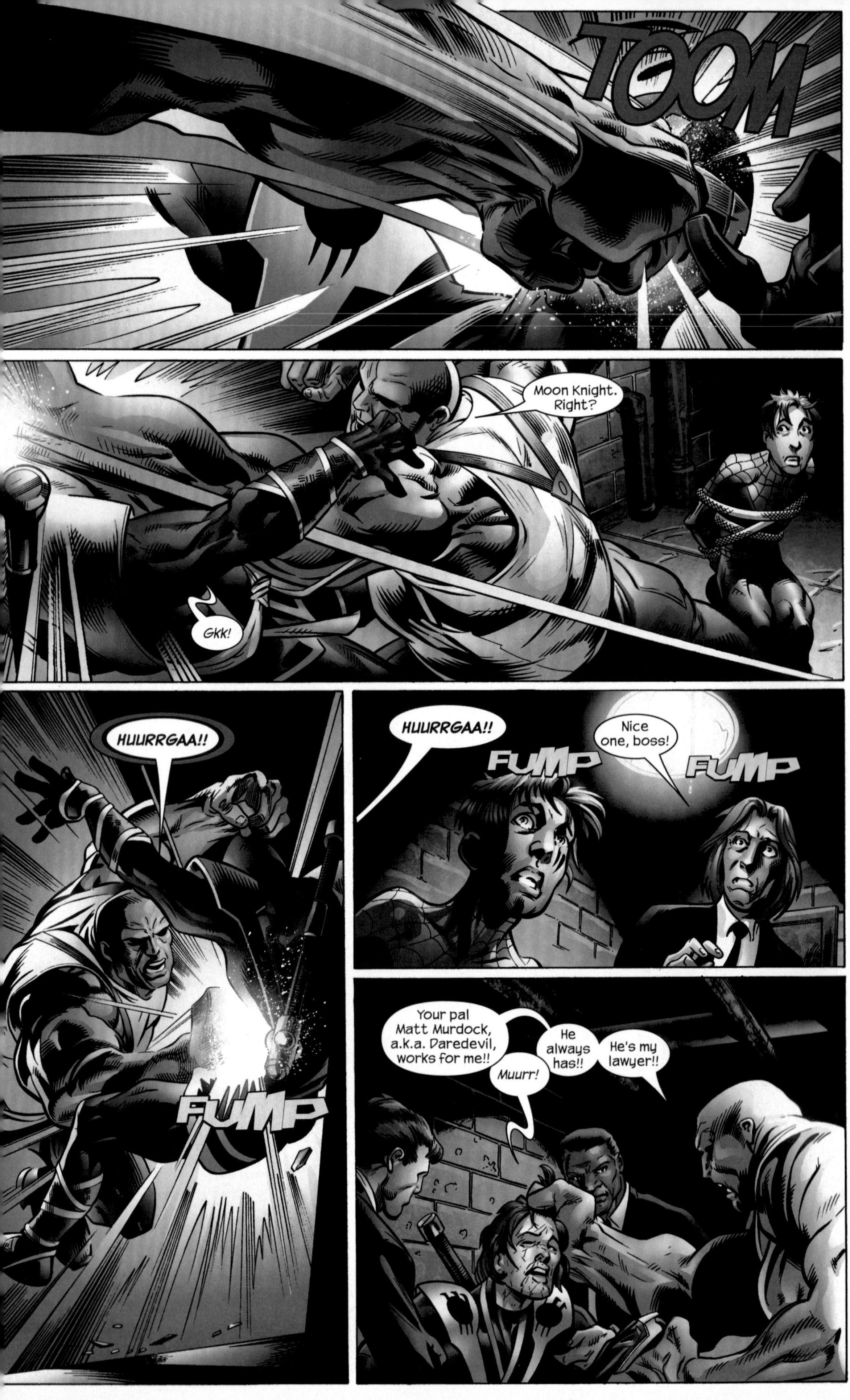
TOOM
Moon Knight. Right?
Gkk!
HUURRGAA!!
FUMP
HUURRGAA!!
Nice one, boss!
FUMP
FUMP
Your pal Matt Murdock, a.k.a. Daredevil, works for me!!
He always has!!
He's my lawyer!!
Muurr!

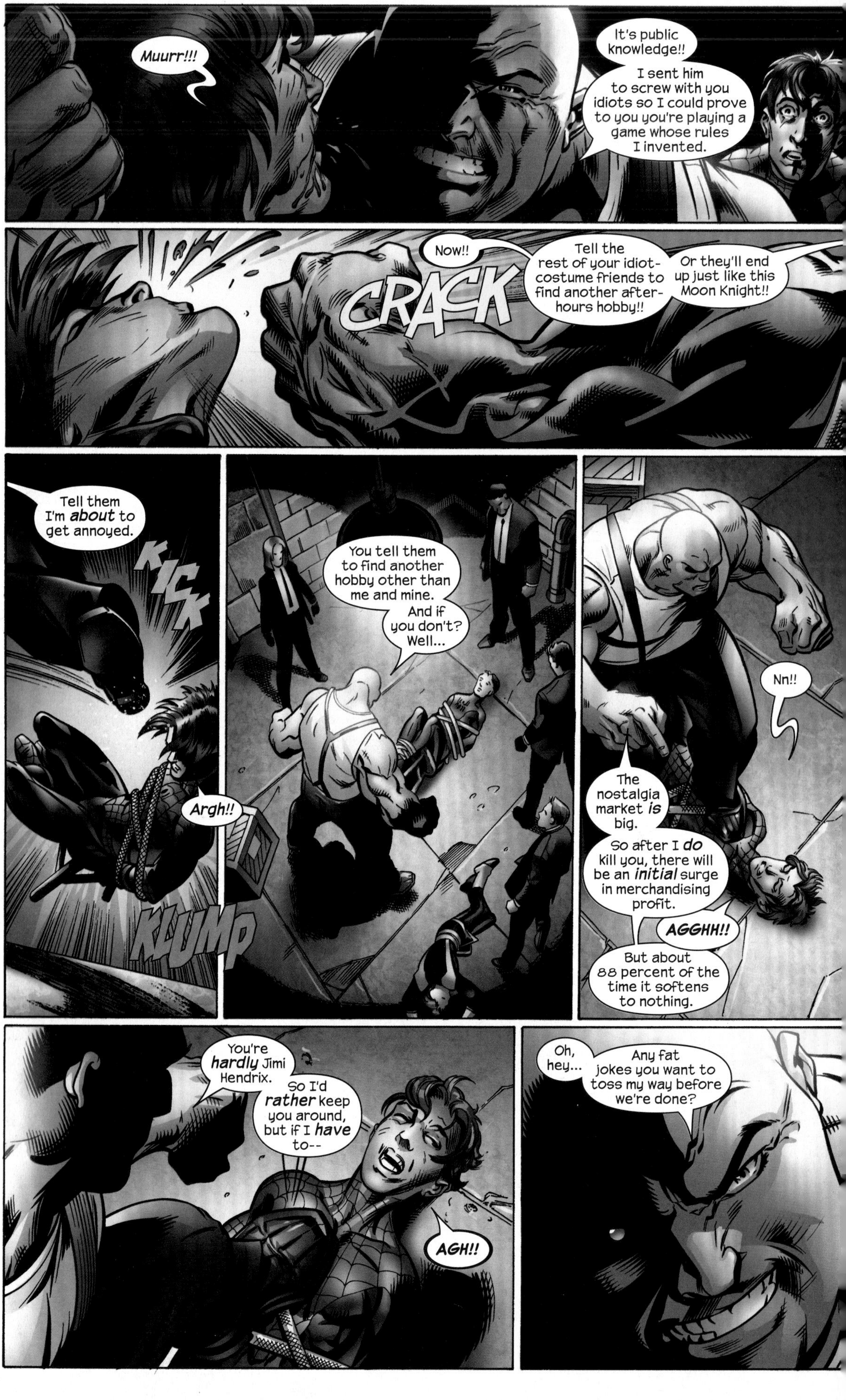
Muurr!!!
It's public knowledge!!
I sent him to screw with you idiots so I could prove to you you're playing a game whose rules I invented.
Now!!
CRACK
Tell the rest of your idiot-costume friends to find another after-hours hobby!!
Or they'll end up just like this Moon Knight!!
Tell them I'm *about* to get annoyed.
KICK
Argh!!
KLUMP
You tell them to find another hobby other than me and mine.
And if you don't? Well...
Nn!!
The nostalgia market *is* big.
So after I *do* kill you, there will be an *initial* surge in merchandising profit.
AGGHH!!
But about 88 percent of the time it softens to nothing.
You're *hardly* Jimi Hendrix.
So I'd *rather* keep you around, but if I *have* to--
AGH!!
Oh, hey...
Any fat jokes you want to toss my way before we're done?

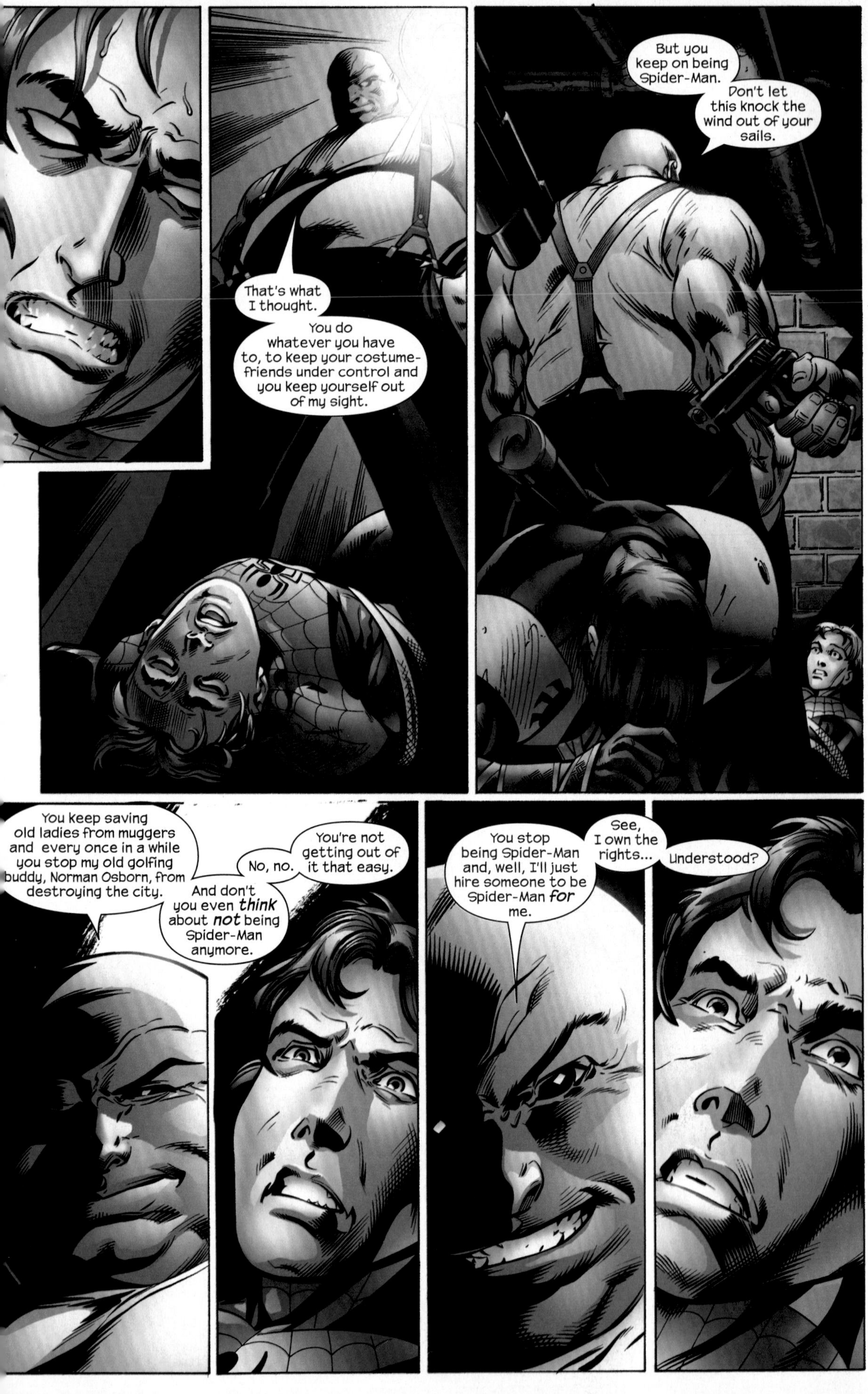
That's what I thought.
You do whatever you have to, to keep your costume-friends under control and you keep yourself out of my sight.
But you keep on being Spider-Man.
Don't let this knock the wind out of your sails.
You keep saving old ladies from muggers and every once in a while you stop my old golfing buddy, Norman Osborn, from destroying the city.
No, no.
You're not getting out of it that easy.
And don't you even *think* about *not* being Spider-Man anymore.
You stop being Spider-Man and, well, I'll just hire someone to be Spider-Man *for* me.
See, I own the rights...
Understood?

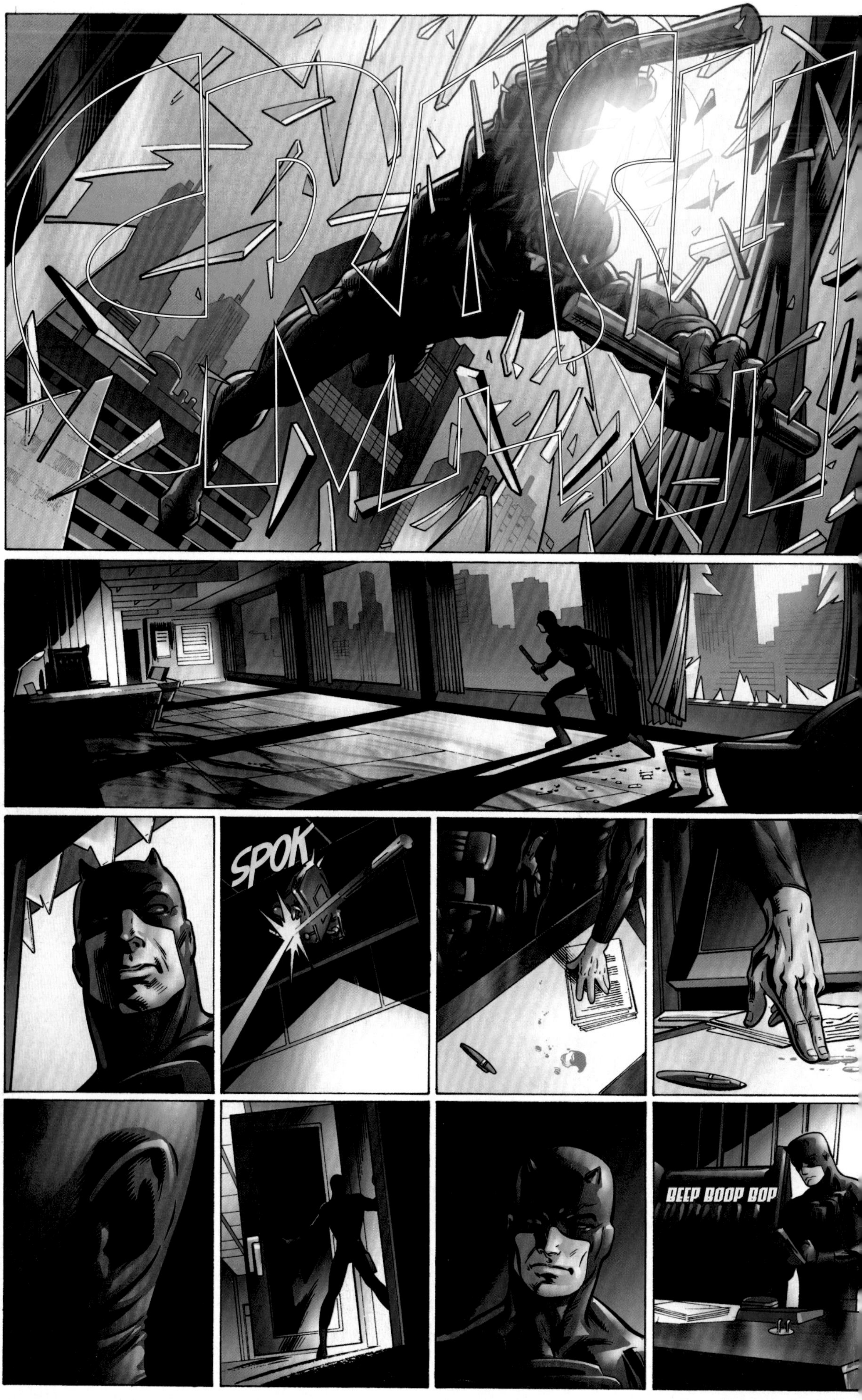
CRASH
SPOK
BEEP BOOP BOP

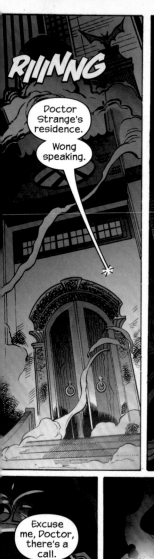

RIIINNG

Doctor Strange's residence. Wong speaking.

Wong, I need to speak to the doctor.

The Doctor is meditating.

It's important.

I'm sorry, the Doctor is meditating.

This is--

(oh brother)

--this is *Daredevil*. It's important.

Excuse me, Doctor, there's a call.

Can't you see I'm *meditating*?

Yes, sir. It's important.

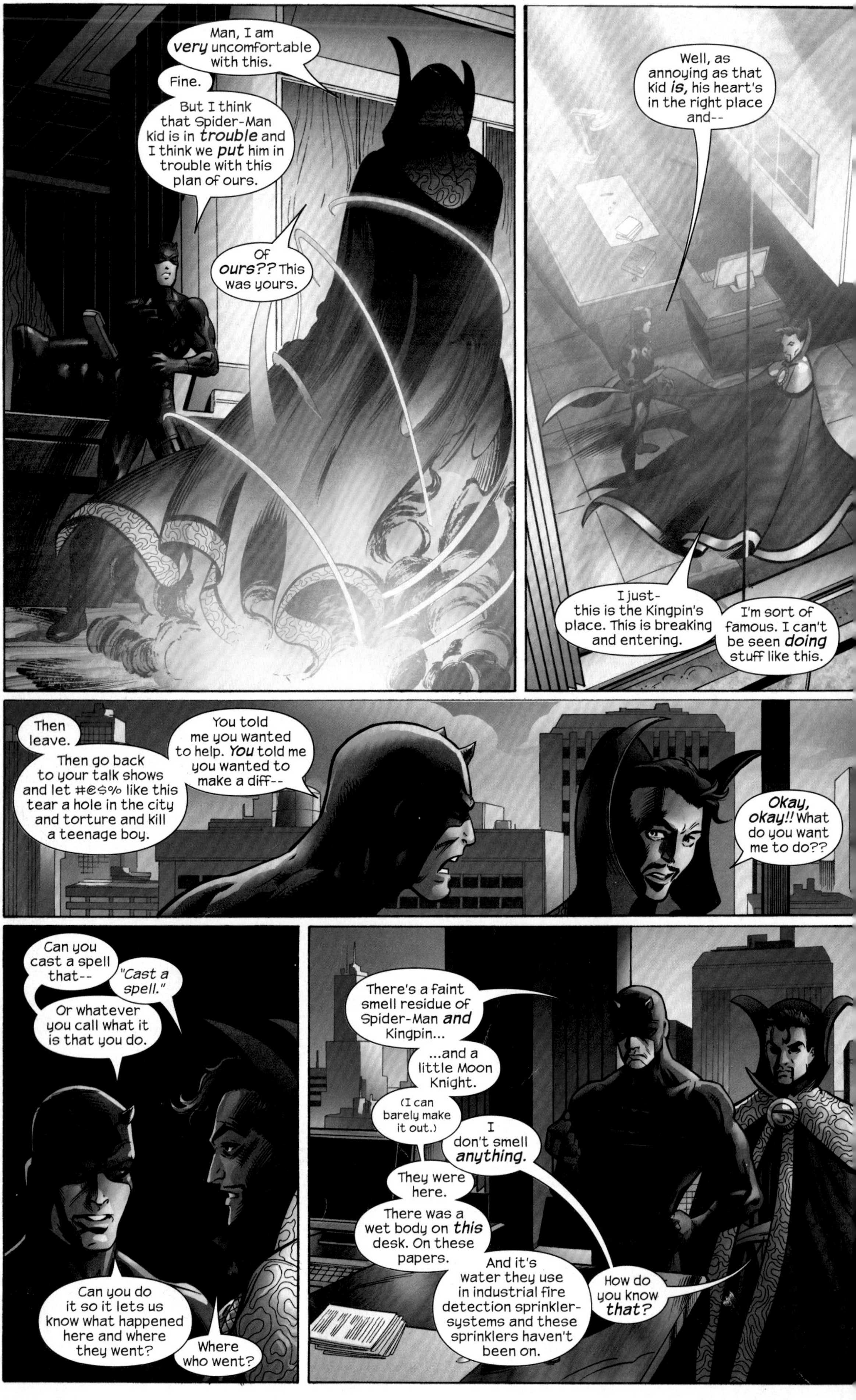
Man, I am *very* uncomfortable with this.
Fine.
But I think that Spider-Man kid is in *trouble* and I think we *put* him in trouble with this plan of ours.
Of *ours??* This was yours.
Well, as annoying as that kid *is*, his heart's in the right place and--
I just- this is the Kingpin's place. This is breaking and entering.
I'm sort of famous. I can't be seen *doing* stuff like this.
Then leave.
Then go back to your talk shows and let #@$% like this tear a hole in the city and torture and kill a teenage boy.
You told me you wanted to help. *You* told me you wanted to make a diff--
*Okay, okay!!* What do you want me to do??
Can you cast a spell that--
*"Cast a spell."*
Or whatever you call what it is that you do.
Can you do it so it lets us know what happened here and where they went?
Where who went?
There's a faint smell residue of Spider-Man *and* Kingpin...
...and a little Moon Knight.
(I can barely make it out.)
I don't smell *anything.*
They were here.
There was a wet body on *this* desk. On these papers.
And it's water they use in industrial fire detection sprinkler-systems and these sprinklers haven't been on.
How do you know *that?*

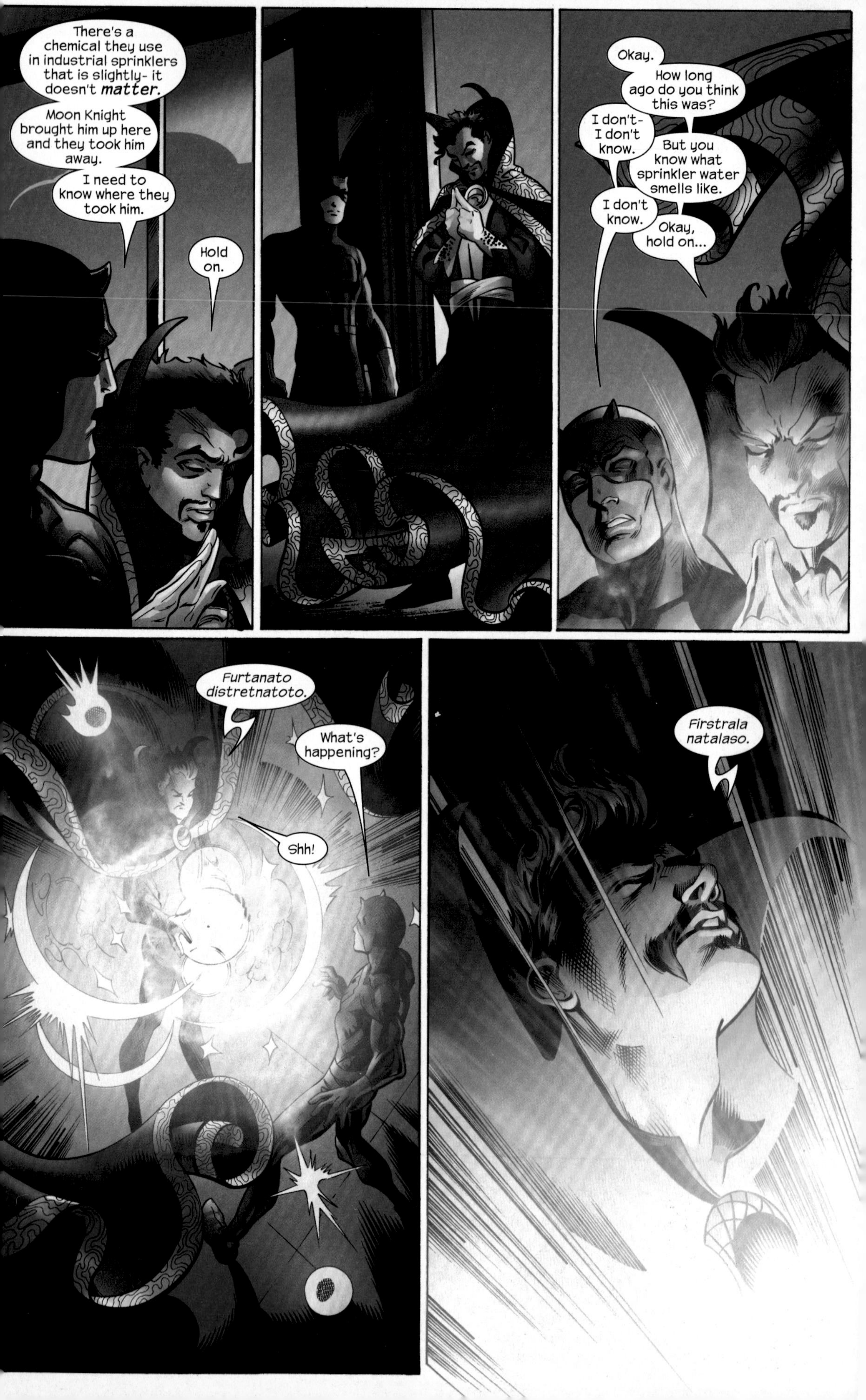
There's a chemical they use in industrial sprinklers that is slightly- it doesn't ***matter***.
Moon Knight brought him up here and they took him away.
I need to know where they took him.
Hold on.
Okay.
How long ago do you think this was?
I don't- I don't know.
But you know what sprinkler water smells like.
I don't know.
Okay, hold on...
*Furtanato distretnatoto.*
What's happening?
Shh!
*Firstrala natalaso.*

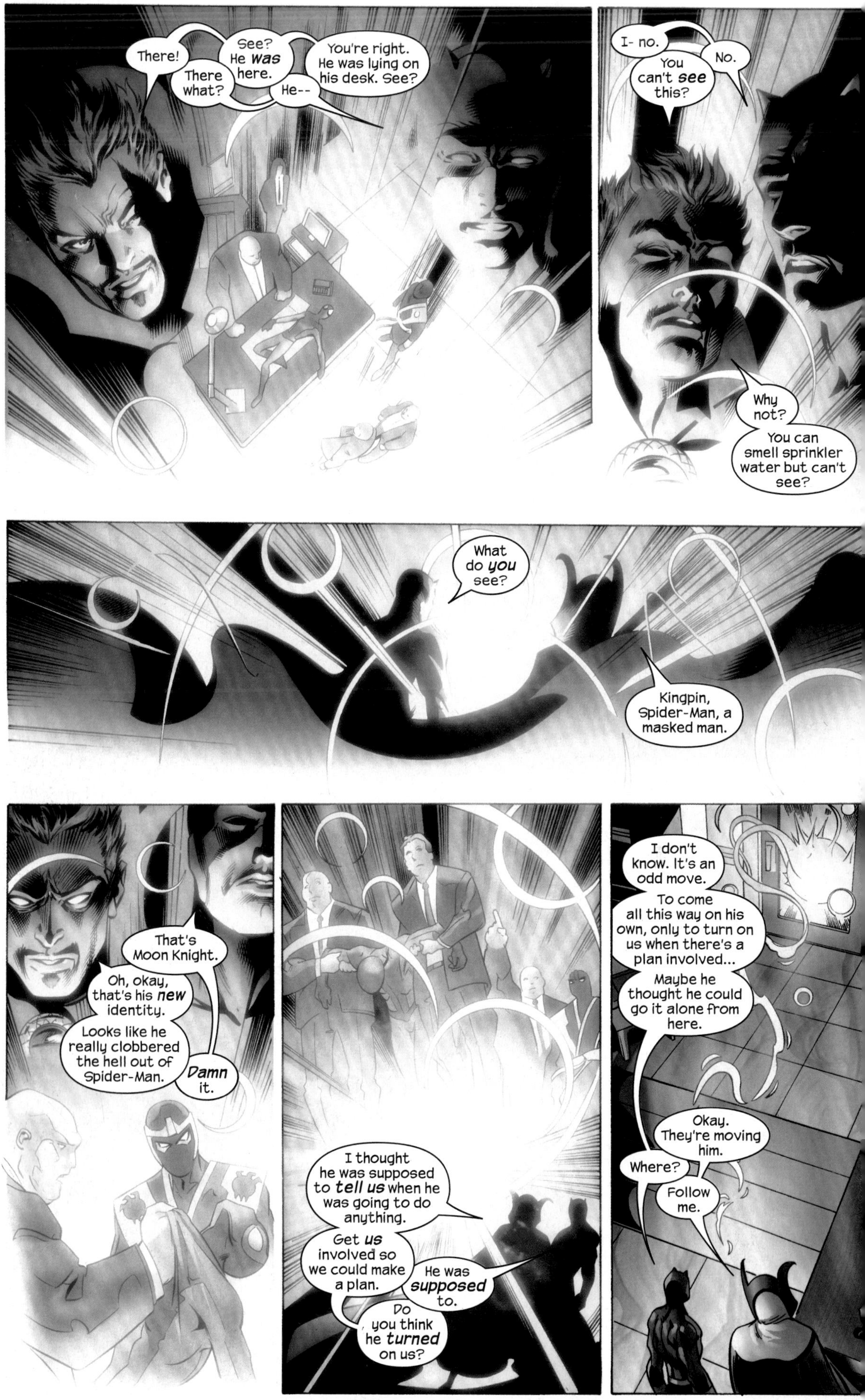
There!
There what?
See? He was here.
You're right. He was lying on his desk. See?
He--
I- no.
You can't see this?
No.
Why not?
You can smell sprinkler water but can't see?
What do you see?
Kingpin, Spider-Man, a masked man.
That's Moon Knight.
Oh, okay, that's his new identity.
Looks like he really clobbered the hell out of Spider-Man.
Damn it.
I thought he was supposed to tell us when he was going to do anything.
Get us involved so we could make a plan.
He was supposed to.
Do you think he turned on us?
I don't know. It's an odd move.
To come all this way on his own, only to turn on us when there's a plan involved...
Maybe he thought he could go it alone from here.
Okay. They're moving him.
Where?
Follow me.

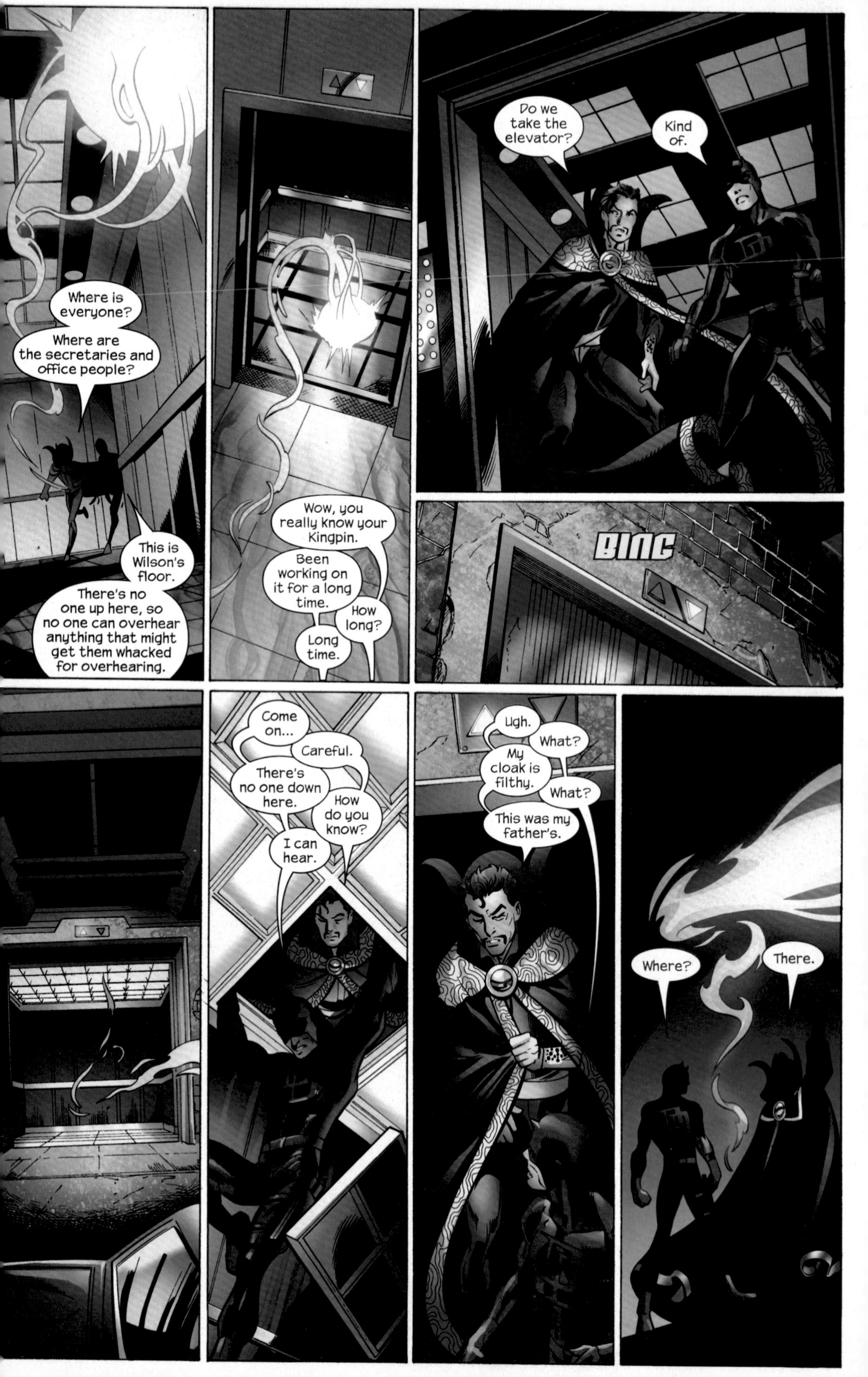
Where is everyone?
Where are the secretaries and office people?
This is Wilson's floor.
There's no one up here, so no one can overhear anything that might get them whacked for overhearing.
Wow, you really know your Kingpin.
Been working on it for a long time.
How long?
Long time.
Do we take the elevator?
Kind of.
BING
Come on...
Careful.
There's no one down here.
How do you know?
I can hear.
Ugh.
What?
My cloak is filthy.
What?
This was my father's.
Where?
There.

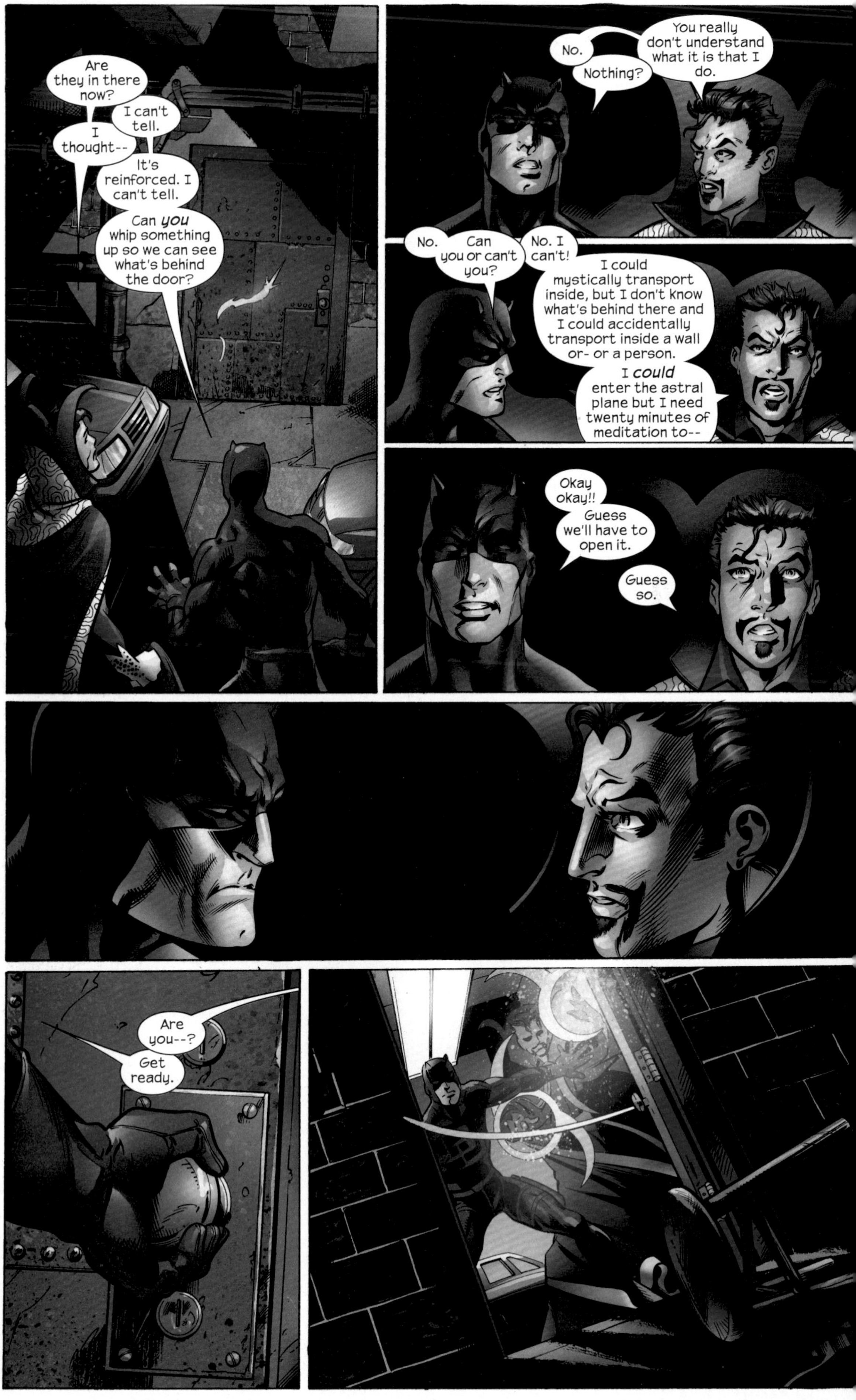

Are they in there now?
I can't tell.
I thought--
It's reinforced. I can't tell.
Can *you* whip something up so we can see what's behind the door?
No.
Nothing?
You really don't understand what it is that I do.
No.
Can you or can't you?
No. I can't!
I could mystically transport inside, but I don't know what's behind there and I could accidentally transport inside a wall or- or a person.
I *could* enter the astral plane but I need twenty minutes of meditation to--
Okay okay!!
Guess we'll have to open it.
Guess so.
Are you--?
Get ready.

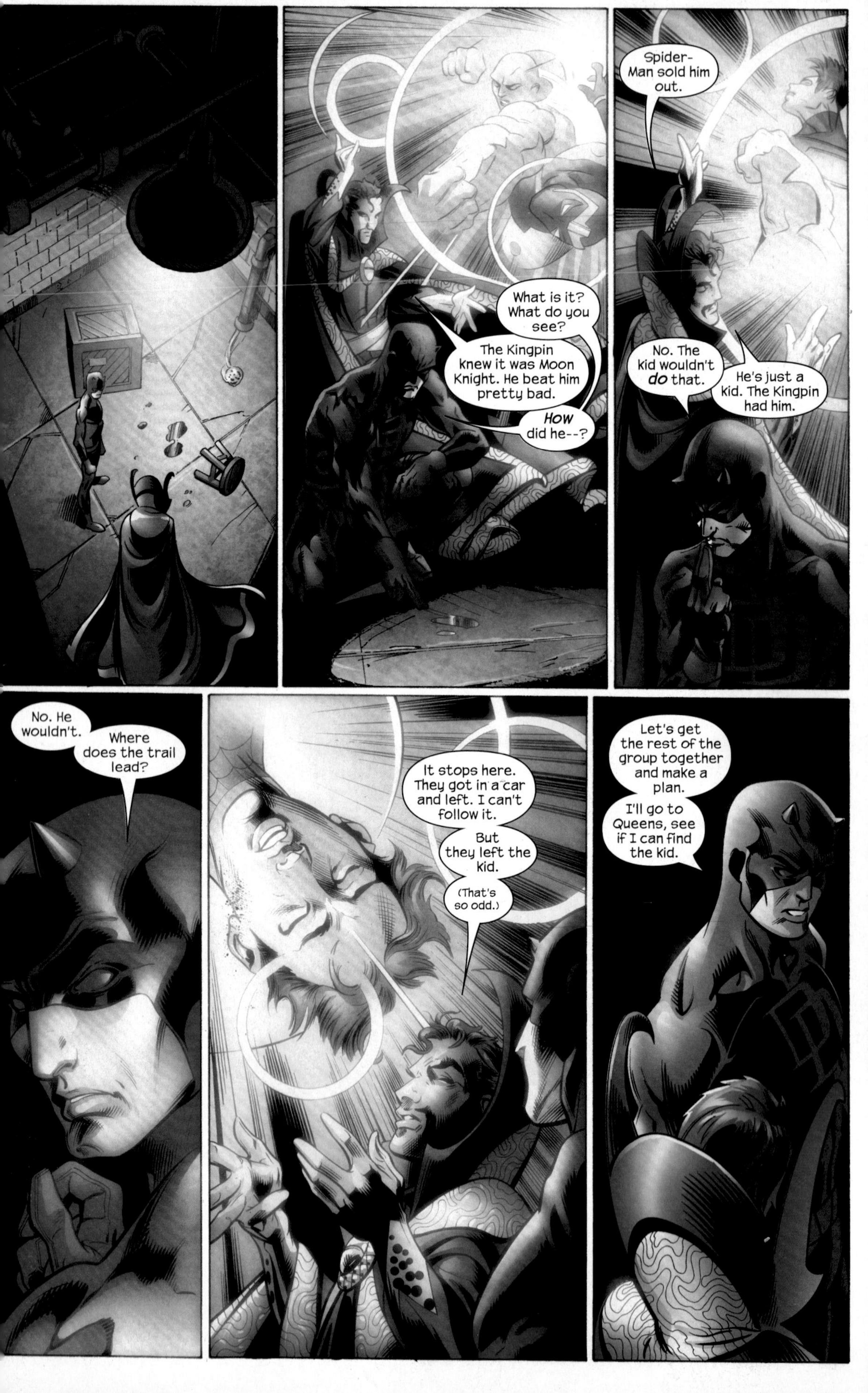
What is it? What do you see?
The Kingpin knew it was Moon Knight. He beat him pretty bad.
HOW did he--?
Spider-Man sold him out.
No. The kid wouldn't DO that.
He's just a kid. The Kingpin had him.
No. He wouldn't.
Where does the trail lead?
It stops here. They got in a car and left. I can't follow it.
But they left the kid.
(That's so odd.)
Let's get the rest of the group together and make a plan.
I'll go to Queens, see if I can find the kid.

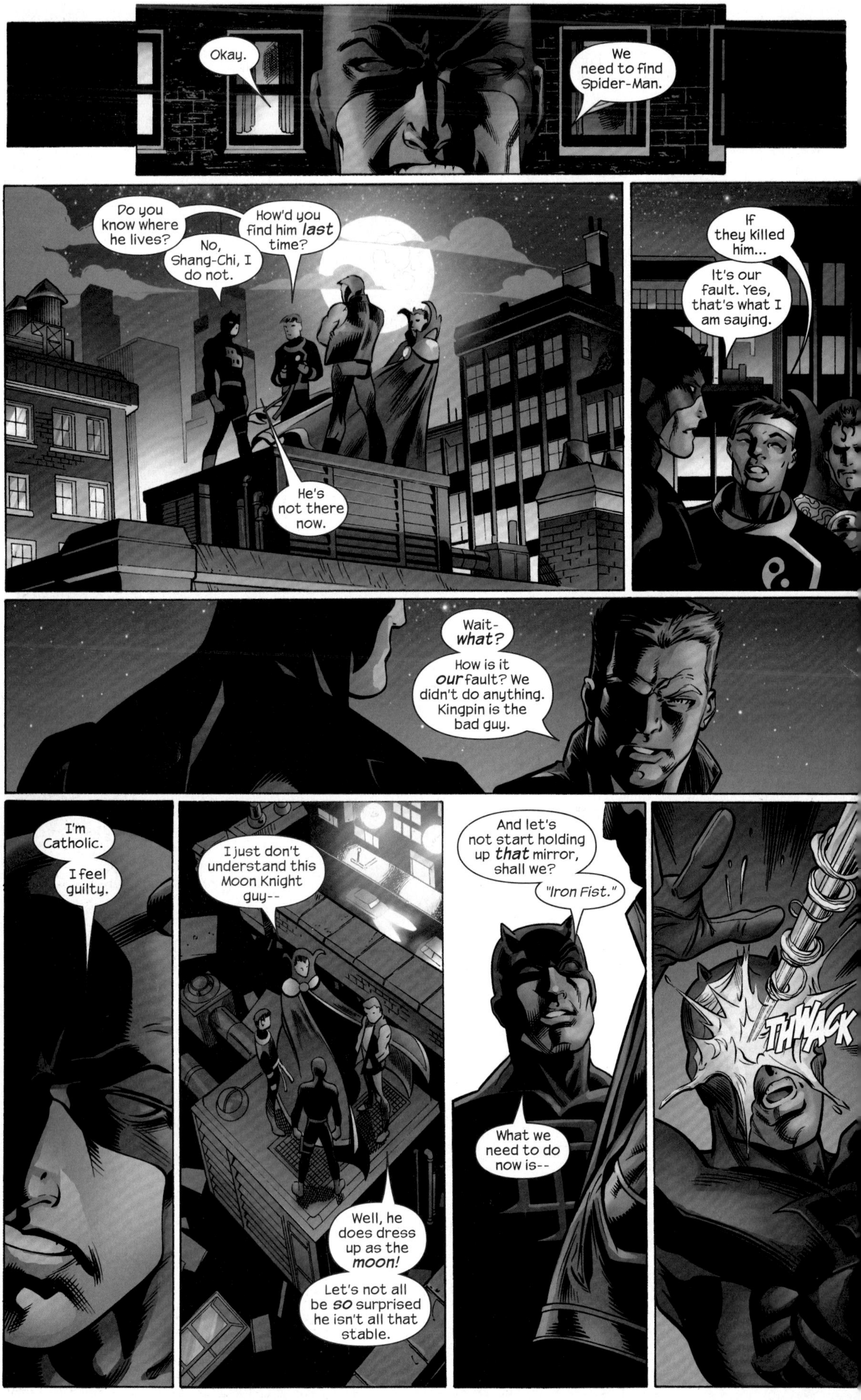
Okay.
We need to find Spider-Man.
Do you know where he lives?
How'd you find him last time?
No, Shang-Chi, I do not.
He's not there now.
If they killed him...
It's our fault. Yes, that's what I am saying.
Wait- what?
How is it our fault? We didn't do anything. Kingpin is the bad guy.
I'm Catholic.
I feel guilty.
I just don't understand this Moon Knight guy--
Well, he does dress up as the moon!
Let's not all be so surprised he isn't all that stable.
And let's not start holding up that mirror, shall we?
"Iron Fist."
What we need to do now is--
THWACK

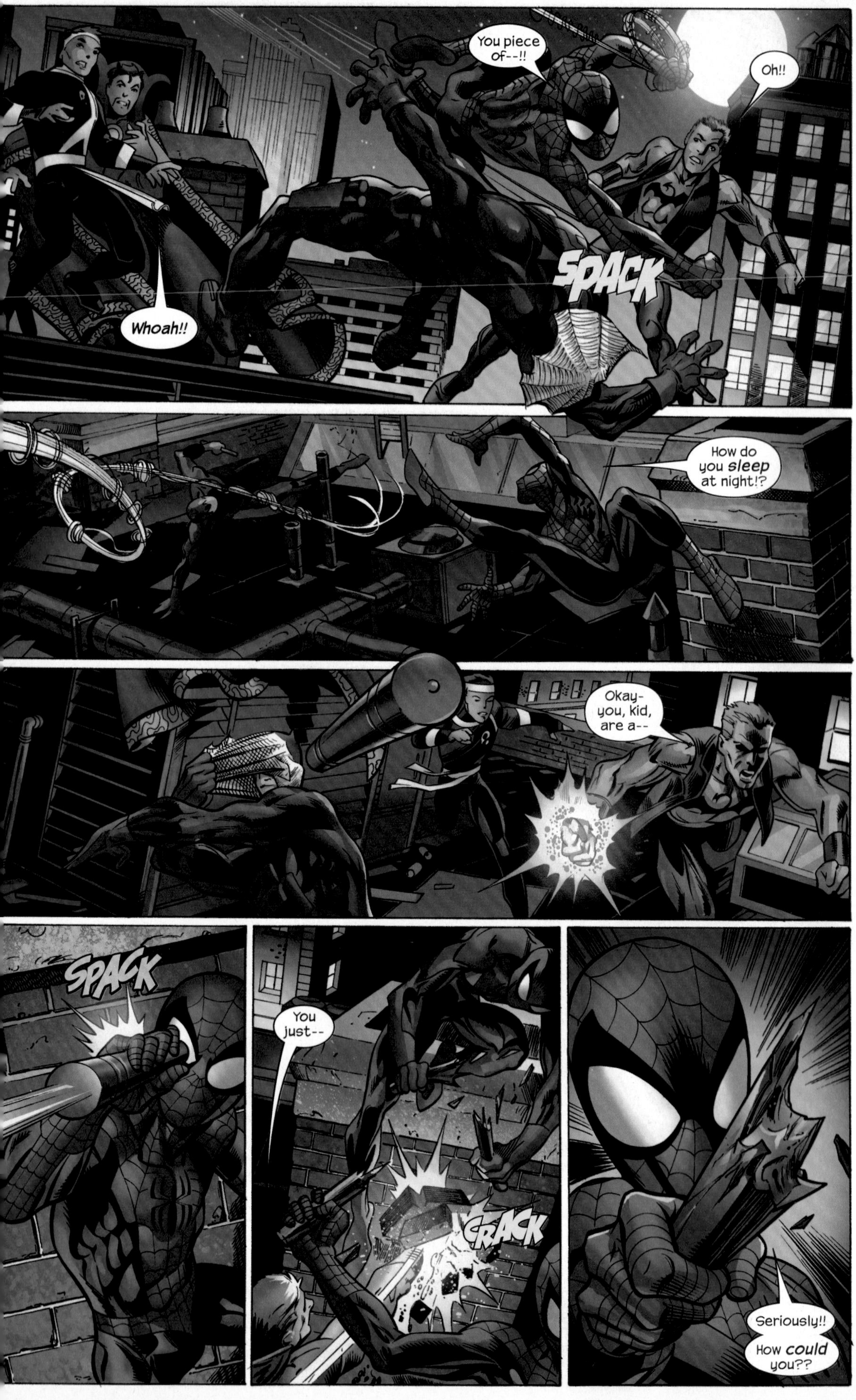
You piece of--!!
Oh!!
SPACK
Whoah!!
How do you sleep at night!?
Okay-you, kid, are a--
SPACK
You just--
CRACK
Seriously!!
How could you??

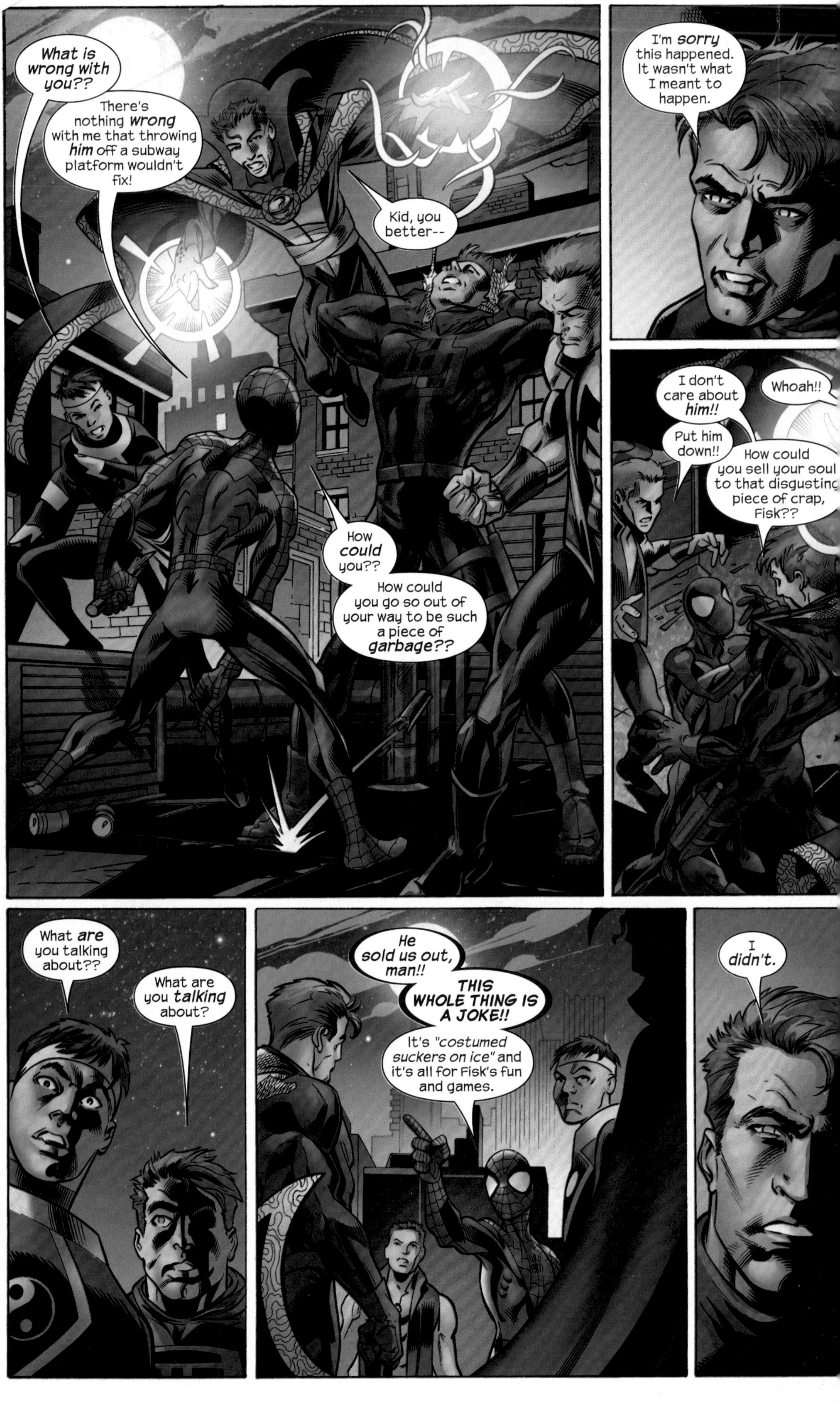
What is wrong with you??
There's nothing wrong with me that throwing him off a subway platform wouldn't fix!
Kid, you better--
How could you??
How could you go so out of your way to be such a piece of garbage??
I'm sorry this happened. It wasn't what I meant to happen.
I don't care about him!!
Whoah!!
Put him down!!
How could you sell your soul to that disgusting piece of crap, Fisk??
What are you talking about??
What are you talking about?
He sold us out, man!!
THIS WHOLE THING IS A JOKE!!
It's "costumed suckers on ice" and it's all for Fisk's fun and games.
I didn't.

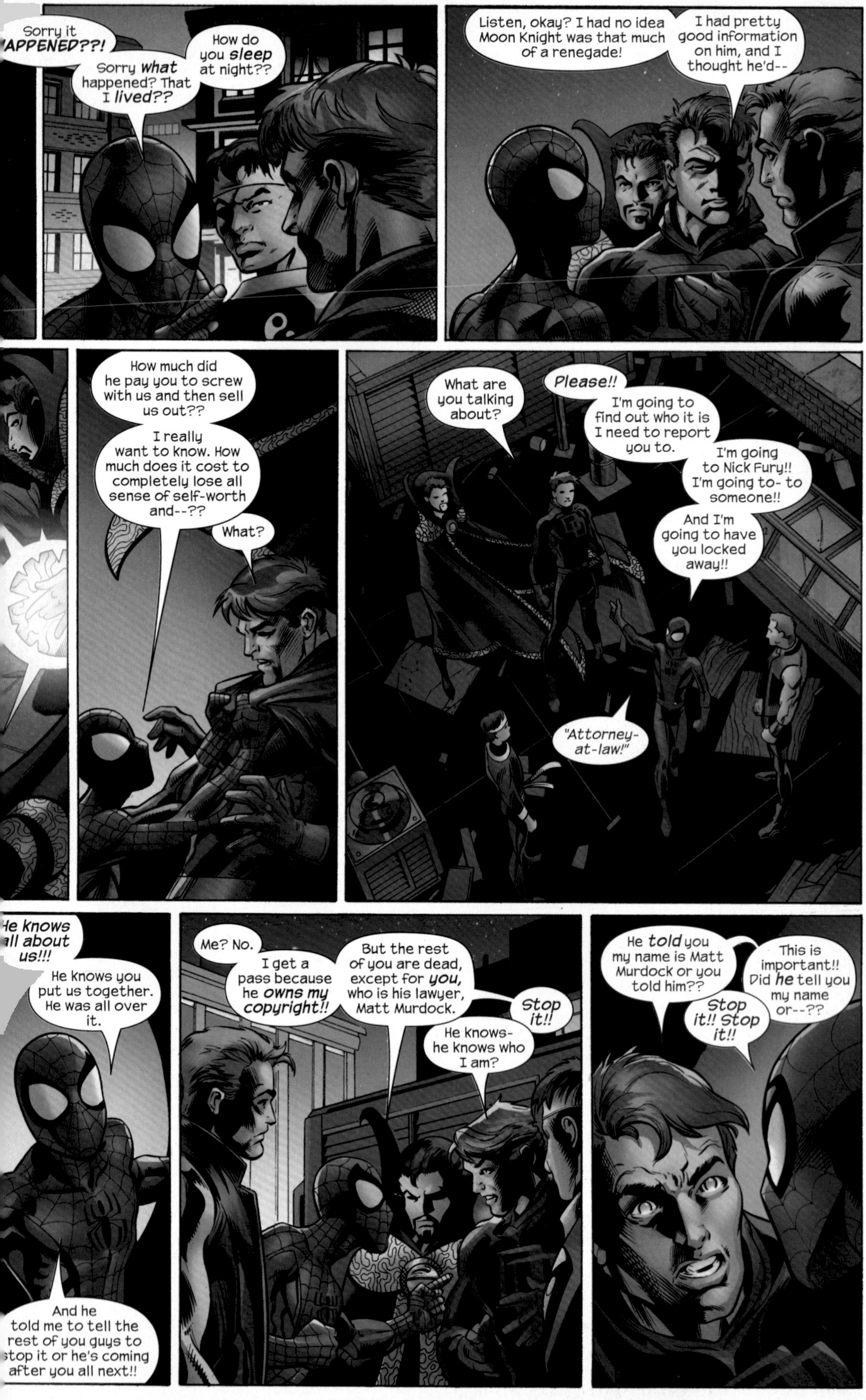

Sorry it
APPENED??!
Sorry what happened? That I lived??
How do you sleep at night??
Listen, okay? I had no idea Moon Knight was that much of a renegade!
I had pretty good information on him, and I thought he'd--
How much did he pay you to screw with us and then sell us out??
I really want to know. How much does it cost to completely lose all sense of self-worth and--??
What?
What are you talking about?
Please!!
I'm going to find out who it is I need to report you to.
I'm going to Nick Fury!! I'm going to- to someone!!
And I'm going to have you locked away!!
"Attorney-at-law!"
He knows
ll about us!!!
He knows you put us together. He was all over it.
And he told me to tell the rest of you guys to stop it or he's coming after you all next!!
Me? No.
I get a pass because he owns my copyright!!
But the rest of you are dead, except for you, who is his lawyer, Matt Murdock.
Stop it!!
He knows- he knows who I am?
He told you my name is Matt Murdock or you told him??
This is important!! Did he tell you my name or--??
Stop it!! Stop it!!

FABOOM

Let's go!!

There's no one there.

It's closed for the night. Everyone went home.

Let it burn.

Whoah!!

What was that?!!

My law office.

What?

But-- The fire department is on its way.

I'm not going to run around my office screaming at the wind.

Because that's *exactly* what he wants me to do.

He killed my father.

I don't know if you can relate to this at all but--

--but this man- in his rise to power- killed my father because he wouldn't throw a boxing match.

He *killed* my father.

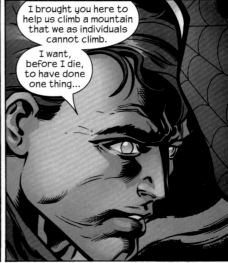

I brought you here to help us climb a mountain that we as individuals cannot climb.

I want, before I die, to have done one thing...

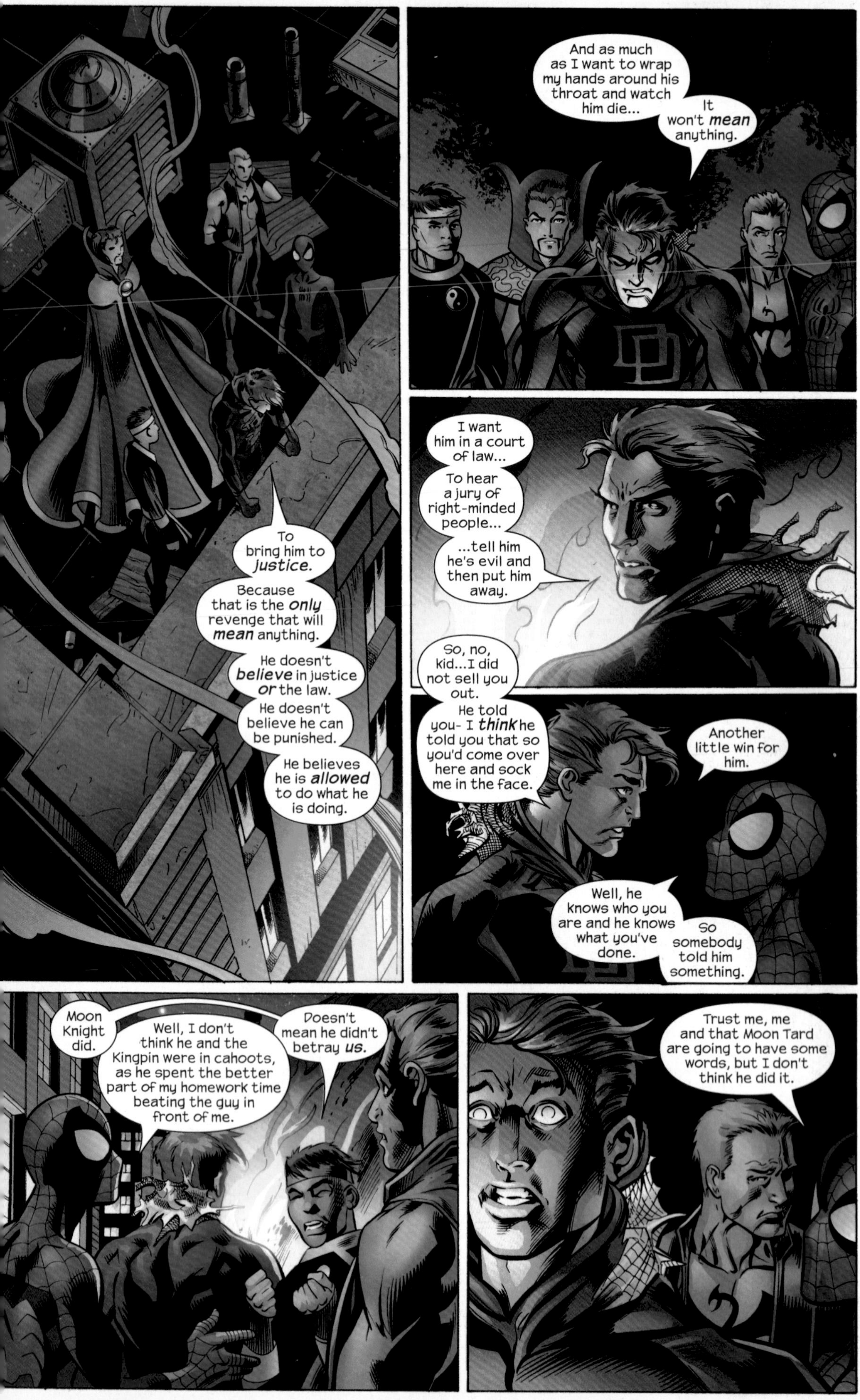
To bring him to *justice.*
Because that is the *only* revenge that will *mean* anything.
He doesn't *believe* in justice *or* the law.
He doesn't believe he can be punished.
He believes he is *allowed* to do what he is doing.
And as much as I want to wrap my hands around his throat and watch him die...
It won't *mean* anything.
I want him in a court of law...
To hear a jury of right-minded people...
...tell him he's evil and then put him away.
So, no, kid...I did not sell you out.
He told you- I *think* he told you that so you'd come over here and sock me in the face.
Another little win for him.
Well, he knows who you are and he knows what you've done.
So somebody told him something.
Moon Knight did.
Well, I don't think he and the Kingpin were in cahoots, as he spent the better part of my homework time beating the guy in front of me.
Doesn't mean he didn't betray *us.*
Trust me, me and that Moon Tard are going to have some words, but I don't think he did it.

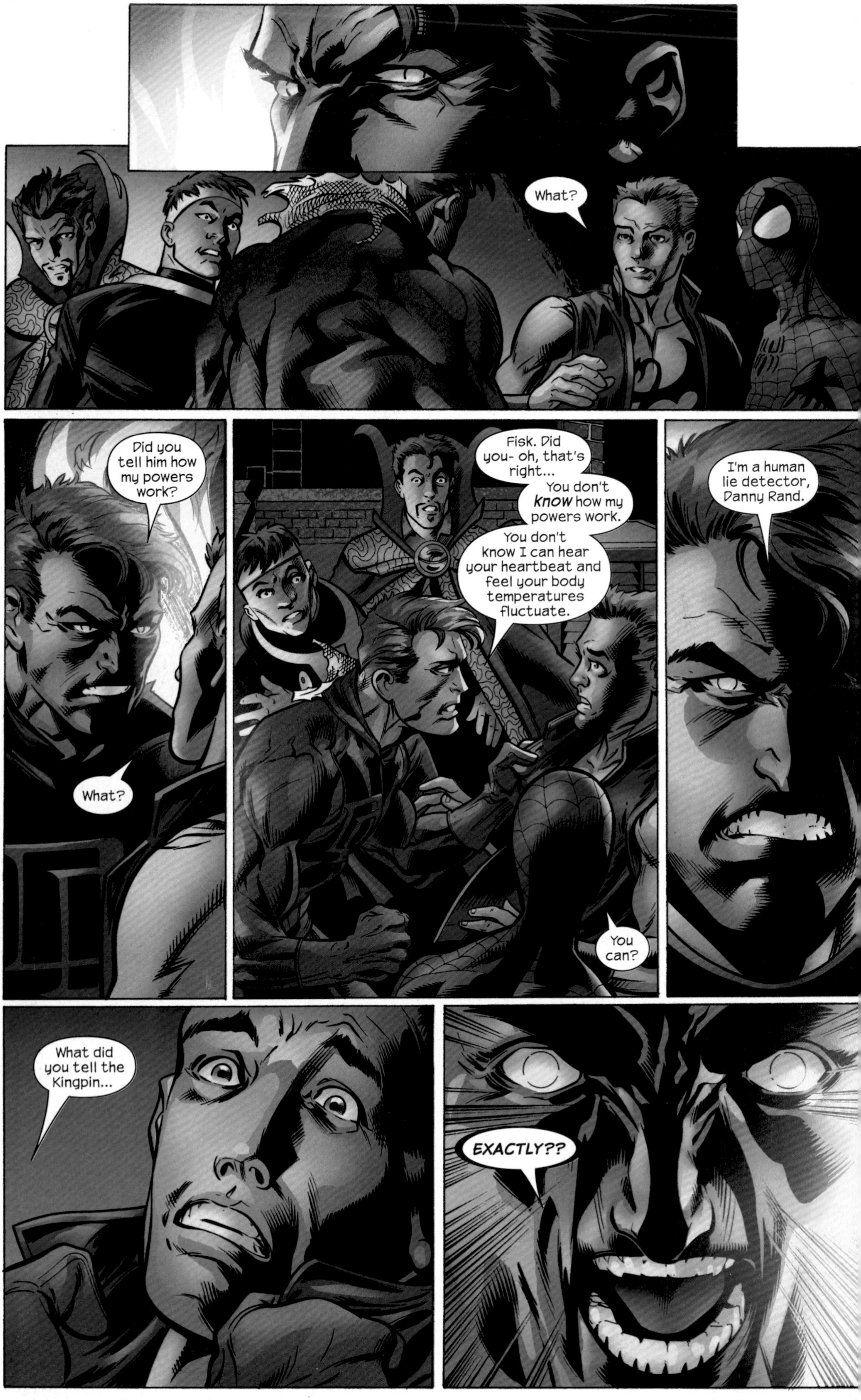
What?
Did you tell him how my powers work?
What?
Fisk. Did you- oh, that's right...
You don't *KNOW* how my powers work.
You don't know I can hear your heartbeat and feel your body temperatures fluctuate.
You can?
I'm a human lie detector, Danny Rand.
What did you tell the Kingpin...
EXACTLY??

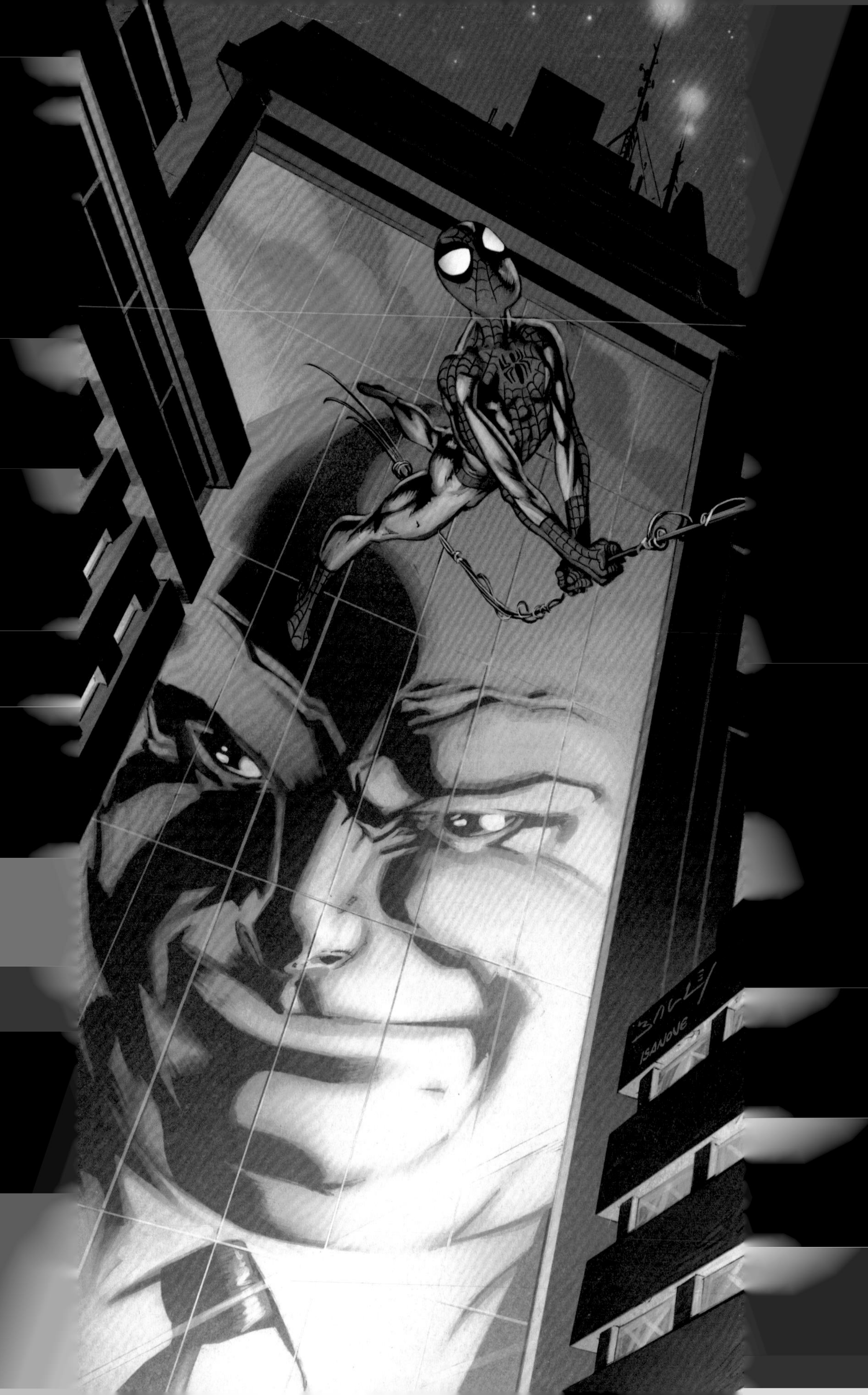

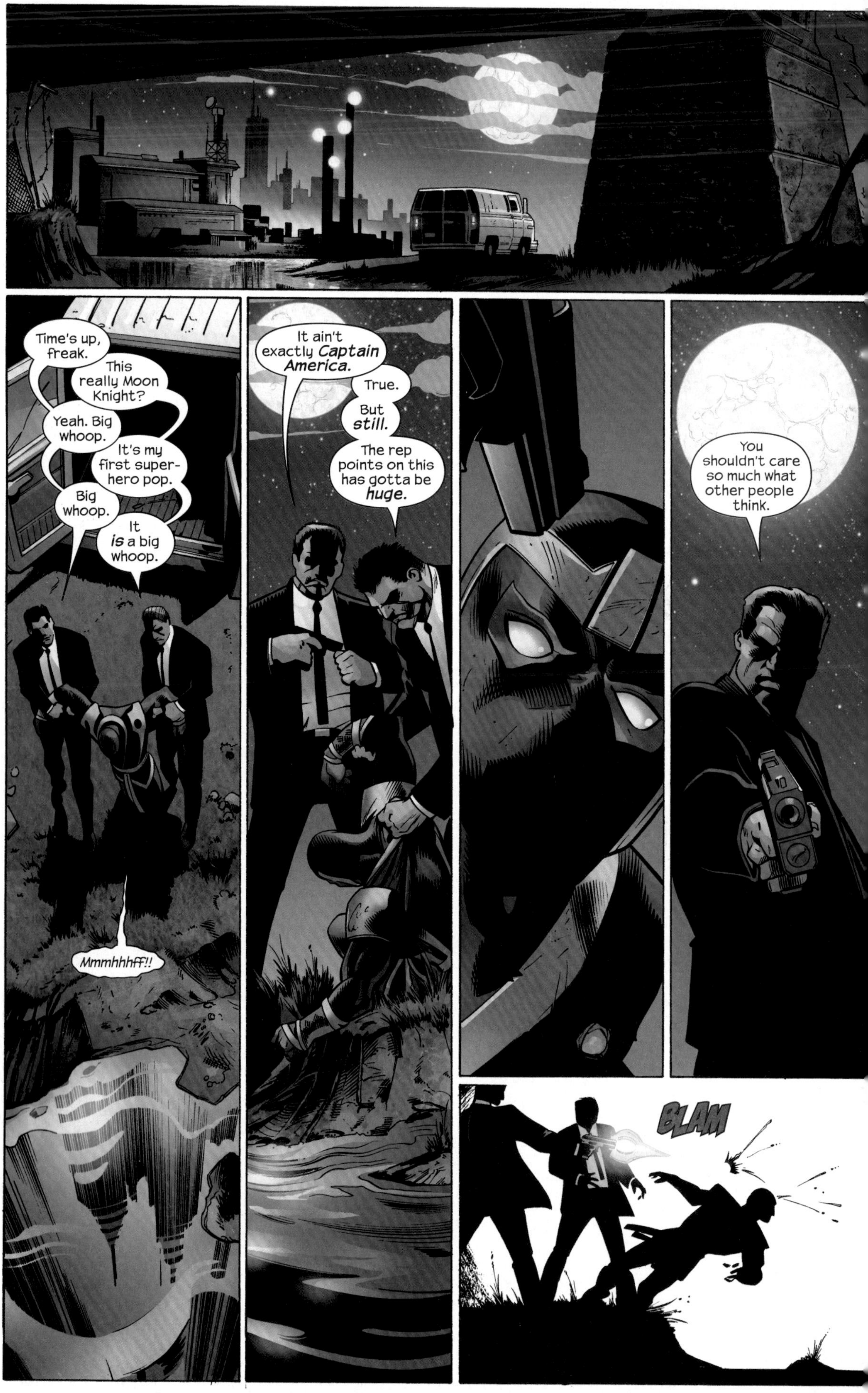

Time's up, freak.
This really Moon Knight?
Yeah. Big whoop.
It's my first super-hero pop.
Big whoop.
It *is* a big whoop.
*Mmmhhhff!!*
It ain't exactly *Captain America.*
True.
But *still.*
The rep points on this has gotta be *huge.*
You shouldn't care so much what other people think.
BLAM

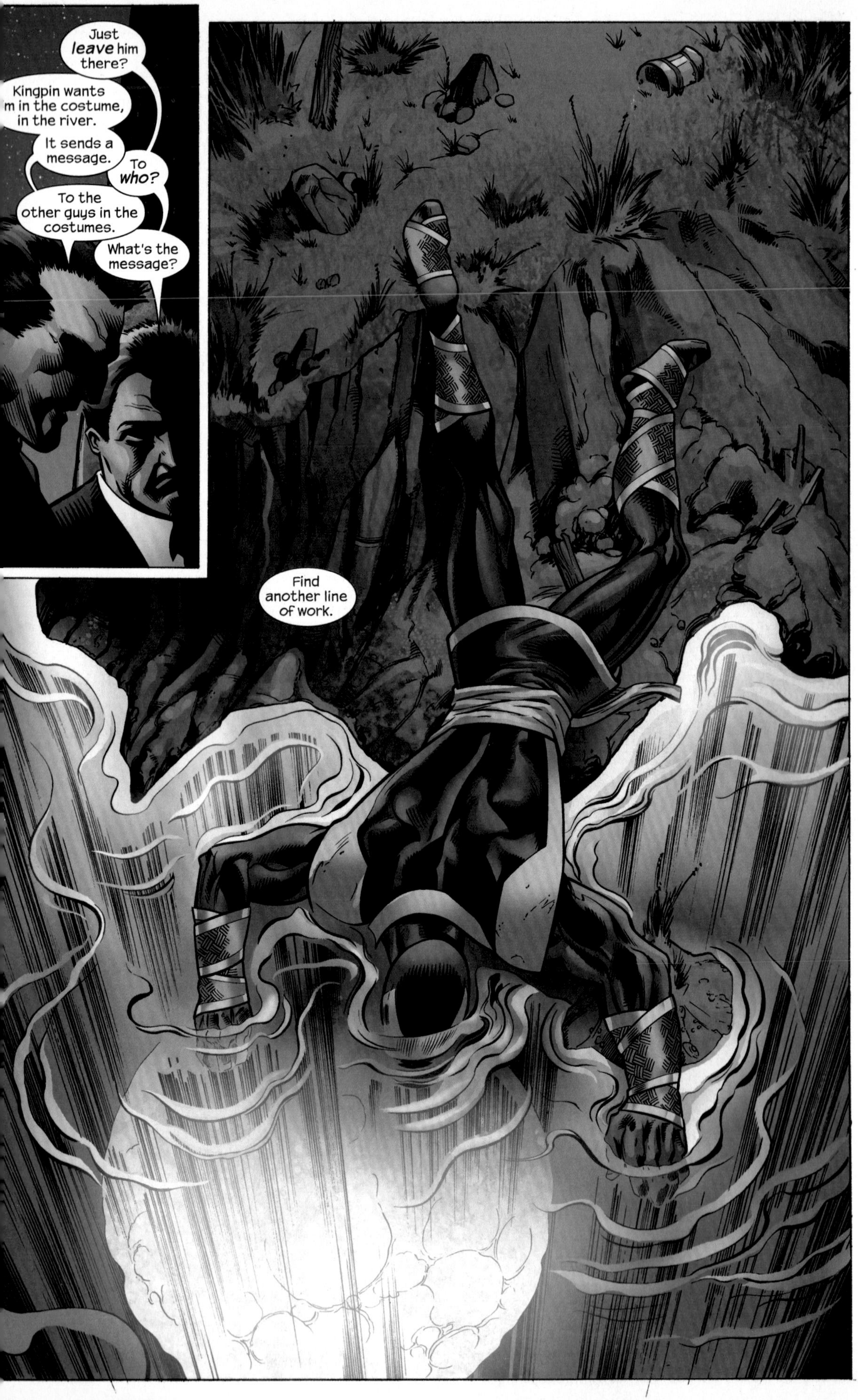
Just leave him there?
Kingpin wants m in the costume, in the river.
It sends a message.
To who?
To the other guys in the costumes.
What's the message?
Find another line of work.

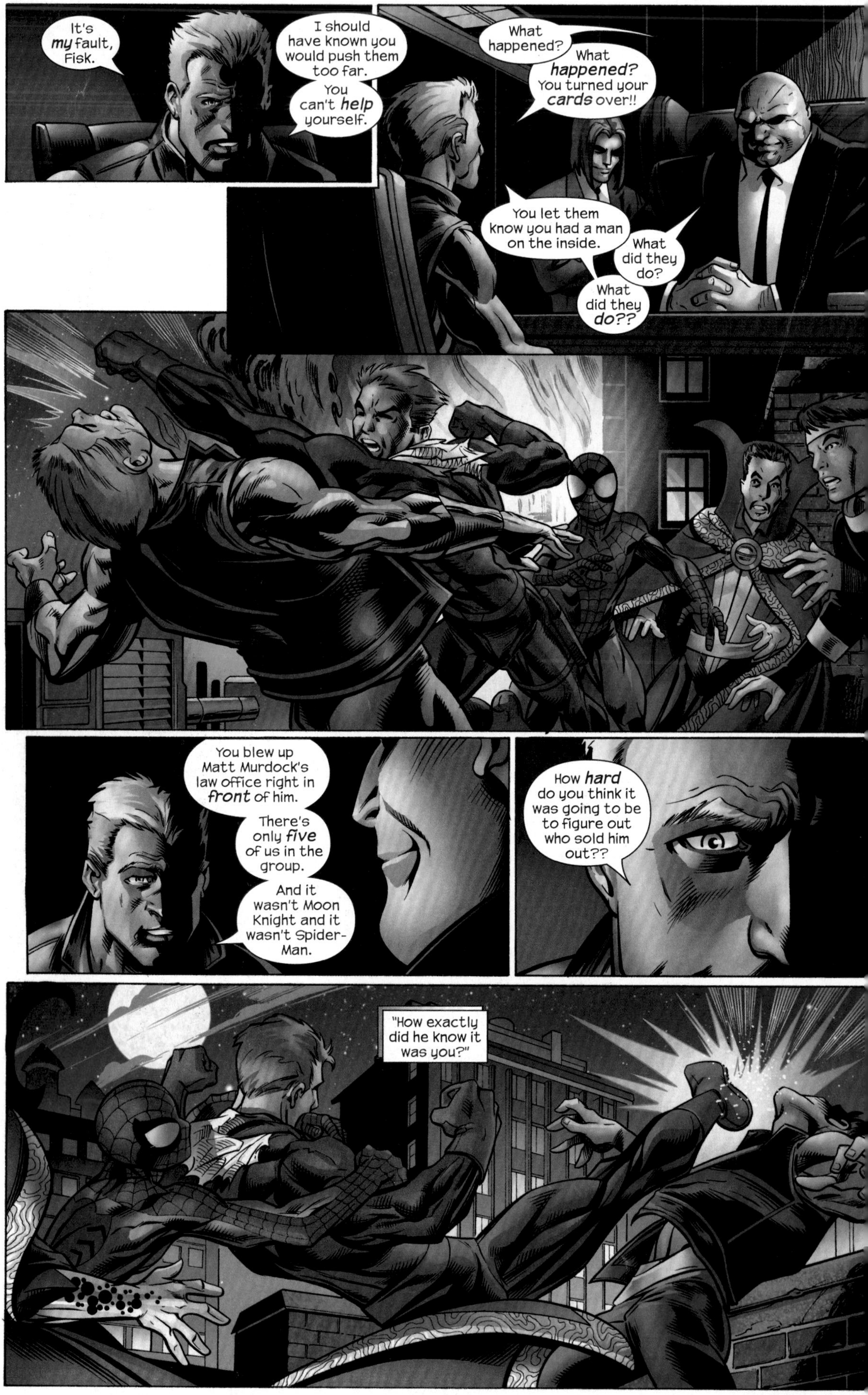
It's my fault, Fisk.
I should have known you would push them too far.
You can't help yourself.
What happened?
What happened? You turned your cards over!!
You let them know you had a man on the inside.
What did they do?
What did they do??
You blew up Matt Murdock's law office right in front of him.
There's only five of us in the group.
And it wasn't Moon Knight and it wasn't Spider-Man.
How hard do you think it was going to be to figure out who sold him out??
"How exactly did he know it was you?"

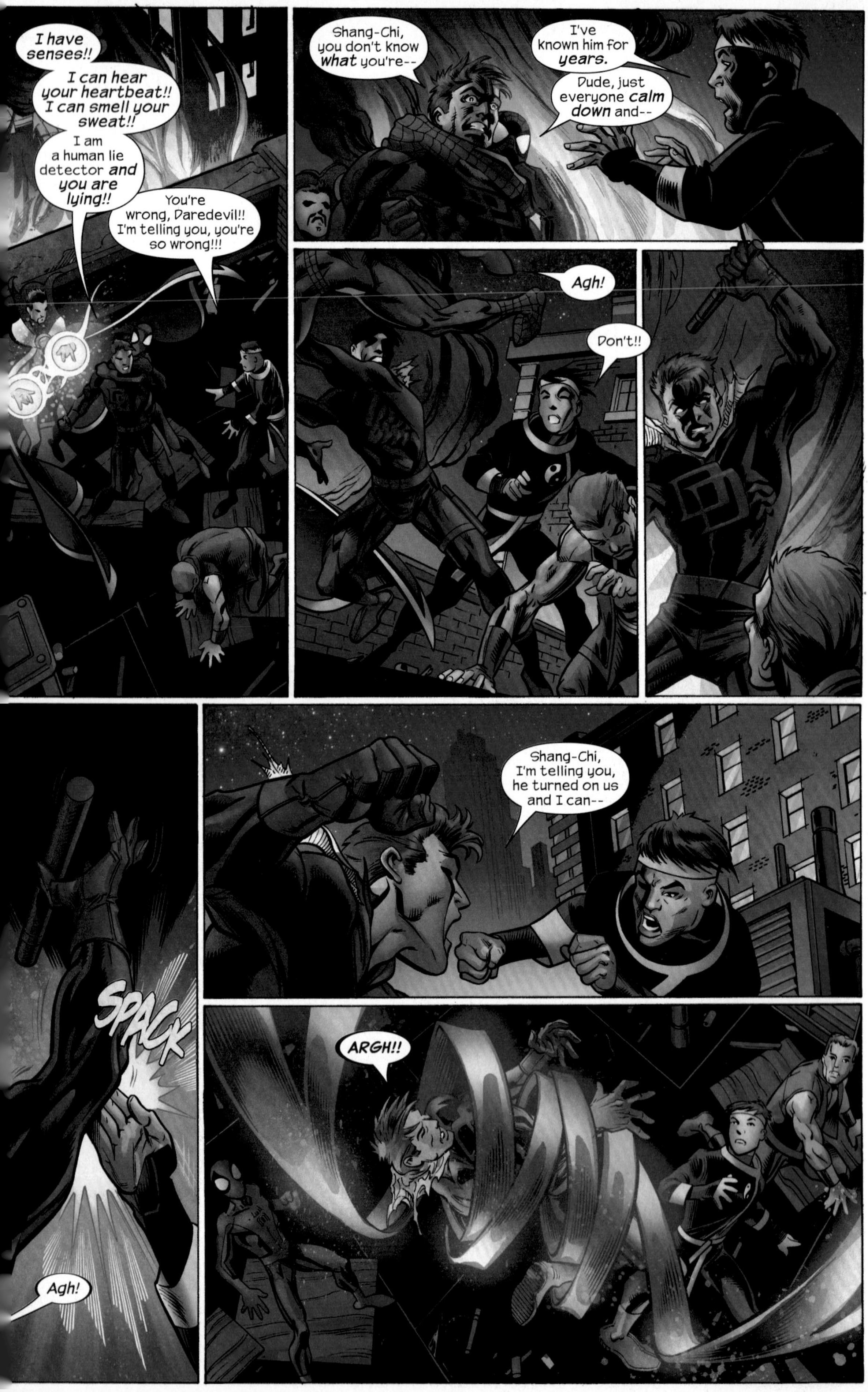
I have senses!!
I can hear your heartbeat!! I can smell your sweat!!
I am a human lie detector and you are lying!!
You're wrong, Daredevil!! I'm telling you, you're so wrong!!!
Shang-Chi, you don't know what you're--
I've known him for years.
Dude, just everyone calm down and--
Agh!
Don't!!
Shang-Chi, I'm telling you, he turned on us and I can--
SPACK
Agh!
ARGH!!

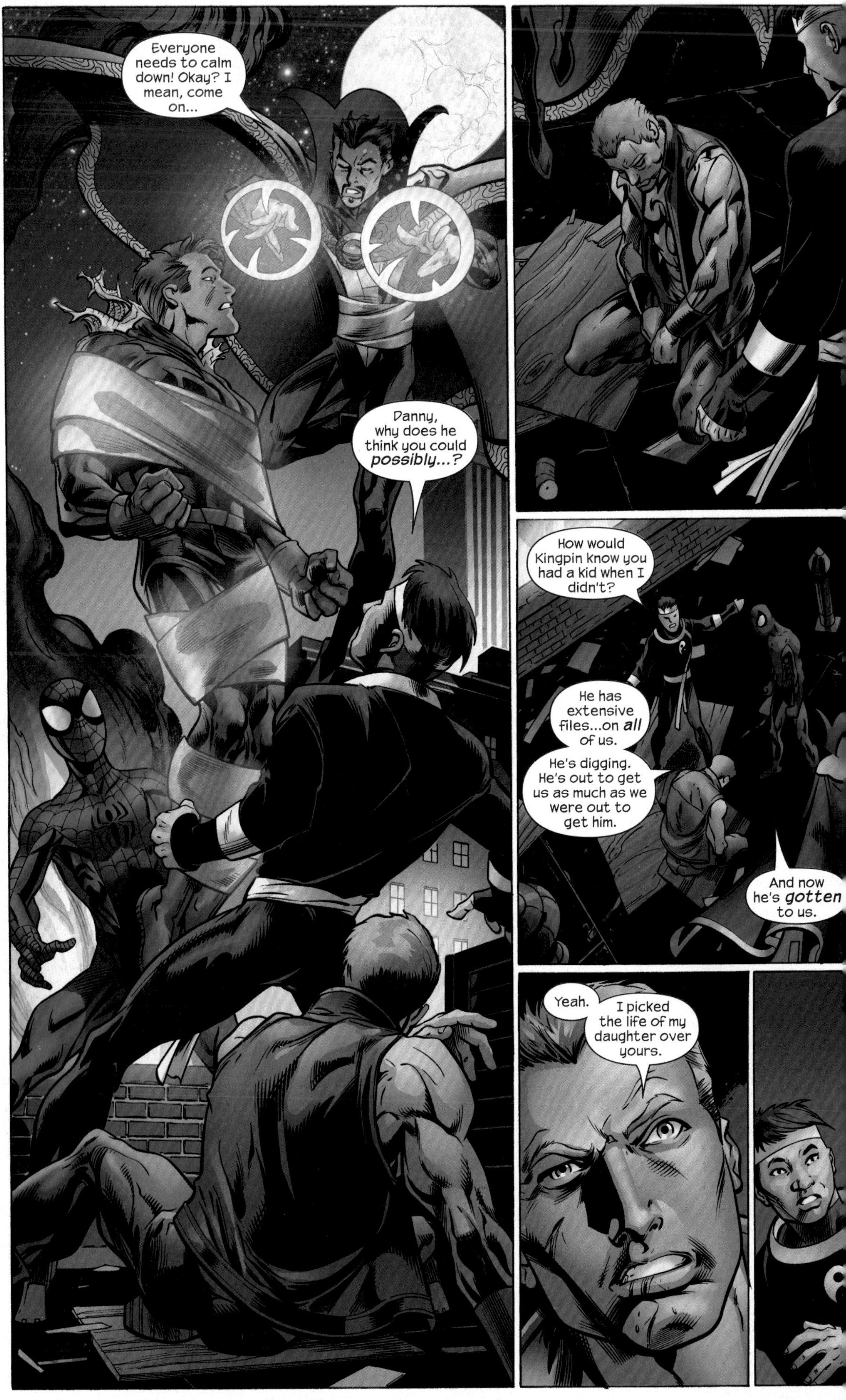
Everyone needs to calm down! Okay? I mean, come on...
Danny, why does he think you could *possibly...?*
How would Kingpin know you had a kid when I didn't?
He has extensive files...on *all* of us.
He's digging. He's out to get us as much as we were out to get him.
And now he's *gotten* to us.
Yeah.
I picked the life of my daughter over yours.

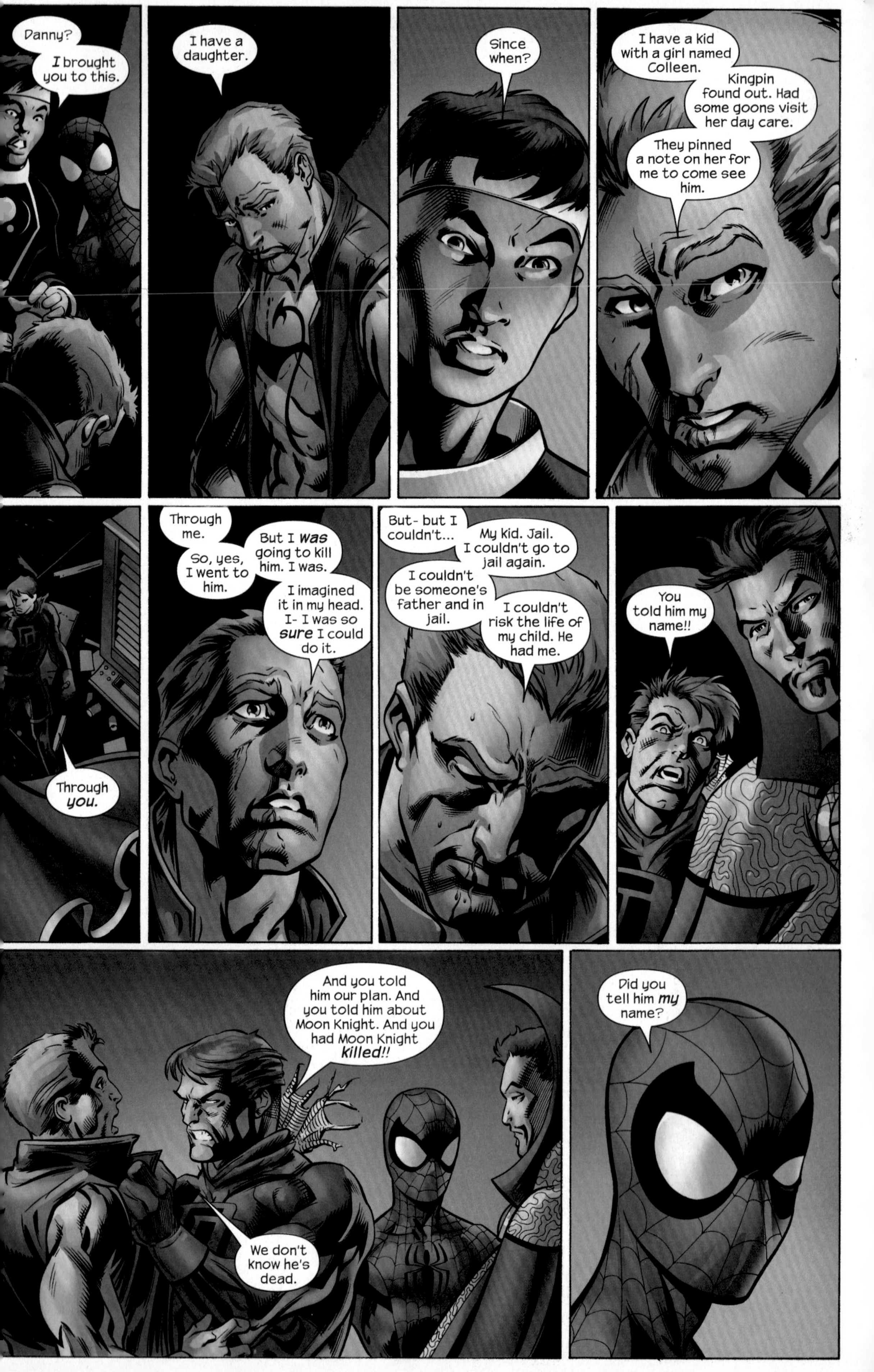
Danny?
I brought you to this.
I have a daughter.
Since when?
I have a kid with a girl named Colleen.
Kingpin found out. Had some goons visit her day care.
They pinned a note on her for me to come see him.
Through you.
Through me.
So, yes, I went to him.
But I was going to kill him. I was.
I imagined it in my head. I- I was so sure I could do it.
But- but I couldn't...
My kid. Jail. I couldn't go to jail again.
I couldn't be someone's father and in jail.
I couldn't risk the life of my child. He had me.
You told him my name!!
And you told him our plan. And you told him about Moon Knight. And you had Moon Knight killed!!
We don't know he's dead.
Did you tell him my name?

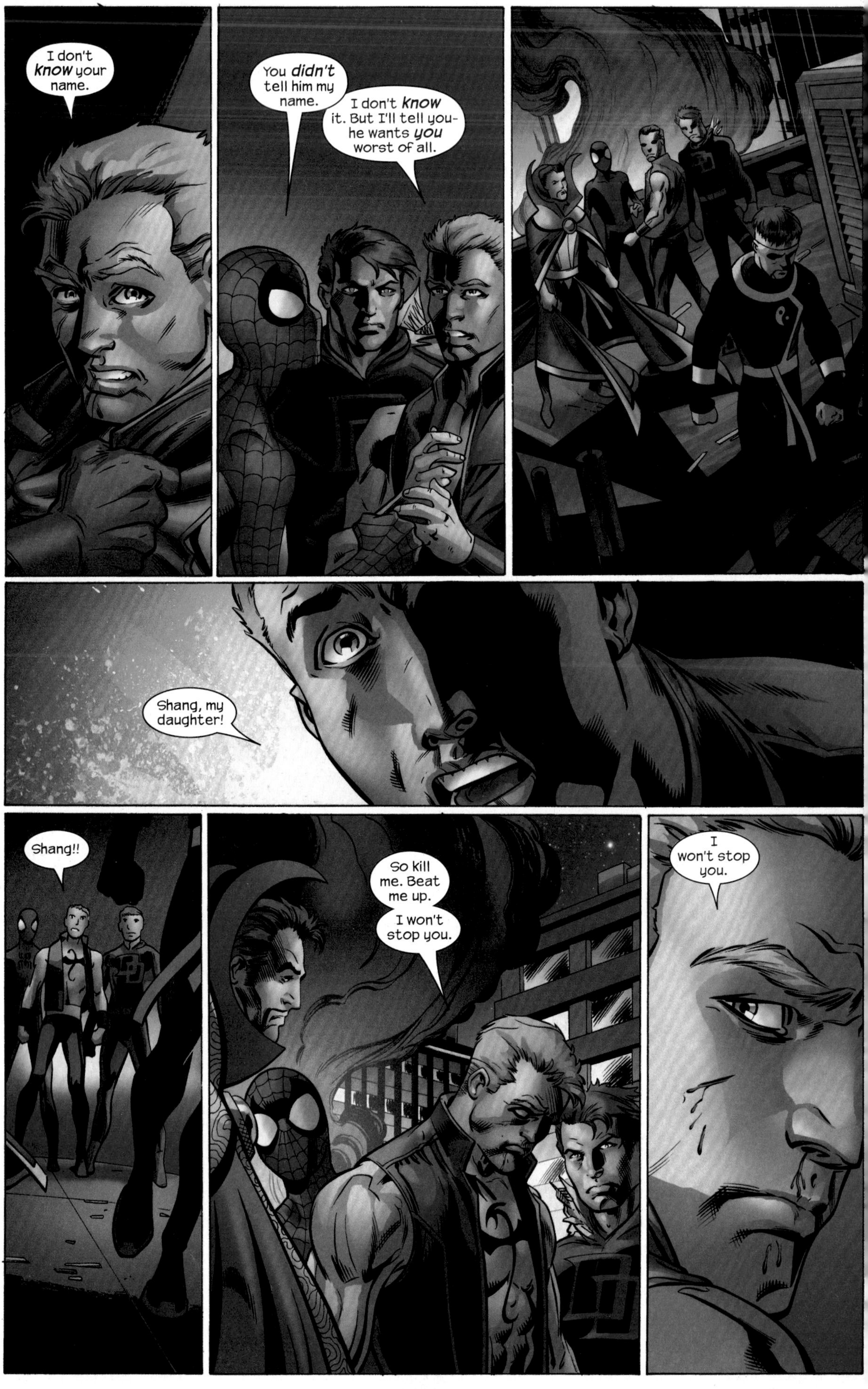
I don't KNOW your name.
You didn't tell him my name.
I don't KNOW it. But I'll tell you- he wants YOU worst of all.
Shang, my daughter!
Shang!!
So kill me. Beat me up.
I won't stop you.
I won't stop you.

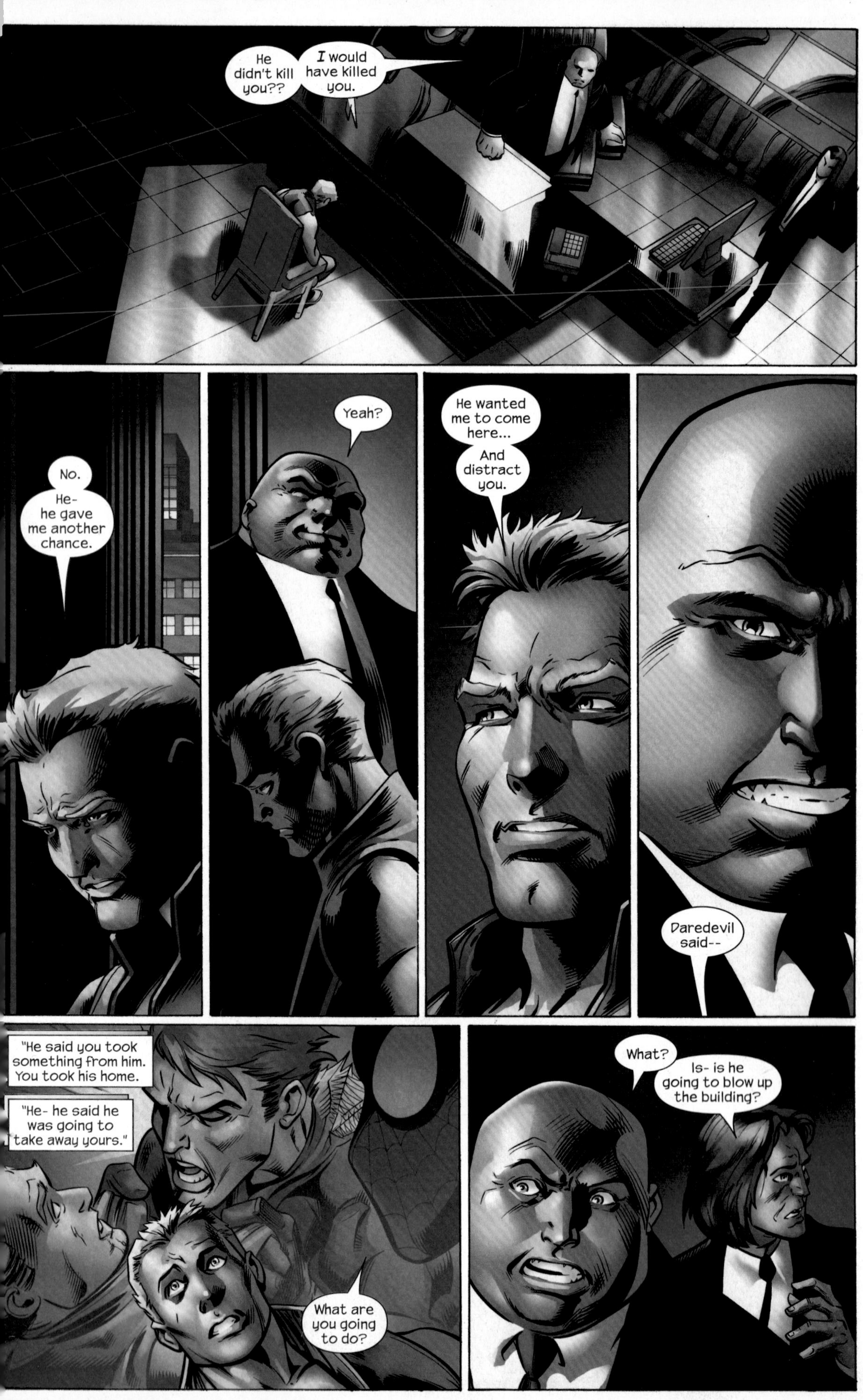
He didn't kill you??
I would have killed you.
No.
He- he gave me another chance.
Yeah?
He wanted me to come here...
And distract you.
Daredevil said--
"He said you took something from him. You took his home.
"He- he said he was going to take away yours."
What are you going to do?
What?
Is- is he going to blow up the building?

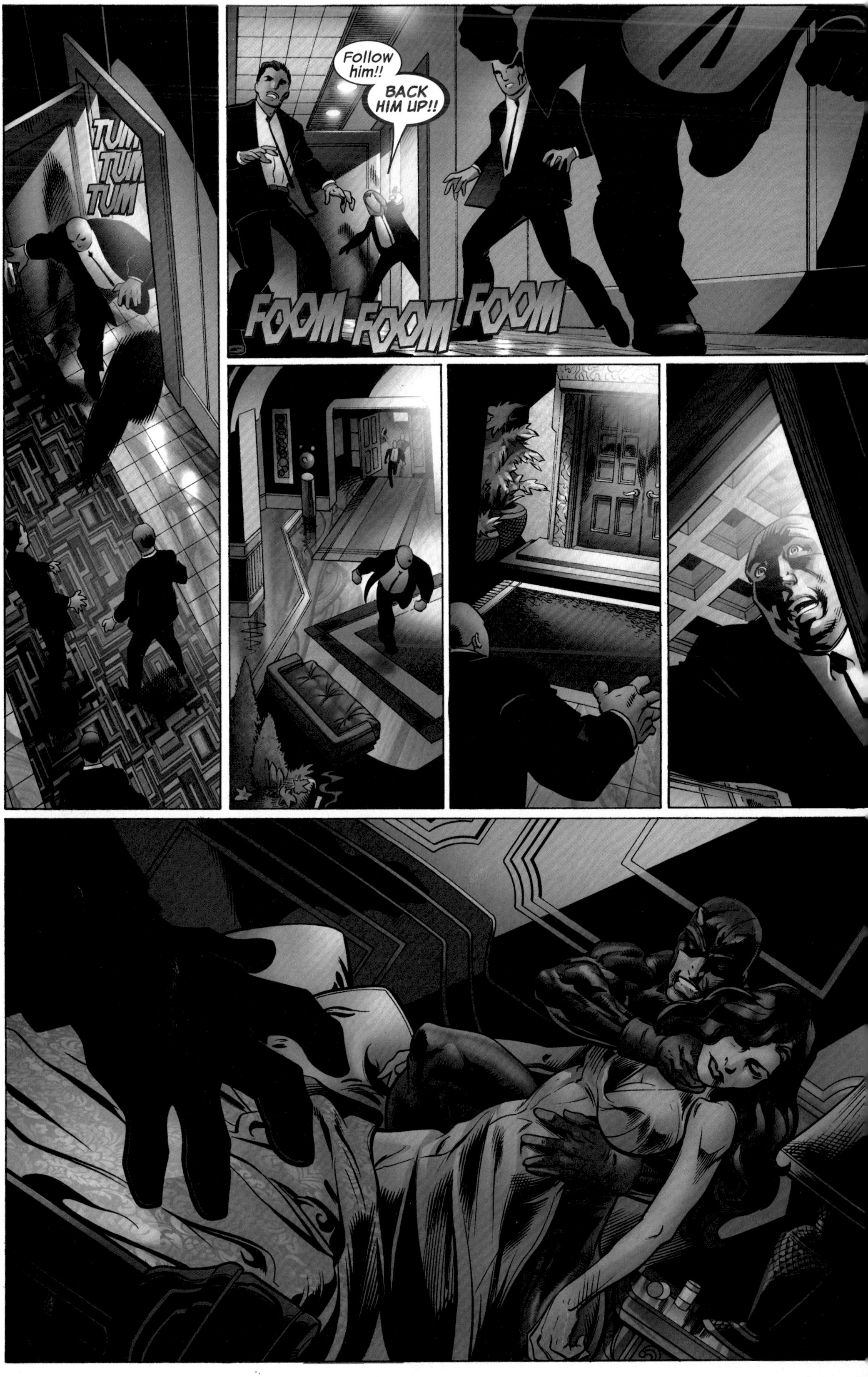
TUM
TUM
TUM
Follow him!!
BACK HIM UP!!
FOOM FOOM FOOM

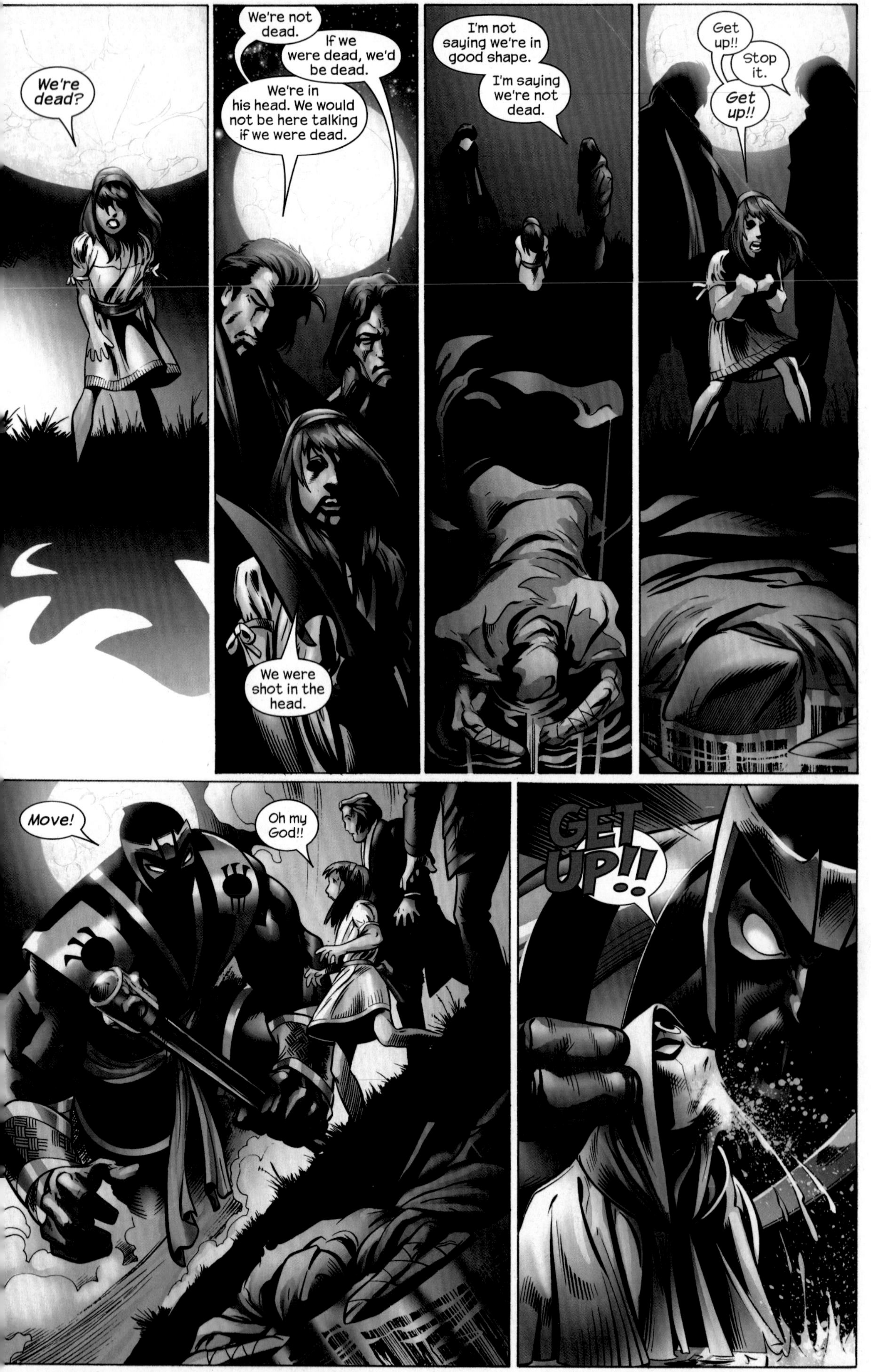
We're dead?
We're not dead.
If we were dead, we'd be dead.
We're in his head. We would not be here talking if we were dead.
We were shot in the head.
I'm not saying we're in good shape.
I'm saying we're not dead.
Get up!!
Stop it.
Get up!!
Move!
Oh my God!!
GET UP!!

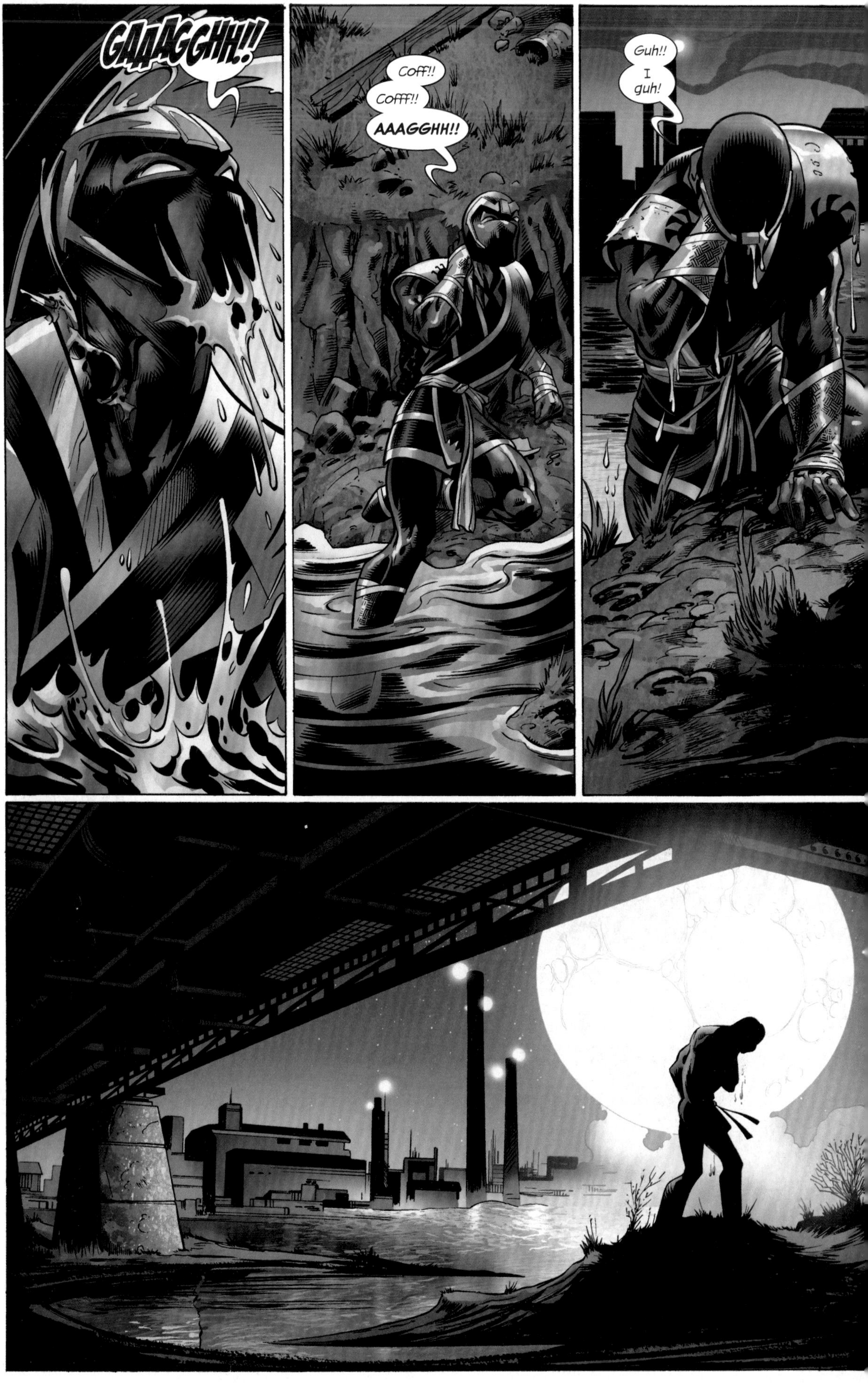
GAAAGGHH!!
Coff!!
Cofff!!
AAAGGHH!!
Guh!!
I
guh!

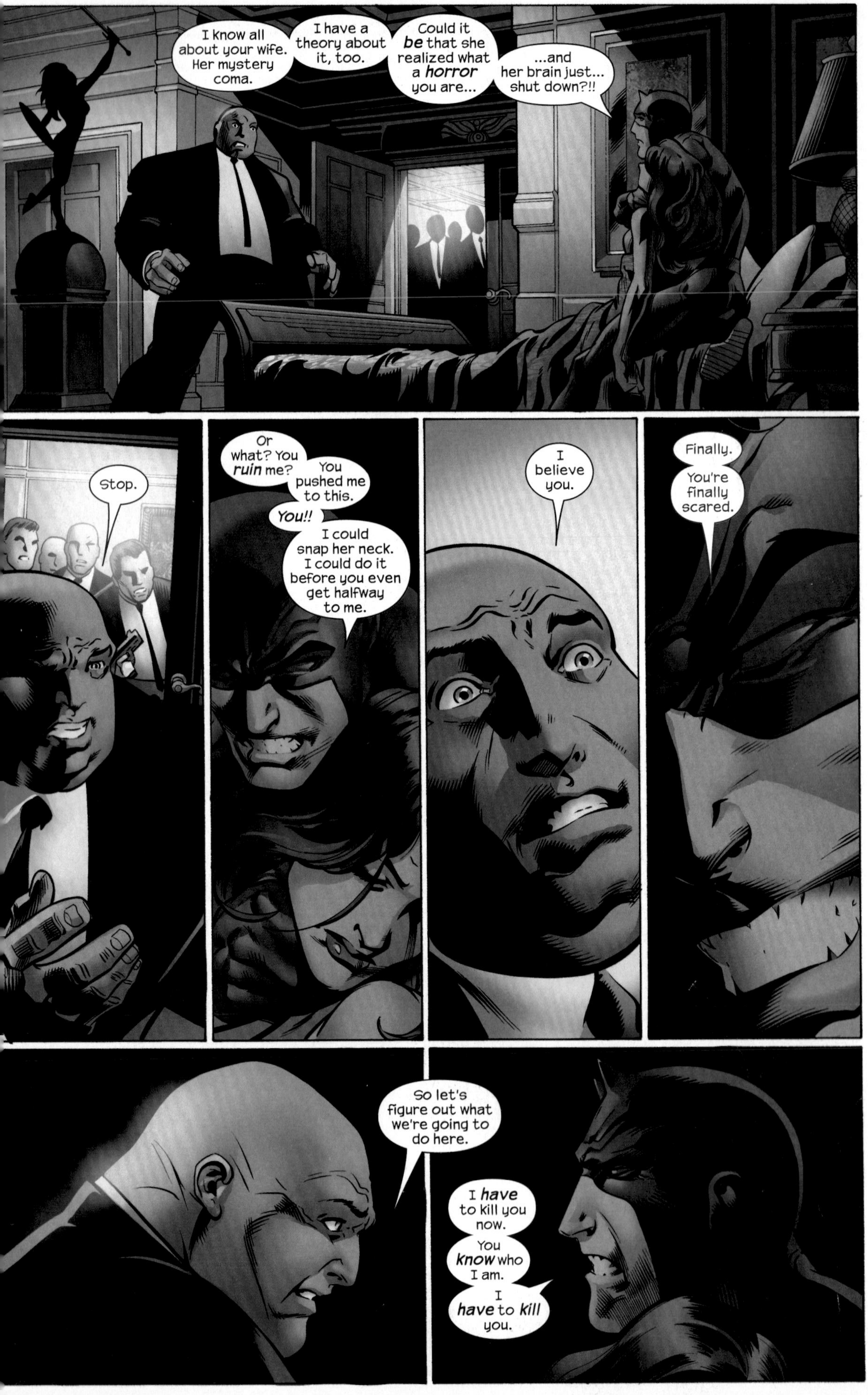

I know all about your wife. Her mystery coma.
I have a theory about it, too.
Could it *be* that she realized what a *horror* you are...
...and her brain just... shut down?!!
Stop.
Or what? You *ruin* me?
You pushed me to this.
*You!!*
I could snap her neck. I could do it before you even get halfway to me.
I believe you.
Finally.
You're finally scared.
So let's figure out what we're going to do here.
I *have* to kill you now.
You *know* who I am.
I *have* to *kill* you.

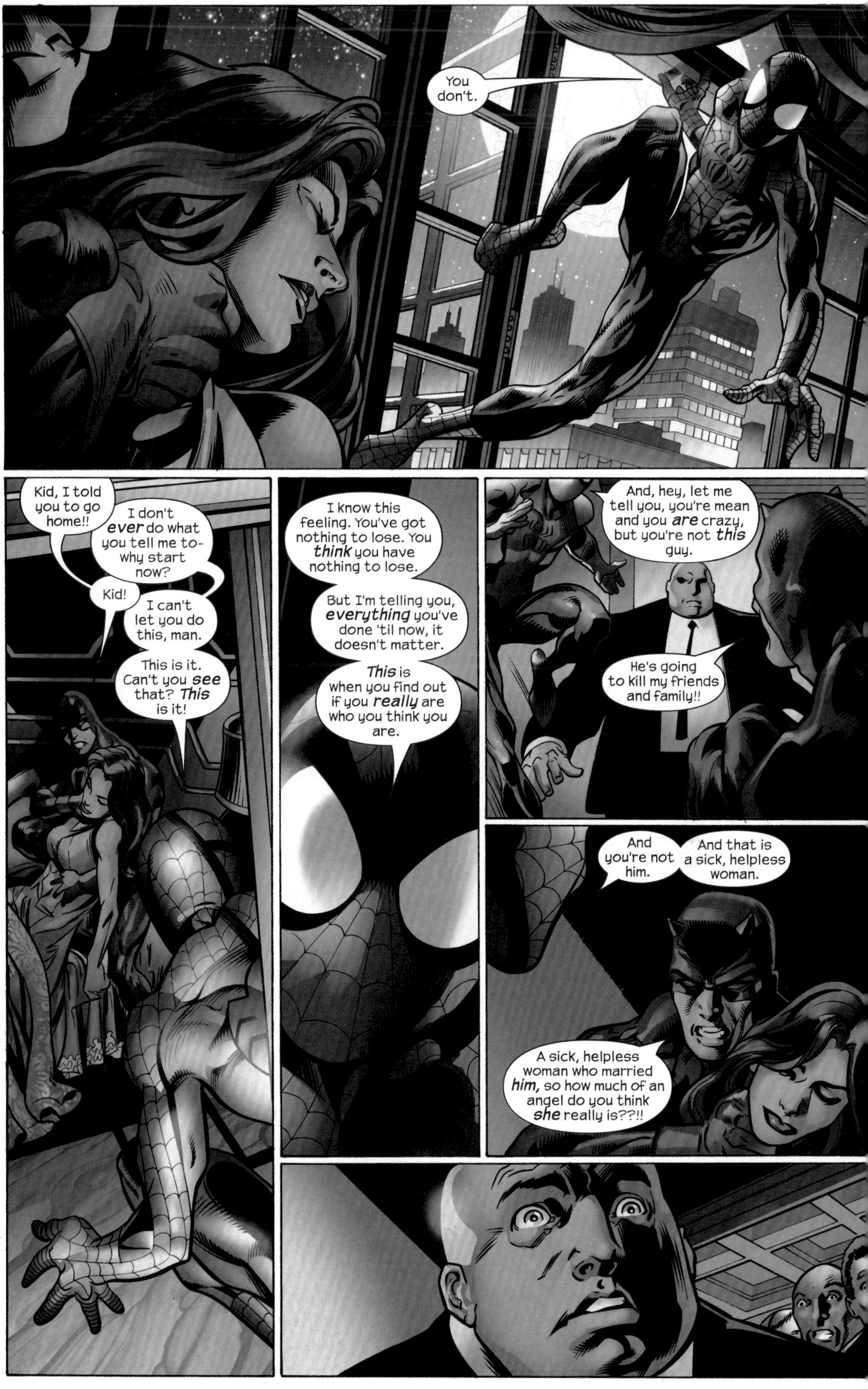

You don't.
Kid, I told you to go home!!
I don't ever do what you tell me to- why start now?
Kid!
I can't let you do this, man.
This is it. Can't you see that? This is it!
I know this feeling. You've got nothing to lose. You think you have nothing to lose.
But I'm telling you, everything you've done 'til now, it doesn't matter.
This is when you find out if you really are who you think you are.
And, hey, let me tell you, you're mean and you are crazy, but you're not this guy.
He's going to kill my friends and family!!
And you're not him.
And that is a sick, helpless woman.
A sick, helpless woman who married him, so how much of an angel do you think she really is??!!

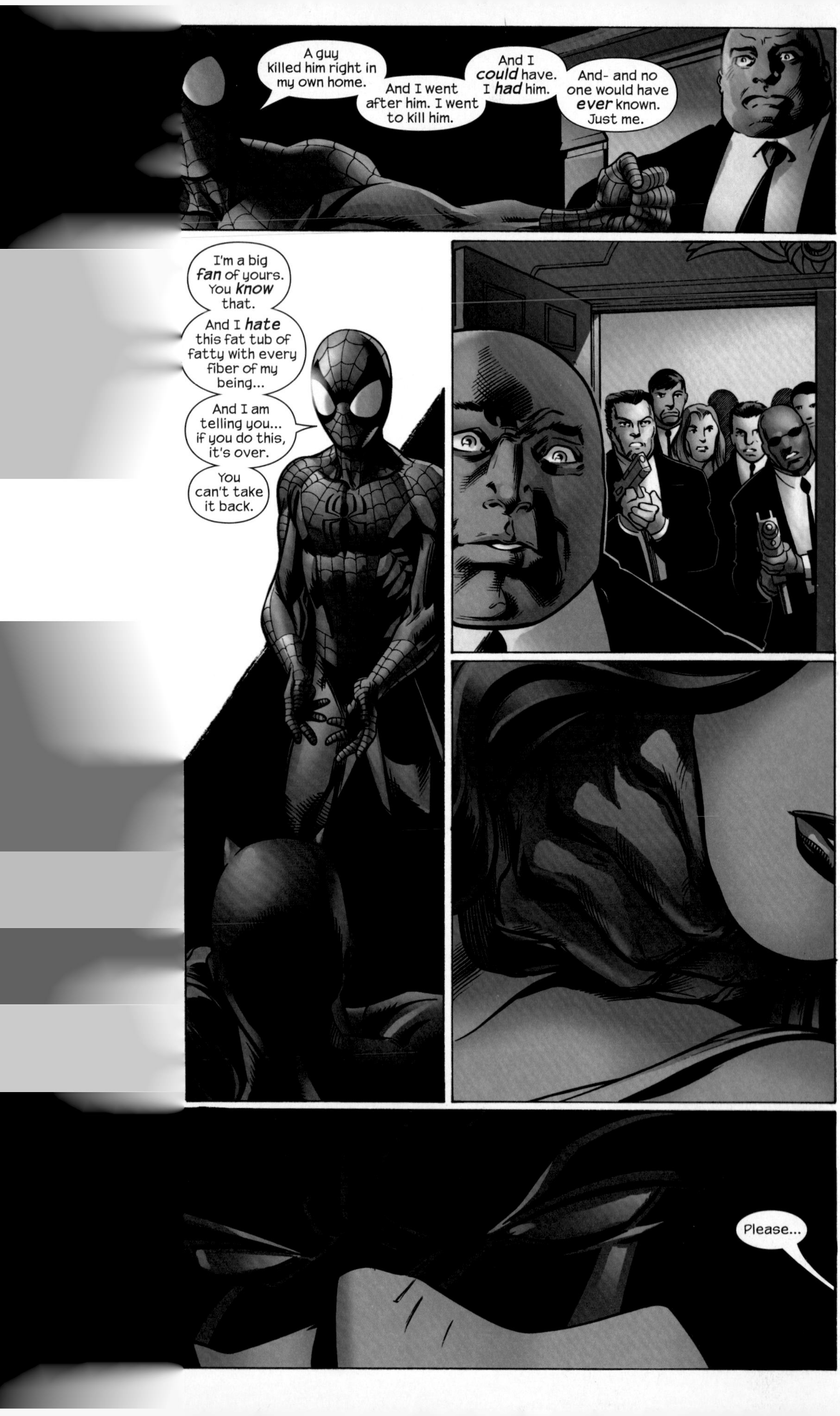
A guy killed him right in my own home.
And I went after him. I went to kill him.
And I could have. I had him.
And- and no one would have ever known. Just me.
I'm a big fan of yours. You know that.
And I hate this fat tub of fatty with every fiber of my being...
And I am telling you... if you do this, it's over.
You can't take it back.
Please...

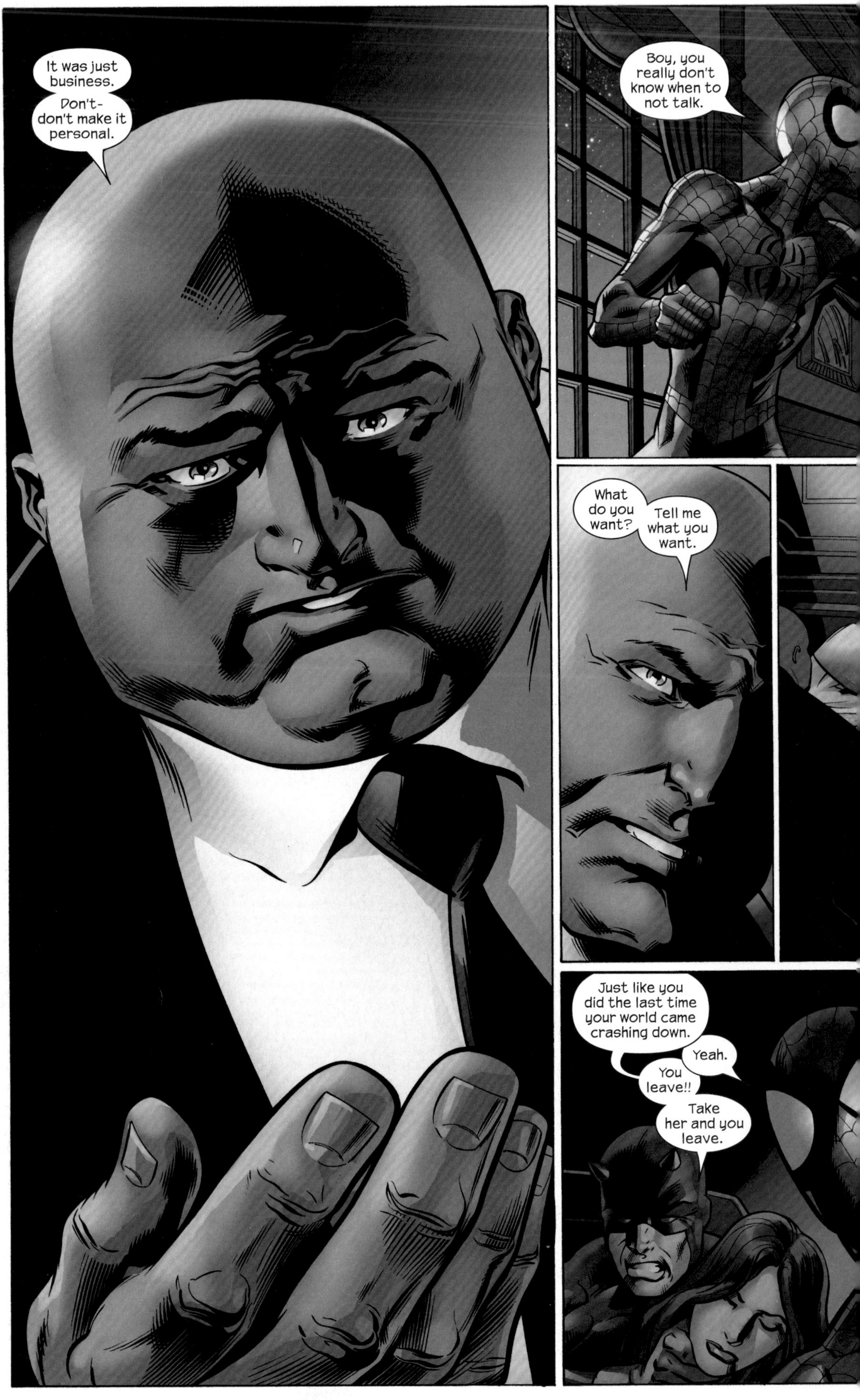
It was just business.
Don't- don't make it personal.
Boy, you really don't know when to not talk.
What do you want?
Tell me what you want.
Just like you did the last time your world came crashing down.
Yeah.
You leave!!
Take her and you leave.

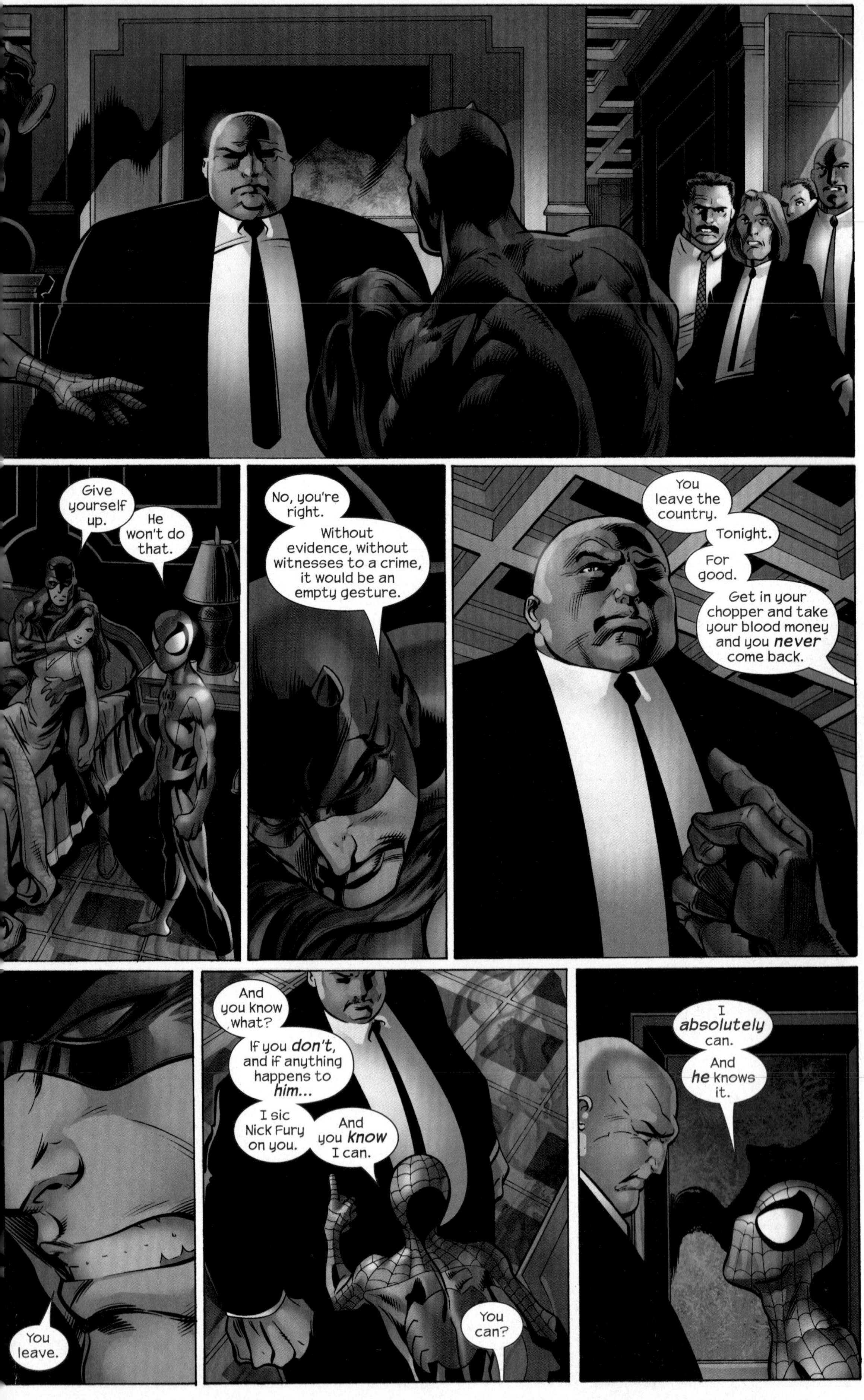
Give yourself up.
He won't do that.
No, you're right.
Without evidence, without witnesses to a crime, it would be an empty gesture.
You leave the country.
Tonight.
For good.
Get in your chopper and take your blood money and you never come back.
You leave.
And you know what?
If you don't, and if anything happens to him...
I sic Nick Fury on you.
And you know I can.
You can?
I absolutely can.
And he knows it.

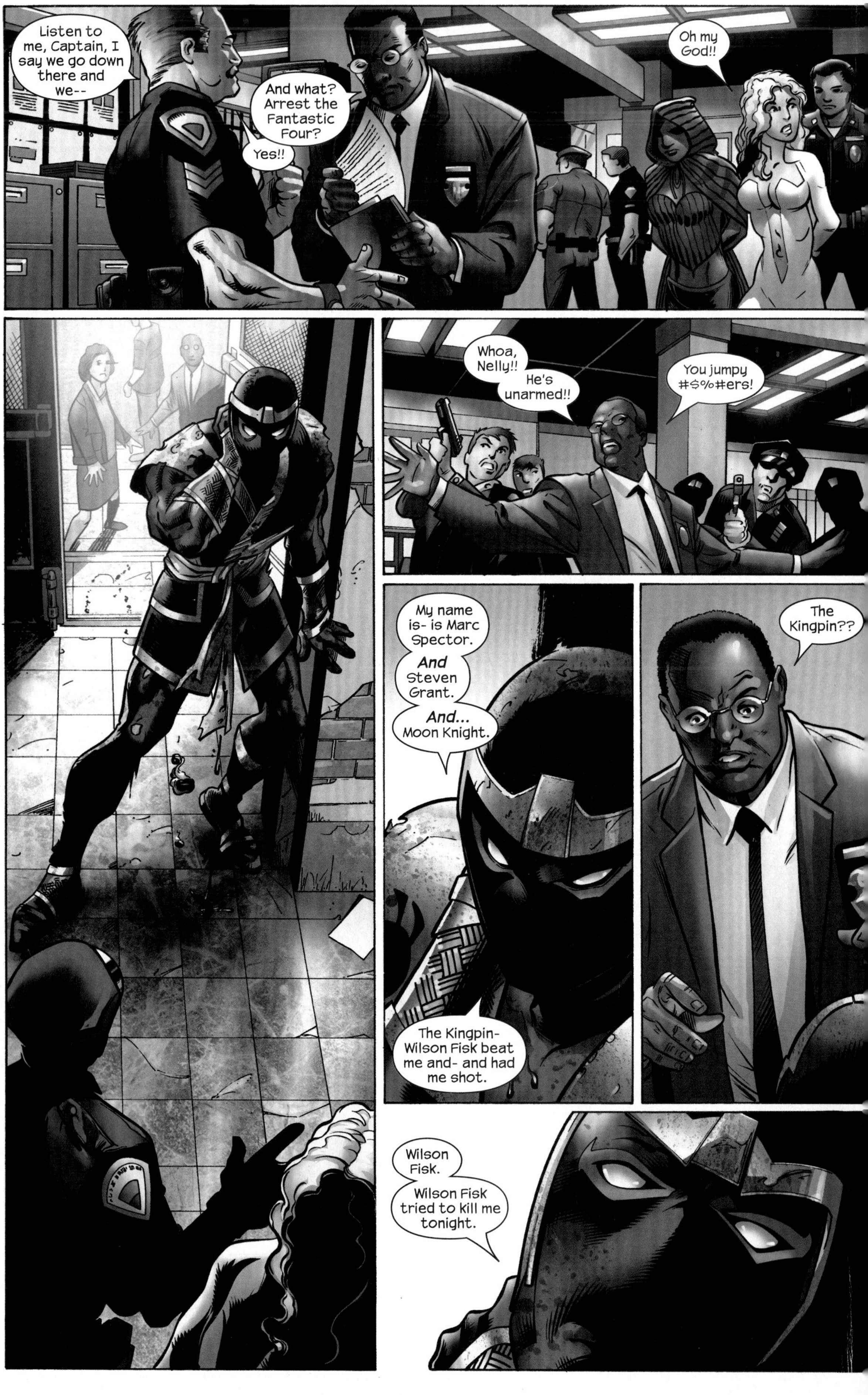

Listen to me, Captain, I say we go down there and we--
And what? Arrest the Fantastic Four?
Yes!!
Oh my God!!
Whoa, Nelly!!
He's unarmed!!
You jumpy #$%#ers!
My name is- is Marc Spector.
And Steven Grant.
And... Moon Knight.
The Kingpin- Wilson Fisk beat me and- and had me shot.
The Kingpin??
Wilson Fisk.
Wilson Fisk tried to kill me tonight.

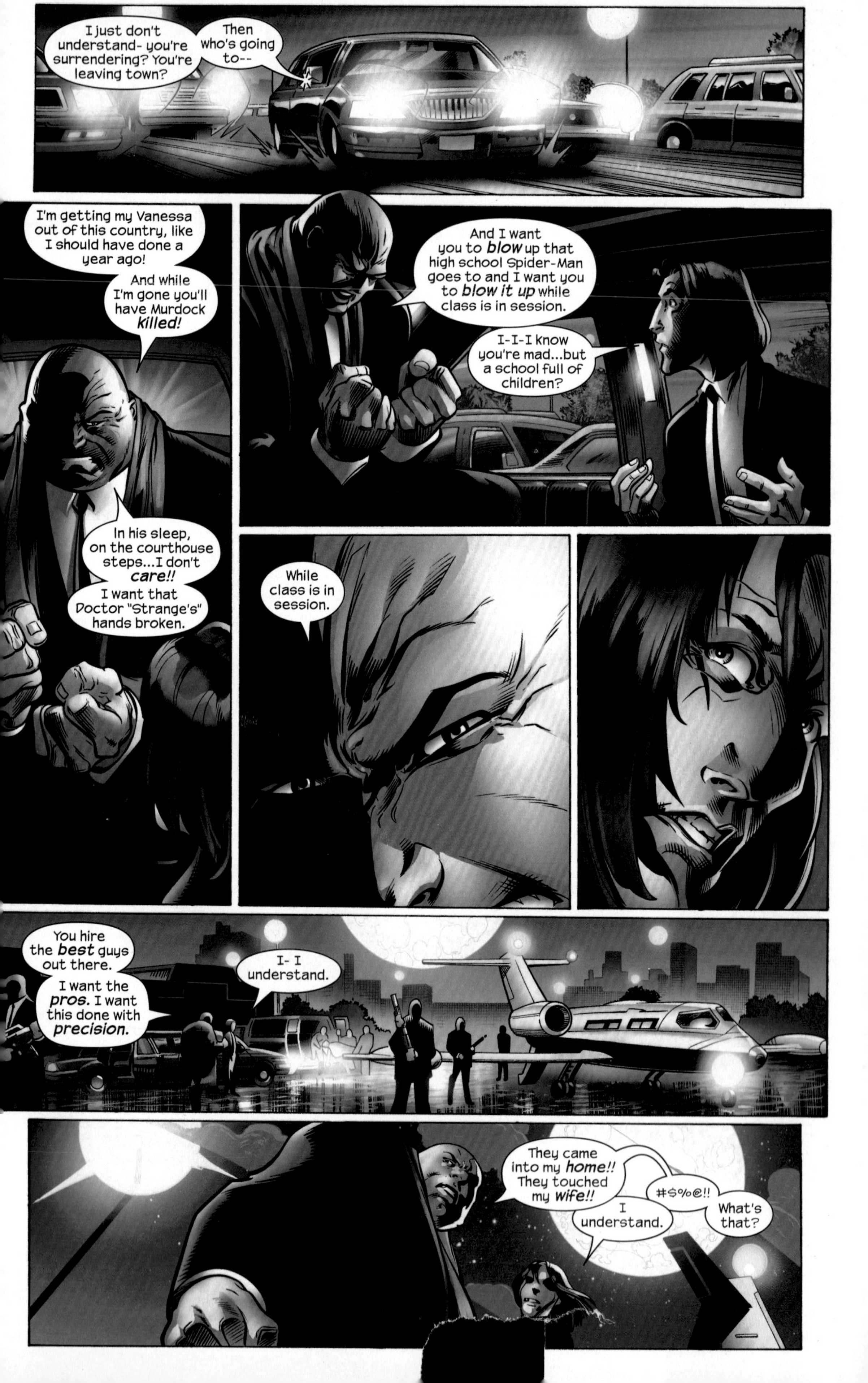
I just don't understand- you're surrendering? You're leaving town?
Then who's going to--
I'm getting my Vanessa out of this country, like I should have done a year ago!
And while I'm gone you'll have Murdock killed!
In his sleep, on the courthouse steps...I don't care!!
I want that Doctor "Strange's" hands broken.
And I want you to blow up that high school Spider-Man goes to and I want you to blow it up while class is in session.
I-I-I know you're mad...but a school full of children?
While class is in session.
You hire the best guys out there.
I want the pros. I want this done with precision.
I- I understand.
They came into my home!! They touched my wife!!
I understand.
#$%@!!
What's that?

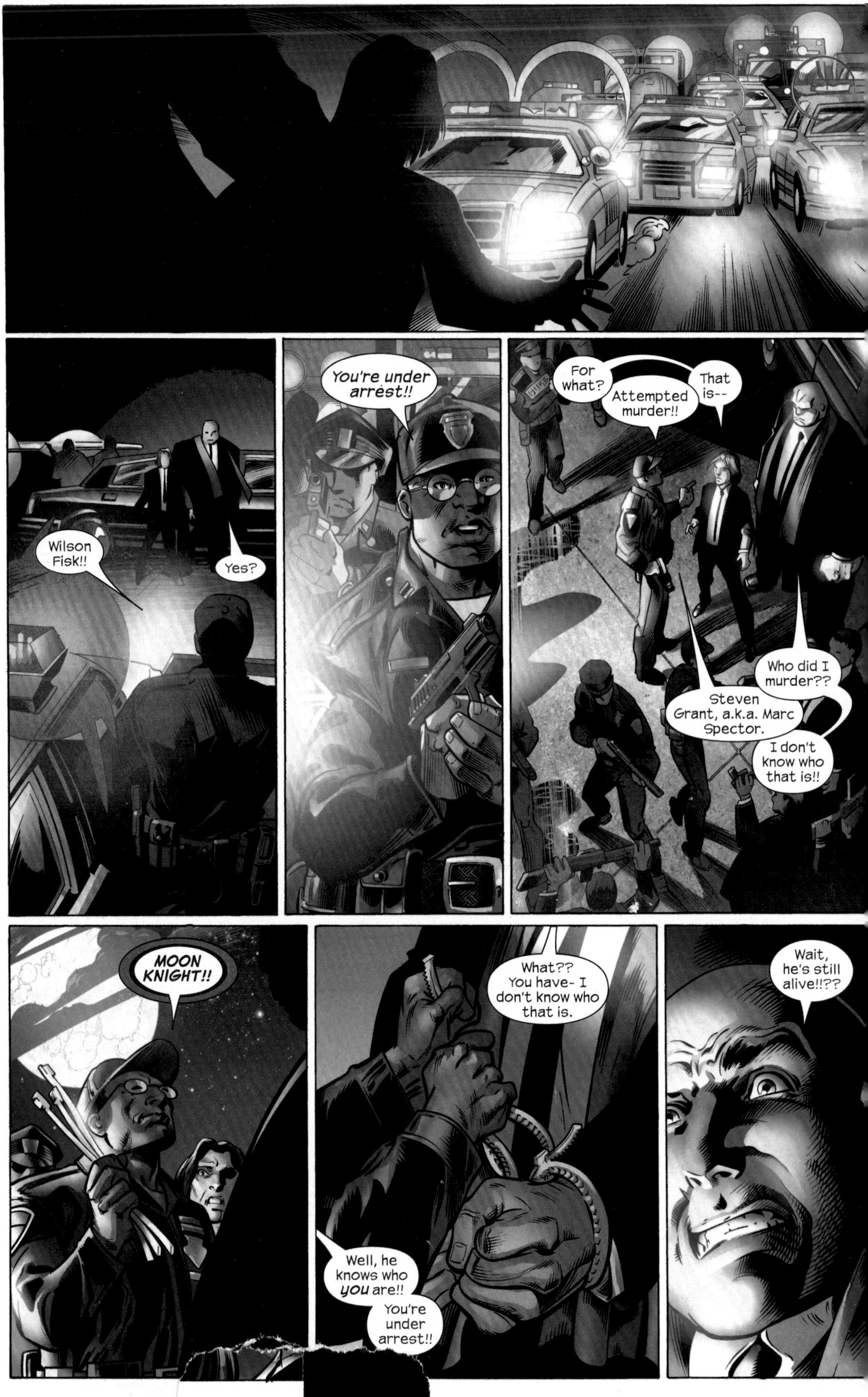
Wilson Fisk!!
Yes?
You're under arrest!!
For what?
That is--
Attempted murder!!
Who did I murder??
Steven Grant, a.k.a. Marc Spector.
I don't know who that is!!
MOON KNIGHT!!
What?? You have- I don't know who that is.
Well, he knows who YOU are!!
You're under arrest!!
Wait, he's still alive!!??

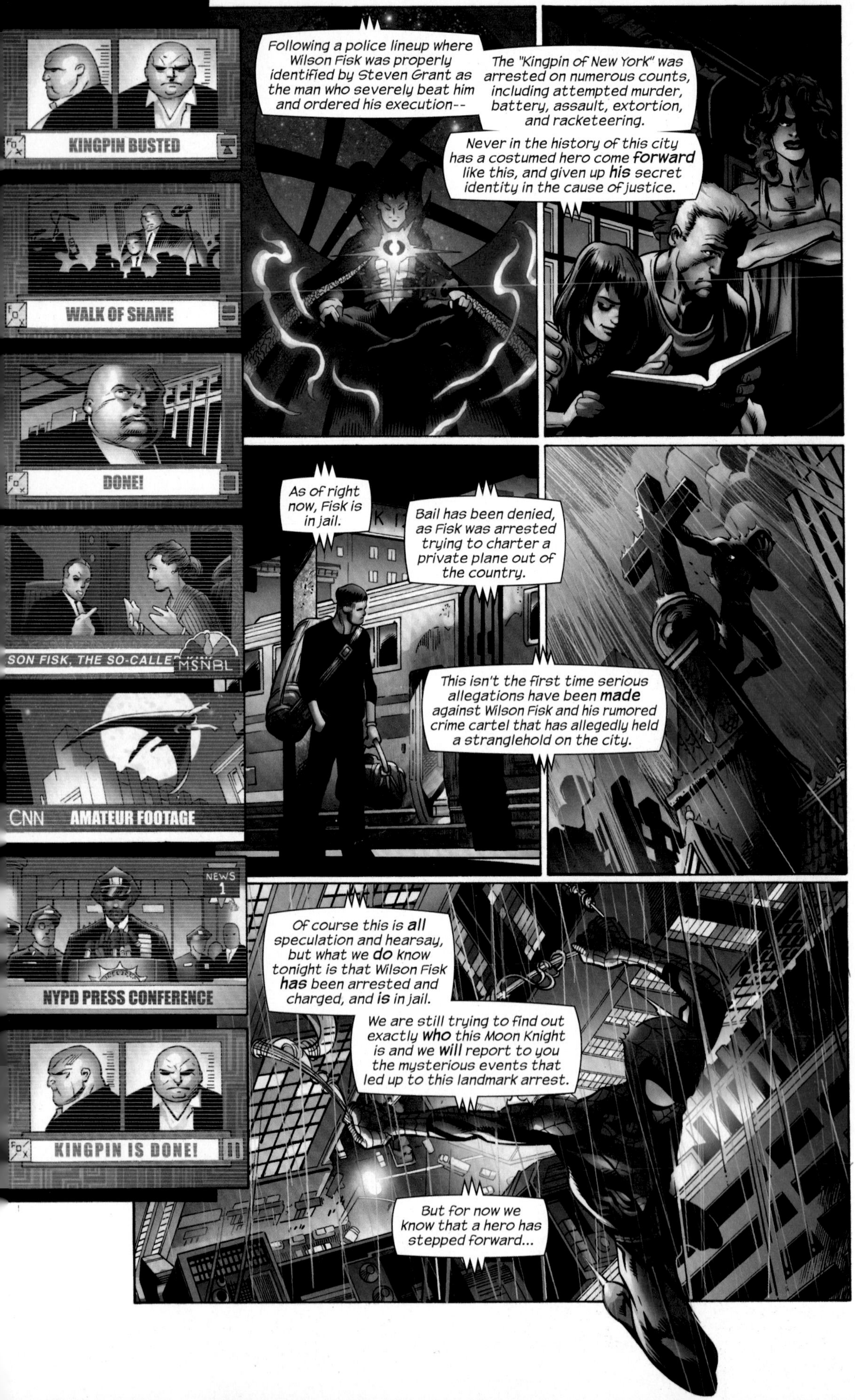
KINGPIN BUSTED
WALK OF SHAME
DONE!
SON FISK, THE SO-CALLE
MSNBC
CNN
AMATEUR FOOTAGE
NEWS 1
NYPD PRESS CONFERENCE
KINGPIN IS DONE!
Following a police lineup where Wilson Fisk was properly identified by Steven Grant as the man who severely beat him and ordered his execution--
The "Kingpin of New York" was arrested on numerous counts, including attempted murder, battery, assault, extortion, and racketeering.
Never in the history of this city has a costumed hero come forward like this, and given up his secret identity in the cause of justice.
As of right now, Fisk is in jail.
Bail has been denied, as Fisk was arrested trying to charter a private plane out of the country.
This isn't the first time serious allegations have been made against Wilson Fisk and his rumored crime cartel that has allegedly held a stranglehold on the city.
Of course this is all speculation and hearsay, but what we do know tonight is that Wilson Fisk has been arrested and charged, and is in jail.
We are still trying to find out exactly who this Moon Knight is and we will report to you the mysterious events that led up to this landmark arrest.
But for now we know that a hero has stepped forward...

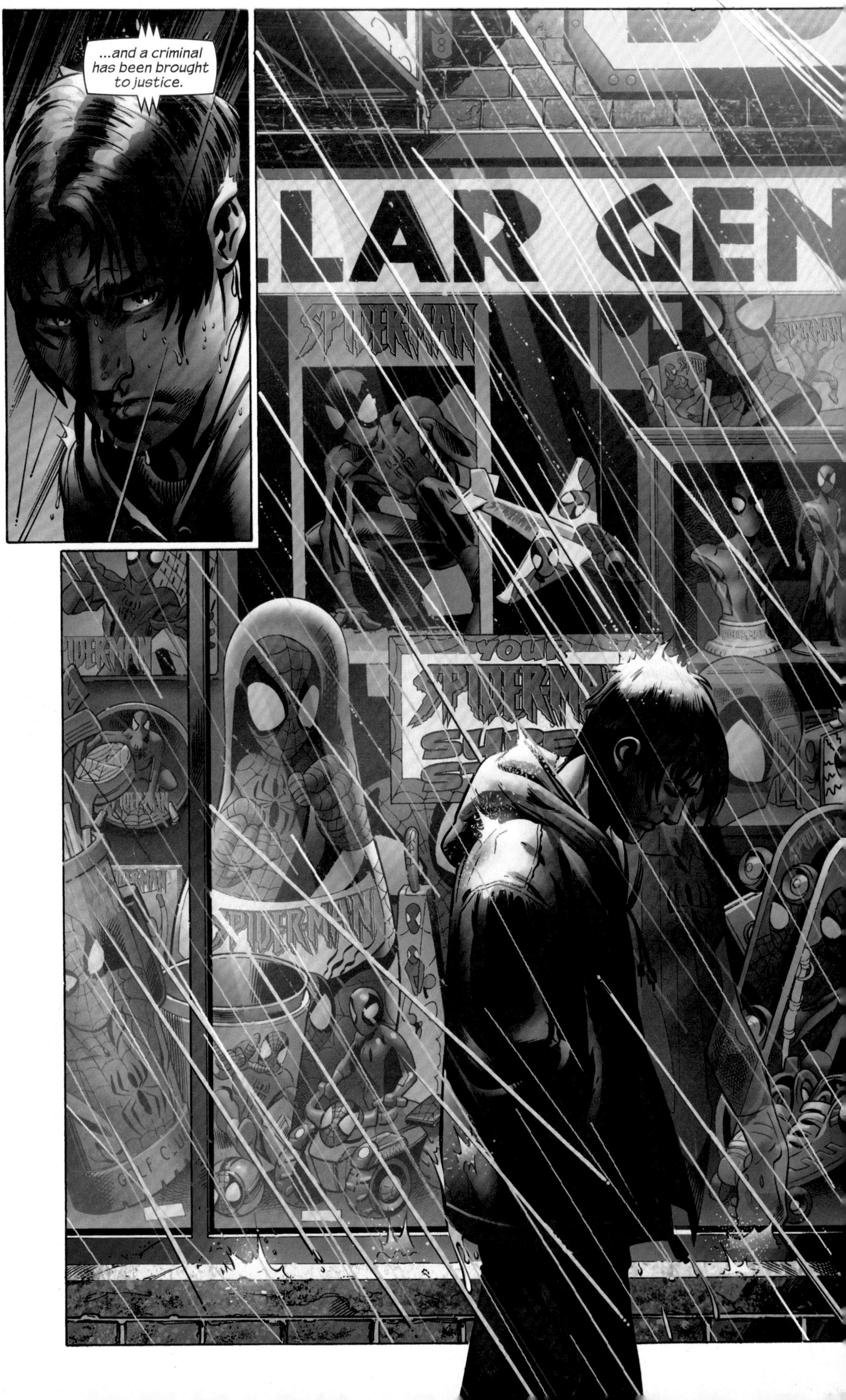
...and a criminal has been brought to justice.
LLAR GEN
SPIDER-MAN
SPIDER-MAN
SPIDER-MAN
YOUR
SPIDER-MAN
SPIDER-MAN

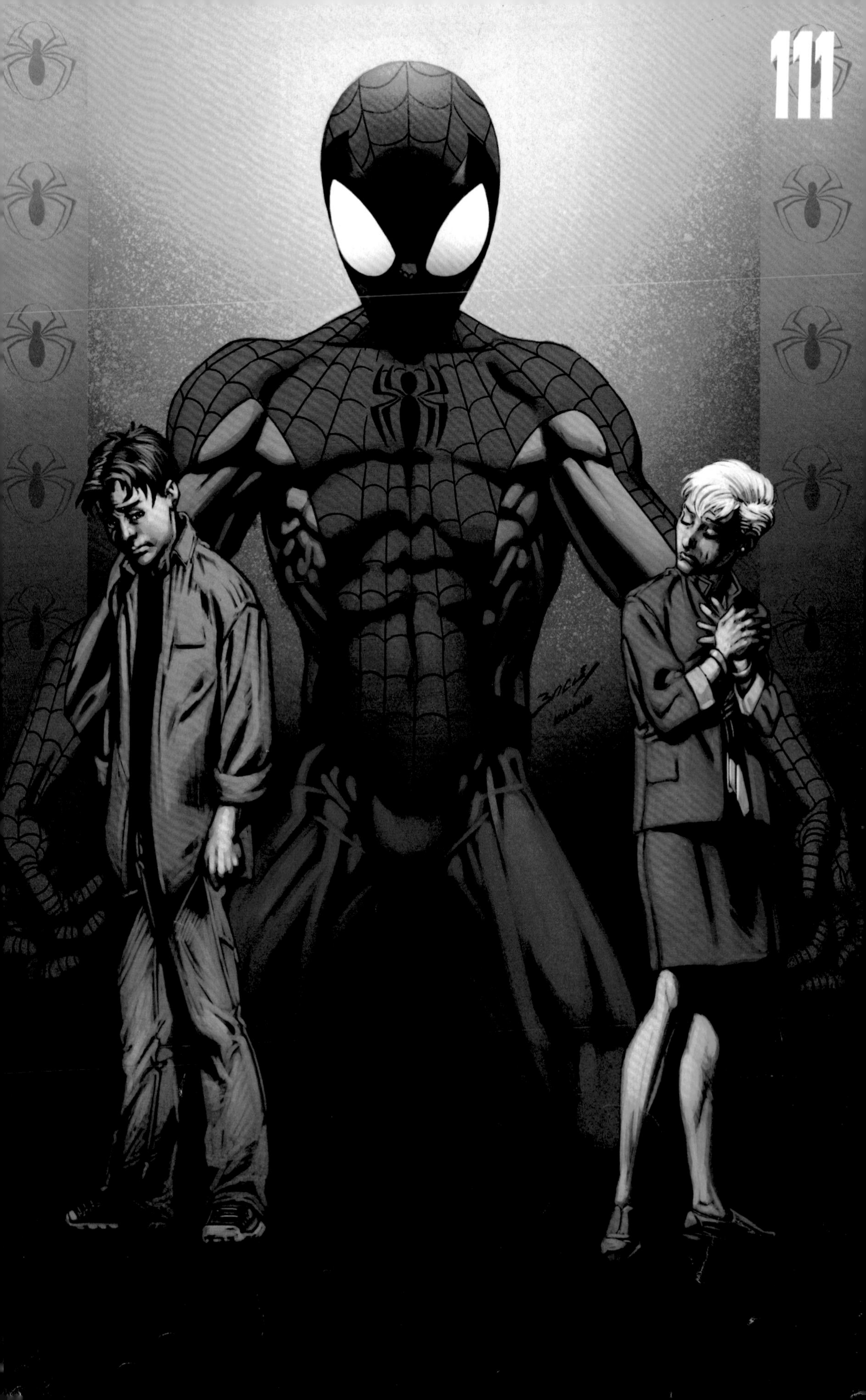
111

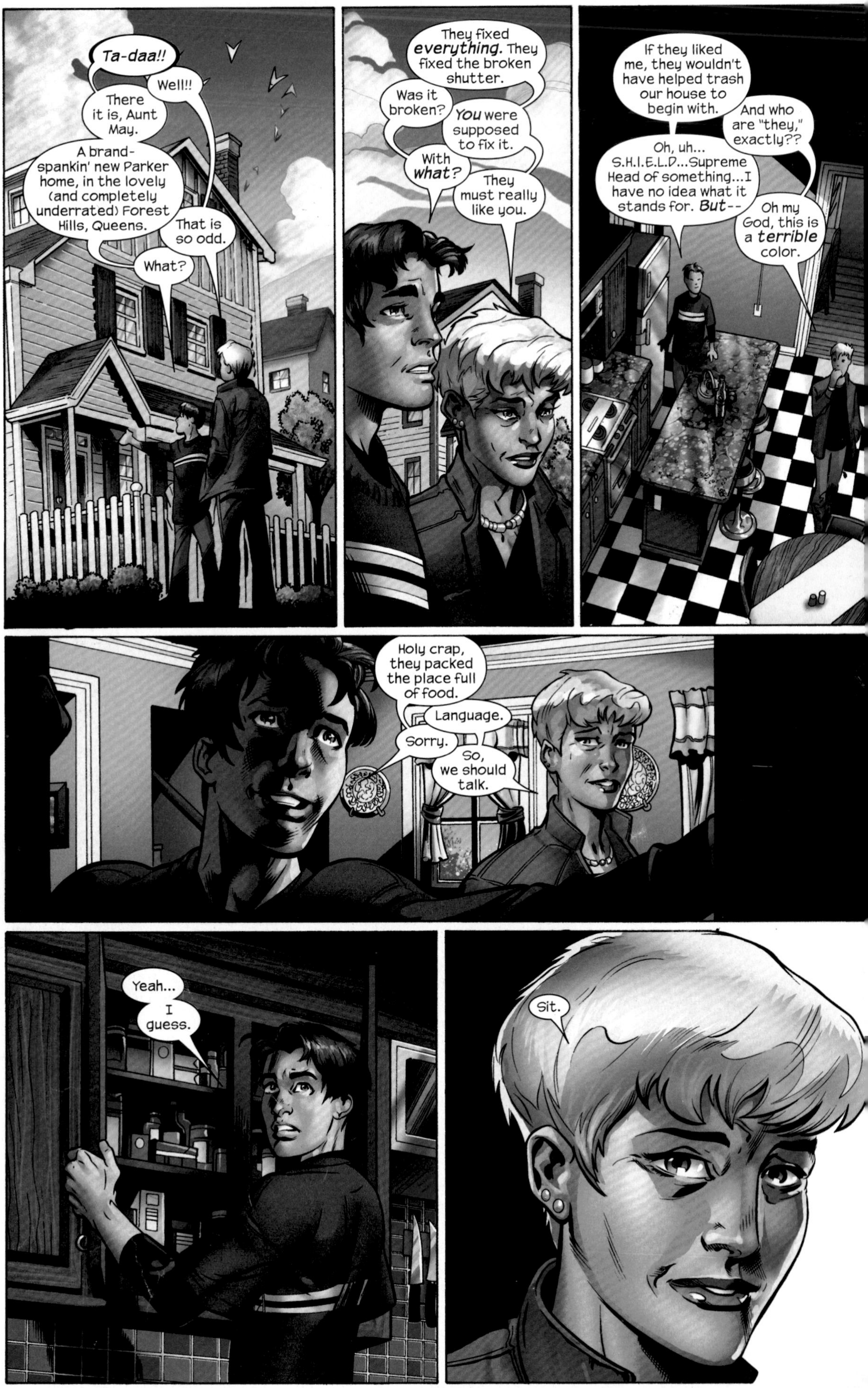
Ta-daa!!
Well!!
There it is, Aunt May.
A brand-spankin' new Parker home, in the lovely (and completely underrated) Forest Hills, Queens.
That is so odd.
What?
They fixed everything. They fixed the broken shutter.
Was it broken?
You were supposed to fix it.
With what?
They must really like you.
If they liked me, they wouldn't have helped trash our house to begin with.
And who are "they," exactly??
Oh, uh... S.H.I.E.L.D...Supreme Head of something...I have no idea what it stands for. But--
Oh my God, this is a terrible color.
Holy crap, they packed the place full of food.
Language.
Sorry.
So, we should talk.
Yeah... I guess.
Sit.

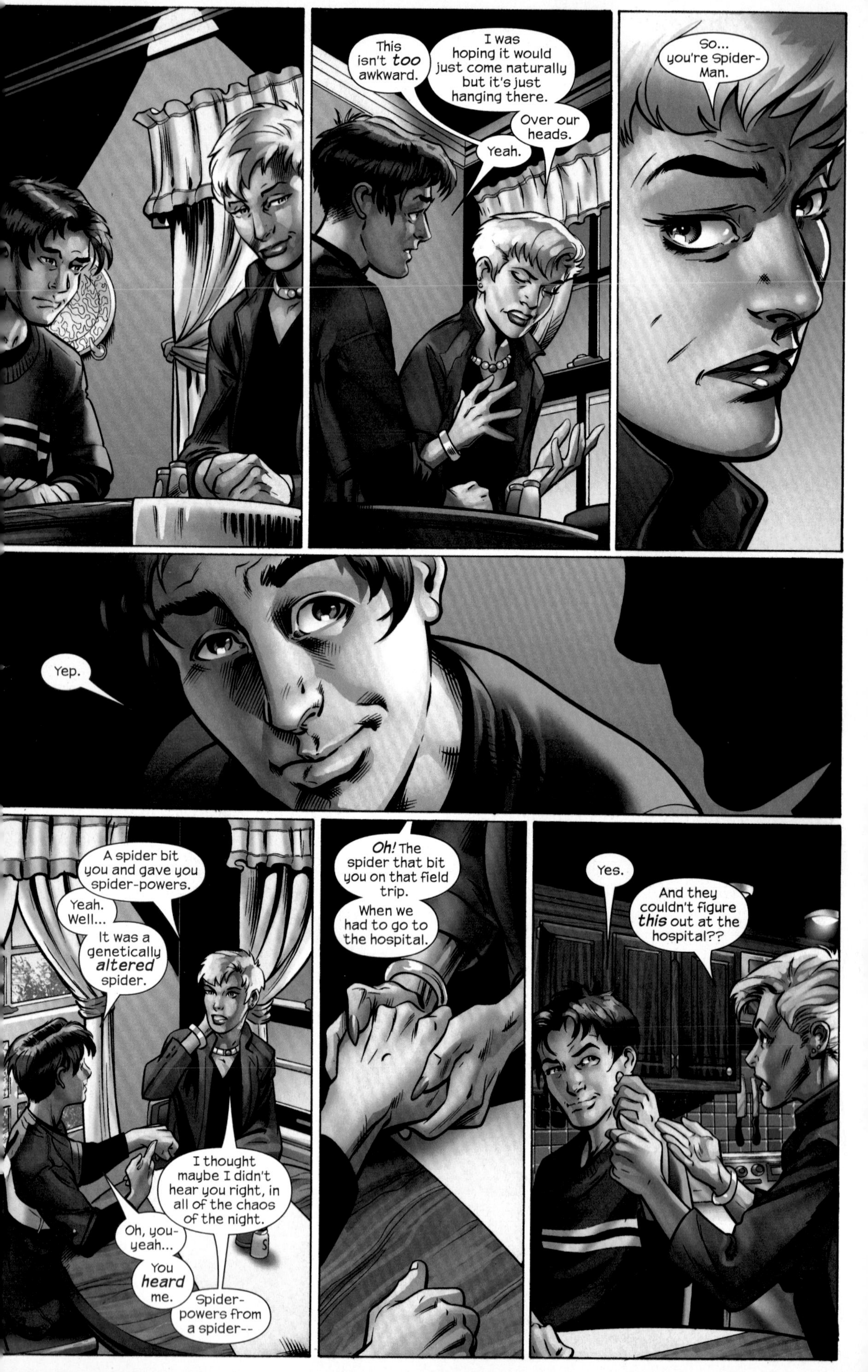
This isn't *too* awkward.
I was hoping it would just come naturally but it's just hanging there.
Over our heads.
Yeah.
So... you're Spider-Man.
Yep.
A spider bit you and gave you spider-powers.
Yeah. Well...
It was a genetically *altered* spider.
I thought maybe I didn't hear you right, in all of the chaos of the night.
Oh, you-yeah...
You *heard* me.
Spider-powers from a spider--
*Oh!* The spider that bit you on that field trip.
When we had to go to the hospital.
Yes.
And they couldn't figure *this* out at the hospital??

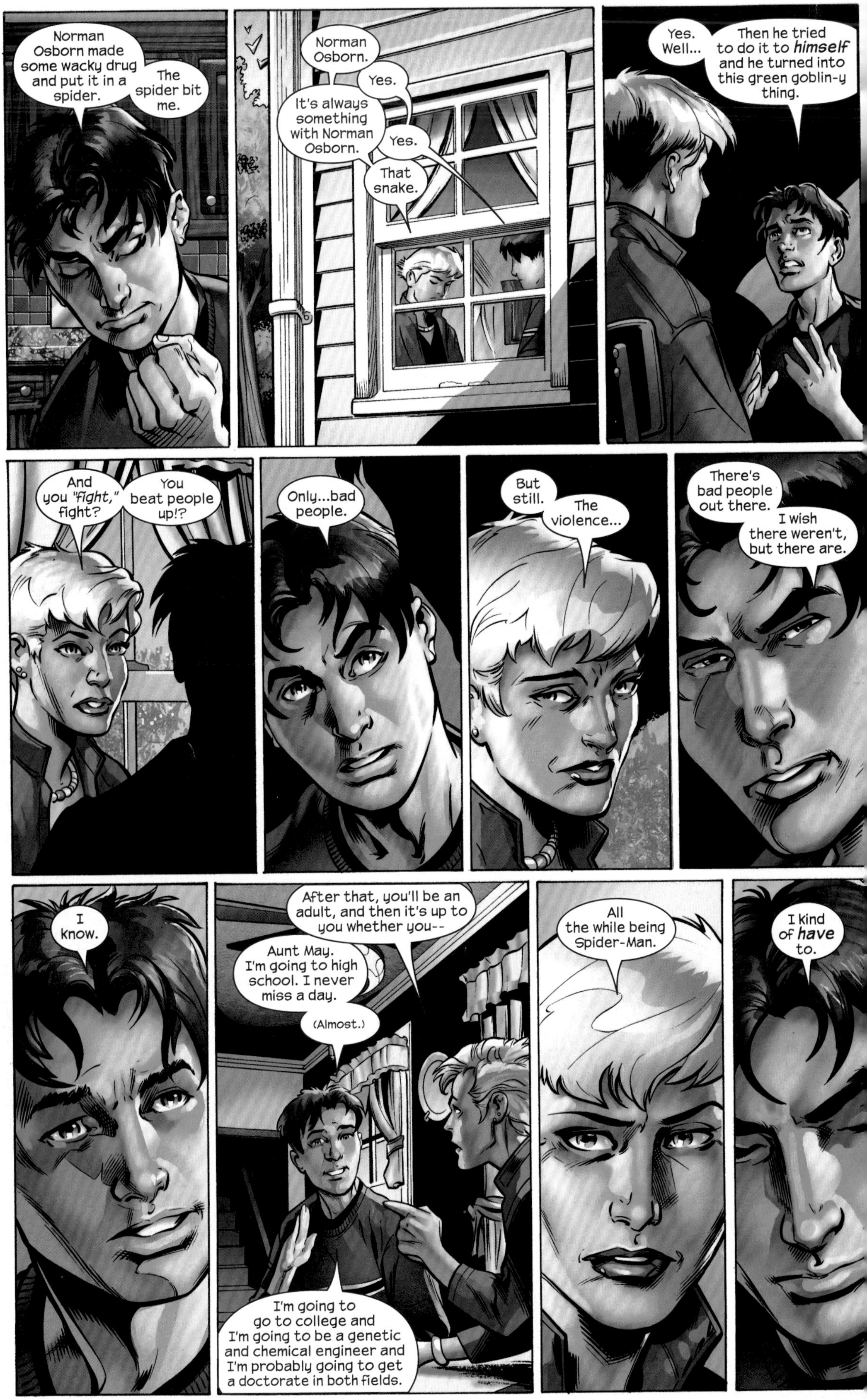
Norman Osborn made some wacky drug and put it in a spider.
The spider bit me.
Norman Osborn.
Yes.
It's always something with Norman Osborn.
Yes.
That snake.
Yes. Well...
Then he tried to do it to *himself* and he turned into this green goblin-y thing.
And you *"fight,"* fight?
You beat people up!?
Only...bad people.
But still.
The violence...
There's bad people out there.
I wish there weren't, but there are.
I know.
After that, you'll be an adult, and then it's up to you whether you--
Aunt May. I'm going to high school. I never miss a day.
(Almost.)
I'm going to go to college and I'm going to be a genetic and chemical engineer and I'm probably going to get a doctorate in both fields.
All the while being Spider-Man.
I kind of *have* to.

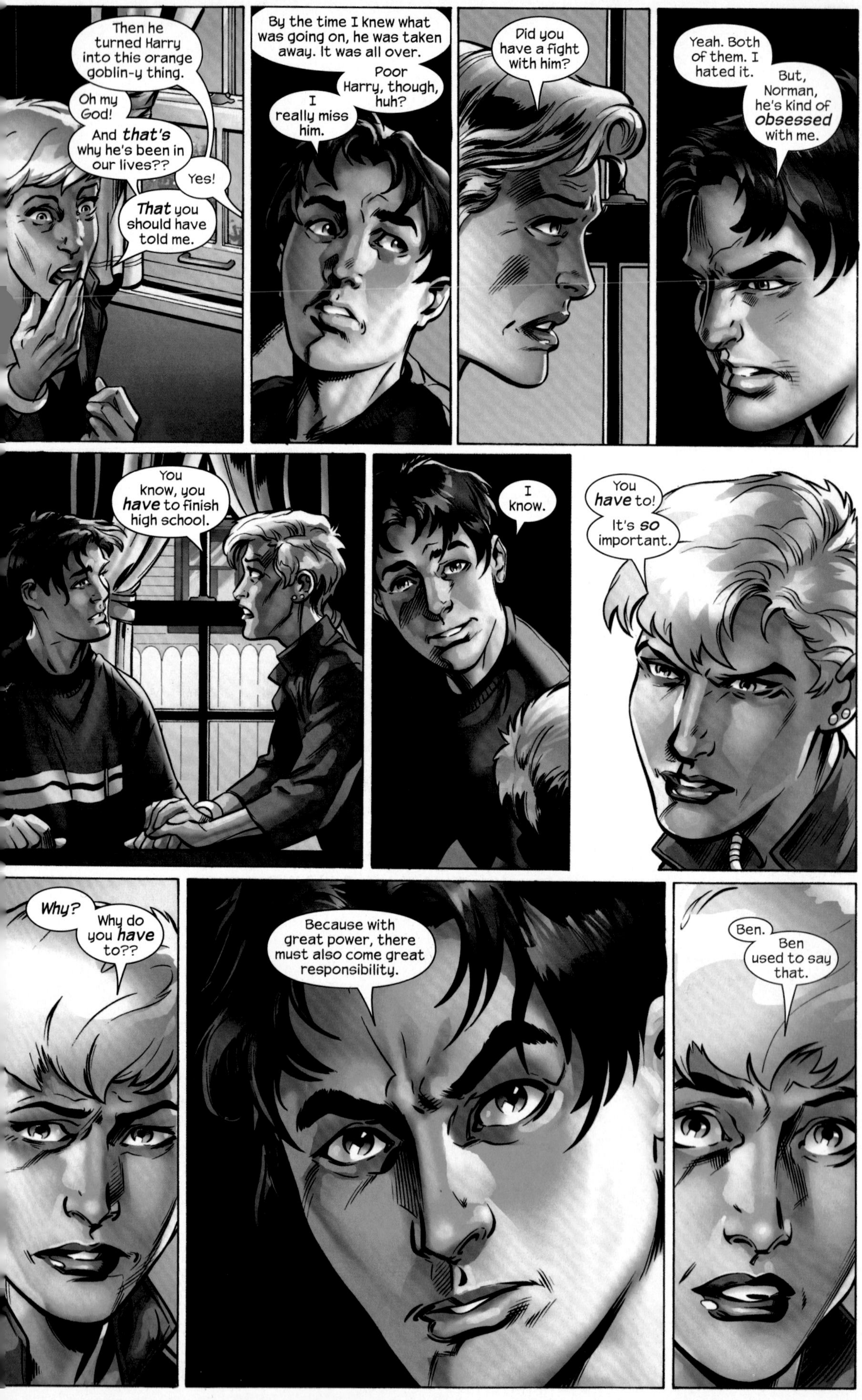

Then he turned Harry into this orange goblin-y thing.
Oh my God!
And *that's* why he's been in our lives??
Yes!
*That* you should have told me.
By the time I knew what was going on, he was taken away. It was all over.
Poor Harry, though, huh?
I really miss him.
Did you have a fight with him?
Yeah. Both of them. I hated it.
But, Norman, he's kind of ***obsessed*** with me.
You know, you ***have*** to finish high school.
I know.
You ***have*** to!
It's ***so*** important.
***Why?***
Why do you ***have*** to??
Because with great power, there must also come great responsibility.
Ben.
Ben used to say that.

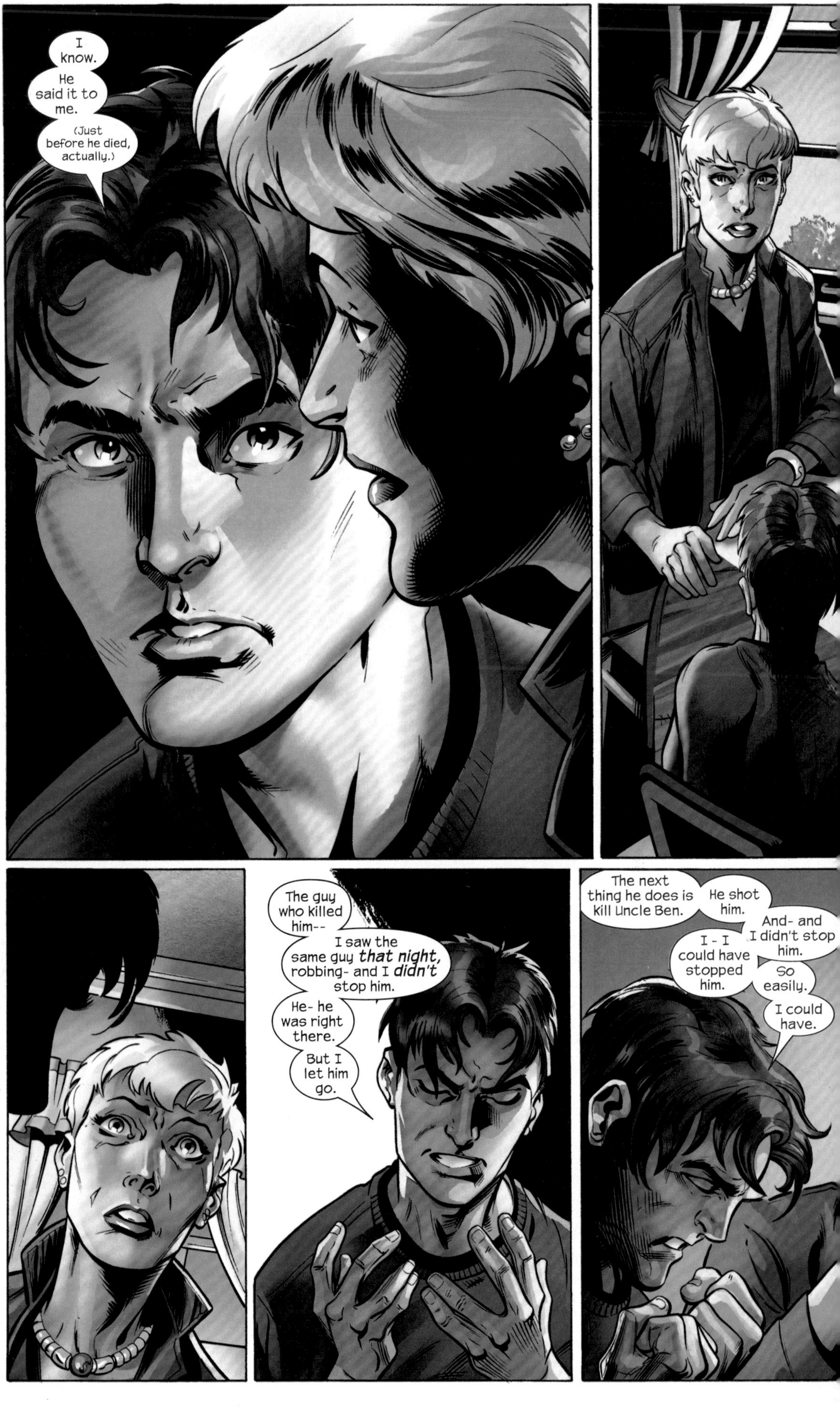
I know.
He said it to me.
(Just before he died, actually.)
The guy who killed him--
I saw the same guy *that night*, robbing- and I *didn't* stop him.
He- he was right there.
But I let him go.
The next thing he does is kill Uncle Ben.
He shot him.
And- and I didn't stop him.
I - I could have stopped him.
So easily.
I could have.

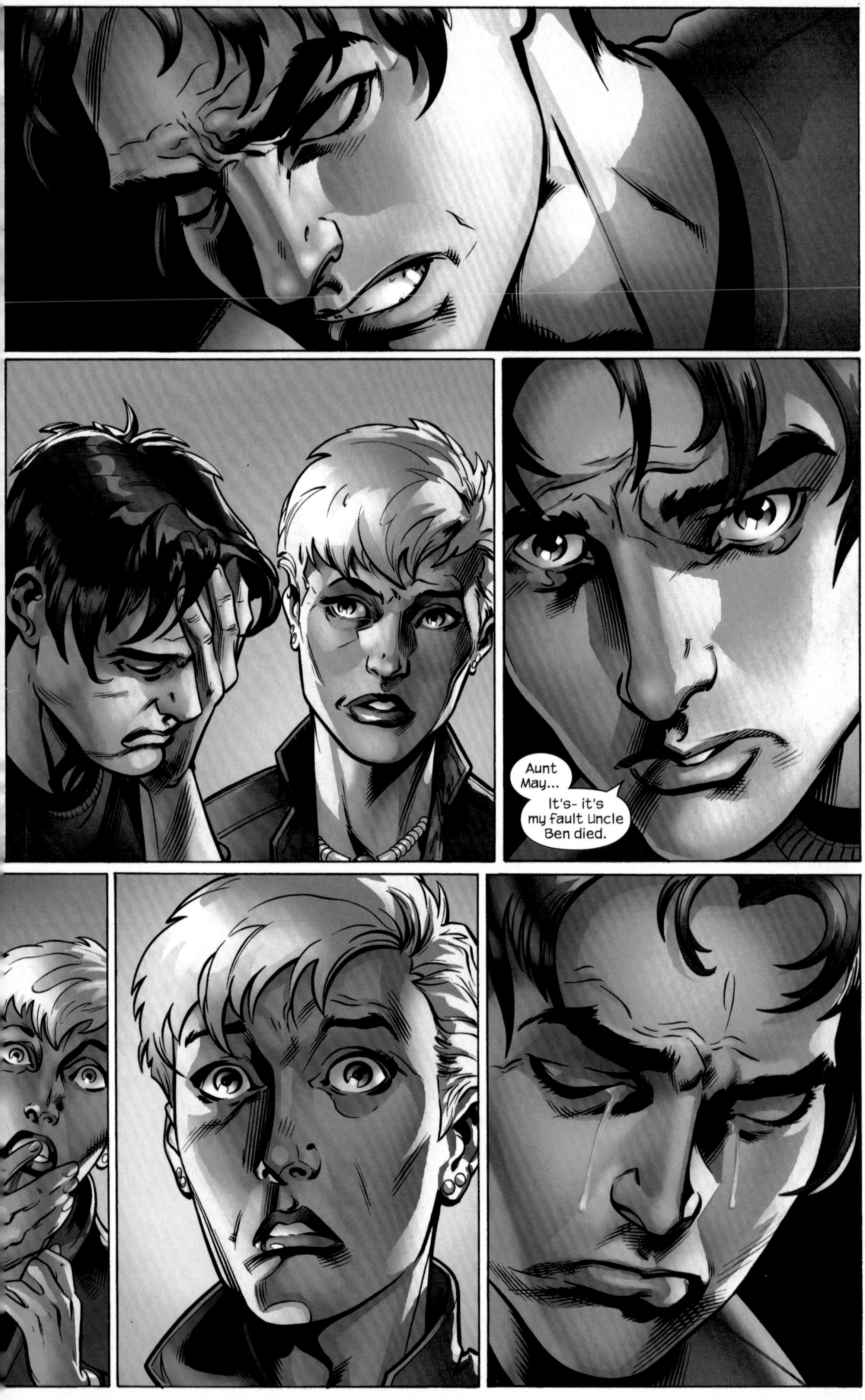
Aunt May...
It's- it's my fault Uncle Ben died.

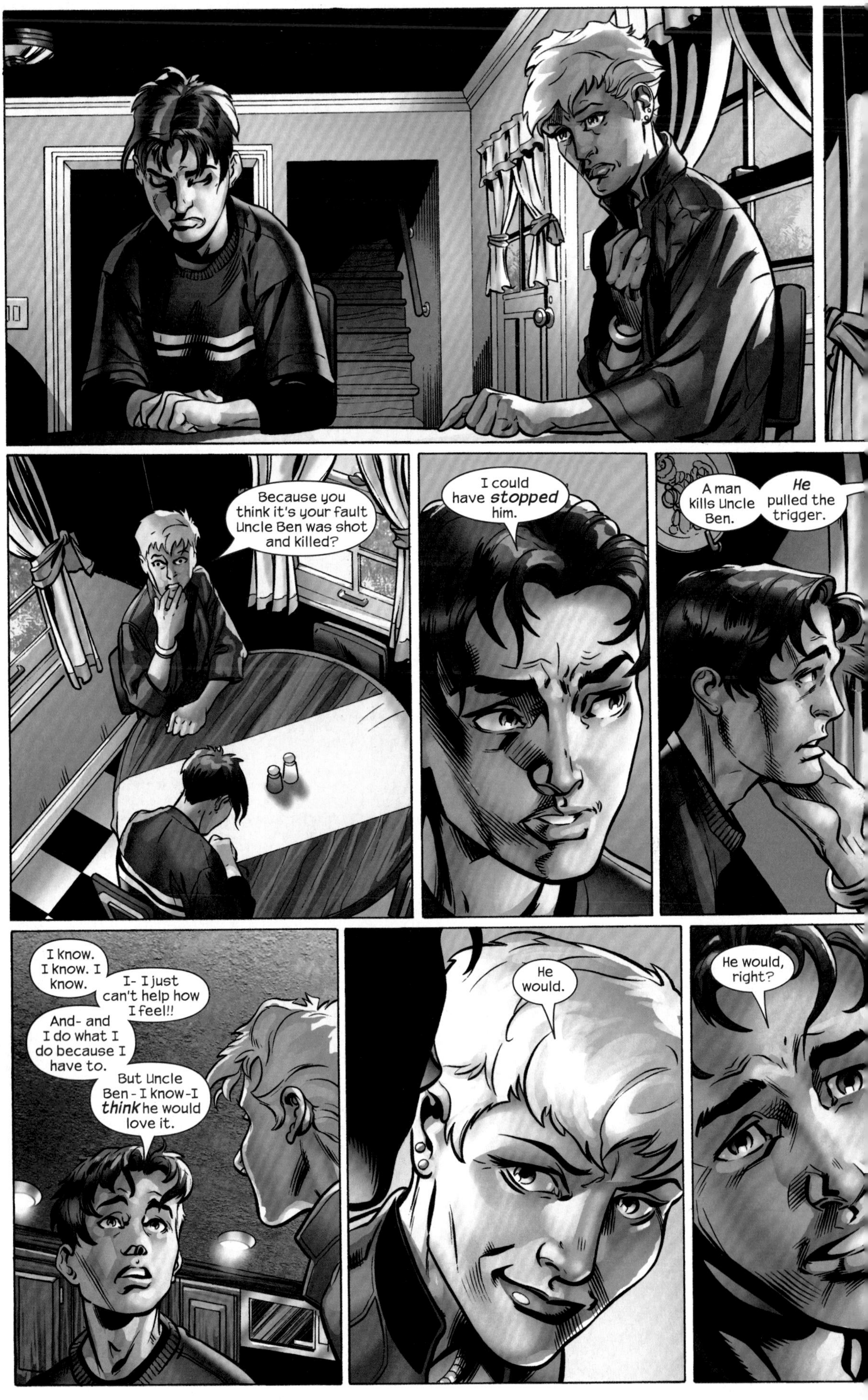

Because you think it's your fault Uncle Ben was shot and killed?
I could have *stopped* him.
A man kills Uncle Ben.
*He* pulled the trigger.
I know. I know. I know.
I- I just can't help how I feel!!
And- and I do what I do because I have to.
But Uncle Ben - I know-I *think* he would love it.
He would.
He would, right?

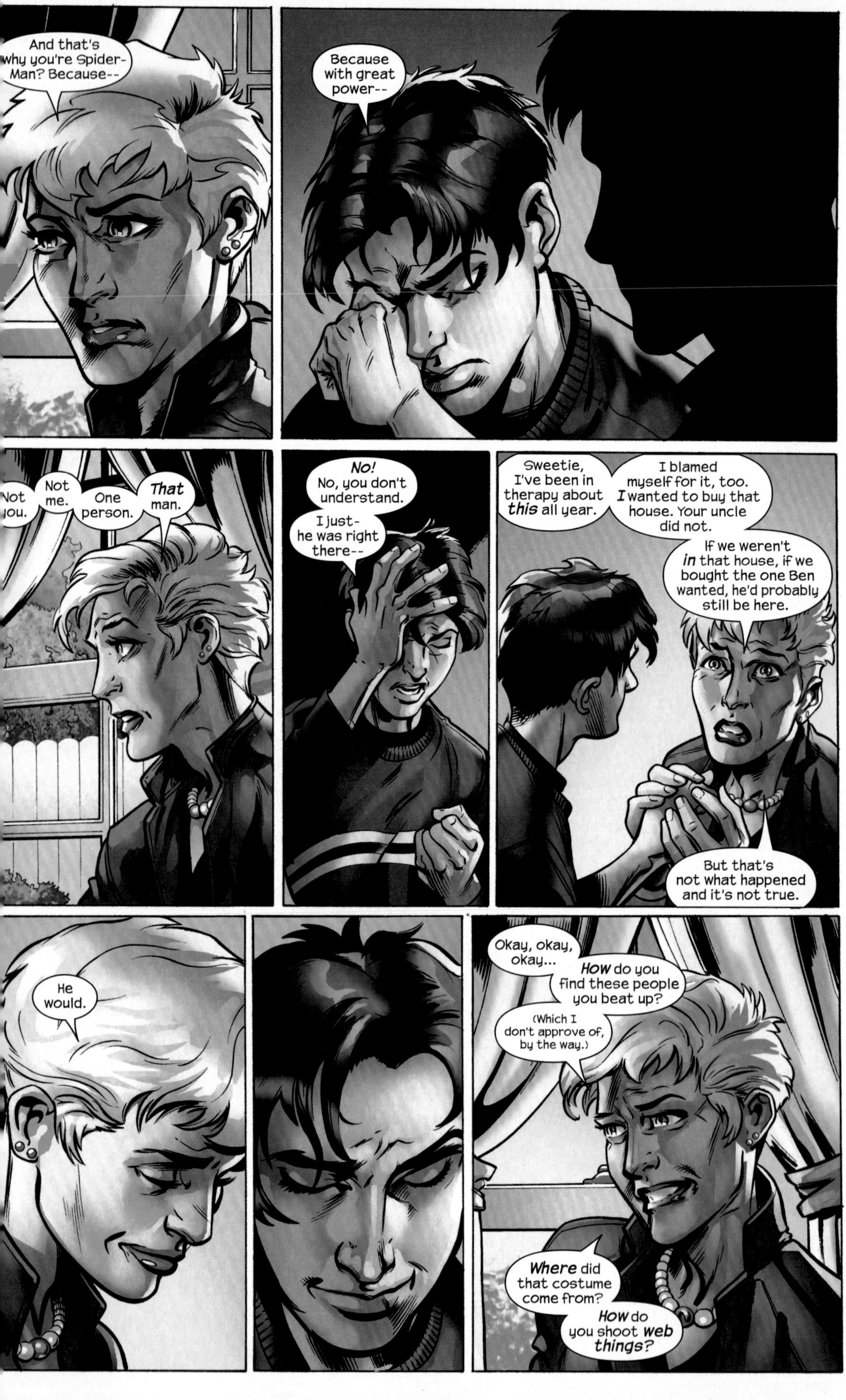

And that's why you're Spider-Man? Because--
Because with great power--
Not you.
Not me.
One person.
That man.
No! No, you don't understand.
I just- he was right there--
Sweetie, I've been in therapy about this all year.
I blamed myself for it, too. I wanted to buy that house. Your uncle did not.
If we weren't in that house, if we bought the one Ben wanted, he'd probably still be here.
But that's not what happened and it's not true.
He would.
Okay, okay, okay...
How do you find these people you beat up?
(Which I don't approve of, by the way.)
Where did that costume come from?
How do you shoot web things?

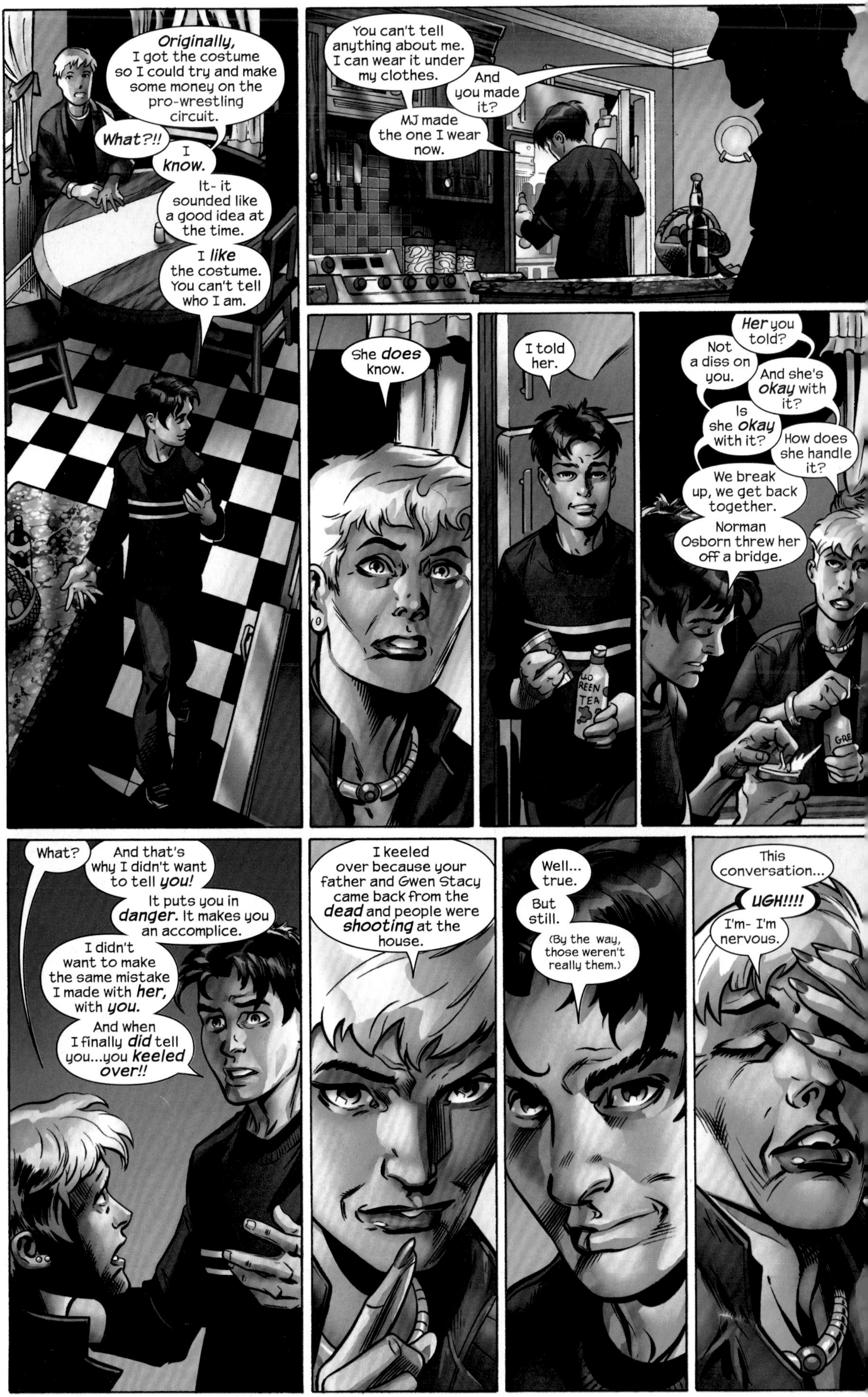

Originally, I got the costume so I could try and make some money on the pro-wrestling circuit.
What?!!
I know.
It- it sounded like a good idea at the time.
I like the costume. You can't tell who I am.
You can't tell anything about me. I can wear it under my clothes.
And you made it?
MJ made the one I wear now.
She does know.
I told her.
Her you told?
Not a diss on you.
And she's okay with it?
Is she okay with it?
How does she handle it?
We break up, we get back together.
Norman Osborn threw her off a bridge.
What?
And that's why I didn't want to tell you!
It puts you in danger. It makes you an accomplice.
I didn't want to make the same mistake I made with her, with you.
And when I finally did tell you...you keeled over!!
I keeled over because your father and Gwen Stacy came back from the dead and people were shooting at the house.
Well... true.
But still.
(By the way, those weren't really them.)
This conversation...
UGH!!!!
I'm- I'm nervous.

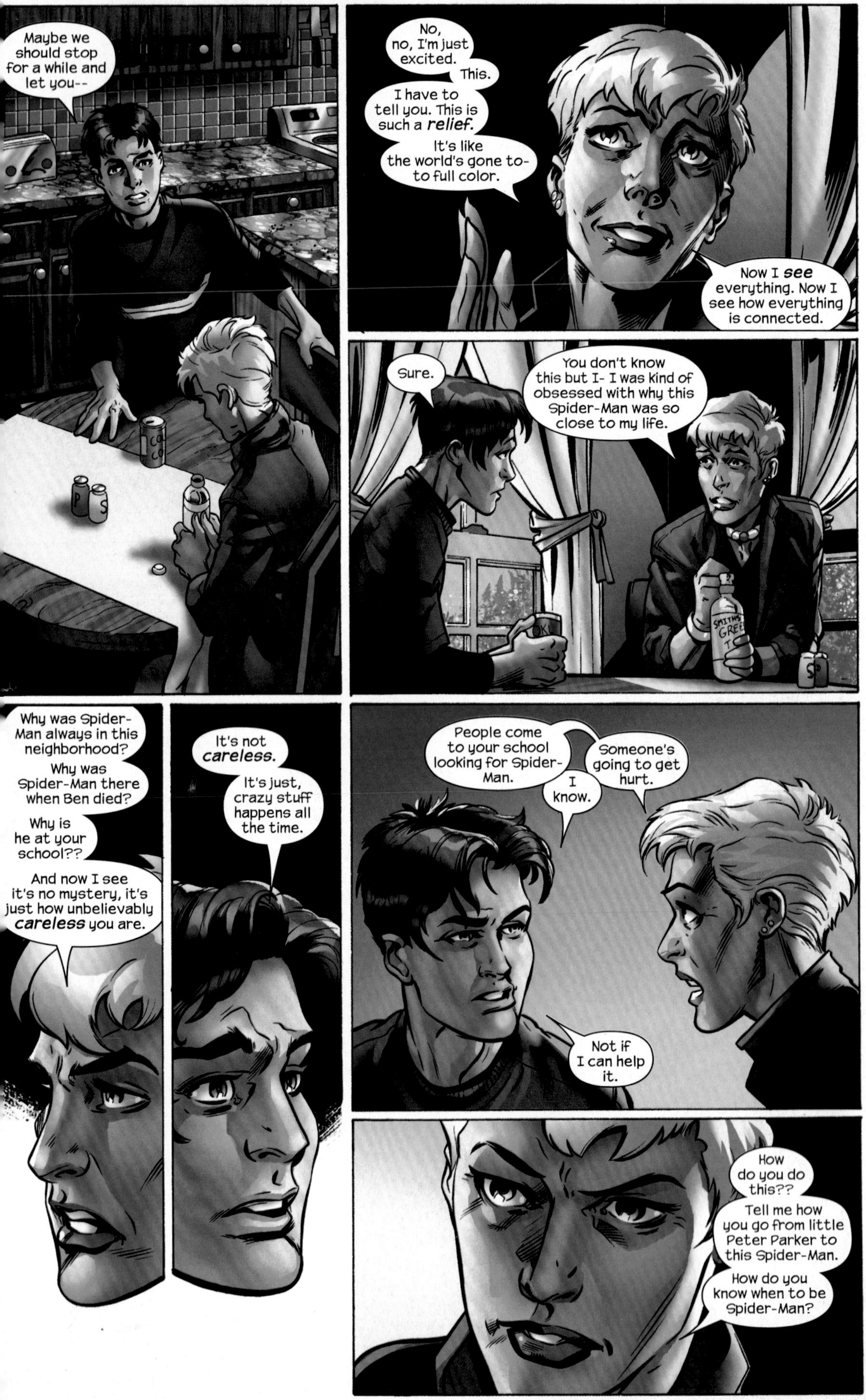
Maybe we should stop for a while and let you--
No, no, I'm just excited.
This.
I have to tell you. This is such a *relief.*
It's like the world's gone to-- to full color.
Now I *see* everything. Now I see how everything is connected.
Sure.
You don't know this but I- I was kind of obsessed with why this Spider-Man was so close to my life.
Why was Spider-Man always in this neighborhood?
Why was Spider-Man there when Ben died?
Why is he at your school??
And now I see it's no mystery, it's just how unbelievably *careless* you are.
It's not *careless.*
It's just, crazy stuff happens all the time.
People come to your school looking for Spider-Man.
Someone's going to get hurt.
I know.
Not if I can help it.
How do you do this??
Tell me how you go from little Peter Parker to this Spider-Man.
How do you know when to be Spider-Man?

*PETER PARKER:*
Well, um, well... I can tell you what happened today.

*AUNT MAY:*
***Today?!*** You were being Spider-Man ***today,*** before you came and got me from the hospital??

*PETER PARKER:*
Well...yeah.

*AUNT MAY:*
I thought you were ***working!***

*PETER PARKER:*
I was. I was at the *Daily Bugle*.

*AUNT MAY:*
You ***do*** work there.

*PETER PARKER:*
You've ***seen*** my paycheck. I ***do*** work there and it's a great job. I ***love*** it there.

There's always something really intense going on.

And- and- and smart people arguing about morals and ethics and integrity that most of them feel they have to ***not*** live by, or the paper will fold.

I love it there. I'm serious. If it wasn't for science, I so could see myself being a journalist.

*AUNT MAY:*
Maybe you ***will*** be one.

*PETER PARKER:*
Maybe. But the ***other*** thing I love about that place is that it's this ***hub*** of information for me.

Anything going on in the city...***anything.*** And the paper knows about it in two seconds.

A bank robbery, a monster tearing up Times Square, vampires...

*AUNT MAY:*
***Vampires??***

*PETER PARKER:*
What***ever*** is going on, I know all about it.

And the place is so huge that I can sneak out and try to do something to help without anyone really ever noticing I'm gone.

Most of the time I get there before the cops.

And a lot of the time ***I'm*** in and out of there before the reporter who got assigned the story can even physically ***get*** across town to get to it.

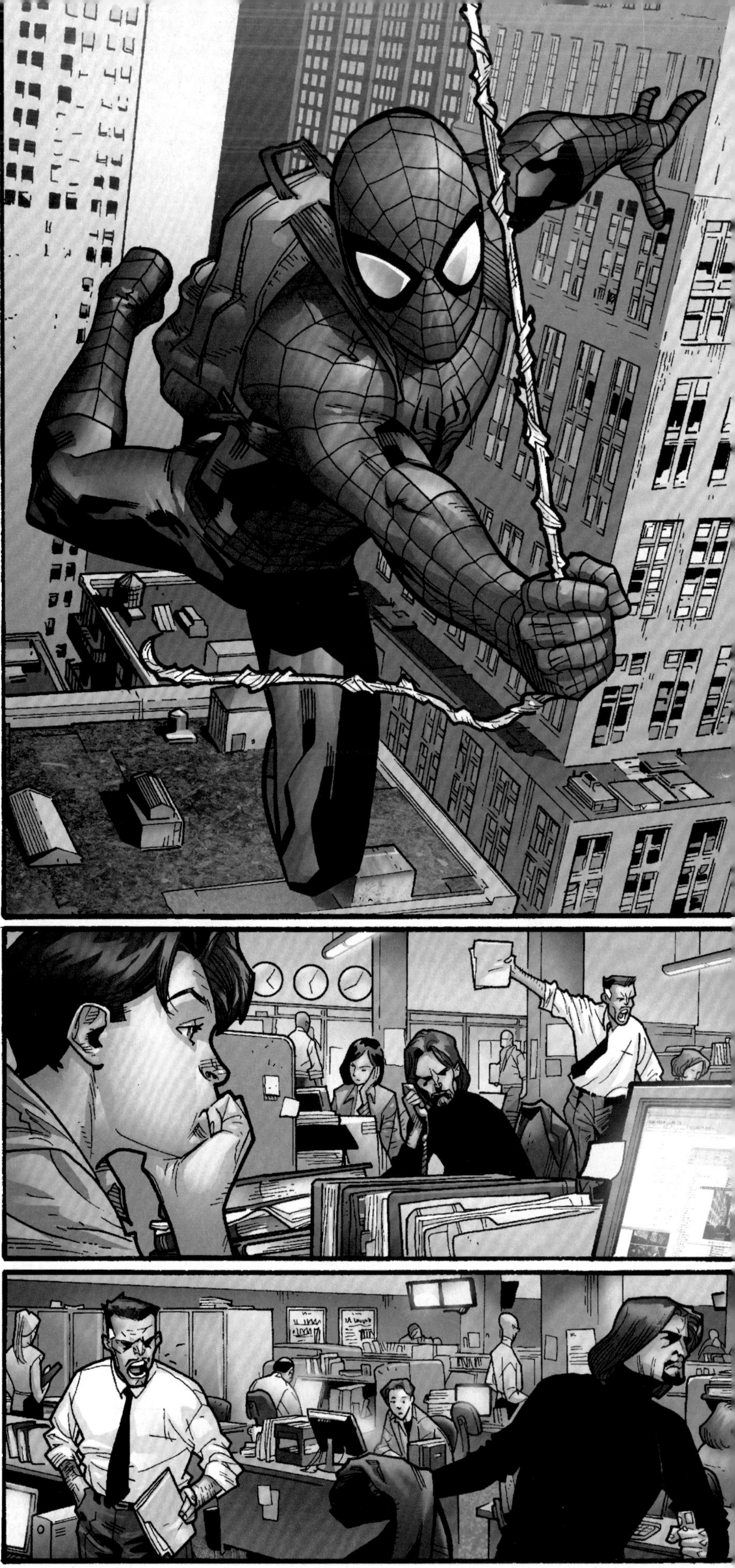

*PETER PARKER:*
Today's adventure was about someone flipping out in an industrial complex, and there were hostages and all kinds of bedlam of some sort.

But what caught my ear about this was it was happening at ***Roxxon Industries.***

*AUNT MAY:*
What's Roxxon Industries?

*PETER PARKER:*
Exactly! They're a pharmacological-industrial-conglomerate-complex, and every fourth time I've had to put my costume on in the last five months, it's been about ***them.***

Either someone's trying to ***assassinate*** the guy who owns Roxxon, or a big, flying birdman is trying to ***blow up*** Roxxon, or some silver lady gets hired by Roxxon to find me.

It's all this ***Roxxon*** stuff.

And I don't know why!!

I don't know what's going on or who exactly is involved, all I know is that this Roxxon company is always at the center of shenanigans!

*AUNT MAY:*
What do you think it is??

*PETER PARKER:*
I think that the rich people who own Roxxon are up to shenanigans and getting away with it because everyone.is so focused on Norman Osborn and Otto Octavius that no one is paying attention to Roxxon.

***Or*** Roxxon paid a bunch of people to look the other way.

Or that Roxxon is in cahoots with our government and getting a free pass.

But what matters is they're up to shenanigans and people are getting hurt.

By the time I got across town, it was already bedlam there, chaos...

Cops, fire trucks, people screaming. The media was blocks away...

I didn't know what I was diving into, but I knew there were people in there and...

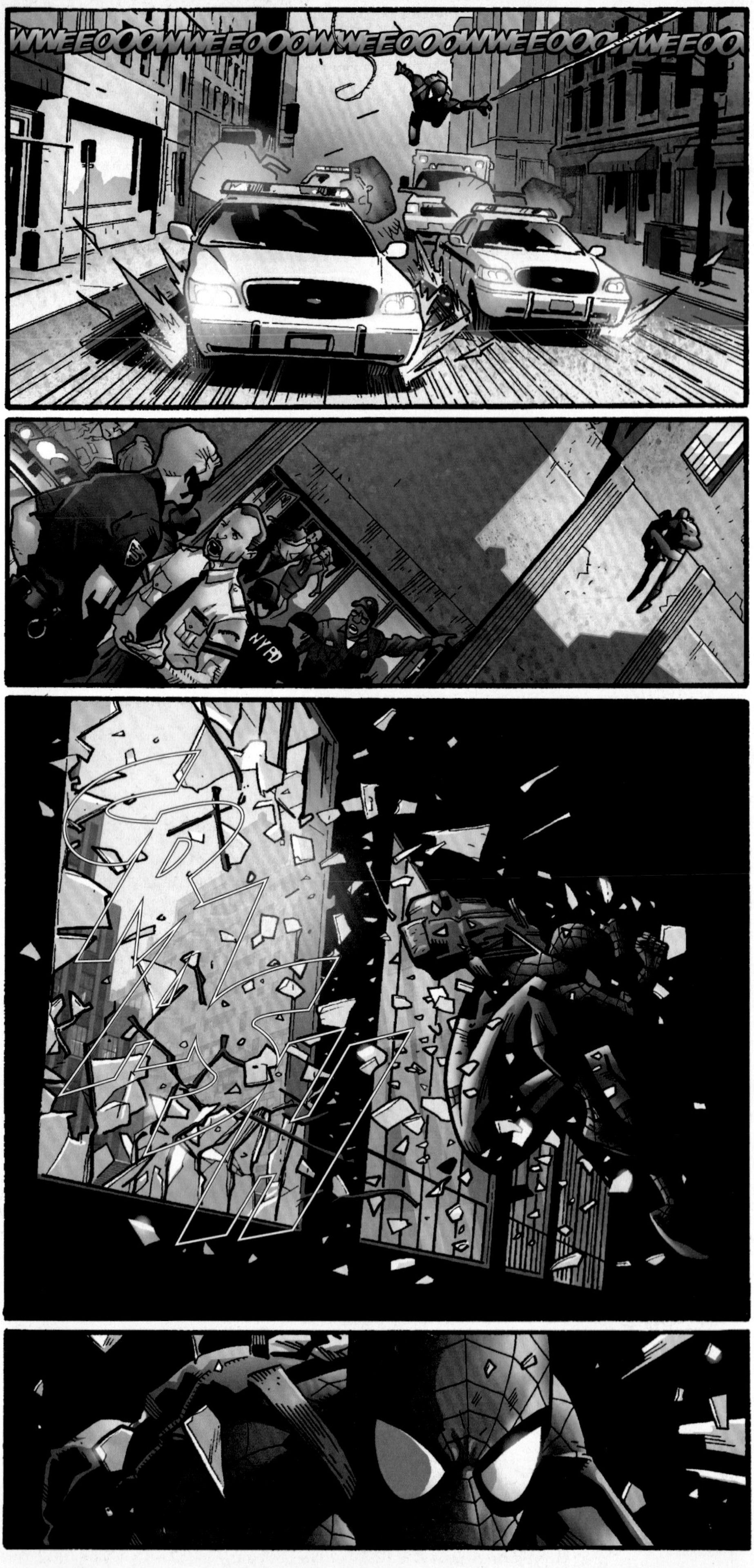
WWEEOOOWWEEOOOWWEEOOOWWEEOOO

*PETER PARKER:*
Honestly, I didn't know ***what*** I was looking at.

*AUNT MAY:*
What happened?

*PETER PARKER:*
Well, first the place was just trashed. People were screaming.

And in the middle of this gorgeous, high-tech laboratory, that was ***so*** trashed it hurt my young scientist heart, was this guy who was made out of- of ***floating black-and-white.***

*AUNT MAY:*
I don't understand.

*PETER PARKER:*
I don't know how else to describe it. There were these floating ***spots*** of black all over his body.

And- and his body seemed- I don't think he was wearing clothes.

All white, chalk-white, with black spots cascading and moving over him and into each other like a human-lava-lamp kind of thing.

It was freaky. He was a man made up of spots.

*AUNT MAY:*
So you just ***hit*** him.

*PETER PARKER:*
Well, no, first I tried asking him what was up, but my spider-sense went off.

*AUNT MAY:*
***Spider-sense??***

*PETER PARKER:*
Oh yeah. I have a ***sense.*** A- a buzzing- it warns me there's danger.

It helps me dive out of harm's way.

And it ***went off,*** which meant *"game on."* So I tried to put a stop to it before it all went crazi***er.***

*AUNT MAY:*
And--

*PETER PARKER:*
And that's when things got crazier.

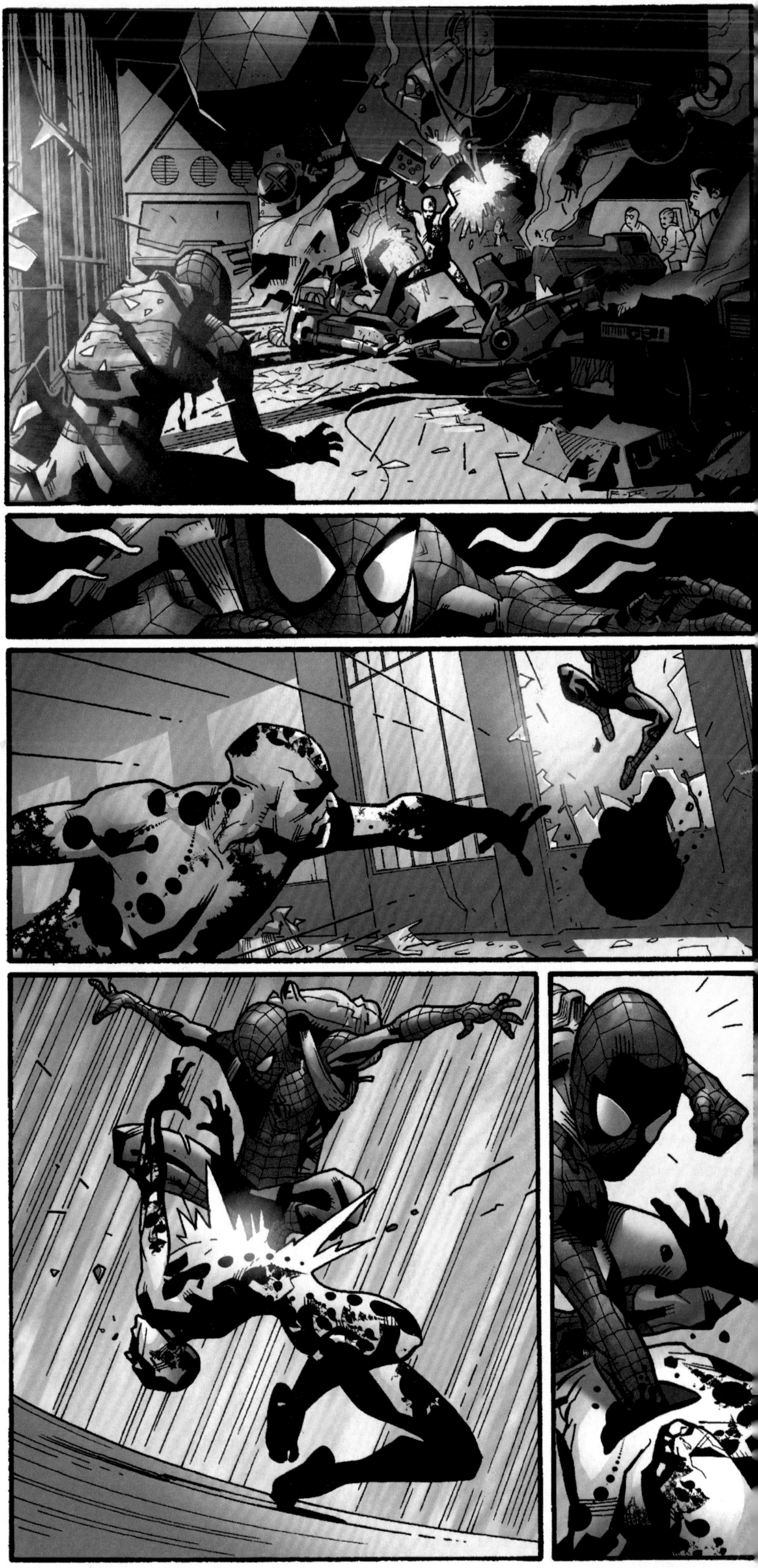

*PETER PARKER:*
These spots.

These black spots.

He controlled them and they seemed to be maybe little black holes, or little doors of antimatter, or little--

I don't know- he could toss black spots onto things and push objects and himself through them.

*AUNT MAY:*
I- I can't even fathom what you're talking about--

*PETER PARKER:*
***I know.*** I know. That's my point.

You'd need to be a genius doctor of particle physics to even know the terms that describe what was ***happening*** and how they ***defied*** all of those terms and laws.

*AUNT MAY:*
Black spots?

*PETER PARKER:*
I'm standing ***here*** and- and he's standing all the way ***over there*** and I'm trying to find out what is happening and all of a sudden I'm being punched in the back of the head...by ***him!***

*AUNT MAY:*
What?

*PETER PARKER:*
Yes, by the same guy, he's over there, and he's punching me like he's standing right behind me.

I was getting ***vertigo*** from it.

Like, the brain's not used to ***seeing*** things like this.

It doesn't know how to register it.

*AUNT MAY:*
But your spider-sense...

*PETER PARKER:*
Tells me I'm in danger.

It doesn't tell me exactly ***what*** I'm in danger from.

*AUNT MAY:*
So he was hitting you, he was hitting you just for trying to help him.

*PETER PARKER:*
To be fair, he doesn't know what I am, either, and it didn't look like he wanted help.

And I wasn't so much trying to ***help*** him as to ***stop*** him from maybe hurting the people in there.

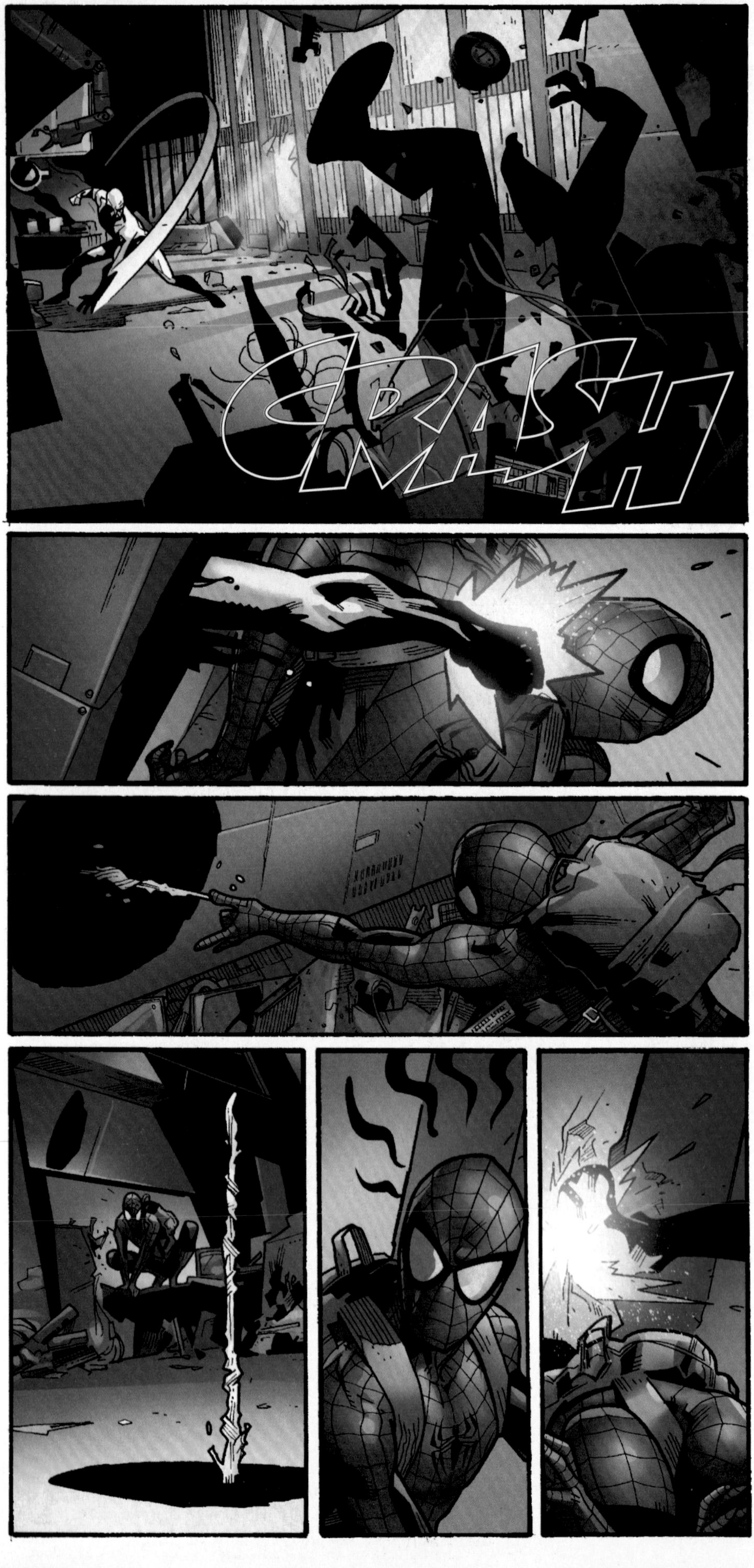
CRASH

*AUNT MAY:*
But still- how did he ***get*** that way with the black spots?

*PETER PARKER:*
I asked.
He kicked me.

*AUNT MAY:*
So you have no idea what this was about even...

*PETER PARKER:*
Well, at first I didn't, but there was this nice, terrified lab assistant under one of the tables who kept yelling out things like:

"Frank, please... it was an accident!

"We would never have done this to you on purpose!!

"Please, let's think about the scientific ramifications of blah blah blah..."

So basically they did this to him, or he did it to himself by accident.

Either way, he was freaking out.

People were in danger.

*AUNT MAY:*
So you beat him up.

*PETER PARKER:*
I can tell you're not comfortable hearing about this part...

...so let's skip it.

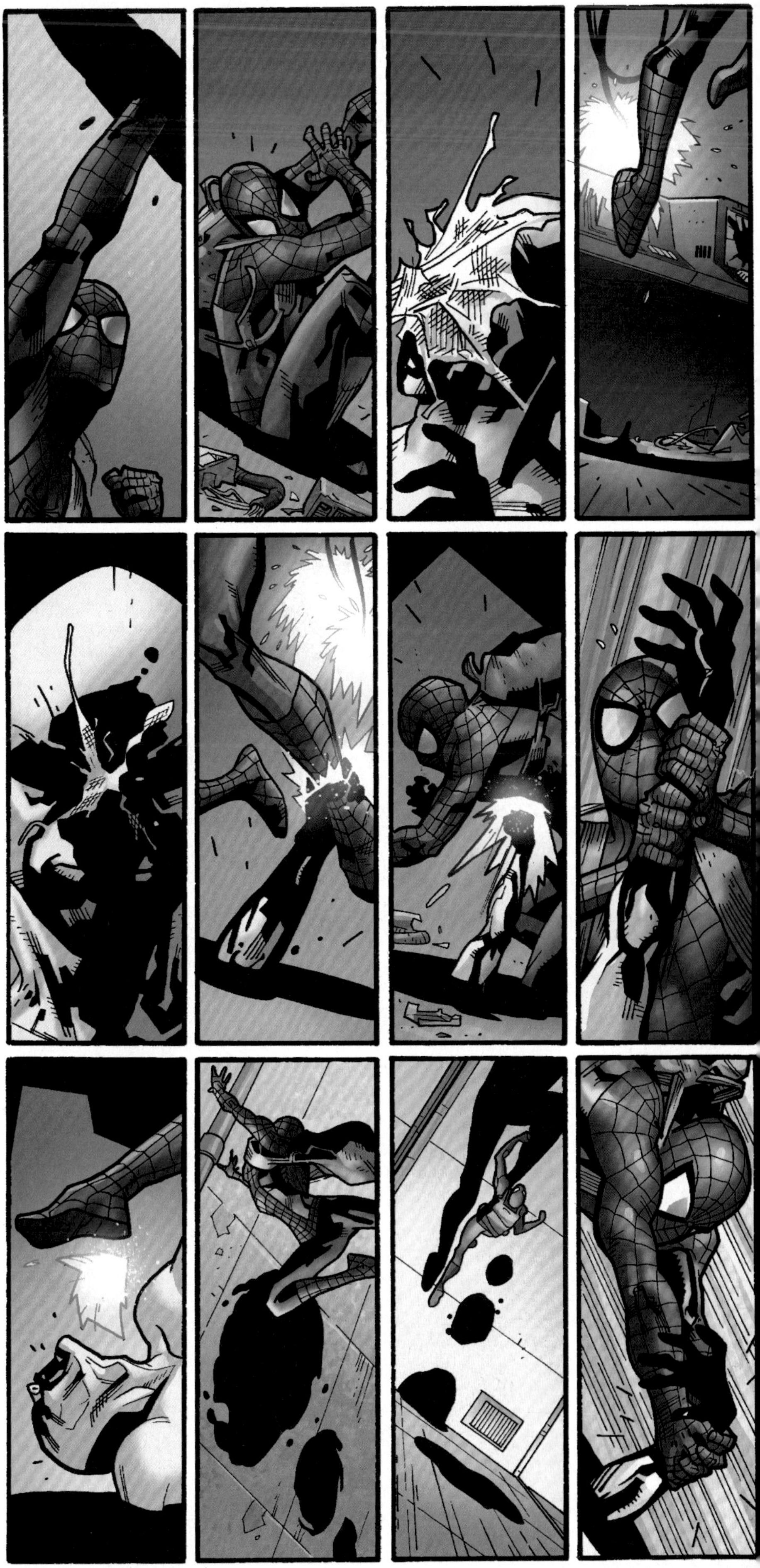

*PETER PARKER:*
But I saved the day.

(I guess.)

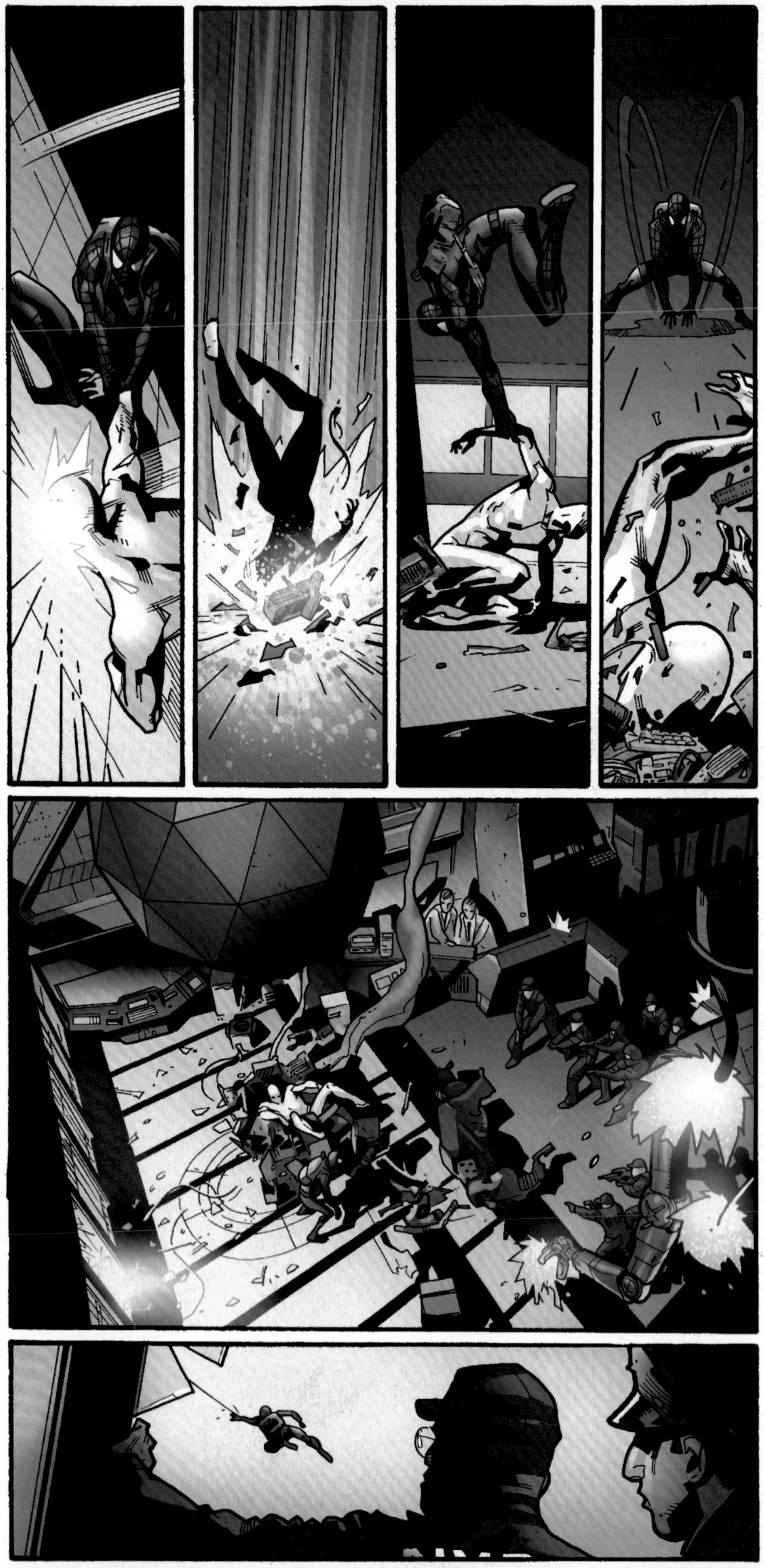

And as usual, the cops barged in, pulled their guns on me and I ran away.

*AUNT MAY:*
Why do they pull their ***guns*** on you?

*PETER PARKER:*
Because everyone is ***freaked out,*** and I'm there in a costume and, hey!!

*AUNT MAY:*
That happens ***all the time?***

*PETER PARKER:*
That happens ***every*** time.

*AUNT MAY:*
They ***shoot*** at you??

*PETER PARKER:*
Listen, I'm not trying to upset you--

*AUNT MAY:*
They shoot at you?? You save them and they ***shoot at you??***

*PETER PARKER:*
Um, let's save that part of it for another time.

The point is there was this guy who defied all laws of physical space who almost pulled me into a black hole of an abyss--

*AUNT MAY:*
This is all- what does it all mean?

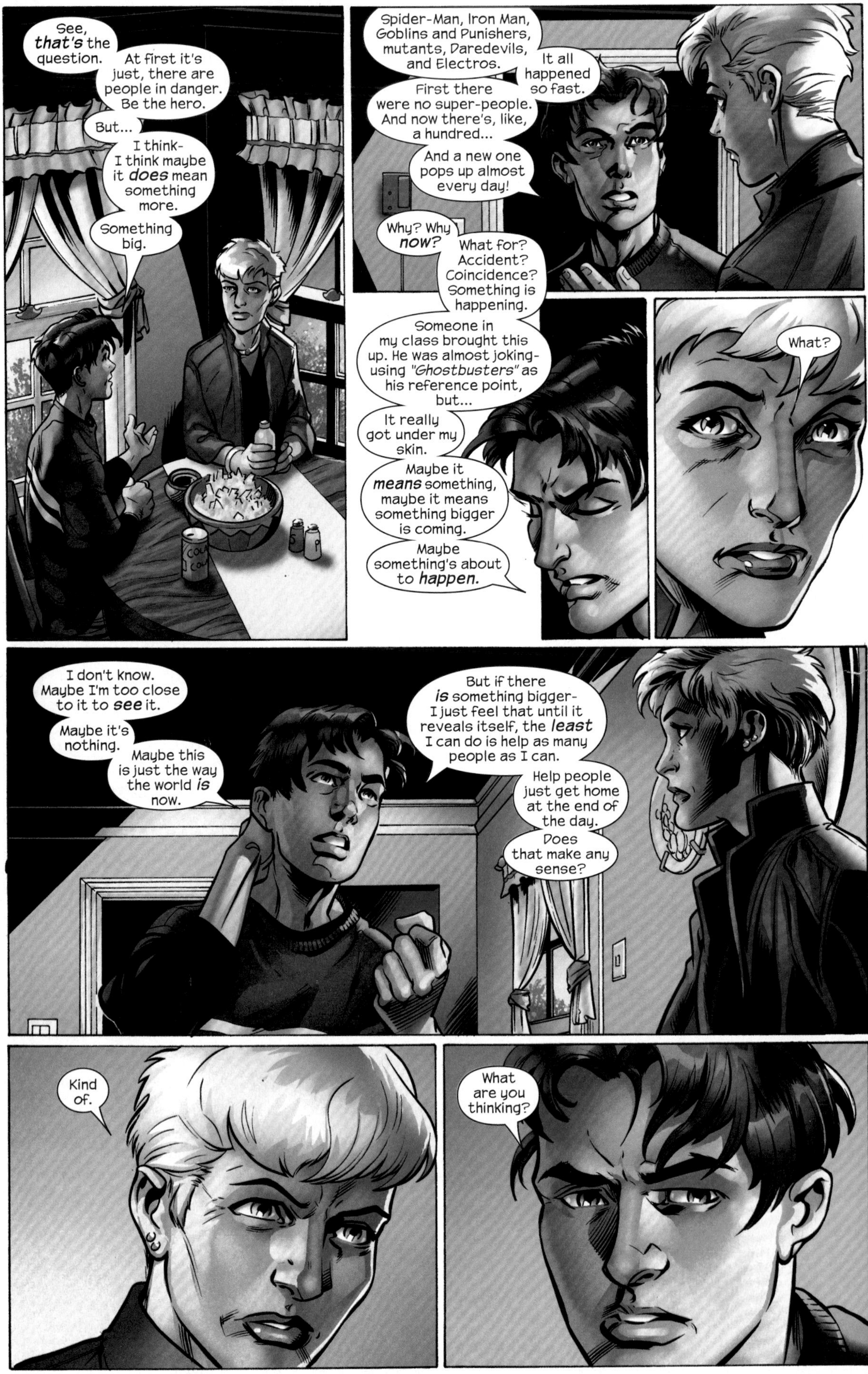
See, that's the question.
At first it's just, there are people in danger. Be the hero.
But...
I think- I think maybe it does mean something more.
Something big.
Spider-Man, Iron Man, Goblins and Punishers, mutants, Daredevils, and Electros.
It all happened so fast.
First there were no super-people. And now there's, like, a hundred...
And a new one pops up almost every day!
Why? Why now?
What for? Accident? Coincidence? Something is happening.
Someone in my class brought this up. He was almost joking- using "Ghostbusters" as his reference point, but...
It really got under my skin.
Maybe it means something, maybe it means something bigger is coming.
Maybe something's about to happen.
What?
I don't know. Maybe I'm too close to it to see it.
Maybe it's nothing.
Maybe this is just the way the world is now.
But if there is something bigger- I just feel that until it reveals itself, the least I can do is help as many people as I can.
Help people just get home at the end of the day.
Does that make any sense?
Kind of.
What are you thinking?

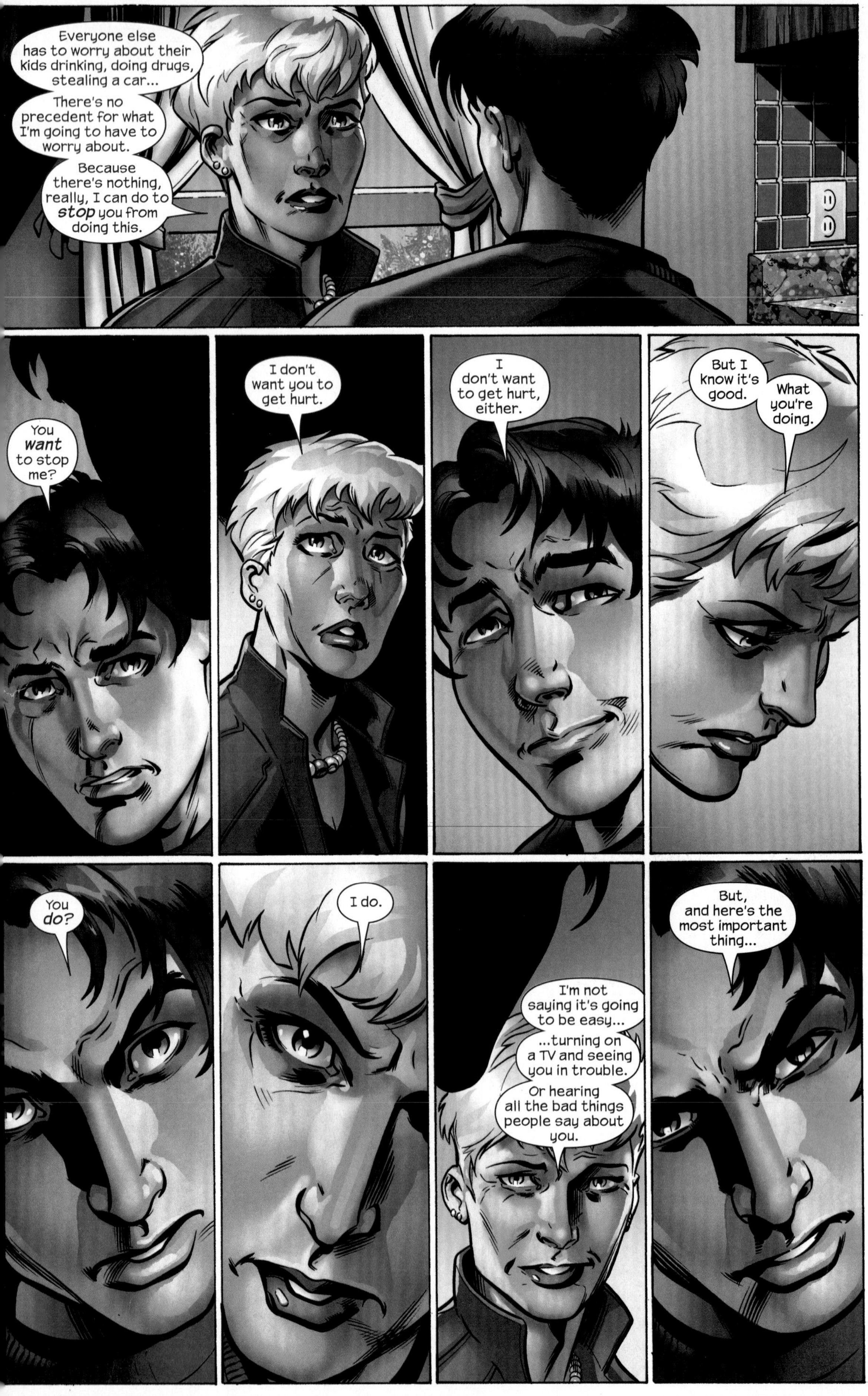
Everyone else has to worry about their kids drinking, doing drugs, stealing a car...
There's no precedent for what I'm going to have to worry about.
Because there's nothing, really, I can do to *stop* you from doing this.
You *want* to stop me?
I don't want you to get hurt.
I don't want to get hurt, either.
But I know it's good.
What you're doing.
You *do?*
I do.
I'm not saying it's going to be easy...
...turning on a TV and seeing you in trouble.
Or hearing all the bad things people say about you.
But, and here's the most important thing...

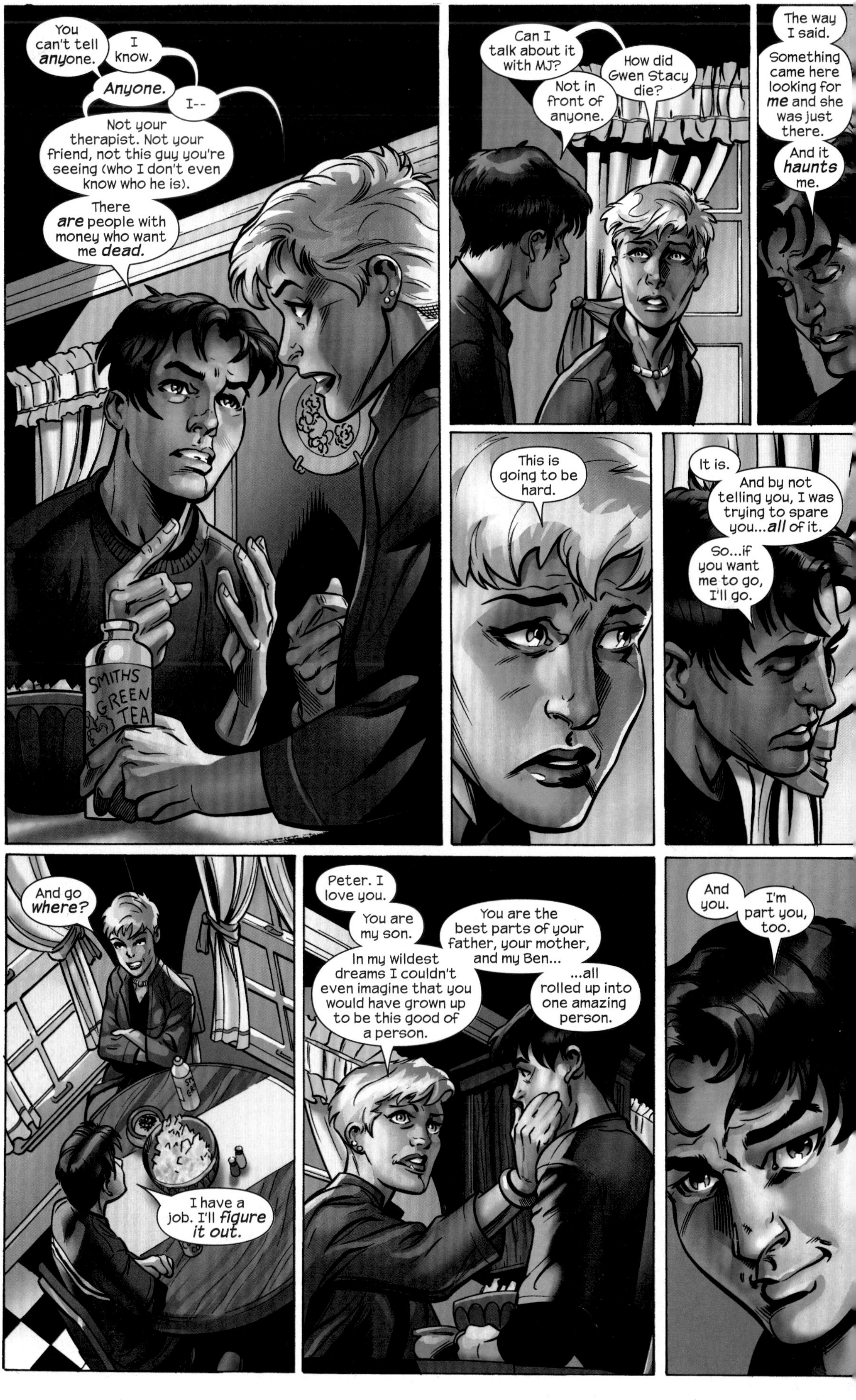
You can't tell anyone.
I know.
Anyone.
I--
Not your therapist. Not your friend, not this guy you're seeing (who I don't even know who he is).
There are people with money who want me dead.
SMITHS GREEN TEA
Can I talk about it with MJ?
Not in front of anyone.
How did Gwen Stacy die?
The way I said.
Something came here looking for me and she was just there.
And it haunts me.
This is going to be hard.
It is.
And by not telling you, I was trying to spare you...all of it.
So...if you want me to go, I'll go.
And go where?
I have a job. I'll figure it out.
Peter. I love you.
You are my son.
In my wildest dreams I couldn't even imagine that you would have grown up to be this good of a person.
You are the best parts of your father, your mother, and my Ben...
...all rolled up into one amazing person.
And you.
I'm part you, too.

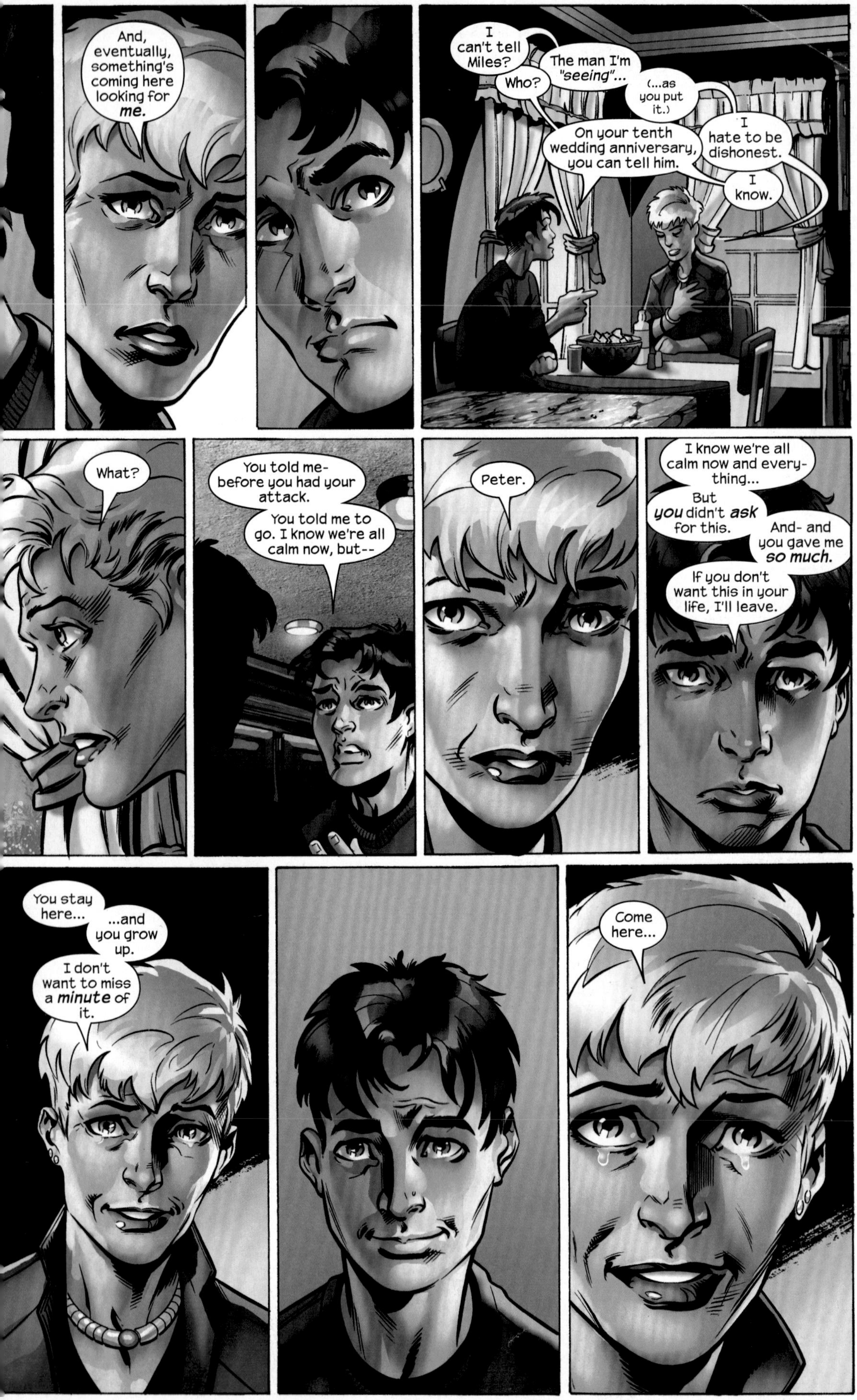
And, eventually, something's coming here looking for *me.*
I can't tell Miles?
Who?
The man I'm *"seeing"*...
(...as you put it.)
On your tenth wedding anniversary, you can tell him.
I hate to be dishonest.
I know.
What?
You told me- before you had your attack.
You told me to go. I know we're all calm now, but--
Peter.
I know we're all calm now and every- thing...
But *you* didn't *ask* for this.
And- and you gave me *so much.*
If you don't want this in your life, I'll leave.
You stay here...
...and you grow up.
I don't want to miss a *minute* of it.
Come here...

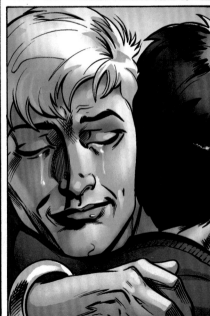

Okay, I have a million more questions, but...

I'm going to go lie down.

Sure. I'll wake you for dinner.

What are you going do to?

I don't know, go to MJ's, do some homework...